NEW DIRECTIONS IN THE STUDY OF
CHINA'S FOREIGN POLICY

New Directions in the Study of China's Foreign Policy

*Edited by Alastair Iain Johnston
and Robert S. Ross*

STANFORD UNIVERSITY PRESS

STANFORD, CALIFORNIA 2006

Stanford University Press
Stanford, California

Printed in the United States of America on
acid-free, archival-quality paper

LIBRARY OF CONGRESS CATALOGING-IN-PUBLICATION DATA

New directions in the study of China's foreign policy / edited by Alastair Iain
Johnston and Robert S. Ross
    p. cm.
 Includes bibliographical references and index.
  ISBN 0-8047-5362-8 (cloth : alk. paper)—ISBN 0-8047-5363-6 (pbk. :
alk. paper)
   1. China—Foreign relations—1976– I. Johnston, Alastair I. II. Ross,
Robert S.
DS779.27.N49   2006
327.51—dc22   2006007045

Original Printing 2006

Last figure below indicates year of this printing:
15   14   13   12   11   10   09   08   07   06

Typeset by G & S Typesetters, Inc. in 10/12.5 Sabon

To Allen S. Whiting
Scholar, Practitioner, Mentor

Contents

List of Figures and Tables

Contributors

Allen Carlson is assistant professor in Cornell University's Government Department. He is the author of *Unifying China, Integrating with the World: Securing Chinese Sovereignty During the Reform Era* (Stanford University Press, 2005). He also recently co-edited (with J. J. Suh and Peter Katzenstein) *Rethinking Security in East Asia: Power, Identity and Efficiencies* (Stanford University Press, 2004). In addition, he has published articles in the *Journal of Contemporary China* and *Pacific Affairs*.

Thomas J. Christensen is professor of politics and international affairs at Princeton University. He received his B.A. in history from Haverford College, M.A. in international relations from the University of Pennsylvania, and Ph.D. in political science from Columbia University. Before arriving at Princeton in 2003, he taught at Cornell University and the Massachusetts Institute of Technology.

Yong Deng is associate professor in political science at the U.S. Naval Academy at Annapolis, Maryland. His scholarly works on Chinese foreign policy include two edited volumes, *In the Eyes of the Dragon: China Views the World* (co-editor, 1999) and *China Rising: Power and Motivation in Chinese Foreign Policy* (co-editor, 2005). He has also published in academic journals, including *Political Science Quarterly*, *China Quarterly*, and *Pacific Affairs*, as well as in several edited volumes.

John Garver is professor with the Sam Nunn School of International Affairs at Georgia Institute of Technology. His research specializes on Chinese foreign relations, and he has written many books and articles in that area. His most recent research has dealt with China-India and China-Iran relations. He has set up and directed student programs in both China and greater East Asia for Georgia Tech.

Avery Goldstein is professor of political science and associate director of the Christopher H. Browne Center for International Politics at the University of Pennsylvania and senior fellow at the Foreign Policy Research Institute in Philadelphia. He is the author of *Rising to the Challenge: China's Grand Strategy and International Security* (Stanford University Press,

2005), *Deterrence and Security in the 21st Century: China, Britain, France, and the Enduring Legacy of the Nuclear Revolution* (Stanford University Press, 2000), and *From Bandwagon to Balance-of-Power Politics: Structural Constraints and Politics in China, 1949–1978* (Stanford University Press, 1991).

Peter Hays Gries is assistant professor of political science at the University of Colorado, Boulder, and director of the Sino-American Security Dialogue. He is author of *China's New Nationalism: Pride, Politics, and Diplomacy* (University of California Press, 2004) and co-editor of *State and Society in 21st Century China: Crisis, Contention, and Legitimation* (RoutledgeCurzon, 2004), as well as author of over a dozen journal articles and book chapters.

Alastair Iain Johnston is the Laine Professor of China in World Affairs in the Government Department at Harvard University. Johnston is the author of *Cultural Realism: Strategic Culture and Grand Strategy in Chinese History* (Princeton University Press, 1995), and co-editor of *Engaging China: The Management of an Emerging Power* (Routledge, 1999). He has written on socialization theory, strategic culture, China's participation in international institutions, Chinese nuclear doctrine and arms control, and Party-Army relations in China, among other topics.

Samuel S. Kim (M.I.A. and Ph.D., Columbia) is adjunct professor of political science and senior research scholar at the Weatherhead East Asian Institute, Columbia University. He is the author or editor of twenty-one books, including, most recently, *The International Relations of Northeast Asia* (ed., Rowman & Littlefield, 2004) and *The Two Koreas in the Global Community* (forthcoming).

Margaret M. Pearson is professor of government and politics at the University of Maryland, College Park. She received her Ph.D. in political science from Yale University. Her publications include the books *Joint Ventures in the People's Republic of China* (Princeton University Press, 1991) and *China's New Business Elite: The Political Results of Economic Reform* (University of California Press, 1997), as well as articles in *World Politics, China Journal, Modern China, China Business Review*, and other journals.

Robert S. Ross is professor of political science at Boston College, associate, John King Fairbank Center for East Asian Research, Harvard University, and senior advisor, Security Studies Program, Massachusetts Institute of

Technology. His current research focuses on Chinese security policy and U.S.-China relations, in particular Chinese use of force and deterrence in East Asia. His recent publications include *Normalization of U.S.-China Relations: An International History* (Asia Center, Harvard University, 2001), of which he was co-editor.

Michael Yahuda is professor emeritus of international relations at the London School of Economics and visiting scholar at the Sigur Center for Asian Studies, Elliott School of International Affairs, George Washington University. He enjoys an international reputation as a specialist on the international relations of East Asia. He has published more than 150 journal articles and book chapters and is the author of six books, the latest being *The International Politics of the Asia-Pacific* (1996; rev ed., RoutledgeCurzon, 2004).

Editors' Preface

This volume is dedicated to Allen Whiting. The contributors are junior and senior scholars who share a commitment to building the field of China's foreign policy and who share an approach to the subject that blends theory and evidence in a way that originated with Whiting. Beginning with his early writings, Whiting combined empirical research with a theoretically rich and policy-relevant analysis of China's international behavior. In short, the contributors join us in a tribute to Whiting as the founding father of Chinese foreign policy studies.

Whiting's work teaches us that China specialists need to understand not only Chinese history and politics but also international politics and the enduring sources, both domestic and international, of the international behavior of the Chinese state. His 1960 classic *China Crosses the Yalu: The Decision to Enter the Korean War* established the norm of using empirical research to support analytic conclusions regarding the sources of Chinese foreign policy, of Chinese deterrence signaling, and of misperceptions in the U.S.-China conflict. His second book on China's use of force, *The Chinese Calculus of Deterrence: India and China*, developed a comparative analysis for understanding Chinese deterrence behavior. His work on the domestic sources of Chinese policy-making is equally insightful. In *China Eyes Japan*, he combined theoretically informed analysis with documentary research and interviews in China and Japan to explain the historically derived cognitive sources of Sino-Japanese conflict. His work on Chinese nationalism similarly reflects his appreciation of domestic political and societal factors in foreign policy.

That scholars can and should serve the public interest is demonstrated by Whiting's career as a policy analyst and government advisor. His work with the Council on Foreign Relations and the Rand Corporation showed that scholars can inform the public and contribute to policy-making. Whiting served in government during the mid 1960s, when the United States was struggling with the seemingly interminable conflict in Vietnam and casting about to understand the political convulsions in China. After he left government, Whiting continued to serve American foreign policy. In 1969, he played a pivotal role in calling the attention of the White House to the escalating military conflict along the Sino-Soviet border and its implications for U.S.-China relations. Henry Kissinger later recalled in a letter to

Whiting: "When you served as a consultant to the Department of State in the Nixon administration I, too, benefited from your knowledge of the Pacific region. I particularly remember the time you came to San Clemente to brief me on the Sino-Soviet border dispute. It was a most impressive briefing and helped significantly to shape my own thinking about how the United States should react."

Thus, we honor Allen Whiting for having launched Chinese foreign policy as a field of study and having sustained it with a record of scholarship and public service that continues to inform new research agendas and to serve as a model for the civic-minded scholar.

NEW DIRECTIONS IN THE STUDY OF
CHINA'S FOREIGN POLICY

1 *Introduction*

Robert S. Ross and Alastair Iain Johnston

This volume reflects an effort to take stock of the field of Chinese foreign policy and to consider potential avenues of new research. It is a collaborative effort by scholars of different generations and many academic perspectives who share an interest in and commitment to explaining Chinese foreign policy and to using systematically gathered and analyzed evidence. It is not intended to be a comprehensive survey of the field of Chinese foreign policy, which is simply too large and diverse for one volume to be able to cover all the topics, draw on all the relevant theories, and include all the first-rate scholars in the field. Rather, scholars were chosen in an attempt to represent current research in Chinese foreign policy from multiple theoretical perspectives and methodologies and multiple academic generations. To some degree, the timing of the volume is also worth noting: it appears at a point in history when the integration of the People's Republic of China (PRC) with regional and global economic and political institutions has never been greater, and when a narrowing range of tropes of unease about "rising China" are coming to dominate policy and pundit discourses both in the United States and elsewhere. Not only is there greater demand today for information about China's foreign policy, but scholars are able, in principle, to supply greater amounts of sophisticated analysis.

The chapters were first presented at a conference held at the John King Fairbank Center at Harvard University in December 2002.[1] The volume is organized into three subfields of Chinese foreign policy. Part I examines Chinese security policy, including Chinese use of force, policy toward conflicts of interests affecting war and peace, and China's strategy as a rising power. Owing to greater access to Chinese analysts, decision-makers, and documents, these chapters draw on a wider range of materials about the sources and effects of Chinese security policy than was available in the earlier days of the field.[2] Part II considers China as an actor in multilateral institutions and China's response to emerging global trends, including evolving conceptions of sovereignty and the emergence of globalization. These topics are relatively new for the field,[3] reflecting the fact that since the late 1980s, China has advanced more rapidly into international institutional life than any other major state moving from a similar position of isolation. Part III presents new research on domestic-foreign linkages, considering the impact of trends in public opinion and of Chinese identity on China's policy toward major powers. This is a very new subfield, because access to public attitudes has been severely restricted in authoritarian China, and the impact of public opinion on foreign policy has never been considered relevant. With rapid urbanization, marketization, and the diversification of political, economic, and foreign policy preferences, this seems to be changing.[4]

The Study of Chinese Security Policy

Robert Ross examines the role of deterrence and use of force in Chinese foreign policy. His Chapter 2, "Comparative Deterrence: The Taiwan Strait and the Korean Peninsula," places these two theaters of deterrence in the context of the theoretical literature on effective deterrence and on the sources of unstable deterrence and unintended war, enabling comparative analysis of the two theaters and estimates of the likelihood of war in East Asia. Regarding Korea, Ross assesses North Korean deterrence of U.S. use of force for either regime change or denuclearization, and U.S.–South Korean deterrence of North Korean use of force for unification. Regarding the Taiwan Strait, he considers Chinese deterrence of a Taiwan declaration of independence, an "act of war," and U.S. deterrence of Chinese initiation of use of force for unification. Using deterrence theory and concepts of credibility, capability, and expected utility, he considers the effectiveness of mutual deterrence dynamics in each region. He also compares these two deterrence theaters regarding incentives for first strikes and the implications for crisis instability and unintended war. Ross argues that although there is effective mutual deterrence on both the Korean peninsula and in the Taiwan Strait so that the status quo is preferred to use of force by all of the otherwise revisionist states, the distinct weapons capabilities of the actors in each theater and the distinct geography of each theater create distinct crisis dynamics. He argues that these differences have made the Korean peninsula a more probable military threat than the Taiwan Strait since the end of the Cold War, and that the Korean peninsula will remain a more likely source of war than the Taiwan Strait.

Thomas Christensen's Chapter 3, "Windows and War: Trend Analysis and Beijing's Use of Force," examines conditions under which China has used force since 1949. Working within international politics theories of preemptive and preventive war, Christensen applies the concept of "closing windows" to provide a comprehensive explanation for all post-1949 cases of Chinese use of force. He argues that Chinese leaders have used force to achieve international political objectives, despite the absence of a clear "red-line" provocation, when they perceive a closing window for China to achieve its strategic objectives, to deter an adversary from becoming more aggressive, or to create favorable long-term strategic trends. Christensen also argues that domestic conditions have consistently contributed to Chinese use of force, not because domestic instability can contribute to Chinese threat perception but because Chinese leaders have seen use of force as an appropriate instrument to achieve their domestic political objectives. Christensen further establishes that Chinese leaders have used force to reverse a deteriorating international situation even when China faced a more powerful and committed adversary, suggesting that China may be an especially difficult state to deter. Christensen's analysis of the patterns in Chinese use of force suggests a relatively pessimistic outlook for relying on deterrence to maintain stability in the Taiwan Strait. Based on past PRC behavior, he warns that although Taiwan might not offer a red-line provocation by declaring de jure independence, mere continued Taiwan movement toward de jure independence could produce sufficient Chinese concern about a closing window to elicit use of force, even should Chinese leaders expect intervention by superior U.S. forces.

John Garver's Chapter 4, "China's Decision for War with India in 1962," presents an analysis of Chinese use of force against India in 1962. This case study integrates many of the issues addressed by Ross and Christensen to explain a major Chinese use of force. Drawing on voluminous new materials, the chapter analyzes the sources of Chinese threat perception, Chinese deterrence strategy, and China's decision to use force. Following the works of Allen Whiting and Neville Maxwell, Garver concurs that India's border policy challenged China's territorial integrity and that the Chinese failure to deter Indian forward deployment across the McMahon Line reflected low Indian assessment of China's resolve to use force and the constraints of Indian domestic politics on Nehru's ability to moderate India's broader policy. But, in contrast to Whiting and Maxwell, Garver argues that China's subsequent use of force against India reflected not simply China's imperative to defend its territorial integrity but rather primarily reflected heightened Chinese threat assessment resulting from Mao Zedong's misperception that Indian border policy reflected Nehru's contribution to the CIA-assisted 1959 uprising in Tibet and his determination to promote Tibetan separatism. Psychologically, Mao was simply unable to grasp Nehru's actual moderate intention to promote Tibetan autonomy within Chinese sovereignty and the domestic situational constraints on Nehru's Tibet and border policies. Mao thus developed a worst-case assessment of Nehru's intentions. Garver concludes that although China's victory over India established Chinese resolve and compelled India to adopt a more cautious China policy, Mao's misperception of Nehru's intentions also inflicted significant costs on China, including long-term hostility with a determined and more modern Indian army and development of anti-China Soviet-Indian cooperation.

Chapters 5 and 6 analyze Chinese policy toward two key issues affecting Chinese security—developments on the Korean peninsula and trends in Sino-Japanese relations. Avery Goldstein's Chapter 5, "Across the Yalu: China's Interests and the Korean Peninsula in a Changing World," examines contemporary Chinese policy toward the Korean conflict. He stresses that during the Cold War, ideology, territorial security, and alignment with Soviet power against U.S. capabilities dominated Chinese policy. In contrast, although in the post–Cold War era, U.S. power remains at the heart of PRC assessments of trends on the peninsula, in the absence of the option of alignment with a great power, Beijing has had to accommodate U.S. power, while seeking gradual development of greater Chinese capabilities and minimization of domestic political instability. These demands require Beijing to seek a peaceful international environment, including peace on the Korean peninsula, even as management of domestic instability and concern about U.S. capabilities require vigilance against U.S. policy and an enduring commitment to the survival of the North Korean government. This analytical indeterminacy requires development of a framework for forecasting the future of China's Korean policy. Goldstein develops four "stylized scenarios" and assesses each in terms of its implications for China's pursuit of its multiple interests on the Korean peninsula, especially vis-à-vis the United States. He then applies two conceptual frameworks to assess the likely course of Chinese policy among these four futures. First, he builds on Whiting's concepts of Chinese threat perception and deterrence behavior, stressing that linkage between internal instability and heightened PRC threat perception, on the one hand, and the role of force in diplomatic signaling in Chinese deterrence efforts, on the other, may affect crisis outcomes. Second, he considers the impact of China's Korean policy on U.S.-China management of the rise of China, stressing that the very indeterminacy in PRC policy creates space for a negotiated solution, which can facilitate a peaceful power transition.

Michael Yahuda's Chapter 6, "The Limits of Economic Interdependence: Sino-Japanese Relations," also adopts a conceptual approach to the trends in a bilateral Chinese foreign policy. He considers the impact of increasing Sino-Japanese economic interdependence on the trends in the bilateral relationship. Observing that Sino-Japanese relations have become more contentious just as economic cooperation has increased, contrary to the expectations of the international political economy literature, Yahuda considers what factors have been responsible for this countervailing trend. Like

Goldstein, he argues that the end of the Cold War in East Asia has transformed the security preferences of each country. In the absence of the constraints imposed by the Soviet Union, each country has developed more assertive and independent security policies. Simultaneously, each country has also been increasingly intolerant of the changes in the other's policies. Yahuda explains this development and the resulting tension in relations by observing each country's inability to appreciate the impact of its changing security policies, especially the growth in respective military capabilities, on the other's security, that is, its inability to appreciate the impact of the security dilemma in international politics, so that each develops a worst-case perspective on the other's intentions. He explains these mutual worst-case analyses by developments in domestic politics. Following Whiting's analysis of Sino-Japanese relations in the 1980s, he finds that anti-Japanese nationalism in Chinese education has fostered widespread Chinese misperceptions about Japanese behavior. Moreover, generational change in China and Japan has given rise to leaders with limited knowledge of the other's culture and society. The result is that security perspectives, informed by domestically informed misperceptions, have offset the potentially positive effects of increased economic interdependence.

Part I concludes with Deng Yong's Chapter 7, "Reputation and the Security Dilemma: China Reacts to the China Threat Theory," which discusses China's management of its rising power status, considered in the context of Beijing's implicit appreciation of the impact of the security dilemma in international politics. Whereas Yahuda suggests that Chinese leaders are insensitive to the impact of Chinese policy on Japanese security, Deng argues that the Chinese leadership is aware that China's reputation in other countries can be a major factor in their assessments of Chinese intentions and in their corresponding response to China's rising capabilities. In particular, perceptions of a "China threat" can lead other countries to adopt belligerent policies toward China that might disrupt Beijing's ability to focus on economic development and to enhance Chinese security in a peaceful international environment. Thus, Chinese diplomacy has actively tried to neutralize China threat arguments. First, it accuses proponents of the China threat of having a Cold War mentality of containment, seeking to delegitimate China's critics. Second, it has tried to foster a benign image of itself. One aspect of this is China's public diplomacy to define its own reputation in world affairs. Deng explains that China's development of its "peaceful rise" diplomacy aims to undermine China threat arguments. Another aspect of its rising power diplomacy is its extensive participation in multilateral institutions, including in arms control and nonproliferation institutions. Deng concludes with the observation that China's recognition of the importance of reputation for security dilemma dynamics is indicative of the fundamental changes in Chinese foreign policy that have taken place since the Maoist era, when China primarily depended on a reputation for military resolve to influence the behavior of potential adversaries.

China and Globalization

Part I of this volume thus considers the impact of China's international strategic environment on Chinese policy. Part II is also concerned with China's response to its international environment, but the focus is on China's response to globalization, including the globalization of norms of limited sovereignty, humanitarian intervention, and economic cooperation.

Allen Carlson's Chapter 8, "More Than Just Saying No: China's Evolving Approach to Sovereignty and Intervention Since Tiananmen," examines in depth perhaps the most sensitive challenge of globalization—China's gradual compromise of its long-term commitment to absolute sovereignty in response to its determined exposure to the deepening and increasingly global norm of humanitarian intervention. Although Carlson acknowledges the role of material interests in Chinese behavior, he explains the evolution in Chinese thinking on sovereignty by focusing on the susceptibility of Chinese foreign policy elites to international norms through "social learning." He argues that Chinese participation in international society has led to internalization of hitherto unacceptable ideas. His empirical work examines changes in Chinese attitudes toward sovereignty as they relate to the legitimacy of security and humanitarian international intervention in a state's domestic affairs. Carlson argues that even as interest calculations clearly drove China's initial moderation of its stand on absolute sovereignty in the early 1990s, China's changing policy also encouraged underlying ideational change among Chinese foreign policy elites that sustained and even deepened the trend in China toward acceptance of the concept of limited sovereignty well into the decade. By the first decade of the twenty-first century, despite enduring Chinese concern that Western democracies, in particular the United States, have used the concept of limited sovereignty to suit their narrow national interests, the global norm of humanitarian multilateral intervention in protection of human rights, expressed in the very language used by Western foreign policy elites, had become widespread in Chinese foreign policy circles, and Chinese government attitudes toward multilateral intervention had become increasingly flexible.

Margaret Pearson's Chapter 9, "China in Geneva: Lessons from China's Early Years in the World Trade Organization," turns to China and the global economy, in particular to Chinese participation in the WTO and its impact on global trade. Similar to Carlson's investigation of China's stance toward the norms of sovereignty and nonintervention, Pearson examines China's stance toward the WTO's formal rules and informal norms in the early and critical period after December 2001. But whereas Carlson stresses growing Chinese socialization into evolving norms of sovereignty, Pearson, while open to the suggestion that China may become "socialized" into WTO norms, stresses that calculations of economic interest drive cooperative, norm-acceptant Chinese policy. Rather than actively promoting the revisionist agenda of developing countries, China works with the handful of states at the center of power in the WTO; it aligns with coalitions of developed states that promote policies favorable to greater PRC access to international markets, including the markets of developing countries. Thus, on agriculture issues, it has aligned with the United States to promote open markets. On textiles, although it opposes U.S. protectionist efforts, it has maintained a low profile, even when its preferences favor the interests of developing countries. Insofar as the WTO norms enable agenda stetting and negotiations to be dominated by the economic powers and their interest in maintaining the existing trade order, since 2000, China has avoided revisionist behavior and has accommodated itself to well-established WTO rules and norms. Underscoring Samuel Kim's observation that globalization and the development of so-called intermestic actors have undermined the policy-making authority of the central government, Pearson observes that China's ability to assume leadership in the WTO will depend on its ability to forge a consensus position among competing domestic interests prior to conducting negotiations with its international trading partners.

Samuel Kim's Chapter 10, "Chinese Foreign Policy Faces Globalization Challenges," steps back and addressees the big picture—the multiple challenges China faces as it engages globalization and the wide range of international institutions that are the agents of globalization. He observes that after many years of criticizing globalization as a threat to Chinese sovereignty and as a plot to foment domestic instability, by the early 1990s, Chinese leaders had acknowledged that both domestic stability and Chinese international security required China to participate in globalization, that China could not be a revisionist power. Since then, China has fully engaged economic, security, and political globalization. But Kim observes that whereas economic globalization and membership in the WTO have been relatively easy for China to manage, insofar as the growth of the Chinese economy, of exports, and of foreign investment have made China a winner in economic globalization, China has had to make important trade-offs in other sectors. For example, engagement with globalization has required China to come to terms with evolving norms of sovereignty. As a member of the UN Security Council, China has acceded to numerous multilateral security arrangements. It has also compromised its position on intervention in a state's sovereign affairs, increasingly supporting UN peacekeeping operations since the late 1990s. Kim observes that whereas participation in globalization has enhanced Chinese national power and its ability to defend its external sovereignty, the associated weakening of national boundaries has simultaneously undermined China's internal sovereignty. Domestic groups with competing international interests, intermestic actors, require Chinese leaders to engage in domestic negotiations before they can successfully negotiate at the international level. Moreover, the central government's diminishing control over localities and of cross-border information flows poses a long-term challenge to political stability.

Domestic Politics and Chinese Foreign Policy

The chapters in the second part of this volume argue that Chinese participation in globalization has necessarily eroded the boundary between China's domestic politics and its foreign policy. Part III directly addresses this issue and the domestic sources of China's international behavior. In particular, it seeks to assess the impact of the erosion of the Chinese central government's authority over society and the corresponding implications of the influence of mass attitudes on China's foreign policy.

Peter Gries's Chapter 11, "Identity and Conflict in Sino-American Relations," examines the role of "othering" in Chinese nationalism and thus its impact on China's involvement in international conflict, in particular in conflict with the United States. Like Carlson in Chapter 8, Gries acknowledges the important role of material interests in shaping foreign policy and also argues that a constructivist approach employing social identity theory can reveal the substance of Chinese nationalism and its contribution to conflict. Examining the writings of China's more vocal nationalists, Gries develops a "hard test" to argue that Chinese nationalism is not necessarily a source of Chinese belligerence. Following the research on social identity theory, he argues that China's in-group identity does not require a zero-sum policy framework that promotes hostility toward the out group, so that nationalism is an indeterminate source of competitive, conflict-prone attitudes toward the United States. Gries's case studies are the 1999 U.S.-China tension over the U.S. bombing of the Chinese embassy in Belgrade and the 2001 U.S.-China tension over the crash of a Chinese surveillance plane after its collision with an American EP-3 intelligence aircraft near Hainan Island. Whereas conflict over the embassy bombing continues to fester in China, the EP-3 incident was fully resolved. The difference, Gries explains, was that whereas U.S. policy in both cases undermined China's positive self-identity, in the latter case, creative ambiguity in U.S.-China diplomacy enabled both sides to "save face," while enabling China to escape zero-sum dynamics in its nationalist out-group competition with the United States.

Iain Johnston's Chapter 12, "The Correlates of Beijing Public Opinion Toward the United States, 1998–2004," addresses broader themes in public attitudes toward key international actors and the potential long-term implications for China's role in international politics and its policy toward the United States. Taking advantage of a variety of social science methodologies and seven years of polling of Beijing-area residents, he presents the first randomly sampled, nongovernmental time-series analysis of Chinese public opinion on foreign policy issues, with controls for various socioeconomic and demographic variables. Johnston observes that repeated short-term mini crises in U.S.-China relations have contributed to a gradual decline of "warmth" toward the United States among Beijing residents. But Johnston's findings also suggest that wealth, education, and travel abroad may help offset these trends to some degree. Thus insofar as China's exposure to globalization contributes to the expansion of an educated middle class and to greater cross-border information flows resulting from travel and news reports about international politics, the foreign policy preferences of this group will tend to be relatively less anti-American and nationalistic. Moreover, greater income levels, education, and travel all tend to diminish Chinese tendencies toward "othering," in which a positive Chinese self-identity is paired with a negative characterization of the United States. Johnston acknowledges the many limitations in the polling data and the limited role that public opinion continues to have in Chinese policy-making. Yet his analysis since 1998 of the opinions of Beijing-area residents suggests that reduced central government control over society, including that resulting from globalization and democratization, may not necessarily lead to greater anti-American nationalism and heightened U.S.-China conflict.

Conclusions

The research in this volume should not be considered as either definitive or all-encompassing. Rather, it simply reflects an effort to consider the study of Chinese foreign policy from multiple dimensions, including different research agendas and diverse methodologies and research materials. It is the hope of all the contributors that the volume will be considered a gesture of their appreciation of the work of their predecessors, who first established the importance and viability of the field of Chinese foreign policy studies, and whose work contributed to the richness and sophistication of current research. They also hope that the volume may make a modest contribution to the future development of the field.

Notes

1. We are grateful to Elizabeth Economy, Joseph Fewsmith, Steven Goldstein, Roderick MacFarquhar, Alan Romberg, and Ezra Vogel for serving as discussants and for their valuable contributions to the conference and to the quality of the chapters in this book, as well as to David Zweig for sharing his research on China's reverse brain drain. We also wish to thank the Fairbank Center for providing the funding and administrative support for the conference, which was the Fairbank Center's way of honoring Allen S. Whiting, owing to the fact that he had been unable to deliver the prestigious Reischauer Lecture the year before.

2. The earlier literature on Chinese security behavior is too rich to cite here. But some of the pioneering work—research that tried to mainstream Chinese foreign policy behavior by applying standard analytical constructs such as deterrence theory, rational actor models of decision-making, and a realism-influenced focus on China's pursuit of power within different regional and global configurations of power and interest—include Allen S. Whiting, *China Crosses the Yalu: The Decision to Enter the Korean War* (1960; Stanford: Stanford University Press, 1968); Peter Van Ness, *Revolution and Chinese Foreign Policy: Peking's Support for Wars of National Liberation* (Berkeley: University of California Press, 1970); Allen S. Whiting, *The Calculus of Chinese Deterrence: India and Indochina* (Ann Arbor: University of Michigan Press, 1975); J. D. Armstrong, *Revolutionary Diplomacy: Chinese Foreign Policy and the United Front Doctrine* (Berkeley: University of California Press, 1977); and Melvin Gurtov and Byong-Moo Huang, *China Under Threat: The Politics of Strategy and Diplomacy* (Baltimore: Johns Hopkins University Press, 1980).

3. In contrast to the work on Chinese security, there are very few pioneering works on which to build this new research. The most obvious of these are Samuel Kim, *China, the United Nations and World Order* (Princeton, N.J.: Princeton University Press, 1979); Gerald Chan, *China and International Organizations* (Hong Kong: Oxford University Press, 1989); and Harold K. Jacobson and Michel Oksenberg, *China's Participation in the IMF, the World Bank, and GATT* (Ann Arbor: University of Michigan Press, 1990).

4. This research is new in the sense that it tries to analyze the impact of ideology, historical memory, and collective identity in society, not primarily among the decision-making elites in the Chinese system. But this work, too, stands on the shoulders of giants in Chinese foreign policy, scholars who have taken ideational variables seriously in their own work. See Allen S. Whiting, *China Eyes Japan* (Berkeley: University of California Press, 1989) and "Chinese Nationalism and Foreign Policy After Deng," *China Quarterly*, no. 142 (June 1995): 295–316, www.people.fas.harvard.edu/~johnston/GOV2880/whiting.html (accessed 27 September 2005); Steven I. Levine, "Perception and Ideology in the Study of Chinese Foreign Policy," and Steven M. Goldstein, "Nationalism and Internationalism: Sino-Soviet Relations," both in *Chinese Foreign Policy: Theory and Practice*, ed. Thomas W. Robinson and David Shambaugh (Oxford: Clarendon Press, 1994), 30–46 and 224–65, respectively; and Michel Oksenberg, "China's Confident Nationalism," *Foreign Affairs* 65, 3 (1987): 501–23.

Part **One**

SECURITY STUDIES

2 *Comparative Deterrence*

THE TAIWAN STRAIT AND THE KOREAN PENINSULA

Robert S. Ross

In the 1990s, the United States was involved in two confrontations in East Asia involving the People's Republic of China. In 1994, it contended with North Korea, the PRC's immediate neighbor and ally, over Pyongyang's nuclear weapons program, and in March 1996, it contended with the PRC over Beijing's military activities in the Taiwan Strait. The difference between these two incidents presents a puzzle. Former Secretary of Defense William Perry characterized the confrontation on the Korean peninsula as a crisis in which the United States risked war, but he was also clear that the 1996 Taiwan Strait confrontation was not a crisis.[1] Why is it that the United States did not experience a crisis in a direct military confrontation with China, a major power possessing considerable naval and air force capabilities, contending over a vital interest, Taiwan's sovereignty relationship with mainland China, but did experience crisis decision-making when it directly confronted North Korea, a small state with a weak and backward military, and only indirectly confronted China, over a prospective North Korean nuclear weapons program?

The solution to this puzzle does not lie in the respective capabilities of China and North Korea in weapons of mass destruction. In the mid 1990s, China possessed a small yet credible nuclear capability deployed on intercontinental ballistic missiles (ICBMs) capable of reaching the continental United States and on shorter-range missiles capable of targeting U.S. regional allies, including Japan. In 1994, North Korea did not possess nuclear weapons, but it possessed a significant arsenal, possibly including chemical and biological weapons, and a large land force that could cause great destruction in South Korea, as well as to U.S. forces deployed in South Korea. War with either country could be catastrophic.

The argument of this paper is that in the mid 1990s, effective mutual deterrence existed both on the Korean peninsula and in the Taiwan Strait.

None of the protagonists preferred war to maintaining the status quo, and all of the protagonists believed that their adversaries possessed sufficient resolve to use force to resist a challenge to the status quo. From this perspective, the risk of war and thus the propensity for crisis escalation should have been the same in each case. Nonetheless, despite these similar conditions, there were different outcomes, reflecting the difference in mutual deterrence in the two cases. Whereas there was mutual stable deterrence in the Taiwan Strait, there was mutual unstable deterrence on the Korean peninsula.

Following the conceptual work of Thomas Schelling, this paper argues that crisis dynamics and the propensity for escalation reflected the unique character of each deterrence dyad.[2] Whereas the protagonists in the Taiwan theater possess effective deterrence capabilities, these same capabilities do not have significant offensive potential, so there exists mutual stable deterrence. In contrast, the deterrence capabilities of the adversaries on the Korean peninsula also possess significant offensive capabilities, creating mutual fear of incurring a debilitating first strike. The resulting intense security dilemma dynamics create pressures for each side to prepare for war and to consider the merits of a preemptive strike. Thus, there is mutual yet unstable deterrence on the Korean peninsula, explaining the propensity for crisis escalation and the potential for unintended war.

The first part of this paper discusses the sources of effective mutual deterrence and unstable mutual deterrence. The second part argues that there is mutual deterrence in both the Korean and Taiwan theaters. The third part assesses the sources of stable and unstable deterrence in each theater. The final part considers the policy implications for the United States of the distinct deterrence dynamics of each dyad.

Deterrence and the Taiwan and Korean Conflicts

In the Taiwan theater, mutual deterrence involves U.S. deterrence of Chinese use of force for unification and Chinese deterrence of a formal Taiwan declaration of independence. In the Korean theater, mutual deterrence depends on U.S. deterrence of North Korean use of force for unification of the Korean peninsula under Pyongyang's rule and North Korean deterrence of U.S. use of force for unification under Seoul's rule or for denuclearization of North Korea. In each deterrence relationship, effective deterrence requires the status-quo state to possess the retaliatory capability to inflict costs that outweigh the benefits to a country that might use force to change the status quo and the reputation for resolve to make its retaliatory threats credible.

Effective deterrence thus requires that all of the actors value peace more than costly forceful revision of the status quo. This is clearly the case. China has not used force to unify Taiwan for over fifty years, and although Taiwan has moved closer to declaring formal independence, its leaders have thus far judged the risk to be too great. Similarly, the protagonists on the Korean peninsula have preferred peace to war since 1953. The question for the future is whether changes in capabilities or domestic political conditions have altered this assessment for any of the actors and thus the deterrence dynamics in either or both of the two theaters.

But even should each of the actors be deterrable by the costs of war, they must also have sufficient respect for their opponent's resolve to make their retaliatory threats credible. Credibility in part reflects interests. Sometimes, the deterrer's interests are so high that its credibility is not in doubt. At other times, its interests are so low that reputation cannot enhance credibility, regardless of capabilities. In between lurks the extended deterrence problem, where uncertainty about the deterrer's interests and resolve can determine the credibility of threats.[3]

The United States faces the extended deterrence problem in its effort to deter Chinese and North Korean use of force against Taiwan and South Korea, respectively. In the 1950s and 1960s, U.S. policymakers feared that if the U.S. deterrent of a Soviet invasion of western Europe was undermined by the questionable credibility of its retaliatory threats, the U.S. ability to deter conventional use of force by a nuclear-armed China was even less certain, because U.S. interest in the East Asian status quo was not as strong as its interest in the European status quo.[4] Washington's extended deterrence problem in East Asia is no different today than it was during the first half of the Cold War.

China also faces an extended deterrence problem. Its commitment to defend its North Korean ally is necessarily not as strong as its commitment to defend its own territory. The questionable credibility of its commitment to maintain a buffer state on its northern border in part explains its failure to deter U.S. expansion of the Korean War to northern Korea in the 1950s. Many U.S. leaders believed that China would not go to war if Washington established its determination to use force to unify Korea under southern rule.[5] In contemporary East Asia, China's reputation for resolve to defend its ally affects U.S. willingness to risk war to eliminate the North Korean regime.

Perceptions of the resolve of Taiwan and North Korea also affect deterrence. In North Korea's case, the issue is not the leadership's willingness to defend North Korea and its regime from attack, but whether the regime possesses sufficient legitimacy to survive during a war, and whether its people will defend the country from attack. To the extent that there is doubt regarding Pyongyang's ability to resist, deterrence must rest on an assured destruction capability. Taiwan's resolve also reflects the extent to which the people of Taiwan will resist a mainland attack. Taiwan's democratic government is legitimate, but it is unclear whether the people of Taiwan will maintain their resistance to unification in a war, given the high costs of war to other important Taiwanese interests, China's overwhelming superiority in size and likely war-fighting endurance, and the common culture and increasing societal ties connecting the people on the two sides of the Strait.

The capabilities and credibility of the status-quo state interact with the revisionist state's interest in challenging the status quo to create the "expected cost" of the use of force and thus the effectiveness of deterrence. Leaders must balance the credibility of a threat to retaliate with the likely costs of retaliation when addressing the expected cost of use of force. Thus, high costs of war can offset low credibility of retaliation. This was the source of effective nuclear deterrence in the mutually assured destruction relationship between the United States and the Soviet Union.[6] In contemporary East Asia, the high cost of war can compensate for a status-quo power's questionable resolve, as in extended deterrence threats or when doubts about resolve can reflect domestic politics, creating a high expected cost of use of force and thus effective deterrence.

Deterrence can be effective in both East Asian theaters, but nonetheless unstable if any of the protagonists fears that a surprise attack would lead to very high costs or to defeat. Unstable deterrence can reflect the influence of geography, weapons technologies, and defense strategies on first-strike capabilities, creating heightened security dilemma dynamics as the offensive potential of military capabilities and actions designed to deter or defend create fears of attack and thus spiraling preparations for war.[7] This is the critical distinction between the Korean and Taiwan theaters. There is effective mutual deterrence in both theaters, but heightened security dilemma dynamics undermine the contribution of deterrence to peace on the Korean peninsula, but do not do so in the Taiwan Strait.

Deterrence in the Taiwan Strait

Peace in the Taiwan Strait requires mutual deterrence—both China and Taiwan must be deterred from challenging the status quo. Deterring China requires U.S. possession of the capabilities and credibility necessary to persuade Beijing that the expected cost of U.S. retaliation would be greater than the benefits of using force for unification. Deterrence of Taiwan requires sufficient Chinese capabilities and resolve to persuade Taipei that the expected costs of a Chinese retaliation would be greater than the benefits of formally declaring independence for Taiwan.

CAPABILITIES AND CREDIBILITY: DETERRING CHINA

Effective U.S. deterrence of Chinese use of force requires that Chinese leaders understand that the United States possesses the capabilities and resolve to make Chinese use of force too costly to other Chinese interests. They must understand that China lacks sufficient capabilities to incorporate Taiwan and deter costly U.S. intervention.

Chinese military analysts argue that the most fundamental change in U.S. conventional capabilities since the end of the Cold War is that the United States no longer faces adversaries with superior or even equal conventional power. During the Cold War, when the United States confronted adversaries with effective conventional forces, it depended on its nuclear forces for extended deterrence. Today, U.S. extended deterrence relies on the overwhelming superiority of the United States in high-technology conventional weaponry, so that Washington can de-link extended deterrence from reliance on nuclear weapons. PRC military analysts further concluded from the U.S. victories in the 1991 Gulf War and the 1999 war in Kosovo not only that high-technology weaponry had become the most important factor in warfighting, but that the elements of high-technology warfare "to a very high degree determine the outcome of war." Thus, superiority in "precision-guided weapons of greater variety and higher performance" results in "battlefield control."[8] Moreover, the U.S. military's rapid deployment capabilities allow it to project force "as soon as needed" for any regional contingency, further reducing U.S. dependency on nuclear missiles for retaliation.[9]

U.S. conventional military superiority also benefits from superiority in information warfare. In the era of information warfare, "military combat 'transparency' [*toumingdu*] . . . has already become an effective form of . . . combat." The superior power can blind the adversary by destroying its information systems, thus immobilizing its war-fighting capabilities and establishing information dominance. Indeed, a fundamental element of contemporary deterrence is "information deterrence" (*xinxi weishe*). Some Chinese military specialists argue that superior information capabilities can create an "information umbrella" (*xinxi san*) that not only can substitute for the nuclear umbrella but is superior to it. Information deterrence is the "finest result" of "defeating the enemy without fighting." It seeks "bloodless confrontation to achieve military victory."[10] It is a "peace umbrella" (*heping san*).[11]

The conventional superiority of the United States enhances its ability to deter war. First, if nuclear extended deterrence had failed during the Cold War, the United States could not have used its nuclear capabilities to retaliate without exposing itself to universal condemnation. Today, because collateral damage to an adversary would be relatively small, there are reduced

U.S. misgivings about punishing potential challengers.[12] As one military analyst concluded, "the usability of conventional deterrence forces is far greater than that of nuclear deterrence forces" and the credibility of U.S. extended deterrence commitments to intervene in local conflict is thus higher than in the past.[13]

Second, if deterrence fails, the United States can achieve its objectives through victory on the battlefield. Conventional deterrence failure therefore has the unintended effect of enhancing the credibility of subsequent U.S. deterrence threats. This was the effect of deterrence failure against Iraq and the subsequent U.S. victory in the Gulf War. Presumably, U.S. deterrence failure and subsequent military actions first against Serbia and then against al-Qaeda terrorists and their Afghan host government have had a similar effect in enhancing the credibility of the U.S. retaliatory threats.[14]

Third, if nations do not submit to U.S. demands, Washington can use conventional forces to carry out "assured destruction," which in the past would have depended on nuclear weapons. U.S. offensive conventional capabilities enable the United States to abandon the strategies of limited war and gradual escalation it unsuccessfully employed in the Vietnam War. Should deterrence fail, U.S. strategy calls for the rapid and decisive introduction of U.S. forces, facilitating victory in the shortest possible time in the initial stages of the war.[15]

Chinese leaders acknowledge that U.S. capabilities would be particularly effective against Chinese forces operating in the Taiwan theater. A senior Chinese military officer has lectured his troops that China's likely adversary in a local war would possess high-technology equipment that could neutralize China's ability to rely on manpower to defeat the enemy. A civilian analyst has noted that in a war in China's coastal region, it would be difficult for the People's Liberation Army (PLA) to take advantage of its superior numbers as it did during the Korean War, and that the adversary could "make full use of its superiority in air and naval long-range, large-scale, high-accuracy weaponry."[16] A military analyst was more direct, explaining that not only would such superior capabilities seriously restrict China's ability to seize and maintain sea control around a "large island," but would also pose a major threat to coastal political, economic, and military targets in China.[17] Experts at China's Air Force Command College have concluded that an "air-attack revolution" has occurred and that a "generation gap" exists between the high-technology air-attack capabilities of the United States and the "stagnant" air defense capabilities of less advanced countries, causing a "crisis" in air defense. Despite ongoing modernization of Chinese capabilities, fundamental PRC inferiority has not changed. In July 2005, Chinese General Zhu Chenghu observed that China has "no capability to fight a conventional war against the United States."[18]

Beijing must assume that the prospect of victory in a conflict with the United States would be close to nil and that the costs of war and defeat would be massive, even if China could defeat Taiwan and compel it to concede. Once war began, the United States could target China's large but backward navy. Even China's advanced Russian destroyers equipped with highly capable missiles would not contribute to its war-fighting capability, because they lack sufficient standoff range to challenge U.S. offensive forces. Indeed, U.S. capabilities would be even more effective in targeting Chinese surface assets at sea than they have been in targeting enemy assets in deserts, as in the 1991 Gulf War, the 2001 war in Afghanistan, and the 2003 war in Iraq.[19] War with the United States would also compel China to switch to a wartime economy, requiring reallocation of resources away from civilian infrastructure development to large-scale acquisition of outdated military hardware and would cost it access to international markets, capital, and high technology. The resulting economic dislocations would defer China's ability to achieve great power status well into the second half of the twenty-first century.[20] Most important, the combination of a military defeat over Taiwan and a domestic economic crisis would challenge the leadership's top priority—continued leadership of China by the CCP. Nationalism and economic performance, the twin pillars of CCP legitimacy, would collapse, bringing Party rule down with them.

Thus, China assumes that if the United States intervened in a mainland-Taiwan war, the costs of defeat would be catastrophic. It also assumes that the United States has the resolve to intervene in a mainland-Taiwan war and to impose such costs. Chinese civilian and military analysts understand that U.S. domestic politics has encouraged the growth in U.S. arms sales to Taiwan since the early 1990s and will constrain the administration's options during a mainland-Taiwan conflict. They also acknowledge that the March 1996 U.S. deployment of two carriers to the vicinity of Taiwan during PRC military maneuvers and missile launches was a "strong military signal" of U.S. readiness to intervene in a war over Taiwan.[21] The carrier deployment strongly coupled the U.S. commitment to defend Taiwan to the credibility of its commitments to its allies in East Asia. Since then, Chinese leaders have assumed that a war with Taiwan means a war with the United States. As one observer noted, "What many, many people realize is that the effectiveness of [U.S.] deterrence . . . must markedly exceed that of 1996, so that the likelihood of U.S. military intervention is even more notable, with a likely corresponding escalation in the deterrence dynamics."[22] Another analyst has warned that the possibility of U.S. intervention means that any Chinese actions could encounter "unexpectedly serious consequences."[23] Overall, Chinese decision-makers acknowledge that China cannot deter costly U.S. intervention in a Taiwan-mainland war.[24]

Chinese analysts also realize that U.S. forces can wage war while remaining out of range of enemy forces and can use precision-guided munitions to target leadership command-and-control centers to shorten the war and further reduce casualties, thus enhancing American resolve to use force. Chinese studies of the 1991 Gulf War concluded that high-accuracy, long-range weaponry was the decisive factor in the U.S. victory. One Chinese military analyst, summing up the impact of high technology on warfare, argued that "whoever possesses the newest knowledge and technology can thus grab the initiative in military combat and also possess the 'killer weapon' to vanquish the enemy."[25]

Beijing possesses considerable respect for U.S. resolve, but it may believe that Taiwan lacks resolve to fight a war against the mainland. Chinese leaders may calculate that a rapid barrage of missile and air attacks against Taiwan in combination with the deployment of special forces could quickly devastate Taiwan's resolve to resist, leading to political collapse and rapid Taiwan capitulation to Beijing's political demands that it acknowledge the mainland's sovereignty over Taiwan. Such a fait accompli strategy might enable Beijing to end the hostilities with a political victory before U.S. intervention, leaving Washington the unattractive option of engaging PRC forces in order to reverse Taiwan's compromise over a political issue of little consequence to U.S. security interests.[26]

But Beijing can have little confidence in the coercive capability of its missiles. Beijing may have deployed as many as 700 DF-15 missiles across from Taiwan by 2005.[27] But Chinese missiles and aircraft have only limited coercive capability. The United States dropped approximately 22,000 bombs in its wars in Yugoslavia and in Afghanistan, including over 12,000 precision-guided bombs in the latter case. Yet in both cases, U.S. missile and air assaults did not cause enough destruction to cause rapid political surrender. In 2003, the United States used cruise missiles to oust the Saddam Hussein government, but it could not weaken his army's ability to wage protracted warfare. Chinese missiles, despite significant improvement since 1995, still lack the accuracy of U.S. missiles.[28] Thus, a Chinese missile-based fait accompli strategy might wreak havoc in Taiwan, but Beijing cannot have high confidence that it would cause Taiwan to accede to even symbolic political unification. If Taiwan did not surrender, the humiliation would devastate the CCP's domestic legitimacy and significantly undermine its staying power. If Taiwan fought back and inflicted high casualties on the mainland military, the humiliation would be even greater. Should Chinese leaders then decide that they had no choice but to prosecute a long-term war for unification, the CCP would face the likelihood of U.S. intervention, military defeat, domestic humiliation, and collapse.

Moreover, China cannot be confident that it could bring a war to rapid conclusion before U.S. intervention. Chinese analysts are generally impressed with post–Cold War U.S. rapid response capabilities. The United States possesses significant forward military presence of the U.S. military in East Asia. In addition to U.S. aircraft deployed in Japan, the United States has transferred aircraft carriers and attack submarines to the Pacific theater, developed nuclear-powered guided missile submarines for East Asia, and stationed cruise missiles on Guam, as well as fighter aircraft, bombers, and unmanned reconnaissance aircraft. It is also gaining increased access to naval facilities in Japan, Singapore, and the Philippines. U.S. rapid response capabilities have thus greatly improved.[29] Finally, given the difficulty of surprise and U.S. satellite and signal intelligence capabilities, additional U.S. deployments would also likely be present at the outbreak of war.[30]

Beijing acknowledges the high cost of a U.S.-China war, respects U.S. resolve, and is necessarily uncertain of its coercive capabilities and of Taiwan's resolve. Accordingly, Chinese military officers and civilian analysts urge caution and promote reliance on "peaceful unification" though long-term development of China's economy and modernization of its military. "Smooth economic development" is China's most fundamental interest and most important national security strategy. It is also the most effective way to assure Chinese territorial integrity. As long as China's economy continues to develop, time is on its side.[31] As one Chinese analyst has argued, China has already waited 100 years to achieve unification and should be prepared to wait another 50 years.[32] In the meantime, as long as Chinese deterrence of Taiwan is effective, China can achieve peaceful unification through long-term economic and military modernization.[33]

CAPABILITIES AND CREDIBILITY: DETERRING TAIWAN

Peace in the Taiwan Strait also requires deterring a formal Taiwan declaration of independence. This task falls to China. Beijing must possess sufficient capability and credibility to impose costly retaliation against a Taiwan challenge to the status quo. Effective deterrence of a Taiwan declaration of independence by the PRC does not depend on its ability to defeat Taiwan, but rather on its ability to punish it. PRC punishment capability rests on the combination of the mainland's missile and aircraft capability and Taiwan's economic and political vulnerability to mainland use of force. China's medium-range missiles are not very accurate and possess minimal war-fighting capability. Minimal hardening of Taiwan's defense facilities would negate their pure military value.[34] Nonetheless, in combination with penetration of Taiwan air space by the Chinese air force, Chinese missiles have significant punishment capability. Overnight, Taiwan's economy would contract, and unemployment would skyrocket as its stock market plummeted and capital fled the island. In the first three months of 1996, when China massed its troops across the Strait from Taiwan and carried out military exercises nearby, the Taiwanese stock market fell by 25 percent, even though the government spent U.S.$1.6 billion to reduce the decline. Loss of confidence in the Taiwan dollar and panic buying of the U.S. dollar required the Taiwan government to intervene in capital markets.[35] Moreover, Chinese missiles are inexpensive and in close proximity to Taiwan, so that over the long term, missile-defense systems will not be able to offset Taiwan's vulnerability to PRC missiles.[36]

In addition to targeting Taiwan with its SRBMs, the mainland could also declare a blockade around the island. Although the Chinese navy and air force would lack the ability to militarily enforce a blockade against U.S. military intervention, the mere announcement of such a blockade and PRC threats of economic sanctions against any of its trading partners that continued to trade with Taiwan would not only dramatically curtail commercial shipping to Taiwan but also cut off most of Taiwan's remaining foreign trade.

Finally, the mainland could directly retaliate against Taiwan's economic interests. As Taiwan has increased its economic involvement in the mainland economy, it has been losing its economic autonomy and ceding leverage over its continued prosperity to the mainland. In 2001, the combined Chinese–Hong Kong market surpassed the U.S. market as Taiwan's most important export market. In 2002 and in 2003, Taiwan's exports to the mainland increased by more than 25 percent, while Taiwan's exports to the United States declined. And in 2003, more than 35 percent of Taiwan's exports went to the China–Hong Kong market, while Chinese exports to Taiwan amounted to only 6.4 percent of total Chinese exports.[37] Moreover, in 2002, the mainland became the leading production center of overseas Taiwan investors. Nearly 55 percent of Taiwan overseas investment is located on the mainland and Taiwan's largest corporations, including its high-technology manufacturers, have invested in the mainland. These investment trends create an additional source of PRC leverage over Taiwan's economy.[38]

Cross-Strait economic trends are creating societal ties that the mainland can use for political purposes. More than one million Taiwanese now have residences on the mainland, where they have established separate Taiwan communities, complete with elementary schools. More than 500,000 Taiwanese live in the Shanghai area alone.[39] More than 30,000 Taiwan companies have manufacturing facilities there. In 2002, a Taiwan bank opened its first branch office in China, Chinese and Taiwanese state-owned energy corporations developed a joint venture for oil exploration, and Chinese firms began recruiting Taiwan financial and technology experts.[40] Should Taiwan declare independence, the mainland could retaliate by curtailing trade, freezing investments, and threatening the livelihood of citizens of Taiwan living in China.

Chinese military and economic retaliation against a Taiwan declaration of independence and the ensuing international and domestic crisis would inevitably cause political instability on Taiwan. In a mainland-Taiwan war, not only would Taiwan's economy suffer, but the survival of Taiwan's democratic political system would be in jeopardy. Thus, the cost to Taiwan of mainland retaliation against a declaration of independence would be the loss of its economic prosperity and of its democracy.

The mainland's threat to retaliate against a declaration of independence is credible. As noted above, the result of China's fifty-year commitment to unification is that the political legitimacy and survival of the Chinese leadership is attached to its commitment to resist Taiwan independence. As one Chinese analyst argues, "no Chinese politician, strategist, or anyone else will dare to abandon the objective of making Taiwan return and the unification of the motherland."[41] Failure to respond to a declaration of independence would also challenge China's international reputation to defend other vital interests, affecting border security and independence movements around its periphery. But the mainland also has developed a reputation for resolve regarding the Taiwan issue. Despite the risk of U.S. intervention and of a U.S.-China crisis, in March 1996, the PLA launched DF-15 missiles into coastal waters within the vicinity of Kaohsiung, Taiwan's major port city, to underscore its will to oppose Taiwan independence and thus reverse the trend in U.S. policy toward Taiwan and Lee Teng-hui's independence policy. Senior Taiwan political and military officials concur that a declaration of independence would lead to war with the mainland.[42]

The deterrent effect of mainland capabilities and credibility is reflected in Taiwan's domestic politics. Since 1997, in public opinion surveys commissioned by the Taiwan government, support for an immediate declaration of Taiwan independence has declined since the high of 7.4 percent in mid 1998. The consistent low level of support for immediate independence reflects widespread understanding on Taiwan that mainland retaliation would be both costly and likely. Indeed, Taiwan voters have routinely signaled their opposition to pro-independence politicians. Since Taiwan's first competitive election in 1989, on all but one occasion, the pro-independence party has not won a majority of the votes in either presidential or legislative elections. The sole exception was the 2004 presidential election, in which Chen Shui-bian won 50.02 percent of the vote in an outcome heavily influenced by an alleged attempt to assassinate him the day before the election. Prior to the alleged assassination attempt, almost all public opinion polls had predicted defeat for Chen. Most recently, the inability of the Democratic Progressive Party (DPP) to win a majority of seats in the Legislative Yuan in the December 2004 election and its losses in the December 2005 city and county government elections reflected in great part voters' dissatisfaction with his mainland policy.[43] Since then, visits to the mainland and the strong statements in opposition to Taiwan independence by opposition party leaders have been widely supported by the electorate.

Deterrence on the Korean Peninsula

As with the Taiwan Strait, peace on the Korean peninsula requires mutual deterrence. Deterring North Korea depends on U.S. possession of the capabilities and credibility necessary to persuade Pyongyang that the expected cost of U.S. intervention in a north-south war would be greater than the benefits of using force for unification. Deterrence of the United States and South Korea from using force to eliminate the Pyongyang government or its nuclear weapons capability requires that the expected cost of North Korean retaliation be high enough to persuade them to accept the status quo.

CAPABILITIES AND CREDIBILITY: DETERRING NORTH KOREA

North Korean commentary does not use the language of deterrence to discuss contemporary military trends. Nor does North Korea publish detailed analyses of contemporary military affairs or of the likely course of a war on the Korean peninsula. Nonetheless, North Korea's assessment of the U.S. military makes it clear that North Koreans share Chinese respect for U.S. ability to intervene in post–Cold War regional conflicts.

North Korean commentators concur with Chinese analysts that the United States faces no opponent in the Third World that can limit its use of force, its "tyranny and military hegemony." This is a "very dangerous development," Song Mu-kyong asserts, because it enables the United States to use force "as it sees fit" and to carry out "armed intervention at any time."[44] Pyongyang further understands that the source of U.S. post–Cold War supremacy is its development of high-technology weaponry. North Korean analysts observe that modern warfare is "three-dimensional" and that it relies on long-range weaponry, such as missiles, to carry out offensive operations. These analysts point to such advances as stealth air and naval technologies, including radar-elusive vessels equipped with long-range missiles, and laser weaponry as reflecting Washington's quest for domination.[45]

Moreover, North Korea understands that the forward military presence of the United States enables it to "carry out armed intervention at any time," and that since the end of the Cold War, the United States has been expanding its deployment in East Asia. In the aftermath of the U.S. war against the Taliban, North Korean commentaries observed that the United States is trying to consolidate its supremacy in East Asia to better prepare to cope with a Korean "contingency."[46]

Pyongyang also acknowledges the security consequences of North Korea's extreme technological backwardness. An editorial in the Korean Workers' Party newspaper put it bluntly. "Now is the age of science and technology. We cannot even take a step forward." Thus, whether North Korea can "possess up-to-date science and technology . . . in a short period of time is a serious question decisive to the future of the nation."[47] Key to North Korea's interest in science and technology is its preoccupation with information technologies. "Everything depends on the ideological point of view. In the new century, we cannot do anything at all without the knowledge of information technology. Nor can we remain loyal to the party and leader."[48] Another author observed, "We are living in a century where the national strength of each country is guaranteed by science and technology, which is developing at an unimaginably rapid rate."[49] Thus, "how to develop military science and technology is a crucial issue to national defense." Because a "bloody competition is taking place in the science and technology sector world wide . . . , it is impossible to have one's own strong military capability without improved science and technology."[50] Given the gravity of North Korea's strategic circumstances, it is "incumbent upon the North Korean revolutionary party and people to build up their own military force more firmly than ever before." Thus, they should focus on developing science and technology to help arm the military with "sophisticated weapons and defend the sovereignty of their country."[51]

The leadership's recognition of North Korean technological inferiority has led to fundamental changes in Pyongyang's approach to ideology, economic development, and foreign trade. Whereas in the past, North Korea's economic isolation reflected its ideological commitment to self-reliance, today it also reflects the U.S. blockade of science and technology. North Koreans must "smash" this blockade, Kim Chong-son asserts, or they will not be able to "free themselves from backwardness even after 100 years."[52] Similarly, whereas the doctrine of self-reliance once implied economic autarchy, Pyongyang now sees self-reliance as an objective requiring development of high-technology capabilities through imports from advanced economies. In the contemporary era, where there is no science and technology, "there is no self reliance." To build a strong economy "on the principle of self-reliance by no means signifies doing economic construction with the door closed up." Rather, only by "introducing" modern science and technology "positively" can self-reliance be strengthened.[53] From their observation of the experience of other developing countries, North Korean commentators have learned that developing countries "import the relevant technology and make great efforts on understanding, absorbing, and developing the technology."[54] These changes explain North Korea's recent introduction of early Chinese-style economic reforms, including limited use of the market and creation of special economic zones for foreign investment.[55]

North Korea can hold little hope of withstanding an encounter with U.S. forces. Even should Pyongyang's ground forces be able to occupy much of South Korea, U.S. air and naval power would be able to inflict devastating assaults on the primitive and undernourished North Korean army, so that North Korea's ability to hold South Korean territory is doubtful. Moreover, its air force, missiles, and artillery could not provide assistance to its ground forces, because U.S. air and naval platforms could target North Korean assets while remaining out of range of its air defense systems. The North Korean military might be able to impose significant costs on South Korea, but the United States would retain the military capabilities to inflict rapid defeat on the North Korean military and high costs on its economic system.

Moreover, paralleling the Chinese situation, North Korean military defeat would not only frustrate Pyongyang's effort to unify the peninsula under communism but would lead to the fall of the North's Korean Workers' Party and to Korean unification under southern rule. In North Korea's case, the end of Party rule would result not only from loss of legitimacy and the economic dislocations following military defeat, but also from likely U.S. and South Korean determination to achieve an unnegotiated end to the war based on unconditional surrender.

North Korea also respects the credibility of U.S. retaliatory threats. First, Pyongyang must contend with Washington's fifty-year security commitment to the defense of South Korea. This commitment is reflected in U.S. participation in the Korean War, the subsequent and ongoing U.S. military presence in South Korea, and the United States–Republic of Korea Mutual Defense Treaty. Because none of these signals of commitment exist in the U.S.-Taiwan relationship, North Korea's assessment of U.S. resolve to defend South Korea is likely much greater than China's assessment of U.S. resolve to defend Taiwan.

Second, the U.S. reputation for resolve is bolstered by North Korea's evaluation of U.S. willingness to use force in the post–Cold War era. According to North Korean commentary, American use of force to overthrow the Taliban government was simply the latest post–Cold War example of the U.S. effort to rid the world of countries that resist its will. Moreover, each U.S. victory fuels its ambition and its readiness to wage war. After the war in Afghanistan, Washington was "flush with victory" and had set its sights on the "axis of evil."[56] The "danger of new war is growing all the more by the day," the North Korean paper *Nodong Sinmun* commented in 2002.[57] North Korean commentary warns that North Korea is prepared to defend itself and, unlike the Taliban, will retaliate with "unimaginable fire of punishment."[58] Changes in U.S. defense doctrine indicating readiness to use nuclear weapons against states developing weapons of mass destruction suggest even greater U.S. resolve. Pyongyang argued that Asia was the most contentious region in the world, and that the Korean peninsula was the "dangerous ignition point for nuclear war in Asia." North Korea was the "first target of the U.S. nuclear attack plan," according to Kim Chong-son.[59]

Thus, both North Korea and China believe the United States has the commitment and capabilities necessary to make credible its retaliatory threats. But whereas in the Taiwan theater, Beijing understands that the United States can rely on its long-range missiles and advanced aircraft to limit its casualties, North Korea's ability to use its ground forces to inflict significant casualties on the United States may undermine the credibility of the American commitment to defend South Korea. This difference between the two theaters is not trivial. Nonetheless, another difference between the two regions is also significant. Whereas in the Taiwan theater, U.S. deterrent forces remain outside the theater, thus suggesting the possibility of mainland-Taiwan war that does not involve the United States, in the Korea theater, U.S. troops are at the front line, so that U.S. credibility to defend South Korea is enhanced by the presumed U.S. resolve to retaliate against an attack on its own forces. U.S. forces play the role of a "trip wire." In addition, the large U.S. civilian presence in Seoul and elsewhere in South Korea means that Pyongyang cannot avoid inflicting significant collateral damage on U.S. citizens.

Complementing the U.S. retaliatory capabilities and resolve is South Korea's own development of a retaliatory capability. Since the 1990s, Seoul has acquired over 100 U.S.-made advanced 300-kilometer-range ground-to-ground guided missiles and 29 launchers. Since then, it has begun the acquisition of U.S. joint direct attack munitions (JDAMs), which the United States used in Afghanistan in 2001 and has used in Iraq since 2003.[60] The deployment of these missiles will give South Korea an independent and survivable retaliatory capability that can reach over a North Korean invasion force to target Pyongyang's command and control facilities and its defense facilities.

Thus, in the early twenty-first century, American and also South Korean credibility to use force in defense against a North Korean attack is greater than ever before. The result for North Korea is thus similar to that for China—the combination of high costs plus high credibility of retaliatory threats creates a high expected cost for the use of force. Thus, just as Beijing no longer advocates the "liberation" of Taiwan, but now stresses peaceful unification, Pyongyang's commentary no longer advocates the forceful removal of the U.S. presence from the peninsula and the "liberation" of South Korea, but stresses deterrence of U.S. use of force and defense against the unification of Korea by the U.S. military. As with China's attitude toward Taiwan, North Korea has waited over fifty years to "liberate" South Korea and is prepared to wait another fifty years.

CAPABILITIES AND CREDIBILITY: DETERRING
SOUTH KOREA AND THE UNITED STATES

Deterring war on the Korean peninsula also requires that the United States and South Korea be deterred from using force against North Korea. The effectiveness of North Korea's deterrence posture, based upon its assured destruction retaliatory capability, is evident from U.S. assessments of Pyongyang's capabilities and resolve, from its assessment of the risk of war, and from its caution in crisis situations.

North Korean capabilities make the cost of war prohibitively high for both South Korea and the United States, and no strategy, including a massive surprise attack, can create sufficient confidence that this cost can be reduced to an acceptable level. Pyongyang's only plausible strategy to defend against an invasion is to go on the offensive, and just as South Korea has deployed the bulk of its forces between the demilitarized zone and Seoul (which is some 30 miles from the DMZ), North Korea has deployed most of its forces—over 700,000 soldiers and two thousand tanks—south of its capital (which is 85 miles from the border). It lacks both the infrastructure to enable dispersed forces to coordinate a rapid response against a focused attack and the ability to turn back an attack from deep within its territory. As General James R. Clapper, former deputy director of the U.S. Defense Intelligence Agency, observed, North Koreans "think that the best defense is a good offense."[61]

Complementing Pyongyang's conventional defense strategy is its conventional and WMD-based deterrent capability. Its forward deployment of its conventional forces deters invasion by threatening to make a ground attack on North Korea very costly. Between Pyongyang and the demilitarized zone, North Korea has deployed approximately 8,000 artillery systems, including 500 long-range systems, armed with one million tons of ammunition. The U.S. Department of Defense estimates that this artillery could sustain a barrage on South Korea of up to 500,000 rounds an hour for several hours. Augmenting North Korea's conventional deterrent is its deployment of chemical munitions in its artillery systems. Beginning in the late 1980s, as North Korea experienced increasing military inferiority vis-à-vis South Korea, it developed chemical weapons. By the late 1990s, Pyongyang had stockpiled up to 5,000 metric tons of chemical agents. Approximately 10 percent of its forward-deployed artillery shells are deployed with chemical weapons. North Korea is also assumed to have the ability to produce biological weapons.[62]

Deployed at the front lines, North Korea's WMD capability is a destructive trip wire that poses a credible "use it or lose it" retaliatory threat of widespread civilian and military casualties in South Korea, even should North Korea be unable to avoid rapid political collapse after a U.S. retaliatory attack. Thus, in 1994 Washington could not discount Pyongyang's threat to turn Seoul into a "sea of fire" if United States carried out a preventive strike against North Korea's nuclear facilities. The U.S. Department of Defense estimated that in the first ninety days of an ensuing war, there would be over 50,000 U.S. casualties and nearly 500,000 South Korean casualties.[63]

North Korea's nuclear program and its ballistic missile program possess a similar deterrent threat. Pyongyang began its nuclear weapons program in the late 1980s, just as the collapse of Soviet power undermined the balance of power on the peninsula and Moscow was normalizing relations with Seoul.[64] By 1994, North Korea had extracted sufficient enriched uranium to produce two nuclear bombs. In 2005, U.S. officials reported that it had extracted sufficient plutonium to make six nuclear bombs.[65] In June 2003, as U.S.–North Korean tension escalated, Pyongyang declared that it was actively developing a nuclear deterrent to counter U.S. aggression. In August, it said that it planned to declare itself a nuclear power, and that it was prepared to carry out a nuclear test.[66] Although North Korea has yet to conduct a nuclear test, and there is uncertainty regarding North Korean possession of a delivery vehicle, the United States cannot assume that war on the Korean peninsula will not escalate to North Korean use of nuclear weapons.

North Korea's deterrent capability is enhanced by the credibility of its retaliatory threat. Pyongyang's past willingness to use terrorism, special operations, and low-level force against the South Korean leadership reflects its willingness to create crises and risk war even in the absence of threats to regime survival. Its style of crisis diplomacy, including its frequent readiness to heighten tension and threaten war, further contributes to its reputation for recklessness.[67] Indeed, mirroring North Korea's perception of the resolve in U.S. defense policy to carry out a preemptive strike, the United States and South Korea perceive in North Korean behavior the resolve necessary to use force for unification, much less in response to an attack. As a "rogue state" and a member of the "axis of evil," North Korea is assumed to have a ready inclination to use force.[68]

Finally, China's interest in maintaining secure borders contributes to deterrence of U.S. use of force. One of the "lessons of history" from the Korean War is that a U.S. troop presence near Chinese borders will provoke Chinese intervention and a very costly war for the United States.[69] This makes the risk of war with North Korea even more dangerous for the United States, and deterrence thus more reliable.

Stable and Unstable Deterrence

Effective deterrence exists both in the Taiwan Strait and on the Korean peninsula, but whereas it is stable in the former case, in the latter, it is unstable. The difference lies in the distinct geographic deployments of the protagonists and the implications for security dilemma dynamics.

Instability in deterrence is characterized by a propensity for unintended crisis escalation and for unintended war. This occurs when a status-quo state is vulnerable to a debilitating first strike, so that it experiences pressure to prepare for war rather than risk being caught unprepared. Stable deterrence, on the other hand, reflects confidence on the part of both states that the outcome of a war would not be determined by a surprise attack. In these circumstances, each of them can observe its counterpart's actions with greater patience, rather than prepare for possible imminent attack. Thus, crises are slower to develop and unintended war less likely. Mutual deterrence can be effective yet unstable. Two states may be deterred from using force by their opponent's retaliatory threat, but if each state's deterrent posture includes first-strike capabilities, each may nonetheless respond to the other's efforts at deterrence with preparations for war, thus contributing to a crisis spiral.

In the U.S.-China dyad in the Taiwan Strait, there is relatively minimal security dilemma pressure for unintended crisis escalation. The United States has little apprehension that a surprise PRC attack on U.S. naval forces would determine the outcome of the war, for China lacks the capability to launch an attack that would deny the United States time to protect sufficient forces to maintain a powerful retaliatory capability. Although China has increasingly been relying on Russian submarines to enable it to threaten U.S. surface ships and to develop an access-denial capability, this capability does not allow a decisive first-strike capability. The security of the U.S. surface fleet reflects China's intrinsic inability as a land power to contend with the naval forces of an advanced maritime power. It also reflects its backward economy and technology. Given U.S. information warfare dominance and China's limited targeting ability, U.S. surface vessels will be relatively secure from Chinese capabilities for many years. Thus, Chinese capabilities that deter Taiwan independence do not have a first-strike capability against U.S. forces.

Moreover, China's development of its naval power projection capability will be limited by enduring budget constraints reflecting its political geography. Whereas the United States can continue to prioritize naval spending for the indefinite future, Chinese defense policy will have to hedge against the emergence of adversaries along its land border, including the inevitable revival of Russian power in Central Asia.[70] The limits to Chinese naval spending and the considerable head start the United States possesses in both quantity and quality in the U.S.-China naval balance ensure long-term U.S. maritime superiority and, thus, continued stable deterrence in the Taiwan Strait.

The security of U.S. deployments in East Asia against a surprise Chinese attack enables the United States to respond to Chinese mobilization of deterrent capabilities that also allow for a coercive fait accompli strike against Taiwan without contributing to crisis escalation. U.S. aircraft based on Okinawa can come to Taiwan's defense without extensive defensive preparations suggesting offensive planning. The United States can also deploy its power-projection naval forces to the region to "observe" Chinese actions without placing these forces on high alert, thus contributing to conflict control.

Just as U.S. naval forces are secure from a surprise Chinese attack, China is secure from a surprise U.S. attack. Although the United States possesses capabilities that can inflict considerable costs on China, Chinese leaders do not fear that a surprise attack will determine either the outcome of war or the fate of the regime. China's mere size offers it security from air attack. The United States significantly depleted its stockpile of cruise missiles in its war in Kosovo, but the impact on Serbian will or war-fighting capability was minimal.[71] China's ability to absorb such an attack is far greater. Moreover, China's DF-15 missile launchers are mobile, so that they can be protected from attack, preserving China's ability to retaliate against a Taiwan declaration of independence.[72] Defeating China requires engaging it on the mainland. But as the U.S. experience in both the Korean and Vietnam wars revealed, the United States possesses minimal ability to project war-winning power onto the East Asian mainland.

The security of U.S. and Chinese capabilities explains each side's composure during the 1996 March confrontation in the Taiwan Strait. China launched DF-15s in the vicinity of Taiwan, and the United States responded by deploying two aircraft carriers within 200 miles of the Chinese coast. Nevertheless, Secretary of Defense Perry confidently observed that a Chinese attack on Taiwan would be " a dumb thing." China, he said, did "not have the capability" to invade Taiwan. Although Perry believed that China had the ability to "harass" Taiwan, he observed that "it does not make any sense. . . . I do not expect China to be attacking Taiwan."[73] Perry told Vice Foreign Minister Liu Huaqiu that Chinese missile firings were a "threat to American interests" and that the United States "had more than enough military capability to protect its vital national security interests in the region."[74] Although Chinese forces could conceivably have been used against U.S. maritime forces, U.S. policymakers did not expect war and did not believe that there was a crisis.

China was equally composed. Although the United States deployed two aircraft carriers to the vicinity of Taiwan and possessed considerable forward-presence air power on Okinawa, China did not perceive the U.S. response to its political use of force as posing an imminent threat of a decisive first strike. Hence, it did not heighten the readiness of Chinese forces in response to U.S. deployments. To the extent that Beijing may have shortened its military show of force, it responded to the political costs of its confrontation with the United States, not the risk of war.[75]

Mutual deterrence in the Taiwan Strait is effective and stable. But on the Korean peninsula, there is unstable mutual deterrence. The likelihood of crisis escalation and unintended war is greater, reflecting each side's vulnerability to a surprise attack and the likelihood that a surprise attack could determine the outcome of the war.

In contrast to the character of the Chinese deterrent forces in the Taiwan Strait, North Korean and U.S. capabilities that deter use of force and defend against an invasion also possess offensive, first-strike capabilities. Both countries have deployed land-based forces and weapons systems to serve as a trip-wire deterrent, yet trip wires do not only contribute to deterrence. Trip-wire deployments close to a border also create a first-strike capability that contributes to an adversary's fear of attack. The resulting security dilemma dynamics are thus a critical factor in threat perception on both sides of the demilitarized zone.

North Korea's forward-deployed ground forces and tanks pose the threat of a blitz warfare strategy. According to retired General John Tilelli, the former commander of U.S. forces in South Korea, the "tyranny of proximity" of Pyongyang's massive forward deployment of artillery systems and chemical weapons enables North Korea to carry out destructive shelling of both U.S. and South Korean forces and the civilian population in Seoul.[76] Should North Korea launch a surprise massive first strike, there would be extraordinarily high casualties among both the military and civilian populations. Moreover, the ensuing associated panic and widespread destruction in South Korea could also make an effective retaliatory attack difficult. U.S. and South Korean infantry and land-based aircraft might be immobilized, limiting the initial U.S. reprisal to shelling from naval-based capabilities.[77]

North Korea experiences similar pressures for rapid mobilization. The overwhelming military superiority of the United States, including its long-range high-accuracy attack weaponry, suggests a capability to launch preemptive strikes against command and control centers. A surprise U.S. attack might not only immobilize the North Korean military command but also cause the collapse of the North Korean communist leadership. The Bush administration's doctrine of preemptive war further contributes to North Korean fear of a surprise attack.

In these strategic circumstances, there is intense pressure for crisis escalation on both sides of the border. General Leon J. LaPorte, commander of U.S. forces in South Korea, explained that due to the "proximity and lethality" of North Korean capabilities, U.S. forces "must be 'ready to be able to fight tonight.'"[78] In these insecure circumstances, North Korean military moves designed to signal deterrent credibility will be readily seen by the United States as potentially dangerous preparations for a first strike, thus eliciting corresponding military mobilization and spiraling crisis dynamics. During the June 1994 crisis, as the United States prepared to mobilize its forces for a possible strike against North Korea's nuclear facilities, the Clinton administration feared that its own military preparations might elicit a North Korean preemptive strike, even though the United States had not yet decided to use force. Such fears were warranted—North Korea had begun to mobilize its forces just as the United States was evaluating its deployment options. Former President Jimmy Carter's diplomatic intervention during his visit to Pyongyang on 16 June 1994 did not forestall an imminent U.S. attack, but it did defuse a developing crisis that might well have quickly escalated into unintended war.[79] Thus, in 1994, the mere preparation for deployment of U.S. forces had elicited heightened tension and a dangerous U.S.–North Korean crisis in a way that China's actual military deployments and missile and naval exercises in the Taiwan Strait in 1996 had not.

The 2003 Korean crisis reflected similar elements of crisis instability. Whereas the Clinton administration had considered positioning forces near North Korea to prepare to attack North Korean facilities, in 2003, the Bush administration actually deployed U.S. forces near North Korea to try to coerce Pyongyang to abandon its nuclear weapons program. In February, it positioned equipment for launching precision-guided missiles near North Korea and placed B-1 and B-52 bombers on alert for deployment to Guam. In March, it deployed these bombers to Guam, immediately following President Bush's warning that he was prepared to use force to end North Korea's nuclear program. In addition, U.S. and South Korean forces carried out large-scale war games, using F-117 Stealth fighters for the first time in seven years. Following the exercises, these fighters remained deployed in South Korea. During the exercises, U.S. forces also increased their aerial and naval reconnaissance of North Korea. According to North Korean sources, in March, the United States carried out more than 220 espionage flights against North Korea. In the aftermath of the initial phase of the air war in Iraq, Washington transferred three aircraft carriers from the Iraq theater to the Pacific theater, so that it had altogether four carriers deployed within range of the Korean peninsula in April 2003. Two of the carriers returned to the United States, but two remained in the region within range of North Korea.[80] Then, in May, Washington announced that it would augment its capabilities on the Korean peninsula by immediately deploying an advanced Stryker Brigade Combat Team to South Korea, facilitating rapid and flexible application of U.S. medium and heavy weaponry. Washington also announced that it would deploy advanced Apache military helicopters and PAC-3 missiles in Korea.[81]

The United States accompanied its increased military deployments with signals that it was prepared to initiate use of force against North Korea. In September 2002, the Bush administration released its report on U.S. national security, which explicitly stated that preemption was an effective response to threats of nuclear proliferation.[82] Following U.S. use of force against Iraq in March 2003, North Korea seemed the likely next target of U.S. preemptive use of force. In February, President Bush repeatedly warned North Korea that "all military options were open" to deal with its nuclear program. In March, he warned that if U.S. efforts "don't work diplomatically, they'll have to work militarily." Other U.S. officials warned that North Korea should learn a lesson from U.S. use of force against Iraq.[83] In May, U.S. Defense Department officials explained that the United States was deploying its forces in Northeast Asia to be able to carry out an attack on the North Korean leadership similar to the attack that it had just launched against the Iraqi leadership.[84]

In this context, both U.S. and North Korean forces prepared to be attacked. U.S. forces were at the "highest stage of readiness." According to a U.S. defense official, there was no way for them "to be any more prepared." Echoing General LaPorte's remark in 2002, General George Coggins, the operations officer for U.S. forces in South Korea, reported that U.S. soldiers were "ready to fight tonight if we have to."[85] North Korea was similarly prepared for war. As the United States made the final preparations for war against Iraq, North Korean president Kim Jong Il went into seclusion for fifty days near the Chinese border, apparently fearing that he might be the target of a U.S. attack. U.S. forces prepared to interdict North Korean vessels suspected of carrying components of weapons of mass destruction, and Pyongyang warned that its forces were at "full combat readiness." Pyongyang declared that it was "closely watching" U.S. preparations "with a high degree of vigilance."[86]

U.S. concern for the North Korean "tyranny of proximity" and North Korean fear of U.S. high-technology capabilities and alleged readiness to use force combined to cause mutual fear of a first strike. Each side feared that a first strike would have devastating consequences, so that each side was on heightened alert and prepared to go to war at any time. Thus, relatively minor incidents could have easily been interpreted as the first step in an attack and escalated to all-out war. In February 2003, North Korea fired an anti-ship missile into the sea between the Korean peninsula and Japan, the first such test in three years. In February, too, its military aircraft entered South Korean airspace for the first time in twenty years. In March, North Korean military aircraft intercepted a U.S. reconnaissance plane. The North Korean aircraft came within fifty feet of the U.S. plane and tailed it for over twenty minutes. Then, in July, South Korean and North Korean forces exchanged machine-gun fire over the demilitarized zone.[87]

The instability of the Korean peninsula is underscored by prior cases in which fear of first strikes elicited preparation for war. According to the North Korean defector Hwang Jang Yap, during three prior U.S.–North Korean incidents, the north was on the brink of war. It was in crisis mode during the 1968 *Pueblo* incident, involving North Korean capture of a U.S. intelligence collection ship, the 1969 EC-12 incident, and the 1976 Panmunjom incident, involving the murder of two U.S. military officers. In each case, Pyongyang placed its troops on high alert and transferred civilian populations in preparation for a war.[88] Similarly, according to General Clapper, the annual U.S.–South Korea Team Spirit military exercise causes heightened threat perception in Pyongyang, because the North Korean leadership cannot be sure that the exercises are not a prelude to a devastating first strike.[89] The high-technology conventional superiority of the United States and its preemptive strategy have increased the threat to Pyongyang of attack and thus further intensified the dilemma of security instability.[90] The United States and South Korea are similarly predisposed to prepare for attack during military incidents with North Korea. In addition to fearing a North Korean surprise attack during the 1994 crisis, during the 1976 Panmunjom incident, Washington heightened the alert status of U.S. military forces and deployed military aircraft to South Korea from Idaho.[91]

The potential for crisis escalation is intrinsic to the strategic structure of the opposing forces on the Korean peninsula. The contrast with the Taiwan theater is clear. Despite annual and increasingly larger and more sophisticated PRC military exercises in the Taiwan Strait since 1996, there has not been corresponding tension in U.S.-China relations. Since the 1950s, there has not been any tension in the Taiwan Strait similar to the repeated crises on the Korean peninsula.

The deterrence relationship between North Korea and the United States is similar to other crisis-prone relationships. The frequencies of crises in Europe during the Cold War reflected, in part, American concern that a Soviet conventional first strike might quickly overwhelm NATO forces, leading to heavy allied casualties and the difficult U.S. choice between either using nuclear weapons or accepting defeat. The onset of World War I reflected similar escalation dynamics. General concern throughout Europe that a first strike could decisively determine the outcome of a war contributed to rapid mobilization, crisis escalation, and war.[92]

Nonetheless, there is a critical distinction between Europe before World War I and the contemporary Korean peninsula. Crisis escalation in 1914 reflected Austrian and German fear of a Russian offensive. German support for Austria required Berlin to mobilize for war in response to Russian mobilization for war against Austria. Alliance dynamics combined with security dilemma dynamics to contribute to unintended war. On the Korean peninsula, although China and North Korea are allies, they do not share the same security dilemma concerns regarding U.S. capabilities. Whereas U.S. deterrent and defensive deployments threaten North Korea with first-strike capabilities, thus requiring Pyongyang to mobilize rapidly during periods of heightened tension, U.S. deployments do not pose a similar threat to China.

The moderate security dilemma in U.S.-China relations on the Korean peninsula has two important and positive implications for crisis escalation and unintended war. First, Chinese leaders can observe U.S. preparations for war against North Korea without carrying out a corresponding mobilization of China's own ground forces. Given China's overwhelming numerical superiority in ground forces, even should the United States escalate the war to China's borders, or even into Chinese territory, Beijing can be confident that it can repel the attack and defeat U.S. forces on the Korean peninsula.[93] Such confidence explains Chinese patience before it mobilized its forces and then engaged U.S. troops following U.S. entry into the Korean War in 1950.[94] Similarly, in 1994, despite the crisis in U.S.–North Korean relations, although China warned the United States not to attack North Korean nuclear sites, there is no evidence that China prepared its forces for war. And during the 1976 Panmunjon incident, the Nixon administration was not concerned about possible Chinese or Soviet intervention should the United States retaliate militarily against the killing of the two U.S. officers.[95] Thus, a crisis on the Korean peninsula can be contained within U.S.–North Korean relations, reducing the potential for a great power war. In this respect, the implications of U.S. mobilization for deterrence on the Korean peninsula for China is similar to the impact of Chinese mobilization for deterrence in the Taiwan Strait for the United States. In these two scenarios, the third-party great power can observe its potential great power adversary prepare for war without contributing to a spiral crisis.

Second, because China can exercise restraint during a U.S.–North Korea crisis, North Korean leaders cannot be confident that they will have Chinese support in a war with the United States, or that Chinese mobilization might deter a U.S. offensive. Thus, Pyongyang has to exercise greater caution and diplomatic flexibility in a crisis than, for example, Austria prior to World War I, which drew support for its diplomatic intransigence vis-à-vis Serbia and Russia from German mobilization for war against Russia.

Conclusions

There is effective mutual deterrence in both the Taiwan and Korean theaters. No country values revising the status quo higher than the expected cost of use of force. Nonetheless, because of very different deployment patterns and geographies, the security dilemma dynamics in the two theaters are very different. In the Taiwan Strait, the United States can rely on offshore platforms that minimize U.S. vulnerability to a first strike from Chinese forces. In contrast, although North Korea cannot rival China as a military power, its conventional capabilities and its chemical weapons capability present a far greater offensive threat to the United States than Chinese capabilities. This is because defense of South Korea has required U.S. ground force deployments close to the North Korean border. Whereas the United States is relatively secure in its confrontation in the Taiwan Strait with China, the world's second most powerful country, without the protection of water, the United States is vulnerable to a first strike from North Korea, one of the world's poorest and most backward countries.[96]

These distinct dynamics create very different prospects for conflict management. In the Taiwan Strait, there may well be future confrontations similar to those in 1996, because China may once again use its military in response to developments in Taiwan's mainland policy or in U.S.-Taiwan relations, and the United States may respond with its own political use of force. But, as in the past, there is minimal likelihood that such confrontations will escalate into a true great power crisis. Stable mutual deterrence reduces pressures for both unwanted escalation and unintended war.

In addition, the peripheral role of U.S.-Taiwan relations in U.S. deterrence of Chinese use of force allows the United States to manage relations with Taiwan with relatively minimal attention to the implications for stability. Thus both the Clinton and George W. Bush administrations could criticize Taiwan's moves toward independence without undermining U.S. deterrence of Chinese use of force. In this respect, the U.S. relationship with Taiwan in cross-Strait deterrence is similar to China's relationship with North Korea in deterrence on the Korean peninsula, with similar policy consequences. Chinese confidence in U.S. respect for China's threat to retaliate against U.S. troops in Korea has enabled China to manage potentially destabilizing North Korean policy without undermining its deterrence of U.S. use of force. Thus, Beijing has allowed relations with Pyongyang to deteriorate as it has cooperated with the United States to curtail North Korea's nuclear program, improved relations with Seoul, and pressured North Korean leaders to reform their economic system.

Moreover, China's confidence in its deterrent capability allows it to discount the importance of U.S. defense ties with Taiwan. In the past, China worried that U.S. arms sales to Taiwan or improved U.S.-Taiwan diplomatic relations might encourage Taiwan independence by suggesting that the United States would defend Taiwan against mainland retaliation. But the combination of mainland missiles and Taiwan's economic vulnerability has increasingly undermined the value to Taiwan of the U.S.-Taiwan defense relationship. For all its power, the United States can defend Taiwan against neither missiles nor economic sanctions. Thus, many Chinese foreign policy analysts now argue that effective Chinese deterrence of Taiwan independence through credible and assured destruction threats means that "time is on China's side," and Chinese leaders can more easily tolerate provocative U.S. policies with regard to Taiwan.[97]

In contrast to the constructive trends in the Taiwan theater, the Korean peninsula is likely to remain far more dangerous than the Taiwan Strait, despite efforts at conflict management. If the Taiwan issue is the world's most likely source of a great power war, the Korean peninsula is and will remain the world's most likely source of major war.[98]

In contrast to the Taiwan Strait, developing policy to promote greater stability on the Korean peninsula is inherently difficult. The tendency of states to focus on capabilities rather than on intentions and the massive deployments on both sides of the demilitarized zone mean that the United States and South Korea and North Korea will all experience intense pressure to make policy based on worst-case assumptions. As Deputy Director of the Central Intelligence Agency John McLaughlin observed, it might be "foolish" for North Korea to use force, but it also "would be foolish to make that assumption. . . . We can ill-afford to ignore capabilities."[99] North Korean leaders would agree—U.S. capabilities require preparation for war.

In this context, it is likely that confidence-building measures that focus on intentions, such as nonaggression agreements and normalization of relations, will be rejected by both the United States and North Korea; the risks of being seduced by false promises are extraordinarily high. Rather than focus on intentions, management of the security dilemma on the Korean peninsula must focus on the capability-induced instability there. Fear of surprise attack and corresponding pressure for crisis escalation can be reduced by measures such as advance notice of military exercises, holding them far from border regions, and exchanging observers of exercises. Such measures will require persistent U.S. efforts at engagement of the North Korean leadership.[100] There is little risk that such efforts will signal lack of U.S. resolve, and they might well reduce the high cost of unintended war.

Notes

1. Ashton B. Carter and William J. Perry, *Preventive Defense: A New Security Strategy for America* (Washington, D.C.: Brookings Institution Press, 1999), chs. 3 and 4.

2. Thomas C. Schelling, *The Strategy of Conflict* (New York: Oxford University Press, 1963), ch. 9; Thomas C. Schelling, *Arms and Influence* (New Haven, Conn.: Yale University Press, 1966), ch. 6.

3. Richard K. Betts, *Nuclear Blackmail and Nuclear Balance* (Washington, D.C.: Brookings Institution Press, 1987); Patrick M. Morgan, "Saving Face for the Sake of Deterrence," in *Psychology and Deterrence*, ed. Robert Jervis, Richard Ned Lebow, and Janice Gross Stein (Baltimore: Johns Hopkins University Press, 1985), 125–35; Schelling, *Arms and Influence*, chs. 2 and 3, and *Strategy of Conflict*, ch. 8. There is debate in the theoretical literature regarding the role of reputation in deterrence. See Alexander L. George and Richard Smoke, *Deterrence in American Foreign Policy: Theory and Practice* (New York: Columbia University Press, 1974), 559–60; William W. Kaufmann, "The Requirements of Deterrence," in *Military Policy and National Security*, ed. id. (Princeton, N.J.: Princeton University Press, 1956), 23–29; Glenn H. Snyder and Paul Diesing, *Conflict Among Nations: Bargaining, Decision Making, and System Structure in International Crises* (Princeton, N.J.: Princeton University Press, 1977), 185–88; Jonathan Mercer, *Reputation and International Politics* (Ithaca, N.Y.: Cornell University Press, 1996).

4. For a discussion of the Cold War deterrence problem in East Asia, see, e.g., Schelling, *Arms and Influence*, 49–50, 63–66, 82–83; Glenn H. Snyder, *Deterrence and Defense: Toward a Theory of National Security* (Princeton, N.J.: Princeton University Press, 1961), ch. 4; Henry A. Kissinger, *The Necessity for Choice: Prospects of American Foreign Policy* (New York: Harper & Brothers, 1960), ch. 2.

5. See Allen S. Whiting, *China Crosses the Yalu: The Decision to Enter the Korean War* (1960: Stanford: Stanford University Press, 1968).

6. On expected cost and similar concepts, see Snyder, *Deterrence and Defense*, 29; and George and Smoke, *Deterrence in American Foreign Policy*, 60, 525–26. See also Robert Jervis, "Deterrence and Perception," in *Strategy and Nuclear Deterrence*, ed. Steven E. Miller (Princeton, N.J.: Princeton University Press, 1984), 58–59; and Bruce Bueno de Mesquita, *The War Trap* (New Haven, Conn.: Yale University Press, 1981); Robert Jervis, *The Illogic of American Nuclear Strategy* (New York: Columbia University Press, 1984), 46–47.

7. Schelling, *Strategy of Conflict*, ch. 9; Snyder, *Deterrence and Defense*, 97–110; Stephen Van Evera, *Causes of War: Power and the Roots of Conflict* (Ithaca, N.Y.: Cornell University Press, 1999), 35–44. On the security dilemma, see Robert Jervis, "Cooperation Under the Security Dilemma," *World Politics* 30, 2 (January 1978): 167–215; Stephen Van Evera, "Offense, Defense, and the Causes of War," *International Security* 22, 4 (Spring 1998): 5–43.

8. Su Yanrong, chief ed., *Gao jishu zhanzheng gailun* [An overview of wars under high-technology conditions] (Beijing: Guofang Daxue Chubanshe, 1993), 7; Hu Guanping, "Kexue jishu shi diyi zhandouli" [Science and technology are the primary combat power], *Zhongguo Junshi Kexue*, no. 3 (2000): 85.

9. Yao Yunzhu, *Zhanhou Meiguo weishe lilun yu zhengce* [Postwar U.S. deterrence theory and policy] (Beijing: Guofang Daxue Chubanshe, 1998), 162, 168–69, 173–74; Zhai Xiaomin, *Lengzhanhou de Meiguo junshi zhanlue* [American military strategy after the Cold War] (Beijing: Guofang Daxue Chubanshe, 1999), 73, 81, 93.

10. On information and deterrence, see Strategic Research Department, Academy of Military Science, *Zhanlue xue* (2001 edition), 237–38; Chen Bojiang, "Xinxi shidai Meiguo junshi liliang jianshe yu yunyong de jishuhua" [Buildup and use of U.S. military strength in the information age], *Zhongguo Junshi Kexue*, no. 2 (1999): 146; Chen Bojiang, "Cong 'he wupin san' dao 'xinxi san'" [From "nuclear weapons umbrella" to "information umbrella"], *Guangming Ribao*, 23 January 2001, www.gmw.com.cn/o_gm/2001/01/20010123/GB/01^18674^0^GMC1-218.htm (accessed 17 October 2005); Zhao Xijun, "'Bu zhan er quren zhi bing' yu xiandai weishe zhanlue" ["Victory without war" and modern deterrence strategy], *Zhongguo Junshi Kexue* 5 (2001): 60; Yuan Zhengling, "Shilun changgui weishe" [On conventional deterrence], *Zhongguo Junshi Kexue* 4 (2001): 91; and Zhao Zhongqiang and Peng Chencang, *Xinxi zhan yu fan xinxi zhan: zema da* [Information war and anti-information war: how to fight] (Beijing: Zhongguo Qingnian Chubanshe, 2001), 375. See also Michael Pillsbury, *Chinese Views of Future Warfare* (Washington, D.C.: Institute for National Strategic Studies, National Defense University, 1997), pt. 4.

11. Military Teaching Department, General Staff Department, Chinese People's Liberation Army, *Junshi gao jishu zhishi jiaocai* [Teaching materials on knowledge about military high technology], 2d ed. (Beijing: Jiefangjun Chubanshe, 1996), 148–49. "If our networks can outperform the other guy's networks, we can win the battle without ever firing a shot," Vice Admiral Timothy LaFleur, commander of the U.S. naval surface forces in the Pacific, is quoted as saying (Sharon Weinberger, "Future Littoral Ships Could Wage Information Warfare, Official Says," *Aerospace Daily*, 17 July 2002).

12. Yao, *Zhanhou Meiguo weishe lilun yu zhengce*, 177–78.

13. Ibid., 172, 177–78.

14. Ibid.; Zhai, *Lengzhanhou de Meiguo junshi zhanlue*, 82–83; and Wang Qiming and Chen Feng, eds., *Daying gao jishu jubu zhanzheng: junguan bidu shouce* [Winning high-technology local war: required reading handbook for military officers] (Beijing: Junshi Yiwen Chubanshe, 1997), 405–6. Strategic Research Department, Academy of Military Science, *Zhanlue xue* (2001 edition), 235–36. For a comparison of the role of high technology in the Gulf War and the Kosovo War, see, e.g., Gao Qiufu, ed., *Xiaoyan wei san: Kesuowo zhanzheng yu shijie geju* (The smoke did not disperse: the war in Kosovo and the world structure) (Beijing: Xinhua Chubanshe, 1999), 280–83. See also Chen Zhou, *Xiandai jubu zhanzheng lilun yanjiu* [A study of modern local war theories] (Beijing: Guofang Daxue Chubanshe, 1997), 153. For an early analysis of the U.S. war in Afghanistan, see this assessment in a PRC-owned Hong Kong newspaper: Tian Xin, "Afghan War Assaults Chinese Military Theory," *Wen Wei Pao*, 4 February 2002, in Foreign Broadcast Information Service (hereafter cited as FBIS), CPP20020204000032.

15. Yao, *Zhanhou Meiguo weishe lilun yu zhengce*, 178–80; Chen, *Xiandai jubu zhanzheng lilun yanjiu*, 155; Teaching Department of the Chinese Communist Party Central Party School, *Wuge dangdai jianggao xuanbian* [A compilation of five contemporary lectures] (Beijing: Zhonggong Zhongyang Dangxiao Chubanshe, 2000), 243.

16. Zhang Wannian, *Dangdai shijie junshi yu Zhongguo guofang* [Contemporary world military affairs and China's national defense] (Beijing: Junshi Kexue Chubanshe, 1999), 183–84; Chu Shulong, "Zhongguo de guojia liyi, guojia liliang, he guojia zhanlue" [China's national interest, national strength, and national strategy], *Zhanlue yu Guanli*, no. 4 (1999): 15.

17. Liu Yijian, *Zhi haiquan yu haijun zhanlue* [Command of the sea and strategic employment of naval forces] (Beijing: Guofang Daxue Chubanshe, 2000), 146. See also Zhang Wannian, *Dangdai shijie junshi yu Zhongguo guofang* [Contemporary world military affairs and China's national defense] (Beijing: Zhonggong Zhongyang Dangxiao Chubanshe, 2000), 100. Chinese comparison of the Gulf War and the war in Kosovo underscores that deserts do not provide the cover necessary to defeat information dominance. The implication for China's surface fleet is clear. See Zhao and Peng, *Xinxi zhan yu fan xinxi zhan*, 42–44.

18. "Kongjun zhihui xueyuan zhuanjia tan—21 shiji de fangkong geming" [Air Force Command College experts discuss—the twenty-first-century revolution in air defense], *Jiefang Junbao*, 16 May 2001, 9; Yu Kaitang and Cao Shuxin, eds., *Tezhong kongxi mubiao yu duikang lilun yanjiu* [Theoretical research on special air-attack targets and counterattack] (Beijing: Guofang Daxue Chubanshe, 2000); Wang Houqing and Maj. Gen. Zhang Xingye, chief eds., *Zhanyi xue* [Military campaign studies] (Beijing: Guofang Daxue Chubanshe, 2000), ch. 12; Wang and Chen, eds., *Daying gao jishu jubu zhanzheng*. Zhu Chenghu's observation is in the *New York Times*, 15 July 2005, 8. See also Kenneth W. Allen, "China and the Use of Force: The Role of the PLA Air Force," forthcoming.

19. On the impact of U.S. intervention on the outcome of a war, see David A. Schlapak, David T. Orletsky, and Barry A. Wilson, *Dire Strait? Military Aspects of the China-Taiwan Confrontation and Options for U.S. Policy* (Santa Monica, Calif.: Rand Corporation, 2000), 38–45. On the PRC's navy, see Bernard D. Cole, *The Great Wall at Sea: China's Navy Enters the Twenty-First Century* (Annapolis, Md.: Naval Institute Press, 2001). On the PRC's air force, see Kenneth W. Allen, "PLA Air Force Operations and Modernization," in *People's Liberation Army After Next*, ed. Susan M. Puska (Carlisle, Pa.: Strategic Studies Institute, U.S. Army War College, 2001), 189–254; Allen, "China and the Use of Force."

20. On this point, see Shi Yinhong, "Guanyu Taiwan wenti de jixiang bixu zhengshi de da zhanlue wenti" [Several great strategic issues regarding the Taiwan issue that must be squarely faced], *Zhanlue yu Guanli*, no. 2 (2000): 30; and the discussion by Jia Qingguo in An Wei and Li Dongyan, *Shizi lukou shang de shijie: Zhongguo zhuming xuezhe tantao 21 shiji de guoji jiaodian* [World at the crossroads: famous Chinese scholars explore central international issues of the twenty-first century] (Beijing: Zhongguo Renmin Daxue Chubanshe, 2000), 393.

21. Zhang Zhaozhong, "Meiguo junshi zhanlue zhuanxiang yatai zhendui shei?" [At whom is the U.S. military strategy's move toward the Asia-Pacific aimed?],

Beijing Qingnian Bao, 30 August 2001, www.people.com.cn/GB/junshi/192/3514/ 3646/20010830/547897.html (accessed 29 September 2005).

22. Shi Yinhong, "Kunnan yu xuanze: dui Taiwan wenti de sikao" [Difficulty and choice: thoughts on the Taiwan issue], *Zhanlue yu Guanli*, no. 5 (1999): 4; Shi Yinhong, "Meiguo dui Hua zhengce he Taiwan wenti de weilai" [U.S. policy toward China and the future of the Taiwan issue], *Zhanlue yu Guanli*, no. 6 (2000); Zhang, "Meiguo junshi zhanlue zhuanxiang yatai zhendui shei?"; and author interviews with Chinese government foreign policy analysts, civilians, and military officers, 2000.

23. Wang Yizhou, "Mianxiang 21 shiji de Zhongguo waijiao," 21. See also the comments by Yan Xuetong and Jia Qingguo, in An and Li, *Shizi lukou shang de shijie*, 388–89.

24. Author interview with a Chinese military officer, 2001.

25. Guo Dafang, "Kexue jishu shi gao jishu jubu zhanzheng shouyao de zhisheng yinsu" [Science and technology are the first factor in subduing the enemy in high-technology local war], *Zhongguo Junshi Kexue*, no. 6 (2000): 146; Chen Youyuan, "Junshi jishu geming yu zhanyi lilun de fazhan" [The revolution in military technology and the development of campaign theory], and Zhan Xuexi, "Xiandai zhanyi tedian" [Analysis of the characteristics of contemporary campaigns], in Campaign Teaching and Research Office, Research Department, National Defense University, *Gao jishu tiaojian xia zhanyi lilun yanjiu* [Research on theory of local war under high-technology conditions] (Beijing: Guofang Daxue Chubanshe, 1997), 21, 54–56; Wang and Chen, *Daying gao jishu jubu zhanzheng*, 502; Wang Baocun, "Shixi xinxi zhan" [On information warfare], *Zhongguo Junshi Kexue*, no. 4 (1997): 103; Yao, *Zhanhou Meiguo weishe lilun yu zhengce*, 169; Zhao and Peng, *Xinxi zhan yu fan xinxi zhan*, 44–47; and Liu Aimin, "Xinxihua zhanzheng tezheng tantao" [Inquiry into the characteristics of the information transformation of war], *Zhongguo Junshi Kexue*, no. 3 (2000): 72.

26. On fait accompli strategies, see T. V. Paul, *Asymmetric Conflicts: War Initiation by Weaker Powers* (Cambridge: Cambridge University Press, 1994); and Paul K. Huth, *Extended Deterrence and the Prevention of Local War* (New Haven, Conn.: Yale University Press, 1988).

27. Central News Agency, 1 March 2005, in FBIS, CPP20050301000214.

28. And these numbers pale compared to the number of bombs dropped during the Gulf War. The figures are from Michael O'Hanlon, "A Flawed Masterpiece," *Foreign Affairs* 81, 3 (May–June 2002): 52. On the accuracy of the DF-15, see Shirley A. Kan, *China: Ballistic and Cruise Missiles* (Washington, D.C.: Congressional Research Service, Library of Congress, 2000), 11–12. For an analytical assessment of the effectiveness of bombing for coercion, see Robert A. Pape, *Bombing to Win: Air Power and Coercion in War* (Ithaca, N.Y.: Cornell University Press, 1996).

29. Owen R. Cote Jr., *The Future of the Trident Force: Enabling Access in Access-Constrained Environments* (Cambridge, Mass.: Security Studies Program, Massachusetts Institute of Technology, 2002); and U.S. Department of Defense, *Quadrennial Defense Review Report* (Washington, D.C.: U.S. Department of

Defense, 2001), www.defenselink.mil/pubs/qdr2001.pdf (accessed 27 September 2005); James Dao, "Army to Move Some Weapons Out of Europe," *New York Times*, 31 August 2001, 16; Richard Halloran, "America Realigns Military Forces," *Straits Times*, 11 June 2005. On U.S. force requirements, see Schlapak, Orletsky, and Wilson, *Dire Strait?* 38–39. For Chinese attention to these trends, see Cai Wei, "Mei haijun zhunbei jinnian xiaji jiang sansou luoshanji ji he jianting bushu dao guandao" [This summer the U.S. Navy will deploy three Los Angeles class nuclear submarines to Guam], *Huanqiu Shibao* [Global Times], 9 May 2002, 17; Yang Lei, "U.S. Strategy Is Pointed Straight at Asia," *Renmin Ribao* (Guangzhou South China News Supplement), 3 April 2001, in FBIS, 3 April 2000; Wu Qingli, "At Whom Is the U.S. Asia-Pacific Strategic Spearhead Pointed," *Renminwang*, 29 March 2002, in FBIS, 31 March 2002; Richard Halloran, "Checking the Threat That Could Be China," *Japan Times*, 12 June 2005.

30. See, e.g., *Renminwang*, 19 August 2001, in FBIS, 21 August 2001; and Central News Agency, 11 August 2001, in FBIS, August 13, 2001.

31. Zhang, *Dangdai shijie junshi yu Zhongguo guofang* (2000), 76–77; Chu, "Zhongguo de guojia liyi, guojia liliang he guojia zhanlue," 16–17; Shi, "Guanyu Taiwan wenti de jixiang bixu zhengshi de da zhanlue wenti," 31; Wang, "Mianxiang 21 shiji de Zhongguo waijiao," 21; and interviews with Chinese military officers and civilian analysts, 2001 and 2002.

32. Ye Zicheng, "Zhan yu he, jiaogei Taiwan dangju xuan" [War and peace, give the choice to the Taiwan authorities], *Huanqiu Shibao*, 22 October 1999.

33. Shi, "Kunnan yu xuanze: dui Taiwan wenti de sikao," 4; Zhang, *Dangdai shijie junshi yu Zhongguo guofang* (1999), 203–4, and *Dangdai shijie junshi yu Zhongguo guofang* (2000), 75; discussion by Jia Qingguo, in An and Li, *Shizi lukou shang de shijie*, 393–94. This is also the conclusion of Yan Xuetong, "Dui Zhongguo anquan huanjing de fenxi yu sikao" [Analysis and thoughts on China's strategic environment], *Shijie Jingji yu Zhengzhi* [World Economics and Politics], no. 2 (2000): 10.

34. On Taiwan's defense policy, see Michael D. Swaine, *Taiwan's National Security, Defense Policy, and Weapons Procurement Processes* (Santa Monica, Calif.: Rand Corporation, 1999).

35. Edward Gargan, "Long-Term Forecast for Taiwan Remains Upbeat," *New York Times*, 22 March 1996, 35; Sheila Tefft, "Taiwan Moves to Restore Shaken Investor Confidence," *Christian Science Monitor*, 1 April 1996, 9; Steven Mufson, "China-Taiwan Conflict 'In Remission, Not Resolved,'" *Washington Post*, 22 April 1996, 17.

36. James M. Lindsay and Michael E. O'Hanlon, *Defending America: The Case for Limited National Missile Defense* (Washington, D.C.: Brookings Institution Press, 2001), 123–30. On Taiwan's diminished interest in missile defense, see James Mulvenon, *Missile Defenses and the Taiwan Scenario*, Report No. 44 (Washington, D.C.: Henry L. Stimson Center, 2002); *Lien-ho Pao*, 27 July 2002, in FBIS, 29 July 2002.

37. The 2002 trade statistics are from the Taiwan Board of Foreign Trade; Central News Agency, 15 September 2002, FBIS, CPP20020915000025; 28 September 2002,

FBIS, CPP20020928000044; and 7 August 2002, FBIS, CPP20020807000167. The investment statistics are in Central News Agency, 7 August 2002, FBIS, CPP20020807000167, and 21 October 2002, FBIS, CPP20021022000004; Zhongguo Xinwenshe, 3 January 2004, FBIS, CPP20040103000056.

38. The investment statistics are in Central News Agency, 7 August 2002, FBIS, CPP20020807000167, and 21 October 2002, FBIS, CPP20021022000004. For a discussion of historical cases in which trade dependency created leverage affecting security policy, see Albert O. Hirshman, *National Power and the Structure of Foreign Trade* (Berkeley: University of California Press, 1980).

39. Zhongguo Xinwenshe, 3 January 2004, FBIS, CPP20040103000056; interview with official from Taiwan's Mainland Affairs Council, January 2004.

40. Mark Landler, "Money Might Not Be Able to Buy Political Ties, Either," *New York Times*, 9 December 2001, 4; "Taiwan and China Ink Landmark Oil Exploration Pact," Reuters, 16 May 2002; "Mainland to Hire Hi-Tech, Financial Experts from Taiwan," Agence France-Presse, 24 May 2002.

41. Wang, "Mianxiang 21 shiji de Zhongguo waijiao," 20.

42. Interviews with Taiwan military and civilian officials, 2002, 2004.

43. Interviews in Taiwan with DPP and KMT officials, January 2005; *Taipei Times*, December 4, 2005, at http://www.taipeitimes.com/News/front/archives/2005/12/04/2003282889 (accessed December 5, 2005).

44. Song Mu-kyong, "Domination and Unilateralism Is the Road to Isolation and Destruction," *Nodong Sinmun*, 3 March 2002, in FBIS, 14 March 2002.

45. Kim Chong-son, "One's Own Military Power Must Be Strong," *Nodong Sinmun*, 26 October 2002, in FBIS, 28 October 2002; "U.S. Imperialist Warmongers Who Are Heated Up in Arms Buildup," Pyongyang Central Broadcasting System, 27 April 2002, in FBIS, 27 April 2002.

46. Cho T'aek-pom, "Military Maneuvers Aimed at Domination of Asia," *Nodong Sinmun*, 13 September 2001, in FBIS, KPP20010924000058; Song, "Domination and Unilateralism."

47. Editorial, "Let Us Effect a New Leap in the Construction of a Powerful State While Seizing Science and Technology," *Nodong Sinmun*, 23 January 2002, FBIS, KPP20020123000024.

48. Editorial, "Following the Lead of Our Great Party, Let Us Go Construct Even More Splendidly Our Fatherland's Information Industry," *Kwahak-ui Segye*, 5 October 2001, in FBIS, KPP2002011000096.

49. M. A. Kim Ch'ol-ryong, "On World Trends in the Development of Science and Technology," *Ch'ollima*, 2 June 2002, in FBIS, KPP20020705000030.

50. Kim Chong-son, "One's Own Military Power Must Be Strong," *Nodong Sinmun*, 26 October 2001, in FBIS, KPP20011028000044.

51. *Nodong Sinmun*, 26 October 2001, in FBIS, KPP20011026000094. This is clearly a controversial policy that has aroused strong opposition. For the argument that North Korea must rely on its indigenous capabilities for defense, see "Military-First Politics is a Powerful Weapon in Our Era's Anti-Imperialist Struggle," *Nodong Sinmun*, 1 April 2002, in FBIS, KPP2002040100003.

52. Kim Chong-son, "Imperialists' Mean Maneuvers for Scientific and Economic Blockades," *Nodong Sinmun*, 14 August 2002, in FBIS, KPP2002082800008.

53. Kim Un-chu, "Major Tasks over Self-Reliance," *Nodong Sinmun*, 28 February 2002, in FBIS, KPP20020316000042. See also editorial, "Let Us Thoroughly Implement the Slogan of Self-Reliance in Accordance with the Demand of the New Century," *Nodong Sinmun*, 9 May 2002, in FBIS, KPP20020515000124.

54. Kim Ch'ol-ryong, "On World Trends."

55. For a discussion of recent North Korean reforms, see, e.g., Norimitsu Onishi, "2 Koreas Forge Economic Ties To Ease Tensions on Their Own," *New York Times*, 8 February 2005, 1; Howard W. French, "North Korea Experiments, with China as Its Model," ibid., 28 March 2005, 6.

56. Song, "Domination and Unilateralism."

57. Commentary, "Reckless Act Aimed at Preemptive Attacks," *Nodong Sinmun*, 24 June 2002, in FBIS, KPP20020624000060.

58. Commentary, "The U.S. Imperialist Must Not Run Recklessly Amuck," *Nodong Sinmun*, 9 December 2001, in FBIS, KPP20011209000033.

59. Kim Chong-son, "Korean Peninsula Is Most Dangerous Starting Ground for Nuclear War by U.S. Imperialists," *Nodong Sinmun*, 21 March 2002, in FBIS, KPP20020329000060.

60. *Chosun Ilbo*, 24 April 2005, at http://english.chosun.com/w21data/html/news/200504/200504240006.html (accessed 29 September 2005). The North Korean reaction is in Korean Central News Agency, 7 January 2002, in FBIS, KPP20020107000025. The JDAMs are reported in *Yonhap*, 26 May 2002, http://english.yna.co.kr/Engnews/20050526/610000000020050526185122E8.html (accessed 2 December 2005).

61. For a discussion of North Korean vulnerability to a first strike and the corresponding role of its forward deployment strategy, see David Kang, "North Korea's Military and Security Policy," in *North Korean Foreign Relations in the Post-Cold War Era*, ed. Samuel Kim (New York: Oxford University Press, 1998), 171–75; Leon V. Segal, *Disarming Strangers: Nuclear Diplomacy with North Korea* (Princeton, N.J.: Princeton University Press, 1998), 20–21. Also see U.S. Department of Defense, *2000 Report to Congress on the Military Situation on the Korean Peninsula* (Washington, D.C.: U.S. Department of Defense, 2000), for a discussion of the defensive elements in North Korean deployments.

62. On North Korea's WMD program, see Chung Min Lee, "Coping with the North Korean Missile Threat: Implications for Northeast Asia and Korea," in *Emerging Threats, Force Structures, and the Role of Air Power in Korea*, ed. Natalie Crawford and Chung-in Moon (Santa Monica, Calif.: Rand Corporation, 2000), 225–30; Kyoung-Soo Kim, "North Korea's CB Programs: Threat and Capability," *Korean Journal of Defense Analysis* 14, 1 (Spring 2002).

63. Marcus Noland, *Avoiding the Apocalypse: The Future of the Two Koreas* (Washington, D.C.: Institute for International Economics, 2000), 148–49. For a discussion of the likely casualties in Seoul from a North Korean chemical weapon attack, see Bruce Bennett, "The Emerging Ballistic Missile Threat: Global and Regional Implications," in *Emerging Threats*, ed. Crawford and Moon, 198–99. On U.S. and South Korean efforts to prepare for North Korean chemical warfare, see U.S. Department of Defense, *Annual Report to Congress and Performance Plan* (Washington, D.C.: U.S. Department of Defense, 2002); testimony of General Rich-

ard B. Meyers, commander, Pacific Air Forces, Subcommittee on Military Readiness, House Armed Services Committee, 6 March 1998, www.house.gov/hasc/testimony/105thcongress/3-6-98myers.htm (accessed 17 October 2005); *Korea Times*, 15 May 1998, in FBIS, dreas05161998000007; *Korea Times*, 15 August 1997, in FBIS, dreas08151997001662.

64. For a discussion of the origins and motivations in North Korea's nuclear weapons program, see Alexander Platkovskiy, "Nuclear Blackmail and North Korea's Search for a Place in the Sun," in *The North Korean Nuclear Program: Security, Strategy and New Perspectives from Moscow*, ed. James Clay Moltz and Alexander Y. Mansourov (New York: Routledge, 2000), 93–100.

65. See the statement by Secretary of Defense Donald Rumsfeld, U.S. Department of Defense briefing, 17 October 2002. See also David E. Sanger, "U.S. Not Certain if Pyongyang Has the Bomb," *New York Times*, 17 October 2002; David S. Cloud and David E. Sanger, "U.S. Aide Sees Arms Advance by North Korea," ibid., 28 April 2005, 1. For a discussion of U.S. intelligence on North Korean nuclear capabilities, see Jonathan Pollack, "The United States, North Korea, and the End of the Agreed Framework," *Naval War College Review* 61, 3 (Summer 2003): 11–49.

66. Korea Central News Agency, 18 June 2003, in FBIS, KPP20030618000072; David E. Sanger, "North Korea Says It Seeks to Develop Nuclear Arms," *New York Times*, 10 June 2003, 10; David E. Sanger, "North Korea Says It Has Made Fuel for Atom Bombs," ibid., 15 July 2003; Joseph Kahn and David E. Sanger, "North Korea Says It May Test an A-Bomb," ibid., 29 August 2003, 9; Korean Central Broadcasting Station, 20 August 2003, in FBIS, KPP20030820000050.

67. On North Korea's crisis diplomacy, see Scott Snyder, *Negotiating on the Edge: North Korean Negotiating Behavior* (Washington, D.C.: United States Institute of Peace, 1999).

68. David C. Kang, "The Dog that Didn't Bark: Why North Korea Hasn't Attacked in Fifty Years and What International Relations Theorists Can Learn" (unpublished paper) discusses the fact that North Korea's reputation for risk-taking serves deterrence but does not reflect its intentions to use force. For a discussion of various North Korean high-risk activities, see Don Oberdorfer, *The Two Koreas: A Contemporary History* (New York: Basic Books, 1997).

69. For a discussion of the impact of the Chinese intervention in the Korean War on U.S. policy in the Vietnam War, see Yuen Foong Khong, *Analogies at War* (Princeton, N.J.: Princeton University Press, 1992); Robert D. Schulzinger, "The Johnson Administration, China, and the Vietnam War," in *Re-examining the Cold War: U.S.-China Diplomacy, 1954–1973*, ed. Robert S. Ross and Jiang Changbin (Cambridge, Mass.: Harvard University Asia Center, 2001).

70. For a Chinese discussion of enduring PRC naval inferiority, see Liu Yijian, "Zhongguo weilai de haijun jianshe yu haijun zhanlue" [China's future naval construction and naval strategy], *Zhanlue yu Guanli*, no. 5 (1999): 99–100. This argument is developed in Robert S. Ross, "The Geography of the Peace: East Asia in the Twenty-First Century," *International Security* 23, 4 (Spring 1999): 81–118.

71. Peter G. Gosselin, "Crisis in Yugoslavia: U.S. is Low on Cruise Missiles,"

Los Angeles Times, 30 April 1999, 29; "Postwar Review Found Fewer Serb Weapons Hit in Kosovo," *Washington Post*, 9 May 2000, 17.

72. On the likelihood of survival of PRC mobile short-range missile launchers, see Alan Vick, Richard Moore, Bruce Pirnie, and John Stillion, *Aerospace Operations Against Elusive Ground Targets* (Santa Monica, Calif.: Rand Corporation, 2001).

73. Secretary of Defense William Perry's comments at the National Press Club, Washington, D.C., 28 February 1996. For a discussion of U.S. and Chinese motives during the 1996 confrontation, see Robert S. Ross, "The 1995–96 Taiwan Strait Confrontation: Coercion, Credibility, and Use of Force," *International Security* 25, 2 (Fall 2000): 87–123.

74. Carter and Perry, *Preventive Defense*, 95.

75. Note that China canceled two of its planned missile tests. It did not target the closure zone of the east side of Taiwan. These tests would have been the most provocative, for firing missiles into this zone would have required it to send the missiles directly over Taiwan. Interview with Robert Suettinger, director of Asian affairs, National Security Council. Also see Patrick Tyler, *A Great Wall: Six Presidents and China* (New York: Public Affairs, 1999), 31, which notes that China readied "more than a dozen missiles" for firing.

76. Vernon Loeb and Peter Slevin, "Overcoming North Korea's 'Tyranny of Proximity,'" *Washington Post*, 20 January 2003, 16.

77. For U.S. military discussion of a possible North Korean strategy for war, see the paper presented to the Army War College workshop on Competitive Strategies, 12–14 June 2000, by Stephen Bradner, special advisor to the commander-in-chief of the UN Command in Korea, www.npec-web.org/essay/Bradner.htm (accessed 29 September 2005). For a discussion of North Korea's ability to surprise U.S. and South Korean forces, see Michael McDevitt, "Engagement with North Korea: Implications for the United States," in *North Korea's Engagement—Perspectives, Outlook, and Implications*, ed. U.S. National Intelligence Council (Washington, D.C.: National Intelligence Council, 2001).

78. See General LaPorte's response to advance questions posed by the Senate Armed Forces Committee in preparation for his confirmation hearing on 26 April 2002, at http://www.globalsecurity.org/military/library/congress/2002_hr/laporte426.pdf (accessed December 5, 2005).

79. Carter and Perry, *Preventive Defense*, 129–31. See also Segal, *Disarming Strangers*, 95, 122.

80. Doug Struck, "Observers See Rising Risk of U.S.–N. Korea Conflict," *Washington Post*, 28 February 2003, 14; Bradley Graham and Doug Struck, "U.S. Officials Anticipate More Provocations by North Korea," *Washington Post*, 3 March 2003, 12; Doug Struck, "War Games on Korean Peninsula Upset North," *Washington Post*, 23 March 2003, 10; Korea Central News Agency, 1 April 2003, in FBIS, KPP20030401000074; Bradley Graham and Doug Struck, "U.S., Asian Allies Face Tough Choices," *Washington Post*, 25 April 2003, 18.

81. Agence France-Presse, 31 May 2003, in FBIS, JPP20030531000047; *Yonhap*, 31 May 2003, in FBIS, AFS KPP20030531000068; *Yonhap*, 7 August 2003, in FBIS, AFS KPP20030807000014; *Yonhap*, 31 May 2003, in FBIS, AFS

KPP2003053I000020. For a discussion of the Stryker Brigade, see Alan Vick, David Orletsky, Bruce Pirnie, and Seth Jones, *The Stryker Brigade Combat Team: Rethinking Strategic Responsiveness and Assessing Deployment Options* (Santa Monica, Calif.: Rand Corporation, 2002).

82. See the report at www.whitehouse.gov/nsc/nssall.html (accessed 2 December 2005).

83. David E. Sanger, "U.S. Sees Quick Start of North Korea Nuclear Site," *New York Times*, 1 March 2003, 1; David E. Sanger and Thom Shanker, "U.S. Sending Two Dozen Bombers in Easy Range of North Koreans," ibid., 5 March 2003, 1; Michael Wines, "Warning to North Korea on Nuclear Arms," ibid., 12 April 2003, 5.

84. Thom Shanker, "Aftereffects: Korea Strategy," *New York Times*, 12 May 2003, 17.

85. Howard French, "Heightened Tension Touch South Korea Troops," *New York Times*," 23 February 2003, 16; Struck, "War Games on Korean Peninsula Upset North."

86. Shanker, "Aftereffects: Korea Strategy"; Korea Central News Agency, 20 June 2003, in FBIS, KPP20030620000034; Pyongyang Broadcast Station, 6 July 2003, in FBIS, KPP20030706000015.

87. Struck, "Observers See Rising Risk of U.S.–N. Korean Conflict"; Eric Schmitt, "North Korean MIG's Intercept U.S. Jet on Spying Mission," *New York Times*, 4 March 2003, 1; Bradley Graham and Glenn Kessler, "N. Korea Tails U.S. Spy Plane," *Washington Post*, 4 March 2003, 1; "North and South Koreans Exchange Gunfire," *New York Times*, 17 July 2003, 6.

88. See the report of his testimony at http://nis.go.kr/english/democratic .hwang1.html (accessed 29 September 2005). See also Oberdorfer, *Two Koreas*, 79.

89. Segal, *Disarming Strangers*, 21.

90. See North Korea's discussion of U.S. preemptive strategy in Commentary, "Reckless Act Aimed at Preemptive Attacks," *Nodong Sinmun*, 24 June 2002, in FBIS, KPP20020624000060, 24 June 2002.

91. Oberdorfer, *Two Koreas*, 78.

92. See, e.g., Jack Snyder, *The Ideology of the Offensive: Military Decision Making and the Disasters of 1914* (Ithaca, N.Y.: Cornell University Press, 1984); Steven M. Miller, Sean M. Lynn-Jones, and Stephen Van Evera, eds., *Military Strategy and the Origins of the First World War*, rev. ed. (Princeton, N.J.: Princeton University Press, 1991).

93. Interviews with senior Chinese military analysts, June 2003.

94. Whiting, *China Crosses the Yalu*; Thomas J. Christensen, *Useful Adversaries: Grand Strategy, Domestic Mobilization, and Sino-American Conflict, 1947–1958* (Princeton, N.J.: Princeton University Press, 1996), ch. 5.

95. Oberdorfer, *Two Koreas*, 76; Segal, *Disarming Strangers*, 118.

96. The contribution of water to U.S.-China relations is developed in Ross, "Geography of the Peace."

97. Interview with Chinese foreign policy analysts, October 2002.

98. General Thomas Schwartz said that North Korea is "the country most likely to involve the United States in a major war." See his testimony before the Armed

Forces Committee, U.S. Senate, 7 March 2000. Also see the testimony of R. James Woolsey, director of central intelligence, before the Committee on National Security, U.S. House of Representatives, 12 February 1998.

99. See John McLaughlin, speech at Texas A&M University, 17 April 2000, http://www.cia.gov/cia/public_affairs/speeches/ddci_speech_04172001.html (copy in author's possession).

100. For an analysis of U.S. policy options that favor cautious engagement, see Victor D. Cha, "Hawk Engagement and Preventive Defense on the Korean Peninsula," *International Security* 27, 1 (Summer 2002): 40–78.

3 *Windows and War*

TREND ANALYSIS AND BEIJING'S USE OF FORCE

Thomas J. Christensen

If the history of the People's Republic of China (PRC) is any guide, there is reason to be concerned about the possibility of conflict across the Taiwan Strait sometime in the first two decades of the twenty-first century. War is hardly inevitable, however, and at the time of this writing, conflict appears rather remote in the near term. If policies in Beijing, Taipei, and Washington are managed well, the two sides of the Strait can handle their differences peacefully and avoid conflict. Good management will not necessarily be easy, however, and will require both vigilance and an understanding of what factors are most likely to lead to cross-Strait conflict. Excessive optimism can be as dangerous as excessive pessimism, because the former can lead us to ignore problems that might spark a conflict and thereby fail to remedy them in time. An understanding of the factors that have led to the use of force in PRC history could help us avoid that pitfall in the future.

Some analysts believe that cross-Strait relations and the U.S. deterrent role in those relations are quite stable now and should remain so long into the future. The optimistic logic flows as follows. The United States can rather easily deter conflict by maintaining military superiority over the PRC. For its part, Taiwan can avoid provoking a mainland use of force against the island and its offshore interests by simply avoiding a declaration of permanent legal independence from the Chinese nation. Given the costs of conflict with the mainland to the island, such a declaration seems unlikely. Without a bright-line provocation such as a declaration of independence, the PRC would not dare to use force against Taiwan. In addition to the economic and political costs of belligerence to the mainland, the PLA lacks the ability to invade and subdue the island quickly, if at all. More important, once the United States became involved in the conflict, the PLA would be facing a massively superior military. In other words, since it would be difficult, if not impossible, for the PRC to finish the job and resolve the Taiwan problem once and for all at acceptable costs, Beijing will not use force except under the most dire circumstances.[1]

The logic of these arguments is very tight and is rooted in a rich tradition of deterrence theory. But the study of PRC strategic history offered below suggests that deterrence and stability in cross-Strait relations might not be quite as simple to maintain as the optimistic scenario allows. In episodes that have been largely lauded as strategic successes in PRC historical writings, CCP leaders have used force—sometimes against superior foes or their allies—because they feared that, if they did not, the PRC's strategic situation would only worsen further. They often have done so in anticipation of a future bright-line provocation rather than waiting for the provocation to occur. Moreover, on several occasions, they have used force to affect and shape long-term political and security trends in the region and at home, not to resolve security problems permanently. In the contemporary Taiwan setting, this history suggests that the PRC might use force even if the United States has military superiority, even if Taiwan has not formally declared legal independence, and even if the PLA lacks the ability to resolve the Taiwan question permanently through the use of force against the island and its interests. If this is true, what we need to know is whether the CCP views long-term trends as dangerous or beneficial to PRC security and whether the use of force might be seen as the best way, however dangerous, to slow, halt, or reverse long-term trends that appear to CCP elites to be running against the PRC's security interests.

In this chapter I briefly review the PRC's strategic history from 1949 to 1979 for the purpose of uncovering certain relevant patterns in Beijing's decisions about the use of force. The lessons about these patterns should provide cautionary warnings about the potential for future conflict across the Taiwan Strait and, by association, across the Pacific. The aspects of PRC strategy and strategic thinking to be studied are:

The use of trend analysis by CCP elites and the belief that, if force is not used in the near term, a dangerous window of vulnerability might be opening or a window of opportunity to accomplish some goal might be closing permanently.

The use of force against superior foes or their allies in the belief that enemy superiority and aggressiveness will only grow if force is not used.

The use of force without a clear, bright-line provocation, in anticipation that if force is not used, such a provocation will take place, perhaps on terms more advantageous to the enemy.

The use of force to shape long-term trends in security politics rather than to resolve a security problem once and for all. In these instances, force is seen as therapeutic rather than curative.

In some of the cases I discuss below, only one or two of the phenomena listed above were present. For example, in the Korean War and in the Vietnam War, CCP leaders applied windows logic for their decision to enter the conflicts, but they clearly sought full victory in both wars at the onset of their intervention. In those cases, warfare was seen as a solution to a security problem, not just as a political tool to make the problem more tractable. In other cases, such as the 1954 Taiwan Strait crisis and the 1969 border conflict with the USSR, all of the factors above are found, including the use of force primarily as a method of shaping longer-term international security trends.

From my case studies, I conclude that the PRC has used force most frequently when it perceived an opening window of vulnerability or a closing window of opportunity. A key element of Beijing's "windows logic" has been its estimation not only of changes in adversaries' aggressiveness or military might in comparison to China's own, but also political trends in China's own alliances and in the alliances formed among China's actual or potential enemies. Chinese elites have paid careful attention to trends in the domestically generated power capabilities of China and its adversaries and to the political and military trends within PRC alliances and anti-PRC alliances in the region. Another consistent concern has been the potential domestic political costs of acquiescence and the potential domestic political benefits of belligerence to the CCP regime, given certain trends in international politics and certain challenges facing the CCP leadership at home.

Chinese elites only sometimes believed that they clearly had the upper hand in the military arena before choosing to use force. In some cases, they merely surmised that trends were working against them and that however dangerous and disadvantageous armed conflict might be in the short term, forgoing force would be even more dangerous. Leaders decided that the use of force could serve political purposes and reverse or halt perceived trends that were not in China's favor, even if, in the short term, military victory as traditionally conceived was not possible given the military and political circumstances Beijing faced. In other cases, CCP elites hoped to eliminate an enemy in a particular theater permanently through the use of force.

This is not to say that the PRC is particularly prone to use force or that CCP leaders are particularly eager for conflict, but rather that the reasons that the PRC has used force in the past would not always appear obvious to the casual observer, who might not expect a weaker actor to lash out at much stronger states or those stronger states' allies. In my conclusion, I briefly review related points that I have made in other publications regarding the real danger of conflict over Taiwan in the second half of this decade. Some of the lessons of the PRC's historical use of force may be critically important today in assessing the stability of relations across the Taiwan Strait.

Theoretical Writings on Power Shifts, Windows of Opportunity and Vulnerability, and the Causes of War

Before turning to the cases, it is important to recognize that the concepts I am using in this article, windows of opportunity and windows of vulnerability, are part of a hotly contested literature in the international relations theory literature: theories of preventive or preemptive wars. The theories are simple: proponents of them argue that wars are sometimes, or even often, caused by leaders who fear that if they do not act militarily in the short term, their long-term security objectives will be even more threatened by an increasingly powerful or aggressive enemy or alliance of enemies. Before the most recent war in Iraq, critics argued that such wars "almost never happen," to quote one, and that even in cases where windows logic is purported to have affected outcomes, the importance of those variables is at best unclear.[2]

Although I reject this critic's conclusion, there are indeed some real problems in the existing literature on windows logic and preventive war. There has been too much focus in this literature on the great powers and on whether or not one country was overtaking another in overall national power prior to a war.[3] For our purposes, this approach suffers from two major limitations. First, by focusing on power competitions between actual or near-peer competitors, the literature often misses the question of whether or not leaders in weaker states might believe that war in the short term is preferable to war in the longer term, despite the risks of taking on enemies that they view as militarily stronger than their own state in the near term. A second problem with the literature, recognized by its critics, is that wars are almost never purely caused by naked power considerations. I agree with this proposition, but in many political relationships, there are ample reasons for rivalry, distrust, and conflict outside of trends in the relative capabilities of the potential foes. But given existing or predictable occasions for tensions, shifts in that balance can lead one side or the other to act now, rather than later, and can preclude patient diplomacy if one actor perceives an opening window of vulnerability or a closing window of opportunity either in the short term or the longer term.[4] In certain relationships, such as America's relationship with China on the Taiwan issue, political provocations occur fairly regularly. The question is, which provocations, under what conditions, will lead a nation (for our purposes, the PRC) to use force? In such an analysis, windows logic is an important factor in precipitating conflict, but it is hardly the only factor.

Korea, 1950

The classic case of Chinese "windows" logic was Mao Zedong's decision to enter the Korean War in October 1950. Much has been written
about the decision, and controversy still revolves around the issue among
political scientists and diplomatic historians.[5] But it appears clear from the
documentary record from China and the former Soviet Union that Mao
eventually decided to enter the Korean War reluctantly and largely because
of the perceived long-term threat that would be posed by the permanent stationing of U.S. forces in North Korea. This portrayal of Mao as being driven
by PRC security concerns is accurate despite evidence to the contrary such
as Mao's support for Kim Il Sung's initial invasion of the south, Mao's
preparation for war even before General Douglas MacArthur's Inchon
landing, and Mao's very aggressive strategy once he entered the war.

In Mao's eyes, the Americans appeared increasingly strong and aggressive after they entered the Korean War in late June, inserted the Seventh
Fleet into the Taiwan Strait at that time, and then crossed the 38th parallel
with U.S. troops in October. Mao and other Chinese elites viewed fighting
the Americans as highly risky, but Mao and his field general Peng Dehuai
argued successfully to their colleagues that doing so was preferable to waiting to fight the Americans later, following a buildup of American forces in
Korea and Taiwan. Mao and Peng believed that, if the PRC were to allow
American troops to remain in both Taiwan and North Korea, the United
States might build up its forces and attack China at some later time of its
choosing. It is important then to recognize the critical role played by President Harry Truman's decision on 27 June 1950 to use the U.S. Navy to
block the Taiwan Strait, apparently reversing the president's assertion in his
speech of 5 January 1950 that Washington did not intend to intervene in the
Chinese Civil War. From Mao's sometimes almost paranoid perspective,
this did more than just demonstrate increased American hostility to his
regime, it showed that the United States was building a circle of alliances
around China, from French Indochina to Taiwan to Korea.[6] Moreover, by
linking up with Taiwan, the United States was lending encouragement to
Mao's domestic enemies at a time when American forces in Korea could tie
down large numbers of PLA forces at the border, rendering them incapable
of suppressing domestic foes.[7] Those foes in turn would be encouraged by
the rollback of communism in Korea and the stabilization of a permanent
opposition regime on Taiwan. Even if the United States did not attack
Manchuria soon after occupying all of Korea, in Mao's and Peng's minds,
a U.S. presence there would create a negative and worsening long-term
trend in PRC security. Unless China acted in the near term, that attack on
China would occur on a timetable most suitable to Washington.[8] Mao and

Peng were careful to avoid fighting on the enemy's timetable precisely because they viewed the world in terms of windows of opportunity and vulnerability.

In early October, just after MacArthur showed his hand by demanding the surrender of North Korean forces north of the 38th parallel (1 October) and just days before he actually ordered UN forces to cross into North Korea (7 October), Mao and Peng apparently needed to convince some very worried high-level comrades that taking the fight to the Americans was a good idea, despite the risks. They ultimately succeeded in doing so, apparently because of the specter of American troops coming north and because of Mao's and Peng's arguments about long-term windows of vulnerability if the PRC remained passive while being encircled by the United States and a revitalized Japan. In his briefing to his division commanders just before entering Korea, Peng pointed out that the United States and its allies were overextended in October 1950 and, while the Americans were mobilizing, it would take the United States until June 1951 to draft and train 500,000 additional troops. He said that this had been the reasoning used by those in the Politburo who decided that fighting a war sooner rather than later was the right decision, despite China's own lack of full readiness.[9] As Peng explained to his leading officers: "Our preparations [for war] are insufficient, [but] the enemy's preparations are also [currently] insufficient, especially the American imperialists' preparations are insufficient."[10] Mao and Peng's argument to the Politburo for action was that a combination of geography and Chinese military backwardness made ground warfare the most desirable option to employ against the Americans. Waiting to fight would also allow the Americans to bring more force to bear against more economically developed targets. So, part of the winning argument for war in Beijing was that fighting a war in the short term would be less painful than fighting a larger war later, a clear example of windows logic.[11] Mao was hardly confident of success, nor did he believe that China clearly had the upper hand in the near term. Rather, Mao and Peng believed the local political and military balance of power might easily worsen over time if the PRC did not take action soon. For our purposes, it is important to note that Mao intentionally took on a superior foe out of fear that his enemy's superiority would only grow, and that the PRC's security would be further compromised if action were not taken.

From the above, we can see how "windows logic" based on assessment of current and future security trends in the region and in domestic political stability encouraged Mao's CCP to get into the war in the first place and then shaped how and when China fought. It was actually China's weakness and the bleaker prospects for the future if the Americans were left unmolested in Korea and Taiwan that made China enter the war. Moreover,

China's perceived weakness and Beijing's fear that things would be even worse if the PRC did not act decisively made China's war strategy very aggressive.

The fundamental importance of this windows logic in Beijing's strategy in late 1950 has been clouded by three facts: Mao's advance approval of Kim Il Sung's initial invasion of South Korea in June 1950 and support for Vietnamese communists before the outbreak of the war; Mao's preparation for war before MacArthur's Inchon landing; and the discrepancies between Russian and Chinese archival materials from October 1950.

Mao's support for communist expansion in Vietnam and Korea before the Korean War broke out might call into question the portrayal of Mao as a defensive actor concerned with closing windows of vulnerability. The simple answer to this question is that Mao was both aggressive and defensive, ideological and highly concerned about his new nation's defense. Despite his ideological leanings and his desire to spread revolution when the opportunity presented itself, he was not eager to fight the Americans in Korea. In fact, his indecision apparently delayed the crossing of the Yalu because he was wracked with doubts about the dangers of a war for his weak military and his new regime. Mao reportedly paced the floor for sixty hours (10–12 October) before sending the final order for troops to prepare to cross the Yalu.[12]

Mao had indeed given a verbal nod to Kim Il Sung's initial push south in spring 1950. There are two potential reasons why. First, Stalin had cleverly cornered Mao with responsibility for the decision by approving the very confident Kim's plan on the condition that Mao also approve it. This would mean that Mao's refusal would make Beijing responsible for pouring cold water on Kim's plan. According to one authoritative Chinese account, Mao was very wary about Kim's plan, because he was not as confident as Kim and Stalin that the invasion would score a quick victory that would preclude an effective American response of some kind. But Stalin's maneuvers put Mao in a bad position, and Mao agreed to approve Kim's gambit even though he felt Kim was overconfident and that conflict in Korea threatened the achievement of China's core goal of regaining Taiwan.[13] Another interpretation of events, based in part on Soviet archival material, is that, to a large degree, Mao shared Kim's view that the United States likely lacked the strength and resolve to respond in Korea in a timely fashion. According to one Russian source, Mao believed that the United States would not expend its overstretched resources on "such a small area" as Korea. Instead, he worried that the United States might dispatch Japanese forces to the area.[14] In this way, America's nascent alliance with Japan and its attempt to rebuild its former foe entered Chinese calculations in the earliest phases of the Korean War.

There is probably some truth in both versions of Mao's calculations. Nobody was quite as aggressive and confident as Kim Il Sung, who took months in late 1949 and early 1950 to persuade Stalin to support his plan and only succeeded in late January, after Truman's speech on noninterference in the Chinese Civil War on 5 January 1950 and Secretary of State Dean Acheson's speech to the Press Club on 12 January 1950 suggesting that the United States would not defend Korea.[15] So, to say Mao had more reservations than Kim is not saying much. Still, the United States had abandoned the Chinese mainland in 1949, had apparently written off Taiwan and South Korea in January 1950, and had very limited firepower in the region, as demonstrated by MacArthur's struggles both before and after Inchon. As the Chinese scholar Shi Yinhong argued recently, a combination of the communist allies' overconfidence, in the face of an apparent lack of U.S. resolve, and PRC obligations to the communist alliance led to Mao's disastrous failure to restrain Kim Il Sung.[16] So, especially given the diplomatic pickle that Stalin and Kim had placed him in, it might have seemed relatively wise to offer verbal support for Kim's plan to attack South Korea. One thing seems fairly certain from the available evidence. Mao did not expect the United States both to enter Korea with a large number of troops quickly and to intervene in the Taiwan Strait. And it was this surprising combination of events, not either in isolation, that created Mao's perceived window of vulnerability in October 1950.[17]

The fact that Mao prepared to enter the war before Inchon also suggests to some that the UN crossing of the 38th parallel was not critical to China's decision, and that China was not behaving reactively out of windows logic. In fact, one of the critics of preemptive war theory focuses on this point to show that this "classic case" of preemptive war was likely nothing more than clear-cut PRC ideological expansionism.[18] This argument disregards the contentious meetings within China leading up to the final decision and various documents from July and August in both the Soviet and Chinese archival collections available in the West. Those documents show the crossing of the 38th parallel and the need to defend North Korea, not a desire to "liberate" South Korea per se, as the key triggers for expansion of the war by Beijing. Most important, the argument resting on PLA planning before Inchon to demonstrate Mao's early commitment to war does not take into account that Mao fully expected MacArthur to drive north of the 38th parallel and was preparing accordingly before Inchon. He would have been surprised if the Americans had stopped, and he needed to plan in case they did not. Moreover, for various reasons including the greater difficulty of launching offensives against American defensive positions if they had been as far south as the 38th parallel and China's reliance on Soviet assistance for any offensive against American defensive positions, it is hard to imagine escalation of the war if the Americans had stopped at the 38th parallel. Such escalation would have required massive Chinese assets, which in turn would have required massive Soviet support for a plan that, on both political and military grounds, would have been much more risky than engaging American forces that were overextended, closer to China (providing for shorter Chinese logistics lines), and in terrain that was more favorable to the Chinese.[19]

As for the reliability of Chinese sources on these questions and their consistency with Soviet archival sources, it should be noted that the document collections from the Soviet and Chinese archives are largely compatible and the discrepancies can largely be explained by Mao and Peng's need to convince the Politburo in early October that their call for an aggressive strategy was justified. A telegram from Mao to Stalin in the Chinese archives, dated 2 October 1950, which was apparently never sent, because it does not bear the stamp that telegrams routinely received after being sent, portrays a decisive Mao preparing for war. However, a telegram to Stalin from the Soviet embassy on the same date, found in the Soviet archives, portrays Beijing as extremely reluctant, with Mao citing resistance to war in his own Politburo.[20] Some combination of Mao's personal standing in the Party, the persuasiveness of Mao's and Peng's geostrategic arguments with reference to an American encirclement campaign involving Korea and Taiwan, and the threat posed by the U.S. crossing of the 38th parallel on 7 October helped Mao and Peng win the day. On 8 October, Mao initially decided to enter the war with the backing of the Politburo and alerted both Stalin and Kim Il Sung to that fact. He then planned a strategy in Korea on which both Soviet and Chinese archival documents concur. Between 10 and 13 October, he also had last-minute second thoughts before he reached the final decision to enter and reconfirmed his commitment to enter on 13 October in the telegram to Zhou Enlai cited above. Again, there is no apparent contradiction between the two document sets either on that issue or about Mao's war plans outlined in the telegram of 14 October to Zhou Enlai in Moscow.[21]

Mao saw both windows of opportunity in Korea in early 1950 and windows of vulnerability later in the year. He was an offensive and defensive actor calculating trends in his own alliance and in the alliance of his main adversary, the United States. His combination of offensive and defensive motives made him particularly difficult, although not necessarily impossible, to deter.

Taiwan, 1954–1955

In late summer 1954, Mao also believed international forces were shifting against the PRC and would perhaps permanently prevent Beijing from attaining its goal of reunification with Taiwan and elimination of his

Civil War enemy, Chiang Kai-shek's Kuomintang (KMT). In this case, Mao used limited force to send a message to the United States and to Chiang about the costs of forming a formal alliance. This case fits all of the criteria discussed above. Mao's analysis of long-term trends led him to attempt to alter those trends through the use of force. He used force not directly, after a bright-line provocation, but rather in anticipation of provocative actions to follow. He did not try to resolve the problem once and for all through military means, but rather to create a security situation that would be somewhat better than the one he predicted would result if the PRC were to remain passive.

According to well-connected PRC scholars, Mao was concerned about two trends that he believed augured a more stubborn "Taiwan problem" if the PRC did not take action. The first was a diplomatic trend in the region, partially supported by Beijing's own diplomacy in Korea and Vietnam: the settlement of Asian civil wars by internationally recognized demilitarized zones and political separation lines that created the appearance of two geographically distinct legitimate governments in Korea and Vietnam. Such an outcome, if it were going to become a precedent, clearly ran counter to Mao's desire to unify his country under CCP leadership and to gain diplomatic recognition of Beijing as the sole legitimate government of all of China.

The second trend was the expansion of American alliances in the region to include actors antagonistic to communism around China's periphery. The United States had failed to set up anything akin to NATO in East Asia. The Eisenhower administration, in its efforts to create the Southeast Asia Treaty Organization (SEATO), appeared poised to change that. The problem for Mao on this score was twofold: first, a stronger and tighter alliance among anti-communists in Asia was clearly aimed at containing communist China and preventing China from reaching its regional goals, especially regarding Taiwan; second, and more important, Beijing was gravely concerned that the Republic of China (ROC) on Taiwan would be included in the alliance system, thus strengthening and encouraging Chiang militarily and politically. Moreover, this linkage between the United States and Taiwan would occur at a time when China was recovering from the Korean War and Chiang still had strong irredentist claims on the mainland, which could only be fulfilled with American support. In the past, when the United States had upgraded its military relations with Chiang's ROC, he had quickly become more belligerent, accelerating harassment of the mainland and seizing tiny offshore islands just off the mainland coast.[22] But most important to Mao in 1954, inclusion of Taiwan in an alliance would seem to lock the United States permanently into the Chinese Civil War, with long-term implications for reunification and the mainland regime's security, because the United States would be providing assistance to anti-communist forces on Taiwan that wanted to use military means and subversion to over-throw Mao's regime.[23]

Although it actually backfired and, if anything, only hastened the U.S.-ROC Mutual Defense Treaty, the PLA's artillery assault on the offshore islands, which began in September 1954, was designed to send a signal to both Taipei and the United States. The intended political message of the attack was that China would not stand idly by as Washington and Taipei tied the military knot and, more abstractly, to remind the United States that remaining involved in the Chinese Civil War by supporting Chiang Kai-shek would be both costly and risky.

In January, the PLA attacked and seized the offshore island of Yijiang-shan off of Zhejiang, and in February, the PLA took the Dazhens, also off of Zhejiang, after they were evacuated by ROC troops. According to He Di, the Yijiangshan and Dazhens attacks were really more of military than of political significance, because they provided good practice for a weak PLA amphibious capability. Although the islands were very far from Taiwan and weakly defended, they had provided a base for irritating harassment and blockade activities by the ROC. But Mao had apparently recognized that full-scale invasion of the most important ROC offshore garrisons on the islands of Quemoy and Matsu was impractical, given their strong forti-fications and the PLA's weak amphibious forces. The motivation for the ar-tillery attacks on those islands, which sparked the crisis with the United States, was apparently largely political.[24] It is hardly clear, however, that Mao would have wanted to seize all of the offshore islands, even if he had believed the PLA to be more able to do so. As part of Fujian province, the offshore islands of Quemoy and Matsu provide a notional political bridge between Taiwan and the mainland. Cutting that bridge, especially with no hope of taking Taiwan itself soon thereafter, would serve the perceived American goal of permanently wresting Taiwan away from the mainland.

According to Colonel Xu Yan of the National Defense University, in ad-dition to the international political objectives discussed above, there was also a domestic dimension to the operations in 1954–55. As a revolution-ary, Mao emphasized the psychology of struggle as necessary for his popu-lace to meet the domestic goals set by the Party. The land reform campaign and the pacification of western China were carried out during the Korean War and, according to Xu, Mao believed that the successful implementation of the First Five Year Plan (1953–57) would be assisted by reminding the population that the international environment was hostile and that struggle was needed for the PRC to meet its goals. Although I see less hard evidence of this in the 1954–55 case, it would clearly become a theme in the 1958 Taiwan Strait crisis, itself a result of long-term strategic thinking, albeit of a different sort.[25]

In his sometimes surprisingly frank 1992 open-source book, *Jinmen zhi zhan* (The battle over Quemoy), Xu Yan sums up the factors discussed above when he writes:

Beginning in July 1954, the Central Committee, [and] Mao Zedong at the same time, placed "liberation of Taiwan" and the coastal islands question in prominent positions, demanding that the PLA increase its struggle in the coastal regions. This decision made at this time was the result of comprehensive consideration of multiple factors [such as] the international situation, the struggle across the Taiwan Strait, and domestic political mobilization and economic construction, etc. The main reason for the prominence of the Taiwan issue was the result of the 1954 Geneva conference . . . [Mao's] first consideration was the international strategic situation's influence on the question of re-unification of the motherland. At that time, the separation of Korea into north and south had been fixed and completed, [and] the result of the cease-fire in Indochina was also a dividing line [separating] north and south Vietnam. The United States was also mustering together Britain, France, Australia, the Philippines, New Zealand, Thailand, and Pakistan in preparation for signing the Southeast Asia Treaty Organization, whose purpose was to contain China. At the same time, it [the United States] was plotting the solidification [*gudinghua*] of the separation of the two sides of the Taiwan Strait. The need to stress the "liberation of Taiwan" was an expression of the CCP's resolute position on unification of the motherland and the smashing of plots to divide China. In addition to this . . . under conditions of armistice in Korea and the Geneva conference's decision for a cease-fire, [Mao] was unwilling to allow the peaceful influences to slacken the national people's fighting spirit [*quanguo renmin douzhi*]. And that is not even to mention that at that time, the U.S. military was still illegally occupying the Chinese territory of Taiwan, constituting a major threat to the new China, and the Taiwan KMT also had continuously harassed the mainland.[26]

Xu goes on to say that Mao's decision in summer 1954 did not represent a decision for large-scale military attack across the Taiwan Strait (*da guimo de duhai zuozhan*) but rather Mao's efforts to affect real or perceived negative trends in international politics and domestic politics by use of coercive diplomacy.

The 1958 Taiwan Strait Crisis

The assaults on Quemoy and Matsu in August–October 1958 were similar to those in 1954–55 in some ways and not in others. China used force in a demonstrative way against the offshore islands of Quemoy (Jinmen) and Matsu (Mazu) for what appeared to be political purposes. As before, Mao apparently did not seem overly dedicated to the mission of seizing the islands or even to driving all ROC forces off of them, despite the sometimes ferocious intensity of the shelling.[27] Because it was typhoon season, it was a particularly poor time to plan an amphibious attack on either Quemoy or Matsu. The artillery forces alone suffered mightily from wind and rain in August 1958.[28] Mao's commander in the field, Ye Fei, reported that Mao had never given him orders to prepare for seizing the islands, so he had not taken certain actions consistent with such a plan, such as softening up the defenses on the islands with large-scale bombing.[29] Moreover, at one point late in the crisis, when the artillery blockade appeared to be having a real effect on the islands and the United States was urging withdrawal of ROC forces there, Beijing encouraged the forces to stay and even offered to bring supplies to them if they needed them.[30]

But if Mao's goals in late summer and early fall 1958 were limited and largely political, what political situation was he addressing? It is possible that Mao was employing a straightforward windows logic following the introduction of new weapons systems to Taiwan, such as the nuclear-capable Matador missile, deployed to Taiwan in the second half of 1957. In fact, some leading scholars have asserted that Mao did perceive an increasing threat to the mainland from growing U.S.-Taiwan cooperation since summer 1957.[31] Running somewhat counter to this argument is evidence that Mao did not see the United States or Taiwan as particularly threatening in summer 1958.[32]

My interpretation is that Mao was indeed responding to a shift in the international distribution of power, but that he was most concerned with a shift within his own alliance and the long-range implications for China if it were not reversed.[33] After Sputnik, Beijing elites became concerned that the increasingly powerful Soviet Union was becoming less dependent on China and less supportive of its revolutionary allies now that it appeared to have a home-based deterrent against its main enemy.[34] In Mao's eyes, Moscow also appeared to be more assertive toward China in hopes of gaining a higher degree of control over its weaker ally. Mao viewed as evidence of this trend Nikita Khrushchev's foot-dragging on certain weapons transfers and especially his request for joint naval fleets and Soviet submarine radio stations on Chinese soil, which Mao regarded as an "assault" (*jingong*) on China's sovereignty.[35] Although this was a response to a changing balance of power, it was not of the same kind, however, as that noted above in the case of Korea or in some of the cases discussed below.

These concerns about Soviet power and bullying contributed to Mao's desire for a stronger, more self-sufficient China, which he pursued through his own hopelessly utopian program of the Great Leap Forward. In order to mobilize his population and urge them to make the significant sacrifices necessary to implement his Great Leap strategy, Mao wanted to recreate the spirit of sacrifice found in the 1930s base camps of the anti-Japanese war. In order to do so, he manufactured a carefully controlled international crisis and directly connected the danger of war with the United States and the need to liberate Taiwan with his domestic economic and social programs.[36]

Mao wanted to achieve political goals, including mobilizing his population for the Great Leap, and, most probably, to demonstrate foreign policy independence from the USSR, which was not informed in advance of the attack. It also could not hurt to remind the Americans, the KMT, and the world that the Civil War was not over and that the division of China was not considered acceptable in Beijing. Most Chinese histories of this event published in the reform era include all of these motives in their analysis, suggesting that the desire to preclude further solidification of the U.S.-ROC alliance was at least one of the motives behind the shelling of Quemoy and Matsu in early fall 1958.[37]

There are certain aspects of the case that match the analysis offered above quite well. Unlike in the case of the Korean War, in the shelling in 1958, Mao clearly did not want war with the United States and did not see his military campaign as a permanent solution to the Taiwan issue. Force was used to send a political message. As in the 1954–55 case, Mao seemed concerned to avoid escalation with the Americans, and Lin Biao even entertained the idea of warning the Americans in advance to ensure that no U.S. advisors on the islands were inadvertently hit (the notion was rejected by Mao).[38] Mao also strictly restricted air activity over the islands so as to avoid engaging American aircraft.[39] Despite these precautions, when one notes the hair-raising U.S. contingency plans in the crisis, including tactical nuclear strikes on PRC targets, one realizes that Mao ran real risks. The political use of limited force always raises the prospect of escalation, even if such escalation is not intended.[40] This is an important lesson for the analysis of contemporary cross-Strait relations.

India, 1962

It is difficult to find many references to windows logic in the relatively large secondary literature in China about this case. The main reason is that aggressive Indian actions are portrayed fairly universally as driving events. But there is at least one sense in which windows logic applies: Chinese analysts ascribe to Indian leaders a window of opportunity logic in explaining why Nehru provoked the conflict. In internally circulated Chinese analysis of the case, Nehru is in fact portrayed as being driven by false hopes related to a perceived window of opportunity that did not exist. Chinese authors argue that Nehru misread the meaning of global trends in the Cold War and China's growing isolation from both the USSR and the United States. Nehru's India is portrayed as becoming more aggressive on border issues between 1959 and 1962 because of Soviet military aid to India and because of Indian leaders' false belief that India's status as a neutral power in the Cold

War would deter a Chinese military response to Indian incursions. An internally circulated book argues that, in addition to trying to divert popular resistance to New Delhi outward, Nehru was guilty of false application of windows-of-opportunity thinking: "India's government incorrectly judged the situation: it believed the serious difficulties in the Chinese economy were insurmountable; China's Tibet and Xinjiang regions were unstable; the United States was supporting the Taiwan KMT's preparations for raids on the southeast coast, tying down [*qianzhi*] the PLA's main forces [*zhuyao li-liang*]; China's western border defense vacuum was an opportunity to seize [*you ji kecheng*]; the United States and Soviet Union and such countries supported India and opposed China, so China was isolated without help."[41] Another internally circulated text states that Nehru believed that "China would not dare risk the danger of American and Soviet intervention and launch a counterattack against India."[42] The military historian Xu Yan reports that in fall 1962, Mao judged the major reasons for India's obstreperous behavior to be a desire to divert domestic troubles by creating a conflict, an attempt to obtain foreign aid from the West, a desire to attack China's prestige in the Third World, and the general belief in Indian strategic circles that China would not dare counterattack, given its domestic problems and international isolation. Mao believed the last of these factors was the most important driver of Nehru's policy.[43]

Whether or not Chinese elites themselves saw closing windows of vulnerability is much less clear. As John Garver points out, Mao and others were concerned about Indian designs on Tibet, where India wanted to create a buffer state (*huan chong guo*) between it and its Asian rival to the east.[44] Those Indian designs became all the more important to China as Sino-Soviet relations worsened. Strategically important roads ran between western Tibet and Xinjiang province, thus potentially linking the many PLA forces in Tibet with those facing Soviet troops in the northwest. There is one problem with a straightforward window of vulnerability argument in the Sino-Indian war case. In the Chinese literature, PLA and CCP leaders are often portrayed as relatively confident and calm in the face of Indian salami tactics, waiting for the enemy to launch a larger-scale assault so that the PLA could implement Mao's doctrine of second-strike dominance (*houfa zhiren*).[45] Such a strategy also meshed with Mao's international goal of having the PRC seem to be the victim in the dispute to Third World onlookers.[46]

But a more complicated windows argument about the need to shut down the perception in New Delhi of an opening window of opportunity seems quite supportable from the available evidence. There were objective reasons for the misperceptions ascribed to the Indian leadership about China's weaknesses: China was isolated from both superpowers, although neither was likely to enter the conflict on India's side either, particularly since the brief war broke out during the Cuban missile crisis. China's economy was indeed in shambles after the Great Leap. And Taiwan recently had appealed unsuccessfully to the United States for assistance in invading the mainland, given the CCP's domestic and international weakness. If Nehru misread the relationship between Taipei and Washington as different than it was, so must have Mao, as late as June 1962, when he assembled large numbers of troops along China's southeast coast in order to defend against a possible KMT assault.[47]

In his 1975 classic *The Chinese Calculus of Deterrence: India and Indochina*, Allen Whiting traces a series of domestic and international concerns among the Chinese leaders, beginning in early 1962, and shows some explicit links between these concerns and the problem of India in the months leading up to the crisis. We lack the kind of smoking-gun documentary evidence and memoirs regarding the fight with India that we have in other cases. Such documentation would be helpful in more directly establishing Mao's desire to reverse dangerous international and domestic trends by using force. But Whiting's research on China's official statements about its security concerns in the first few months of 1962 is thorough and paints a picture of a China with security perceptions that fit the approach offered above. Foreign forces are viewed as preparing to exploit China's economic weaknesses and vulnerabilities and to promote separatism in Taiwan and Tibet. Japan in particular is seen as conspiring with the United States to cause the downfall of the KMT and to promote Taiwan's independence, and the United States is viewed as upgrading its security relationship with Taiwan in preparation for war.[48] In May, all of these domestic and international factors were linked to the problems in India by Foreign Minister Chen Yi.[49]

Unfortunately, we do not have such evidence from October 1962, but it seems hard to believe that Beijing was so concerned about trends in the international situation in spring and had such a dramatic turnaround in its consciousness within six months. This having been said, Mao was almost certainly more confident about the Taiwan issue in the near term after the United States restrained Chiang in Summer 1962, but the issue was hardly solved on a permanent basis. However, according to Taylor Fravel, the initial planning for the India campaign was done by Zhou Enlai in concert with senior military commanders in May, when the threat from Taiwan still seemed quite real. Zhou asked the military to prepare a military strategy by the end of June.[50] So China's basic strategy toward India in 1962 was formed before the threat from Taiwan had dissipated.

It is quite possible that Chinese leaders saw the use of decisive but measured force in the Himalayas primarily as a way of sending a political message, not only to New Delhi, but to Taipei, Washington, and Moscow as well. This is, however, difficult to prove or disprove without more documentary evidence. Moreover, by almost all accounts, India was so aggressive and overextended in its deployments that one could hardly have expected China to do anything but counterattack.[51] So it is hard to sustain the argument that sending a signal to third parties was the main purpose of the Chinese operations. China's use of force was nonetheless clearly more defensive and political than it was rooted in a desire to expand Chinese territory, because China quickly and unilaterally ceded much of the territory that the PLA gained in its utter rout of Indian forces on the latter's side of the Sino-Indian border's line of control.

Vietnam, 1964–1969

China's use of force from 1964 to 1969 had complex causes, ranging from China's assessment of international security trends to its desire to compete with the Soviet Union for the hearts and minds of international communists, especially in the Third World. The combination of national security concerns and ideology made Mao much more aggressive in supporting revolution in Vietnam and much less eager for a peaceful settlement of the war there, for example, than we would have expected had he only been interested in national security traditionally conceived.[52] That having been said, although it was not the only important factor or perhaps even the most important factor, Mao's assessment of international security trends did apparently affect his decisions to increase the number of troops the PRC sent to Vietnam and the amount of material aid transferred to the Vietnamese communists both before and after the Gulf of Tonkin Incident and Pleiku. As in Korea, Mao's intervention in Vietnam was based on the goal of driving the Americans out of the country, so the goals were not primarily political, as they were in the Taiwan crises in the 1950s and in the 1962 case.

It is very difficult to imagine that the Vietnamese communists could have carried out their revolutionary plans in the south without Chinese assistance, particularly prior to the U.S. escalation in 1964–65 and the Soviet assistance to Vietnam that followed it. In fact, as a CCP Party history argues, basically all of the Vietnamese communist matériel was supplied by China in the first half of the 1960s, aside from weapons captured from the enemy.[53] Perhaps of equal importance, China offered its own territory as a strategic "rear area" if the United States were to invade the north.[54] Even before the Gulf of Tonkin Incident, Mao announced to the North Vietnamese chief of staff his intention to send "volunteers" into Vietnam.[55] On

10 July 1964, just one month before the Gulf of Tonkin Resolution, Zhou Enlai bolstered Vietnamese communist spirits by making a clear commitment to assist North Vietnam in the event of a U.S. invasion of China's ally. He said: "If the United States is resolved to expand this war, by invading the Democratic Republic of Vietnam, or directly sending in forces, bringing the flames of war to China's side, we cannot just stand idly by [*zuo shi bu guan*]. That is to say, if they want to fight a Korean-style war, we shall prepare for it."[56]

Mao's support for the Vietnamese communists was based both on ideological goals Mao set in competition with the USSR and on national security concerns not shared by the more distant Soviet Union. Arguably, before the August 1964 Gulf of Tonkin Incident, the former were more important than the latter. Mao did discuss the American threat and the need to prepare for it earlier in the year, but he did not expect a direct American invasion of North Vietnam, let alone China, anytime soon.[57] He said that the United States was spread too thin militarily and would have to rely on intermediate allies, such as Japan and West Germany, to take the fight to communist countries other than the Soviet Union. He believed the U.S. strategy was to be the "last to join an international war." As for China, he believed that the U.S. strategy was based more on "peaceful evolution" than military conquest.[58] Despite such a moderate threat assessment, in June, Mao himself offered "unconditional support" to a Vietnamese military General Staff entourage.[59]

The Gulf of Tonkin Incident in August 1964 and the U.S. reaction to it would change Beijing's perception of the Vietnam War and the trends in U.S. security policy. On 6 August, one day after U.S. Navy aviators bombed North Vietnam, the CCP Central Committee resolved that "America's infringement [*qinfan*] against the Democratic Republic of Vietnam is an infringement against China." It pledged to make "assistance to Vietnam our top priority. We must handle all Vietnam's requests with the utmost seriousness, conscientiousness, and activism." The statement goes on to say that China must facilitate the delivery of supplies to communists in South Vietnam as well.[60]

In order to boost Vietnamese morale, China made early significant promises of support. In April 1965, Liu Shaoqi promised Le Duan that the Chinese would "do our best to support" the Vietnamese communists in their request for "some volunteer pilots, volunteer soldiers . . . and other volunteers, including road and bridge engineering units."[61] Responding to the specter of a U.S. buildup on its southwestern periphery, Beijing greatly increased military assistance to the Vietnamese communists in 1965. From 1965 to 1971, 320,000 Chinese troops would rotate through the Vietnamese theater, reaching a one-time peak of 170,000 in the theater in 1967–68.

Among the Chinese forces, arguably the most important were 150,000 air defense troops. Beijing claims that it supplied U.S.$20 billion worth of assistance from 1950 to 1978, 90 percent of it in outright grants, outfitted 2 million Vietnamese troops, laid hundreds of kilometers of strategically important railroad lines, and provided 300 million yards of cloth, 5 million tons of food, and 3,000 kilometers of oil pipeline. China suffered thousands of casualties, both dead and wounded, in Vietnam.[62]

As in Korea, and unlike in the 1950s Taiwan Strait crises, Mao sought military victory for the communist forces in Vietnam. He was not just making a political statement, because he did not initially want to settle for a cease-fire line. Instead, Beijing continued to assist in Hanoi's efforts to "liberate" the south. In May 1965, Mao supported Ho Chih Minh's plan to use Chinese road engineers in the north to free up Vietnamese personnel for action in the south. Mao also supported building roads through Laos, and, in preparation for escalation of the war, he even told Ho that "because we shall fight large-scale battles in the future, it would be good if we also build roads to Thailand."[63] In August 1966, Zhou Enlai even decided to send 100 specially trained personnel into South Vietnam to serve in "command staffs, logistics, chemistry, engineering, [and] political training."[64] In late 1967, just weeks before the Tet offensive, Mao promised again that China would be a "reliable rear area" for Hanoi should it find itself in greater trouble after taking the fight to the south.[65] All of these measures were designed to encourage the Vietnamese communists to eschew peace deals with the United States and South Vietnam, as was preferred at the time by the ideologically less fervent and geographically more distant Soviet Union.

China's actions in Vietnam are not usually considered among the cases of Chinese use of force. Arguably, China's material and political support for the Vietnamese communists was more important than its personnel in the war. But if the statistics cited above are indeed correct, China's intervention in the Vietnam War was massive at times and significantly raised the costs and dangers of American involvement in the war. Although ideology and Sino-Soviet competition played a heavy role in China's Vietnam War strategy, especially in Mao's many efforts from 1965 to 1969 to scuttle peace talks between Hanoi and Washington, it is also fairly clear that his initial suspicions about the Americans and his surprise at the large-scale insertion of U.S. ground troops from 1965 to 1968 affected the intensity of his support for the Vietnamese communists.

But just as his initial shock at the American escalation made him most concerned about his southern flank, Mao relatively quickly determined that the likelihood was low of escalation of the Vietnam War to include American crossing of the 17th parallel with ground forces. As a result, his view of the threats facing China shifted gradually from south (the United States) to north (the USSR) in the years 1965–69. In fact, as early as March 1965, Mao told foreign audiences that he was so concerned about Soviet-American collusion in Vietnam peace negotiations that he was preparing for the possibility of a joint U.S.-Soviet assault on China.[66] So, Mao's concerns about the USSR increased in 1968–69, but they were not new.

The Road to Zhenbaodao in 1969

Sino-Soviet differences over the proper course of war and diplomacy in Vietnam in 1965–68 turned into direct Sino-Soviet tensions in this period, which reached a boiling point in 1968. With the Soviet invasion of Czechoslovakia, which Moscow sought to justify by proclaiming the so-called Brezhnev Doctrine, Sino-Soviet rivalry within the communist camp turned into Sino-Soviet confrontation.[67] The Brezhnev Doctrine had clear implications for China: if the Kremlin reserved the right to use force to overthrow regimes that strayed from orthodox Marxism-Leninism as defined in Moscow, then Cultural Revolution China surely was at risk of attack. There were more than just ideological reasons to worry. Since 1965, the USSR had been gradually building up its forces, not only along the Sino-Soviet border in Xinjiang and Manchuria, but also in Mongolia, a country with which Moscow signed a defense pact in 1965. By 1967, several Soviet divisions were in Mongolia alone.[68] At the same time, when assessing the broader international environment, it appears that Mao became increasingly convinced that the Americans were not going to escalate in Vietnam in the near term, and that the threat on China's southern flank was therefore diminishing.[69]

Most of the recent scholarship on China's role in the Sino-Soviet border clashes seems to support the earlier wisdom of Allen Whiting and Thomas Robinson. Fighting seemed to have started on Zhenbaodao (Damansky) Island, in the Ussuri River, in March 1969 after a Chinese ambush of Soviet forces in disputed territory.[70] In terms of the analysis offered above, politics were in command in this case, and trend analysis led to the use of force against a superior foe. The PRC was using force to try to alter long-term trends that were running against Beijing's security interests. Force was used to teach the USSR a lesson and demonstrate China's resolve. It was not used to resolve the Sino-Soviet tensions at the border once and for all, or to prevent an imminent Soviet invasion, which nobody, least of all Mao, expected at the time of the attack. Rather, Mao's concerns were more about the longer-term future. Mao seems to have expected and feared that an increasingly powerful Soviet military presence in East Asia might be the precursor of an eventual Soviet attack on China. Given the crushing of the Prague Spring, political trends seemed to confirm this view of the world. So, in a manner consistent with his actions in 1954 and, to a lesser degree, 1962, Mao used force against the Soviets.[71] Yang Kuisong argues that, as in the earlier cases, Mao worked hard to prevent escalation, because he was not seeking a wider war. "Beijing's leaders, Mao in particular, had no further military aims than to teach the Soviets a bitter lesson, so that Moscow would stop further military provocations on the Sino-Soviet border," Yang contends.[72]

The use of force almost certainly had a domestic component as well, as it did in Korea and the Taiwan Strait crises in the 1950s, especially the 1958 crisis. Yang emphasizes this factor—the need to restore Party and national unity at home following three years of Cultural Revolution—alongside his argument regarding the "pedagogical war" incentives. In a provocative article about the case, Lyle Goldstein dismisses the strategic argument altogether, pointing to the lack of an objective Soviet threat to China in the theater before the Zhenbaodao incident. Instead, Goldstein focuses exclusively on the domestic mobilization aspects of the conflict.[73] Goldstein believes that Mao was simply attempting at this time to rein in the excesses of the Cultural Revolution and to unify the CCP at the April 1969 Ninth Party Congress. The 1969 border clash, then, was a diversionary conflict, not a preventive one, because Mao could not have seen the Soviet forces in the theater before the conflict as particularly threatening. In his Ph.D. dissertation, Taylor Fravel takes issue with Goldstein's account, arguing that evidence from China strongly suggests that Chinese elites saw the Soviet forces as increasingly threatening, even if an objective military assessment might dismiss the notion that Soviet forces might be used in an offensive against China anytime soon. Fravel stakes out his position in a way that is reminiscent of Whiting's work on Chinese perceptions, asserting that "even though China maintained numerical superiority [locally in 1969], China's leaders viewed the dramatic increase in Soviet deployments as representing a sharp and adverse decline in their ability to secure the border and project power over disputed areas. How China's leaders perceived the balance is as important as the actual balance."[74]

There may be a way to resolve this debate without dismissing either the international or domestic explanations, but rather by integrating them. If Mao was worrying about affecting long-term Soviet trends in a way consistent with windows logic and not simply preempting a perceived imminent threat, it would only make sense for Mao to attack prior to a larger-scale Soviet buildup and while Moscow still seemed preoccupied in Europe, rather than to wait for the Soviet threat in East Asia to grow further before attacking. In that sense, contra Goldstein, the lack of full Soviet preparations for an offensive in spring 1969 is evidence for, not against, the preventive logic offered above. Moreover, as a longtime practitioner of the tactic of using external conflict to bring about internal Party unity, Mao might very well have calculated that a carefully circumscribed conflict with the USSR would create the sense of emergency in high-level Party circles that he deemed necessary to unify the CCP during and after the critically important Ninth Party Congress, which was necessary if China were to counter growing Soviet pressure and, perhaps, to prepare for eventual rapprochement with the United States. Consistent with this thesis, Yang Kuisong reports that, as in 1958, Mao urged millions of Chinese to rally in protest, this time against the Soviet revisionists rather than the American imperialists. There may be a way to synthesize the two apparently quite different aspects of Yang's thesis. One of the things that made China appear weak in Soviet eyes, and actually made China weak in fact, was its internal turmoil. Mao might have seen a need to "internally balance," to use political science terminology, by unifying and mobilizing his society to counter the long-term threat from the USSR. Attacking the Soviet forces on Zhenbao Island sent a tough signal before Moscow was fully ready and willing to retaliate massively against China in East Asia. Mao then used the heightened tensions for longer-term mobilizational purposes, as he had done in sparking a crisis with the United States in 1958.

Yang Kuisong's account, however, provides a potentially sobering future lesson for Chinese leaders who would emulate Mao by "teaching a lesson" to a superpower spread thin in multiple regions and distracted elsewhere. Yang argues that Mao was shocked by the intensity of the Soviet response both in terms of a near-term war scare and the fast-paced military buildup on the Chinese border that followed. Mao had not expected such a concerted response so soon, especially when it occurred far from European Russia, where the main Soviet forces and logistics bases were. In the end, these tensions did not escalate and did have one good result for China: they sped rapprochement with the United States, allowing China to break out of its isolation. But in an unusually frank and brave thesis, Yang rejects the notion that Mao knew that this would be the outcome, and insists that he badly miscalculated the Soviet response in dangerous ways.[75] Yang's account seems both balanced and plausible.

The Xisha Islands (Paracels), 1974

This case does not deserve a great deal of attention, perhaps, but the PRC's use of force to seize the Xisha Islands from the Republic of Vietnam is a fine example of windows logic. In this case, the term "window of opportunity" might apply better than "window of vulnerability," but they are really two sides of the same coin. In 1974, it was fairly clear that the American position in Vietnam was weak and getting weaker. Also, the Sino-American rapprochement meant that the United States would not actively intervene if PLA forces attacked Vietnamese forces around the Paracels. Moreover, China wanted to settle the dispute before North Vietnam successfully "liberated" the south. Chinese relations with the Vietnamese communists had worsened in the early 1970s as Hanoi turned increasingly to the USSR for assistance, and as Sino-Soviet relations remained chilly at best. In any event, China was more likely to win the Xisha dispute against the weak, noncommunist Republic of Vietnam than against a strong communist Vietnam backed by the Soviet bloc. Although the aim of the use of force here was to seize territory militarily, rather than to send a message, doing so fits the pattern described earlier: a window was open and was quickly closing. If force were not used to seize the islands at this point, it would be much more difficult to do so in the future.[76]

Vietnam, 1979

Perhaps the most difficult case of China's use of force to study is the 1979 "pedagogical war" against Vietnam. On two trips to China in 2001 and 2002, I attempted to find interesting new materials on this topic, but was told in interviews that such materials are very hard to acquire and that even CCP historians do not have access to most of the details of the decision-making process. One CCP international security analyst confided to me that this might be because the military effort was largely a failure, and the CCP not only avoids airing its dirty laundry before outsiders, on security politics, it does not freely air that laundry within the Party either.[77]

From viewing the international setting at the time and how it must have appeared to the Chinese elite, the post-Mao CCP elites' decision to use force fits the window of vulnerability logic offered here. Relations with the USSR remained extremely tense in 1978, and the competition with Moscow was intensifying on several scores. Soviet relations with Vietnam had improved markedly since Hanoi successfully unified Vietnam under its rule. As Harlan Jencks argues: "The [recently signed] Soviet-Vietnamese treaty threatened a considerable increase of Soviet military aid to the SRV [Socialist Republic of Vietnam], but the Soviet military presence in Vietnam was still fairly small in mid-February 1979. Chinese leaders probably saw time working against them in this respect, and therefore wanted to strike sooner rather than later."[78] The Chinese were also seeking a counter to Vietnamese power in Southeast Asia by supporting the Khmer Rouge in Cambodia. And, in December 1978, Vietnam launched a massive invasion of Cambodia with the purpose of overthrowing Pol Pot's regime. So the Chinese attack was almost certainly designed to slow or even reverse Vietnam's invasion of Cambodia.

King Chen offers the most detailed account of the December 1978 Plenum Party meetings at which a conditional decision to use force against Vietnam was made. Vietnam would be subject to attack if Hanoi did not back down on Cambodia and in border conflicts with China. Although his story is compelling, we cannot be certain of Chen's sources. Chen argues that Deng Xiaoping was extremely concerned about the situation in Cambodia and about the Soviet-Vietnamese encirclement campaign more generally. Chen reports that Deng also argued to the CCP elite that the costs of invasion would be limited, and that any failures that might occur could be beneficial in convincing intransigent domestic forces of the necessity for the reform and modernization programs that were being launched at the same plenum.[79]

In terms of windows of opportunity, the recent diplomatic normalization with the United States might have given Deng confidence that he could take such actions without spoiling the warming trends with Washington and without sparking a war with the USSR. It is fairly clear that during his trip to Washington and Tokyo in January 1979, Deng sought at least tacit approval of his attack in Vietnam in both capitals, and he certainly behaved as if he had received it.[80] Moreover, Taiwan was on the defensive diplomatically, and could not gain U.S. backing for an attack even it had been considering one. So, there was little or no danger that action in Vietnam would leave dangerous vulnerabilities to ROC attack along China's southeast coast.[81]

Harlan Jencks argues that, on the military side, February was a logical time for an invasion of Vietnam. The rainy season in April would complicate an invasion of Vietnam and the spring thaw in the north would make a Soviet counterattack against China's northern border less feasible than it would be in winter. So by attacking in very late winter, China was jumping through a weather window that maximized its own chances of success, while minimizing the time that the USSR would have to mobilize an attack against China.[82]

One last window of opportunity or vulnerability might have been at work. Deng was about to launch a massive reform program under the banner of the Four Modernizations. Deng knew that military modernization was only the fourth of the four modernizations, and that he planned to cut the size of the military and the military budget radically. It is quite possible that Deng wanted to address the Vietnam security problems before the military became distracted in this reform process.[83]

In discussions with American security specialists inside and outside the government in 1978, Beijing laid out a windows of vulnerability argument about the dangerous behavior of Vietnam and the need for China and the

West to "break up the timetable of Soviet strategy." The Chinese need for long-term peace during the nascent reform era, rather than making China less belligerent in the short term, made it more so. Nayan Chanda argues that this was the case because "China could buy time by preempting the enemy plan at an early stage."[84]

There had been other major irritants in Sino-Vietnamese relations before the invasion. These included a cutoff of Chinese aid, border disputes, and Hanoi's inhumane treatment and expulsion of ethnic Chinese in Vietnam. But these incidents appear epiphenomenal: the underlying causes of these disputes and the military conflict itself seem to have been geopolitics and Chinese fear of encirclement. In fact, according to Nayan Chanda, the poor treatment of ethnic Chinese in Vietnam was viewed in Beijing not so much as a violation of those citizens' human rights but as a sign that Vietnam was taking instructions from Moscow about how to prepare for an encirclement campaign against China.[85] As Robert Ross argues persuasively, Soviet actions in South and Southeast Asia and the development of the Soviet Pacific Fleet in the 1970s were the strategic backdrop for China's view that Moscow and Hanoi were colluding to encircle China and limit China's influence in its own backyard.[86]

As in the Korean War case, China chose to take action on land rather than at sea. But unlike in the case of the Korean War, and more like many other cases discussed above, there is no evidence that China had expansive goals of defeating enemy forces throughout the country or of changing the territorial status quo. This is true despite the very large scale of the Chinese invasion.[87] Instead, force seems to have been intended more to alter political trends and send political messages. The invasion probably had two aims: on the political side, to send a coercive message to Hanoi that its pro-Soviet and anti-Chinese behavior was unacceptable and would be costly, thus reversing the negative political trends in the region; and on the military side, to draw sufficient Vietnamese military strength away from Cambodia and to give Pol Pot a chance to regroup and better counter the Vietnamese invasion. Neither result was achieved. Soviet-Vietnamese relations would only tighten in the remaining years before Gorbachev transformed Soviet foreign policy. The new Soviet Pacific Fleet moved into the U.S.-built naval base at Cam Ranh Bay, and, as the invasion of Afghanistan later in the year demonstrated, Moscow was hardly deterred from future adventures on China's periphery. And, although there is some evidence that Vietnam did begin to shift forces from the Cambodian theater upon news of the Chinese invasion, the war was short, and the Vietnamese border defense forces in place did quite well, so that the establishment of a pro-Vietnamese regime in Phnom Penh was not greatly delayed. Of course, if one is assessing the success of a campaign designed to affect long-term trends, one can use counterfactual reasoning to deem the effort a success by comparing it to a hypothetical projected future in which China had not used force in Vietnam. Would the security situation in Southeast Asia and along the northern border with the Soviet Union and Mongolia have been even worse from China's perspective had Beijing not responded vigorously to the Vietnamese invasion of Cambodia and the budding Soviet-Vietnamese alliance? Robert Ross argues that the campaign, however militarily clumsy, might indeed have served the PRC's security interests for this reason.[88]

For our purposes, the important lessons of this case are that, like Mao, the post-Mao Chinese leadership took significant risks to launch a war for largely political, rather than territorial, objectives. Although one might code the Vietnamese invasion of Cambodia as a "bright-line provocation," the attack on Vietnam was about broader objectives than simply reversing Vietnamese gains there. Those objectives were based primarily on an assessment of negative and positive trends in the alliances and alignments of China's friends and enemies, and on Beijing's desire to alter those trends before the PRC's long-term interests were harmed. As in other cases, the need for a long-term peaceful environment encouraged shorter-term belligerence. In particular, the domestic political challenges involved in the reform process probably only made the use of force more rather than less likely. Finally, although Vietnam was not itself militarily superior, and CCP elites probably perceived it as even weaker than it was, Vietnam was aligned with the much more powerful Soviet Union, so China was running real risks by attacking. In 1979, the reputation of the United States for resolve and assertiveness in international affairs was hardly at its peak, thus rendering Beijing's belligerence against a new Soviet ally all the more risky.

Conclusions: Taiwan and Trend Analysis in the Contemporary Era

A brief overview of the 1995–96 Taiwan crisis shows how the PRC used force coercively in response to views of long-term trends in Taiwan politics and in U.S.-China relations.[89] China was concerned about President Lee Teng-hui's diplomatic assertiveness, the potential implications of Washington's granting Lee a visa to visit the United States, the politically charged nature of Lee's public speeches and statements while in the United States, and the prospect of a long-term trend in Taiwanese domestic public opinion in the direction of legal independence for Taiwan. One can easily see that President Lee's visit to the United States fell far short of a declaration of independence, yet it sparked a militarized crisis, including PLA missile launches and surface exercises. Chinese interlocutors in 2002 stated that a similar visit by Taiwan's current president, Chen Shui-bian, to Washington would require a show of force that exceeded in scope that of 1995–96.[90]

I have written about the potential impact on Chinese trend analysis from 1993 to the present in several articles. This is not the place to present those findings, but rather to establish some links to the themes discussed above.[91] Since 1996, Chinese security analysts have been concerned about various trends in U.S. security policy, in cross-Strait relations, and in domestic politics in Taiwan. PRC analysts ascribe great influence to the United States in cross-Strait relations, so one of the key factors that determine whether their trend analysis is pessimistic or optimistic is their attitude toward U.S. security policy. They ask: what is the nature of the U.S.-Taiwan political and defense relationship, and what is the relative likelihood that Washington is moving toward unconditional support for Taiwan's security, even in cases where Taiwan were to take provocative diplomatic steps to spark a crisis or conflict? Along these lines, CCP security elites worry about the Bush administration's efforts to sell weapons to Taiwan, even though they appreciated the tough tone that the Bush administration adopted when President Chen Shui-bian made statements suggesting Taiwan's national sovereignty.[92] Beijing also pays careful attention to trends in the U.S.-Japan alliance and other U.S. defense relationships in the region, especially those with implications for war in and around Taiwan.

In general, since 11 September 2001, Chinese analysts have recognized that the United States is intent on avoiding provoking a fight with China. Washington would like Beijing's cooperation in the global war on terror and on related proliferation issues, such as the North Korean nuclear crisis. Even without positive incentives for cooperation, Beijing realizes that the United States has other fish to fry, in Afghanistan, Iraq, and elsewhere.

PRC analysis of Taiwan domestic politics is centrally important to Beijing's trend analysis. The electoral fortunes of traditionally pro-independence parties on Taiwan have been a major focus of attention in Beijing, especially as Taiwan prepares to revise its constitution over the next few years. The election and reelection of the pro-independence Democratic Progressive Party President Chen Shui-bian in 2000 and 2004 made Beijing very nervous about long-term trends, but there are factors pulling in the opposite direction that reassure Beijing: these include the inability of traditionally pro-independence or "pan-Green" parties to gain a majority in Taiwan's legislature (the Legislative Yuan) in 2004 and the restraining influence this electoral outcome will have on the constitutional revision process scheduled for 2005–8.

An important cause of Beijing's confidence is the weakness of the Taiwan economy and Taiwan's increasing economic dependence on the mainland. Trade across the Taiwan Strait is in the tens of billions of dollars, is growing,

and strongly favors Taiwan in terms of the trade balance. This creates political leverage for the PRC. More important still, Taiwanese citizens have
invested as much as $100 billion in the mainland, and hundreds of thou-
sands of Taiwanese citizens now have residences in the Shanghai area alone.
China's increasing economic and diplomatic importance to other actors in
the region and the United States has also bolstered Beijing's confidence that
few, if any, important countries would be eager or even willing to line up
against Beijing on the Taiwan issue.

In military affairs, China's quickly growing, but still limited, coercive capacity against Taiwan counsels patience, at least until the PLA has absorbed
and trained with some of the imported and locally produced weapons systems procured for Taiwan scenarios. Especially since 1999, Beijing has
expended greater resources and greater attention on developing coercive
options against Taiwan. This effort takes time, however, and it appears that
the PRC is capitalizing on the budgetary malaise in Taiwan to improve its
relative coercive capacity against the island, while Taiwan struggles to
respond. However, concerns remain in Beijing about certain long-term
military trends, including increased coordination between the U.S. military
and its Taiwanese counterpart, strengthening of the U.S.-Japan alliance,
and the prospect of the introduction into the region of future upper-tier,
theater-navy-wide ballistic missile defenses once these systems are fully
developed.

If, at a time when China had developed more robust military options
against Taiwan than it currently has, PRC elites were to become very concerned about these trend lines (as they were in early 2000) and frustrated
that factors like Taiwan's economic dependence on the mainland and PLA
coercive capacity were not producing Taipei's accommodation, then Chinese use of force for largely political purposes seems quite possible, even if
Taiwan had not yet declared legal independence and even if Beijing elites did
not believe that they could resolve the Taiwan issue on their own terms by
using force.

Fortunately, there are usually many "ifs" in any pessimistic scenario about
how cross-Strait relations could lead to conflict. The situation is far from
hopeless, as long as the United States can mix credible threats of intervention and arms transfers to Taiwan with credible political assurances that it
will not use its superiority now or in the future to promote Taiwan independence. This should bolster deterrence across the Taiwan Strait. By analyzing the PRC's historical uses of force, I have tried in this chapter to demonstrate that maintaining peace across the Taiwan Strait may not be as simple
as some might believe. Americans should not be overly confident about
the safety of Taiwan or of American forces in the region by reference to U.S.
military superiority or Taiwan's ability to defeat a D-Day–style invasion.

Instead, they should ask themselves how to reduce China's ability to hurt American forces, coerce America's friends and allies, and damage Taiwan's economy. At the same time, they should be asking what diplomatic steps, military improvements, alliance policies, and diplomacy toward Taiwan and the mainland best meet the paradoxical demands of deterring mainland adventurism while reassuring Beijing that the United States is not backing China into a corner on the Taiwan issue by encouraging the forces of Taiwan independence over time.

This balance in U.S. policy might prove tricky to find, especially as PLA coercive capacity grows during this decade. Deterring coercion is harder than deterring invasion and requires a much higher level of superiority for U.S., Japanese, and Taiwan forces in combination. We should expect a security competition between China's coercive capabilities and the increasingly coordinated defensive capabilities of Taiwan, the United States, and, perhaps, Japan. Taiwan might even try to break out of this race by going offensive and creating a deterrent of missiles and weapons of mass destruction of its own. This would not happen overnight, however, and judging from the history of PRC use of force, we should not expect the PLA to wait until those capabilities are up and running to strike Taiwan and try to force a political deal.

The optimists are correct that peace is still more likely than war, and the problems that exist in cross-Strait relations can be resolved. But for Washington to play a constructive role in this process and increase the likelihood of peace, U.S. security analysts need to understand the ways in which PRC security analysts consider present and future trends in military affairs, economics, and politics when devising security strategies.

Notes

1. For the most thorough and theoretically informed presentation of the case for optimism and the likely future effectiveness of the traditional U.S. deterrent posture in cross-Strait relations, see Robert S. Ross, "Navigating the Taiwan Strait: Deterrence, Escalation Dominance, and U.S.-China Relations," *International Security* 27, 2 (Fall 2002): 48–85.

2. The most comprehensive review of the literature on preventive war is Jack S. Levy, "Declining Power and the Preventive Motivation for War," *World Politics* 40 (October 1987): 82–107. The best analysis of both preemptive wars and preventive wars, and the best defense of the theories about them, is Stephen Van Evera, *Causes of War: Power and the Roots of Conflict* (Ithaca, N.Y.: Cornell University Press, 1999), chs. 3 and 4. The assertion that preemptive wars "almost never happen" comes from Daniel Reiter, "Exploding the Powderkeg Myth: Preemptive Wars Almost Never Happen," *International Security* 20 (Fall 1995): 5–34.

3. For classic examples of power transition theory, see A. F. K. Organski and Jacek Kugler, *The War Ledger* (Chicago: University of Chicago Press, 1980); and Robert Gilpin, *War and Change in International Politics* (Cambridge: Cambridge University Press, 1981).

4. The clearest statement of this argument is Van Evera, *Causes of War*, ch. 3.

5. The pioneering and still classic account of Mao's calculations in the second half of 1950 is Allen Whiting, *China Crosses the Yalu: The Decision to Enter the Korean War* (1960; Stanford: Stanford University Press, 1968); also see Thomas J. Christensen, *Useful Adversaries: Grand Strategy, Domestic Mobilization, and Sino-American Conflict* (Princeton, N.J.: Princeton University Press, 1996), ch. 5. For arguments that Mao was more aggressive and ideologically driven than either Whiting or I argue, see Chen Jian's excellent book *China's Road to the Korean War: The Making of Sino-American Confrontation* (New York: Columbia University Press, 1994). Other prominent works include Sergei Goncharov, John Lewis, and Xue Litai, *Uncertain Partners: Stalin, Mao, and the Korean War* (Stanford: Stanford University Press, 1993), esp. chs. 3–4; Shuguang Zhang, *Deterrence and Strategic Culture: Chinese-American Confrontations, 1949–58* (Ithaca, N.Y.: Cornell University Press, 1992); and Shuguang Zhang, *Mao's Military Romanticism* (Lawrence: University of Kansas Press, 1995).

6. For relevant evidence and argumentation, see "Talk at the Eighth Meeting of the Central People's State Conference," 28 June 1950, in *Jianguo yilai Mao Zedong wengao* [The manuscripts of Mao Zedong since the founding of the nation] (Beijing: Zhongyang Wenxian Chubanshe, 1987–), 1: 423; Hong Xuezhi, *Kang Mei yuan Chao zhanzheng huiyi* [Recollections of the war to resist U.S. aggression and to aid Korea] (Beijing: Liberation Army Literature and Art Publishing, 1990), 1; Chai Chengwen and Zhao Yongtian, *Banmendian tanpan* [Panmunjon negotiations] (Beijing: Liberation Army Press, 1989), 81–82; Chen Jian, *China's Road to the Korean War*, 132; Peng Dehuai, "Talk to the Meeting to Mobilize Cadres of Division Commander and Above of the People's Volunteer Army," 14 October 1950, in *Peng Dehuai junshi wenxuan* [Selected military writings of Peng Dehuai] (Beijing: Zhongyang Wenxian Chubanshe, 1988), 322; and Hao Yufan and Zhai Zhihai, "China's Decision to Enter the Korean War: History Revisited," *China Quarterly*, no. 121 (March 1990): 94–115, at 103–8; Christensen, *Useful Adversaries*, ch. 5.

7. See "Telegram to Zhou Enlai: 13 October 1950," in *Jianguo yilai Mao Zedong wengao*, vol. 1; on the prohibitive expense of standing defenses at the Yalu, see Hao and Zhai, "China's Decision," 104.

8. Peng Dehuai, *Memoirs of a Chinese Marshal* (Beijing: Foreign Languages Press, 1984), 473; and Hao and Zhai, "China's Decision," 103–8.

9. Peng, "Talk to the Meeting to Mobilize Cadres," in *Peng Dehuai junshi wenxuan*, 321.

10. Ibid.

11. See Peng, *Memoirs*, 473–74, and Christensen, *Useful Adversaries*, ch. 5.

12. For Mao's tortured decision, see Chen, Jian, "The Sino-Soviet Alliance and China's Entry into the Korean War" (working paper of the Cold War History Project, Woodrow Wilson International Center, Washington, D.C., 1991); Zhang, *De-*

terrence and Strategic Culture, ch. 4; and Michael Hunt, "Beijing and the Korea Crisis," *Political Science Quarterly* (Fall 1992): 453–78; Peng Dehuai also reports sleepless nights in early October regarding the prospect of entering the war, see Peng, *Memoirs*, 473.

13. Shen Zhihua, *Mao Zedong, Si Dalin yu Chao zhan: Zhong Su zui gao jimi dang'an* [Mao Zedong, Stalin and the Korean War: the top secret Sino-Soviet archives] (Hong Kong: Cosmos Books, 1998), 218–20; and Chen Jian, *China's Road*, 112.

14. Kathryn Weathersby, "New Findings on the Korean War," *Cold War International History Project Bulletin*, no. 6–7 (Winter 1995–96). This obsession with Japanese intervention on Mao's part is also noted by the most recent open-source Chinese scholarship on the war by Song Liansheng, which reports more frankly about the events of spring 1950 than any previous work I have read, open or internally circulated. Song reports that, from late 1949 through 1950, China's main concern about foreign intervention in Korea was with Japanese forces fighting at the behest of the United States. Mao's initial commitment to assist Kim if his invasion plan went badly was premised on the notion that 20–30,000 Japanese troops might enter the fray. Song Liansheng, *Kang Mei yuan Chao zai hui shou* [Looking back again on the Korean War] (Kunming: Yunnan People's Press, 2002), 42–43.

15. Kathryn Weathersby, *Soviet Aims in Korea and the Origins of the Korean War, 1945–50*, Working Paper No. 8 (Washington, D.C.: Cold War International History Project, Woodrow Wilson International Center for Scholars, 1993).

16. "PRC Scholar Shi Yinhong on Gains, Losses, Winners, Losers in Korean War" (in Chinese), Beijing Qianlong Wang online text, 28 July 2003, in Foreign Broadcast Information Service (hereafter cited as FBIS), CPP20030730000190.

17. For an excellent review of the reasons for Mao's underestimation of American power, resolve, or both, see Chen, *China's Road*, 126–28, which posits that Mao was not so much stunned by the hypothetical prospect of eventual war between China and the United States as he was by the speed and intensity of the American response in 1950.

18. Reiter, "Exploding the Powderkeg Myth."

19. Russian documents reveal that in Sino-Soviet discussions of the conditions for escalation and of Stalin's desire for China to enter the war as early as July, defending against a breach of the 38th parallel by American forces was always primary in the thinking of both Chinese and Russian leaders. For discussion of these documents, see Christensen, *Useful Adversaries*, 158–59.

20. For this telegram, see Alexandre Mansourov, "Stalin, Mao, Kim, and China's Decision to Enter the Korean War, September 16–October 15, 1950: New Evidence from the Russian Archives," *Cold War International History Project Bulletin*, no. 6–7 (Winter 1995–96): 94–119, at 114–15.

21. For a fuller review of the two document collections and their general compatibility with the thesis that Beijing entered the war reluctantly because of a fear of inaction and despite a recognition of the very high risks, see Christensen, *Useful Adversaries*, 163–70. For Mao's 14 October telegram, see "Telegram to Zhou Enlai on

the Principles and Deployments of the People's Volunteer Army as It Enters Korea for Combat," in *Jianguo yilai Mao Zedong wengao*, 1: 560–61, translated in *Useful Adversaries*, app. B.

22. Xu Yan, *Jinmen zhi zhan* [The battle over Quemoy] (Beijing: Zhongguo Guangbo Dianshi Chubanshe, 1992), 159.

23. He Di, "The Evolution of the People's Republic of China's Policy Toward the Offshore Islands (Quemoy, Matsu)," in *The Great Powers in East Asia, 1953–60*, ed. Warren I. Cohen and Akira Iriye (New York: Columbia University Press, 1990), 222–45; and Thomas Stolper, *China, Taiwan, and the Offshore Islands* (Armonk, N.Y.: M. E. Sharpe, 1985), 19–27; Gerald Segal, *Defending China* (Oxford: Oxford University Press, 1984), ch. 7.

24. See He, "Evolution," 226.

25. Xu Yan, *Jinmen zhi zhan*, 159. Xu's argument directly contradicts a leading work on the offshore islands problem in the West. Given Mao's domestic agenda, "external crisis then would only be a distraction," Stolper, *China, Taiwan*, 18, writes.

26. Xu Yan, *Jinmen zhi zhan*, 173–74.

27. I argue these points in greater detail in Christensen, *Useful Adversaries*, ch. 6.

28. Ye Fei, *Ye Fei huiyilu* [The memoirs of Ye Fei] (Beijing: Liberation Army Press, 1988), 651; and Xu Yan, *Jinmen zhi zhan*, 216.

29. Ye Fei, *Ye Fei huiyilu*, 656–63.

30. Jonathan Pollack, "Perception and Action in Chinese Foreign Policy, Vol. 1: The Quemoy Decision" (Ph.D. diss., University of Michigan, 1976), 237.

31. Zhang, *Deterrence and Strategic Culture*, ch. 8; and Gong Li, "Tension Across the Taiwan Strait," in *Re-examining the Cold War: U.S.-China Diplomacy, 1954–73*, ed. Robert S. Ross and Jiang Changbin (Cambridge, Mass.: Harvard University Asia Center, 2001), 156–57.

32. Christensen, *Useful Adversaries*, 225–27.

33. Ibid., ch. 6.

34. See, e.g., the account of Mao's Russian-language interpreter on how Sputnik hurt Sino-Soviet relations by making Khrushchev less accommodating to Beijing. Li Yueran, *Waijiao wutaishang de xin Zhongguo lingxiu* [The leaders of new China on the diplomatic stage] (Beijing: Liberation Army Press, 1989), 177–78.

35. See Mao's reflections on the requests in 1959 in "An Outline Concerning the International Situation," 12 September 1959, in *Jianguo yilai Mao Zedong wengao*, 8: 599–603.

36. Christensen, *Useful Adversaries*, ch. 6.

37. See, e.g., Xu Yan, *Jinmen zhi zhan*, and Gong Li, in *Re-examining the Cold War*, ed. Ross and Jiang.

38. Ye, *Ye Fei huiyilu*, 650–56.

39. See Mao's telegram of 18 August 1958 to Peng Dehuai, "Comments Concerning the Cessation of Military Exercises at Shenzhen and Preparation for Attack on Quemoy," in *Jianguo yilai Mao Zedong wengao*, 7: 348.

40. See Christensen, *Useful Adversaries*, 195–96; George Eliades, "Once More unto the Breach: Eisenhower, Dulles, and Public Opinion During the Offshore

Islands Crisis of 1958," *Journal of American–East Asian Relations* 2, 4 (Winter 1993): 343–67.

41. *Zhong Yin bianjiang ziwei fanji zuozhan shi* [The battle history of the self-defense counterattack on the Sino-Indian border] (Beijing: Academy of Military Sciences, 1994), 2. These findings are consistent with the coverage of the Chinese literature by John W. Garver, *Protracted Contest: Sino-Indian Rivalry in the Twentieth Century* (Seattle: University of Washington Press, 2001), 58–61.

42. Chen Pingsheng, chief ed., *Yindu junshi sixiang yanjiu* [Research on Indian military thinking] (Beijing: Academy of Military Sciences, 1992), 47–48 (internally circulated).

43. Xu Yan, *Zhong Yin bianjie ziwei fanji zuozhan de lishi zhenxiang* [The real history of the self-defense counterattack warfare at the Chinese-Indian border], in *Junshi miwenlu* [Secret military records] (Beijing: Beijing Shifan Daxue Press, 1993), 36–71, at 48.

44. Garver, *Protracted Contest*, 58–61.

45. *Zhong Yin bianjing ziwei fanji zuozhan shi*, 181, 253.

46. Xu Yan, "Zhongyin bianjie," 48.

47. Stolper, "China, Taiwan, and the Offshore Islands," 132. The crisis deescalated when the United States sent reassurances to Beijing that it did not support a KMT attack on the mainland, but the CCP must still have been wary of American promises, particularly from Kennedy, whom Beijing portrayed as more aggressive than Eisenhower. Allen S. Whiting, *The Chinese Calculus of Deterrence* (Ann Arbor: University of Michigan Press, 1975), 34–35.

48. Whiting, *Chinese Calculus*, 34–65; also see Segal, *Defending China*, 149.

49. Whiting, *Chinese Calculus*, 63.

50. Taylor Fravel, "The Long March to Peace: China and the Settlement of Territorial Disputes" (Ph.D. diss., Stanford University, 2003), ch. 6. Consistent with Fravel's account, Xu Yan states that the Central Military Commission ordered the restoration of military patrols near the McMahon Line in early June 1962. Xu Yan, "Zhong Yin bianjie," 44–45.

51. For critical accounts of Indian strategy, see Neville Maxwell, *India's China War* (London: Jonathan Cape, 1970); and Brigadier J. P. Dalvi, *Himalayan Blunder: The Curtain-Raiser to the Sino-Indian War of 1962* (Bombay: Thacker, 1969).

52. I cover these topics in greater depth in Thomas J. Christensen, "Worse Than a Monolith: Disorganization and Rivalry in East Asian Communist Alliances and U.S. Containment Challenges, 1949–69," *Asian Security* 1, 1 (January 2005): 80–127.

53. Guo Ming, ed., *Zhong Yue guanxi yanbian sishinian* [Forty-year evolution of Sino-Vietnamese relations] (Nanning: Guangxi People's Publishers, 1992), 69 (internally circulated).

54. Chen Jian, "China's Involvement in the Vietnam War, 1964–69," *China Quarterly*, no. 142 (June 1995): 360.

55. Li Danhui, "Sino-Soviet Relations and the Aid Vietnam, Resist America War," *Dangshi Yanjiu Ziliao*, no. 251 (June 1998): 7 (internally circulated).

56. *Zhou Enlai nianpu: 1949–76 (zhong)* [Zhou Enlai's chronicle: 1949–76 (vol. 2)] (Beijing: Zhongyang Wenxian Chubanshe, 1997), 10 July 1964, 655.

57. Qiang Zhai, *China and the Vietnam Wars, 1950–1975* (Chapel Hill, N.C.: University of North Carolina Press, 2000), 140–41.

58. Li Danhui, "Sino-Soviet Relations," 3–5.

59. For Mao's June 1964 statement, see Qu Aiguo, "Zhongguo zhiyuan budui yuan Yue kang Mei junshi xingdong gaishu" [A narrative of the military activities of the Chinese volunteer units in the Assist Vietnam Oppose America War], in *Junshi Shi Lin* [Military History Circles], no. 6 (1989): 40.

60. *Zhou Enlai nianpu*, vol. 2, 6 August 1964, 663.

61. Liu Shaoqi and Le Duan, Beijing, 8 April 1965, in 77 *Conversations Between Chinese and Foreign Leaders on the Wars in Indochina, 1964–1977*, Working Paper No. 22, ed. Odd Arne Westad et al. (Washington, D.C.: Cold War International History Project, Woodrow Wilson Center for Scholars, 1998) (hereafter cited as 77 *Conversations*), 83. Also see Zhou Enlai, Nguyen Van Hieu, and Nguyen Van Binh, Great Hall of the People, Beijing, 16 May 1965, ibid., 83–84.

62. See Guo Ming, ed., *Zhong Yue guanxi sishinian*, 68–72; Wang Xian'gen, *Zhongguo mimi da fabing: yuan Yue kang Mei shilu* [China's secret large dispatch of troops: the real record of the war to assist Vietnam and resist America] (Ji'nan: Ji'nan Publishers, 1992), esp. the back cover; and Yang Gongsu, *Zhonghua renmin gongheguo waijiao lilun yu shixian* [The theory and practice of PRC diplomacy], a limited edition Beijing University textbook, 1996 version, 341 (internally circulated).

63. Mao Zedong and Ho Chi Minh, Changsha (Hunan), 16 May 1965, in 77 *Conversations*, 84–85

64. Zhou Enlai and Pham Van Dong, Hoang Tang, Beijing, 23 August 1966, in 77 *Conversations*, 96–97.

65. "Zhujia Yuenan nanfang minzu jiefang lianxian chengli qi zhounian de dianbao" [Telegram celebrating the seventh anniversary of the establishment of the National Liberation Front of South Vietnam], 19 December 1967, in *Jianguo yilai Mao Zedong wengao*, 12: 458–59.

66. See, e.g., Zhang Baijia, "Mao Zedong yu Zhong Su tongmeng he Zhong Su fenlie" [Mao Zedong and the Sino-Soviet alliance and the Sino-Soviet split] (MS presented to the Chinese Communist Party Central Party History Research Office's International Scholars Research Forum, Beijing, October 1997), 7.

67. Thomas Robinson, "China Confronts the Soviet Union: Warfare and Diplomacy Along China's Inner Frontier," in *Cambridge History of China*, vol. 15, ed. Roderick MacFarquhar and John K. Fairbank (Cambridge: Cambridge University Press, 1991), 250–51.

68. Ibid., 256–57.

69. For the shift of concern from the United States to the Soviet Union, see Li Danhui, "Sino-Soviet Relations and the Aid Vietnam, Resist America War."

70. See, e.g., Robinson, "China Confronts the Soviet Union," 257. Soon after the clash, Allen Whiting correctly assessed Mao's largely defensive motives and concerns about Soviet aggression in a critically important meeting with Henry Kissinger that got Kissinger thinking in terms of rapprochement with China. For a description of this timely analysis by Whiting and by sections of INR at the State Department,

where Whiting had previously worked, see William Burr, "Sino-American Relations, 1969: The Sino-Soviet Border War and Steps Toward Rapprochement," *Cold War History* 1, 3 (April 2001): 73–112. Recent works that emphasize the importance of international pressures, a combination of international and domestic factors, or just domestic factors all assert that Mao intentionally set a trap for the Soviet forces. For an account emphasizing international pressures on Mao and his preemptive response, see Gong Li, "Chinese Decision Making," in *Re-examining the Cold War: U.S.-China Diplomacy, 1954–73*, ed. Robert S. Ross and Jiang Changbin (Cambridge, Mass.: Harvard University Asia Center, 2001), 327–31; for a mixed account emphasizing the preemptive warning calculus and the need to mobilize the Party and nation after three years of the Cultural Revolution, see Yang Kuisong, "The Sino-Soviet Border Clash of 1969: From Zhenbao Island to Sino-American Rapprochement," *Cold War History* 1, 1 (August 2000): 21–52; for the pure domestic argument, see Lyle J. Goldstein, "Research Report: Return to Zhenbao Island: Who Started Shooting and Why Does It Matter," *China Quarterly*, no. 168 (December s2001): 985–97.

71. Gong Li, "China's Decision Making," 327–31. Citing William Whitson's classic, *The Chinese High Command* (New York: Praeger, 1973), Thomas Robinson offers this possible explanation for Chinese behavior, which he considers a likely component but not exclusive factor in China's strategy. He writes of this hypothesis: "whenever the Chinese Communists perceived a superior force about to attack, the proper strategy (learned through bitter experience during the Shanghai-Kiangsi-Yenan days) was to preempt the situation at a place and time of one's own choosing, thus throwing the enemy off balance and perhaps even preventing his coming ahead at all" (Robinson, "China Confronts the Soviet Union," 263).

72. Yang, "Sino-Soviet Border Clash," 30.

73. Goldstein, "Research Report."

74. Fravel, "China's Long March to Peace," 45.

75. Yang, "Sino-Soviet Border Clash," esp. 35–37.

76. For a detailed review of this case, see Segal, *Defending China*. Segal's account fully fits a windows logic, with China worrying on the one hand that newfound oil deposits in the South China Sea would bring international actors into the dispute over the Paracels and that the Republic of Vietnam's impending demise would make it more difficult later than then to "solve the problem."

77. Not-for-attribution interviews, 2001/2002.

78. Harlan W. Jencks, "China's 'Punitive' War on Vietnam: A Military Assessment," *Asian Survey* 19, 8 (August 1979): 804.

79. King C. Chen, *China's War with Vietnam: Issues, Decisions, and Implications* (Stanford, Calif.: Hoover Institution Press, 1987), esp. 87–93.

80. On this issue, see Banning Garrett, "China Policy and the Strategic Triangle," in *Eagle Entangled: American Foreign Policy in a Complex World*, ed. Kenneth Oye (London: Longman, 1979), 228–61; and Chen, *China's War with Vietnam*, 92.

81. Jencks, "China's 'Punitive' War on Vietnam," 804.

82. Ibid.

83. China would cut 2 million troops from its 6-million-person military of 1978,

and defense budgets would be cut so sharply in the next few years that they would not return to 1978 levels until the mid 1990s, after years of double-digit increases beginning in the early 1990s.

84. Nayan Chanda, *Brother Enemy: The War After the War* (San Diego: Harcourt Brace, 1986), 259. The quotation is from Dr. Michael Pillsbury.

85. Ibid., 256.

86. Robert Ross, *The Indochina Tangle: China's Vietnam Policy, 1975–79* (New York: Columbia University Press, 1988), chs. 7–8.

87. For the most comprehensive coverage of the military aspects of the war to date, see Edward O'Dowd, "The Last Maoist War" (Ph.D. diss., Princeton University, 2004).

88. Ross, *Indochina Tangle.*

89. For excellent coverage of this case, see Allen S. Whiting, "China's Use of Force, 1950–96, and Taiwan," *International Security* 26, 2 (Fall 2001): 103–31; Ross, "Navigating the Taiwan Strait"; and Andrew Scobell, *China's Use of Force: Beyond the Great Wall and the Long March* (Cambridge: Cambridge University Press, 2004).

90. As one high-ranking military officer stated in a discussion in 2002, the PLA response would not necessarily include an attack on the island of Taiwan itself but would exceed in intensity the exercises of 1995–96. He therefore predicted a major crisis with the United States if such a visit were to occur.

91. For a few of those articles, see "Chinese Realpolitik," *Foreign Affairs* 75, 5 (September–October 1996): 37–52; "China, the U.S.-Japan Alliance, and the Security Dilemma in East Asia," *International Security* 23, 4 (Spring 1999): 49–80; "Posing Problems Without Catching Up: China's Rise and the Challenges for U.S. Security Policy," *International Security* 25, 4 (Spring 2001): 5–40; "China," in *Strategic Asia, 2002–2003: Asian Aftershocks*, ed. Aaron L. Friedberg and Richard Ellings (Seattle: National Bureau of Asian Research, 2002), 51–94; and "The Contemporary Security Dilemma: Deterring a Taiwan Conflict," *Washington Quarterly* 25, 4: 7–21.

92. Author interviews in Beijing and Shanghai, January 2003; Thomas J. Christensen and Michael Glosny, "Sources of Stability in U.S.-China Security Relations," in *Strategic Asia, 2003–2004*, ed. Richard Ellings and Michael Wills (Seattle: National Bureau of Asian Research, 2003). For further discussion of these issues, see my contributions to nos. 6, 7, and 8 of the *China Leadership Monitor*, online at www.chinaleadershipmonitor.org (accessed September 29, 2005).

4 *China's Decision for War with India in 1962*

John W. Garver

Why Did China's Leaders Decide for War Against India?

Why did the People's Republic of China (PRC) go to war with India in 1962? What were the reasons for that war from the standpoint of China's leaders? What were the considerations that led the PRC's leaders to opt for large-scale use of armed force then? And how accurate were the views held by China's leaders? These are the questions this chapter addresses.

The 1962 war with India was long the PRC's forgotten war. Little was published in China regarding the process through which China decided for war—unlike in the case of the Korean War, the Indochina wars, the conflicts over the offshore islands in the 1950s, and even the 1974 Paracel Island campaign. Foreign analysts such as Neville Maxwell and Allen Whiting, writing in the early 1970s, were thus compelled to rely on inferences drawn from Chinese public statements.[1] This situation began to change during the 1990s, when a half dozen Chinese publications on the 1962 war appeared. On the Indian side, the publication in 2002 of India's long-classified official history of the 1962 war offered additional new and authoritative material.[2] While these sources are far from complete, they do offer sufficient new materials to warrant a revisiting of China's road to the 1962 war.

This study will postulate two major, interrelated sets of reasons why China's leaders decided for war with India in 1962.[3] Ordered in the chronological fashion in which they preoccupied China's leaders, these two sets of factors were:

1. A perceived need to punish and end perceived Indian efforts to undermine Chinese control of Tibet, which were seen as aimed at restoring the pre-1949 status quo ante there.

2. A perceived need to punish and end perceived Indian aggression against Chinese territory along the border.

This study is also concerned with the accuracy of Chinese perceptions in these two areas. It will attempt to ascertain whether China's decision for war was based, to some degree, on misperceptions rather than on accurate assessment of the situation. I argue that in terms of deterrence along the border, Chinese perceptions were substantially accurate. Chinese perceptions regarding Indian policy toward Tibet, however, were substantially inaccurate.

The historiography of any war is politically sensitive, because it touches on the question of which nation bears responsibility and thus the implicit moral onus for initiating war. The 1962 war is especially sensitive in this regard, and its historiography figures prominently in the contemporary political psychology of Sino-Indian relations—on both sides of that relationship. While a scholar should ideally be oblivious to the requirements of any such pressures, this ideal is hard to realize in practice. Fortunately for a scholar who feels deep empathy with both sides in the 1962 war, this study argues that the two sides share responsibility for that war. India's policies along the border, and especially the Forward Policy adopted in November 1961, were seen by China's leaders as constituting incremental Indian seizure of Chinese-controlled territory, and there is little basis for deeming that view inaccurate. Chinese perceptions of Indian policies toward Tibet were fundamentally erroneous, however, and those Chinese misperceptions contributed substantially to the 1962 war. Hence *both sides* bear the onus for the 1962 war, China for misconstruing India's Tibetan policies, and India for pursuing a confrontational policy on the border.

Regarding the border, this study tests the Whiting-Maxwell hypothesis regarding China's road to the 1962 war by drawing on recently available Chinese accounts of the decision-making process in the People's Republic of China. Broadly speaking, Whiting and Maxwell reached the same conclusion: China's resort to war in 1962 was largely a function of perceived Indian aggression. As noted earlier, Maxwell and Whiting were forced to rely largely on inferences drawn from official Chinese statements at the time of the 1962 war. Newly available Chinese materials allow us to go "inside" the Chinese decision-making process in a way that was not possible in 1962. This offers a useful testing of the Whiting-Maxwell thesis.

Maxwell and Whiting stressed the role of Beijing's concerns regarding Tibet in the formation of Chinese perceptions of foreign threat in 1962. They generally took Chinese perceptions as a given, however, and were not concerned with exploring their objective accuracy. "It is not the purpose of this study to evaluate the accuracy of Chinese charges [against the United

States]," Whiting said regarding Chinese perceptions of U.S. policy, but he went on to note: "Preconceptions can act as filters for selecting relevant evidence of intention as well as determinants of bias in assessing the degree of threat to be anticipated."[4] I argue that this was indeed the case with Mao's authoritative judgments about Indian motives.

Two concepts from psychology are useful for understanding the Chinese perceptual filters that linked Tibet and the 1962 war: fundamental attribution error and projection. Attribution involves an individual's inferences about why another person acts as he or she does. It is a process beginning with the perception of another person in a particular social context, proceeding through a causal judgment about the reasons for the other person's behavior, and ending with behavioral consequences for the person making the judgment. A fundamental attribution error occurs when one person incorrectly attributes particular actions to the internal motives, character, or disposition of another individual, rather than to the characteristics of the situation in which that individual finds him- or herself. Commission of a fundamental attribution error entails systematic underestimation of situational determinants of the other's behavior, determinants deriving, above all, from the political and social roles of an individual and compulsions on the individual arising in particular situations due to those roles. Instead of recognizing that other individuals act as they do because of their particular roles and the requirements of particular situations, observers may attribute their behavior to personal motives or interior disposition. Social psychologists have found this to be very common. There is a pervasive tendency to attribute the behavior of others to interior motivations, while attributing one's own behavior to situational factors.[5] Below I argue that Mao committed a fundamental attribution error by concluding that Nehru was seeking to seize Tibet from China.

Projection involves transference by one individual onto another of responsibility for events deriving, in fact, from actions of the first individual. It is very difficult for people to deal with the dissonance arising from the fact that their actions were inept or created pain for themselves and others. Rather than accept the blow to self-esteem and the psychological discomfort that comes from that acceptance of responsibility, individuals will often assign responsibility to some other individual. Thus the person actually responsible is able to reach the comfortable conclusion that he or she was not responsible. The fact that people suffered was not due to one's own actions, but to the actions of some other person. In this way, the positive self-concept of the first individual is maintained. Below, I argue that India became the main object of Chinese projection of responsibility for the difficulties that Chinese rule encountered, and in fact Chinese themselves created, in Tibet circa 1959.

A premise of the argument developed below is that what leaders think matters. Some realists find it satisfactory to look only at interests and policies, black-boxing or ignoring the specific psychological processes through which leaders arrive at their determinations about interests and policies. It is not necessary or possible to engage this fundamental issue here. But it should be stipulated that the argument below rests on the premise that particular policies derive from specific sets of beliefs and calculations linked to those beliefs, and that different sorts of beliefs and calculations might well lead to different policies.

Tibet and the 1962 War: The Chinese View of the Root Cause

A starting point for understanding the Chinese belief system about the 1962 war is recognition that, from the Chinese point of view, the road to the 1962 war begins in Tibet. Although Chinese deliberations in 1962 leading up to the war were closely tied to developments on the border, Chinese studies of the 1962 war published during the 1990s link Indian border policies to Tibet and insist that Indian border policies derived from an Indian effort to weaken or overthrow Chinese rule over Tibet. Chinese studies of the 1962 war insist that an Indian desire to "seize Tibet," to turn Tibet into an Indian "colony" or "protectorate," or to return Tibet to its pre-1949 status, was the root cause of India's forward policy and the 1962 war. These contemporary assertions mirror the views of China's leaders circa 1962. In other words, Chinese beliefs about the nature of Indian objectives regarding Tibet deeply colored Chinese deliberations regarding India's moves along the border.

There is unanimous agreement among Chinese scholars that the root cause of the 1962 war was an Indian attempt to undermine Chinese rule and seize Tibet. The official PLA history of the 1962 war argues that India sought to turn Tibet into a "buffer zone" (huanchongguo). Creation of such a buffer zone had been an objective of British imperial strategy, and Nehru was perceived as a "complete successor" to Britain in this regard. Nehru's objective was seen as the creation of a "great Indian empire" in South Asia by "filling the vacuum" left by the British exit from that region. According to the PLA history, Nehru regarded control of Tibet as essential for "mastery over South Asia" and "the most economical method for guaranteeing India's security."[6] A study by Xu Yan, professor at the PLA's National Defense University and one of China's foremost military historians, follows the same line of argument: Nehru aspired and worked consistently throughout the 1950s to turn Tibet into a "buffer zone." According to Xu, Nehru had

imbibed British imperialist ideology and believed that India should dominate neighboring countries. He quotes Nehru and other early Congress
Party leaders about their aspirations that India should lead and organize the
Indian Ocean region. Regarding Tibet, Nehru aspired to turn that region
into a "buffer zone" between China and India. This was Nehru's consistent
objective throughout the 1950s. The "decisive factor" in the deterioration
of Sino-Indian relations, according to Xu Yan, was Nehru's policy of "protecting" the Tibetan "splittists" after the Lhasa rebellion of March 1959.[7]

An article by Wang Hongwei of the Chinese Academy of Social Science,
and one of China's senior India hands, presents a similar view. Prior to 1947,
Britain's objective, Wang argues, was to bring Tibet within its "sphere of influence." Britain sought "Tibetan independence" and continually attempted
to instigate Tibet to "leave China" (tuoli Zhongguo). Nehru was deeply influenced by this British thinking, Wang argued, through education in Britain
and by assimilation of the mentality of the British ruling class. In 1959, the
Indian government "supported the Tibetan rebels," permitted them to carry
out "anti-China activities" on Indian territory, and even gave some Tibetan
rebels military training. Simultaneous with this, India advanced claims on
Chinese territory.[8] Implicitly but clearly, the purpose of India doing this was
to achieve Tibetan "independence" by instigating Tibet to "leave China."

One of the most extensive and nuanced Chinese accounts of events leading up to the 1962 war is by Zhao Weiwen, a longtime South Asian analyst
of the Ministry of State Security. Zhao's account of the road to war also begins with Tibet and attribution of aggressive motives to Indian policy
moves. From 1947 to 1952, Zhao writes, "India ardently hoped to continue
England's legacy in Tibet."[9] The "essence" of English policy had been to
"tamper with China's sovereignty in Tibet to change it to 'suzerainty' thereby
throwing off the jurisdiction of China's central government over Tibet under the name of Tibetan 'autonomy.' "[10] By 1952, however, the PLA's victories in Korea, in Xikang province (later to become the western part of
Sichuan province), the conclusion of the 17-point agreement of May 1951,
the PLA's occupation of Tibet, and Beijing's forceful rejection of Indian efforts to check the PLA's move into Tibet had forced Nehru to change
course. Nehru now began direct talks with Beijing over Tibet. There were,
however, "right-wing forces" in India who "refused to abandon the English
legacy" in Tibet and who pressured Nehru in 1959. Moreover, Nehru himself "harbored a sort of dark mentality," the exact nature of which is not
specified, but which presumably included aggressive designs on Tibet.[11]
These factors led Nehru to demonstrate an "irresolute attitude" in 1959.
On the one hand, he said that Tibet was a part of China and that he did not
want to interfere in China's internal affairs. On the other hand, he permitted
all sorts of "anti-China activities and words" aimed against China's exercise

of sovereignty over Tibet. Zhao is more sensitive than other Chinese analysts to the domestic political pressures weighing on Nehru in 1959. Yet even she suggests that Nehru's "dark mentality" led him to give free rein to "anti-China forces" in an attempt to cause Tibet to "throw off the jurisdiction of China's central government."

The attribution to India by contemporary Chinese scholars of a desire to seize Tibet mirrors—as we shall see below—the thinking of Chinese leaders who decided to launch the 1962 war. This is probably due to the fact that published scholarship in China is still expected to explain and justify, not to criticize, the decisions of the Chinese Communist Party, at least on such sensitive matters as war and peace.

Indian Policy Toward Tibet

Assessment of the accuracy of Chinese views regarding Indian policy toward Tibet depends on ascertaining what actually transpired in Indo-Tibetan-Chinese relations in the years prior to the 1962 war. A brief review is thus requisite.

Indian policy toward the PRC takeover was complex. On the one hand, New Delhi opposed Beijing's military occupation of Tibet. In 1949 and 1950, India covertly supplied small amounts of arms to the Tibetan government.[12] During the same period, and while the PLA was preparing to move into Tibet, the Indian government sought via diplomatic protests to the new PRC government to prevent or limit PLA occupation of Tibet. Beijing rejected these Indian protests with stern warnings. New Delhi also initially sought to uphold Indian rights in Tibet inherited from Britain and embodied in treaties with the old Republic of China. These rights included trading missions, representative offices, telecommunications facilities, and small military contingents to guard these facilities in several Tibetan towns. Beijing viewed these rights as products of imperialist aggression against China and unilaterally abrogated the treaties upon which they were based. By 1952 or so, Nehru had accepted China's views of these old treaties and of India's derivative special rights in Tibet. Many in India, including a number of very prominent individuals, though not initially Nehru, were concerned about the fate of Tibet's Buddhist-based and Indian-influenced civilization under rule by the Chinese Communist Party. Nehru became increasingly sensitive to these "sentimental," "cultural" (terms Nehru used) interests in Tibet as the years passed.[13]

On the other hand, India actually helped China consolidate its control over Tibet. In October 1950, India refused to sponsor a Tibetan appeal to the United Nations. When El Salvador sponsored such an appeal, India played a key role in squashing it. Many governments, including those of the United States, Britain, and many Middle Eastern countries, were willing to follow India's lead on this issue, and India's opposition to the Tibetan appeal to the United Nations was, in fact, a major reason for its nonconsideration.[14] New Delhi also turned down U.S. proposals in 1950 for Indo-U.S. cooperation in support of Tibetan resistance to China.[15] India also played a key role in persuading the young Dalai Lama not to flee abroad and try to rally international support for Tibet, but to return to Tibet and reach an accommodation with China's communist government—an accommodation that occurred with the 17-point agreement of May 1951. Then in 1954, India formally recognized China's ownership of Tibet as part of an effort to reach a broader understanding with China. Again, most countries recognized India's leadership on this matter. After the 1954 agreement between China and India regarding Tibet, the Indian government encouraged the Dalai Lama and his local Tibetan government to assert its autonomy under the 17-point agreement. Perhaps most important of all, until mid 1959, India allowed trade with Tibet to continue unimpeded. Prior to the mid 1950s, when new PLA-built roads into Tibet were opened, India's supply of foodstuffs, fuels, and basic goods was essential to restraining inflation in Tibet created by demand for these commodities due to the introduction of large numbers of Chinese soldiers and construction workers into a region with a subsistence economy.

In mid 1957, the U.S. Central Intelligence Agency (CIA) began covert assistance to rebels in the Kham region of southeastern Tibet. Assistance rendered through this CIA program was actually quite limited, totaling only 250 tons of munitions, equipment, and supplies between 1957 and 1961.[16] But CIA operations came to the attention of Chinese intelligence and thus became a concern of China's government. Tibetan refugees who found asylum in northern Indian cities (especially Darjeeling, Kalimpong, and Gangtok) in the 1950s also in various ways supported resistance movements inside Tibet. Covert operatives from various countries, including the United States, Nationalist China, and the PRC, were also active in those cities. By late 1958, Beijing began demanding that India expel key leaders of the Tibetan resistance based in India and suppress activities supporting opposition to Chinese policies within Tibet. Nehru sought a middle course, restricting Tibetan activities but refusing to expel Tibetan leaders. A key question, to which we shall return below, is how much Nehru knew about CIA operations in 1957–61.

Once the Tibetan national uprising began in Lhasa on 10 March 1959, India did not wash its hands of Tibetan affairs, as Beijing insisted it do. Rather, Indian media and elected Indian politicians, including Nehru and virtually every other Indian politician, expressed greater or lesser sympathy with Tibet's struggle. Beijing condemned a large number of Indian moves that it said encouraged the rebellion, including the Indian consul general in Lhasa's meeting with demonstrating Tibetans in the early days of the Lhasa uprising; granting asylum to the Dalai Lama; having official contact with the Dalai Lama; treating the Dalai Lama as an honored guest; permitting the Dalai Lama to meet with the media and foreign representatives; not quashing the Dalai Lama's appeal to the United Nations; granting asylum to ten thousand or so Tibetan refugees who followed the Dalai Lama to India; concentrating those refugees in camps near the Tibetan frontier; not suppressing "anti-China activities" conducted in those refugee camps; permitting or encouraging negative commentary by Indian newspapers about China's actions in Tibet; Nehru raising the "Tibet issue" in India's parliament and making critical comments about China's policies in Tibet; Nehru permitting the Indian parliament to discuss Tibet; allowing "anti-China activities" by protesters in Indian cities; not punishing Indian protestors for defacing a portrait of Mao Zedong; instigating an "anti-China campaign" in the Indian press; restricting trade between India and Tibet; and allowing the Dalai Lama to speak of "a Tibetan government in exile." All these acts, in China's view, constituted "interference in the internal affairs of China."[17] Beijing saw these Indian actions as ways in which New Delhi was attempting to "seize Tibet."

CCP Leaders' Perceptions of Indian "Expansionism" in 1959

As noted earlier, the uniform belief of PRC historians of the 1990s that India wanted to seize Tibet mirrors the beliefs of China's leaders in 1959. In the aftermath of the uprising that began in Lhasa on 10 March 1959, the CCP decided to dissolve the Tibetan local government, assert its own direct administration, and begin implementing social revolutionary policies in Tibet. On 25 March, "central cadres" met in Shanghai to discuss the situation in Tibet. Mao gave his views of the situation. India was doing bad things in Tibet, Mao Zedong told the assembled cadres, but China would not condemn India openly at the moment. Rather, India would be given enough rope to hang itself (*guo xing bu yi*—literally, "to do evil deeds frequently brings ruin to the evil doer"). China would settle accounts with India later, Mao said.[18]

Three weeks later, as thousands of Tibetans fled into India, where outraged Indian and international sympathy welcomed them, Mao intensified the struggle against India. On 19 April, Mao ordered the Xinhua News Agency to issue a commentary criticizing unnamed "Indian expansionists."

Mao personally revised the draft commentary.[19] Four days later Mao ordered a further escalation. *Renmin Ribao* (*People's Daily*) should now openly criticize Nehru by name, Mao directed. When Mao was presented with the draft, he rejected it. The draft missed the point, Mao said. The target should not be "imperialism" but "Indian expansionists" who "want ardently to grab Tibet" (*wangtu ba Xizang nale guochu*).[20] Days later, on 25 April, Mao convened a Politburo Standing Committee meeting and immediately asked about the status of the revised editorial criticizing Nehru. He then directed that the criticism should "be sharp, don't fear to irritate him [Nehru], don't fear to cause him trouble." Nehru had miscalculated the situation, Mao said, believing that China could not suppress the rebellion in Tibet and would have to beg for India's help. Here Mao implied that Nehru was pursuing a strategy of fomenting rebellion in Tibet in hopes that Beijing would solicit Indian help in dealing with that rebellion. The objective was to maintain Sino-Indian friendship, Mao said, but this could only be achieved via unity through struggle. Nehru's incorrect ideas had to be struggled against.[21] Implicit in Mao's comments was the notion that Nehru's instigation was responsible for the rebellion in Tibet.

The polemic ordered and revised by Mao appeared on 6 May 1959 under the title "The Revolution in Tibet and Nehru's Philosophy."[22] The main charge leveled against India was conduct of an "anti-China slander campaign" being waged by Nehru and the Indian media over events in Tibet. Nehru's main offense against China was what he was *saying* about Tibet, and the encouragement those words gave to rebels in Tibet. In his comments, Nehru denied "that a handful of upper-strata [Tibetan] reactionaries are responsible for the rebellion in Tibet, describes the just action of the Chinese people in putting down the rebellion as a 'tragedy' and expresses sympathy for the rebellion. Thus, he commits a most deplorable error," according to the article. The "vociferous self-styled sympathizers of the Tibetan people" in fact "sympathize with those who for generations oppressed, exploited, and butchered the Tibetan people"—with the "big serf-owners" who tortured and oppressed the Tibetan people under the "cruelest and most savage serfdom in the world." Nehru was spreading such "slanders" against China in Tibet via speeches to the Indian parliament and interviews with Indian newspapers. This "slander campaign" against China had to cease. If it did not, China would hit back: "So long as you do not end your anti-Chinese slander campaign, we will not cease hitting back. We are prepared to spend as much time on this as you want to. We are prepared too, if you should incite other countries to raise a hue and cry against us. We are also prepared to find all the imperialists in the world backing you up in the clamor. But it is utterly futile to try to use pressure to interfere in China's internal affairs and salvage the odious rule of the big serf-owners in Tibet."

Nehru's sympathy for the Tibetan serf-owning class stemmed from the "dual character" of the Indian "big bourgeoisie," which by its class nature "has a certain urge for outward expansion." Thus Nehru and the Indian "big bourgeoisie" strove "to prevent China from exercising full sovereignty over its territory in Tibet." They wanted Tibet to have "a kind of semi-independent status," to be a "sort of buffer zone between China and India."

It is significant that Nehru's most egregious offense was his words. It was these words that were reflective of his "philosophy," of his inner nature, of his class character, of his role as a representative of the Indian "big bourgeoisie" and its ambitions for expansion in Tibet. Mao's close involvement in the drafting of this document makes clear that it fully represented Mao's own views.

The same day that *Renmin Ribao* published this commentary, Zhou En-lai outlined Chinese views for an assembly of socialist country representatives in Beijing. In doing so, Zhou underlined the links between Nehru's words, his "class nature," and his counterrevolutionary objectives in Tibet. Nehru and people from the Indian upper class, Zhou explained, "oppose reform in Tibet, even to the extent of saying that reform is impossible." Their motive in doing this was to cause "Tibet to remain for a long time in a backward state, becoming a 'buffer state' between China and India." "This is their guiding mentality, and also *the center of the Sino-Indian conflict*," Zhou said (emphasis added). "A section of the Indian upper class had inherited England's old policy of saying Tibet is an 'independent country,' saying that China only has 'suzerainty,' or saying Tibet is a 'protectorate.'" All these formulations were violations of China's sovereignty, Zhou said. Nehru and company claimed sympathy for the Tibetans, but "Actually, they sympathize with the serf-owners. Their objective is to cause Tibet not to advance, not to reform, to become a 'buffer country,' to remain under India's influence, and become their protectorate." This was "Nehru and company's" "basic class reaction."[23]

The question of responsibility for the crisis in Tibet figured prominently in the contentious talks between Mao Zedong and Soviet leader Nikita Khrushchev in Beijing on 2 October 1959. After a complete disagreement over Taiwan, Khrushchev turned to India and Tibet, saying: "If you let me, I will tell you what a guest should not say—the events in Tibet are your fault. You ruled in Tibet, you should have had your intelligence [agencies] there and should have known about the plans and intentions of the Dalai Lama" [to flee to India]." "Nehru also says that the events in Tibet are our fault," Mao replied. After an exchange over the flight of the Dalai Lama, Khrushchev made the point: "If you allow him [the Dalai Lama] an opportunity to flee to India, then what has Nehru to do with it? We believe that the events in Tibet are the fault of the Communist Party of China, not Nehru's fault." "No, this is Nehru's fault," Mao replied. "Then the events in Hungary are not our fault," the Soviet leader responded, "but the fault of the United States of America, if I understand you correctly. Please, look here, we had an army in Hungary, we supported that fool [Hungarian Premier Mátyás] Rákosi—and this is our mistake, not the mistake of the United States." Mao rejected this: "The Hindus acted in Tibet as if it belonged to them."[24]

The proposition that an Indian desire to seize Tibet underlay Indian actions continued to be central to Chinese thinking in the weeks prior to the 1962 war. On 16 October 1962, two days before the Politburo approved the PLA's plan for a large-scale "self-defensive counterattack" against India, General Lei Yingfu, head of the PLA's "war-fighting department" (*zuo zhan bu*), reported to Mao on why India had six days previously launched a major operation to cut off Chinese troops atop Thagla Ridge. Lei had been appointed to head an ad hoc small group established to probe the motives and purposes behind Indian actions. Tibet headed Lei's list of five major Indian motives. "Nehru has consistently wanted to turn China's ethnically Tibetan districts into India's colony or protectorate," Lei reported to Mao. Lei adduced various Indian actions of 1950, 1956, and 1959 to substantiate this proposition. In March 1959, Lei reported to Mao, Nehru "incited the Dalai Lama group to undertake rebellious activity of openly splitting the motherland." Nehru "always wanted to use the strength of a minority of Tibetan reactionaries to drive China out of the Tibetan areas of Tibet, [western] Sichuan, and Qinghai." When Nehru saw this "plot" of using Tibetan reactionaries to split China had failed, he "sent Indian forces to aggress against China's borders." "Yes," Mao said as he nodded in agreement with Lei's conclusions about Tibet, "Nehru has repeatedly acted in this way."[25]

Typically, Mao Zedong stated the matter most directly and forcefully. Speaking to a visiting delegation from Nepal in 1964, Mao told his foreign visitors that the major problem between India and China was not the McMahon Line but the Tibet question. "In the opinion of the Indian government," Mao said, "Tibet is theirs."[26]

The Erroneous Nature of Chinese Perceptions of Indian Policy Toward Tibet

The fact that China's leaders saw Indian efforts as attempts to "grab Tibet," to turn Tibet into "a buffer zone," to return Tibet to its pre-1949 status, to "overthrow China's sovereignty," or to cause Tibet to "throw off the jurisdiction of China's central government" does not necessarily mean that those perceptions were accurate. In fact, this core Chinese belief was wrong. This belief, which Chinese analysts explain underpinned China's decision for war in 1962, was, in fact, inaccurate. It was a deeply pernicious

Chinese misperception that contributed powerfully to the decision for war in 1962.

The Indian government indisputably *was* attempting to influence events inside Tibet, as well as relations between the Tibetan local government and Beijing. What is in question is not Indian actions, but the motives and purposes that lay behind those actions.

Nehru's policies derived not from a desire to seize Tibet or overthrow Chinese sovereignty there, but from a desire to uphold Tibet's autonomy under Chinese sovereignty as part of a grand accommodation between China and India—an accommodation that would, Nehru believed, make possible a global partnership between India and China. Nehru envisioned a compromise between Chinese and Indian interests regarding Tibet, with Chinese respect for Tibetan autonomy combined with Indian respect for Chinese sovereignty over Tibet. This accommodation would, Nehru believed, provide a basis for a broad program of cooperation between China and India on behalf of the peoples of the developing countries and against the insanity of a nuclear-armed bipolar Cold War. Nehru believed that by demonstrating India's acceptance of China's ownership and military control of Tibet while simultaneously befriending China on such issues as the war in Korea, the PRC's admission to the United Nations, the peace treaty with Japan and transfer of Taiwan to the PRC, Indochina, and decolonization and the Afro-Asian movement, China could be won to cooperation with India. The two leading Asian powers would then create a new axis in world politics. In terms of Tibet, Nehru hoped that China would repay India's friendship and consolidate the Sino-Indian partnership by granting Tibet a significant degree of autonomy.[27]

A series of moves by Nehru in 1959 contradicts the proposition that he sought to undermine China's rule over Tibet. Nehru stated repeatedly and publicly that Tibet was part of China and that events there were a Chinese internal affair. When he granted asylum to the Dalai Lama in March 1959, he believed, on the basis of earlier comments by Zhou Enlai regarding such a possibility in 1950, that Beijing would not regard it as an unfriendly act. After the Dalai Lama's flight to India, Nehru initially thought the Tibetan leader could work out a deal with Beijing restoring a degree of autonomy and permitting his return to Lhasa—as had been the case in 1951. After the Dalai Lama's 1959 flight to India, Nehru urged the Tibetan leader to avoid speaking of independence, saying that such a goal was "impractical." Instead, Tibet should seek mere autonomy, Nehru said. India refused to support, and indeed actively discouraged, a Tibetan appeal to the United Nations in 1959 and 1960—as it had in 1950. New Delhi urged Britain and other states not to open contacts with the Dalai Lama and worked to obstruct the Dalai Lama's efforts to establish such contacts. Even after the

U.S. State Department stated in February 1960 that the United States believed the principle of self-determination should apply to the Tibetan people, India did not welcome this move. These moves do not suggest a policy of seeking to overthrow China's control over Tibet. As Tsering Shakya concluded, Nehru's handling of Tibet during 1959–60 (and indeed all the way to the 1962 war, according to Shakya), amounted to an effort to placate Beijing at the expense of the Dalai Lama and Tibetan independence.[28]

Nehru believed that India had certain "cultural" and "sentimental" interests in Tibet by virtue of several thousand years of intimate interaction between the two countries and the fact that Tibet's unique culture had been deeply influenced by India. These interests were very limited, Nehru believed, and could best be achieved by respect for China's sovereignty over Tibet. Nehru had explained India's interests, and their limited nature, to Zhou Enlai in 1956, and believed that Zhou had been quite reasonable and even generous in his recognition of them. That agreement accommodating Chinese and Indian interests regarding Tibet was to be the foundation for Sino-Indian partnership in Asia and the world. Then came Beijing's discarding of Tibetan autonomy in 1959.

Nehru believed that he and Zhou Enlai had reached a meeting of the minds, an "agreement," in 1956 whereby India agreed to recognize China's sovereignty over Tibet in exchange for China's granting of a significant degree of autonomy to Tibet. This "agreement," according to Nehru, accommodated India's "sentimental," "cultural" interests in Tibet, and China's security and sovereignty concerns in that region, and thus provided a foundation for Sino-Indian partnership. India's encouragement of Tibetans' efforts to uphold their autonomy in the 1950s were, Nehru believed, in accord with China's promises to uphold Tibet's autonomy. During the mid 1950s, Zhou Enlai had been remarkably understanding of India's cultural interests in Tibet, or so it seemed to Nehru. India's various moves to strengthen Tibetan autonomy in the mid 1950s (tutoring the Dalai Lama on the 17-point agreement and the ways he could use it to uphold Tibet's autonomy, etc.) had been in accord with the Sino-Indian agreement. Following the uprising in Lhasa in March 1959, however, China's destruction of Tibetan autonomy "broke" this agreement.[29] In 1959, Beijing still had its half of the bargain (Indian recognition of China's sovereignty over Tibet) but had demolished India's part (Tibetan autonomy). Yet Nehru's response was to press Tibet to forgo claims to independence or appeal to the United Nations. Only under the mounting pressure of Indian public criticism, and sharp polemics from Beijing, did Nehru begin to adopt a more sympathetic attitude toward the Dalai Lama and the Tibetan resistance to Beijing. Nehru's clear if implicit objective was to return Tibet to its *pre-1959, not pre-1949,* status quo ante.

Nehru was dismayed in 1959 by Beijing's breaking of what he believed was the agreement between him and Zhou Enlai regarding Tibetan autonomy. He was dismayed too that Beijing apparently did not value India's friendship highly enough to respect its side of the bargain with India. Nehru's strategy was not to oust China from Tibet but to press China to compromise with the modest and limited Indian "cultural and sentimental" interests in that region, a compromise that would permit broad Sino-Indian cooperation on the world scene. Nehru's objective, in other words, was not to "seize Tibet" or deny Chinese sovereignty over Tibet. It was to persuade Beijing to respect India's limited interests in that region within the framework of Indian support for China's sovereignty over Tibet.

A second Indian objective (other than upholding India's "cultural" interest) in Tibet can be reasonably inferred: minimizing the threat posed to India by Chinese military forces in Tibet positioned on India's northern borders. While Nehru and other Indian leaders were not explicit about this, such a concern almost certainly helped inspire their desire to maintain Tibetan autonomy. An autonomous Tibet would be one with fewer Chinese soldiers and Chinese military bases. Again, this does not equate to a desire to "seize Tibet" or cause Tibet to "leave China." Rather, persuading Beijing not to militarize Tibet required reassuring Beijing that India respected and would help uphold China's sovereignty over Tibet, and that there was, consequently, no reason for China to militarize that region. As Nehru told Sadar Vallabhai Patel in late 1949, when Patel pointed out to Nehru the adverse consequences for India of China's impending military occupation of Tibet, since there was not very much that India (or any country for that matter) could do to prevent China from asserting sovereignty over Tibet, it was best for India to recognize Chinese sovereignty and work to secure India's interests within that framework.[30] Rather than challenging Chinese sovereignty over Tibet, it is more accurate to say that Nehru sought to persuade Beijing to respect Indian interests regarding Tibet by assuring Beijing of India's acceptance of China's sovereignty over Tibet and convincing Beijing of the benefits that would accrue to China if it compromised with India over Tibet, thereby winning Indian friendship. Nehru's hope was that Beijing would repay India's friendship by keeping the Chinese military presence in Tibet low.

There were also powerful domestic pressures working on Nehru in 1959. Criticism of Nehru's policy of befriending and placating China began to mount in 1958 as Indians became aware that China rejected the legitimacy of the McMahon Line. With China's fierce repression of the Tibetan resistance in 1959, domestic Indian criticism of Nehru's China policies became intense. Nehru struggled to respond to this mounting criticism of his handling of relations with China. He explained the political reality in comments to parliament on 4 May: failure to grant the Dalai Lama asylum would have won the support of only a "few thousand" Indians, while "hundreds of millions" welcomed the granting of asylum. It was simply "impossible" not to grant asylum, Nehru explained.[31] Tibetan refugees streaming into India after March 1959 offered firsthand accounts of Chinese vicious repression that were further sensationalized by India's media. There was widespread revulsion in India at China's bloody and brutal repression in Tibet. As Jaiprakash Narayan, one of India's foremost Gandhians, put it in mid 1959: "Tibet may be a theocratic state rather than a secular state and backward economically and socially, but no nation has the right to impose progress, whatever that may mean, upon another nation."[32]

Ascertaining the exact relation of Nehru to Tibetan resistance, both armed and nonviolent, and to U.S. covert operations is crucial for determining the accuracy of Chinese perceptions. Regarding nonviolent Tibetan resistance, the evidence is fairly clear: Nehru, and India, did give low-key support to such resistance. Nehru's statements to parliament in 1959, plus his comments to Intelligence Bureau chief B. N. Mullik in the mid 1950s, indicate that Nehru saw strong but nonviolent and unarmed Tibetan resistance to unlimited Chinese rule in Tibet as one way to help maintain a substantial and genuine degree of Tibetan autonomy—while recognizing and accepting Chinese sovereignty over Tibet.[33]

Regarding Nehru's attitude toward *armed* Tibetan resistance to Chinese rule, and his knowledge of covert CIA operations in support of that armed resistance, the evidence is, unfortunately, unequivocal. The closest study of India's decision-making process during this period, by Steven Hoffman, concluded: "It is unclear how much India's government knew in 1958 or 1959 about the major CIA program" to support the Tibetan armed resistance.[34] Nor does the official Indian history of the 1962 war, published in late 2002, shed any light on this question. Mullik maintained in his memoir that Nehru told him that *armed* Tibetan resistance would be suicidal and counterproductive and insisted that peaceful, nonviolent resistance was the best way. Tsering Shakya also concluded that Nehru and other Indian leaders were not aware until after the 1962 war of the extent of U.S. activities in support of Tibetan armed resistance. They had assumed, Shakya concludes, that Chinese Nationalist airplanes had been making the various mysterious flights protested by Beijing.[35] On the other hand, John Knaus, the CIA field officer in charge of covert support for the Tibetan rebels in the late 1950s and early 1960s, points to a communication from an official of the Indian Home Office regarding fighting inside Tibet and the Tibetan insurgents' need for arms. The U.S. government might be interested in this information, the Indian told the U.S. representative. Knaus calls this a "signal" to the United States from Nehru.[36] Kenneth Conboy and James

Morrison, in a study based on interviews of U.S. participants in those covert operations, concluded that Nehru and Mullik, at least, knew the general parameters of and tacitly condoned U.S. covert operations in Tibet.[37]

This author's guess is that that Nehru, Mullik, and perhaps a few other people in the Indian government understood at least the broad contours of U.S. covert operations into Tibet but chose to turn a blind eye to them. Given the scope of U.S. activities among the Tibetan refugee community at that juncture, and given India's good domestic intelligence services, anything else seems improbable. But even if we stipulate that Nehru knew of and turned a blind eye to U.S. covert operations in Tibet, it does not necessarily follow that the Indian objective was to seize Tibet or overturn Chinese sovereignty there. A far more economical explanation, and one in line with Nehru's conciliatory handling of the Tibet issue outlined above, and also congruent with the evidence of Nehru's hope of striking a grand bargain with China, is that Nehru's objective was to create a set of pressures that would induce Beijing to accommodate India's interests in Tibet. In other words, Nehru's turning a blind eye to U.S. covert activities was probably a way of persuading Beijing of the wisdom of securing Indian cooperation in upholding Chinese sovereignty.

It is clear that Nehru sought to persuade and pressure Beijing to grant Tibet a degree of genuine autonomy. It is also probably true that Nehru sought to limit the level of Chinese military presence in Tibet for the sake of India's own security. It is an insupportable leap from these elements of Indian policy to the conclusion that India sought to overthrow or undermine Chinese rule over Tibet. The proposition that because India recognized and acted on interests within Tibet, it was ipso facto attempting to undermine Chinese sovereignty is untenable, although this proposition certainly constitutes one element of the Chinese belief system.

Narrower elements of the Chinese belief system were also clearly inaccurate. The proposition that Nehru sympathized with Tibet's "serf-owning class" and wanted to maintain Tibet's traditional sociopolitical system unchanged is palpably wrong. Nehru deemed himself a socialist, a secularist, and, in religious terms, an agnostic. He had little sympathy for the reactionary, religion-based political system of Tibet. He was also deeply cognizant of the urgent need for reform of Tibet's traditional structures. Indeed, it was partially because of that recognition that he concluded circa 1950 that the CCP would be able to consolidate its rule over Tibet. To some degree, Nehru's conciliatory approach to Beijing's rule over Tibet in the mid 1950s was based on active sympathy with the CCP's mission of progressive reform in Tibet. In sum, the conclusion that Nehru desired to maintain Tibet's traditional system, to keep Tibet poor, or to prevent progress in Tibet was simply wrong.

China's leaders erred in attributing to Nehru a desire to seize Tibet from China, transforming it into an Indian protectorate or colony. Once "expansionist" motives were attributed to Nehru and judged to arise out of his "basic class character," "British influences," or "dark psychology," it followed that China would have to struggle against and punish Nehru and his ilk. A determination that Nehru sought a balanced compromise of Chinese and Indian interests regarding Tibet within the framework of Indian support for Chinese sovereignty, and for the sake of Sino-Indian global cooperation, would have led to a very different Chinese course of action.

This fundamental attribution error must be laid at Mao's door. It was he who first determined, at the central meeting on 23 April 1959, that "Indian expansionists" wanted to "seize Tibet." Mao completely dominated China's foreign policy decision-making process by 1959. Once Mao made that determination, China's other leaders were compelled to chime in. Indeed, even today, China's scholars are still compelled to affirm Mao's erroneous judgment.

The consequence of Mao's fundamental attribution error regarding Nehru was compounded by projection onto India of responsibility for Tibetan resistance to Chinese rule. Confronted with strong Tibetan resistance to Chinese policies in Tibet, Mao and his comrades responded by blaming that resistance on Indian "expansionist" machinations. This too was faulty thinking.

It is certainly true that demonstrations of Indian sympathy such as conveyed by Nehru's comments in March–April 1959 did, to some degree, encourage Tibetan resistance to the dictates of Beijing. Far more fundamental, however, were such factors as those analyzed by Tsering Shakya in his monumental study of Tibet's history: the introduction of large numbers of PLA soldiers and road construction crews into Tibet and the increased demand for foodstuffs and inflation that followed; the socialist reforms—especially collectivization of agriculture—introduced in ethnically Tibetan regions of western Sichuan and the flood of refugees into Lhasa those reforms produced; the civilizational clash between CCP atheism and Tibet's deep religiosity; and perhaps most important of all, the pervasive sense of unease Tibetans felt as they watched more and more Han Chinese pour into the Tibetans' ancestral land, where Han had previously been scarce.[38] These factors weighed far heavier than anything India may or may not have done.

Chinese leaders felt very strongly that road building, socialist reforms, suppression of religion, and other Chinese measures in Tibet were "correct" and "progressive." This very strong Chinese sense of self-righteousness prevented them from recognizing the responsibility of their own actions for producing the rebellion against Chinese rule. How could "correct" and "progressive" policies rouse rebellion against them—unless there were outside machinations? It was cognitively impossible for Mao and his comrades to recognize that their own policies had produced a popular rebellion against them.

Chinese misperceptions of Indian motives in 1959 were linked to the border conflict of 1961–62 (discussed in the next section) in two ways. First, Mao's beliefs about Nehru's desire to "seize Tibet" structured the Chinese interpretation of Indian border policies—especially the forward policy. A more accurate understanding of Nehru's increasingly desperate effort to maintain his cooperative, friendly policies toward China might have produced a more conciliatory Chinese response to the forward policy. If the forward policy had not been seen—as Mao saw it—as part of an effort to "seize Tibet," but as arising from a desire on the part of Nehru to demonstrate toughness and resolve in the face of mounting domestic criticism, the Chinese rebuff of November 1962 might not have been deemed necessary.

The second link between Mao's misperceptions of 1959 and the border conflict of 1961–62 was that Beijing's strident polemics and diplomatic protests in 1959–60 helped propel Nehru toward a more forceful border policy. Beijing's strident denunciations of Nehru's policies in spring 1959 contrasted sharply with Nehru's equivocation during the same period. This discrepancy fueled the mounting chorus of criticism of Nehru's "weakness" and "naïveté" that drove him toward the forward policy. If Beijing had responded to Tibetan events in 1959 not by polemicizing against Nehru, but by lauding and courting him, by finding a few face-saving sops for him regarding Tibetan "autonomy" that Nehru could use in fending off his domestic critics, Nehru might not have felt compelled to prove his toughness on the border issue. Instead of adopting the forward policy, he might have stood by a still-not-discredited friendship policy.

China's Response to India's Forward Policy

If Chinese perceptions regarding India's Tibet actions and policies were deeply flawed, the same cannot be said about Chinese views of India's forward policy. Succinctly stated, the orthodox scholarly view in this regard, established by Maxwell and Whiting, is that, in deciding for war, China's leaders were responding to an Indian policy of establishing Indian military outposts in territory claimed by both India and China but already under effective Chinese military occupation, the purpose being to expel Chinese forces from territory claimed by India. Evidence from recently published Chinese and Indian histories substantiates this traditional view.

Because war is a continuation of policies, it is important to understand the evolution of Chinese policies toward the Indo-Tibetan border. The crucial background was Nehru's rejection of a Chinese proposal—subtly and unofficially but nonetheless effectively raised by Zhou Enlai during his April 1960 visit to India—that China drop its claims in the eastern sector in exchange for India dropping its claims in the western sector. Such a swap would have given each side legal right to territory already in its possession and most important to each nation's security. Nehru rejected the swap proposal and insisted that China abandon its claim in the east *and* withdraw from Aksai Chin in the west. The grounds for Nehru's position was a belief that there already existed a legally based boundary between India and Tibet going back to the 1914 Simla conference. The question, for Nehru, was whether China would respect that legal and already existing boundary. Chinese leaders, on the other hand, saw the Simla agreement as without legal or moral basis. It had been rejected by China's central government in 1914 and had been implemented by British force majeure during China's century of national humiliation. China was nonetheless willing to accept the McMahon Line as the basis of a settlement, as was intimated by Zhou to Nehru during discussions in 1956 and 1957. By doing this, however, China believed it was making a substantial concession that reasonably required an Indian quid pro quo in Aksai Chin. In the words of the official Indian history, Nehru "did not agree to barter away the Aksai Chin area, under illegal occupation of China, in return for China giving up its unreasonable claim to Indian territory south of the McMahon Line."[39] From the Chinese point of view, the offer of an east-west swap was eminently fair and took into consideration the interests of both countries. Its rejection by Nehru was, China's leaders felt, entirely unreasonable.

Three rounds of border talks were held in 1960 following two visits by Zhou to India. Those talks soon deadlocked. Zhou's repeated visits to India were seen by Beijing as further tokens of Chinese sincerity. Then in February 1961, India published in full its final report on the talks, along with an English translation of the Chinese report to India. New Delhi hoped that publication of this voluminous documentary record would cause China to "adopt a reasonable attitude."[40] Beijing saw it as a further Indian effort to force China to accept an unreasonable and unfair settlement. When Indian representatives found no change in China's position, New Delhi became uninterested in further talks. This led Beijing to charge, in March 1962, that India "refused to hold negotiations." New Delhi replied that while it was prepared for negotiations, Chinese withdrawal from Aksai Chin was "an essential step for the creation of a favorable climate for negotiations . . . regarding the boundary."[41]

Unlike with Chinese perceptions of India's Tibetan policies in 1959, there is no basis for concluding that Chinese views of India's border policies were inaccurate. In part this is due to the difference between evaluating an empirical proposition (i.e., what motives lay behind Nehru's Tibetan policies?) and a normative question (i.e., were Beijing's offers of a border settlement fair and reasonable?). Normative propositions are intrinsically subjective. It should perhaps be noted, however, that had Nehru accepted Zhou's 1960 offer of an east-west swap, he (Nehru) could very probably have carried Indian public opinion with him—and avoided war. Thus Nehru's rejection of Zhou's package-deal solution and his insistence on Chinese abandonment of Aksai Chin must be seen as crucial steps on the road to the 1962 war.

Nehru's insistence on Chinese abandonment of Aksai Chin established a link in Chinese minds between the border issue and China's ability to control Tibet. The road built via that desolate but low snow-fall plateau was then very important to PLA logistic capabilities in Tibet.[42] Chinese abandonment of that road would have significantly diminished PLA capabilities in Tibet, further increasing pressure on Beijing to compromise with India regarding Tibet. Whether this was, in fact, Nehru's intention we do not and probably never will know. There is, however, no evidence indicating that this was, in fact, India's objective. Steven Hoffman traced Nehru's concern with Aksai Chin to a vision of India's historic boundaries adversely compromised by British colonial bureaucrats.[43] The recently declassified official Indian history of the 1962 war also attributes the Indian fixation on Aksai Chin to "national sentiments" roused by "loss of national territory."[44] Very probably, the powerful but inaccurate Chinese belief about India's desire to "seize Tibet" led to an incorrect Chinese conclusion that Nehru's insistence on Aksai Chin was part of a grand plan to achieve that purpose.

The Militarization of the Border Conflict

The military forces of both sides began pushing into remote and previously mostly unoccupied mountainous frontier regions in 1958 and 1959. Beijing's greater public assertiveness in challenging the McMahon Line in 1958, combined with growing Indian awareness of China's road building in Aksai Chin, led India to begin pushing Indian forces into forward regions. As for China, following the Lhasa uprising in March 1959, the PLA launched an "all-out war" against the Tibetan rebels. The first objective of the operation was to seal the border between the Lokka region of Tibet southeast of Lhasa and India's North Eastern Frontier Agency (NEFA) and Bhutan. By August, the PLA had sealed the border.[45] That brought Chinese forces into forward areas.

The first incident of bloodshed on the Sino-Indian border occurred at Longju on the Lokka-NEFA frontier on 25 August 1959. That clash apparently occurred, or at least escalated, at the initiative of the Chinese side, but without the authorization of China's central authorities. Khrushchev discussed this incident with Mao and Zhou during his early October 1959 visit to Beijing. He was dismayed with the spiraling tension in Sino-Indian relations and wanted an explanation of the 25 August incident. Both Zhou Enlai and Mao assured him that the Chinese handling of that incident had been at the initiative of the local commander and without central authorization, and that China desired peaceful resolution of the border problem.[46]

In September, just before Khrushchev's visit, Chinese leaders had met in Hangzhou, Zhejiang province, to consider how to avoid further bloodshed on the border with India. Mao, Zhou, PRC President Liu Shaoqi, Beijing mayor and Politburo member Peng Zhen, Mao's secretary Hu Qiaomu, and General Lei Yingfu participated. The meeting began with a report by Lei on the border situation. Lei recounted repeated calls from frontline commanders for "rebuff" (huanji) of India's "blatant aggression" against China. Mao became somewhat exasperated at this and observed that conflict was inevitable as long as soldiers of the two sides were "nose to nose." He therefore proposed a mutual withdrawal of 20 kilometers. If India was unwilling to do this, Mao suggested, China should unilaterally withdraw. "Meeting participants unanimously supported Chairman Mao's suggestion," according to Lei Yingfu.[47] Thus, Chinese forces were ordered to withdraw 20 kilometers from what China felt was the line of actual control and to cease patrolling in that forward zone. Further Chinese measures to decrease tension on the border were adopted in January 1960 (prohibiting target practice, food gathering, exercising, etc., within the forward zone). Tension declined for twenty-three months.

It began to spiral up again in November 1961 when India started implementing its forward policy. According to the official Indian history, before 1961 a "wide corridor of empty area" separated Chinese forward outposts from Indian outposts. But Chinese forces were steadily pushing forward their posts "occupying more and more of the empty area." In an effort to prevent further Chinese advances by demonstrating "that the remaining area was not empty," Indian forces were ordered to "push forward." The assumption underlying this critical decision was that the Chinese were not likely to use force against Indian outposts "even if they were in a position to do so."[48] Under the new policy, Indian forces were ordered to "patrol as far forward as possible from our [India's] present position toward the International Border as recognized by us . . . [and] prevent the Chinese from advancing further and also to dominate any Chinese posts already established on our territory." As Whiting observed, this new policy "sowed the seeds of conflict." [49] When Indian forces initially began implementing the forward policy, Chinese forces withdrew when they encountered the newly advanced Indian outposts. This encouraged the Indian side and led to the further acceleration of the forward policy. According to the official Indian history. "A large number of Indian posts were established quickly."[50]

Shortly after Indian forces began implementing the forward policy, Mao Zedong convened a Central Military Commission (CMC) meeting in Beijing to consider China's response.[51] Mao had earlier asked the Tibet and the Xinjiang military regions for proposals, and those were apparently on the table when the central meeting convened. Mao compared India's forward policy to a strategic advance in a game of Chinese chess in which one side pushes pawns across the centerline of the board, a line known as the Han-Chu boundary, in reference to the frontier between those two ancient Chinese states: "Their [India's] continually pushing forward is like crossing the Han-Chu boundary. What should we do? We can also set out a few pawns, on our side of the river. If they don't then cross over, that's great. If they do cross, we'll eat them up [a chess metaphor meaning take the opponent's pieces]. Of course, we cannot blindly eat them. Lack of forbearance in small matters upsets great plans. We must pay attention to the situation."[52]

In line with Mao's comments, the CMC ordered China's border forces to resume patrols within the zone 20 kilometers north of the McMahon Line—patrols suspended since October 1959. Accelerated construction of roads to forward areas was also ordered. As the crisis built, Mao Zedong took personal charge of the "struggle with India." Mao stressed to PLA Chief of Staff Luo Ruiqing that the firing of the Chinese "first shot" must be personally approved by himself, Mao Zedong.[53]

On 26 February 1962, Beijing delivered a lengthy and conciliatory-sounding note to India. The note called for negotiations to reach a peaceful settlement of the boundary problem. India's reply came on 13 March. It reiterated India's standard position that Chinese withdrawal from Aksai Chin was an essential precondition for negotiations.[54]

A while later Mao met again with Lin Biao, then vice chair of the CMC and minister of defense, Zhou Enlai, and Luo Ruiqing. Again the topic was the situation being created by implementation of India's forward policy. Zhou Enlai first reported on India's rejection of China's many diplomatic proposals for negotiations. Lin Biao then reported that Indian forces continued to set up outposts next to Chinese outposts, continued to dispatch patrols into forward areas, and continued to fire on Chinese border defense personnel. Mao noted that it would be hard to make Nehru change course: "A person sleeping in a comfortable bed is not easily roused by someone else's snoring," he commented. After discussion, the CMC decided that the PLA absolutely should not retreat before Indian advances. When Indian forces established outposts encircling Chinese positions, Chinese forces should build even more outposts counter-encircling the new Indian positions. In this fashion, Chinese and Indian positions would develop in an interlocking, zigzag fashion. But Chinese forces were also to seek to avoid bloodshed. They were absolutely not to fire without orders from above. In this fashion a situation of "armed coexistence" would develop. Mao's comment on this situation was: "Nehru wants to move forward and we won't let him. Originally, we tried to guard against this, but now it seems we cannot prevent it. If he wants to advance, we might as well adopt armed coexistence. You wave a gun, and I'll wave a gun. We'll stand face to face and can each practice our courage."[55]

Following this meeting, further orders went out to the Tibet and Xinjiang military regions accelerating construction of new PLA outposts and roads. All levels of the PLA and frontier forces were ordered to report developments immediately, and it was reiterated that lower levels absolutely could not decide matters on their own. At all costs, troops and units were to avoid actions that would cause a further worsening of the border situation. Chinese forces were also ordered to conduct propaganda work toward Indian soldiers, calling out to them on encounters to urge them to stop their aggression against China, extolling the traditional friendship between China and India, and recounting the efforts of the Chinese government to achieve a peaceful resolution of the border issue.[56]

Chinese border forces also abandoned their initial policy of withdrawing when encountering new Indian posts. Chinese forces began standing their ground. According to the official Indian history, "When some Indian posts, for example in the Galwan valley [in Aksai Chin] were established outflanking the Chinese posts, the Chinese attitude changed and became more threatening." Rather than withdraw as previously, Chinese forces countered the Indian move by building positions surrounding the new Indian post and cutting off its supply routes to rear areas.[57]

As Whiting and Maxwell maintained, Chinese leaders believed they were defending territory that they believed was legitimately Chinese and had already been under de facto Chinese occupation for some time when Indian forces arrived on the scene. To fail to contest India's forward policy would be to acquiesce to continual Indian "nibbling" of Chinese territory, resulting, finally, in unilateral Indian establishment of a new de facto line of control between Indian and Chinese territory.

China's abandonment of the initial policy of withdrawal in the face of Indian advances, in favor of the tougher policy of armed coexistence, "clearly showed that the basic assumption behind the Forward Policy decision [that the Chinese would withdraw rather than use force] was no longer valid, and a serious reappraisal of the new situation should have been undertaken" by India. "This reappraisal, however, never took place and the situation was allowed to drift," according to the official Indian history.[58] Instead of reexamining the assumptions of the forward policy, Indian leaders made that policy still more aggressive. Rather than merely seeking to preempt Chinese occupation of vacant land, "It was now decided to push back the Chinese posts they already occupied."[59]

In April 1962, India accelerated implementation of the forward policy in the eastern sector, apparently because Nehru believed that the situation there favored India more.[60] More Indian posts were built on commanding heights near existing PLA outposts, and aerial and ground reconnaissance was increased. This produced a "strongest protest" from China's foreign ministry. "Should the Indian government refuse to withdraw its aggressive posts and continue to carry out provocation against the Chinese posts," the note said, "the Chinese frontiers will be forced to defend themselves."[61] India pushed forward with implementation of the forward policy in spite of China's protests. On 5 May 1962, the first officially protested exchange of gunfire occurred. Another Chinese protest followed on 19 May: unless India "desists immediately" from intrusions into the Longju region, it said, "the Chinese Government will not stand idly by."[62] By the end of June, the Indian Foreign Office reported that Indian forces had brought under Indian control over 2,000 square miles of territory since the beginning of the forward policy.[63] Moreover, in July 1962, Indian Army Headquarters "gave discretion to all post commanders to fire on the Chinese if their [Indian] posts were ever threatened."[64]

Egregious Indian miscalculation regarding China's willingness to resort to military force underlay the increasingly assertive Indian policies that unfolded between November 1961 and October 1962. There was a virtual consensus among Indian leaders that China would not respond with military force to Indian advances, and that if it did, any military response would be extremely limited. A Chinese resort to large-scale military force was deemed impossible. This conclusion was established by Nehru and Defense Minister Krishna Menon, not challenged by Indian military leaders, and, in the judgment of the official Indian history, became unchallengeable political orthodoxy.[65] In spite of a clear Indian recognition of China's military superiority in the frontier regions, Indian leaders reached the conclusion that China's superiority was irrelevant. If India demonstrated firm intent, China would back down. In the words of the Indian chief of General Staff regarding the final order to Indian forces in September 1962 to drive Chinese forces from atop Thagla Ridge: "experience in Ladakh had shown that a few rounds fired at the Chinese would cause them to run away."[66]

Since our concern is with China's decision-making process, we need not delve into the origins of this monumental Indian miscalculation. It is important to note, however, the twofold impact of this Indian assumption on China's thinking. First, it deeply offended Chinese nationalist pride. China had "stood up," as Mao said when proclaiming the establishment of the People's Republic in October 1949. It would no longer be bullied by foreign powers. The PLA had fought the United States in Korea and performed creditably, at least in the judgment of China's leaders. Yet here was India acting as though the PLA would turn tail and run rather than fight to defend Chinese territory and honor. Apparently, India had not yet learned the lesson that the Americans had learned in Korea—to respect the power of the new China. The second implication of India's apparent disdain for Chinese power was that a very strong jolt would probably be necessary to cause Indian leaders to acquire a sober appreciation of Chinese power. The gradual hardening of China's response to India's forward policy—ceasing withdrawal when confronted by Indian advances and adoption of a policy of "armed coexistence," acceleration of China's own advance, building positions surrounding, threatening, and cutting off Indian outposts, steady improvement of PLA logistic and other capabilities in the frontier region, increasingly strong and direct verbal warnings, and by September 1962, outright but small-scale PLA assaults on key Indian outposts—did not cause India to abandon its illusion of Chinese weakness. The final Chinese decision to inflict a big, painful defeat on Indian forces derived substantially from a sense that only such a blow would cause India to begin taking Chinese power seriously.

The Final Five Months

While India's forward policy was gathering steam in mid 1962, Beijing received indications that a war between China and India would not draw in other powers. First, Beijing secured indications from Washington that the United States would not support a Nationalist Chinese attack on mainland China. In late May 1962, Premier Zhou Enlai recalled Ambassador Wang Bingnan from vacation and ordered him to return to his post in Warsaw to ascertain U.S. intentions regarding the Nationalist Chinese invasion then being ostentatiously prepared on Taiwan. (Ambassadorial talks in Warsaw were then the main venue for U.S.-PRC interactions.) The crisis in Laos was still raging, and Zhou was concerned that Laos might serve as a corridor for a possible Nationalist attack. Were Washington to support a Nationalist invasion, a conflict between India and China might become linked to that invasion, possibly touching off a larger conflagration across China's entire southern border. Thus Wang was "extremely relieved" when he heard from his U.S. counterpart in Warsaw on 23 June that the United States did not desire war with China and would not, "under present circumstances" support a Nationalist Chinese invasion of the mainland. Wang later learned that this information played a "very big role" in China's decision-making process.[67]

Next, the war raging in Laos between Laotian communists supported by Hanoi and Beijing and anti-communists supported by the United States was put on hold by a de facto partition of that country. On 23 July, exactly a month after the Warsaw ambassadorial meeting, the major powers signed an agreement at Geneva "neutralizing" Laos. The end of intense fighting in Laos, plus a U.S. pledge not to introduce its military force into Laos (part of the "neutralization" agreement) reduced the prospect that U.S or U.S.-supported Nationalist Chinese forces might attack China via Laos. This development increased the prospect that a war between China and India would remain limited.

During the Geneva conference on Laos, Beijing also made another effort to halt the Indian advance via diplomatic means. Zhou Enlai directed China's representative, Foreign Minister General Chen Yi, to seek out India's representative, Defense Minister Krishna Menon, and urge him to find ways of preventing the border situation from further deteriorating. This would be advantageous not only to Sino-Indian relations but to the peace of the whole world, Zhou told Chen to tell Menon. Chen Yi was one of the PLA's most combat-experienced PLA generals, having had years of experience fighting Japanese and Nationalist forces with considerable success. One can imagine the meeting in Geneva between this hard-headed general and the idealistic Krishna Menon, who believed in the persuasiveness of moral opinion. On 23 July, the two men met. Chen asked Menon what ideas the "honorable Indian government" had about solving the Sino-Indian border problem. Menon replied that, in India's view, there was no border problem between China and India. The location of the boundary was very clearly displayed on Indian maps. Implicit in this was the notion that the way to a solution lay in Chinese withdrawal from all territory claimed by India. Moreover, this message was conveyed in an arrogant tone of voice, according to the Chinese account. Chen Yi then said that Indian forces were steadily advancing into Chinese territory, and could it be that the Indian representative did not know this? Menon replied that the movements of Indian troops were taking place on Indian territory. He did not wish to argue, Chen said, but the border problem was a "big one," and the two sides should sit down and calmly discuss it. Chen proposed that he and Menon issue a joint communiqué announcing future talks on the "problem of preventing border conflict." Menon declined this proposal but said he would report the matter to his government. The next day Chen flew back to Beijing to report to Zhou Enlai.[68]

After hearing Chen Yi's report, Zhou commented, "It seems as though Nehru wants a war with us." Yes, Chen replied. Menon had showed no sincerity regarding peaceful talks, but "merely intended to deal in a perfunctory way with China." "At least we made the greatest effort for peace,"

Zhou reportedly replied. "Premier," Chen replied, "Nehru's forward policy is a knife. He wants to put it in our heart. We cannot close our eyes and await death." "We need to discuss the matter with the Chairman," Zhou concluded.[69]

Around July 1962, Mao issued a "twenty-character directive" in response to India's "forward policy." The CMC later embodied Mao's directive in a decision that provided the "general direction" until several weeks before the October war. According to Mao's directive, the PLA should "absolutely not give ground, strive resolutely to avoid bloodshed, interlock [with Indian forces] in a zigzag pattern, and undertake a long period of armed coexistence."[70] To implement this new "general direction," Luo Ruiqing issued orders to the Xinjiang military region specifying twenty-two measures that PLA frontline troops were to follow. If Indian forces advanced on PLA positions, PLA forces would give warning and urge the Indian forces to withdraw. If the Indian forces did not heed these warnings, the warnings could be repeated two, three, or even more times. Only if Indian forces advanced to within fifty meters of PLA positions and Chinese forces "could not survive without self-defense," would PLA forces "prepare for self-defense." If the enemy then withdrew, PLA forces would not seek to block that withdrawal.

It is not clear whether Luo's twenty-two measures authorized Chinese soldiers to fire on Indian forces closing in a threatening fashion within fifty meters of Chinese forces. Reading between the lines, Xu Yan's account implies that it did. But that is only implicit. It may be that PLA forces were ordered to prepare to fire but not authorized actually to open fire unless first fired upon by Indian forces. In any case, firefights intensified. On 9 July, following deployments the previous day by an Indian platoon cutting off a PLA position in the Galwan valley of the western sector, a *Renmin Ribao* editorial delivered another warning: "The Indian Government should rein in at the brink of the precipice."[71] According to Xu Yan, some Indian forces interpreted PLA restraint under the July CMC guidelines as weakness. The result, according to Xu, was repeated provocations against PLA outposts. In one such "provocation" on 21 July, Indian forces opened fire first on Chinese forces manning a "newly constructed" outpost. Chinese forces returned fire. After a twenty-minute firefight, the Chinese had suppressed Indian fire. The PLA then ceased fire and allowed the Indian forces to withdraw.[72] The same day, 21 July, *Renmin Ribao* further intensified China's warnings to India: China would wage a "tit-for-tat" struggle with India in the eastern sector, the article said. It also indirectly raised the possibility of a PLA advance south of the McMahon Line and even the eviction of Indian forces from India's entire NEFA.[73]

These Chinese warnings did not cause Nehru to halt the forward policy or agree to unconditional talks on the border dispute. Beijing noted a speech by Nehru to the Lok Sabha (House of the People), the popular body of the Indian parliament, on 13 August in which he reiterated that the precondition for negotiations was China's complete withdrawal from all Indian territory it had "unilaterally occupied," that is, Aksai Chin. An Indian note of 22 August formally presented the same demands. From Beijing's perspective, this "closed the door to negotiations."[74]

Chinese leaders spent considerable time in mid 1962 analyzing Nehru's objectives in attacking China. Three main reasons were identified. First, Nehru wished to direct outward internal contradictions within India. Second, he hoped to win international, and especially U.S., support. Third, he hoped to "attack China's prestige in the Third World." Pursuit of these objectives by attacking China was based on the belief, Mao concluded, that China would not hit back.[75] Notably absent from this Chinese understanding of Nehru's motives was the proposition that Nehru believed that through the forward policy, India was recovering legitimately Indian territory arbitrarily and illegally occupied by China. Again Chinese leaders simply failed to understand Nehru's motives and attributed far-fetched motives to him deriving from his evil class nature.

In August, Lei Yingfu received CMC orders to inspect and report on the situation in the western sector of the Sino-Indian border. Lei's report concluded that PLA forces "without firing could no longer prevent Indian forces from advancing further."[76] When considering Lei's report, the CMC also noted among Indian public opinion and political personages a rising chorus for the "expulsion of Chinese aggressors from Indian territory."

The situation in the rugged terrain in the Tawang tract east of the Tibet-Bhutan-NEFA tri-border juncture was growing increasingly tense. There the massive Thagla Ridge dominated the local terrain at the forward line of actual control. Indian forces had established an Indian outpost at Dhola at the southern base of Thagla in June 1962 as part of the forward policy and as part of a plan to push Chinese forces from atop Thagla Ridge.[77] Chinese forces responded by entrenching themselves atop that ridge in August, according to the official Indian history.[78]

By early September, Beijing was warning New Delhi that if India "played with fire," it would be "consumed by fire."[79] On 8 September, a force of 800 Chinese soldiers descended from the Thagla heights to surround the Indian post at Dhola. Neither side opened fire for twelve days, but this display of overwhelming Chinese power was a clear warning that China would resist the Indian advance. As Whiting demonstrated, there was careful calibration of Chinese verbiage conveying warnings, plus implementation of corresponding moves on the ground designed to give substance to the verbal warnings. Within India, the Chinese military demonstration before Dhola "gave rise to strong public clamor to throw the Chinese out from

Thagla Ridge," in the words of the official Indian history. The Indian government "in its fond belief did not expect serious retaliation from the Chinese and it assumed that whatever mild reaction came from the Chinese, the Indian Army would be capable of neutralizing it." Thus "the Government of India ordered the Army to rid the Thagla Ridge of the Chinese as early as it was [prepared to do it and the Army] accepted the task—both having based their decision on the unmilitary assumption that the enemy would not react strongly and that mere starting of military activity by India would make the Chinese vacate the Thagla Ridge."[80] On 18 September, an Indian government spokesman announced the government's intention of driving Chinese forces from the Dhola area at the base of Thagla.[81] Indian Army efforts to achieve that objective led to clashes at Dhola on 20 and 24 September.

The increasingly tense armed confrontation at Thagla Ridge forced Mao and other Chinese leaders to reconsider the earlier policy of armed coexistence in late September. The policy had not halted the Indian advance. Mao and other Chinese leaders now began considering administering a large-scale and "painful" military rebuff to Indian forces. Nehru had mistaken China's policy of restraint for weakness, they believed. A number of factors had apparently contributed to an Indian judgment that China would not counterattack, Mao and his comrades concluded. Chinese security concerns were centered on the Pacific coast and regarded the United States and Chiang Kai-shek, while China also faced internal economic difficulties, and Chinese-Soviet relations had soured. China had relatively few troops in Tibet, having withdrawn most of its forces after the successful repression of the Tibetan rebellion circa 1960. On these grounds, China's leaders surmised, Nehru had concluded that China would not counterattack in response to India's forward policy, but would merely issue protests.[82] In these circumstances, a sharp, major blow was necessary to disabuse Nehru and force him to stop his aggression against China.

Nehru's insistence on pushing the forward policy rendered ineffective China's previous policy of very limited use of force. Confronted with continual Indian attacks, the previous policy of defending Chinese positions with "little blows" no longer worked. Even if Chinese "little blows" in one place forced Indian forces there to retreat, Indian attacks elsewhere would continue. This might cause the entire border region to become unstable. A large and punishing blow was thus necessary. The PLA should strive for a "big blow," for a "war of extermination" (*jianmie zhan*). In Xu Yan's characterization of the thinking of China's leaders: "If we strike, we must strike in a big fashion, moreover wage a war of extermination, resolutely hit the wolf and make it hurt. Only in this way can we completely destroy his aggression and cause the aggressors to receive their proper punishment.

Moreover, we can guarantee that for a long time to come [the aggressors] will not dare to come again to conduct aggression against China's borders."[83]

In early October (probably on the 6th), China's leaders met to review the escalating conflict with India. Deputy CMC Chair Lin Biao led with a briefing on the situation. Reports from both the Tibet and the Xinjiang military regions indicated continual Indian advance and firings on Chinese outposts in both the eastern and western sectors. Ten Chinese personnel had been killed or wounded, Lin reported. Yet Chinese forces had strictly followed the principle of not firing the first shot, and "have throughout not fired." Even more serious, India was concentrating military forces in both sectors and had deployed artillery to positions threatening Chinese outposts and camps. The situation was rapidly worsening, according to Lin. Reports by PLA intelligence units indicated that Indian forces might undertake an attack on Thagla Ridge on 10 October.[84] After hearing Lin's report, Mao commented: "It seems like armed coexistence won't work. It's just as we expected. Nehru really wants to use force. This isn't strange. He has always wanted to seize Aksai Chin and Thagla Ridge. He thinks he can get everything he desires."[85] Then Mao declared himself for war:

We fought a war with old Chiang [Kai-shek]. We fought a war with Japan, and with America. With none of these did we fear. And in each case we won. Now the Indians want to fight a war with us. Naturally, we don't have fear. We cannot give ground, once we give ground it would be tantamount to letting them seize a big piece of land equivalent to Fujian province. . . . Since Nehru sticks his head out and insists on us fighting him, for us not to fight with him would not be friendly enough. Courtesy emphasizes reciprocity.

Zhou signaled his concurrence: "We don't wish for a war with India. We have always striven in this direction [of avoiding war]. We wanted India to be like Nepal, Burma, or Mongolia, and solve border problems with us in a friendly fashion. But Nehru has closed all roads. This leaves us only with war. As I see it, to fight a bit would have advantages. It would cause some people to understand things more clearly."[86] Mao concurred: "Right! If someone does not attack me, I won't attack him. If someone attacks me, I shall certainly attack him."

Apparently following this consensus among Mao, Zhou, and Lin, a larger meeting of military leaders was convened in the western outskirts of Beijing. Participants included Mao, Zhou Enlai, Chen Yi, Lin Biao, Marshals Ye Jianying and Liu Bocheng, Chief of Staff General Luo Ruiqing, Vice Chief of Staff General Yang Chengwu, head of the PLA General Political Department General Shao Hua, head of the General Logistic Department General Qiu Huizuo, the commander of the Tibet military region, Lieutenant

General Zhang Guohua, and the commander of the Xinjiang military region, Major General He Jiachan.[87] Mao opened by indicating that war had already been decided upon, and that the purpose of the meeting was to consider problems associated with it. Mao explained: "Our border conflict with India has gone on for many years. We do not want war and originally sought to solve it through peaceful negotiations. But Nehru is not willing to talk and has deployed considerable forces, insistently demanding a fight with us. Now it seems not to fight is not possible. If we fight, what should be our method? What should the war look like? Please everyone contribute your thoughts on these policy issues."[88]

Mao then asked Chen Yi to brief the group on the "diplomatic struggle." Chen traced the problem to 1954, when India had published an official map showing the McMahon Line as a definitive national boundary. At present, Chen said, India "occupies or claims" 1,250,000 square kilometers of Chinese territory. Forty-seven Chinese personnel had been killed or wounded in attacks by Indian forces on the border. China had devoted considerable diplomatic effort to achieving a negotiated settlement, Chen said, but "Nehru is not willing to sit down and talk, and moreover has adopted a provocative forward policy. . . . It seems we can only meet him [Nehru] on the battlefield."[89]

Mao then placed the projected war in a broad historical context. "A war between China and India is truly a most unfortunate event," Mao said. He had recently been reading books on Indian history and was struck by the friendly, beneficial interactions between China and India from the seventh to ninth centuries. After some discussion of those interactions, Mao turned to the history of China-India wars, of which there had been "one and a half." The first war, Mao said, had been in A.D. 648, when a Tang dynasty emperor had dispatched troops to assist the legal claimant to a throne to a subcontinental kingdom—after the other claimant had killed thirty members of a Tang diplomatic mission. A Tang-strengthened force defeated the usurper, who was captured and sent to the Tang capital Chang'an, where he lived out his life. The "half war" came in 1398, said Mao, when Timurlane captured Delhi. This was a great victory, but was followed by the slaughter of over 100,000 prisoners and looting of all precious metals and gems across the land. This was a "half war" because Timurlane and his army were Mongols from both Inner and Outer Mongolia. Mongolia was then part of China, making this attack "half" Chinese. Two key points followed from this history, according to Mao. First, the PLA had to secure victory and "knock Nehru to the negotiating table." Second, Chinese forces had to be restrained and principled.[90]

After Yang Chengwu reported on the military situation in the border regions, Mao called on Ye Jianying to tell the meeting about his impressions of the Indian Army commander, General B. M. Kaul. Ye had met Kaul during a 1957 visit to India. Even though Kaul had apparently served in the Burma Theater during World War II, Ye said, the Indian commander had no actual combat experience. He also seemed to be a very rigid, if impressive-looking, soldier. Still, he was one of India's most outstanding commanders. "Fine," Mao interjected, "he'll have another opportunity to shine." Mao concluded the meeting by warning that China would find itself internationally isolated during the coming war, but that this would not be the decisive factor. The United States and the Soviet Union would, of course, oppose China's action. So too would many other "uninformed countries." Chiang Kai-shek might "adopt measures." But China needn't fear this isolation, Mao said. As long as the frontline troops fought well, "We shall be in an advantageous position. . . . It's better to die standing, than to die kneeling." If China fought successfully and in an awe-inspiring way, this "will guarantee at least thirty years of peace" with India.[91]

On 6 October, New Delhi rejected a Chinese proposal of 3 October to start peaceful negotiations to settle the border issue. Xu Yan terms this a "final effort to secure peace" and asserts that its rejection by India, together with Nehru's declared intent to continue the forward policy, led Mao and the CMC to begin "final consideration" of a large-scale counterattack against India.[92]

On 6 October, Mao and the CMC decided in principle for a large-scale attack to severely punish India.[93] The same day, PLA Chief of Staff Luo Ruiqing received a directive from the CCP center and Chairman Mao authorizing a "fierce and painful" attack on Indian forces. "If Indian forces attack us, you should hit back fiercely . . . [you should] not only repel them, but hit them fiercely and make them hurt."[94] The 6 October directive also laid out the broad directions of the projected offensive. The main assault was to be in the eastern sector, but Chinese forces in the western sector would "coordinate" with the eastern assault.

The CMC staff was then directed to draw up detailed operational plans for a campaign to expel Indian troops from the area north of the traditional, customary boundary (that is, China's claim line at the southern foothills of the Himalayas) in the eastern sector. It was in the process of this staff work that the idea of terminating the war by a unilateral Chinese halt, cease-fire, and withdrawal was developed. In view of "practical difficulties associated with China's domestic situation," the operational plan developed by the CMC staff proposed that after achieving military objectives, Chinese forces would disengage and end the fighting as quickly as possible.[95]

Chinese leaders began finding other reasons for war with India. They observed an increasingly "hegemonist attitude" by India toward its smaller neighbors, Nepal and Pakistan. In this way, India's relations with these countries "became connected to" the border conflict. On 29 September, for example, Indian "armed personnel" provoked an incident on the border with Nepal. When the Nepali government expressed anger over the incident, the Chinese government issued a statement of "firm support" for Nepal's "protection of national sovereignty." Beijing noted that some Indians went so far as to suggest that India act to prevent Nepal from becoming a "Chinese satellite." Toward Pakistan, too, Beijing detected a more aggressive Indian policy. In early October, an armed conflict erupted on the East Pakistan–Indian border, which continued with artillery and automatic weapons fire for twelve days. [96] It seemed to Mao and his comrades that Indian hegemonism was increasingly running amok. In spite of sympathy for Nepal and Pakistan, however, punishing Indian "hegemonism" toward its small neighbors was probably not a major motive for the 1962 war. Rather, this was an example of the common tendency of people facing a difficult decision to seek out and "pile up" reasons substantiating their preferred solution. Doing this mitigates somewhat, at least cognitively, the recognized negative costs of the favored solution.

In deciding for war with India, Mao recognized many difficulties and dangers. Nehru enjoyed great international status, and India was a leader of the nonaligned movement and a prestigious advocate of nonviolence. Both the United States and the Soviet Union were courting India and Nehru. India saw itself as the leader of the "third force" in the world. India's military inferiority to China would play into Indian efforts to depict China as the aggressor. (Indian military forces were about one-sixth of China's, according to China's calculations.) Even among "some Afro-Asian countries," there would be some "misunderstanding." These costs were more than offset, however, by the long-term gains of inflicting a severe if limited defeat on India.

On 8 October, the CMC ordered several additional divisions in the Chengdu and Lanzhou military regions to move into Tibet. All these forces were veteran, high-quality units. Most had previously participated in anti-rebel operations in Tibet and were therefore acclimated to combat operations at high altitudes. The PLA judged Indian forces inferior to the Chinese in combat and war-fighting capability. But uncertainty about Indian military strength led the CMC to concentrate larger forces than might otherwise have been necessary.[97]

Even as the PLA moved toward war with India, Mao continued to mull over vexing problems. Should China permit Indian forces to advance a bit farther into Chinese territory under the forward policy, thereby making clearer to international opinion that China was acting in self-defense? What should be the focus of PLA attack? The major piece of territory in dispute between China and India was Aksai Chin in the west. This suggested focusing the Chinese offensive there. But geographic circumstances for China were worst in the west. Roads to that region "were not convenient" for the PLA. India's geographic situation in the west was also difficult, making it hard for India to concentrate large forces there. The Chinese objective of inflicting a big, painful defeat on India that would cause it to sober up meant that a "big battle" was required.[98] A powerful Chinese offensive that met only thin Indian forces would not fulfill that political objective. The east, where India could more readily rush in large reinforcements, better served Chinese objectives in this regard. It was also in the eastern sector that Nehru insisted that the McMahon Line was an "established fact." Focusing the Chinese offensive there would hit at Nehru's "hegemonist attitude" and compel India to accept the fact that negotiation with China was the only way to achieve a complete settlement of the territorial issue.[99]

A "strategy small group" set up in the CMC staff paid considerable attention to problems of conduct of the war. Marshal Liu Bocheng headed that group. On 10 October, Liu laid out four "opinions" regarding the upcoming war. Liu was one of China's leading military strategists and one of China's foremost exponents of mobile warfare.[100] The crux of success in the coming war, Liu argued, was "concentration of local superiority to achieve a swift war and swift decision." It was absolutely vital to concentrate superior matériel, weapons, and forces in one locality to wage a quick battle and achieve a quick decision. The PLA must also absolutely fight well. Victory in the war was a matter directly connected to the prestige of the Chinese army and nation, Liu warned.[101] It was thus essential to deploy crack troops. The upcoming fight would not be against border police, but against India's best regular forces, which had participated in World War II. The PLA could not be arrogant in this situation. Nor could it rely on such "mechanistic" tactics as infiltration, isolation, and encirclement. Such measures would not produce victory. The correct approach was to "kill, wound, and capture the enemy" by "gnawing the flesh off their bones," that is by attacking fiercely.[102]

On 9 October, the anticipated Indian offensive to evict Chinese forces from atop Thagla Ridge began. The Chinese positions were deemed too powerful for direct assault, so Indian forces moved to outflank them by seizing a previously unoccupied peak to the west of and outflanking Thagla.[103] According to Xu Yan, on the evening of 9 October, over a hundred Indian soldiers crossed the stream flowing along the base of Thagla, and closed on a Chinese outpost. The next morning Indian forces opened fire on the Chinese. In response a full PLA battalion (about a thousand men) assaulted the Indian advance force. Eleven Chinese soldiers were killed and twenty-two wounded in the firefight.[104] The intensity of the Chinese response led Indian leaders to delay further offensive operations in the Thagla region, although not to alter the fixed policy of eventually driving Chinese forces from the ridge. On 12 October, Nehru told the press that Indian forces were still under orders to "free our country" from Chinese occupation—a comment embroidered on considerably by Indian newspapers.[105] Indian forces continued "aggressive patrolling" and "harassing fire."[106]

In Xu Yan's view, this Indian attack signaled the beginning of relatively large-scale fighting in the eastern sector.[107] The fact that the Indian side had shot first created a advantageous political situation for China. Chinese leaders also noted that Nehru had made public comments on 12 October (just prior to a trip to Ceylon) about ordering Indian forces to clear Chinese forces from all "Indian territory." This too made clear Nehru's "stubborn and war-mongering attitude," according to Xu.[108]

Shortly after the start of the Indian move to outflank Thagla, Zhou Enlai appointed Lei Yingfu and Luo Ruiqing to research and report on the reason for India's "expanded offensive" against China. On 16 October, Lei reported to Mao. Lei laid out five key reasons for India's new offensive posture. The first was a desire to turn Tibet into "a colony or a protectorate" of India—the core Chinese belief discussed earlier. Other reasons adduced were a desire to gain increased U.S. and Soviet military assistance by becoming a part of their anti-China campaign; a desire to "achieve hegemony in Asia" by using anti-China activities to increase India's status with poor and small countries of the Third World; and a desire to divert class and national contradictions within India. The final and probably most important reason adduced by Lei's group was a belief that China was "bluffing." Lei returned repeatedly to the notion that Nehru believed that China "was weak and could be taken advantage of" and "barks but does not bite." Because of U.S.-Soviet-Indian "encirclement" of China, compounded by China's "economic difficulties," Nehru believed "that no matter how they attack us, we shall not hit back." Mao agreed with Lei's analysis: "It seems like it is indeed that sort of a situation. In this case, we cannot but fight a war. Well, since Nehru says we only 'bark but don't bite,' we absolutely must fight. We have no other choice. We might as well go along with him [in fighting a war]."[109]

On 16 October, the same day Lei Yingfu reported to Mao, the CMC formally decided to "annihilate" (jianmie) Indian forces that had aggressed against Chinese territory in the east.[110] This decision apparently involved approval of the war plan drafted by the CMC staff.

When China's leaders made their second crucial 16 October decision for war, they had in hand indications of Soviet support. On 8 October, Beijing had formally notified Moscow that India might launch an attack on China, forcing China to respond. On 14 October, China's ambassador in Moscow, Liu Xiao, had secured guarantees from Khrushchev that if there were a Sino-Indian war, the USSR would "stand together with China." A neutral attitude on the Sino-Indian border conflict was impossible, the Soviet leader said. If China were attacked, it would be an act of betrayal to declare neutrality.[111] Chinese leaders attributed this Soviet support, and the stark reversal of earlier Soviet policy of neutrality in the Sino-Indian dispute it entailed, to a Soviet desire for Chinese support in the event of war with the United States over Cuba.[112] The Cuban missile crisis would not erupt until 22 October, when President Kennedy announced the U.S. discovery of Soviet missiles in Cuba and the U.S. naval blockade of the island. It seems, however, that Moscow had earlier given Beijing some glimpse of the plan to deploy missiles to Cuba. According to Moscow's timetable, the new deployment of missiles to Cuba was not to be made public, and the anticipated crisis to erupt, until mid November, after the U.S. midterm elections.[113] Thus Chinese leaders may have anticipated a Soviet-U.S. confrontation in late November, coinciding with the second, expanded stage of the projected punitive war against India, unleashed, in fact, on 18 November.

Approaching winter also forced China's decision. The best time for military operations in the Himalayas was July–September. By October, the weather was already becoming cold, and heavy snowfalls were possible. The Tibet military district reported that once such snowfalls began, the PLA would encounter "great difficulties" in moving supplies and reinforcements across the high passes to frontline Chinese forces.[114] Major PLA action would have to come soon or be deferred to mid 1963. On the other hand, PLA intelligence made it apparent that the military balance in the front regions currently weighed heavily in China's favor. In terms of number of troops, heavy weapons, and communications, the PLA held a distinct advantage. Indian forces were short even of winter clothing and food.[115] Were China to postpone the attack by six months, however, the Indian forces might become better prepared.

On 17 October, the CMC cabled the appropriate orders to the Tibet military district. PLA forces were ordered to "exterminate the Indian aggressor forces."[116] On 18 October, the CMC met yet again to give formal approval to the decision for a "self-defensive counterattack war" (*yi chang ziwei fanji zuozhan*).[117] Participants in the meeting included Mao, Zhou, Liu Shaoqi, Deng Xiaoping, Luo Ruiqing, and Marshals Liu Bocheng, He Long, and Xu Xiangqian.[118]

On 18 October, the decision for war was approved by an expanded Politburo meeting. In attendance were Mao, Zhou, Liu Shaoqi, Zhu De, Deng Xiaoping, Chen Yi, He Long, Luo Ruiqing, Yang Shangkun (then Deng Xiaoping's assistant and in charge of organizational matters for the Central Committee), Tibet MR Commander Zhang Guohua, General Wang Shangrong (a professional soldier and Long March participant, then head of the Operations Department of the PLA), the diplomats Zhang Hanfu and

Qiao Guanhua, and General Lei Yingfu.[119] The meeting opened with a statement by Zhou that from many different aspects, it was apparent that China could not but launch a "self-defensive counterattack" against India as quickly as possible. Mao seconded Zhou's "opinion," but warned of the need not to underestimate India's military forces. General Zhang Guohua, designated to command the upcoming attack, reassured Mao in this regard. Finally, the PLA's war plan was approved. The attack was set for 20 October.[120]

The PLA offensive launched on that day in the Tawang region continued for only four days, culminating in the seizure of strategically located Tawang on 23 October. In the western sector, the offensive continued until 27 October. Chinese forces then halted, and a three-week lull followed. Allen Whiting was probably correct in his surmise that this hiatus was intended to provide an opportunity for Indian leaders to rethink their approach and abandon their forward policy. The weeklong PLA offensive that began on 20 October, followed by a pause, was in line with the gradual escalation of Chinese moves under way since early 1962. The 20 October offensive was a step considerably more forceful than the encirclement and then attack on the Dhola outpost in September, but a measure considerably more limited than the massive assault that came in November. Yet there is nothing in the new Chinese sources that directly substantiates the hypothesis that the three-week lull was intended by the Chinese as opportunity for an Indian drawback. Currently available Chinese sources do not indicate another decision for war after the 6 and 16 October decisions. It seems that those decisions were for a multistage war. Indian forces would first be given a sharp and bloody warning, after which Chinese forces would halt and reorganize for their next offensive. If India did not change its frontier policy after this warning, and if there were no indications of U.S. intervention, the next stage, a massive assault on the southern fringe of the Himalayas, would follow.

Roderick MacFarquhar raises the important point that Nehru could and should have used the early November lull to reorient Indian policy.[121] By then it was abundantly clear that the key assumption underlying the forward policy—that China would not go to war over the border—was wrong. The realities of the military balance, that is, the PLA's clear superiority over Indian forces in the frontier region, should also have been clear. Given this, it was unfortunate that Nehru did not order suspension of Indian offensive operations and find a way of starting boundary negotiations, as Zhou Enlai proposed on 24 October, the day after the first phase of the Chinese offensive ended. Had Nehru reoriented Indian policy in early November, the next phase of the war very probably could have been avoided.

In fact, Indian offensive operations to oust the Chinese from both the Tawang and Walong areas of the NEFA resumed on 14 November.[122] Chinese forces responded by launching a massive, preplanned offensive on 18 November, and Indian defenses in the east rapidly crumbled. PLA forces would not halt until Chinese soldiers looked out from the Himalayan foothills to the broad valley of the Brahmaputra River.

Internal Mobilization and International Confrontation

It is now pretty well established that Mao's domestic mobilization concerns occasionally helped inspire his preference for confrontational international policies. Thomas Christensen has demonstrated this in the cases of Mao's 1950 decision for war with the United States in Korea and his 1958 decision to bombard the offshore islands.[123] A similar dynamic may have been operating in 1959 and again in 1962. In early 1959, when he decided to launch a polemical struggle against Nehru, Mao was struggling to push the agricultural collectivization movement to a new high. In fall 1962, as Mao was guiding his comrades toward war with India, he was also striving to revive "class struggle" in agricultural policy as part of a broader effort to reverse the post–Great Leap retreat from collectivized agriculture.[124] On the other hand, there is a danger of overdetermining an event, and the border conflict, viewed on the Chinese side through the prism of Tibet, certainly seems adequate to explain the 1962 war. In any case, both the highly selective Chinese sources on the 1962 war available thus far and constraints of space associated with a single book chapter do not allow testing of the internal mobilization hypothesis here.

Conclusions

There was an underlying reason why China's leaders decided for war in 1962: a belief that India's leaders did not appreciate the fact that the People's Republic of China was a "new China," that had "stood up" and, unlike pre-1949 "old China," could no longer be "bullied" and "humiliated" by foreign powers. Indian leaders believed that China would not strike back, but would back down before Indian provocations, or so China's leaders concluded. Indian leaders did not respect the new China but arrogantly believed they could impose their will on it, just as Britain, India's imperial mentor, had done repeatedly in the nineteenth century. Indian leaders were unaware of the power and determination of the new China.

This image of India was linked, I believe, to a fundamental asymmetry of Chinese and Indian worldviews regarding the role of military power in world affairs, an asymmetry symbolized perhaps by the meeting of Chen Yi and Krishna Menon at the 1962 Geneva conference. China's leaders saw military power as playing a central role in politics, both domestic and international. When and how to use military power were a matter of pragmatic calculation for them. (This is exemplified by the prominent role of combat veterans such as Liu Bocheng, Lin Biao, Chen Yi, and even Mao, Deng, and Zhou, in China's decision-making.) Nehru and Menon, on the other hand, believed that war among major powers was an obsolete phenomenon. World moral opinion would constrain potential aggressor states. And certainly among the African and Asian states that had shared the common experience of national oppression, resort to war was unthinkable. Thinking along these lines led India to disregard the realities of power in the Himalayas and to conclude that China would not resort to war against India. China's hardheaded leaders took India's disregard for China's power as disdain. They took the Indian belief that China would not fight as a belief that China was weak and would back down before assertive policies.

Was China's resort to war in 1962 prudent? Did it achieve its policy objectives at an acceptable cost? The official PLA history of the 1962 war stresses that "quickly achieving peaceful, stable borders in the west" (*ba xibu bianjiang diqu xunsu wending xialai*) was the objective of the 1962 war. This goal was to be achieved by inflicting a painful defeat on India, thus demonstrating the futility and danger of aggressing against borders defended by the PLA and forcing India to abandon the forward policy. Sharp military defeat would also "compel India to again [*sic*] sit down at the negotiating table and solve the Sino-Indian border problem." This too would "achieve peaceful stability along the western borders."[125]

The harsh defeat inflicted on India in 1962 did, in fact, cause Indian leaders to look much more soberly and respectfully at Chinese power. India did in fact swiftly abandon the earlier policy of using military force to challenge Chinese control of disputed territory. After 1962, Indian leaders were, in fact, much more cautious in dealing with China and more respectful of China's power. The reality of Chinese power also ultimately led New Delhi to resume border negotiations with China still in possession of Aksai Chin—although it would take twenty-seven years for this to happen.

These Chinese gains were secured at great cost. The PLA's drive to the southern foothills of the Himalayas had a profound effect on Indian opinion. China became an Indian nemesis second only to Pakistan. Even forty-some years after the war, this sentiment remains significant in India. The experience of 1962 made India deeply skeptical of Chinese professions of friendship and more wary of the expansion of Chinese security ties with neighboring South Asian countries. What Indians view as China's "betrayal" of India's desire for friendship in the 1950s has made India far less responsive to Chinese diplomatic friendship offensives and more determined to keep China out of places like Nepal and Bangladesh. Fear of the Chinese rooted in 1962 was a major factor impelling India to keep open its nuclear weapons options and then, in 1998, openly to acquire nuclear weapons. There also exists in Indian military culture a desire for payback against China to erase the humiliation of 1962. The trauma of 1962 impelled New Delhi into close strategic alignment with the Soviet Union in the 1960s and 1970s, a development "encircling" China with Soviet power. Even in the 2000s, when India began developing a military partnership with the United States, the defeat of 1962 was a remote but distinct factor in India's deliberations. India also began serious military modernization after the 1962 defeat, and this would eventually change the equation of military power between the two countries. One component of the new military capabilities developed by India was a highly trained, professionally led, and militarily very potent Tibetan armed force of roughly 10,000 men, the Special Frontier Force.[126] Given the decisive impact of the 1962 war on increasing Indian hostility to China, it is quite plausible that had China not opted for war with India, or had perhaps opted for a far less powerful and traumatic assault, China and "China's Tibet" would today face far less of a threat from India.

Notes

1. Neville Maxwell, *India's China War* (New York: Random House, 1972); Allen S. Whiting, *The Chinese Calculus of Deterrence: India and Indochina* (Ann Arbor: University of Michigan Press, 1975).

2. P. B. Sinha, A. A. Athale, with S. N. Prasad, chief eds., *History of the Conflict with China, 1962* (New Delhi: History Division, Ministry of Defence, Government of India, 1992), published online by the *Times of India*, December 2002, www.bharat-rakshank.com (accessed 21 December 2002).

3. There was a third set of factors underlying China's road to the 1962 war—a perception of U.S.-Indian-Soviet collaboration against and encirclement of China. Considerations of space require limitation to consideration of the first two factors, which were, I believe, rather more important than the third.

4. Whiting, *Chinese Calculus of Deterrence*, 36, 34.

5. See *Encyclopedia of Sociology*, ed. Edgar Borgatta and Rhonda J. V. Montgomery (New York: Macmillan, 2000), 1: 194; 4: 2751.

6. *Zhong Yin bianjiang ziwei fanji zuozhanshi* [History of the Sino-India border self-defensive war] (Beijing: Junshi Kexue Chubanshe, 1994), 37–40. This official PLA history of the 1962 war labors at considerable length to demonstrate that India's aggressive intentions and actions precipitated the 1962 confrontation and provides copious details of PLA military operations. Yet it gives very short shrift to the actual process through which China's leaders decided to resort to war. Only 4 out of 567 pages deal with China's decision-making process. Still, these few pages

provide important information when pieced together with other equally fragmentary accounts.

7. Xu Yan, *Zhong Yin bianjie zhi zhan lishi zhenxiang* [True history of the Sino-Indian border war] (Hong Kong: Cosmos Books, 1993), 28, 29–30, 50, 53. This is the most important Chinese work thus far on the 1962 war. It is significant that Xu's work was published in Hong Kong rather than in the PRC. The work deals at considerable length with China's actual decision-making process. Xu apparently had access to primary documents, although he does not reference those sources.

8. Wang Hongwei, "Zhong Yin bianjie wenti de lishi beijing yu 1962 nian Zhong Yin bianjie zhanzheng" [Historical background of the Sino-Indian border problem and the 1962 Sino-Indian border war], *Ya Tai Ziliao* [Asia-Pacific materials], no. 1 (18 March 1989): 1–13.

9. Zhao Weiwen, *Yin Zhong guanxi fengyun lu (1949–1999)* [Record of the vicissitudes of India-China relations (1949–1999)] (Beijing: Shi Shi Chubanshe, 2000), 103. Zhao is one of China's authoritative India hands. From 1950 until the mid 1990s, she worked for the analytical branch of China's Ministry of State Security, the China Institute for Contemporary International Studies and its organizational predecessors.

10. Zhao Weiwen, *Yin Zhong guanxi fengyun lu*, 110.

11. Ibid., 129.

12. Tsering Shakya, *The Dragon in the Land of Snows: A History of Modern Tibet Since 1947* (London: Pimlico, 1999), 13, 26.

13. Regarding India's Tibet policies, see ibid. and Claude Arpi, *The Fate of Tibet: When Big Insects Eat Small Insects* (New Delhi: Har-Anand, 1999).

14. Arpi, *Fate of Tibet*, 338–43.

15. Shakya, *Dragon in Land of Snows*, 21–23.

16. John K. Knaus, *Orphans of the Cold War: America and the Tibetan Struggle for Survival* (New York: Public Affairs, 1999), 155. See also Kenneth Conboy and James Morrison, *The CIA's Secret War in Tibet* (Lawrence: University of Kansas Press, 2002).

17. Zhao Weiwen, *Yin Zhong guanxi fengyun lu*, 124–29. These Indian transgressions are also enumerated in Yang Gongsu, *Xin Zhongguo duiwai zhengce* [New China's foreign policies] (MS), 68–69. Yang was foreign affairs assistant to the PLA in Tibet in the 1950s. He was later China's ambassador to Nepal. Yang charges the Indian consul general in Lhasa with encouraging Tibetan demonstrators to draft a statement of demands that eventually became a Tibetan declaration of independence, and with promising to convey such a statement of demands to the Indian government. In testimony to the Indian parliament, Nehru denied this and said that the consul had merely talked with Tibetans who had pushed their way into the consulate building, had explained that he could not render any assistance, and had declined to become involved in their protests in any concrete way. See Institute of National Affairs, Delhi, *Dalai Lama and India: Indian Public and Prime Minister on Tibetan Crisis* (New Delhi: Hind Book House, 1959), 75. This volume contains Nehru's various comments to parliament about Tibetan developments in 1959.

18. Wu Lengxi, *Shi nian lunzhan, 1956–1966: Zhong Su guanxi huiyilu* [Ten-

year polemical war, 1956–1966: a memoir of Sino-Soviet relations] (Beijing: Zhongyang Wenxian Chubanshe, 1999), 1: 195. Wu Lengxi was the head of the Xinhua News Agency as well as general editor of *Renmin Ribao* at the time. He was also the Politburo's record keeper for relations with the Soviet Union. His two-volume memoir is an extremely rich source for scholars. See my review in *China Quarterly*, no. 173 (March 2003): 197–213.

19. Wu Lengxi, *Shi nian lunzhan*, 197.

20. Ibid., 198.

21. Ibid., 198–99.

22. Editorial department of *Renmin Ribao*, "The Revolution in Tibet and Nehru's Philosophy," 6 May 1959, in *Peking Review*, 12 May 1959, 6–15.

23. *Zhou Enlai waijiao wenxuan* [Selected diplomatic documents of Zhou Enlai] (Beijing: Zhongyang Wenxian Chubanshe, 1990), 268–76.

24. "Memorandum of Conversation of N. S. Khrushchev with Mao Zedong, Beijing, 2 October 1959," *Cold War International History Project Bulletin* [Woodrow Wilson International Center for Scholars, Washington, D.C.], no. 12–13 (Fall–Winter 2001), 266.

25. Lei Yingfu, as told to Chen Xianyi, *Zai zuigao zongshuaibu dang sanmo— Lei Yingfu jiangjun huiyilu* [Serving on the staff of the high command: memoir of General Lei Yingfu] (Nanchang: Baihuazhou Wenyi Chubanshe, 1997), 207.

26. "Mao Zedong sixiang wansui" [Long live Mao Zedong thought], in *Miscellany of Mao Tse-tung Thought* (1949–1968), 2. Joint Publications Research Service (JPRS), no. 61269 (20 February 1974), 573.

27. Apri, *Fate of Tibet*, 320–47, 392–98; Shakya, *Dragon in Land of Snows*, 52–184.

28. Shakya, *Dragon in Land of Snows*, 215, 219, 232, 233.

29. Nehru returned repeatedly during his parliamentary testimony in 1959 to this theme of a two-part agreement. See Nehru's statements to parliament, 30 March 1959, 27 April 1959, and press conference on 5 April 1959, all in Institute of National Affairs, Delhi, *Dalai Lama and India*, 80, 103, 105, 120–21.

30. Correspondence between Nehru and Patel over Tibet is in R. K. Jain, *China and South Asian Relations, 1947–1980* (Brighton, Eng.: Harvester Press, 1981), 1:41–47.

31. Institute of National Affairs, Delhi, *Dalai Lama and India*, 127.

32. B. N. Mullik, *My Years with Nehru: The Chinese Betrayal* (Bombay: Allied Publishers, 1971), 221.

33. Ibid., 70, 180, 182.

34. Steven A. Hoffman, *India and the China Crisis* (Berkeley: University of California Press, 1990), 38.

35. Shakya, *Dragon in Land of Snows*, 215, 282.

36. Knaus, *Orphans*, 159.

37. Conboy and Morrison, *Secret War*, 95–96, 155–56.

38. Shakya, *Dragon in Land of Snows*.

39. Sinha et al., eds., *History of the Conflict with China, 1962*, 56.

40. Ibid.

41. Ibid., 72.

42. See John Garver, *Protracted Contest: Sino-Indian Rivalry in the Twentieth Century* (Seattle: University of Washington Press, 2001), 79–86.

43. Hoffman, *India and the China Crisis*, 23–30.

44. Sinha et al., eds., *History of the Conflict with China, 1962*, 412.

45. *Zhongguo renmin jiefangjun liushinian dashiji (1927–1987)* [Record of sixty years of major events of the PLA, 1927–1987] (Beijing: Junshi Kexue Chubanshe, 1988), 579–80.

46. "Memorandum of Conversation of N. S. Khrushchev with Mao Zedong" (cited n. 24 above), 266, 268.

47. Lei Yingfu, *Zai zuigao zongshuaibu dang sanmo*, 202.

48. Sinha et al., eds., *History of the Conflict with China, 1962*, xx.

49. Whiting, *Chinese Calculus of Deterrence*, 46.

50. Sinha et al., eds., *History of the Conflict with China, 1962*, xx.

51. Chinese accounts of the 1962 war are almost entirely devoid of specific dates for specific decision-making events. With several exceptions, reference to meetings is by very general terms like "later" or "in mid 1962." I have therefore tried to order reported meetings by the context of other events discussed by the book at the time of the reported meeting, or by matters discussed in the meeting themselves.

52. *Zhong Yin da zhan jishi* [Record of events in the big China-India war], ed. Shi Bo (Beijing: Da Di Chubanshe, 1993), 182.

53. Xu Yan, *Zhong Yin bianjie zhi zhan lishi zhenxiang*, 110.

54. Whiting, *Chinese Calculus of Deterrence*, 51.

55. *Zhong Yin da zhan jishi*, ed. Shi Bo, 183–84.

56. Ibid., 184.

57. Sinha et al., eds., *History of the Conflict with China, 1962*, xx.

58. Ibid.

59. Ibid.

60. Ibid., 415–16.

61. Whiting, *Chinese Calculus of Deterrence*, 55.

62. Ibid., 58.

63. D. K. Palit, *War in High Himalaya: The Indian Army in Crisis, 1962* (New Delhi: Lancer, 1991), 177–78.

64. Sinha et al., eds., *History of the Conflict with China, 1962*, xx.

65. Ibid., xx, 415–17. Also 428–29n9.

66. Ibid., 430n13.

67. Wang Bingnan, *Zhong Mei huitan jiunian huigu* [Recollections of nine years of Sino-American talks] (Beijing: Shijie Zhishi Chubanshe, 1985), 85–90.

68. *Zhong Yin da zhan jishi*, ed. Shi Bo, 185–86.

69. Ibid., 187–88.

70. Xu Yan, *Zhong Yin bianjie zhi zhan lishi zhenxiang*, 87.

71. Whiting, *Chinese Calculus of Deterrence*, 78.

72. Xu Yan, *Zhong Yin bianjie zhi zhan lishi zhenxiang*, 88.

73. Whiting, *Chinese Calculus of Deterrence*, 82.

74. Xu Yan, *Zhong Yin bianjie zhi zhan lishi zhenxiang*, 91. This corresponds to Whiting's judgment in *Chinese Calculus of Deterrence*, 92.

75. Xu Yan, *Zhong Yin bianjie zhi zhan lishi zhenxiang*, 113.

76. Ibid., 91–92.

77. Sinha et al., eds., *History of the Conflict with China, 1962*, 415. A map of this region is available in Palit, *War in High Himalaya*, 239.

78. Sinha et al., eds., *History of the Conflict with China, 1962*, 94.

79. Whiting, *Chinese Calculus of Deterrence*, 95–96.

80. Sinha et al., eds., *History of the Conflict with China, 1962*, 415, 417.

81. Ibid., 95.

82. Xu Yan, *Zhong Yin bianjie zhi zhan lishi zhenxiang*, 103–4.

83. Ibid., 110.

84. *Zhong Yin da zhan jishi*, ed. Shi Bo, 188.

85. Ibid., 189.

86. Ibid.

87. Sun Shao and Chen Zhibin, *Ximalaya shan de xue: Zhong Yin zhanzheng shilu* [Snows of the Himalaya mountains: the true record of the China-India war] (Taiyuan: Bei Yue Wenyi Chubanshe, 1991), 95. As far as I can ascertain, this was China's first book-length study of the 1962 war. Although it is not a scholarly book—it lacks reference notes and is written in an often-breezy style—it was authored by two longtime PLA soldiers and to date provides the fullest, most direct account of Mao Zedong's thinking about the road to war with India. The book was banned shortly after its appearance. CASS's Wang Hongwei gives an account of a CMC meeting in "mid October" with some quotations using the exact same language as Sun Shao and Chen Zhibin, but omitting not only quotation marks and precise dates but also the more offhand comments by Mao quoted in the Sun-Chen book. Omitted too in Wang's account are the negative comments by Ye Jianying about Kaul. Wang Hongwei, *Ximalaya shan qingjie: Zhong Yin guanxi yanjiu* [The Himalayas sentiment: a study of Sino-Indian relations] (Beijing: Zhongguo Zangxue Chubanshe, 1998), 228–30. It may well have been Sun and Chen's too full and direct quotations of Mao, plus reportage of Ye Jianying's negative evaluation of Kaul's abilities, that were deemed inappropriate for open publication and led to the volume's ban.

88. Sun Shao and Chen Zhibin, *Ximalaya shan*, 96.

89. Ibid., 97.

90. Ibid., 97–98.

91. Ibid., 99–100.

92. Xu Yan, *Zhong Yin bianjie zhi zhan lishi zhenxiang*, 104.

93. Ibid.

94. *Zhong Yin bianjiang ziwei fanji zuozhanshi*, 179.

95. *Zhong Yin da zhan jishi*, ed. Shi Bo, 189.

96. Xu Yan, *Zhong Yin bianjie zhi zhan lishi zhenxiang*, 106.

97. Ibid., 109.

98. Ibid., 111.

99. Ibid.

100. Howard L. Boorman and Richard C. Howard, eds., *Biographical Dictionary of Republican China* (New York: Columbia University Press, 1967), 1: 404–5.

101. Xu Yan, *Zhong Yin bianjie zhi zhan lishi zhenxiang*, 111–12.

102. *Zhong Yin bianjiang ziwei fanji zuoshanshi*, 180–81.

103. Sinha et al., eds., *History of the Conflict with China, 1962*, 98–100.

104. Xu Yan, *Zhong Yin bianjie zhi zhan lishi zhenxiang*, 112.

105. Roderick MacFarquhar, *The Origins of the Cultural Revolution: The Coming of the Cataclysm, 1961–1966* (Oxford: Oxford University Press; New York: Columbia University Press, 1997), 3, 308, attributes major significance to Nehru's comments to the press. Nehru's comments certainly confirmed established Chinese suspicions about Nehru, but I suspect that the aggressive Indian actions over the previous week weighed more heavily in Chinese evaluations.

106. Sinha et al., eds., *History of the Conflict with China, 1962*, 102.

107. Xu Yan, *Zhong Yin bianjie zhi zhan lishi zhenxiang*, 112.

108. Ibid.

109. Lei Yingfu, *Zai zuigao zongshuaibu dang sanmo*, 209.

110. *Zhong Yin bianjiang ziwei fanji zuozhanshi*, 179.

111. Liu Xiao, *Chu shi Sulian ba nian* [Eight years as ambassador to the Soviet Union] (Beijing: Zhonggong Dangshi Ziliao Chubanshe, 1986), 121.

112. Xu Yan, *Zhong Yin bianjie zhi zhan lishi zhenxiang*, 114.

113. MacFarquhar, *Origins of the Cultural Revolution*, 3, 314–18.

114. Xu Yan, *Zhong Yin bianjie zhi zhan lishi zhenxiang*, 104.

115. Ibid., 107.

116. Ibid., 114.

117. Ibid.; *Zhong Yin bianjiang ziwei fanji zuozhanshi*, 179.

118. *Zhong Yin bianjiang ziwei fanji zuozhanshi*, 180.

119. Biographic information is from Donald W. Klein and Anne B. Clark, *Biographic Dictionary of Chinese Communism, 1921–1965*, 2 vols. (Cambridge, Mass.: Harvard University Press, 1971).

120. Lei Yingfu, *Zai zuigao zongshuaibu dang sanmo*, 209–10.

121. MacFarquhar, *Origins of the Cultural Revolution*, 3, 309.

122. Sinha et al., eds., *History of the Conflict with China, 1962*, 171–74, 242–47.

123. Thomas Christensen, *Useful Adversaries: Grand Strategy, Domestic Mobilization, and Sino-American Conflict, 1947–1958* (Princeton, N.J.: Princeton University, 1996).

124. MacFarquhar, *Origins of the Cultural Revolution*, 3, 261–318.

125. *Zhong Yin bianjiang ziwei fanji zuozhanshi*, 178.

126. Conboy and Morrison offer a good account of the evolution of this force in *Secret War*.

5 *Across the Yalu*

CHINA'S INTERESTS AND THE KOREAN PENINSULA
IN A CHANGING WORLD

Avery Goldstein

Half a century after military conflict in Korea decisively inaugurated the Cold War, and forty years since Allen Whiting's seminal work about China's intervention in Korea introduced an analytical approach for interpreting Beijing's security policy, much has changed.[1] The Cold War has ended, and the regime in the People's Republic of China (PRC) today is dramatically different from the one that charted the country's foreign policy under Mao Zedong. Yet despite these significant changes, in at least two key respects, there is continuity: the Cold War persists on the Korean peninsula in the form of a divided nation led by two regimes, each armed against the threat they believe the other poses; and, the Chinese Communist Party (CCP) retains the reins of power in Beijing. Given this mixture of change and continuity, can Whiting's analysis of China's decision to cross the Yalu in the fall of 1950, and his subsequent generalizations about Beijing's practice of signaling and coercive diplomacy in the Maoist era still illuminate the Korea policies of a quite different Chinese leadership, operating in dramatically different international circumstances?[2] The answer suggested below is that, with substantial modification to account for historical change, Whiting's work indeed remains helpful, insofar as it identifies strategic beliefs that continue to shape thinking among the CCP's top leaders, focuses on the way such beliefs shape perceptions of events in Korea, and suggests the sorts of signals about China's interests in Korea that one might anticipate.[3]

The chapter is divided into four sections. The first section briefly identifies important differences between the early Cold War era and the contemporary period. The second section more closely examines several key considerations shaping China's Korea policy after the Cold War. The third section suggests four highly stylized scenarios depicting different futures for the Korean peninsula and their implications for China's foreign policy, especially its most important bilateral relationship with the United States. The fourth section returns to several broad insights from Whiting's work about China's strategic practice and suggests how, with substantial modification, they may helpfully illuminate China's choices and perhaps the consequences of choice as events in Korea unfold. The chapter concludes by briefly looking at the Korea question in the context of concerns about China's rise and its implications for international politics in the twenty-first century.

Yesterday and Today

THE MID TWENTIETH CENTURY

In 1950, three broad considerations molded China's perception of the Korea problem—national interest, ideology, and international structure. China's Korea policy at the time is most convincingly explained by the concerns of the Chinese Communist Party about its ability to consolidate its hold on newly acquired national power and to turn its attention to the daunting tasks of domestic development. Mao might have believed that his approval of the Stalin-Kim plan to initiate war in Korea carried little risk of escalation to a wider conflict and potentially great benefits for China if a communist buffer state dominated the peninsula.[4] But once the United States decided to lead UN military forces in responding to the North Korean attack on South Korea, and especially once the determined counterattack began to succeed in reversing the tide of the war, any optimism in Beijing was replaced by grave concerns about the potentially serious threat to the PRC's own political and territorial integrity. A straightforward realpolitik assessment rooted in national interests, therefore, readily explains Beijing's decision to intervene in Korea after attempts to dissuade the United States from continuing its military advance toward the Chinese border went unheeded.[5]

That said, ideological considerations were also an important component of China's calculus in 1950, especially since Marxist ideology as interpreted by Mao Zedong played a key part in defining national interests and identifying security threats to them. Mao's decision to "lean to one side" and ally with the Soviet Union, his support for Kim's attack on South Korea after Stalin gave him a green light, and his subsequent willingness to dispatch Chinese forces to engage the forces of "capitalist-imperialism" reflected not just the universal concerns any state has about a hostile power's military stationed on its doorstep. It also reflected the particular concerns of a communist state whose leader had a deeply rooted ideological conviction about the inevitability of conflict between the socialist and imperialist camps.

The bipolar structure of the Cold War international system reinforced the realpolitik and ideological considerations driving China's Korea policy in 1950. At a time when the militarily superior American superpower's hostility was deepening (and included ambitious talk of rolling back communist gains since World War II), a thoroughly outgunned China's fate might well rest on the kind of support it could only get from the world's other superpower, the Soviet Union. Bipolarity, then, created a strong incentive for China to cultivate Soviet support, which was enshrined in the alliance formed in February 1950. But even though the USSR had signed a formal treaty, the international condition of anarchy meant that its pledge was necessarily problematic. And bipolarity, though providing a powerful incentive for China to seek Soviet backing, also exacerbated this uncertainty, which inevitably accompanies such international commitments. Moscow could afford to renege on the promise it was undertaking if its self-interest so dictated, since the Sino-Soviet alliance was a pledge between unequal partners. Both parties recognized that the alliance was vastly more important to China's security than it was to that of the Soviet Union.[6] Therefore, to minimize the risk that their patron might well fail to live up to its treaty obligation, China's leaders sought to increase the political and military costs the USSR would pay for abandoning its partner. Mao's public deference to Stalin's leadership and his plea for the socialist bloc to stand up to rapacious U.S. imperialism in the postwar world both served this purpose.[7] In this light, China's willingness to shoulder the risks and burdens of fighting in Korea were part of Beijing's effort to demonstrate loyalty to Moscow and vividly underscore the threat the United States posed to all socialist states. By bolstering solidarity in the Soviet-led socialist camp, China's leaders hoped to increase the dependability of the security umbrella the Sino-Soviet alliance provided.

THE EARLY TWENTY-FIRST CENTURY

As China considers its policy toward Korea in the twenty-first century, the situation is obviously quite different along each of the three dimensions just discussed. First, the sense that the most fundamental national interest, state survival, faced a serious military threat, in part emanating from the northeast, no longer prevails. Beijing remains concerned about the possible problems an unfavorable disposition of forces in Northeast Asia might present, but the notion of a foreign power attacking the Chinese mainland to realize the goal of regime change (arguably a dubious proposition in the 1950s) is not even a remote possibility today. Although China may still be decades from achieving the status of a peer competitor to the world's surviving superpower, its military modernization has already yielded conventional and especially nuclear forces that confront even the most powerful adversary's military or civilian population with the risk of unacceptable punishment if it challenges China's vital interests.[8] Because of the dangers inherent in any such confrontation, the most plausible threats to survival that leaders in Beijing face at the start of the twenty-first century are no longer external military pressures. Instead, internal problems resulting from the dislocations of rapid economic development and the shortcomings of an archaic political system pose the sorts of dangers most likely to worry China's leaders today, even as they consider how to deal with the evolving situation on the Korean peninsula.

Second, Marxist ideology is no longer a major influence on China's foreign policy. This change, of course, was evident well before the end of the Cold War. While the actual significance of ideology as a determinant of choice in the 1950s and 1960s is debatable, by the 1970s, Beijing's fear of Soviet domination made China's top priority when discerning friends and enemies a nearly pure realpolitik calculus covered with an ideologically correct, but flimsy, fig leaf under Mao Zedong and especially under Deng Xiaoping.[9] In the post–Cold War era, the notion of rivalry between socialist and capitalist camps has simply lost all relevance. As a consequence, ideology no longer provides a reason for Beijing to hope that Korea will be unified under the leadership of a socialist ally. Moreover, Beijing's interest in peace and stability on the Korean peninsula takes precedence over reunification, now described as a goal to be achieved "eventually, peacefully, gradually, and without outside interference."[10] When, to Pyongyang's chagrin, Beijing and Seoul normalized relations in 1992, and especially as economic ties between South Korea and China boomed afterward, it became clear that the PRC's leaders no longer see an ideological affinity with the North's Korean Workers' Party that implies a significant obligation.[11] Instead, China's foreign policy toward the peninsula has been tailored to meet China's national interests (a peaceful environment conducive to economic development in which neighboring states do not become pawns of any foreign power hostile to the PRC) rather than to meet the obligations of the 1961 treaty with Pyongyang, signed when ideology underpinned a relationship of fraternal communist parties allegedly as close as "lips and teeth."[12] Thus, although China still has interests in Korea and concerns about the fate of the North Korean regime, these concerns are no longer rooted in the ideologically defined vision of an expanding socialist camp that had encouraged Beijing's risk-acceptant behavior in 1950.

Third, the structure of the international system has shifted from bipolarity to unipolarity. China can no longer leverage the support of a more powerful ally to counter the challenges posed by the United States. While China's conventional and nuclear forces do continue to provide a robust deterrent against threats to the security of the PRC, China's interests are expanding and now include protecting vital trade routes and ensuring access to valuable natural resources. Beijing's ability to ensure these larger interests, which extend beyond simply protecting the physical security of the country's borders, however, is still tightly constrained by the reality of vastly superior American capabilities deployed in Asia and elsewhere. Despite very real improvements that have resulted from its recent push for military modernization, China's forces remain at a substantial relative disadvantage.[13]

With neither arms nor allies to provide the clout to counter a preponderant United States if it poses a challenge, China's approach to ensuring its interests has been to accommodate the stark realities of American power, while pursuing capabilities that will eventually loosen this constraint on Beijing's options. Especially since the late 1990s, when China's leaders accepted that unipolarity would not soon give way to multipolarity, Beijing has sought to (1) husband its resources, while patiently attempting to lay the economic and technological foundations necessary for it to emerge as a first-class military power in the mid twenty-first century; (2) selectively focus its current military planning on the most pressing threats to its vital interests; and (3) forestall new threats that would require the country to shoulder a heavier military burden and divert investment to producing immediate results at the expense of comprehensive, long-term modernization.[14]

With these considerations in mind, since the mini-crisis of 1995–96, China's strategists have given top priority to the possible need to use force in the Taiwan Strait—a scenario in which China anticipates facing American intervention.[15] Beijing, therefore, has a strong interest in ensuring that tensions on the Korean peninsula do not require it to incur the additional costs of preparing to simultaneously fight on a second front where the United States might be engaged. Beijing would be loath to consider simply redeploying forces from the Taiwan Strait to the northeast. Taiwan is a more vital interest for the CCP, having become a litmus test of its nationalist credentials, which are crucial to the regime's political survival. Beijing would be unlikely to compromise its military readiness in this theater as a response to developments in Korea, especially since China's interest in Korea is much less clearly defined and, in any event, that country, unlike Taiwan is not a visible test of the regime's ability to assert control over what it claims is national territory.[16] Thus, resource constraints and political priorities together encourage Beijing to minimize the possibility of conflict in Korea reemerging as a major planning contingency, because this would significantly increase the military burden Beijing must shoulder.

In the present circumstances, then, three key considerations are relevant to China's policy toward the Korean peninsula. First, survival concerns are mainly concerns about the political fate of the CCP regime, and especially possible internal threats to it, rather than fear of direct external threats to the country's political or territorial integrity. Second, because internal stability is the chief security concern, foreign policy is tailored to maximize the prospects for the success of China's ongoing program of economic development. This has the twin political payoffs for the CCP of maintaining support among those Chinese who see the regime serving their material interests and, by providing the foundation for growing international economic and military clout and strategic self-reliance, building support among those Chinese who take pride in the prospect of their country rising to the position of a true great power. Given these concerns, Beijing has a strong interest, one it repeatedly invokes, in maintaining a peaceful international environment conducive to its modernization. China's policy favoring efforts to foster peace and stability on the Korean peninsula serves its interest in minimizing the risk of political tensions and military conflicts that would complicate international trade and investment.[17] And, third, if military conflict in Korea seemed more likely, or if the North Korean state were replaced with a heavily armed U.S. ally on China's border, prudence would require Beijing to divert resources to fortifying the northeastern frontier, compounding the economic burden and military challenges it already faces in managing the situation in the Taiwan Strait.

China's Foreign Policy and Korea

In the post-Marxist era, the legitimacy of China's communist regime rests on two pillars. One is its ability to deliver on the promise of growing prosperity for the Chinese people. The other is the regime's ability to stand up to hostile or meddling foreign powers that might challenge the CCP's credentials as guardians of China's international interests. These twin pillars link China's domestic and foreign policy agendas in ways that pose something of a dilemma for the country's leaders. On the one hand, they have to figure out how to champion policies in Asia that meet the nationalist aspirations the regime has nurtured. On the other hand, they must do this in a way that does not provoke tensions with the United States and other advanced industrial powers whose negative reaction could jeopardize China's integration with the international economy, a process that since the late 1980s has become essential for the regime's ability to continue building prosperity at home.[18]

These potentially conflicting imperatives require a delicate and difficult balancing act for Beijing in Korea and elsewhere. China's participation in the armed conflict that froze the current division of the Korean peninsula clearly established Beijing's commitment to the survival of the Democratic People's Republic of Korea (DPRK), a commitment sealed by a steep investment of Chinese blood and treasure. China's involvement in the Korean

War subsequently assumed great symbolic significance for the CCP. Since the early 1950s, it has often been invoked as evidence of the competence and determination of communist Chinese leadership. To buttress the nationalist credentials of the CCP among those Chinese who do not embrace the party's Marxist ideological trappings, China's leaders have highlighted the stark contrast between the result of its Korean intervention and the repeated humiliations Chinese regimes had suffered at the hands of foreigners over the preceding century. The demonstrated ability of the Chinese "People's Volunteers" to stand up to the might of the world's greatest power and fight the Americans to a draw has remained a point of pride for Beijing.

The historical legacy of the PRC's involvement on the Korean peninsula in the 1950s means that decisively abandoning the decades-long commitment to North Korea would be a costly and difficult choice for Beijing. Even if it did not entail risking the sorts of devastating domestic political ramifications that would accompany abandonment of the CCP's pledge to recover Taiwan, it would generate controversy within the leadership.[19] Nevertheless, the end of the Cold War has changed the meaning of China's commitment to the DPRK. No longer rooted in the rivalry between two camps defined by ideological preferences, Beijing's interest in the fate of the DPRK today is mainly rooted in Beijing's post–Cold War concerns. The desirability of maintaining (or the acceptability of changing) the status quo on the Korean peninsula is linked to Beijing's concerns about domestic political stability and also about the implications of having the military of the world's sole superpower poised near the PRC's borders.

China's support for any settlement in Korea will be strongly influenced by its underlying nervousness about preponderant American power and the constraints it poses. The situation on the Korean peninsula is now tied to three Chinese concerns about the post–Cold War strategic policy of the United States—the continuing large-scale forward deployment of American military forces in East Asia, to which Washington made a firm public commitment in the mid 1990s; the recasting of bilateral alliances in Asia to cope with post-Soviet challenges to peace and security (in Beijing's view, implicitly aimed at worries about an anticipated China threat); and the deployment of missile defenses. Fluctuating tensions on the Korean peninsula after 1990 provided a clear rationale for U.S. Asia policy bearing on these matters, but it was a rationale that China found implausible. It viewed American forward military deployments, reinvigorated U.S. alliances (especially with Japan), and missile defenses allegedly geared toward a North Korean contingency as dangerous, because their real purpose might actually be to prepare for future contingencies involving a more powerful China.[20] Most worrisome was the prospect that this Korea-focused, post–Cold War U.S. military posture in Northeast Asia might be tapped to influence events in the theater where Sino-American disagreements were already potentially explosive—the Taiwan Strait.

Yet opposing U.S. policy in Asia has not been the guiding principle for China's leaders since the end of the Cold War. Beijing's main emphasis has instead been on the need to ensure an international environment conducive to China's daunting modernization effort, on which the regime's legitimacy largely rests. This consideration places a premium on containing tensions with, rather than countering threats from, the United States and its Asian allies, who are key economic partners for China. In this respect, Korea is not just a troubled, divided country that provides a rationale for disconcerting U.S. military polices in the region and a challenge for China's leaders; the peninsula also offers distinctive opportunities from which they can benefit.

Since the end of the Cold War, Beijing has established a remarkably solid political and a mutually beneficial economic relationship with South Korea.[21] It therefore has little reason to support a North Korean agenda that would entail killing the southern golden goose. China's economic incentives to ensure peace on the peninsula have instead encouraged Beijing to craft a Korea policy that on balance facilitates cooperation with the United States. As noted below, Washington and Beijing surely have different perspectives on what would be the optimal future for Korea. Yet both have a strong short-term interest in managing tensions there in ways that reduce the likelihood of a devastating armed conflict, incentives that became manifest in convening the four-party talks during the 1990s to promote dialogue and reduce tensions on the peninsula.[22] Indeed, this shared interest in maintaining peace and promoting prosperity in the region has made the Korea issue one of the most important reasons both Beijing and Washington have worked hard to contain tensions in their bilateral relations since the mid 1990s. American leaders have routinely cited the need to cooperate on Korea when explaining the importance of sustaining a sound working relationship with China. Despite their ostensibly divergent approaches to U.S. policy in Asia, the Clinton and Bush administrations have both subscribed to this view. President Clinton cited China's usefulness for managing the potential dangers in Korea as a benefit that would result from his administration's effort to develop a "constructive strategic partnership" with Beijing. And although the Bush administration has rejected the term "strategic partnership," it too has emphasized the benefit of working with Beijing to contain tensions in Korea as the United States tries to build a somewhat different "candid, cooperative and constructive relationship" with China.[23]

In sum, then, China has mixed interests in its dealings with the United States over Korea: an enduring, if now more limited, commitment to the security of the DPRK; concerns about the way American military capability

ostensibly geared toward a Korean contingency might threaten China's regional interests; and an incentive to benefit economically from good relations with the Republic of Korea (ROK) and the United States. These mixed
interests preclude easy forecasts about China's policy toward the Korean
peninsula. One way to begin sorting out the complexity is to think about
these interests in the context of four broad, and intentionally simplified,
scenarios for Korea's future.

Four Korean Futures

SCENARIO 1: STATUS QUO PLUS

Under this scenario, the DPRK remains weak and largely isolated but
poses no imminent threat to its neighbors. In such circumstances, the risk
of intense crisis or war remains at a modest level. The American military
maintains its major presence in South Korea, geared toward the contingency of action (either defensive or preemptive) against a dangerously unpredictable North Korea. This U.S. military posture, the development and
deployment of missile defenses, and the nurturing of the security alliance
with Japan are all credibly justified in terms of the need to hedge against
a deterioration of the situation on the peninsula.[24] This military posture
also facilitates a thinly veiled U.S. strategy of crypto-containment, aimed at
a potential China threat, but does so in a context that neither requires
the United States to commit to this purpose nor China to react to this
possibility.[25]

SCENARIO 2: STATUS QUO MINUS

Under this scenario, the DPRK remains weak and isolated but appears a more imminent threat, demonstrating an enhanced capacity to deliver
weapons of mass destruction by means of ballistic missiles and adopting
more bellicose rhetoric and behavior. The protracted ratcheting up of tensions with the United States after October 2002 (when Pyongyang con-
fessed to a secret program to enrich uranium that violated the spirit, if not
the technical letter, of the 1994 Agreed Framework) seemed to be creating
just this sort of situation. Halting multilateral talks among North Korea,
the United States, China, South Korea, Japan, and Russia failed to alleviate
concerns about Pyongyang's apparent determination to field a nuclear
deterrent.[26]

The underlying dynamic driving this more dangerous scenario would
most likely be the one that Victor Cha has outlined, in which a desperate regime in Pyongyang overestimates the probability that aggressive behavior

will improve its survival prospects.[27] Under such circumstances, the risks of crisis and conflict grow and China would find it more difficult to maintain its current straddling posture. If the crisis became acute, and especially if it resulted in the actual use of military force initiated by the United States, Beijing would most likely conclude that it had to lend some sort of support to North Korea.[28] This expectation reflects the competitive aspect of the broader Sino-American relationship. Although Beijing might care little about North Korea per se, it would see such an emerging Korean crisis or conflict as a zero-sum contest in which China's self-interests, both reputational and intrinsic, were at stake. If the United States were allowed to prevail in a showdown with the DPRK while Beijing stood aside, America's international stature would grow at China's expense; the experience would visibly demonstrate China's inability to parry U.S. post–Cold War international dominance even in Beijing's own front yard. The Korean peninsula, after all, is not the Balkans or the Persian Gulf, where geographic distance allows China the option of remaining relatively detached. Inaction during an intense Korean crisis would not only undercut China's international stature but also besmirch the domestic political credentials of the CCP as the leader of a proudly resurgent China.[29] In addition, a U.S.-imposed solution could result in a changed military situation that represented meaningful gains for the United States at China's expense; such an outcome would effectively reactivate Korea as an important security concern, a front whose military importance had declined since the 1950s relative to China's other major post–Cold War concerns (especially Taiwan, but probably even disputed claims in the South China Sea).

Beijing, therefore, would have strong incentives to forestall a resolution of any Korean crisis or conflict that had the potential to cause such damage to China's interests. Choosing how to respond, however, would be excruciatingly difficult. Strong support for North Korea in a confrontation with the United States would not only harm China's economic ties with the United States, Japan, and South Korea in the short term, but would also almost certainly result in a more explicit American strategy in Asia defined by containment of China. Adopting a hands-off approach would have its own risks for Beijing, including the reputational and military costs just mentioned, as well as the risk that the regime would be vulnerable to a domestic challenge from an increasingly nationalistic public outraged at what would be seen as yet another post–Cold War American humiliation of China, or perhaps from a faction in the military or Party who viewed the current leadership group as feckless.[30] China's role since early 2003 in dealing with the increased tensions that followed North Korea's defiant stance on its nuclear program reflected the challenge this tough balancing act poses. On the one hand, Beijing refused to support the imposition of economic sanctions that might strangle the economically desperate DPRK and increase the already huge number of Korean refugees in China's northeast. On the other hand, Beijing quietly pressured Pyongyang to agree to compromise in talks with Washington designed to discover a diplomatic resolution.

SCENARIO 3: SERIOUS REFORM

Under this scenario, the DPRK emulates China's reform strategy, whose logic requires extensive engagement with the international economy. As in China, the leaders in North Korea would be expected to combine economic reform with tight control of political challenges at home, but to the extent that Pyongyang sees economic development as the key to regime survival, its military posture would become more relaxed. Bellicose rhetoric and weapons development programs that frighten potential investors and trade partners would be forsaken.[31] The result of such a reform process would be a situation on the Korean peninsula that best suited China's interests. Beijing could position itself as role model for the North, continue as economic partner with the South, and work to undermine the U.S. justification for its Cold War–style military presence in northeast Asia. The CCP would be able to enjoy the fruits of its open economic policy and at the same time serve its nationalist agenda, insofar as the regime's stature would benefit from the perception that it was playing a leading role in solving a long-standing international problem.[32]

In short, such reforms in North Korea would advance China's reputational as well as its intrinsic interests. Under this scenario, it is the United States, rather than China, that would confront tough choices—most broadly between a reduced military role in the region and a more explicit redefinition of its purpose as a hedge against a potential China threat. Missile defenses (in the theater or deployed in North America, but with an East Asian orientation), having lost their North Korean rationale, would be seen as insurance against a possible U.S.-China confrontation (most likely to emerge from a dispute about Taiwan). The United States would be hard pressed to avoid creating the impression that its alliance with and heavy troop presence in the ROK, and perhaps even Japan, though cast in terms of "regional peace and stability," were not aimed at contingencies involving China, rather than contingencies involving what would appear to be an increasingly cooperative, reformed regime in North Korea.[33]

SCENARIO 4: TRANSFORMATION

Under this scenario, the DPRK disappears and the peninsula is unified under Seoul's leadership. Although such an outcome would most likely result from unpredictable and unforeseen events, one can imagine at least two ways they might unfold that would not entail the implausible scenario of an ROK military conquest.[34] One would be a peaceful settlement negotiated by leaders in Pyongyang who anticipated an imminent loss of control and collapse, possibly as a consequence of a failed attempt at opening and reform of the sort described above. Another would be a much more disruptive collapse in which some element of the North Korean security apparatus cuts a deal with South Korea and imposes it on the rest of the elite.[35] However it might come to pass, such a transformation resulting in a unified Korea would profoundly affect Chinese and American interests in the region, but in ways that would depend on the nature of the new regime.

As long as the U.S.-ROK security alliance holds, the end of the DPRK as a separate state would immediately put an American ally on China's border.[36] At a minimum, this proximity would increase Beijing's uncertainty about the military challenges with which it would have to prepare to cope, even if it is unlikely that the United States would take the provocative step of aggressively repositioning any forces that remain on the peninsula much closer to the Yalu River separating China and Korea.[37] America's freedom of maneuver in northeast Asia would be increased, while China's would be decreased. During any Sino-American confrontation in the Taiwan Strait or the South China Sea, U.S. military planners would no longer have to keep one eye on a possible second front activated by the regime in Pyongyang. If it wanted to preserve American uncertainty about a second front, China would have to incur the burden of allocating significant military resources to its far northeast. And even if it responded in this way, such forces could only represent a threat to punish the Americans and their allies in Korea (much as China can threaten Japan); they would not reconstitute the current risk, however small, that conflict in Korea could result in unification under a regime hostile to U.S. interests. China, in short, would have lost the benefits of the complication that North Korea presents for American military planning in East Asia.

The end of the DPRK as a separate state would also heighten China's insecurity, because it would echo the events of 1989–91, when most communist regimes collapsed and the future of the surviving handful seemed doubtful. As in the early 1990s, China would react with alarm. The most likely immediate response would be some version of the siege mentality that prevailed following the double-whammy of China's own widespread antigovernment protests in spring 1989 and the subsequent demise of European and Central Asian communist governments. As in the early 1990s, the CCP would buttress political controls at home and seek to protect itself against what it labels the threat of "peaceful evolution" from abroad—the political price China's leaders reluctantly accept as necessary in order to enjoy the benefits of participation in the international economy.[38] The likely American celebration of the end of the North Korean communist dictatorship, undoubtedly including a reprise of President Clinton's theme of being "on the right side of history," would almost certainly add an ideological challenge to the potential military-strategic challenge China would perceive.

Washington, of course, would also have to recast its security policies in northeast Asia in the aftermath of the collapse of the DPRK. It is conceivable that hard choices could be sidestepped simply by citing the need for continuity as a hedge against unspecified threats to stability and peace in the region.[39] This, however, seems unlikely to suffice. Ambiguity may suit diplomatic communiqués, but force procurement, contingency planning, and military exercises require thinking about the dangers that the United States and its allies would be preparing to confront. Invoking the global war on terrorism to justify an American presence in the region, though less vague, would also do little to explain a continuing major military foothold in northeast Asia, especially large numbers of U.S. troops in Korea. Instead, a fundamental question, once North Korea was off the table, would most likely be the extent to which basic continuity in the American military posture in Asia could be justified without making explicit what has thus far been mostly implicit—contingency planning for conflict with China.[40] In short, while Korean unification under Seoul's leadership would be a welcome development for many reasons, it would present substantial challenges for U.S. interests in Asia. By providing a sound rationale for American regional security policy, North Korea has in many ways been a "useful adversary" for Washington.[41]

Indeed, it is even conceivable that unification could prove to be less troublesome for China than the United States, because Beijing's ties with Seoul have improved so significantly since 1992. A scenario under which China might very well tolerate the peaceful unification of Korea under Seoul's leadership is simply no longer as far-fetched as it once might have been. Beijing might, after all, deflect the potentially dangerous ideological implications of the DPRK's demise by describing it as a result of Pyongyang's failure to "seek truth from facts" during the arduous process of building socialism that the CCP has mastered. And Beijing might also be able to deflect the potential military challenges of proximate U.S. power by convincing Seoul that the tangible mutual economic benefits of bilateral ties with China far exceed the speculative benefits of continuing a nettlesome military relationship with the United States that, absent the DPRK, would serve only as a hedge against an unlikely China threat. Beijing might then not only succeed in avoiding the dangers of unification suggested above. It might even welcome unification under Seoul's leadership if it were seen as creating a more stable and friendly regime on the Korean peninsula that no longer risked embroiling China in dangerous disputes with the United States.

Whiting's Hypotheses Revisited

The preceding sections have examined China's interests in Korea and how they might shape Beijing's policies under four different scenarios for the future of the peninsula. Against this background, I next revisit and, with modification, apply several of Whiting's insights into China's foreign policy behavior, especially its practice of deterrence.[42] In some respects, the principles Whiting identified in a quite different context have clear implications for interpreting China's current Korea policy. In other respects, the relevance of these principles is more speculative, but nevertheless potentially helpful for anticipating future developments.

INTERNAL-EXTERNAL SECURITY LINKAGE

The need to deter threats increases as the domestic situation worsens. In contrast to the early Cold War period, contemporary Chinese concerns about Korea that link domestic and international security are more likely to be political than military. Domestic political insecurities provide incentives for the CCP leaders to worry about the implications of developments on the peninsula that could exacerbate challenges to regime stability within the PRC. This is relevant in three areas: (1) links between the reactivation of a serious security challenge along China's northeastern frontier and the political dangers it implies for the regime if it must divert substantial national resources from civilian to military spending, thereby slowing the pace of China's economic development, which, as noted above, has been crucial to political stability since 1989; (2) links between the survival of the DPRK and demands for an accelerated pace of political reform in China that the CCP has routinely rejected (a concern that could be prominent under the "transformation" scenario); and (3) links between the problem of illegal Korean immigration and the dangers of social unrest within China that have accompanied painful economic reforms to which the CCP is committed (a concern that could be prominent under the "status quo plus" scenario).

Fallout from a DPRK collapse.   As happened following the events of 1989–91, and especially following the collapse of the Soviet Union, the demise of the DRPK could well intensify debate about the long-term viability of Leninist systems, raising potentially troublesome questions for China's leaders, comparable to those they faced in the early 1990s.[43] Put differently, the dangers of instability that China's leaders believe they confront reflect not only the domestically generated problems of economic modernization but also pressures for change linked to the outside world. The latter include direct foreign criticism of China's authoritarian political practices, as well as the indirect effects from expanded access to information about the experiences of other countries (including other failed communist states) that enables China's citizens to form their own opinions (positive and negative) about the appropriateness of political arrangements in their country.[44] A DPRK collapse would probably increase the pressures for political change in China. To the extent that China's leaders feel insecure about their grip on power, then, they have an interest in forestalling the rapid collapse of the regime in Pyongyang.[45] Beijing not surprisingly has tried to encourage a modus vivendi between North and South Korea that prolongs the life of the DPRK, while urging Pyongyang to create more favorable conditions for regime survival by embracing its own version of the "market-Leninist" model of reform that the CCP has pioneered (China's preferred outcome described in the "serious reform" scenario).

Recast in terms of Whiting's internal-external hypothesis, the weaker and more besieged the CCP feels, the more likely it is that it will insist on arrangements in Korea that preserve a significant role for the regime in Pyongyang. Conversely, the stronger and more secure China's CCP leaders are, the wider the range of political arrangements for the future of the peninsula they may be willing to consider.

Fallout from Korean refugees. Beijing's sensitivity to the links between internal and external security are also manifest in the problem of economic refugees and political asylum seekers arriving in China from Korea. The influx of refugees from the economic hardships that have plagued the DPRK since the early 1990s exacerbates China's own problems with a large "floating population" and chronic underemployment that has accompanied the downsizing of inefficient state-owned industry. China's northeast (the country's industrial heartland in the old centrally planned economy) is not only the destination for illegal Korean immigrants, it is also plagued by some of the most serious socioeconomic problems resulting from the painful reform of the state-owned industrial sector. Moreover, these problems are likely to become more acute as Chinese industry is subjected to growing pressure from foreign competitors under the terms of accession to the World Trade Organization. Korean immigration, therefore, threatens to worsen the difficulties confronting an already troubled region of the PRC.

Recast in terms of Whiting's internal-external hypothesis, the more severely disruptive the social consequences of economic adjustments within China, the more likely it is that (1) Beijing will take a hard line in response to the threat Korean economic refugees pose to China's stability, and (2) Beijing will strengthen its effort to get Pyongyang to make changes that will reduce the desperation that drives North Koreans to take the risky gamble on a better life in China as illegal aliens.

Aside from the challenge of absorbing an influx of economic refugees, China faces the materially less imposing but politically more embarrassing problem of North Koreans who seek political asylum in the diplomatic compounds of China's cities as a route for escaping to the ROK.[46] Each such case puts Beijing in a tight spot. The CCP leaders face competing considerations: an interest in adhering to their principled position of absolute respect for state sovereignty and noninterference in the domestic affairs of the others (i.e., respecting the jurisdiction of the DPRK over its citizens under the terms of the extradition treaty with China), respect for the sovereignty of the states whose diplomatic compounds have been breached, and a clear international humanitarian consensus that militates against returning the asylum seekers to the harsh punishment they may suffer in the DPRK. Moreover, the visibility these asylum cases achieve, to a limited extent in domestic media but to a greater extent in foreign media to which many politically engaged Chinese have access, necessarily draws attention to the grave risks these people have taken in order to escape the repressive policies of a failing communist state. That subtext aggravates the unresolved tension between international opinion that increasingly pushes for a universal conception of human rights and the perspective of a CCP regime that puts a higher priority on order than freedom and justifies its approach by asserting a "hard" view of state sovereignty in which each country determines its own citizens' rights according to distinctive national conditions.[47]

Recast in terms of Whiting's internal-external hypothesis, with respect to both economic refugees and political asylum seekers, then, the more secure China's central leadership and the lower its anxiety about domestic instability, the less likely it is that it will see these externally generated problems as a serious threat, and the more likely it is to adopt a flexible posture in addressing them. In the early 2000s, a relatively secure CCP has on balance demonstrated considerable flexibility and pragmatism in its handling of even the more difficult problem of Koreans seeking political asylum. Relying on quiet diplomacy and face-saving solutions (such as sending Korean political refugees to a third country rather than permitting them to go directly to the ROK), Beijing has thus far been able to accommodate international pressure for humanitarian treatment, while avoiding the most blatant affront to Pyongyang and minimizing the danger that such incidents could trigger domestic debates about the legitimacy of foreign intervention in cases of human rights violations within a sovereign state, specifically one led by a repressive communist regime.[48]

ACTIONS, NOT JUST WORDS

Deterrence requires a belligerent posture that is made credible by actions and not just rhetoric. If China's leaders perceive a growing risk that trends on the Korean peninsula are inimical to their interests—either because of what developments portend for future military dispositions in the region or because of the political implications discussed above—Whiting's hypothesis suggests that they might conclude that it is necessary to take dramatic action to signal concern and prevent a further deterioration of the situation. This hypothesis, most relevant to the "status quo minus" and "transformation" scenarios described in the previous section, highlights an important possibility for an unintended and potentially dangerous outcome. It indicates that China's leaders, even if their goal is only to bolster the status quo in Korea, may under certain conditions decide to adopt a belligerent posture. If so, would others, especially the United States, correctly discern China's purposes?

The international relations literature about the "security dilemma" and the "spiral model of conflict" explains why attempts to deter can sometimes instead intensify conflict.[49] Even if Beijing's rhetoric and possible actions (e.g., reviving closer military ties with the DPRK, undertaking a military buildup in China's northeast) were actually intended to maintain the status quo in Korea, Americans might wonder if they were evidence of a long-range Chinese strategy aimed at forcing the United States out of a natural "sphere of Chinese influence." Contemporary concerns among many in the U.S. government about a rising China's international aspirations, and among many in the CCP regime about an American interest in precluding the emergence of any great powers to rival U.S. hegemony (the complementary worries that "power-transition theorists" identify in such dyads throughout history), prime both sides for an acute form of the security dilemma generating spirals of conflict. Under such circumstances, belligerent signals from China, even if only intended as deterrents, are likely to be viewed with alarm in the United States. It is possible that American concerns might be mitigated if China's signals were sent during a period when bilateral relations were relatively good. But unavoidable uncertainty about China's intentions and, more important, the recognition that its intentions could change in the future, especially as China's capabilities increase, would provide the United States with incentives to hedge its bets in ways likely to amplify mutual suspicion. Under the sort of circumstances that would prompt Beijing to send such a strong deterrent signal, even a clear understanding that it might trigger increased tensions with the United States would probably not discourage China's leaders from taking steps they viewed necessary to preserve the status quo in Korea.

The likelihood that trends in Korea might so alarm Beijing that it would choose to send sharp deterrent signals is indeterminate, as are the consequences that would follow. But in one respect, the policy implication of Whiting's observation about China's use of belligerent signals for deterrence is clear: if China responds to changes in Korea by adopting a harder line, analysts would be wise to carefully parse the words and actions that Beijing employs. It would be especially important to focus not simply on their belligerent form but also to consider the substance of the message they were designed to convey about matters such as the future disposition of military forces on the peninsula, foreign ties to the rival Korean states, or the nature of a post-unification regime. Whiting's analysis of the West's experience in interpreting signals in 1950 serves as a cautionary tale. Beijing's belligerence was at least partly misconstrued, both before the "People's Volunteers" intervened (when warnings were readily discounted as the fiery rhetoric to be expected from an ideologically motivated revolutionary regime) and after (when China's actions were simplistically interpreted by many in the West as part of a communist strategy of aggression rather than at least partly a Chinese strategy of preventive defense).[50]

TIMING IS ESSENTIAL

To deter successfully, warn early enough to be effective, ideally early enough to prevent the threat from arising, rather than attempting to eliminate the threat after it has emerged. "Bureaucratic and political pressures" make it more difficult to persuade others to abandon objectionable positions to which they have become publicly committed (because this may mean a substantive concession and also a loss of face) than it is to influence their deliberations beforehand.

Whiting's position here echoes the arguments Thomas Schelling set forth in proposing a useful distinction between deterrence (a strategy employing threats to preserve the status quo) and "compellence" (a strategy employing threats to alter the status quo or restore the status quo ante). Schelling, like Whiting, provides convincing reasons why the latter is often so much more difficult to practice.[51] According to this logic, CCP leaders have incentives to adopt a proactive stance on Korea's future, especially if the status quo appears unstable, and to lay down markers about their "bottom line." Such clarification needs to be undertaken early enough to discourage others from promoting political or military arrangements in Korea that Beijing deems unacceptable (a prominent concern under the second and third scenarios above) by indicating the risk that they will trigger a hostile Chinese response. The more China's leaders become worried about the political fate of the DPRK, the more likely it is that they will assert the limits of their tolerance with respect to both the process (e.g., no outside interference) and outcome (e.g., limits on the size and location of U.S. forces stationed on the peninsula) of reunification.

China's statements about the Korean peninsula since the early 1990s have consistently emphasized the importance of "independent and peaceful reunification" (*zizhu heping tongyi*) and the principle that no state should establish military bases in a foreign country.[52] These statements should probably be understood as signals intended to discourage the ROK and the United States from entertaining the belief that Beijing would tolerate the unification of Korea under American auspices, especially if it means a major U.S. military presence that could be moved farther north. This concern has deep roots. In the post–Cold War era, Beijing's dissatisfaction with the implications of enduring unipolarity makes it more likely to worry that the United States will attempt to exploit its present dominant international position to lock in, if not expand, its military presence on the peninsula.[53] While this is partly a manifestation of Beijing's broader concerns about the constraining consequences of continued U.S. preponderance in the Western Pacific, it also reflects specific concerns about the future purposes of the U.S.-ROK alliance in the event the North Korean threat no longer provides a basis for its continuation. As noted above, under such circumstances, an enduring U.S.-ROK alliance would most plausibly appear to be a hedge against China, part of a containment strategy linking Korea with other American bilateral security agreements in East Asia in a chain of encirclement. In fact, such concerns are already apparent in some Chinese analyses that see the U.S. invocation of "the North Korea threat," like references to "the China threat," as a flimsy pretext devised to justify a continuing strong U.S. military presence in East Asia.[54]

Understanding China's interests may reduce the chances that the signals it sends about them will be misunderstood, but the risk cannot be eliminated. Problems may arise not only from the difficulty in receiving and interpreting the message, but also from the challenges China faces in formulating the way to signal its concerns. As Whiting's work details, in late summer 1950, even relatively explicit attempts to warn Washington that Beijing saw a serious threat to China's vital interests that it was determined to protect were ineffective. In the quite different circumstances of the early twenty-first century, China is much less likely to rely on such blunt threats to try to influence events on the peninsula. China's leaders may recognize the advantages of adopting a proactive approach sending deterrent signals to discourage unacceptable outcomes in Korea rather than waiting to respond to changes after they have taken shape. But they may also believe that the costs of such an approach in present circumstances outweigh this narrowly defined deterrent benefit. Chinese threats aimed at shaping events on the Korean peninsula would risk alarming and alienating at least three trade partners (the ROK, Japan, and the United States) that are crucial to the CCP's modernization program. In addition, such threats would be likely to prompt concerted military cooperation among these and other regional actors who have thus far been reluctant to accept the argument that it is more important to contain than to engage China.

If relying on signals to convey deterrent threats is problematic for Beijing, failing to signal China's concerns about events in Korea would also carry risks, though different ones. Reticence might benefit China by enhancing its reputation as a responsible regional actor with which others can safely trade, and which they need not cooperate to contain. If the status quo endures, or a new status quo emerges that does not pose problems for Beijing, then the benefits of Chinese restraint might be substantial. If China's leaders believe there is a significant risk that events in Korea could be moving in unacceptable directions, however, then silence may have the costly effect of encouraging others to assume Beijing's indifference and to overestimate its willingness to tolerate changes it in fact would not accept, changes that would actually prompt China to respond in ways that would then be both surprising and alarming.[55]

Conclusions

Miscalculation and misinterpretation are far from trivial concerns in international politics. In 1950, miscalculating the credibility (for the United States) or clarity (for Beijing) of deterrent signals about Korea resulted in a costly war and resulted in a protracted period of intense Sino-American hostility. The danger in the twenty-first century is that miscalculation over Korea could contribute to igniting a new Cold War based on the perception of sharply clashing interests between a dominant United States and a rising China. Although both share a short-term interest in peace and stability in Korea, their preferences about the peninsula in the longer term differ. The U.S. vision is one that seeks a resolution of tensions in Korea consistent with preserving regional security arrangements that Washington designed and has cemented in place over the past half century. China's vision is one that seeks a resolution consistent with Beijing playing an increasingly influential role in molding a post–Cold War security architecture that is less U.S.-centric.[56]

As such, differences about the future of the Korean peninsula look like one of a number of Sino-American issues that may reflect what international relations scholars generally describe as the problems associated with rising great powers.[57] Much of this literature examining the relations between an emerging challenger and a dominant power has suggested that the process is likely to trigger major wars. War allegedly results either when a nervous hegemon, attempting to prevent its displacement, attacks the ambitious challenger or when the challenger, determined to improve its position, attacks a dominant state that refuses to redraw the international order so that it better reflects the changing distribution of power. On both empirical and theoretical grounds, however, this worrisome power-transition argument is problematic and the implications for China's posture toward the Korean peninsula are unclear.

Although catastrophic war has sometimes been the outcome of the dynamics the power transition literature identifies, not all such great power shifts throughout history fit the disaster scenario. Neither the Anglo-American experience in the first half of the twentieth century nor the Soviet-American experience in the second half fits the mold. Thus, history alone does not conclusively demonstrate a law-like pattern indicating that the United States and China are inevitably on a collision course, with disagreements about problems like Korea intensifying the rivalry. Moreover, in addition to doubts raised by the mixed empirical evidence, there are doubts about the logic at the core of power-transition theory—that peace prevails during periods of hegemonic stability, and wars occur as a dissatisfied, rising challenger catches up with and seeks to supplant the dominant state. Robert Powell's careful formalization of the bargaining dynamics informally portrayed in most descriptions of power transition demonstrates that the outcome of the process is logically indeterminate.[58]

Whether the challenger or the hegemon chooses to resort to war as an alternative to a peaceful adjustment of the international order (either prior to or at the moment of an actual transition) depends on the willingness and ability of the dominant state to make concessions that the rising state will find satisfactory in light of the changing distribution of power. The abstract bargaining relationship is clear and can be modeled with precision. But applying the model to particular cases is difficult because it requires knowledge about each state's preferences and estimates of relative power, interests, and resolve, as well as the efficiency with which each updates such information as their relationship unfolds over time. Sometimes fears about the consequences of allowing a potential rival to grow more powerful prompt a state to opt for war while it retains an advantage (as may have been the case with Germany in 1914, when it worried about being overtaken by Russia). Or dissatisfaction with the concessions the dominant state is prepared to make can lead a rising power to strike first, hoping it can improve its bargaining position (perhaps Japan in 1941). But at other times, diplomacy may suffice (as in the Anglo-American and Soviet-American cases mentioned above). The point that Powell's elegant and inevitably simplified model underscores is that there is no logical basis for a claim that war must result from these sorts of interactions, even at the decisive crossover moments on which the power transition literature focuses.

The practical importance of Powell's work is just as significant as the theoretical. From the perspective of his more heavily qualified understanding of the consequences of shifts in the distribution of power, signals from

Beijing about its interests and intentions with respect to Korea's future are part of the information that the United States will use to "screen" China as a rising power and to assess its willingness to accommodate Beijing's demands for greater influence. The good news about the prospects for accommodation between China and the United States on the future of Korea is that neither side is already committed to a position that significantly narrows the range of acceptable compromises (as may be the case with disagreements about Taiwan). Thus, the process of bargaining about the future of Korea as China's power rises need not contribute to growing Sino-American tensions. Interaction in addressing problems engaging both countries' interests may even provide opportunities for each to demonstrate the extent of its flexibility and to assess the other's ability and willingness to compromise. The bad news is that flexibility also means uncertainty and perhaps dangerous inattentiveness if positions evolve while each party is focused on more pressing matters—for the United States, the war on terrorism; for China, managing tensions in the Taiwan Strait. A process of tacit bargaining during which each side relies on signals that may be overlooked or misinterpreted could then result in a drift toward incompatible positions from which it may later be tough to climb down. If so, Korea would become a problem that contributes to intensifying tensions resulting from China's rise, rather than an issue on which the United States and China demonstrate the possibility of peaceful adjustment. In this respect, the Korean nuclear crisis in the early twenty-first century may turn out to be a blessing in disguise if it encourages Beijing and Washington to pay closer attention to each other's interests in Northeast Asia and to think carefully about the risks that each is prepared to run in support of them. Events on the peninsula and the reactions they evoke from China and the United States seem certain to play an important role in defining the security architecture of East Asia for the twenty-first century.

Notes

1. I thank Chen Cheng, Tang Wei, and Wang Yanbo for their research assistance in the writing of this chapter.

2. Allen S. Whiting, *China Crosses the Yalu: The Decision to Enter the Korean War* (1960; Stanford: Stanford University Press, 1968); id., *The Chinese Calculus of Deterrence: India and Indochina* (Ann Arbor: University of Michigan Press, 1975); id., *The Chinese Calculus of Deterrence: India and Indochina*, Michigan Papers in Chinese Studies, No. 4 (Ann Arbor: Center for Chinese Studies Publications, 1981, 2001).

3. On similarities and differences across the cases from the Maoist era that informed Whiting's generalizations, see Whiting, *Chinese Calculus of Deterrence*,

196–99. Drawing lessons from the past is a difficult and imprecise business, for policymakers as well as for scholars. See Ernest R. May, *"Lessons" of the Past: The Use and Misuse of History in American Foreign Policy* (New York: Oxford University Press, 1973); Robert Jervis, *Perception and Misperception in International Politics* (Princeton, N.J.: Princeton University Press, 1976), esp. ch. 6; Yuen Foong Khong, *Analogies at War: Korea, Munich, Dien Bien Phu, and the Vietnam Decisions of 1965* (Princeton, N.J.: Princeton University Press, 1992). This chapter, however, does *not* use "lessons of the past" or "analogical explanations" as a framework for interpreting China's contemporary Korea policy; it focuses instead on China's interests and the situational constraints (both international and domestic) its leaders confront. Although events in Korea might trigger the invocation of historical lessons that would subsequently shape Beijing's response, the experience that would be deemed relevant is uncertain. Beijing could, for example, react to an intense crisis on the Korean peninsula that included the prospect of American military involvement by drawing on "lessons of 1950." Alternatively, it might view a new Korean crisis as another instance of a distinctive pattern of U.S. interventionism in the post–Cold War unipolar world that Chinese analysts have emphasized since the mid 1990s. In short, it may be the lessons of the *recent* past, rather than the distant history of the early Cold War, that would dominate the minds of the makers of foreign policy in Beijing.

4. A now vast literature reconsidering who among Pyongyang, Moscow, and Beijing favored what and when has emerged as more documents have been declassified. The new evidence does not resolve all controversies about responsibility but does reveal differences between Mao and the other top CCP leaders about the risks China should be willing to run in support of a North Korean attack and then in its response to the UN counterattack. See Shen Zhihua, "The Discrepancy Between the Russian and Chinese Versions of Mao's 2 October 1950 Message to Stalin on Chinese Entry in the Korean War: A Chinese Scholar's Reply," trans. Chen Jian, *Cold War International History Project Bulletin*, no. 8–9 (Winter 1996–97): 237–43; Alexandre Y. Mansourov, "Stalin, Mao, Kim, and China's Decision to Enter the Korean War, September 16–October 15, 1950: New Evidence from the Russian Archives," *Cold War International History Project Bulletin*, no. 6–7 (Winter 1995–96): 94–119; Thomas J. Christensen, "Threats, Assurances, and the Last Chance for Peace: The Lessons of Mao's Korean War Telegrams," *International Security* 17 (Summer 1992): 122–54; Chen Jian, *China's Road to the Korean War* (New York: Columbia University Press, 1994); Zhang Shuguang, *Deterrence and Strategic Culture: Chinese-American Confrontations, 1949–1958* (Ithaca, N.Y.: Cornell University Press, 1992); Zhang Shuguang, *Mao's Military Romanticism: China and the Korean War, 1950–1953* (Lawrence: University Press of Kansas, 1995); Dieter Heinzig, "Stalin, Mao, Kim and Korean War Origins, 1950: A Russian Document Discrepancy," *Cold War International History Project Bulletin*, no. 8–9 (Winter 1996–97): 240.

5. See Zhang, *Mao's Military Romanticism*, 5, 56, 81; Chen, *China's Road to the Korean War*, 93, 94–96; Hao Yufan and Zhai Zhihai, "China's Decision to Enter the Korean War: History Revisited," *China Quarterly*, no. 121 (March 1990): 94–115. On the various signals the Chinese sent during the late summer and early fall

of 1950, as well as the failure of the United States either to grasp their significance or, if it was recognized, to believe in the credibility of the actions Beijing was threatening to take, see Whiting, *China Crosses the Yalu*, esp. ch. 6.

6. The PRC's main contribution to Soviet security reflected geography. As a friendly state on the Soviet Union's Asian borders, China reduced the length of the front along which the United States could pose a direct threat to the USSR from the east. This Chinese contribution to Soviet security was diminished, however, by (1) East Asia's secondary importance for Moscow compared with Europe, (2) the need for the USSR to assist China's program of military modernization, and (3) the anticipation that the real American threat to Soviet security was not likely to be a conventional ground assault but air and missile power.

7. On the ways junior partners in alliances seek to forestall the dangers of abandonment, see Avery Goldstein, "Discounting the Free Ride: Alliances and Security in the Postwar World," *International Organization* 49, 1 (Winter 1995): 39–72; id., *Deterrence and Security in the 21st Century: China, Britain, France and the Enduring Legacy of the Nuclear Revolution* (Stanford: Stanford University Press, 2000), 24–26, 69–77. On China's doubts about Soviet commitment, see Sergei N. Goncharov, John W. Lewis, and Xue Litai, *Uncertain Partners: Stalin, Mao, and the Korean War* (Stanford: Stanford University Press, 1993), 118; see also Zhang, *Deterrence and Strategic Culture*, 31.

8. See Goldstein, *Deterrence and Security in the 21st Century*, 37–41, 90–103.

9. China's tortured attempts to offer a Marxist ideological explanation for Soviet "hegemonism" depended on identifying its roots in the revisionist character of the regime, something that Beijing could no longer comfortably emphasize after 1976 as it rapidly abandoned its own revolutionary Maoist policies.

10. See comments from Jiang Zemin and Li Peng in "Kim Jong-Il Visits China, Meets Jiang," Xinhua, 1 June 2000; "Jiu Zhong-Han guanxi, Zhongguo dui Chaoxian bandao zhengce wenti, Li Peng jieshou Hanguo jizhe caifang" [On China-ROK relations, Li Peng takes questions from visiting ROK reporters about China's policy toward the Korean peninsula and other matters], *Renmin Ribao*, 26 February 1995; "PRC Delegation Offers Suggestions on Korean Peace Accord," Xinhua, 22 January 1999; Su Guiyou and Liu Yusheng, "PRC Report on Koreas, Middle East," *Zhongguo Xinwen She*, 26 January 1998.

11. During his meeting with DPRK leader Kim Jong Il, Jiang Zemin referred to ties between the countries simply as "good neighborly and friendly relations" and expressed his hope that they could advance "bilateral friendly relations" [*Zhong Chao you hao guanxi*] ("Kim Jong-Il Visits China, Meets Jiang"). Even more striking was Li Peng's comment that "China develops relations with the Democratic People's Republic of Korea *and the ROK* on the basis of the five principles of peaceful coexistence" (Qi Deliang, and Tang Shuifu, "Li, Yi Yong-Tok Discuss Economic Ties," Xinhua, 1 November 1994; emphasis added).

12. See Mao Xuncheng, "Chaoxian bandao jushi de fanfu ji qi yuanyin" [The causes of the recurrent situation on the Korean peninsula], *Shanghai Shifan Daxue Xuebao* (March 1996); Tao Wenzhao, "China's Position Towards the Korean Peninsula" (paper presented at the ASEM 2000 People's Forum, Seoul, Korea, 17–20

October 2000); Weixing Hu, "Beijing's Defense Strategy and the Korean Peninsula," *Journal of Northeast Asian Studies* 14 (1995): 50–67; Banning Garrett and Bonnie S. Glaser, "Looking Across the Yalu: Chinese Assessments of North Korea," *Asian Survey* 35 (June 1995): 528–45.

13. Experts continue to disagree about the results of China's military modernization. Most, however, agree that the effort is now focused on Taiwan contingencies, and that despite significant purchases of advanced military equipment from Russia, the gap between Chinese and American military capabilities remains large. See Avery Goldstein, "Great Expectations: Interpreting China's Arrival," *International Security* 22, 3 (Winter 1997–98): 36–73; Thomas J. Christensen, "Posing Problems Without Catching Up: China's Rise and Challenges for U.S. Security Policy," *International Security* 25, 4 (Spring 2001): 5–40; Council on Foreign Relations, *Chinese Military Power*, Report of an Independent Task Force Sponsored by the Council on Foreign Relations Maurice R. Greenberg Center for Geoeconomic Studies (Washington, D.C.: Council on Foreign Relations, 2003), www.cfr.org/pdf/China_TF.pdf (accessed 1 October 2005); U.S. Department of Defense, *Annual Report on the Military Power of the People's Republic of China* (Washington, D.C.: U.S. Department of Defense, 2004), www.defenselink.mil/pubs/d20040528PRC.pdf (accessed September 27, 2005).

14. See Avery Goldstein, *Rising to the Challenge: China's Grand Strategy and International Security* (Stanford: Stanford University Press, 2005).

15. See Robert S. Ross, "The 1995–96 Taiwan Strait Confrontation," *International Security* 25, 2 (Fall 2000): 87–123; Christensen, "Posing Problems Without Catching Up"; Richard K. Betts and Thomas J. Christensen, "China: Getting the Questions Right," *National Interest*, 22 December 2000, 17–29.

16. Korea is arguably not even China's second priority. That is more likely to be territorial disputes in the South China Sea. For an assessment that lists Taiwan, the South China Sea, and the Diaoyu Islands disputes with Japan as the top three priorities, see Craig S. Smith, "China Reshaping Military to Toughen Its Muscle in the Region," *New York Times*, 16 October 2002.

17. See Wang Linchang, "Tang Jiaxuan waizhang baihui Hanguo zongtong Jin Dazhong" [Foreign Minister Tang Jiaxuan calls on ROK President Kim Dae Jung], *Renminwang*, 3 August 2002; Wang Linchang, Xu Baokang, and Zhao Jiaming, "Yearender—Korean Peninsula: Peace Process in Motion and Tense Situation Eased," *Renmin Ribao*, 24 December 1997, Foreign Broadcast Information Service FBIS-CHI-98–012 (hereafter cited as FBIS), Article Id: drchio1121998002156; "Jiu Zhong-Han guanxi" (cited n. 10 above).

18. See Goldstein, *Rising to the Challenge*; Erica Strecker Downs and Phillip C. Saunders, "Legitimacy and the Limits of Nationalism: China and the Diaoyu Islands," *International Security* 23, 3 (Winter 1998): 114–46; Ye Zicheng and Feng Yin, "Dangqian ZhongMei guanxi de ba da tedian" (Eight Key Characteristics of Current Sino-U.S. Relations), *Nanfang Ribao*, 22 February 2002, at www.nanfangdaily.com.cn/zt/zt/009/bush/200202220021.asp (accessed 19 February 2006). For discussion of the importance of international trade and investment for China's continued growth, see Nicholas R. Lardy, *China in the World Economy* (Washington,

D.C.: Institute for International Economics, 1994); id., *Integrating China into the Global Economy* (Washington, D.C.: Brooking Institution Press, 2002).

19. The comments from PLA Chief of the General Staff, Fu Quanyou, in October 2002, reflect the strong opinions still held by some of China's elite: "The traditional China-DPRK friendship personally forged and fostered by Chairman Mao Zedong, Premier Zhou Enlai, Comrade Deng Xiaoping, and President Kim Il Sung is a precious legacy bequeathed by the leaders of the older generation of the two countries. Over the past many years, despite changes in the international situation, China-DPRK friendship cemented with blood has remained unchanged, and has withstood the test of history" (Dong Lixi, "Fu Quanyou Meets with the DPRK People's Army Goodwill Mission," Xinhua, 11 October 2002).

20. On the North Korea threat as a proxy for China, see Wu Xinbo, "U.S. Security Policy in Asia: Implications for China-U.S. Relations," *Contemporary Southeast Asia* 22 (2000): 479–97; Yi Jun, Hua Shan, and Xu Shujun, "Behind the U.S.–South Korea 'RSOI 2001' Exercise," *Jiefangjun Bao*, 30 April 2001, 12, FBIS-CHI-2001–0430, WNC Document No. 0GCNRWY01F5CM5; Zhang Xin and Han Xudong, "Reasons Behind Constant Clashes in Northeast Asia as Viewed from ROK-DPRK Sea Battle," *Liaowang* 28 (2002): 60–61, FBIS-CHI-2002–0718, WNC Document No. 0GZNJ2T00J3S5Q.

21. By the end of the 1990s, China and the ROK had established a "Sino-Korean cooperative partnership oriented toward the twenty-first century." See "Zhu Rongji zongli tong Hanguo zongtong Jin Dazhong juxing huitan" [Premier Zhu Rongji and ROK President Kim Dae Jung hold talks], Xinhua, 18 October 2000; Liu Zhengxue and Wang Linchang, "Zhu Rongji tong Jin Dazhong huitan, shuangfang jiu shuangbian guanxi he diqu wenti jiaohuanle yijian" [Zhu Rongji and Kim Dae Jung hold talks, the two sides exchange opinions on bilateral relations and regional issues], *Renmin Ribao*, 19 October 2000; Hu, "Beijing's Defense Strategy and the Korean Peninsula"; Kay Moeller, "China and Korea: The Godfather Part Three," *Journal of Northeast Asian Studies* 15 (1996): 35–48.

22. See Tao, "China's Position"; Ding Shichuan, and Li Qiang, "Chaoxian bandao heping jizhi ji qi qianjing" [A peace mechanism for the Korean peninsula and its prospects], *Xiandai Guoji Guanxi*, no. 4 (1999): 42–44; Zhang Guocheng, "Quadripartite Talks Enter Substantive Stage," *Renmin Ribao*, 29 January 1999, 6, FBIS-CHI-99-030, WNC Document Number: 0F6JMO503HYFPI; "PRC Outlines 5 Principles to Reduce Tension in Koreas," Xinhua, 22 January 1999. On China's initial reservations about the four-party talks, see "PRC Spokesman: Beijing Hopes for Negotiations on Korea," Agence France-Presse, April 18, 1996, FBIS-CHI-96–076, WNC Document No. 0DQ4PPO047NXHJ; Moeller, "China and Korea," 38.

23. On the evolution of Sino-American relations in this period, see Goldstein, *Rising to the Challenge*, 143–59.

24. For an optimistic assessment of the military balance that had developed by the 1990s on the peninsula, see Michael O'Hanlon, "Stopping a North Korean Invasion: Why Defending South Korea Is Easier Than the Pentagon Thinks," *International Security* 22, 4 (Spring 1998): 135–70.

25. Nevertheless, some Chinese analysts already criticize the "anti-China" pur-

poses of such U.S. military deployments across Asia. See Gao Tian, "U.S. Nuclear Submarines on Guam Target China," *Renminwang*, 19 March 2002; Wu, "U.S. Security Policy in Asia"; Yi, Hua, and Xu, "Behind the U.S.–South Korea 'RSOI 2001' Exercise"; Zhu Feng, "RiChao shounao huitan: Xiaoquan chengle zuida 'ying jia'?" [The Japan-DPRK summit: will Koizumi be the biggest 'winner'?], *Zhongguo Ribao*, 19 September 2002.

26. Despite diplomatic efforts, between 2002 and 2005 North Korea assertively moved toward deploying nuclear weapons. Pyongyang evicted international inspectors, resumed reprocessing plutonium, withdrew from the Nuclear Nonproliferation Treaty, harassed a U.S. spyplane in international airspace, tested short-range missiles (some that might be capable of carrying nuclear warheads), made vague claims about already having a nuclear deterrent, and then bluntly claimed to possess a working nuclear weapon.

27. Victor D. Cha, "Hawk Engagement and Preventive Defense on the Korean Peninsula," *International Security* 27, 1 (2002): 40–78.

28. See Garrett and Glaser, "Looking Across the Yalu," 534. Most Chinese analysts, officers, and officials whom the author interviewed during March 2003 in Beijing indicated that China would oppose U.S. military action against the North but that its support for Pyongyang would be mainly diplomatic. Chinese assistance to the DPRK, if it were forthcoming, would almost certainly not include the PRC's direct military participation.

29. The contrast between China's role on the Iraq and Korea problems in 2003 clearly reflected such geopolitical considerations. Beijing played a minimal role during the debate preceding the U.S.-led military operation against Iraq but was at the same time working hard to encourage the North Koreans and the Americans to find a face-saving way to deescalate tensions and search for a diplomatic solution to the confrontation over the DPRK's nuclear program. China's efforts facilitated a resumption of dialogue brokered by Beijing in April 2003.

30. A string of perceived American humiliations of China since the early 1990s have elicited a sometimes strident nationalist reaction in the media and on the streets. These events included the alleged U.S. role in denying China the 2000 Olympics, the American interdiction and boarding of a Chinese ship (the *Yinhe*) mistakenly thought to be carrying illicit cargo, the U.S. reversal of policy that granted Taiwan's President Lee a visa to visit the United States in May 1995, the bombing of the Chinese embassy in Belgrade in May 1999, and the collision between a U.S. EP-3 surveillance plane and a Chinese fighter jet that resulted in the death of the Chinese pilot. So far, however, nationalist outrage has not split the CCP leadership, which agrees on the broad fundamentals about vital foreign policy issues like Taiwan. See Paul Heer, "A House United," *Foreign Affairs* 79 (2000). See also Allen S. Whiting, "Chinese Nationalism and Foreign Policy after Deng," *China Quarterly* 142 (1995).

31. Until the summer of 2002, this seemed to be a plausible interpretation of the path the North was following. In addition to cultivating better relations with the EU, Kim Jong Il's visit to Shanghai had inspired him to initiate economic reforms in the DPRK, including price reforms and the creation of a Chinese-style special economic zone to facilitate international trade and investment.

32. Thus, China's Korea policy seeks to foster this outcome by prodding the DPRK to reform, pressing the DPRK's adversaries to continue dialogue with Pyongyang, and encouraging the ROK, Japan, the Europeans, and the Americans to engage, rather than isolate, the DPRK and integrate it into the international system. See also Robert J. Saiget, "North Korean Premier in Beijing amid Renewed Nuclear Threats," Agence France-Presse, 22 March 2005, FBIS, NewsEdge Document No. 200503221477.1_2389008b6e6f5d5e; "North Korea This Week, No. 338 (March 31)," Yonhap, 31 March 2005, FBIS, NewsEdge Document No. 200503311477.1_42d30d5f153fc36d.

33. In March 2005, ROK President Roh fueled the simmering debate about the future of the U.S.-ROK alliance when he suggested that Korea might move beyond its historical role as the cockpit of great power conflict and close Cold War alignment with the United States and might instead become an active "balancer" facilitating the resolution of disputes among potential adversaries such as China, Japan, and the United States. See "Roh Stresses S. Korea's Balancing Role in Regional Security," Yonhap, 22 March 2005; An So'ng-kyu, "ROK NSC Official Expounds on 'Balancer Role' in Northeast Asia Interview with Yi Cho'ng-so'k, deputy chief of the National Security Council," JoongAng Ilbo, 15 April 2005.

34. This assumes that the ROK would not attack the DPRK unless blatantly provoked, and that the North recognizes the suicidal consequences of attacking the South.

35. Such a scenario might reflect the expectations of those in the United States who prefer a policy that will trigger "regime change" rather than negotiated nuclear disarmament in the DPRK.

36. The Korean presidential election of 2003, in which the winning candidate was most closely identified with continuing Kim Dae Jung's sunshine policy toward the DPRK, coincided with an upsurge in protests against the U.S. military presence in Seoul and raised questions about the future of the alliance. By late March 2003, however, Pyongyang's nuclear brinkmanship apparently motivated the newly elected South Korean president, Roh Moo Hyun, to reiterate his government's determination to maintain a close security alliance with the United States, including a substantial American troop deployment on Korean soil. See Howard W. French, "Bush and New Korean Leader to Take Up Thorny Issues," New York Times, 21 December 2002; Howard W. French, "Threats and Responses: Asian Arena; Shifting Loyalties: Seoul Looks to New Alliances," ibid., 26 January 2003; Doug Struck, "S. Korean Stresses Alliance, Dismisses Differences with U.S.," Washington Post, 10 April 2003. Yet differences between the United States and the ROK about how best to deal with North Korea, along with the notion of Korea as a regional balancer noted above, reflect continuing uncertainty about the durability of the ROK-U.S. alliance in its current form.

37. In fact, by 2004, the United States was not only redeploying forces southward, away from the DMZ, but also slightly reducing their number as troops were shifted to Iraq.

38. One can imagine a different, but less likely, reaction. Some of China's more cosmopolitan fourth- and fifth-generation CCP leaders might argue that the fate of

the DPRK simply underscores the need to overcome the contradictions between the rapid pace of economic reform and the snail's pace of political reform.

39. As an official U.S. report on its strategy for East Asia stated: "The United States welcomes the public statements of ROK President Kim Dae-Jung affirming the value of the bilateral alliance and the U.S. military presence even after reunification of the Korean Peninsula. The U.S. strongly agrees that our alliance and military presence will continue to support stability both on the Korean Peninsula and throughout the region after North Korea is no longer a threat. . . . Beyond the Peninsula, instability and uncertainty are likely to persist in the Asia-Pacific region, with heavy concentrations of military force, including nuclear arsenals, unresolved territorial disputes and historical tensions, and the proliferation of weapons of mass destruction and their means of delivery serving as sources of instability." From *The United States Security Strategy for the East Asia-Pacific Region* (Washington, D.C.: Office of International Security Affairs, 1998), 62–63.

40. For discussion that hints at this contingency but carefully avoids naming China as a prospective adversary, see U.S. Department of Defense, "Quadrennial Defense Review Report" (Washington, D.C.: U.S. Department of Defense, 2001), www.defenselink.mil/pubs/qdr2001.pdf (accessed 27 September 2005).

41. On the reasons why such adversaries may be useful, see Thomas J. Christensen, *Useful Adversaries: Grand Strategy, Domestic Mobilization, and Sino-American Conflict, 1947–1958* (Princeton, N.J.: Princeton University Press, 1996).

42. For the full set of principles of deterrence that Whiting distilled from China's experiences with confrontations in Korea, India, and Indochina, see his *Chinese Calculus of Deterrence*, 202–3.

43. John W. Garver, "The Chinese Communist Party and the Collapse of Soviet Communism," *China Quarterly*, no. 133 (1993): 1–26.

44. Growing access to Internet-based information is compounding this concern and Beijing's response has been an imperfectly effective attempt to restrict access. See Shanthi Kalathil, "Dot Com for Dictators," *Foreign Policy*, no. 135 (March–April 2003): 43–49. Despite the controls, it is unclear that the regime believes it can any longer prevent China's citizens from learning about major events outside China, even when they may carry potentially subversive connotations about popular opposition to authoritarian rule. China's leading official outlet for news, *Renminwang*, for example, provided ample coverage of the Iraqi people's celebrations of Saddam Hussein's downfall in 2003, as well as the anti-regime mass protests that forced a change of government in neighboring Kyrgyzstan in 2005.

45. The fear of falling communist dominoes would be a distant echo of Mao's concern in the early 1950s that the defeat of North Korea might encourage counterrevolutionaries in Asia. See Christensen, *Useful Adversaries*, 156.

46. See Elisabeth Rosenthal, "More Koreans Give China the Slip, Invading Embassy School," *New York Times*, 4 September 2002; Elisabeth Rosenthal, "U.N. Group Backs North Korean Asylum Seekers in China," ibid., 15 March 2002.

47. China restated its position in 1998 when the PRC signed the International Convention on Civil and Political Rights, saying: "The Chinese Government believes that the principle of the universality of human rights must be respected, but

the specific conditions of each country must also be taken into consideration in observing this principle" (People's Republic of China, Ministry of Foreign Affairs, "The Signing of the International Convention on Civil and Political Rights by the Chinese Government" (17 November 2000), www.fmprc.gov.cn/eng/ziliao/3602/3604/t18041.htm (accessed 1 October 2005).

48. See e.g., Elisabeth Rosenthal, "7 North Koreans Allowed to Leave China," *New York Times*, 29 June 2001, and "North Korean Asylum Seekers Leave China," ibid., 24 June 2002.

49. On deterrence and spirals, see Jervis, *Perception and Misperception in International Politics*. For a discussion that explores reasons why actors often fail to consider alternative explanations for the signals an adversary sends, or for his observed behavior, see Robert Jervis, "Hypotheses on Misperception," *World Politics* 20 (1968): 454–79.

50. See Whiting, *China Crosses the Yalu*, esp. chs. 8 and 9.

51. On the differences between deterrence and compellence, see Thomas C. Schelling, *Arms and Influence* (New Haven, Conn.: Yale University Press, 1966); Goldstein, *Deterrence and Security in the 21st Century*.

52. See Chen Hegao, Li Siyang, and Gao Haorong, "Li Peng weiyuanzhang huijian Jin Dazhong zongtong" [NPC Standing Committee Chairman Li Peng meets with President Kim Dae Jung], Xinhua, 25 May, 2001. Opposition to U.S. forces in Korea was reiterated by China's ambassador to the ROK, Li Bin, in remarks on the tenth anniversary of establishing diplomatic relations between China and the ROK (Kim Ji-ho, "China's Envoy to ROK: US Troops in Korea Must Not Pose Threat to Neighbors," *Korea Herald*, 21 August 2002).

53. Repeated displays of U.S. military superiority in the post–Cold War era have led Chinese analysts to argue that the transition period from unipolarity to multipolarity will be protracted. See Lu Youzhi, "Chongxin shenshi Zhongguo de anquan huanjing" [A fresh examination of China's security environment], *Shijie Jingji yu Zhengzhi* [World Economics and Politics], no. 1 (2000): 56–61; Ye Zicheng, "Zhongguo shixing daguo waijiao zhanlüe shizai bixing" [The imperative for China to implement a great power diplomatic strategy], ibid.: 6–7; Chu Shulong and Wang Zaibang, "Guanyu guoji xingshi he wo duiwai zhanlüe ruogan zhongda wenti de sikao" [Reflections on some important questions about the international situation and our external strategy], *Xiandai Guoji Guanxi*, no. 8 (1999): 17; Xiao Feng, "Dui guoji xingshizhong jige redian wenti de kanfa" [Perspective on several hot issues in the international situation], *Xiandai Guoji Guanxi*, no. 12 (1999): 3; For a summary of changing Chinese views about polarity, see Michael Pillsbury, *China Debates the Future Security Environment* (Washington, D.C.: National Defense University Press, 2000), 13, 15, 25, 28, 58. For Western views of the nature and likely durability of the present unipolar era, see William C. Wohlforth, "The Stability of a Unipolar World," *International Security* 24 (Summer 1999): 5–41, and id. and Stephen G. Brooks, "American Primacy in Perspective," *Foreign Affairs* 81 (July–August 2002): 20–26.

54. See Wu, "U.S. Security Policy in Asia"; Yi, Hua, and Xu, "Behind the U.S.– South Korea 'RSOI 2001' Exercise."

55. China's policy during the standoff over North Korea's nuclear weapons program after 2002 may have reflected an attempt to steer a middle course, simultaneously sending deterrent signals that China's interests could not be ignored, while also offering to play a responsible role in working toward a diplomatic resolution.

56. Yan Xuetong, "Dui Zhongguo anquan huanjing de fenxi yu sikao" [Analysis of and reflections on China's security environment], *Shijie Jingji yu Zhengzhi* [World Economics and Politics], no. 2 (2000): 10; Fang Hua, "Yatai anquan jiagou de xianzhuang, qushi ji Zhongguo de zuoyong" [The current Asia-Pacific security framework, trends, and China's role], ibid.: 11, 14; Chu Shulong, "Lengzhanhou Zhongguo anquan zhanlüe sixiang de fazhan" [The development of China's thinking about security strategy after the Cold War], ibid., no. 9 (1999): 11–13; Xiao, "Dui guoji xingshizhong jige redian wenti de kanfa," 3; Sa Benwang, "Woguo anquan de bianhua ji xin de pubian anquanguan de zhuyao tezheng" [The change in our country's security and the main features of the new concept of universal security], *Shijie Jingji yu Zhengzhi Luntan*, no. 1 (2000): 51; Wang Yiwei, "Dui Tai junshi douzheng dui shijie zhanlüe geju de yingxiang chutan" [A preliminary exploration of the effects on the international strategic situation of military action against Taiwan]," ibid., no. 6 (1999): 28.

57. See A. F. K. Organski and Jacek Kugler, *The War Ledger* (Chicago: University of Chicago Press, 1980); Robert Gilpin, *War and Change in World Politics* (New York: Cambridge University Press, 1981); Paul Kennedy, *The Rise and Fall of the Great Powers* (New York: Random House, 1987). On the application of such arguments to the rise of China, see Goldstein, "Great Expectations," 62–63; id., *Rising to the Challenge.*

58. Robert Powell, *In the Shadow of Power: States and Strategies in International Politics* (Princeton, N.J.: Princeton University Press, 1999).

6 The Limits of Economic Interdependence

SINO-JAPANESE RELATIONS

Michael Yahuda

The principal question that this chapter addresses is why the growing economic interdependence between the People's Republic of China and Japan in the post–Cold War period has failed to prevent a marked deterioration in relations between the two states, especially in the early years of the twenty-first century.[1] Such a development does not accord with general liberal international theory, which claims that deepening economic relations and economic interdependence should lead to recognition of shared interests as bolstered by separate business and other constituencies in each country with a stake in improving relations.[2]

Yet the increased openness of Chinese and Japanese societies and the growth of contacts between the two sets of peoples, as evident from the numbers of student exchanges and visits by tourists, have not led to an improvement of the image that each side has of the other.[3] On the contrary, the relatively positive views of each other in earlier years have been replaced by negative ones. No wonder that many in the foreign policy elites in both countries sense that the gap between them is widening.[4]

I argue that the key to understanding the deterioration in Sino-Japanese relations is the structural change in the international politics of East Asia occasioned by the end of the Cold War. This change has been slow in unfolding, but its impact is extensive, and it has not yet run its course. The change resulting from the end of the Cold War has been far less dramatic or readily visible in Asia than in Europe, which is perhaps why it has not received much attention in the Asian context. No "Berlin Wall" came down, the communist parties of China, North Korea, and Vietnam did not fall from power, and no reconfiguration of alliances took place. Nevertheless the impact of the loosening of the shackles imposed by the Cold War in Asia has been profound. It has led to a repositioning of the regional great powers and has allowed for an intensification of economic development in most of the East Asian countries, especially China. This in turn has helped change the international and regional economies and possibly the regional and international balance of power. In one sense, the American predominance of power has been enhanced, but in another, the American capacity to determine outcomes has been weakened.[5]

The collapse of the Soviet Union also pointed up the bankruptcy of the Soviet (or communist/socialist) economic model and paved the way for intensification of the Chinese embrace of globalization. As elsewhere, globalization had the paradoxical effect of encouraging the development of regional economic groupings, while at the same time bringing about a yearning to redefine more local or national identities. Coupled with the changes in the international political system, the countries of East Asia have been engaged in new attempts to redefine their domestic, regional, and international identities. Thus a new national assertiveness is evident in South Korea, as well as in China and Japan. Each of the three may be seen to be reacting to these changes in accordance with its own particular domestic and external circumstances.

The problem in the case of China and Japan is that their respective nationalist resurgences are developing with the other cast as the putative adversary. Furthermore, China and Japan do not have experience of conducting relations with each on the basis of equality. Before the advent of Europeans in East Asia, China was accepted as superior, even though Japan was fully independent. Following the modernization of Japan after the Meji Restoration of 1868, the tables were turned and Japan became the superior power, as attested by its defeat of China in 1895. Notwithstanding its defeat in 1945, Japan soon began to see itself as superior once again when its economy rose from the ashes of defeat to become in due course second in the world only to the United States. It was not until recent years that the rise of China changed that perception, meaning that for the first time in their respective histories, the two major powers have to conduct relations when neither is prepared to defer to the other. Moreover, the two sides have little if any experience in discussing the management of their strategic relations in depth. Neither appears to take into account the national security interests of the other, and there are no means in place for their leaders to meet on a regular basis to discuss the broader strategic issues. In practice, both sides address these matters through the prism of their relations with the United States—hence the emphasis both sides give to the so-called triangular relationship.[6] However, even if seen within the framework of such a triangle, the Sino-Japanese side is much, much thinner than either that of the United States and Japan or that of the United States and China. I argue, therefore, that the United States will have an important role to play if the deteriorating relations between the two great powers of East Asia are not to threaten regional stability in an area of its abiding security and commercial interests.

This chapter first outlines the depth and far-reaching character of the economic interdependence of the two countries, before going on to explore further how their relationship has been affected by the end of the Cold War. It then considers the specific issues on which the divide between the two has deepened and concludes with a discussion of the strategic agenda that must be addressed if the two are to narrow their differences and reduce the risk of a new confrontation between them that could threaten the stability of the region as a whole.

Economic Interdependence

China's leaders have long claimed that the Sino-Japanese economies are highly complementary. Japan, with its resource-poor advanced high-tech economy, it is argued, should find a natural partner in China, with its resource-rich, more backward, but developing economy. Indeed, it would seem that Chinese expectations have at last begun to bear fruit, because Japan emerged in the 1990s as China's greatest trading partner, and China in the 2000s as the biggest for Japan, surpassing the United States. The value of their mutual trade, according to Chinese figures, grew from around $12 billion in 1990 to $83 billion in 2000 and $168 billion in 2004 (the Japanese figure is $214 billion, because it also includes Hong Kong), when it accounted for more than 22 percent of China's and 20 percent of Japan's total trade. Paralleling this has been a corresponding growth in Japanese investment in China. After being cautious in the 1980s, Japanese companies rapidly increased their investment in China in the 1990s. Again according to Chinese figures, Japanese investment, which in 1991 totaled $579 million, reached $3.2 billion in 1998. By the end of the year 2000, there were 20,340 Japanese direct investment projects in China, with a total agreed investment of $38.6 billion and actual investment of $28.2 billion. Japanese figures put the accumulated investment at the end of 2003 at a total of nearly $40 billion. By the late 1990s, China ranked second only to the United States as a target for Japanese investment.[7]

This is significant, because foreign direct investment (FDI) is often taken as a criterion for assessing economic interdependence (or mutual dependence). Indeed, in this case, the point has been reached where some Japanese fear that Japanese industry is being "hollowed out" because of the transfer of so much manufacturing capacity to China. Closer economic relations, of course, can also give rise to new forms of dispute, as well as being a sign of greater cooperation. Sino-Japanese economic relations have indeed given rise to new sources of friction. But economic disputes are more amenable to settlement than most others. Thus despite their so-called tariff war both sides managed to settle their differences over Chinese exports of a particular kind of mushroom, despite the vigorous opposition of Japan's agricultural lobby.[8]

The deepening economic relationship has been matched by increasing interactions between the two peoples. In 2004, more than 3.3 million Japanese tourists visited China and more than 577,000 Chinese visited Japan. Such visits have grown dramatically in the past few years. For example, both figures marked increases of over 35 percent over the previous year.[9] Educational exchanges have also risen significantly. In 2003, some 13,000 Japanese studied in China and more than 70,000 Chinese students were registered at Japanese institutions of tertiary education. The latter accounted for 64.7 percent of foreign students in Japan. Beyond that, there are more than 220 sister-city relationships between the two countries and an expanding number of NGOs working on a variety of topics and issues in bilateral relations.[10]

The Chinese cliché that "economics are hot and politics are cold" in their relations with Japan contains much truth. The economic and social interactions between the two sides have been increasing rapidly, especially since 2000. But these have led neither to noticeable improvements in political relations between the two sets of leaders nor to better perceptions of each other by Chinese and Japanese. There is little to suggest that particular constituencies have developed in either country that press for protecting the Sino-Japanese relationship. Those in both countries who have spoken in favor of pursuing a new course so as not to alienate their powerful neighbor have been effectively silenced on that score by the strength of apparently nationalistic sentiments. Thus Katutaro Kitashiro, head of the Japan Association of Corporate Executives, publicly called on Prime Minister Junichiro Koizumi to refrain from visiting the Yasukuni Shrine, a Shinto shrine in Tokyo that commemorates Japan's war dead, which is controversial because a number of prominent war criminals are among those enshrined there, as did Yotaro Kobayashi, chairman of Fuji Xerox Co. But they found themselves without support from fellow businessmen when they were assailed in the press and even subjected to physical harassment by extreme right-wingers.[11] Similarly, Ma Licheng, a senior editor of *Renmin Ribao* (*People's Daily*), and Shi Yinhong, a leading academic at the Chinese People's University, were subjected to abuse and hostility for promoting the cause of "new thinking" with regard to Japan.[12] Yet the scale of Sino-Japanese interactions is deep, extensive, and unprecedented.

Even the provision of official Japanese aid to China failed to become a vehicle for improving ties between the two sides. The aid begun in 1979 was extensive. In the period 1979–2000, according to the Japanese Foreign

Ministry, Japanese Official Development Assistance (ODA) to China came to over 5.4 trillion yen, or "more than half of all bilateral assistance" given by OECD countries.[13] However, the Chinese side tended to regard the ODA as something to which it was entitled as a form of war reparations, and in any case, it was aid from which Japanese business benefited by being awarded contracts for many of the projects. For their part, the Japanese complained that the Chinese government withheld the true extent of this aid from its people. It was only following the fence-mending visit of Premier Zhu Rongji in 2000 that the Chinese began to make the figures indicating the true magnitude of the aid from Japan publicly available.

Since 1995, Japanese ODA has reflected another dimension of the interdependence of the two countries that underscores elements of concern rather than cordiality. Japanese ODA is no longer aimed at promoting economic development as such, but has been retargeted to address environmental problems and poverty alleviation. The former stem from Japanese worries about acid rain and dust blown in from China, and the latter reflects Japanese anxieties about potential social instability in China that could also be damaging to Japan.

To be sure, the economic interdependence between China and Japan is crucially important to the relationship as a whole, and the two countries' leaders are particularly conscious of its beneficial significance. It also ensures that both sides can point to underlying positive value in the relationship. Arguably, the economic interdependence acts as a constraint against allowing relations to deteriorate unduly. But so far there is little evidence of these considerations spilling over into other aspects of their relations. Thus, although there are arrangements for military exchanges and security consultations, there is no sign that these have led to serious discussions about the management of security in the region. More indicative of the nature of the relationship is the complaint by a leading official of the Japan Center for International Exchange that there is a "huge lacuna" in the shape of the absence of a system of cooperation involving China and Japan, in particular, and, to a lesser extent, China and the United States.[14]

The Post–Cold War Context

The military threat posed by the Soviet Union to China and Japan ended with the demise of the Soviet Union in 1991. The U.S.-Japan alliance was also cast in a new and ambiguous light, especially as Japanese and American security interests were no longer as closely congruent as before. Indeed, it was possible to argue that as far as China was concerned, Japan faced the dilemma of either being "entrapped" or "abandoned" by the United States, on whom its security depended.[15]

Evidence of the fear of being entrapped into a hostile policy of isolating China appeared soon after the Tiananmen massacre. Japan was the first of the Western allies both to resume loans and to send an incumbent head of government to visit China after the Tiananmen massacre. The fear of "abandonment" was evident in reactions to the "Japan bypassing" practiced by President Bill Clinton in the course of his visit to China in 1998.[16] As seen from China, the U.S.-Japan Security Alliance was acceptable if it did indeed keep the cork in the bottle of Japan's military potential, but it was quite a different matter if the alliance were to serve the purpose of co-opting Japan into becoming an active partner in American regional security objectives.[17] This was precisely what some in China suspected as a result of the 1996 agreement on new guidelines for U.S.-Japan defense cooperation and of Japan's commitment to participate in research into so-called theater missile defense (TMD).[18] If successful, TMD would be able to nullify the Chinese missile threat to Taiwan and thereby deny Beijing what it sees as the only credible means of preventing Taiwan from pursuing the path of independence. The fact that the Japanese have been vague about the geographical applicability of the new guidelines of their military cooperation with the United States has only stoked Chinese fears that Japan still seeks to exercise influence over the fate of Taiwan, which it ruled for fifty years until 1945.[19] These Chinese fears were apparently confirmed by the agreement between Japan and the United States of February 2005, which specifically identified the peaceful resolution of the Taiwan problem as among the twelve listed strategic objectives of the two allies.[20]

More broadly, from a strategic perspective, the end of the Cold War brought to light fundamental problems in the place that Japan and China each envisioned the other occupying in the region and in the wider world. Most Japanese saw their alliance with the United States as central to their strategic security into the indefinite future. Accordingly, they implicitly or explicitly accepted a version of Pax Americana. That ranged in Japanese thinking from a vision of America as the provider of hegemonic stability to a vision of a more liberal order centered on free trade and the promotion of democracy. Moreover, the security alliance with the United States was seen as central both to resisting adverse implications of China's seemingly inexorable rise and, paradoxically, to cultivating a durable, stable relationship with China. The alliance has also been seen as providing China with reassurance against the reemergence of Japan as a military power, while allowing it sufficient space to develop a more political international profile commensurate with its economic standing.

The problem with this Japanese outlook in its various formulations is that it is at odds with the Chinese view, in which American hegemony (benign or otherwise) is the problem rather than the solution. Chinese leaders have made their preference for a multipolar world order, in which their relations with other important countries are conducted through partnerships of different kinds, abundantly clear. These partnerships are to be buttressed by dialogues about security and consultations about economic exchanges conducted in different multilateral fora. While they accept the basics of a liberal order, provided that it is confined to the promotion of free trade in the interests of "peace and development," China's leaders reject intrusive promotion of democracy. The bottom line is the preservation of Communist Party rule.

The end of the Cold War also had a major impact on the domestic politics of the two great neighbors, which in turn accentuated the divisions between them. First, the disintegration of the Soviet Union and the concomitant collapse of the communist economic system as a viable alternative to capitalism provoked profound changes in the way both the Chinese and Japanese political elites positioned themselves at home. Once Deng Xiaoping had prevailed over his more orthodox or leftist colleagues after the Tiananmen disaster, the opening to the international economy and the emphasis on market-led rapid economic growth quickly undermined what support remained for the command economy.[21] The leadership sought to strengthen its legitimacy by reaching out for the support of the people by launching a two-year campaign of "patriotic education," beginning in 1993. In contrast to the campaigns of previous years, this one was notable for the exclusion of socialist themes. Instead, it painted the Communist Party as the savior of the nation in the war against Japan, after which it was able to consolidate Chinese unity.[22]

In Japan, the end of the Cold War led to the effective demise of the opposition Socialist Party and with it of the institutionalized opposition to the alliance with the United States and the main base of support for the commitment to the policies of peace and opposition to reforming the peace Article 9 of the Japanese constitution. By default, the center of gravity in Japanese politics shifted to the right.[23] If the revival of nationalistic sentiments in China identified Japan as the unreconstructed "other," the new national assertiveness in Japan was no longer willing to accept the diplomatic deference to China associated with the "friendship diplomacy" of the 1970s and 1980s.

Second, removed from the constraints of the axis of conflict of the Cold War, in which both China and Japan shared a common adversary in the Soviet Union, both countries began to fashion new approaches to the outside world that were more independently assertive. China first began to cultivate its neighbors in part to escape ostracism by much of the Western world after Tiananmen and in part to explore the new strategic latitude it enjoyed now that any lingering threat from the north had been removed.

This was deemed essential to the encouragement of a more peaceable regional and international environment in which to concentrate on the main task of domestic economic development. Despite the bursting of its speculative economic bubble and the onset of what was to be a ten-year-long period of economic stagnation, Japan nevertheless found that the constraints of its alliance with the United States had loosened to the extent that it had to fashion new foreign policies. For example, it now had to deal with Moscow independently of the United States, and it played an independent role in helping to fashion a peaceful settlement in Cambodia. Indeed, for the first time, Japan actively participated in a UN peacekeeping operation by sending a small contingent to Cambodia.[24] However, as a country that was not used to fashioning independent foreign and strategic policies, Japan soon came under pressure for not contributing militarily to the first Gulf War in 1991 and for its quietist response to the first nuclear crisis with North Korea in 1993–94.[25] Nevertheless, it was at this point that Japan began to assert a claim to a permanent seat on the UN Security Council.[26]

While many Japanese may have been persuaded that they should play a more assertive international and regional role within the framework of the alliance with the United States, many in Beijing demurred. They have been greatly concerned by what they see as the emergence of Japan as a more active partner of the United States in the pursuit of American military strategy in the region. At the same time, the Chinese have expressed their displeasure at every Japanese attempt to chart an independent role for their country. Thus even the participation of Japanese Self-Defense Forces in noncombat roles in UN peacekeeping operations has drawn criticism from China.[27] However, it is not clear what role for Japan would be acceptable to China's leaders, other than remaining politically and strategically quiescent until such time as presumably it would be overshadowed by China. At the same time, it is unclear what role Japan's leaders expect a rising China to play in the region and beyond.

It is clear that the division between the two political systems and the ways in which they define their national identities continue to bedevil Sino-Japanese relations. There is little or no sympathy and understanding on either side for the expectations and aspirations of the other. In this regard, it is instructive to note how many of the observations and findings of Allen Whiting in his study of the nationalistic images and perceptions that shaped Chinese policies toward Japan are still applicable twenty years later.[28] Whiting noted that against all the more favorable mentions of Japan in some official statements and the positive influences of people-to-people exchanges (which have grown exponentially since then), there is "the contrary image of a ruthless aggressor whose rape and plunder of China must not be forgotten and whose potential return to this role is allegedly promoted by the

Japanese in official as well as private circles." He went to observe that the "emotional content of this latter image offset the favorable images and, under . . . [certain] circumstances became dominant in certain sectors, particularly among Chinese university students."[29] Whiting also contrasted the better informed and nuanced accounts of American society and politics that were current in the Chinese media to the rather stereotyped writing that appeared on Japan.[30] That still applies today, as do his points about the significance of the difference between the two political systems, particularly how Chinese behavior exacerbates the problems between the two countries by overstressing the possibility of Japan's return to militarism and the need for perpetual Chinese vigilance. Above all, the high moral tone in which Chinese leaders admonish their Japanese counterparts to recall the past as a guide to the future continues "to stand in contrast to the Japanese proclivity to live in the present with little interest in the past, particularly if it reflects unfavorably on the nation."[31]

Newly assertive Japan has little sympathy for the Chinese demand for unification with Taiwan so as to complete the process of redressing past humiliations and enable China once again to become the great power it feels itself entitled to be by virtue of its history and circumstances. Similarly, the Chinese have little appreciation for the desire of the Japanese to modify their foreign-imposed constitution, however innocuous the proposed change may be. The Chinese officially blasted a draft for reforming the constitution by Japan's Liberal Democratic Party that basically did little more than reaffirm the status quo of retaining an armed force for national defense, affirming the right to collective self-defense, as well as to the use of force when engaging in UN peacekeeping operations, while at the same time maintaining the renunciation of war, the three non-nuclear principles (no production, possession, or introduction of nuclear weapons into Japan). This was hardly a manifesto for radical nationalism, and it still had to face the hurdles of gaining a two-thirds majority in parliament, plus a majority in a nationwide referendum. It was not something that could be determined by a small conclave meeting in secret. Yet on 16 February 2004, the Chinese Xinhua News Agency denounced the draft as "a signal that warrants [the] vigilance of the world, especially various Asian countries that were invaded by Japan in the past . . . Japan is day dreaming to materialize its wild ambitions of becoming a political and military power . . . [when it] will definitely pose a threat to peace in Asia and the world." As mentioned earlier, those within the Chinese elite who tried to pursue a less confrontationist policy toward Japan were rebuffed in 2003. A *Renmin Ribao* editorial on 18 February 2004 seems to have voiced the consensus of the Chinese government, when having surveyed fairly factually the debate about constitutional revision in Japan, it concluded that the fifty years of peace since 1945 had helped Japan become an "economic power" and that "as a responsible member of the East Asia community, it is in its own best interest as well as that of the region that Japan continue its pacifist policies." In other words, while China continues along the path of acquiring a modern military force, as befits the great world power it is destined to be, Japan should occupy a lesser position.

Against this background, it is hardly surprising that the remaining legacy of the Cold War in East Asia has not brought Japan and China closer together in finding means to address their differences. That legacy includes the unresolved problems of Korea and Taiwan and the continued rule of China, North Korea, and Vietnam by communist parties. Even though all of these issues were transformed in the new era, none of them may be said to have led to a closer understanding between China and Japan. China was closely involved in the formal negotiations affecting north-south relations in Korea through the "two + two" arrangements (i.e., the two Koreas, China, and the United States), and it did not respond positively to Japanese (or even Russian) attempts to join in the process. China meanwhile was active behind the scenes both in supporting North Korea and facilitating the American negotiations that led to the 1994 framework agreement. Privately, Chinese diplomats made no secret of their expectation that a unified Korea would come under China's influence at the expense of Japan.[32] Nevertheless, China and Japan share certain basic interests in common in how best to address the immediate problems raised by North Korea's nuclear ambitions. Neither favors policies aimed at forcing a regime change, and still less do they like the idea of a possible military strike at suspected sites of production of nuclear weapons and other weapons of mass destruction (WMD) in North Korea. Yet there is no sign of a coordinated approach, and the two sides were embarrassed by an incident in which Chinese security personnel burst into a Japanese consulate in China's northeast in pursuit of North Korean refugees. Although the matter was swiftly settled, it brought to the fore differences in the importance that the two sides attach to humanitarian values. The democratic transformation of Taiwan increased Japanese sympathy for the island, and the Chinese attempt at intimidation by missile testing in 1996 had the effect of intensifying popular Japanese concerns about the resurgence of China. Chinese protests about the possible application of TMD to Taiwan and about the operational extension of the new U.S.-Japan guidelines to Taiwan waters received little or no sympathy in Japan. Meanwhile, although Japanese have welcomed the continued Chinese emphasis on the priorities of economic growth and development, the underlying concern about the destabilizing effects of rapid economic growth and the decline of the capacity for good governance in China has, if anything, increased.

The multilateral fora established within the region since the end of the Cold War, such as APEC (Asia-Pacific Economic Cooperation) and the ARF (ASEAN Regional Forum), whose formation was very much assisted by Japan, may have played some role in encouraging cooperation within the region, but they have done little to promote closer interactions between Japan and China. They have not served as vehicles for "rehabilitating" Japan in Chinese eyes, nor can the Japanese be entirely satisfied with them as vehicles for consolidating China as a good regional citizen. Indeed, when the financial storm broke in Asia in 1997, many in China blamed Japan for having earlier revalued its currency. Bilateral relations were hardly improved by China receiving much praise, especially from the Americans, for refraining from revaluing its currency, while Japan received opprobrium, despite being the largest international donor to the rescue packages and despite having its proposal to establish an Asian Monetary Fund thwarted by the United States. The lack of coordination between China and Japan became manifest when China turned down the invitation publicly offered by Japan for it to join the Group of Seven (or Eight), then due to meet in Japan. A prominent member of a key think tank in Beijing told me that an important reason for the Chinese refusal was that the invitation came from Japan.[33] A degree of rivalry is also evident between the two major powers in their approach to the regional grouping of the ASEAN + Three (APT—the ten Southeast Asian states, China, Japan, and South Korea) that was formed in December 1997, which serves to limit such progress that has been made toward closer economic integration. A currency swap arrangement has been agreed to, but it has yet to be tested. However, Japan has resisted Chinese suggestions that that the "Three" form a free trade agreement (FTA), preferring instead to form a bilateral one with South Korea.[34] Likewise, Japan has blocked the Chinese suggestion to form an East Asian community based on the APT alone and has successfully urged that Australia and New Zealand and perhaps others be invited too.[35]

Bilateral Differences: The Agenda Extended

In addition to the three long-standing problems in Sino-Japanese relations—the treatment of the historical legacy of Japanese invasion of China; the Taiwan question; and the disputed sovereign claims to the Diaoyu Dao / Sengaku Islands—more points of friction have been added. These include disputes over exclusive economic zones (EEZs) and related drilling rights; Japanese complaints about illegal Chinese surveys of waters adjacent to Japan (notably by a nuclear submarine); Chinese complaints about Japanese Prime Minister Koizumi's visits to the Yakusuni Shrine; and the eruption of violent anti-Japanese demonstrations in China, especially targeted at Japan's quest to become a permanent member of the UN Security Council. No item on this long list of differences has approached a solution and, arguably, their intensity has increased in the post–Cold War period.

Nevertheless, it has been argued on both sides that relations at the governmental level have improved and that whenever problems have threatened to disrupt relations, they have been dealt with fairly rapidly.[36] However, as noted, new issues of substance emerged in the 1990s associated with each side's strategic worries about the other. Identification of China as a potential external threat, first made public in a Japanese Defense White Paper in 1997, was reaffirmed in Japan's National Guidelines of 2005. Chinese security concerns about Japan have been raised by the reinvigoration of the U.S.-Japan Security Treaty, particularly due to Japan's ambiguity about its application to Taiwan and Japan's participation in America's TMD program, which was followed in February 2005 by an explicit mention of the Taiwan issue in a major security statement by the American and Japanese foreign and defense ministers. The Chinese government also claims to see the threat of incipient militarism in Japanese proposals to redefine Japan's peace constitution.

It will be seen that uncertainties in each country about the strategic significance of the perceived growing military clout of the other are the common thread to the problems of the 1990s. This is what gives an edge to Chinese criticisms of activities and statements by right-wing Japanese politicians, ministerial approval of Japanese school textbooks that skate over the excesses of Japanese aggression, and disparaging remarks by ministers and visits by them to the Yasukuni Shrine. In the Chinese view, these illustrate Japan's failure to come to terms with its past history of aggression and war crimes and demonstrate that it is not legitimate for Japan to acquire force projection capabilities. That is regarded as all the more pressing in view of Japan's new commitments in relations with the United States. At the same time, Japanese complaints indicate concern about China's growing ability to project force in the adjacent seas and its readiness to engage in coercive diplomacy, especially with regard to Taiwan. Additionally, there is concern that difficulties in managing the social consequences of rapid economic growth at home may make China more aggressive in the pursuit of its national goals abroad.[37]

These strategic worries have acquired greater salience in view of separate social and political changes in each country that have combined to make each one less receptive to the concerns of the other. The change of generations has brought to the fore leaders in both countries who have little first-hand knowledge of or interest in the other. The late Zhou Enlai had actually lived in Japan, and many of his generation had studied there. Indeed, there was a saying in China that those who had studied in Japan (during the 1890s–1920s) returned as revolutionaries, while those who returned from study in the United States were reformers. Even those who had not visited Japan, like Mao and Deng, nevertheless had a high respect for the capabilities and achievements of the Japanese, notwithstanding the war of aggression. But the subsequent generations of leaders in China, headed first by Jiang Zemin and later by Hu Jintao, had no such experience. On the Japanese side, the postwar leaders who had intimate knowledge of China or were personally affected by a sense of war guilt, such as those who normalized relations with Beijing in 1972, have long since passed on. The current Japanese leadership lacks intimate experience of World War II, which ended some sixty years ago, and is more likely to be affected by the experience of Japan's postwar privations. As a result, the lack of institutionalized patterns of exchange is no longer compensated for by the kind of personal links that matter so much in East Asian political cultures, especially in China and Japan.

Some of these problems became evident in the course of Jiang Zemin's visit to Japan in 1998. Coming hot on the heels of President Clinton's visit to China, which was seen at the time as elevating China's importance to the United States as a potential strategic partner, and shortly after the Japanese prime minister had issued a fulsome apology to South Korea's President Kim Dae Jung, Jiang expected to find a more contrite Japan as a result of the improvement of China's relative position. But not only did the Japanese prime minister fail to issue the expected apology, he also refused to follow Clinton in subscribing to the latter's "three no's policy": no support for "one China, one Taiwan"; no support for Taiwanese independence; and no support for Taiwanese representation in international organizations where sovereignty is a condition of membership.[38] Jiang reacted by publicly hectoring the Japanese, including the emperor, on their failure to atone properly for their past misdeeds. This backfired to such an extent that the following year, Premier Zhu Rongji visited Tokyo and struck a much more conciliatory note. Thereafter, China's leaders were more circumspect in raising the question of historical guilt during their visits to Japan and seemed to use the issue less as a lever to extract concessions from Japan than as a means to counter what they see as a resurgence of nationalism in Japan. Thus Prime Minister Koizumi, who has annoyed Beijing by making a point of visiting the Yakusuni Shrine (albeit not on the key date of the anniversary of the war), has been criticized rather than reviled in the official press and when on the commemoration of the sixtieth anniversary of the end of the war, he was required to visit an anti-Japanese war museum in China, the official Chinese press was relatively mild in the accompanying commentary. It is as if the Chinese drew a lesson from Jiang's earlier visit of not playing up the historical issue too far, lest it spark a nationalist reaction in Japan. But this did not mean that the issue would not be used for domestic purposes at home.

The generational divide is more evident among the young. In China, the overwhelming evidence is that younger people have a negative image of Japan, which may largely be derived from the one-sided accounts of the officially inspired media.[39] In polls published in *Zhongguo Qingnian Bao* (China Youth Daily) in December 1996 and the Japanese newspaper *Asahi Shimbun* in June 1997, respectively, roughly 41 percent of the Chinese respondents either had "bad" impressions of or "disliked" Japan, while from 10 to 17 percent had a "good" impression or "liked" Japan; 44 percent in the one poll and 35 percent in the other had neither good nor bad feelings about the country.[40] As far as Japan is concerned, public opinion swung decisively away from a very positive attitude toward China in the 1980s to a more negative one in the 1990s. For most of the 1980s, more than 70 percent of respondents to official polls had "friendly feelings" toward China, with around 20 percent claiming "unfriendly feelings." By 1996, the ratio for the first time showed that more had unfriendly feelings toward China by a margin of 51:45 percent.[41] Arguably, the latter polls may have reflected responses to the 1996 crisis in the Taiwan Strait, when China launched missiles off the coast of Taiwan. However, polls conducted some five years later, in 2002, on the eve of the thirtieth anniversary of the establishment of diplomatic relations reflected similarly negative views of each other, despite the more upbeat celebratory messages of the two countries' respective leaders: 41 percent of Japanese respondents said relations were going well, as opposed to 46 percent who thought not; 50 percent of Chinese respondents said relations were not good, while only 22 percent were of the opinion that they were fine.[42]

Perhaps more significant is the impression of leading scholars on foreign relations in each country that, generally speaking, there was a lack of interest by the young especially in the culture and contemporary developments of the other country. By comparison, the younger generation in each country was much more interested in developments in the United States. Although they conceded that the products of each country were being bought more extensively in the other, they nevertheless held that that did not lead to a corresponding growth in interest or curiosity about the other. They claimed that intellectual circles in their respective countries were far more familiar with intellectual and academic debates in America and Western Europe than they were with corresponding developments in the other country.[43] Reference has already been made to the relatively large number of Chinese students in Japan, which would suggest a greater interest than implied by the scholars I interviewed. But a closer look suggests that they may not have been so wrong after all. A more telling set of figures as far as intellec-

tual development is concerned is that about 82 percent of the Chinese students in America in 1995 (32,512) were graduate students. Only about
35 percent of all foreign students in Japan were graduate students, and the
Chinese proportion would have been even less. Moreover, there were 9,228
Chinese students carrying out research in the United States, as compared
with only 317 in Japan.[44] There can be little doubt as to the intellectual
dominance of the United States in this regard. This not only illustrates an
important dimension of American "soft power" but also suggests that, despite the animosity felt toward the United States on nationalistic grounds in
China, or indeed in Japan, there is a fundamental reserve in both countries
of understanding of and curiosity about America that is lacking in either
country with regard to the other.

The passing of the Cold War has also given rise to a new national assertiveness in both China and Japan as each seeks to establish a more active
and independent national identity now that the bipolar constraints have
been removed. Japanese self-confidence may have become muted after the
bursting of Japan's bubble economy in the early 1990s and its apparent in-
capacity to break out of the sterile impasse that gripped both its economy
and its politics. Nevertheless, Japan has initiated a number of important
diplomatic and political moves that are indicative of a more internationally
active country. These have been accompanied by debates about foreign and
defense policy that not only call for more political activism but raise the
prospect of a more fundamental change in Japan's international identity.

China's leaders did not challenge Japan's key role in the launching of regional multilateral consultative organizations, notably the APEC and the
ARF. The PRC was pleased to join both, even though it recognized that one
of the objectives of the organizers was to involve China, in the hope that it
would come to accept the restraining norms implicit in regional cooperation.
Doubtless, China's leaders saw positive benefits for them in earning goodwill by joining these essentially consultative organizations, which could not
commit China to do things that it did not wish to do. However, nearly all
of Japan's other initiatives have elicited varying degrees of hostility or skepticism from China. The Chinese, for example, were not happy with the sending of Japanese minesweepers at the end of the Gulf War or the deployment
of members of the Japanese Self-Defense Force to serve with the UN peacekeeping operation in Cambodia, even though the latter were explicitly pro-
hibited from assuming combat roles. Similarly, they responded adversely to
the Japanese dispatch of naval support ships to the Indian Ocean to provide
logistical assistance to the American attack on Afghanistan. The ease with
which the enabling legislation was passed in the Diet also evoked public
criticism in China. Although the Chinese did not openly oppose Japan's bid
to become a permanent member of the UN Security Council, it was clear
that they did not support it. However, the Chinese opposed, and therefore

vetoed, the Japanese proposal to establish a combined force against piracy in the South China Sea.

As we have seen, the new national assertiveness has separately led each side to take a harsher view of the other. In the case of China, the officially inspired education in patriotism has emphasized an interpretation of modern history that treats China as a victim, with the concluding and unresolved chapter focusing on Japanese aggression. As a consequence, indignation about Japan and its alleged failure to express an adequate apology is central to the newfound nationalist ideology of the young, which in turn constrains the Chinese leadership. Having stoked the fires of youthful nationalism as a unifying element at a time when communist ideology has lost meaning and support, China's leaders are now fearful of allowing it full expression. Conscious of instances in modern Chinese history when student demonstrations against alleged humiliations by foreigners ended up being turned against the incumbent government for being too pusillanimous, China's leaders in the 1990s have deliberately prevented students from demonstrating against Japan. But as several prominent Chinese scholars and advisors on foreign affairs pointed out to me in July 2000, the leadership in Beijing has been "too weak" to give a proper lead on the issue. They argue that insufficient recognition is given to Japan's accomplishments in developing its economy and its technology to extremely high levels. A few also deplored the way in which the strength of Japanese feelings about adherence to peace and pursuit of a role as a civilian power was ignored in the official media. At least one professed admiration for Japan as a democracy. A debate was begun at one point in China as to whether the time has come to adopt a more conciliatory approach to Japan. It was argued that the balance of power is shifting in China's favor, partly because of the continued growth of the Chinese economy and partly because of China's newfound partnership with the United States in the "war on terror." Additionally, it was suggested that continued enmity with Japan limits China's capacity to utilize to the full the new activism it has developed in the region's multilateral fora. Moreover, better relations with Japan would contribute significantly to the regional stability China's leaders deem necessary to continuing the economic growth that they regard as fundamental to the survival of Communist Party rule. As against that are the old suspicions about Japan and the revival of Japanese nationalism, with the attendant fear of Japanese militarism. But more significant was the violent public expression of outrage by many young people.[45]

In Japan, with the passing of the war generation, there is a growing impatience with Chinese criticism of Japanese failure to come to terms with its past. Chinese official complaints are seen as instrumental and manipulative, because they always seem to intensify when the Chinese government is pressing demands either for more aid or to prevent Japan from pursuing policies to which it objects. In particular, Japanese have long objected to the way in which the Chinese seize on remarks by unrepresentative right-wingers.[46] But more recently, some intellectuals representing mainstream conservatives and more central opinion have written a controversial new textbook that seeks to find pride in modern Japanese history and see virtue in the Meiji Restoration of 1868 and in the wars against China in 1895 and against Russia in 1905.[47] Such views, of course, still further widen the gap separating Japan from China and other neighboring countries, notably South Korea.

Sino-Japanese relations hit a new low in April 2005, when young Chinese demonstrators in several Chinese cities went on the rampage against Japanese government and private properties. These were instigated in part by outrage at a new round of textbooks approved by the Japanese Ministry of Education that were said to whitewash Japan's war record and, more important, by an attempt to put an end to Japan's bid for a permanent seat on the UN Security Council. Western observers noted that the Chinese authorities approved of the demonstrations and the security forces stood aside as the youths attacked the property.[48] Premier Wen Jiabao, who was in India at the time, made the Chinese official position perfectly clear when he noted that Japan was not qualified to be a permanent member of the Security Council until it had come to terms with its past aggression.[49] The Japanese side did not get the apology or the compensation it sought, but the local authorities where Japanese property had been damaged quietly carried out repairs. The Chinese security organizations then took stringent steps to stop further anti-Japanese demonstrations.[50] If the intention of China's leaders was to demonstrate the strength of popular feelings as a means of strengthening their opposition to Japan's UN bid, they may have succeeded. But the episode damaged the calm, rational diplomatic image that China had been seeking to demonstrate to its neighbors and others. Either the authorities had deliberately stirred up the mob, or they were afraid of what the popular reaction might be if they tried to control it. Neither account put China in a good light. For their part, most Japanese were shocked by the depth of animosity on display, and Japan's leading China specialists thought that only divisions within the leadership could account for the episode.[51]

Some Strategic Conundrums

Currently, the fact that none of the protagonists anticipates military conflict between China and Japan is only possible because of the role played by the United States. The American security alliance with Japan assures the Chinese that the cork remains in the bottle of Japanese "militarism." However, as realists, China's leaders may believe, like Kenneth Waltz, that it is only a question of time before Japan is driven by the logic of international anarchy to become a military power commensurate with its economic power. But China's more immediate security concern regarding Japan is not that it will emerge any time soon as an independent military power in its own right, but rather that it will play a more active security role within the region in support of the United States.

That raises several problems for Chinese strategists. They object to what they see as "American hegemonism," which they perceive as seeking to subvert communist rule at home and contain China's rise abroad. From this perspective, Japan has become the partner of the United States in establishing a ring of containment. But any attempt to weaken the alliance risks accelerating the rise of Japan as an independent military power that could project force throughout maritime East Asia long before China could do so. Meanwhile, in attempting to demonstrate sufficient military strength to exercise coercive diplomacy to intimidate those who favor Taiwan's independence, the Chinese have unwittingly provoked a security dilemma with Japan. Chinese missile exercises against Taiwan in 1995 and 1996 were instrumental in changing the image of China in Japan, and China's fulminations against any form of missile defense as undermining their deterrent drove home to many Japanese that, because of the American bases in Japan, they were a target for China's missiles. That was intensified by the shock of North Korea's testing of a Taepodong missile in 1998 that splashed into the sea after passing over the central island of Japan. As a result, there is greater support in Japan for participating in American research toward the development of a TMD system.

Whether or not the continued presence of American military bases in Japan is sustainable, China's leaders have to think through how a regional order can be made stable. Essentially, three options present themselves. The first is to find a way of establishing a cooperative security framework that accepts the U.S.-Japan alliance as an enduring structure. The second involves coming to terms with the prospect of Japan as a "normal" country that will develop into a military power free of the constraints of the American alliance. The third would result in a rising China that exercises dominance in the region with the acquiescence of a quiescent Japan and a tolerant America. Each one would involve considerable adjustments and mature leadership by the Chinese. They would have to display a greater sensitivity to Japanese concerns and attitudes than they have shown so far.

The first option offers a continuation of the present pattern in one form or another. This is one that has served China well, enabling it to pursue its principal goals of economic growth and development in an international environment in which China has been free of threats of invasion for the first time for at least two hundred years. But it is an option that rubs up against China's nationalist aspirations as expressed in the officially endorsed campaigns of patriotic education. It would call for a leadership that could succeed in promoting the goals and values of cooperative security, as against the realism that has dominated Chinese foreign policy. It would also call for a patriotism that ceased to portray the country as a victim of modern history with an unlimited sense of entitlement from the outside world. It is, however, an option that has gained strength from the new alignment with the United States as partners in the war on terror, which in the wake of the Iraq War has been extended to North Korea. This has provided an opportunity for China to take the lead in working with Japan (alongside South Korea) to persuade the Bush administration to adopt a diplomatic as opposed to a military approach to the North Korean problem. In other words, this option does not condemn China to passivity.

The second option requires even greater adjustment. The removal of American forces from Japan would automatically bring about the multipolar order that China's leaders claim to want. But it would also usher in a balance of power system in the region in which Japan would become a full-fledged independent military power. That would require a transformation of Chinese views of Japan that at present seems almost inconceivable. However, the logic of realism requires the Chinese to think along these lines.

Lastly, the option of Pax Sinica as an alternative to the Pax Americana assumes that China can overcome its massive domestic problems and carry out political reform of sufficient depth as to make it acceptable and even attractive to its neighbors. China's leaders would have to be able to offer incentives and rewards to others rather than continue to make demands on their own behalf. They would have to project their rise in terms of universal ideals and principles.

Even to lay out these alternatives is to show that for the immediate and probably the foreseeable future, China has no alternative but to settle for some version of the first option. Indeed, the Chinese have officially adopted cooperative security as their new security concept.[52] It possible to characterize Chinese debates about foreign policy as between those who look forward to a China that will continue to reform economically, and ultimately politically at home, and integrate more closely with the international economy abroad and those of a more conservative outlook who fear the dilution of Communist Party rule amid growing social dislocation and favor a slower course of reform and a nationalist resistance to integration with the outside world. It is tempting to suggest that much depends on the success of the reformers. But it seems that the prospects for operating successfully within the framework of the Japanese-American alliance depend ultimately on the capacity of China to remain relatively stable while continuing with its rapid economic growth.

Most Japanese cannot envision their immediate future without being bolstered by the alliance with the United States. But they too face difficult choices. On the one hand, there are those who argue that Japan should become more of a "normal" country that lends greater support to American military campaigns based on the right of collective self-defense. On the other hand, there are those who want Japan to emerge as a global "civilian" power and a model and contributor to less-developed countries that promotes human rights, participates in UN peacekeeping operations, and contributes to improving the environment. If the former see the alliance with the United States in security terms, the latter understand it in terms of social relations, friendship, and commitment to common values. The "civilianists" also place the alliance in a balance with a range of multilateral institutions, such as the United Nations, the Asia-Pacific Economic Cooperation, and so on. The crucial difference between the two is their attitude toward China. The "civilianists" favor the cultivation of friendly relations and the promotion of greater social and intellectual links between the two countries. The "normalists" are more wary of the rise of China and assert the need to contain it.[53]

Conclusions

Notwithstanding the close and significant economic interdependence between China and Japan, there is no corresponding spillover into social, intellectual, or security engagement. The result is that the two societies have not come closer together. The recurring disputes about school history textbooks, such as those that emerged in the spring of 2001 and again in April 2005, are not caused by ignorance of each other's processes of decision-making on the issue. They stem from a failure of empathy on both sides. To be sure, there is a particular onus on the Japanese to stop hiding behind legalistic ramparts and confront aspects of their terrible past more openly and offer redress to the many survivors whose wartime suffering at the hands of the Japanese has barely been acknowledged. At the same time, the Chinese should stop using the issue in the pursuit of short-term political gains. The tremendous expansion of economic exchanges has not led to the emergence of constituencies that have publicly taken a stance in favor of promoting closer ties and against manifestations that evoke hostility toward the other country. As we have seen, the contrary seems to be happening: recent trends seem to be driving the two countries farther apart. Fortunately, the two sets of executives appreciate the dangers inherent in a souring of relations and take steps to mend relations whenever they seem in danger of rupture. But in itself that is not enough to build a sound structure for the development of stable relations in the longer term.

The thinness of the Sino-Japanese relationship places an enormous premium upon the United States as the ultimate guarantor of security in

Northeast Asia. Perhaps it is a premium that is greater than either side would like. Given the uncertainties of U.S. policy and policy-making, especially between one administration and the next, neither Beijing nor Tokyo can be confident that the United States will be able to strike a reasoned and consistent balance in its cultivation of relations between these two giants of East Asia.

The growing assertion of nationalist sentiments in both countries continually threatens to distort each side's cultivation of relations with the United States. Even if the spokesman for the Chinese Foreign Ministry can assure all concerned that his country endorses good relations between Japan and the United States, as we have seen, many of his more nationalistically minded fellow citizens (including members of the foreign policy elite) see things differently.[54] Meanwhile, there is an increase in Japanese restiveness about the presence of American troops in their country. In the absence of a clear explanation by the American executive about the moral and strategic principles served by the alliance with Japan and the stationing of troops there, it is entirely possible that the support of the American public for continuing to place them there may erode in the not too distant future.

Traditional concerns about interstate security and about the balance of power may have been overshadowed by the new security agenda of the post–Cold War era. Much emphasis is now given to war against terror, the economic problems of globalization, the problems of intrastate conflict, the collapse of some states and cross-border issues of smuggling of people and drugs by transnational criminal gangs, issues of health, the environment, and so on. But the traditional security issues have not gone away. The failure of the deepening economic interdependence between the two greatest powers of East Asia to bring about closer relations in other dimensions of their relations has had effects that neither could regard as desirable. To cite but one example, the absence of proper strategic understandings between Japan and China constrains them to depend on the security framework provided by the United States. That necessarily reduces their capacity to develop the independence to which each side claims to aspire.

Notes

1. This chapter is based on a paper that was originally prepared for a conference in the summer of 2001. It has been brought up to date and has benefited from having its original series of interviews conducted in Beijing and Tokyo in 2000 augmented by follow-up interviews four years later.

2. For an analysis of theories of interdependence, see Robert O. Keohane and Joseph Nye, *Power and Interdependence: World Politics in Transition* (Boston: Little, Brown, 1997).

3. For an analysis of this key concept with specific reference to Sino-Japanese relations, see Allen S. Whiting, *China Eyes Japan* (Berkeley: University of California Press, 1989).

4. First suggested by interviews conducted in Beijing and Tokyo in the summers of 2000 and then affirmed in 2004.

5. For an excellent overview that attempts to explain developments by using International Relations theory, see Michael Mastanduno, "Incomplete Hegemony and Security Order in the Asia-Pacific," in *America Unrivaled: The Future of the Balance of Power*, ed. G. John Ikenberry (Ithaca, N.Y.: Cornell University Press, 2002), 181–210. See also Michael Yahuda, *The International Politics of the Asia-Pacific* (New York: RoutledgeCurzon, 2004), ch. 8, "the new structure of international relations," 209–41.

6. See, e.g., *Challenges for China-Japan Cooperation*, ed. Kokubun Ryosei (Tokyo: Japan Center for International Exchange, 1998), and Ming Zhang and Ronald N. Montaperto, *A Triad of Another Kind: The United States, China, and Japan* (Basingstoke, Eng.: Macmillan, 1999).

7. The Chinese figures are drawn from the web site of the Chinese Ministry of Foreign Affairs (www.fmprc.gov.cn/eng). An official Chinese source was preferred, as presumably it would have no interest in exaggerating the contribution of Japan to China's economic development. For the Japanese, see David Pilling, "China Surpasses US as Japan's Top Trading Partner," *Financial Times*, 26 January 2005.

8. For an account of Sino-Japanese economic rivalry, see Reinhard Drifte, *Japan's Security Relations with China Since 1989: From Balancing to Bandwagoning?* (New York: RoutledgeCurzon, 2003), 148–51.

9. Japan's National Tourist Organization, www.tourism.jp/english/statistics.

10. Brad Glosserman, "Troubling Signs for Japan-China Relations," *Pac Net* 37 (2 September 2004): 1–2.

11. David Ibison, "Head of Japan Business Group Sides with Japan," *Financial Times*, 25 November 2004; "Koizumi Should Also Fight Terror at Home," editorial, *Asahi Shimbun*, 14 January 2005.

12. Peter Hays Gries, "China's 'New Thinking' on Japan," *China Quarterly*, no. 184 (December 2005): 831–50.

13. Japanese Ministry of Foreign Affairs, www.mofa.go.jp/policy/oda/region/e_asia/china-2.html (accessed 2 October 2005).

14. Wada Jun, "Applying Track Two to China-Japan-U.S. Relations," in *Challenges for China-Japan Cooperation*, ed. Kokubun, 170.

15. For further discussion, see Reinhard Drifte, "US Impact on Japanese-Chinese Security Relations," *Security Dialogue* 31, 4 (December 2000): 449–62.

16. Y. Funabashi, "Tokyo's Depression Diplomacy," *Foreign Affairs* 77, 6 (November–December 1998): 26–36.

17. For discussion of Chinese views of security issues involving Japan, see Banning Garrett and Bonnie Glaser, "Chinese Apprehensions About Revitalization of the U.S.-Japan Alliance," *Asian Survey* 37, 4 (April 1997): 383–402.

18. For a Chinese critique of the new guidelines, see Liu Jiangyong, "China and the Renewal of the US-Japan Security Treaty," in *Japan and China: Rivalry or*

Cooperation in East Asia? ed. Peter Drysdale and Dong Dong Zhang (Canberra: Australia-Japan Research Centre, 2000), 95–114.

19. The official web site of the Chinese Ministry of Foreign Affairs still lists Taiwan as one of the specific issues troubling relations with Japan.

20. U.S. Department of State, "Joint Statement of the U.S.-Japan Security Consultative Committee," 19 February 2005, www.state.gov/r/pa/prs/ps/2005/42490 .htm (accessed 2 October 2005).

21. For an account, see Joseph Fewsmith, *China Since Tiananmen* (New York: Cambridge University Press, 2000).

22. Suisheng Zhao, *A Nation-State by Construction: Dynamics of Modern Chinese Nationalism* (Stanford: Stanford University Press, 2004), 209–47. See also Peter Hays Gries, *China's New Nationalism: Pride, Politics, and Diplomacy* (Berkeley: University of California Press, 2004).

23. Michael J. Green, *Japan's Reluctant Realism: Foreign Policy Challenges in an Era of Uncertain Power* (New York: Palgrave, 2001), 35–75.

24. Ibid., 172–79.

25. Ibid., 203 and 121.

26. Reinhard Drifte, *Japan's Quest for a Permanent Security Council Seat: A Matter of Pride or Justice* (New York: St. Martin's Press, 2000).

27. See the account in ibid., 166–70.

28. Whiting, *China Eyes Japan.*

29. Ibid., 195.

30. Ibid., 189–90.

31. Ibid., 187.

32. Interview with a senior Chinese diplomat in December 1996 in Seoul.

33. Interview with a scholar in the Institute for Asia-Pacific Studies, Chinese Academy of Social Science (CASS), July 1996.

34. Interview with leading official in Japan's Ministry of Foreign Affairs, July 2004.

35. John Ryall, "East Asia Summit Expansion Bid May Feel Friction," *South China Morning Post*, 6 April 2005, and *Tokyo Shimbun*, "Agreement to Expand Participants in East Asia Summit: Japan Aims at Containing China," 7 May 2005.

36. Senior Chinese scholars and officials whom I met in Beijing in July 2000 repeatedly made this point and cited the 1998 visit to Japan by Jiang Zemin as a case in point. They claimed that despite the adverse comments in the media, both governments were satisfied and important agreements were signed. Furthermore, the exchange of prime ministerial visits in 1999 and 2000 ensured that the public perception corresponded to that of the two governments. The same point was repeated, albeit with some qualifications, by my interlocutors in Tokyo.

37. A point made by Japanese interviewees in both 2000 and 2004.

38. See "Clinton Publicly Reiterates U.S. 'Three No's' Principles on Taiwan," www.china-embassy.org/eng/zmgx/zysj/kldfh/t36241.htm (accessed 3 October 2005).

39. See Allen S. Whiting, "China's Japan Policy and Domestic Politics," in *Japan and China: Rivalry or Cooperation in East Asia?* ed. Peter Drysdale and Dong Dong

Zhang (Canberra: Australia-Japan Research Centre, 2000), 19–22. If anything, the depth of feeling in the 1990s seemed to exceed that outlined in the careful account in Whiting, *China Eyes Japan*, 66–79.

40. Osaki Yuji, "China and Japan in Pacific Asia," in *Challenges for China-Japan Cooperation*, ed. Kokubun, citing *Zhongguo Qingnian Bao* (China Youth Daily), 6 December 1996, and *Asahi Shimbun*, 9 June 1997.

41. Osaki Yuji, in *Challenges for China-Japan Cooperation*, ed. Kokubun, 91–92. The author points out that China nevertheless fared reasonably well in comparison to other countries and regions, such as the ASEAN and EU countries and South Korea.

42. The polls were conducted jointly by *Asahi Shimbun* and the Chinese Academy of Social Science in late August– mid September 2002. See the *Asahi Shimbun* web site, www.asahi.com/english/international/K2002092800228.html (accessed 28 September 2002).

43. Author's interviews in July and August 2000.

44. Wada Jun in *Challenges for China-Japan Cooperation*, ed. Kokubun, 178.

45. For the more liberal view, see Wu Xinbo, "U.S. Security Policy in Asia: Implications for China-U.S. Relations," *Contemporary Southeast Asia* 22 (2000): 479–97, and for a more conservative view, see Chong Zi, "Japan Seeks Bigger Military Role," *Beijing Review* 46, 7 (13 February 2003): 11–12.

46. These were evident in the 1970s. See Wolf Mendl, *Issues in Japan's China Policy* (London: Macmillan, for Royal Institute of International Affairs, 1978), 99–102.

47. Tennichi Takahiko, "Debates on Japan's Foreign Policy," in *Challenges for China-Japan Cooperation*, ed. Kokubun, 84.

48. Joseph Kahn, "Chinese Nationalism: Protests Carry a Risk," *New York Times*, 15 April 2005.

49. "Chinese Premier Hits Back at Japan," BBC News, 12 April 2005.

50. Mure Dickie, "Beijing Bid to Contain anti-Japanese Protests," *Financial Times*, 15 April 2005.

51. Bennett Richardson, "Anti Japanese Protests May Signal Power Struggle," *Asia Times*, 3 May 2005.

52. Xiong Guangkai, "The New Security Concept Initiated by China," *International Security Studies*, no. 3 (2000): 1–5. For an evaluation, see my "Chinese Dilemmas in Thinking About a Regional Security Architecture," *Pacific Review* 16, 2 (2003): 189–206.

53. Tennichi Takahiko in *Challenges for China-Japan Cooperation*, ed. Kokubun, 77.

54. See Sun Yixi's briefing of 12 and 14 June 2001, *Beijing Review*, no. 26 (June 18, 2001): 10.

7 Reputation and the Security Dilemma

CHINA REACTS TO THE CHINA THREAT THEORY

Yong Deng

Introduction

The so-called "China threat theory" is essentially foreign attributions to China of a harmful, destabilizing, and even pernicious international reputation. Never before has the People's Republic of China (PRC) had to respond to such persistent denigrations of its international character. Since the mid 1990s, rebuttals of the idea that there is a China threat have permeated official rhetoric and the writings of academics and government-affiliated analysts in China. Concern about the China threat theory has motivated Beijing's foreign behavior, including its strategic choice, reactions to India's nuclear proliferation, and approach to international institutions, such as the World Trade Organization (WTO).[1] It has become a scholarly consensus that contemporary Chinese foreign policy has countered its negative reputation through a commitment to building a cooperative, responsible image in the international society.[2]

Allen Whiting's work suggests that replacing China's image as a "sick man of Asia" with that of a nation standing up to Western powers figured prominently in Mao's foreign policy decision-making. He has shown that Maoist China's calculus of deterrence was characterized by its willingness to pay disproportionate costs on the battlefield to achieve its political aims. Such a demonstrated resolve helped avert the escalation of the Indochina conflict to a full-scale war between China and the United States.[3] Similarly, in the field of international relations, how to establish a reputation for resolve and power is the central concern of state actors in realism and deterrence theory. From these perspectives, it is not immediately clear how refuting the China threat theory contributes to contemporary China's security.

Contemporary Chinese concern about the China threat theory is both important and puzzling. Yet, while there is plenty of literature that examines the origins of and debates about the security challenges posed by rising Chinese power,[4] no comparable effort has been made to explore Chinese reactions. This chapter seeks to fill that gap in the literature. To decipher Chinese sensitivity, I draw on the concept of security dilemma, but make two propositions dissimilar to the standard realist expositions. First, states rely on each other's reputed character to infer intentions and to determine treatment accordingly. The intensity of the security dilemma confronted by the individual state, therefore, varies depending on its social, political reputation and international status. Second, given the clear security stakes involved, the defamed state will be motivated and may succeed to legitimize its power by enhancing its international recognition and acceptance. Hence, there is no reason to believe that the security dilemma is ineluctable. In making these points, my concern is the international politics after the Cold War. In the world of American unipolarity and great power peace, a state's threat reputation leads to social derogation and out-group status, which in turn fuels its threat image. Intensifying threat perception maximizes the security dilemma. Security-conscious Chinese political elites quickly became aware of the security costs of foreign attribution of a dangerous quality to China's international character.

They issued the first official rebuttal in 1995, but trace the origins of the China threat theory to 1992 and earlier. Chinese interpretations lump together variegated negative views, propounded by nonstate actors as well as state actors in the West. For Beijing, even though India was once a principal concern, the three leading progenitors of China threat theory have consistently been the United States, Japan, and Taiwan. Similarly, other versions of the China threat help to project a destabilizing and aggressive image that risks justifying discrimination and motivating hostile balancing against China. These views reflect heightened uncertainties and anxieties about China's security environment and international status.

The security dilemma confronting Beijing will gain momentum if its threat image worsens and material capabilities grow simultaneously. To reverse that dynamic, China has countered the China threat theory by equating it with the mentality of Cold War–style power politics, on the one hand, and by reassuring the international community of China's peaceful intentions, on the other. While Beijing has taken measures to hedge against perceived threats, it also has cultivated legitimacy and acceptance from international institutions, neighboring countries, and other great powers. As a result, China threat theory has subsided in many quarters of the world, but Chinese analysts remain vigilant against its potent persistence. China's struggle to seek international recognition and escape the security dilemma continues.

The chapter first sketches out the conceptual framework on the nexus between reputation and the security dilemma. It then examines Chinese interpretations of the China threat theory. The third section probes the security self-assessment beneath the Chinese views. The fourth section out-lines China's rhetorical and policy responses. Then the chapter evaluates the strength of the reputation-security dilemma argument by comparing it with other alternative explanations. It further offers an assessment of the successes and challenges in Beijing's reputation diplomacy. The chapter con-cludes with brief thoughts on the role of reputation and deterrence in Chinese foreign policy and international relations.

Threat Reputation and the Security Dilemma

Mainstream realism and deterrence theory argue that establishing a reputation for power and resolve to carry out security commitments is paramount in a state's security policy. Typical of this view is Hans Mor-genthau's approach to "prestige." For him, a state's "policy of prestige" is about its "reputation for power," whose purpose "is to impress other na-tions with the power one's own nation actually possesses, or with the power it believes, or wants the other nations to believe, it possesses." The cardinal sin for policymakers is to "be satisfied with a reputation for power which is inferior to the actual power possessed," inasmuch as such a "negative pol-icy of prestige" invites foreign predation.[5]

Similarly, deterrence theory equates reputation with the credibility of a state's resolve to protect its national security interests.[6] For Thomas Schelling, a state's "reputation for action" "consisting of other countries' be-liefs (their leaders' beliefs, that is) about how the country can be expected to behave . . . is one of the few things worth fighting over."[7] Underscoring the security benefits of a tough reputation, neither Morgenthau nor Schelling has much to say about why China would be so terribly upset by the China threat theory. In fact, Schelling contends that "impetuosity, irrationality, and automaticity [sic]" boost deterrence.[8] In this vein, the negative costs of a tough image do not concern those scholars, preoccupied as they are with issues of power struggle and deterrence credibility.

Insofar as it can be used to illuminate the negative security consequences of states' threat perceptions, the notion of security dilemma may offer a ba-sis for understanding Chinese reactions to the China threat theory. Accord-ing to its proponents, the security dilemma is pervasive in the context of in-ternational anarchy in which states, uncertain of each other's intentions, are engaged in the worst-case security planning. They tend to view power and security as zero-sum and in relative terms. Hence a state's supposedly security-enhancing capabilities and behavior become threatening to other states, triggering responses in kind. Such a vicious action-reaction spiral leads to competitive armament and fierce power struggle.[9]

Security dilemma theorists attribute the perpetual source of state insecurity to the anarchic nature of international relations. Under anarchy, there is not much states can do to escape the security dilemma. For Kenneth Waltz, "states have to live with their security dilemma, which is produced not by their wills but by their situations. A dilemma cannot be solved; it can more or less readily be dealt with." And a robust mutual nuclear deterrence is the most states (i.e., great powers for Waltz) can do.[10] Indeed, the Soviet initiative of peaceful coexistence started in the mid 1950s was essentially an attempt to use nuclear deterrence as the "answer" to the USSR's security dilemma vis-à-vis the West.[11]

Based on a similar belief about the structural sources of the security dilemma, Robert Jervis laments: "The central theme of international relations is not evil but tragedy."[12] For him, the acuteness of a security dilemma is due to "the inability to recognize that one's own actions could be seen as menacing and the concomitant belief that the other's hostility can only be explained by its aggressiveness."[13] In other words, the security dilemma persists because anarchy blocks states' "learning" about the mechanics of the security dilemma. And even if states are aware of the danger of escalating mutual hostility, the structural imperative of anarchy is such that, in the words of John Mearsheimer, "little can be done to ameliorate the security dilemma as long as states operate in anarchy." For him, "This situation [of security dilemma–driven great power struggle], which no one consciously designed or intended, is generally tragic."[14]

Jervis does propose that the security dilemma can be alleviated when status quo–oriented states can be confident of the defensive nature of each other's security measures and of their own ability to neutralize any potential military threat. Charles Glaser introduces two additional variables, "greed" and "unit-level knowledge of the state's motives," arguing that states' motivational structure and mutual confidence in each other's intentions also determine the acuteness of the security dilemma they face.[15] These analytical variables have greatly enhanced our theoretical understanding of the key security dynamic in international relations. But at the practical level, defense and offense are notoriously difficult to differentiate. In an environment of mistrust and uncertainty, and when states do not agree on what constitutes each other's legitimate security interests, the offense-defense separation hardly matters. Similarly, it is often impossible to tell the "true" intentions of the states before they translate into action.

Ultimately, before open conflicts break out threat perception and mutual confidence are largely a judgment call. If, according to Jonathan Mercer, "A reputation is a judgment of someone's character (or disposition) that is then used to predict or explain future behavior,"[16] then one can reasonably postulate that states would draw inferences of a state's intentions based on its reputation and would react accordingly. Mercer's definition closely coincides with the standard definition of image by Allen Whiting in Chinese foreign policy studies as the "preconceived stereotype . . . derived from a selective interpretation of history, experience, and self-image." Studies of China's relations with the United States and Japan clearly demonstrate that reputation or preconceived image decisively shapes policy-making in all three capitals.[17]

Thus a state's reputation determines how other states judge its international character and gauge its intentions.[18] A threat reputation will spark hostile reactions and aggravate the security dilemma. According to Stephen Walt, "states that are *viewed* as aggressive are likely to provoke others to balance against them."[19] But what are the sources of threat perception? While they have a material basis, which is emphasized by Walt, threat perception and security dilemmas are ultimately a function of status politics based on mutual identification and categorization.

For our purposes here, a security dilemma exists when a self-perceived security-seeking state is confronted with other states that do not share its definition of security interests and take balancing measures against its power. The more acute the security dilemma, the greater the conflict of security interests.[20] Under certain circumstances, the costs of an unmitigated security dilemma are so unambiguously high that a state will have no difficulty grasping the worsening security dynamics it faces and will attempt to reverse them. For contemporary China, the prospect of confronting a hostile U.S.-led coalition is the worst kind of strategic nightmare. It should not take the security-conscious Chinese political elite long to anticipate and take action to forestall such an eventuality.

In this age of great power peace, a threat reputation would be particularly damaging to an aspiring great power's social standing, and hence to its security interests. After the Cold War, militarized conflict among advanced democratic powers is no longer contemplated or even imagined. A great power "security community" exists, which is distinguished by its members' shared commitment to peace among themselves and to management of global affairs at large.[21] A reputation as a threat would suggest violent Chinese ambitions vis-à-vis the established great power grouping and the international arrangement in which the new great power identity is embedded. Such an out-group status in turn reinforces a threat image and motivates hostile, discriminatory responses. As Jonathan Mercer observes, states tend to attribute the behavior of adversarial, out-group states to dispositional traits, thereby hardening the boundaries that separate "friends" and "enemies" in the first place.[22]

The empirical evidence from the democratic peace literature suggests a near-perfect correlation between social identification and threat perception.

Without shared identity, there is no democratic peace.[23] Liberal and constructivist theorists claim a robust effect of transnational group categorization on threat attribution. They posit that the relevance and intensity of realpolitik calculations in interstate relations depend on the status that states assign each other in terms of in-group–out-group differentiation. And the status effect is wholly consistent with the social psychology insights into group dynamics—attribution of a negative identity to the "other" affirms and magnifies the superior distinctiveness of the in-group identity. Intergroup prejudice explains the persistence of international conflict at both the interstate and transnational group levels.[24]

Despite the robust effect of social identification on threat image, any attempt to establish the direction of the causal arrow would hardly be conclusive. As Dale Copeland observes, group differentiation in international relations starts with some judgment of the character of a state, including threat assessment.[25] Emanuel Adler and Michael Barnett show how the highly integrated peaceful community of democratic states nurtures a collective group identity.[26] Henry Nau simply bases his state categories of enmity and amity toward the United States on the factor of militarized threat—democratic peace leads to shared democratic identity; security threats posed by "others" determine their outlier statuses.[27] Given the insurmountable difficulties in separating the two variables, it seems more fruitful to consider demarcation of group boundaries and threat imputation as symbiotically interactive.[28]

What is clear is that a state's threat reputation hardens its hostile "other" status, which in turn could give rise to what Alexander Wendt dubs "no-holds-barred power politics" directed against it.[29] The China threat theory has not coalesced into an enemy image in the minds of the public and elites in the United States, Japan, or elsewhere. But this discourse, if not countered, could intensify to cause irreparable damage to China's international status and translate into an insurmountable security dilemma. These considerations explain Beijing's ultrasensitivity and aversion to the China threat theory.

"The China Threat Chorus": Chinese Interpretations

Three Chinese versions have been advanced as to the precise timing and genesis of the China threat theory. A *Beijing Review* article attributes its origin to an August 1990 article by a professor at Japan's National Defense Academy.[30] Another account comes from Xu Xin, president of the China Institute for International Strategic Studies and former deputy chief of staff of the People's Liberation Army (PLA). According to Xu, at a Heritage

Foundation symposium on 25 August 1992, the U.S. assistant secretary of defense blamed China for sparking an arms race in the Asia-Pacific region. The notion of a China threat was magnified in the following month by the former U.S. ambassador to China, James Lilley, in Hong Kong, where he openly criticized China's military expansion.[31]

The official version, commonly accepted by Chinese analysts, dates the China threat theory from the end of 1992.[32] A confluence of factors is said to explain its rise. Deng Xiaoping's "Southern Tour" resuscitated China's market reform, leading to the economic rise of a unified China, which lent credence to the fear of China's strength in lieu of the commonplace prognosis of an imminent "China collapse" in the aftermath of the cataclysmic events of 1989. In February that year, China's legislature, the National People's Congress, passed a law that reaffirmed in particular China's territorial claims to the South China Sea Islands. Meanwhile, the United States was contemplating the sale of F-16 fighter jets to Taiwan, and Japan was on the verge of passing a bill that would allow its Self-Defense Forces to participate in UN peacekeeping operations. Both the United States and Japan used China's military threat to achieve their ulterior motives.

The China threat theory has unfolded along both security and economic lines. On the security front, the theory focuses on China's military buildups, irresponsible arms sales, and uncompromising approach to contested territorial claims. A dangerous Chinese expansionism has manifested itself in power, intentions, and behavior, it is argued, and the aggregate material power accruing from the phenomenal growth of the Chinese economy is likely to lead to greater military prowess and aggressive foreign behavior. Moreover, China's economic growth alone means that China will outcompete other countries in areas where it enjoys comparative advantage, particularly in labor-intensive manufacturing industries, and absorb much foreign direct investment that would otherwise go elsewhere. China's growth will thus be attained at the expense of its economic partners. Its mercantilist trade policy will undermine the international liberal economic regimes. And China's surging demand for natural resources also adds fuel to international concerns.

Table 7.1 shows that while security and economic threats are consistent themes, the China threat theory has taken on various other forms, with a multitude of progenitors in Chinese interpretations. The United States, Taiwan, and increasingly Japan represent the most consistent sources of China threat theory. The propagators there fabricated the idea of a China threat to bolster a hostile containment policy toward China, to justify interferences in China's domestic affairs, including Taiwan, to maintain their hegemonic security structure in the Asia-Pacific, and to increase their own military expenditures and enhance their overall defense capabilities. Chinese official

TABLE 7.1
Chinese interpretations of the China threat theory

Variant	Date of Origin (approx.)	Sources	Description
China threat theory	1992–	United States, Japan, Taiwan	China is regarded as a military and economic threat. The rise of these views officially marked the beginning of the most pernicious and persistent China threat theory. The three parties have since led the international smear campaign against China. South Korea was also a progenitor, but has since seen these views die away there.
Japan's China threat theory	1990?–	Japan	Japan has been a main propagator of the China threat theory to keep China down, stoke its own nationalism, and divert international attention from its motivations of remilitarization and lack of remorse for its wartime past.
India's China threat theory	1998–2003	India	India cited the China threat to justify its nuclear tests and non–status quo political and military ambitions.
Cultural sources of China threat	1993–95	Samuel Huntington, United States	Harvard political scientist Huntington's "clash of civilizations" thesis singles out Confucianist China as a threat to the West.
China's food crisis and energy shortage	1995, 2004–5	Lester Brown, United States, et al.	Brown, director of WorldWatch Institute, contended that China couldn't feed its vast population. China's food shortage was bound to trigger a global food crisis. Others argued that China's growing energy demand would motivate Beijing's aggressive policy, particularly toward the South China Sea. The concerns about China's insatiable demand for natural resources were revived in 2004–5.
Greater China superpower	1994–97	Japan, Southeast Asia	The growing economic integration of coastal China, Hong Kong, Taiwan, and overseas Chinese communities was creating a domineering Chinese entity in Asia.
Aggressive Chinese nationalism	1995–	United States, Japan, et al.	Chinese nationalism has led to political conservatism at home and aggressive policy abroad. Rising nationalism has translated into Beijing's military threat to Taiwan, toughening position on Japan over the Diaoyu Islands dispute, and growing anti-American sentiments.
China doesn't matter	1999	Gerald Segal, United States– United Kingdom	Segal argued that China does not deserve great power status and that other great powers need not be accommodative of China's interests.

TABLE 7.1   (*continued*)

Variant	Date of Origin (approx.)	Sources	Description
China's economic threat	2001–	United States, Japan, South Korea, Southeast Asia, and elsewhere	After China's WTO accession, some Asian countries blamed their own economic woes on China's competition. Economic interdependence with China has since lessened their concern. But fear of Chinese growth at the expense of other economies has persisted across the world.
Rising Chinese power, rising Chinese threat	2001	John Mearsheimer, United States	Mearsheimer, a University of Chicago professor, singled out China as the next great power, whose rise is bound to trigger a dangerously destabilizing power transition.
"China collapse theory"	2001–2	Individuals in the West	This represents a new twist to China threat theory, predicting imminent collapse of the Chinese economy and political system.

analysts are particularly concerned about the origins of the China threat theory from the United States. Reflecting hostilities and bias, they argue, various aspects of American China threat theory smear China's image, denigrate the Chinese political system, overstate China's strengths, and assign irresponsible, destabilizing motives to Chinese external behavior.

In the Chinese view, Japan is another highly enthusiastic peddler of the most pernicious brand of China threat theory. As discussed earlier, one Chinese account attributes the origin of the theory to Japan in 1990. Another Chinese author even suggests that the China threat theory was first floated in Japan as early as 1984. Japan's anti-China theme has varied widely, encompassing just about all the concerns about China, including the nuclear, economic, "greater super China," and military threats it represents. Chinese rebuttal directed against Japan took on added vigor in the mid 1990s. Since then, Japan's China threat theory has evolved from being one of the main irritants in Sino-Japanese relations to becoming the overriding Chinese concern vis-à-vis Japan.

India was once a leading originator of the China threat theory. India first became a main progenitor around the time when it detonated nuclear weapons in May 1998. Indian Prime Minister Shri Atal Bihari Vajpayee wrote a letter on 11 May to U.S. President Bill Clinton citing China's nuclear arsenal and the 1962 Sino-Indian war to justify New Delhi's acquisition of nuclear weapons. The most prominent actor in India was its defense minister, George Fernandes, who openly discussed the China threat before and after the nuclear tests.[33] Three years later, Fernandes's remarks ignited another round of Chinese rebuttal, which underscored India's use of the China threat as a "shield" to justify its aggressive arms purchases, expanded missile programs, and great power ambition.[34] But the Indian brand of China threat theory proved ephemeral and has withered remarkably since 2003.

While the United States and Japan have been most responsible for spreading the fear of China, pro-independence advocates in Taiwan have been equally enthusiastic in magnifying the China threat to advance their causes. Most dramatically, President Chen Shui-bian attempted to equate Beijing's military threat with terrorism in the aftermath of the events of 11 September 2001.[35] Other sub-state actors and even individuals in the West have also been singled out as abetting the China threat theory from various perspectives. John Mearsheimer's restatement of a hardcore power politics theory in 2001 reinforces the view about the inevitable military threat a growing Chinese power poses to the status quo powers.[36]

Chinese commentators also take note of the views that link Chinese history and contemporary nationalism to the China threat. In particular, the Harvard University political scientist Samuel Huntington's "clash of civilizations" thesis directed attention to the Confucianist culture as underlying China's military threat.[37] Similarly, legitimate Chinese patriotism and natural antipathy to Western interference were misrepresented by certain individuals as irrational, aggressive nationalism that could translate into anti-Americanism, hegemonic ambitions in Asia, and saber rattling toward Taiwan. The growing economic ties between China and the overseas Chinese communities were even cited as evidence of the malign emergent greater Chinese superpower.[38]

There is another strand of thinking that attributes the China threat to its weaknesses at home and abroad. *Who Will Feed China? Wake-Up Call for a Small Planet*, a 1995 book by Lester Brown, director of the Worldwatch Institute, based in Washington, D.C., contended, for example, that China's vast population threatened to overstrain the world's food supply. A related but more enduring theme has been a concern that China's insatiable demand for natural resources, energy, and living space may generate pressures for an aggressive foreign policy. Gerald Segal's 1999 article "Does China Matter?" in *Foreign Affairs* contended that China's political, economic, and military capabilities were miniscule on the world scale. Beijing should be treated accordingly, and the Western powers should not accommodate Beijing's interests based on an exaggerated estimation of China's international status.[39] Similarly, the "China collapse theory" that seriously questioned China's economic health and institutional viability in 2001–2 was interpreted as reflective of the same hostility and prejudice toward China as in the China threat theory.[40]

China Under Threat

From a Chinese perspective, the China threat theory is simply concocted by hostile forces seeking to threaten China. As such, Chinese interpretations reflect self-assessments of external threats to China's national security. As the preceding section shows, Chinese interpretations have lumped
together wide-ranging negative attributions from abroad that exaggerate
China's alleged non–status quo international impulse, destabilizing potential at home and abroad, and anachronistic worldview. They reflect an acute
sense of insecurity stemming from myriad sources of threat.

Clearly topping China's security concerns is its relationship with the
United States, which holds the keys to China's core national interests in preventing Taiwan's independence, maintaining domestic stability, promoting
economic development, ensuring a manageable international security environment, and ultimately achieving its overriding goal of "national rejuve-
nation." The utmost importance the Chinese elites attach to the United
States is dramatically captured by the prominent think tanker, former director of American Studies at the Chinese Academy of Social Science, Zi
Zhongyun, when she wrote in 1999 that U.S. hegemony "has included two
aspects—'letting those who are with it thrive and prosper,' and 'letting
those who are against it come to their doom' [*shunzhi zechang nizhi ze-
wang*]."[41] Other Chinese commentators may contend that she overstated
the U.S. power and Chinese constraints. But avoiding sustained confrontation with the United States has been the official policy, supported by mainstream Chinese analysts.[42] This has proven to be no easy task. For the PRC,
the unipolar U.S. power has become ever more concentrated and unre-
strained since the mid 1990s. Beijing finds both trends unsettling and frus-
trating as it struggles to define its place in the U.S.-led global order.[43] Thus,
as uncertainties and suspicion have persisted in the bilateral relationship,
Chinese leaders and mainstream analysts have been deeply concerned about
the U.S. threat perception vis-à-vis China.

For the PRC, India is a non–status quo power, insofar as it is deeply dissatisfied with its current international status and entertains great power
ambitions. What worried Chinese strategists most was when India openly
played up the China threat to achieve its political and military goals while
seeking to bandwagon with the United States.[44] Little wonder that the Chinese response to India's nuclear tests in May 1998 showed greater concern
over India's China threat theory than the weapons proliferation itself.
Beijing was specifically galvanized into a fierce reaction by Prime Minister
Vajpayee's letter of 11 May to President Clinton defending the tests and citing the Sino-Indian border conflict in 1962 and the nuclear threat represented
by China to justify Indian's nuclear program, which was made public in the

American media. "Although the Chinese side expressed understanding of India's need to carry out nuclear tests for its security needs, it could not understand why" India would use the China threat to achieve its nuclear ambitions, one leading Chinese India watcher wrote.[45] In addition to fiery rhetorical rebuttal, Beijing launched corresponding diplomatic counterattacks, including spearheading passage of a UN Security Council resolution and allying with the United States to compound denial of India's nuclear status with punitive international isolation.[46]

But mutual animosities diminished significantly after April 2003 when Indian Defense Minister Fernandes, the "number one peddler" of the Indian China threat theory, paid a high-profile visit to Beijing at the height of the SARS (severe acute respiratory syndrome) crisis. The improvement of the bilateral relationship further picked up after Prime Minister Vajpayee's week-long visit to China two months later. Mutual trust has since increased as the two Asian giants have quickly elevated their "cooperative partnership" to a forward-looking "strategic partnership" designed to avoid internecine rivalry.[47]

While India's China threat theory turned out to be manageable, the Japanese version has proved deep-rooted and baneful for the Chinese. Japan's hostility toward China was evident in that while remaining muted on other powers' nuclear testing, Japan "made the loudest noises" over China's limited nuclear tests in the first half of the 1990s. Through the end of the 1990s, Tokyo concocted a China threat, it was argued, as a pretext to increase its own armaments, dodge its historical past, and readjust its international strategy, which notably entailed a tightening of its security alliance with the United States and Japan's decision to join the regional theater missile defense (TMD) system.[48] After the summit between the North and South Korean leaders in June 2000, Japan started to fixate its threat perception on China and the Taiwan Strait. Japan's economic woes, combined with a long-standing unrepentant attitude with respect to its wartime behavior and rising nationalist efforts to abandon the pacific restraints placed on its military and international roles, it is argued, explain its renewed interest in the China threat theory.[49]

Japanese complaints about China's military threat to Taiwan were regarded as interference in Taiwan affairs, reflecting Tokyo's ulterior motives. Taiwan's uncertain role in regional TMD, combined with the new commitment by the United States and Japan to a joint response to "situations in areas surrounding Japan," as stipulated in the revised bilateral defense guidelines in 1997, heightened China's suspicions about the Japanese role. According to the guidelines, the nature and scope of the U.S.-Japan joint action were to be determined on a "situational" basis.[50] Objectively speaking, the attempt at revitalizing the U.S.-Japan alliance reflected a complex host of changes in the alliance itself, Japanese domestic politics, regional security dynamics, and international politics, and was initially prompted by the nuclear crisis on the Korean peninsula in 1993–94. Yet for Beijing, the timing of its conclusion suggested a linkage with the Taiwan crisis in 1995–96 and the alliance's anti-China nature.[51] Japanese refusal to exclude Taiwan from the situational considerations, Chinese pressures notwithstanding, only fueled Beijing's suspicions about Tokyo's motives. Thus, when Japan explicitly joined the United States in pledging to "encourage the peaceful resolution of issues concerning the Taiwan Strait through dialogue" on 19 February 2005, official Chinese observers considered the seemingly mild statement as marking a shift of Japanese policy toward actively using its alliance with the United States and the Taiwan issue to contain China.[52]

For Chinese official and academic commentators, the notion of a China threat is merely a pretext for Japan to remilitarize and to threaten China. "By disseminating these allegations, Japan hopes to divert the attention of the international community and lull the world into letting down its guard so it may quietly achieve its long-coveted goal of becoming a major political and military power."[53] The spread of the China threat theory is seen as being choreographed carefully in tandem with the steps Japan has taken to abandon its historical, constitutional, and international constraints on its military power. The China threat absolves Japan from its responsibility to deal with the war atrocities it committed between 1894 and 1945. It justifies reinterpretations and even possible amendment of Article 9 of the Japanese constitution to relax restrictions on the role of Japan's Self-Defense Forces. It provides a rationale for Japan to strengthen its high-tech military arsenals and even possibly develop nuclear weapons. Citing Japanese sources, one Chinese author claims that Japan "can produce nuclear weapons in seven days. And the nuclear fuel that Japan stores is enough to build 7,500 nuclear warheads."[54] With this technological readiness, all Japan needs to become nuclear-armed is a China threat theory to break through domestic opposition and international restraints.[55] The remarks of the then chairman of Japan's Liberal Democratic Party, Ichiro Ozawa, in April 2002 to the effect that Japan was readily able to develop nuclear weapons and should do so to counter Chinese military might were but another signal of Japan's growing domestic opposition to the country's long-standing "three no's policy" (no development, no possession, and no introduction) on nuclear weapons.[56] Having experienced India's linkage of the China threat to its nuclear tests in 1998, China has become ever more vigilant of any nuclear implications of Japan's China threat theory. Seen in this light, transplanting the China threat into Tokyo's Defense Guidelines released in December 2004 represented an ominous turn in Japan's China threat theory.[57]

Apart from concerns about the policy directions of the United States, Japan, and India, Beijing was also worried about the China threat echoes from all over the region, including Southeast Asia and Central Asia,[58] as these states may bandwagon with major powers to balance against China. The marketability of the notion of the China threat underscored the precarious nature of Beijing's relations with these countries and of its overall security environment.

China's interpretations do not limit China threat theory to the views associated with the state actors. Rather, they are much more expansive. Indeed, the chorus of anti-China voices ranges from views overstating Chinese strengths to views underscoring Chinese weaknesses. Express concerns about the rise of aggressive Chinese nationalism and the power of greater China are denounced, and so is Huntington's view that China represents the challenge of Confucianist civilization. Fears of China's increased economic competitiveness by neighboring countries are refuted, as are various personal views highlighting the flaws and frailties of the Chinese system. For Beijing, these unpalatable views may not directly lead to advocacy of a specific policy inimical to Chinese interests, but they nonetheless tarnish China's image, leading to China's political and psychological estrangement from its neighbors and other major powers. The Chinese responses have shown a keen awareness of the danger that the negative image of China as a threat might mobilize foreign public opinion in support of the isolation of and discrimination against China.

Chinese Responses: Rhetoric and Policy

China issued its first official rebuttal in 1995. Mainstream interpretations, however, trace the rise of the China threat theory to 1992. The lag reflected the policy elites' uncertainties about both the security implications and China's proper response. However, it did not take long before the Beijing leadership learned about the weighty costs of a negative image to China's vital interests. And China's security in the now seemingly enduring American unipolar world must entail a vigorous response to foreign imputation of a violent predisposition to China. The 1995–96 Taiwan crisis and Beijing's disputes with Manila over Mischief Island in the South China Sea in spring 1995 added credibility to the notion of a China threat. Beijing immediately responded by sending several high-ranking military and civilian leaders on foreign trips with the exclusive purpose of rebutting the China threat theory. Official media and academic writings chimed in to reinforce the government position. The themes of rebuttal vary widely.

As regards the notion of China's economic threat, Chinese responses boil down to the arguments that China is still a developing country and its growing competitiveness results from compliance with the market principles. In other words, blame the game, not the players.[59] On the security front, Chinese writers dismiss foreign conjectures about a China threat as a reflection of Cold War mentality, a trick analogous to "a thief crying 'Stop thief' [zeihan zhuozei]," played by those countries to hide their own ambitions while obstructing China's rise.

To defeat the China threat theory, leading strategic thinkers proposed the alternative idea of China's "peaceful rise" (heping jueqi) in late 2003.[60] Designed to provide a credible vision of a cooperative future in China's foreign relations, the concept was soon explicitly endorsed by top Chinese leaders and intensely studied by China's international relations scholars. However, the debate had died down by the summer of 2004, because the idea appeared increasingly to Beijing to be wishful thinking and counterproductive. The ongoing Taiwan crisis and power politics concerns vis-à-vis Japan and the United States quickly raised doubts about the wisdom of elevating the concept of a "peaceful rise" to strategic prominence.

At the substantive level, Chinese responses have focused on debunking the exaggeration of the PRC's material capabilities, misinterpretations of its intentions, and misunderstanding of its policy behavior. The arguments go that despite fast growth of its national power, China still ranks low among the major powers in comprehensive strength, with an even much lower per capita income. In terms of military power, in addition to the significant unilateral troop reduction, China falls far behind the United States in military expenditures and spends less than other powers such as Japan.[61] Chinese writers have debunked extrapolations of China's aggressive intentions from the country's growing power by highlighting its peaceful historical record, associated with the benevolent Confucianist culture, as well as its contemporary embrace of responsibility and interdependence. For them, the PRC's military modernization is purely for legitimate defensive needs. China's foreign policy behavior shows evidence of peaceful intentions, responsibility, and restraint, even on issues including Taiwan, the South China Sea, nuclear tests, and arms sales.[62]

Chinese commentators have devoted equal attention to views originating from nonstate actors and individuals in the West that do not lend themselves to direct policy prescriptions but are damaging to China's overall reputation in the international society. In dealing with these views, Chinese rebuttals were more forceful and showed considerably less interest in any pretense of dispassionate reasoning than their responses to notions of the security and economic threat posed by China associated with state actors. As such, Huntington's civilizational clash thesis, Brown's warning about China's food shortage, and the concerns about aggressive Chinese nationalism were attacked as simply reflective of Western "ignorance" and "bias." Other views objectionable to Beijing were categorized as "malicious belittling and slandering statements" by Western ill wishers.[63] Chinese authors from the conservative political camp even attributed these malign views to racism traceable to the imperialist "Yellow Peril" theory.[64]

Apart from rhetorical rebuttal, China has undertaken corresponding policy responses. Admittedly, the behavioral impact of the China threat theory is much harder to pin down. But analytical reasoning and empirical evidence clearly establish how China's fear of foreign attribution of a threat reputation has shaped its foreign orientations. As was discussed earlier, a threat reputation attached to China, if not countered, could lead to a U.S.-led containment coalition against it, imperiling its core security interests. For the security-conscious Chinese policy elites, it should quickly become clear that to effectively refute the China threat theory, behavioral adjustments must also be made.

The impact of China threat theory on Chinese foreign policy was evident in China's policy toward the WTO. According to the Chinese views, concern about a China threat was a major reason for the tortuous process of China's accession negotiations, particularly with the United States.[65] China's chief negotiator on China's WTO membership, Long Yongtu, repeatedly stated both before and after China's accession that whether the rise of China was viewed as an opportunity or a threat would determine China's international environment. In fact, it was Chinese Premier Zhu Rongji who first popularized the "China opportunity" idea during his visit to the United States in spring 1999.[66] Similarly, other official accounts also consider dispelling notions of a China threat as a major benefit of China's WTO membership.[67] A rationale for seeking China's opening and compliance with the rule-based trade organization was that it would replace China threat theory with China opportunity theory and heslp give the country a more responsible image.[68]

Similar concern to demonstrate positive contributions of China's rise to international security and prosperity has also driven China's broad strategic choices. Indeed, since the mid 1990s, the Chinese government has made vigorous efforts to deepen China's international interdependence, cultivate multilevel, omnidirectional partnerships, and embrace various forms of multilateralism.[69] It has been well documented that image concerns have contributed to China's progress in compliance with the international arms control and disarmament regimes.[70] Similar concern about social recognition as a responsible power was behind Beijing's constructive behavior in the 1997–98 Asian financial crisis, particularly in resisting pressure to devalue its national currency and in contributing to the rescue packages for the hardest-hit neighboring economies.[71] Overall, seeking legitimate power has fundamentally defined the motivational structure in Chinese foreign policy. Both the timing and substance of the systematic set of shifts in Chinese foreign policy suggest a clear linkage of its strategic choice to a concern over the China threat theory.

Escaping the Security Dilemma: Alternative
Explanations and Assessment

Why does China care so much about the China threat theory? One may speculate that China's ultrasensitivity about its less than honorable image may have to do with its self-conception as the paragon of virtues and benevolence in the historically Sinocentric East Asian order.[72] Indeed, Chinese commentators often point to Confucian China's benign history and culture to refute notions of a China threat. But beyond the assertions, there is simply no evidence in either Chinese writings or Western scholarship to establish the historical, cultural impact on contemporary China's preferences or abhorrence with regard to its international image.

Another explanation for the Chinese reactions may be found in the supposed domestic audience effect. Both Maoist and contemporary Chinese leaderships have manipulated ideas of foreign threats for popular mobilization in the interests of their domestic agendas and to shore up the regime's legitimacy.[73] In a similar vein, blaming China's security predicament on hostile foreigners helps divert popular attention away from serious problems in the painful domestic transition. According to this line of reasoning, to the extent that the China threat theory reflects myriad external hostilities, a persistent refutation of the theory perpetuates a sense of national insecurity, which the Beijing regime finds useful to focus the national purpose on maintaining social stability and economic growth. There is some evidence that such a calculation may figure in Beijing's reactions. For example, in his rebuttal, Li Ruihuan, then chairman of the Chinese People's Political Consultative Conference, drew on the bitter experience of a weak China's victimization by imperialist powers and quoted an old Chinese saying, "On hearing the calls of crickets, can you not plant crops?" to urge his domestic audience to "work wholeheartedly with undivided devotion" to build a strong China. In a similar vein, Lu Yuan of the Chinese Academy of Military Science compared the China threat theory to a "whetstone" that can "temper our national will" for great power status.[74] Indeed, there is no distinction in China threat theory over whether the barrage of "character assassinations" was directed against the communist Party-state or the Chinese nation. In Chinese responses, all these hostile foreign voices are lumped together under the rubric of "China threat theory." A vigorous refutation of the smear campaign against China clearly bears upon domestic legitimacy, insofar as it helps mobilize nationalist support for the government. Propaganda targeted at the domestic audience dictates rhetorical tactics to heighten the dangers to the Chinese nation in a perilous world.

With its ideological appeal in question, the CCP relies on Chinese nationalism, which entails negative affirmation by foreign hostile forces trying to keep China down *and* positive affirmation by the Party-state leading China to become strong, wealthy, and respected abroad. This means a highly controlled, carefully calibrated set of reactions to the unfriendly image-projections on China. In this sense, the government has good reasons to keep domestic attention on the stream of China threat theories from Japan, the United States, and Taiwan. However, strident nationalist rhetoric designed for domestic consumption is a far cry from China's foreign policy practices. The domestic legitimacy of the CCP party-state significantly overlaps with international legitimacy, insofar as China's economic modernization and great power recognition necessitate an overall supportive world. Unlike Maoist China where nationalism was mobilized to support aggressive foreign policies, contemporary China has to rein in anti-Western emotions and assuage the fear of China threat in its conduct of international relations. Thus, the regime-legitimating hypothesis has some validity, but it ultimately offers an incomplete explanation. One may also propose that the PRC plays up the China threat theory to paint itself as the innocent victim in international relations. This might have worked with Japan, whose war guilt has defined its China policy. But to the extent that the theory is about an aggressive Chinese image, its utility in putting other countries morally and politically on the defensive is questionable, especially as the PRC has grown so strong.

Thus a full explanation must also consider China's concern about international legitimacy and its fear of a dire security environment to which a threat reputation may lead. Specifically in this age of great power peace, a violent, revisionist reputation would lead to out-group status for China. Such a status escalates the spiral of mutual hostilities and hence the security dilemma. In dealing with out-group nations, in-group nations interpret power in terms of zero-sum logic, and they are likely to be ultrasensitive to power redistribution in favor of a member of the out-group. In contrast, among themselves, they view power as positive-sum, and hence are much less sensitive to power shifts within the group.

From the social categorization literature, we know that the out-group is always the target of negative stereotyping.[75] It follows that China's out-group status would likely lead to continued, selective use of information that reinforces a stereotypical threat image. Chinese reactions to China threat theory show a growing concern about the foreign tendency to impute aggressive intentions to China based on a negative judgment of the character of the Chinese state. A case in point is Li Ruihuan's contention that it is a mistake to view China's growing power as a threat, because "whether a person will harm other people will not depend on the size of his build or strength, but on his moral character and conduct."[76]

The negative image of China in the West has proven remarkably resistant to change. Chinese commentators are frustrated by what they believe to be an unfair and simplistic portrayal of China. They complain that the Western negative image neither appreciates their nation's struggle to balance the difficult tasks of reform, stability, and growth nor recognizes China's progress on both domestic and international fronts.[77] But if a major source of China's image is its less than favorable social position in the international order, it is hard to imagine how without significant status advancement China can qualitatively succeed in projecting a responsible, cooperative image in the West.

In the U.S.-led unipolar world, to be outside the great power peace group is to be disadvantaged in overall security interests. The status factor may also explain the validity of the asymmetry in states' mutual attribution of reputation. Just as social stratification is unequally structured in domestic society, so too are intergroup relations arranged in international hierarchy. As Alexander Wendt and Daniel Friedheim have argued, legitimate power rests on a corresponding hierarchy of reconfigured identities to make non-coerced compliance possible.[78] Due to the gap in both power and legitimacy, the dominant group enjoys greater credibility than the subordinate group in mutual imputation of negative images. Hence China threat theory is quite persistent, while China's counter theories about threats from the United States, Japan, and India have not sold well.

Specifically, Chinese commentary has identified three ways in which the China threat theory may adversely affect China's security: "One, creating political opinion to apply pressures upon China and to meddle in China's domestic affairs. . . . Two, distorting China's image and driving a wedge between China and its neighboring countries to limit China's development. Three, playing the trick of a thief crying 'Stop thief!' to divert public attention and to direct the spearhead at China to maintain their own hegemonic position."[79] What is particularly worrying to Beijing is the danger of the threat attribution delegitimizing China as an international actor. Such denigration would only intensify the fear of rising Chinese power, thereby emboldening the Taiwanese independence movement and sparking armament and alliance-making with the United States directed against China by its neighbors.

The war on global terrorism after the terrorist attacks on 11 September 2001 has helped deflate the China threat theory. A story relayed by Long Yongtu is rather telling in this regard. According to Long, in the morning of 11 September 2001, he was in tough negotiations in Europe with American trade representatives over "the last details of China's WTO accession." The American delegation abruptly left their afternoon meeting (European time) upon hearing the news about the terrorist attacks. Long and his Chinese colleagues feared that China's whole WTO deal might be in jeopardy. To their surprise, the American delegation returned the next day and all "the details hotly discussed at the last meeting" were quickly smoothed over. Long quoted the American representatives as saying: "At this critical moment, a rally of civilized countries is more needed."[80]

Chinese commentators took particular notice of the fact that President George W. Bush attended the unofficial summit meeting at the Asia-Pacific Economic Cooperation (APEC) forum in Shanghai in October 2001. More important, while in Shanghai, he referred to President Jiang Zemin as "the leader of a great nation." Chinese analysts invariably saw in the war on terrorism an opportunity to direct U.S. threat attention away from China and toward unconventional transnational threats.[81] While encouraged by signs that the United States is rethinking its strategic priorities, Chinese analysts are nonetheless skeptical and uncertain as to whether Washington has undertaken a complete reassessment of security threats to embrace China as a strategic partner rather than a potential rival. They continue to consider the U.S. threat perception vis-à-vis China as the root cause of the problems in Sino-American relations. They saw China threat theory reemerge, after only a brief respite, to encompass China's military power, unfair economic practices, policy toward Taiwan, and the EU attempt to lift the arms embargo on China.[82]

Concerted Chinese rhetorical and diplomatic response has, however, achieved important successes in allaying foreign hostilities. China threat theory has diminished overall in places, including notably Europe, Southeast Asia, India, South Korea, and Russia. But China has encountered failures in Japan, Taiwan, and the United States. Alexander Wendt contends that effective strategies of reassurance for a country surrounded by suspicion and fear must entail a wholesale embrace of genuine multilateralism, adoption of democracy (because democracies are seen as inherently more trustworthy than other polities), and "self-binding" or even "self-sacrificing" policy choices.[83] This is a tall order in international relations. With its spectacular growth in material power, the challenge is particularly great for China in its anti-China threat campaign.

Studies in social psychology suggest yet another alternative mechanism for building trust through cooperative pursuit of a commonly desired and only jointly attainable superordinate goal.[84] Such cooperation reduces intergroup rivalry and allows for the pursuit of absolute gains to prevail over considerations of relative gains. Chinese commentators took notice of the changes in the U.S. attitudes toward China resulting from the U.S.-led campaign against global terrorism. After 11 September 2001, China's foreign strategy placed an unprecedented premium on cooperative diplomacy over issues pertaining to interdependence, multilateralism, and transnational and nonconventional threats with a goal to secure increasing international recognition of its great power status.[85]

Conclusions: Reassessing Threat
in Chinese Foreign Policy

Studies of Maoist China's foreign policy have focused on Chinese fear of physical threats in the forms of foreign military attacks and infringement on territorial integrity.[86] Since the early 1990s, an eminently "unconventional" threat to China's security has been the persistent foreign attribution of a dangerously revisionist reputation. Beijing's reactions since the mid 1990s have been marked by an acute sensitivity to international uncertainties about China's intentions and awareness of the danger of an escalating security dilemma fueled by fear of rising Chinese power. In comparison to the past history of the People's Republic, China has shown greater attentiveness in reassuring others and greater responsiveness to others' reassurance in international relations.

The PRC's image-building efforts have overall abated the China threat theory. But the failures and major setbacks in its relations with the United States, Taiwan, and Japan suggest that a tortuous and uncertain path lies ahead in China's struggle to balance power and legitimacy in its foreign policy.

The conventional wisdom established in realist theory and deterrence literature in international relations is that the state's credible resolve to defend its core interests is essential for national security. Viewed in this light, China's ultrasensitivity and wholesale rejection of the China threat theory is puzzling. To the extent that the China threat theory has a direct bearing on China's "general reputation,"[87] it is not clear how Beijing's reactions contribute to the credibility of its policy of deterrence vis-à-vis Taiwanese independence and beyond. What they demonstrate is the role of deterrence and a set of determinants in the use of force in contemporary Chinese foreign policy that do not conform to the patterns set in Maoist China or mainstream realist propositions. The power of China threat theory suggests that the issues of international legitimacy and social reputation deserve careful scholarly inquiry in studies of Chinese foreign policy, great power politics, and international relations.

Notes

I am most grateful to Iain Johnston, Bob Ross, and Allen Whiting for incisive written comments on earlier drafts of the paper. Tom Christensen, John Garver, Peter Gries, Margaret Pearson, Lucian Pye, and other participants at the Harvard conference where the paper was first presented, as well as the anonymous reviewers, also offered helpful comments. For financial support for this research, I thank the Naval Academy Research Council.

1. Avery Goldstein, "The Diplomatic Face of China's Grand Strategy: A Rising Power's Emerging Choice," *China Quarterly*, no. 168 (December 2001): 835–64; John W. Garver, "The Restoration of Sino-Indian Comity Following India's Nuclear Tests," ibid.: 865–89; Susan Shirk, "One-Sided Rivalry: China's Perceptions and Policies Toward India," in *The India-China Relationship: What the United States Needs to Know*, ed. Francine R. Frankel and Harry Harding (New York: Columbia University Press, 2004), 75–100.

2. Alastair Iain Johnston, "International Structures and Chinese Foreign Policy," in *China and the World: Chinese Foreign Policy Faces the New Millennium*, ed. Samuel S. Kim (Boulder, Colo.: Westview Press, 1998); Johnston and Paul Evans, "China's Engagement in International Security Institutions," in *Engaging China: Management of an Emerging Power*, ed. Alastair Iain Johnston and Robert Ross (London: Routledge, 1999), 235–72; Michael D. Swaine and Alastair Iain Johnston, "China and Arms Control Institutions," in *China Joins the World: Progress and Prospects*, ed. Elizabeth Economy and Michel Oksenberg (New York: Council on Foreign Relations Press, 1999), ch. 3; Rosemary Foot, "Chinese Power and the Idea of a Responsible Power," *China Journal*, no. 45 (January 2001): 1–19; Hongying Wang, "Multilateralism in Chinese Foreign Policy: The Limits of Socialization," *Asian Survey* 41, 3 (May–June 2000): 475–91.

3. See Allen S. Whiting, *China Crosses the Yalu: The Decision to Enter the Korean War* (1960; Stanford: Stanford University Press, 1968); id., *The Chinese Calculus of Deterrence: India and Indochina* (Ann Arbor: University of Michigan Press, 1975); and id., "China's Use of Force, 1950–1996, and Taiwan," *International Security* 26, 2 (Fall 2001): 103–31.

4. See, e.g., Denny Roy, "The 'China Threat' Issue: Major Arguments," *Asian Survey* 36 (August 1996): 758–71; Avery Goldstein, "Great Expectations: Interpreting China's Arrival," *International Security* 22, 3 (Winter 1997–98): 36–73.

5. Hans Morgenthau, *Politics Among Nations: The Struggle for Power*, 4th ed. (New York: Knopf, 1967), ch. 6; quotations from pp. 76, 70, 80. Robert Gilpin makes similar points in his *War and Change in World Politics* (New York: Cambridge University Press, 1981), 31–33.

6. See Paul Huth, "Reputations and Deterrence: A Theoretical and Empirical Assessment," *Security Studies* 7, 1 (Autumn 1997): 75–78. For critical reviews of the deterrence literature, see id., "Reputations and Deterrence," ibid.: 72–99; Jonathan Mercer, *Reputation in International Relations* (Ithaca, N.Y.: Cornell University Press, 1996), ch. 1; Dale Copeland, "Do Reputations Matter?" *Security Studies* 7, 1 (Autumn 1997): 33–71.

7. Thomas C. Schelling, *Arms and Influence* (New Haven, Conn.: Yale University Press, 1966), 124. For a similar definition of image, see Robert Jervis, *The Logic of Images in International Relations* (Princeton, N.J.: Princeton University Press, 1970), 5.

8. Schelling, *Arms and Influence*, 40.

9. Robert Jervis, *Perception and Misperception in International Politics* (Princeton, N.J.: Princeton University Press, 1976); id., "Cooperation Under the Security Dilemma," *World Politics* 30, 2 (January 1978): 167–214; and Charles L. Glaser,

"The Security Dilemma Revisited," ibid. 50, 1 (1997): 171–201. For applications of the security dilemma to East Asia, see Thomas J. Christensen, "China, the U.S.-Japan Alliance, and the Security Dilemma in East Asia," *International Security* 23, 4 (Spring 1999): 49–80, and Jennifer M. Lind and Thomas J. Christensen, "*Correspondence: Spirals, Security, and Stability in East Asia*," ibid. 24, 4 (Spring 2000): 190–200.

10. Kenneth Waltz, *Theory of International Politics* (New York: McGraw-Hill, 1979), 187.

11. Graham D. Vernon, "Controlled Conflict: Soviet Perceptions of Peaceful Coexistence," in *Soviet Perceptions of War and Peace*, ed. id. (Washington, D.C.: National Defense University Press, 1981), ch. 7; Adam B. Ulam, *Expansion and Coexistence: The History of Soviet Foreign Policy, 1917–1967* (New York: Praeger, 1968), 509–610.

12. Jervis, *Perception and Misperception*, 66.

13. Ibid., 75.

14. John Mearsheimer, *The Tragedy of Great Power Politics* (New York: Norton, 2001), 36, 3.

15. Glaser, "Security Dilemma Revisited."

16. Mercer, *Reputation in International Relations*, 6.

17. Allen S. Whiting, *China Eyes Japan* (Berkeley: University of California Press, 1989), quotation from p. 18; David Shambaugh, *Beautiful Imperialist: China Perceives America, 1972–1990* (Princeton, N.J.: Princeton University Press, 1991); Jianwei Wang, *Limited Adversaries: Post–Cold War Sino-American Mutual Images* (Hong Kong: Oxford University Press, 2000).

18. Peter J. Katzenstein, "Introduction: Alternative Perspectives on National Security," in *The Culture of National Security: Norms and Identity in World Politics*, ed. id. (New York: Columbia University Press, 1996), 14–17.

19. Stephen Walt, *The Origins of Alliances* (Ithaca, N.Y.: Cornell University Press, 1986), quotation from p. 25; emphasis added.

20. For a succinct argument that security "incompatibility" is driven by the security dilemma, see Jervis, *Perception and Misperception*, 75–76.

21. Robert Jervis, "Theories of War in an Era of Leading-Power Peace," *American Political Science Review* 96, 1 (March 2002): 1–14; Emanuel Adler and Michael Barnett, eds., *Security Communities* (Cambridge: Cambridge University Press, 1998); and Richard Rosecrance, ed., *The New Great Power Coalition* (Lanham, Md.: Rowman & Littlefield, 2001).

22. Mercer, *Reputation in International Relations*.

23. See, e.g., Jack Snyder, "Anarchy and Culture: Insights from the Anthropology of War," *International Organization* 56, 1 (Winter 2002): 36–38; Thomas Risse-Kappen, *Cooperation Among Democracies: The European Influence on U.S. Foreign Policy* (Princeton, N.J.: Princeton University Press, 1995), 32, 223; and Michael E. Brown, Sean Lynn-Jones, and Steven Miller, eds., *Debating the Democratic Peace* (Cambridge, Mass.: MIT Press, 1996).

24. For analyses focusing on transnational group politics, see John M. Owen IV, "Transnational Liberalism and U.S. Primacy," *International Security* 26, 3 (Winter 2002): 117–52; Bruce Cronin, *Community Under Anarchy: Transnational Identity*

and the Evolution of Cooperation (New York: Columbia University Press, 1999); and Christopher Hemmer and Peter Katzenstein, "Why Is There No NATO in Asia? Collective Identity, Regionalism, and the Origins of Multilateralism," *International Organization* 56, 3 (Summer 2002): 575–607. For state-level analyses, see Jonathan Mercer, "Anarchy and Identity," *International Organization* 49, 2 (Spring 1995): 229–52, and Alastair Iain Johnston, *Cultural Realism: Strategic Culture and Grand Strategy in Chinese History* (Princeton, N.J.: Princeton University Press, 1995). Mercer seeks to explain why the state as an in-group pursues relative gains, while Johnston draws on these social psychology insights to illuminate the role of symbolic strategic culture in Ming China.

25. Copeland, "Do Reputations Matter?" 55–61.

26. Adler and Barnett, *Security Communities*, 47–48 and passim.

27. Henry R. Nau, *At Home Abroad: Identity and Power in American Foreign Policy* (Ithaca, N.Y.: Cornell University Press, 2002).

28. See Robert Latham, *The Liberal Moment: Modernity, Security, and the Making of Postwar International Order* (New York: Columbia University Press, 1997), ch. 3 and passim.

29. Alexander Wendt, *Social Theory of International Politics* (Cambridge: Cambridge University Press, 1999), 262. See also Latham, *Liberal Moment*; Cronin, *Community Under Anarchy*.

30. Wang Zhongren, "'China Threat' Theory Groundless," *Beijing Review*, no. 40 (14–20 July 1997): 7–8, in Foreign Broadcast Information Service (hereafter cited as FBIS), FTS19970716000009.

31. Fang Zhi, "Who Threatens Who After All," *Liaowang*, n.d., in FBIS, 21 March 1996, FTS19960321000061.

32. Guan Cha Jia [Observer], "China's Development Is Beneficial to World Peace and Progress—Refuting the 'China Threat' Theory," *Renmin Ribao*, overseas edition, 22 December 1995, 1, 3, in FBIS, FTS1995122000064.

33. Yan Xuetong, "Why Has India Created a 'China Threat Theory,'" *Guangming Ribao* online, 19 May 1998, 3, in FBIS, FTS19980520000644; China Radio International in Mandarin to Northeast Asia, South Pacific, Hong Kong, Macao, and Southeast Asia, 0900 GMT, 21 May 1998, in FBIS, FTS19980521001220.

34. Wang Hui, "India's 'China Threat' Unfair," *China Daily* online, 14 March 2001, in FBIS, CPP20010314000063; Zhao Zhangyun, "Irresponsible Argument," *Renmin Ribao* online, 7 June 2001, 3, in FBIS, CPP20010607000038; Wang Jiaqing, "International Watch: A 'Shield' That Doesn't Hold Water and Can't Stand Refuting," *Jiefangjun Bao* online, 14 June 2001, 5, in FBIS, CPP20010614000020.

35. Liu Hong, "Taiwan Strait Observation: Who is Engaged in Military Terrorism?" *Beijing Renminwang* online, 18 September 2002, in FBIS, CPP200209 18000028; Kong Shengliang, "Chen Shui-bian's Political Show of 'UN Participation' Has Become a Laughing Stock of the International Community," *Renmin Ribao*, overseas ed., online, 16 September 2002, 5, in FBIS, CPP20020916000072.

36. Ren Yujun, "Always Looking For a Fight at Crucial Times, Creating an Enemy Threat," *Huanqiu Shibao* online, 4 September 2001, 1, in FBIS, CPP20010907000052.

37. Liang Lihua, "A Political Myth of Multiple Incarnations: The China Threat Theory," *Dangdai Sichao*, no. 2 (20 April 1998): 57–63, in FBIS, FTS199806020 01171. See also Wang Jisi, ed., *Wenming yu guoji zhengzhi* [Civilizations and international politics] (Shanghai: People's Press, 1995).

38. "James Lilley's Sorrow," *Renmin Ribao*, 1 February 1997, FBIS, FTS19970201000694; Yang Xuejun and Li Hanmei, "Key Factors Affecting Coming Japanese Diplomatic Strategies and Actions," *Zhanlue Yu Guanli*, no. 1 (February 1998): 17–23, in FBIS, FTS19980502000166.

39. Gu Ping, "What Is the Motive for Belittling China?" *Renmin Ribao*, 16 September 1999, 6, in FBIS, FTS 19991023001000.

40. Liu Xiaobiao, "From 'Threat Theory' to 'Collapse Theory,'" *Renmin Ribao* online, 11 June 2002, 3, in FBIS, CPP20020611000045.

41. Zi Zhongyun, "For the Maximum Interests of the Nation, for the Long-term Welfare of the People," *Taipingyang Xuebao*, no. 21 (December 14, 1999): 10–15, in FBIS, CPP20000725000044, 6.

42. John Garver, "Sino-American Relations in 2001: The Difficult Accommodation of Two Great Powers," *International Journal* 57 (Spring 2002): 309, calls this Chinese view "the law of avoidance."

43. Yong Deng, "Hegemon on the Offensive: Chinese Perspectives of the U.S. Global Strategy," *Political Science Quarterly* 116, 3 (Fall 2001): 343–65.

44. Michael Pillsbury, *China Debates the Future Security Environment* (Washington, D.C.: National Defense University Press, 2000), ch. 3. On India, see John Garver, *The China-India-U.S. Triangle: Strategic Relations in the Post–Cold War Era* (Seattle: National Bureau of Asian Research, 2002).

45. Quoted in Garver, "Restoration of Sino-Indian Comity," 869.

46. Ibid.; Shirk, "One-Sided Rivalry"; Yan Xuetong, "Why Has India Created a 'China Threat' Theory," Beijing China Radio International in Mandarin to Northeast Asia, South Pacific, Hong Kong, Macao, and Southeast Asia, 21 May 1998, in FBIS, FTS19980521001220. For the broad context of Chinese reactions, see Ming Zhang, *China's Changing Nuclear Posture: Reactions to the South Asian Nuclear Tests* (Washington, D.C.: Carnegie Endowment for International Peace, 1999).

47. "Chinese Premier, Indian PM Hold Talks," *Renmin Ribao* online, http://english.people.com.cn/200306/23/eng20030623_118736.shtml (accessed 23 June 2003); Fang Zhou, "China, India Forming Strategic Ties," *China Daily*, 18 February 2005, www.chinadaily.com.cn/english/doc/2005-02/18/content_417242.htm (accessed 24 March 2005); "Longxiang gongwu" [The dragon and the elephant dancing together], http://news.sina.com.cn/c/2005-04-15/03536389989.shtml (accessed 19 April 2005).

48. Ji Yu, "Be More Vigilant Against Japanese Militarism," *Beijing Guofang*, 15 September 1996, in FBIS, FTS19966091500350. See also Da Jun, "True Threat Comes from Those Trumpeting 'China Threat,'" *Beijing Review*, 11–17 November 1996, 7–8; Yang Xuejun and Li Hanmei, "Key Factors Affecting Coming Japanese Diplomatic Strategies and Actions," *Zhanlue yu Guanli*, no. 1 (February 1998): 17–23, in FBIS, FTS19980502000166; Ni Feng, "Enhanced US-Japan Security Alliance: Cause for Concern," *Beijing Review* 40, 24 (16–22 June 1997): 7–8, in FBIS, FTS19970616000036.

49. Gu Ping, "New Pretext for Joining the TMD System," *Renmin Ribao* online, 4 August 2000, 6, in FBIS, CPP 20000804000053; "Japanese 'Dream of Military Power,'" *Liaowang*, no. 37 (11 September 2000): 28–29, in FBIS, CPP20000919000054; Tang Tianri, "Japan Seeks New Pretext to Expanding Military Forces," *Liaowang*, 16 July 2001, in FBIS, CPP20010727000031; Sheng Xin, "What Intentions Does Japan Have in Raising Again the 'China Threat' Theory?" *Jiefangjun Bao* online, in Chinese, July 2001, 5, in FBIS, CPP20010723000057.

50. For the complete version of the guidelines, see Michael J. Green and Patrick Cronin, eds., *The U.S.-Japan Alliance: Past, Present, and Future* (New York: Council on Foreign Relations Press, 1999), app. 3, 333–45. For a comprehensive review of Chinese concerns over the new U.S.-Japanese alliance, see Banning Garrett and Bonnie Glaser, "Chinese Apprehensions About Revitalization of the U.S.-Japan Alliance," *Asian Survey* 37, 4 (April 1997): 383–402. For an in-depth assessment of the alliance's security implications, see Christensen, "China, the U.S.-Japan Alliance, and the Security Dilemma in East Asia."

51. Ni Feng, "Enhanced US-Japanese Security Alliance." Japanese accounts seem to support Chinese suspicion. See, e.g., Koji Murata, "Japan's Military Cooperation and Alliances in the Asia-Pacific Region," and Akio Watanabe, "The PRC-Japan Relationship: Heading for a Collision?" in *The Security Environment in the Asia-Pacific*, ed. Hung-Mao Tien and Tun-Jen Cheng (Armonk, N.Y.: M. E. Sharpe, 2000), chs. 4, 5. For an excellent account of the emerging dynamics in Sino-Japanese relations since the mid 1990s, see Michael J. Green, *Japan's Reluctant Realism: Foreign Policy Challenges in an Era of Uncertain Power* (New York: Palgrave, 2001), ch. 3. The objective, according to one key architect of the renewed U.S.-Japan alliance, was to strengthen the U.S. engagement policy toward China. See Joseph Nye Jr., *The Paradox of American Power* (New York: Oxford University Press, 2002), 22.

52. The full text of the "Joint Statement of the U.S.-Japan Security Consultative Committee" can be found at www.state.gov/r/pa/prs/ps/2005/42490.htm (accessed 3 October 2005). For Chinese reactions, see Xiu Chunping, "MeiRi zaixiang 'Taidu' fachu cuowu xinhao" [U.S., Japan send wrong signal to "Taiwan independence" yet again], *Renmin Ribao*, overseas ed., 3 March 2005; Weng Xiang, "US-Japan Joint Statement Has Nothing New, But Very Meaningful," *Zhongguo Qingnian Bao* online, 22 February 2005, in FBIS, CPP20050222000062.

53. Da Jun, "True Threat Comes from Those Trumpeting 'China Threat,'" 8.

54. Tang Tianri, "Japan Seeks New Pretext," 2.

55. Garrett and Glaser, "Chinese Apprehensions," 396–97.

56. Dong Guozheng, "Criticizing Ichiro Ozawa's 'Provocative Remark' on Nuclear Weapons," *Jiefangjun Bao* online, 14 April 2002, 4, in FBIS, CPP20020425000126.

57. Xinhua commentary, "Who Is Japan's New Defense Program Outline Intended to Defend Against?" 11 December 2004, in FBIS, CPP20041211000068; Ding Ying, "Who's Threatening Whom?" *Beijing Review*, 13 January 2005, in FBIS, CPP20050113000057.

58. Allen S. Whiting, "ASEAN Eyes China: The Security Dimension," *Asian Survey* 37, 4 (April 1997): 299–322; Xu Tao, "The Strategic Security Strategy of the

Central Asian Countries and China's Western Security Environment," *Zhanlue yu Guanli*, no. 4 (August 1999): 32–38, in FBIS, FTS19991027000867.

59. Dong Fureng, "On 'Theory of China Threat,'" *Hong Kong Ta Kung Pao* online, 2 February 2002, in FBIS, CPP20020202000017.

60. Song Niansheng, "Heping jueqi, Zhongguo fazhan zhilu" [Peaceful rise: China's road to development], *Huanqiu Shibao* [Global Times], 23 April 2004, 3, www.people.com.cn/GB/paper68/11864/1069451.html (accessed 3 October 2005).

61. Tian Xin, "China Threat Theory Collapses of Itself, as Military Spending of Both US and Japan Has Far Exceeded That of China," *Hong Kong Wen Wei Po*, 6 March 2002, A6, in FBIS, CPP20020306000090.

62. Guan Cha Jia, "China's Development Is Beneficial to World Peace and Progress"; Fang Zhi, "Who Threatens Whom After All?"; Wang Zhongren, "'China Threat' Theory Groundless"; commentary, *Jiefangjun Bao*, 21 January 2002, 5, in FBIS, CPP20020121000008.

63. Wang Zhongren, "'China Threat' Theory Groundless"; Gu Ping, "What Is the Motive for Belittling China?" 2.

64. Peng Huaidong, "From the 'Yellow Peril' to the 'China Threat," *Zhenli de Zhuiqiu*, 11 April 1997, in FBIS, FTS19970602001429.

65. Yue Yang, "China's Opportunity Theory," *Zhongguo Jingji Shibao* online, 12 April 1999, in FBIS, FTS19990422000265.

66. "The Rise of China—A Threat or an Opportunity," *People's Daily* online, at http://english.peopledaily.com.cn/200212/22/eng20021222_108925.shtml (accessed 3 October 2005).

67. See Gong Wen, "Let History Record the 15 Years—Memorandum on the Negotiations for China's WTO Entry," *Renmin Ribao* online, 11 November 2001, 2, in FBIS, CPP20011112000058; He Chong, "Major Significance of China Becoming a WTO Member," in *Hong Kong Zhongguo Tongxun She*, 11 November 2001, in FBIS, CPP20011111000086.

68. Guan Yuanzhi, "China Is Not Stopping Its Efforts to Rejoin the GATT and Face Up to the Asian Financial Crisis in 1998," *Zhongguo Gaige Bao*, 2 March 1998, 3, in FBIS, FTS19980416000855; Long Yongtu, "Join the World Trade Organization, Fuse into the International Community Mainstream," *Guoji Maoyi Wenti*, September 1999, 1–10, 30, in FBIS, FTS19990929000581; "Long Yongtu: Avoiding Disadvantages While Pursuing Advantages of Globalization," *Ji'nan Dazhong Ribao* online, 10 October 2001, in FBIS, CPP20011010000223; Sun Xiaosheng and Yu Jingzhong, "Long Yongtu Says China's Accession to the WTO Creates an Image of a Responsible Power," Beijing Xinhua Hong Kong Service, 23 May 2002, in FBIS, CPP20020524000074.

69. Goldstein, "Diplomatic Face of China's Grand Strategy." See also Yong Deng and Fei-ling Wang, eds., *China Rising: Power and Motivation in Chinese Foreign Policy* (Lanham, Md.: Rowman & Littlefield, 2005).

70. Swaine and Johnston, "China and Arms Control Institutions"; Bates Gill, "Two Steps Forward, One Step Back: The Dynamics of Chinese Nonproliferation and Arms Control," in *The Making of Chinese Foreign and Security Policy in the Era of Reform, 1978–2000*, ed. David M. Lampton (Stanford: Stanford University Press, 2001), ch. 9.

71. Thomas Moore and Dixia Yang, "Empowered and Restrained: Chinese Foreign Policy in the Age of Economic Interdependence," in *Making of Chinese Foreign and Security Policy*, ed. Lampton, ch. 7; Hongying Wang, "National Image Building and Chinese Foreign Policy," in *China Rising*, ed. Deng and Wang, 73–102.

72. Swaine and Johnston, "China and Arms Control Institutions," 134; Samuel Kim and Lowell Dittmer, "Whither China's Quest for National Identity," in *China's Quest for National Identity*, ed. id. (Ithaca, N.Y.: Cornell University Press, 1993), 281.

73. Thomas J. Christensen, *Useful Adversaries: Grand Strategy, Domestic Mobilization, and Sino-American Conflict, 1947–1958* (Princeton, N.J.: Princeton University Press, 1996); Alastair Iain Johnston, "Realism(s) and Chinese Security Policy," in *Unipolar Politics: Realism and State Strategies after the Cold War*, ed. Ethan Kapstein and Michael Mastanduno (New York: Columbia University Press, 1999), ch. 8.

74. Yang Guojun and Wang Dajun, "Li Ruihuan Comments on 'China Threat Theory,'" Xinhua Domestic Service, in Chinese, 13 December 1999, 2, in FBIS, FTS19991213001045; Luo Yuan, "Zhongguo xuyao lilian liuzhong daguo xintai" [China needs to cultivate six types of great power mentality], 21 October 2005, at http://news.xinhuanet.com/world/2005-10/21/content_3662080.htm (accessed 2 November 2005).

75. For evidence from social psychology and applications of group bias to international relations, see Eugene Burnstein, Mark Abboushi, and Shinobu Kitayama, "How the Mind Preserves the Image of the Enemy," in *Behavior, Culture, and Conflict in World Politics*, ed. William Zimmerman and Harold K. Jacobson (Ann Arbor: University of Michigan Press, 1993), 197–229; Mercer, *Reputation in International Relations*, esp. ch. 2.

76. Yang Guojun and Wang Dajun, "Li Ruihuan Comments on 'China Threat Theory.'"

77. Jia Qingguo, "Frustrations and Hopes: Chinese Perceptions of the Engagement Policy Debate in the U.S.," *Journal of Contemporary China*, no. 27 (2001): 321–30; Wu Xinbo, "To Be an Enlightened Superpower," *Washington Quarterly* 24, 3 (Summer 2001): 63–71.

78. Alexander Wendt and Daniel Friedheim, "Hierarchy Under Anarchy: Informal Empire and the East German State," *International Organization* 49, 4 (Autumn 1995): 689–721.

79. Guan Cha Jia, "China's Development Is Beneficial to World Peace and Progress," 5. See also Fang Zhi, "Who Threatens Whom After All?" 4.

80. Chiu Li-ben, Wang Chien-min, and Chi Shuo-ming, commentary, *Hong Kong Yazhou Zhoukan*, no. 41 (8 October 2001): 26–29, in FBIS, CPP20011010000088, 1–2; Duan Silin, "How Long Will Friendship Between China, United States Last This Time?" *Hong Kong Kuang Chiao Ching*, no. 350 (16 November 2001): 6–9, in FBIS, CPP20011116000061, 4–5.

81. Chen Peiyao, "Changes in the US Security Strategy and Adjustments of its China Policy," *Zhongguo Pinglun*, no. 51 (1 March 2002): 6–9, in FBIS, CPP20020307000097; "How to Look at US Strategic Models," *Renmin Ribao* online, 11 January 2002, 7, in FBIS, CPP20020111000046; Duan Silin, "How Long Will Friendship Between China, United States Last This Time?"; Zhang Tuosheng,

"What Will China Do About US Preemptive Action?" *Beijing Shijie Zhishi*, no. 16 (16 August 2002): 24–25, in FBIS, CPP20020906000167.

82. See, e.g., Yuan Peng, "'11 September's Incident and Sino-U.S. Relations,'" *Xiandai Guoji Guanxi*, 20 November 2001, 19–23, 63, in FBIS, CPP20011204000180; Liu Aicheng, "When Will the Cold War Mentality Find Its Resting Place?" *Renmin Ribao* online, 8 June 2004, 3, in FBIS, CPP20040608000036; Huang Qing, "Anyone Who Poses Threat Shall Bear Responsibility," *People's Daily* online, 2 March 2005, http://english.people.com.cn/200503/02/eng20050302_175287.html (accessed 25 March 2005).

83. Wendt, *Social Theory in International Politics*, 360–63.

84. William Kalkhoff and Christopher Barnum, "The Effects of Status-Organizing and Social Identity Processes on Patterns of Social Influence," *Social Psychology Quarterly* 63, 2 (2000): 101. See also Roger Brown, *Social Psychology*, 2d ed. (New York: Free Press, 1986), ch. 17; Burnstein et al., "How the Mind Preserves the Image of the Enemy."

85. See Yong Deng and Thomas G. Moore, "China Views Globalization: Towards a New Great Power Politics?" *Washington Quarterly* 27, 3 (Summer 2004): 117–26.

86. See, e.g., Melvin Gurtov and Byong-Moon Hwang, *China Under Threat: The Politics of Strategy and Diplomacy* (Baltimore: Johns Hopkins University Press, 1980).

87. On general reputation, see Jonathan Mercer, "Reputation and Rational Deterrence Theory," *Security Studies* 7, 1 (Autumn 1997): 100–113, and id., *Reputation in International Relations*, 36–42.

Part **Two**

CHINA AND GLOBALIZATION

8 *More Than Just Saying No*

CHINA'S EVOLVING APPROACH TO SOVEREIGNTY AND INTERVENTION SINCE TIANANMEN

Allen Carlson

In the spring of 1999, vocal Chinese opposition to the American-led NATO operation in Kosovo exposed a set of apparently widening differences between the People's Republic of China and other members of the international system (especially the United States) over the role of sovereignty in international politics, and the place of international intervention within the contemporary international system.[1] According to many Western observers, Beijing's stubbornness on these issues was indicative of its failure to become a more integrated and responsible member of international society.[2] China, by utilizing the rhetoric of nonintervention and protecting sovereignty, appeared to simply be saying "no" to humanitarian intervention and multilateral peacekeeping. Nonetheless, this conclusion has not been supported by a comprehensive empirical investigation into the main characteristics of the Chinese approach to sovereignty and intervention during the 1990s.[3] This chapter is intended to rectify that oversight. In so doing, it challenges much of the conventional wisdom about the intransigence of Beijing's approach to sovereignty and sheds new light on the increasingly complex relationship that has emerged during this period between China and the rest of the international system.

Since 1989, China's position on intervention seems to have been defined by a set of rigid, unyielding principles that strictly limit when Beijing will support the international community's right to intervene: for intervention to be legitimate, it must have UN authorization, take place at the invitation of the target state, and respect sovereignty; force is only to be used when all other options have proven ineffective.[4] The prominence of such principles in official Chinese rhetoric has led many observers to reach the premature conclusion that Beijing opposes all forms of intervention and is wedded to an antiquarian approach to sovereignty. In fact, since the early 1990s, the Chinese have consistently finessed the meaning of these principles in order to create a rhetorical space for China's acquiescence in various "Western"-sponsored UN operations. Moreover, during this period, Beijing did little to oppose multilateral peacekeeping, and its policies have evolved from staking out a position of reluctant participation to one of expanded involvement in peace-keeping and humanitarian intervention. Thus, although Beijing opposed the idea of intervention in principle, Chinese leaders also committed to a series of multilateral endeavors that gradually modified China's approach to peace-keeping and, by extension, sovereignty's role in international politics.

This development, however, was slow in coming. At the start of the 1990s, change in Beijing's stance was retarded by a combination of the clear-cut utility that an invocation of the principle of noninterference had for a gov-ernment facing pronounced challenges to the legitimacy of its rule, and the shadow that the past loss of sovereignty during the "century of humiliation" cast upon contemporary Chinese thinking about the norm.[5] Indeed, from Beijing's perspective, the only benefit to be gained from acquiescing to the wave of international interventions that took place in the early 1990s lay in the extent to which such moves might facilitate a breakout from post-Tiananmen diplomatic isolation, but this consideration proved to be sub-stantial enough to push the Chinese to use their seat in the UN Security Council to cooperate with U.S.-led multilateral initiatives.

While Chinese misgivings about an erosion of sovereignty's role in inter-national politics remained quite pronounced over the course of the decade, during this period two new forces also subtly reframed Chinese delibera-tions on intervention and sovereignty. First, new international norms in-volving intervention (and concurrently the necessity to sometimes trans-gress conventional sovereign boundaries for humanitarian reasons) gained an increasingly broad and deep acceptance among China's foreign policy elites.[6] This process, which Thomas Risse and Kathryn Sikkink have aptly labeled "norms diffusion," that has also been identified as "social learning" led to the emergence within China of more open, flexible interpretations of sovereignty's role in international politics.[7] It also, at least indirectly, opened new terrain in Beijing for the tentative acceptance of multilateral interven-tion. This development was then augmented, during the second half of the 1990s, by the advent of new concerns within China's foreign policy estab-lishment about China's international image and the perception that partic-ipating in humanitarian operations could demonstrate Beijing's willingness to play an increasingly responsible, benign, and cooperative role in interna-tional politics.

This chapter develops these arguments by examining the Chinese re-sponse to the rise of multilateral intervention since the early 1990s. In the first section, I briefly outline the main conceptual and analytical issues pertaining to the task of describing and explaining sovereignty's changing role within the contemporary international system. Section two then examines the way in which the Chinese position on the sovereignty-intervention dynamic changed from the start of the Gulf War through the late 1990s. The third section details the Chinese stance on Kosovo and East Timor, and the evolution of the Chinese approach to sovereignty through the fall of 2001. The fourth section briefly explores China's position on the U.S.-led "war on terrorism" and in Iraq, and the modest expansion of China's involvement in UN peacekeeping operations during this period. The conclusion discusses the implications of the claims made here for our understanding of the broader trajectory of China's rise.

Sovereignty and Intervention: Concepts, Causes, and the China Case

Before describing and explaining the manner in which China's approach to sovereignty and intervention has changed, it is necessary first to reflect briefly on the general relationship between sovereignty and intervention in international politics, and where the words and actions produced by individual states fit within that dynamic. It is also of value to consider the competing arguments put forward in the field of international studies to explain why individual states take particular positions on this nexus. Such considerations then also highlight the importance of more closely examining China's stance on these issues.

To begin with, sovereignty is one of the foundational organizing principles of contemporary international politics. In a general sense, it is comprised of "the recognition of a state's right to exercise final authority over its own affairs," and, as such, it creates a division between the internal affairs of each state and the concerns of the broader international system.[8] In contrast, intervention involves the projection of force by an outside actor, or actors, into the affairs of a sovereign state. Historically, violation of sovereign rights through intervention has been common. Indeed, it is quite obvious that stronger states have long interfered in the affairs of their weaker peers.[9]

Yet the rate at which intervention has occurred is not a constant. Over the past decade, multilateral intervention, especially operations authorized by the United Nations, has become an increasingly common phenomenon in international politics. For example, two-thirds of the fifty-six peacekeeping operations established since 1948 have come into being since 1991 (with thirteen under way in January 2004). In addition, despite annual fluctuations, the total number of peacekeeping personnel rose in a dramatic fashion, peaking in 1993 at over 80,000 military and civilian personnel deployed. Furthermore, the peacekeeping budget mushroomed, reaching U.S.$3 billion in 1995.[10]

At the same time, not all interventions are the same. During the 1990s, UN-authorized interventions moved beyond the limited confines of conventional peacekeeping operations to include peace-building and conflict-prevention activities. Alongside this development, the claim emerged that multilateral intervention has "as its purpose (or at least as one of its principal purposes) the relieving of grave human suffering."[11] Indeed, while humanitarian concerns have not always been the most prominent rationale for intervening since the early 1990s, they have seldom been absent from the rhetoric of those supporting any particular intervention, and they have always been part of the call for international action.

The determination of when this type of intervention is merited, and how it should proceed, has evolved out of a complex interaction between a wide array of actors within the international system. The United Nations itself, international nongovernmental organizations (such as Amnesty International), and the international media are all involved. However, the stance taken by the representatives of states (those intervening, intervened in, and less directly involved) has played the primary role in specifying the balance between sovereignty and intervention during this period.

The actions taken by each of the five permanent members of the UN's Security Council (the United States, Great Britain, France, Russia, and China) are of particular significance, because each of these states has veto power over any proposed UN-sanctioned peacekeeping operation. Beyond votes in the Security Council, each of the relevant parties can also provide a degree of material support for an operation once it has begun. In addition to such policy measures, the efforts of the leaders of each of the five permanent member states to justify (or, for that matter challenge) any given action are of particular importance. In the process of talking about intervention, politicians specify their understanding of sovereignty's role in the international system. At the same time, what foreign policy elites (rather than top leaders) in these states say to each other about both issues plays an important role in specifying the point of intersection between sovereignty and intervention, and under what conditions the former may trump the later, and also helps shape predominant interpretations of the sovereignty-intervention nexus.

Highlighting the importance of the role of actions and words in defining this dynamic draws on the existing work on peacekeeping and humanitarian operations,[12] while the broader literature on sovereignty's role in international politics contains a pair of contrasting claims about why states take particular stances on sovereignty and intervention. On the one hand, rationalist explanations posit that variation in any given state's stance is primarily the product of subtle shifts in the manner in which leaders attempt to realize fairly static interests. Thus, when heads of state are confronted with clearly defined material incentives for compromising sovereignty's role in international politics, they will act accordingly. For example, Stephen Krasner has argued that politicians use sovereignty when it suits their larger interests and disregard it when such interests change due to new incentives (an opportunity to benefit from participation in an international convention or contract) or lack of choice (as the subject of international coercion or imposition).[13] On the other hand, other scholars have argued that change is largely a result of the increasing salience of new boundary-transgressing normative structures and transnational identity constructs that have redefined the way in which elites think about the balance between sovereignty and intervention. This ideational argument hinges on the claim that sovereignty's foundational role in international politics was created and sustained through processes of social interaction between the actors (states) within the system (even as the structure of the system shaped both their interests and identities).[14]

Within the context of this general discussion, China's stance on sovereignty and intervention poses a particularly interesting case for students of international politics and Chinese foreign policy. On the first level, China's position as a permanent member of the Security Council makes it a key actor in determining the fate of any proposed UN peacekeeping mission. In addition, through the 1980s, the Chinese had staked out a particularly narrow interpretation of the international community's right to intervene, a stance predicated upon an interpretation of sovereignty as a virtually sacred right of states. Determining how much Beijing's position changed during the subsequent decade, and the causes underlying the shift (or lack thereof) in the Chinese approach, is then of central importance to understanding how and why the sovereignty-intervention dynamic evolved during this time. On the second level, gauging the extent of change in the Chinese position will provide a crucial yardstick for measuring how far China has been integrated into the international system since the late 1980s, and the degree to which China has been "socialized" into the international community during this period.

The Chinese Stance from 1990 to 1998: From
Limited Approval to Tentative Involvement
in Multilateral Intervention

Between 1989 and 1999, the Chinese government reluctantly began to accept the development of the new interventionist trend in international politics. The first move in this direction came during the prelude to the Gulf

War in 1990. At that time, Beijing supported the initial UN Security Council resolution (UN SC 660) condemning Iraq and demanding an Iraqi withdrawal from Kuwait.[15]

In the aftermath of this first post–Cold War military conflict, Samuel Kim astutely observed that China's initial acquiescence to UN-authorized action against Iraq should be viewed in relation to China's economic and political isolation following the suppression of student-led demonstrations in the spring of 1989.[16] The argument here was that while the international coalition against China had begun to fray before the onset of the Gulf crisis, China remained in a weak and vulnerable position within the international system in the summer of 1990. China's leaders then understood that supporting the fight against Iraq would have a broad set of political and economic benefits for China.

Evidence of such calculations can be seen in the Chinese leadership's relatively transparent wavering on the initial scope of Chinese backing for the war.[17] Indeed, while Beijing insisted that its support for UN SC 660 was based on underlying principles, and the United States argued that there was no linkage between the Chinese vote and Sino-U.S. relations, soon after the resolution was passed by the Security Council (with Chinese approval), the Bush administration took a series of measures to end U.S.-imposed sanctions on Beijing. In other words, China was, at least indirectly, rewarded for its support for a conflict that in principle it could very well have opposed.

Beijing's vote in the Security Council marked an important turning point in the Chinese stance on UN-authorized multilateral operations. However, subsequent Chinese behavior also quickly revealed the depth of Chinese misgivings about intervention. For example, after approving UN SC 660, China abstained on UN SC 678, the key resolution authorizing the use of all means necessary to force Iraq out of Kuwait. In explaining China's decision, China's foreign minister, Qian Qichen, urged that the United Nations use "great caution and avoid taking hasty actions on such a major question as authorizing some member states to take military actions against another member state." But he added that since the resolution drew on UN SC 660, "China will not cast a negative vote."[18] Beijing also abstained on a pair of resolutions (UN SC 687, 688) that created the mechanism for monitoring Iraqi weapons production and established the basis for a no-fly zone over northern and southern Iraq.

Chinese reserve stemmed from both instrumental calculus and ideational factors. Interest-based calculations were clearly evident in the way in which Beijing challenged the validity of the latter pair of Iraq-related resolutions, which it saw as directly undermining the principle of noninterference and, as such, indirectly contributing to the creation of a new, destabilizing international wave of self-determination and separatist movements. More specifically, Chinese foreign policy elites were worried that such trends might erode Beijing's own somewhat tenuous claims to regions and peoples that were pushing against the sovereign boundaries of the PRC. Thus, Wang Kehua, a Chinese Academy of Social Science (CASS) researcher insisted in an article that attacked Lee Teng-hui's apparent support for Taiwanese independence (which Wang argued drew on post–Cold War human rights and self-determination rhetoric), "The nation and sovereignty are inseparable, and state sovereignty is inseparable."[19] Or, as one international legal expert whose editorials were prominently featured in the Chinese media following Tiananmen frankly commented during a personal interview conducted in 1997, "You ask why we placed such emphasis on sovereignty after Tiananmen? Because it was our aim to prevent U.S. interference in Chinese affairs."[20]

These misgivings were not just self-interested, they also drew on the historical memory of past transgressions against China's sovereign rights and an unrelenting commitment to protect contemporary Chinese sovereignty. One prominent example of the way in which Chinese leaders viewed such issues through precisely this type of historical lens can be found in Deng Xiaoping's spring 1990 commentary on the ongoing Western-imposed sanctions China was facing. Deng noted, "I am a Chinese, and I am familiar with the history of aggression against China. When I heard that the seven Western countries, at their summit meeting, had decided to impose sanctions on China, my immediate association was to 1900, when the allied forces of the eight powers invaded China."[21] More specifically, as noted during a 1998 interview with an international relations scholar whose work is seen as being quite influential in foreign-policy-making circles China's historical loss of sovereignty "leads to a certain type of values that lead [the] Chinese to be more concerned with protecting sovereignty in calculating the relationship between national interest and sovereignty."[22]

During the following years, Beijing's half-hearted endorsement of the Gulf War, and the causes underlying it, came to define China's stance on intervention. However, the Chinese position was not static. Indeed, starting in the early 1990s, Beijing also committed a very limited, but expanding, number of personnel to supporting roles in select operations. The first indication of this development came via Chinese pledges to send observers to the UN Truce Supervision Organization (UNTSO) in 1990 and the Iraq-Kuwait Observation Mission (UNIKOM) in 1991. Subsequently, in a higher-profile policy measure, Beijing deployed a large number of observers to the UN Transitional Authority in Cambodia (UNTAC). This force consisted of 800 engineers, who worked on a series of large-scale infrastructure projects in the country.[23] In addition, China sent a group of 20 military observers to the UN mission in Mozambique (ONUMOZ) in 1993 and 1994, to assist with the monitoring of a cease-fire between warring factions, and also contributed a small force to the UN Mission in Liberia (UNOMIL) between 1993 and 1997.[24]

These deployments provided material support for the rhetorical position, and the voting record in the Security Council, that the Chinese were staking out. However, they took place within the context of the expression of increasingly high levels of skepticism in Beijing about the direction in which UN peacekeeping was headed. Thus, while China initially supported the 1992 resolution establishing the UN Protection Force (UNPROFOR) in the former Yugoslavia, it actively opposed the expansion of UNPROFOR's mandate during the ensuing period, especially the 1992 resolution that authorized the use of "all necessary means" for the provision of humanitarian aid in Bosnia. Yet, rather than utilizing its veto power in the Security Council, China simply abstained on the dozens of resolutions on the deteriorating situation in Bosnia and the former Yugoslavia proposed during the following years.

In the same vein, the Chinese first supported the Security Council's 1991–92 initiatives in Somalia. However, once the UN operation became bogged down in Mogadishu the following year, Beijing became increasingly critical of the mission's intrusive nature, and China abstained on each of the subsequent resolutions designed to provide multilateral forces in Somalia with a broader mandate. In addition, Beijing was critical of the limited UN actions proposed to deal with the 1993–94 humanitarian crisis in Rwanda. Thus, China abstained on the main resolution (UN SC 929) on Rwanda that was passed in 1994, emphasizing that the UN move had not garnered any indication of "co-operation and consent" from the parties involved in the conflict there.[25] Beijing also voiced opposition to the UN-authorized, U.S.-led operation in Haiti the same year. Indeed, in explaining his country's abstention on UN SC 940, the Chinese ambassador warned that the actions in Haiti might create a dangerous new precedent in international politics, one that violated basic UN principles and the norms of international law.[26]

In sum, through the mid 1990s, the official Chinese position on multilateral intervention was one of cautious acceptance and incremental change. China continued to oppose the expansion of the "West's" right to intervene in most internal crises, but its opposition was muted, and China participated in a limited fashion in a handful of UN-sponsored peacekeeping operations. At the same time, the initial surge of international support for humanitarian intervention that marked the first half of the decade seemed to crest and recede. This trend, coupled with Beijing's steps toward moderation, suggested that a lessening of differences between Chinese and "Western" policies on intervention was already well under way.

This development was in part fueled by the often overlooked fact that at this time a handful of influential Chinese foreign policy elites were beginning to articulate more flexible, open approaches to sovereignty and intervention than had previously been seen in China. To be sure, much Chinese analysis was simply designed to defend a starkly unyielding interpretation of sovereignty and attack the "West," and especially America, for interfering in other countries' internal affairs.[27] However, even as these charges were highlighted in China's official media, other analysts were cautiously challenging the accuracy of such rhetorical broadsides against intervention. This development was a product of the new normative trends in the "West" that favored intervention, because much of the discussion of these issues within China was driven by attempts to respond to claims being made by Western scholars and politicians about sovereign change. Moreover, while the ties between such analysis and specific policy decisions are difficult to trace, it is also clear that a number of those who advocated the development of more flexible approaches to sovereignty have gained important access to decision-makers and top leaders since the late 1990s.[28] In addition, as I show later in this chapter, such flexibility has, over time and to a limited extent, worked its way into China's official discourse on sovereignty and intervention.

Such views were first expressed in China's legal journals. An early example of this new thinking can be found in Xu Guojin's 1992 contribution to *Zhongguo Faxue* (Chinese Legal Studies) arguing that all states have indirect (*jianjie*) human rights obligations (against genocide, racism, and slavery), and in cases where a state violates such obligations, the international community has the right to act, and this cannot be construed as interfering in the target state's internal affairs.[29] In addition, Li Ming, a legal scholar at Peking University, argued in the same journal that while the UN Charter made it clear that the principle of noninterference was consistent with the protection of human rights, in regard to certain human rights problems, it was still "acceptable to get rid of" such a norm (*keyi paichu bu ganshe yuanze*).[30] The following year Li Buyun, a senior scholar at CASS's Human Rights Research Institute, observed that aspects of the contemporary international human rights system extended beyond domestic political concerns and ideological issues to encompass universally held "moral concepts" (*daode gainian*) and argued that monitoring human rights concerns had both "internal jurisdictional" (*guonei guanxia*) and "international jurisdictional" (*guoji guanxia*) aspects.[31]

By the mid 1990s, similar arguments began to find an outlet in the work of China's growing community of international relations experts. Flexibility about sovereignty and intervention was particularly prominent in the work of Wang Yizhou, a researcher at CASS's Institute of World

Economics and Politics. "In some situations, placing limitations on the practice of sovereignty is related to the unjust and unreasonable international
order, [and] very likely the result of Western countries attempting to develop
a narrow, selfish interest, but on the other hand, the conditions [*sisu*] on
sovereignty reflect the reality of the deepening of the trend toward global
interdependence and international society, reflecting a pressing need to solve
serious global issues," Wang contended.[32]

As important as Wang's guarded acknowledgement of change was, it was
soon surpassed by a round of even more open, flexible analysis, which even
more directly accepted the perceived rise of new humanitarian norms in the
"West." For example, in 1996, Wang Shuliang, a researcher at the Shanghai Academy of Social Science, argued that "the practice of sovereignty is
limited [*xianzhi*] by the protection of human rights."[33] Thus, Wang noted
that if a state failed in respect to human rights principles, it could expect to
be condemned by "international society," and in this case it would be "hard
to use the claim of noninterference" to fend off such criticism.[34] In 1998,
Zeng Lingliang took this argument much further in the pages of *Zhongguo
Faxue* by maintaining that after the end of the Cold War, international law
had increasingly permeated into and decreased the domain of state authority. Thus, it was increasingly clear that in international law, global interests
(*renlei de zhengti liyi*) took precedence over the interests of individual sovereign states. In addition, international humanitarian law had "restricted
[*xianzhi*] state sovereignty."[35]

While such direct admissions about the scope of sovereign change may
strike many observers as being outside the mainstream of Chinese thinking
about sovereignty and intervention, an extensive set of interviews I conducted in Beijing and Shanghai in 1997 and 1998 revealed that Zeng's more
flexible understanding of sovereignty had been broadly accepted within the
Chinese foreign policy community. Indeed, of the 109 individuals interviewed, well over half (58) accepted that at least a limited change had taken
place in sovereignty in the post–Cold War period.[36]

During this period, official Chinese human rights policies exhibited an
unprecedented level of flexibility. China's leaders pledged to sign the two
main human rights treaties and directly endorsed the international human
rights system. Indeed, in October 1998, while speaking to a conference
commemorating the fiftieth anniversary of the Universal Declaration of
Human Rights, Qian Qichen said: "We all recognize the universality of human rights and observe the same international norms on human rights; we
all recognize that no country's human rights situation is perfect, and that
all countries are confronted with a weighty task of further promoting and
protecting human rights."[37] While this statement was noteworthy, the lull
in UN-authorized peacekeeping activities during this period meant that

the Chinese position on these issues (at least in regard to supporting intervention) remained largely untested.

1999–2001: From Kosovo to East Timor and Beyond

In the early stages of the Kosovo conflict, Beijing maintained the same position of reluctant acquiescence that it had advanced in response to previous international crises in the 1990s. Thus, in March 1998, when the earliest of the major Security Council resolutions (UN SC 1160) on Kosovo was proposed, the Chinese delegation voiced its opposition to the motion but opted to abstain on the final vote rather than use its veto power. The Chinese explanation for this stance was firm but not particularly combative. For example, the official statement on the resolution simply noted that the Kosovo matter was "an internal affair" and urged the United Nations to proceed with "caution."[38]

During the following months, Chinese restraint began to unravel as the United States and its European allies became more deeply involved in Kosovo. The first indications of this shift were largely framed in terms of Chinese criticism of the leading role that the six-power Contact Group (France, Germany, Italy, Russia, Great Britain, and the United States) and the Organization for Security and Co-operation in Europe (OSCE) were playing in managing the conflict. Moreover, such warnings quickly became more pronounced through a series of increasingly direct Chinese statements in the Security Council and other UN forums.[39] Once the air war began in 1999, Chinese opposition became even more blunt. Such objections then turned to indignant outrage in May following the unintentional (although within China almost universally viewed as deliberate) NATO bombing of the Chinese embassy in Belgrade. This shift was vividly highlighted by the large-scale popular protests against the bombing that engulfed the U.S. embassy and consulates in China.

For many in the "West," the embassy demonstrations created an enduring image of a Chinese nation at odds with the rest of the international community on the issues of sovereignty and humanitarian intervention. However, only months after anti-U.S., anti-NATO protests paralyzed relations between China and the NATO states (especially the United States), Beijing played a quiet supportive role in facilitating humanitarian intervention in East Timor. Indeed, China voted in favor of both UN resolutions (1264, 1272) that authorized international intervention in the East Timor conflict and issued a number of official statements in support of these votes.[40] In addition, Beijing substantiated its support by deploying a small number of civilian police to the UNTAET mission in September 1999.

The positive Chinese assessment of the international handling of the East Timor crisis underscores the relative continuity in the Chinese position on intervention, despite the fact that Beijing had voiced such strong opposition to the Kosovo operation just months earlier. At the same time, this policy marked the ongoing evolution of Chinese positioning on intervention, in that the international response to the situation in East Timor did not entirely conform to the principled stance that Beijing had previously promoted. For example, the Indonesian "request" for international assistance was less than enthusiastic and was widely seen as the product of fairly intense pressure from the very same Western powers of which China had been so critical during the height of the Kosovo campaign. In addition, while the intervention in East Timor was much more of a UN operation than was Kosovo, it was also obvious that Australia played a central, if not unilateral, role in managing the international response.

As Beijing was enacting such policies, in the aftermath of Kosovo and East Timor, Western scholars began redoubling their efforts to come to terms with the normative, theoretical, and policy implications of humanitarian intervention and engaged in a series of debates over the implications of both actions for sovereignty's role in international politics. Within China during the immediate post-Kosovo period, however, there was little indication of such subtle deliberations and differences of opinion. For example, the NATO operations in Kosovo were universally derided as a form of interference (*ganshe*).[41] In addition, the Chinese discussion of the Balkan conflict was dominated, even before the embassy bombing, by a singular surge of fiercely critical analysis that sharply questioned the legitimacy of the Western concept of humanitarian intervention and staunchly defended the principle of state sovereignty. The tone and tenor of Chinese analysis became even more strident after the bombing. Thus, Fan Guoxiang, director of the China Society for Human Rights Studies and former Chinese ambassador and permanent representative to the United Nations in Geneva, cautioned, "In recent years, some politicians and scholars in big Western nations have put forward 'human rights over sovereignty,' [thus] deliberately misinterpreting, confusing and emptying out the basic concepts of human rights and sovereignty to suit the requirements of hegemony."[42]

Once again, the intransigent side of this type of analysis has tended to attract a great deal of attention in the international media and in secondary literature on Chinese foreign relations. It has generally been accepted as the sole face of the Chinese position on intervention and sovereignty. However, such conventional wisdom overlooks the fact that even within the highly critical analysis outlined above, virtually no scholar questioned the basic premise underlying the rise of multilateral intervention during the 1990s. Even the most trenchant Chinese analysts accepted that the United Nations occasionally has a right, indeed an obligation, to intervene in the affairs of some of its member states.

Into this slight opening in the Chinese discourse, more expansive interpretations of both sovereignty and intervention were introduced during the following years, claims that invariably drew upon the more extensive arguments about change that had been put forward by scholars and politicians in the "West." For example, during an internal workshop on sovereignty held in Hangzhou in the summer of 2001, debate centered on the extent to which sovereignty was changing, rather than whether or not any change was taking place at all.[43] In addition, a more malleable stance on sovereignty found its way into the major Chinese foreign policy journals in 2000 and the first half of 2001. Cheng Shuaihua, a scholar affiliated with Fudan University, argued that if a state "violates its international obligations," it is illegitimate for it to fall back on the claim of defending sovereignty to avoid censure.[44] In addition, Shi Yinhong, who is now at People's University and has gained the reputation of being one of China's top experts in international relations theory, added that international norms on human rights had come to "restrain and intervene" (*xianzhi yu ganyu*) the practice of sovereignty. Moreover, he argued that despite "some problems," this development constituted "an improvement in the level of morality within international politics."[45] Even more directly, Li Zhenguang, a graduate student at Peking University, contended: "The principle of sovereignty cannot be used to violate human rights," nor should it be used as an obstacle to refuse (*jujue*) international society's censure of massive human rights abuses.[46]

Chinese policy on multilateral operations during this period did not endorse such an expansive interpretation of the right to intervene but did reflect a general (albeit still guarded) acceptance in official circles of the general legitimacy of humanitarian intervention in the post–Cold War world order. Thus, in the fall of 2000 at the UN Security Council Summit Meeting, Chinese President Jiang Zemin said: "It is true that peacekeeping operations have contributed to international peace and security. But they are not a panacea."[47] Beijing also pledged to increase its support for the UN's Standby Arrangements System (SAS) and agreed to incrementally increase the level of its financial contributions to UN peacekeeping operations. Furthermore, between the fall of 2000 and the spring of 2001, China sent a limited number of observers to UN operations in Ethiopia (UNMEE), Bosnia (UNMIBH), and the Congo (MONUC) (Peacekeepers in Action).[48] Each of these policies expanded upon Beijing's original, limited approach to multilateral intervention. The former actions normalized Chinese support for peacekeeping by reinforcing inchoate institutional channels for such participation. The latter deployment of observers, while still falling far short of the commitments other UN member states were making to peacekeeping operations, also incrementally normalized Beijing's role in such activities, increasingly making the contribution of personnel more of a routine action, rather than an exceptional policy move. As a Chinese Defense White Paper in 2000 made clear, China was now an active participant in UN peace-keeping, even as Beijing continued to argue for placing relatively strict limits on when and where intervention could be considered legitimate.[49]

Intervention and Sovereignty after 9/11

In the immediate aftermath of the September 11 attacks on the United States, the focus of international peacekeeping and multilateral intervention shifted in a dramatic fashion. At this juncture, the United States placed a much higher emphasis on countering terrorism as the basis for intervening in other states' affairs. More recently, as seen in the lead-up to the war in Iraq, Washington began to underscore the need for the international community to take preemptive measures to defend against the proliferation of weapons of mass destruction (WMD). Although humanitarian concerns have not been extinguished by these developments, such trends have had a broad impact on the fragile norm of humanitarian intervention that has developed over the course of the past decade. In short, the war on terrorism now constitutes the main framework for the enactment of policies on and discourses about the sovereignty-intervention dynamic.

As was the case during the 1990s, China has once again emerged as a peripheral but significant player in this unfolding story. In the initial post-9/11 period, China gave rhetorical support to the U.S.-led war against terrorism. In addition, Beijing voted in favor of the two main Security Council resolutions (UN SC 1368, UN SC 1373) to include the United Nations in such a conflict. In doing so, despite murmurs about the dangers of American military encirclement of China, Beijing implicitly endorsed Washington's plan to use military means to topple the Taliban government of Afghanistan in reprisal for its support of Osama bin Laden. Beijing also is purported to have played a role in helping convince Pakistan, which had long maintained a close relationship with China, to support the U.S. war. Although the Chinese did not then grant the U.S. military the right to use Chinese airspace during the Afghan conflict, China did share intelligence information on terrorism with Washington (via a series of bilateral meetings). In addition, following the collapse of the Taliban, the Chinese pledged $150 million (over a five-year period) for the reconstruction of Afghanistan.[50]

As Beijing was taking these steps in the international arena, within China the response to the U.S.-led war against terrorism, more specifically

Washington's military campaign in Afghanistan, was somewhat divided. On the one hand, initial postings on popular Internet chat rooms, such as the *qiangguo luntan* (strong power forum) sponsored by *People's Daily*, portrayed the United States as the world's biggest terrorist threat and warned that Washington would use the fight against terrorism as a pretext for expanding American hegemony. On the other hand, despite such misgivings, most elites in Beijing argued that it was beneficial for China to work with the United States in supporting the war on terrorism and to accept the war in Afghanistan as an inevitable aspect of this new confrontation.

Interviews conducted in China during the winter of 2001–2 showed broad-based support in foreign policy circles for the conciliatory moves Beijing had made during the previous year (amid residual concerns about protecting sovereignty, and new worries about what post-9/11 international politics would look like). Moreover, virtually all those interviewed concurred that change was taking place in sovereignty's role in international politics. For example, a scholar at Peking University saw an emerging dilemma in the relationship between sovereignty and intervention that eluded simple categorization.[51] An academic at People's University added, "sovereignty is changing in the world community and this influence is felt [in China] through international and transnational institutions."[52] At the Chinese Institute of International Studies, a senior researcher also emphasized that China had been influenced by these developments and argued: "Specific sovereign rights in practice can be ceded to international organizations [*rangbu gei guoji zuzhi*]."[53]

An even more comprehensive understanding of how Chinese views of these issues were changing can be gained from a pair of conferences on sovereignty and intervention held in January 2002, attended by both Chinese and American scholars and co-sponsored by the National Committee on United States–China Relations, the China Reform Forum, and the Shanghai Institute of International Studies.[54] During these meetings, the Chinese participants placed a heavy emphasis on the continuing influence of the historical memory of the "century of humiliation" on China's contemporary stance on sovereignty and intervention. But no Chinese participant objected to the necessity of international involvement to secure human rights when they are under extreme threat.

The Chinese participants agreed that in cases of obviously failed states, and when confronted with humanitarian disasters, the international community has a right to intervene. Moreover, some argued that larger patterns of change had emerged within international politics. For example, Chu Shulong, a prominent specialist in Sino-U.S. relations from Tsinghua University, developed this idea in his paper for the 2002 Beijing International Intervention and State Sovereignty Conference, writing: "Globalization requires a softening of sovereignty and willingness to accept different levels of intervention to promote global regimes which benefit everybody."[55]

Some analysts even acknowledged that the mechanism for intervention became more diverse during the 1990s. They also hinted that while UN leadership in any operation is highly preferable, it is not always an essential attribute of a legitimate and acceptable case of intervention. Many of those who acknowledged such a development also took note of the increasing flexibility of the policies of China and other developing countries in an attempt to accommodate and contribute to emerging trends within the international system. This position was again given its clearest voice in Chu Shulong's contribution to the Beijing conference. He noted that, in a general sense, China's position is "in the period of transition because [of] the change in the world and China itself." He added that China's "returning to [the] international community weakens the traditional concept of national sovereignty and foreign intervention" and concluded that acceptance of such developments "is the global trend that nobody can resist."[56]

Additional unofficial analysis from the post-9/11 period revealed that this more flexible line had finally gained widespread acceptance. For example, even a scholar like Fan Guoxiang, who had previously argued strongly against intervention, now began to gingerly parse the differences between "Western human rights diplomacy" (*xifang renquan waijiao*) and "Western human rights theory" (*xifang renquan lilun*), and. while finding fault in the former, conceded the validity of a few points that had been made in the latter field.[57] At the same time, other analysts publicly advocated even looser interpretations of the sovereignty–human rights dynamic. Zhou Yongkun argued, for example, that sovereignty itself is a "special human right" (*teshu de renquan*), and that it is therefore imperative to realize that to indiscriminately abuse (*lanyong*) the principle of sovereignty to undermine, harm, or block the protection of other human rights is unjustified.[58]

All of these arguments are quite transparent variations on normative declarations by "Western" advocates of humanitarian intervention since the early 1990s. In short, Chinese claims grew out of "argumentative discourse" between elites in China and those in the West who had supported both the idea and practice of intervention.[59] This process included initial blanket Chinese refutations of such a norm and specific multilateral operations, selective interpretations of their meaning, and, finally, more extensive endorsements of their core tenets. As such, it constitutes indirect evidence of social learning.

This being said, Chinese analysis at this juncture also increasingly began to contain more direct reference to the benefits that might accrue to China from more actively participating in UN-authorized operations. While many analysts continued to underscore the potential dangers of multilateral intervention, an increasingly vocal minority argued that by taking a more flexible stance on humanitarian intervention, China could bolster its international image as a responsible power. For example, in 2002, the National Defense University professor Tang Yongshang was quite frank in this regard, arguing that making a more positive contribution to international peacekeeping was both a "responsibility that China should shoulder as a major power [daguo]" and in line with China's basic national interests.[60]

Official discussions of peacekeeping during this period reflected this analytical shift. A spring 2002 statement by the Ministry of Foreign Affairs proclaimed: "As a responsible member of the international community, China stands ready to develop coordination and cooperation with other countries in the field of non-traditional security issues."[61] Later in the year, a top Chinese representative to the United Nations, Zhang Yishan, stated: "China is willing to make its own contribution, together with other Member States, to strengthening the capacity of the United Nations for the prevention of armed conflicts."[62]

Beijing once more followed up on this rhetoric with concrete policy measures. It promised to establish a new training center for civilian police and made additional commitments to the UN's SAS mechanism.[63] Moreover, at the start of 2003, China committed a comparatively large force of engineers (175) to the ongoing UN operation in the Congo.[64] In addition, the Chinese also sent an even larger mission to Liberia. Indeed, the Liberia deployment was the largest Chinese commitment to a UN peacekeeping operation since sending observers to Cambodia in the early 1990s.[65] Perhaps of even greater significance was an action that China did not take; mainly, Beijing refrained from making a vocal stand against the U.S.-led war on Iraq. To be sure, unease about the implications of the impending conflict were pronounced in China, but in the end, the Chinese did not utilize their veto power in the Security Council to prevent the United Nations from partially authorizing this conflict (opposition largely came from Russia and France). Also, while Beijing took note of the failures of the initial attack on Iraq, the Chinese media reported on such difficulties in a relatively subdued manner. Moreover, even as the conflict has dragged on, official Chinese rhetoric has been fairly silent about the shortcomings of the American policy.

Conclusions

In sum, since the early 1990s, a series of multilateral international interventions have occurred, most of which were undertaken with UN Security Council authorization and justified by reference to new humanitarian norms. In the process of attempting to legitimize such operations, the supporters of intervention tended to reinforce, perhaps even create, the very norms to which they were referring. As a result of their efforts, new expectations about the international community's right to intervene grew, and the efficacy of utilizing sovereignty-based rhetoric to denigrate such operations and argue against international action declined.

When China's leaders did not actively move to oppose this development (for a limited set of largely self-interested reasons), they created space for the extension of such norms into the Chinese elite foreign policy community via limited discussions of the conditions under which intervention was justified. This is not to say that such normative forces dictated support for any given intervention in China, or for that matter among core supporters of such moves in the "West." Indeed, over the course of the 1990s, more immediate and pressing national interests repeatedly trumped them. However, over time, it is also apparent that new trends in the international arena eroded the normative obstacles that conventional sovereignty claims posed to intervention (in the name of preventing humanitarian crises and protecting human rights) and helped overcome Chinese reluctance to support multilateral peacekeeping.

The limited changes in Chinese positioning on sovereignty and intervention during this period are particularly interesting when considered with reference to three broader issues. First, the Chinese position on sovereignty and intervention has often been misunderstood. To be sure, Beijing has made its opposition to certain multilateral operations quite clear, and it has consistently proclaimed the sanctity of sovereignty and the centrality of the principle of nonintervention in contemporary international politics. However, China's stance entails much more than simply opposing intervention. Indeed, this chapter has shown that more often than not, Beijing has reluctantly acquiesced to international involvement in a humanitarian crisis, and in recent years, China has even begun to play a more active role in contributing to such operations. While the Chinese remain leery of intervention, they now also accept it as part of the post–Cold War world order. In this sense, China is no longer so much of an outlier when compared with other states in the international system. Indeed, the story of China's reluctant compromises told in this chapter could easily be retold with reference to a broad collection of other states. Nonetheless, China's position on these issues is also unique, because it is the sole permanent member of the UN Security Council that has cultivated a "Third World" and "developing state" identity.[66] Moreover, China's seat in the Security Council ensures that its voice (and vote) on intervention will be heard.

Second, the chapter speaks to the debate that has emerged in recent years over the degree to which China is being "socialized" into the international community through processes of adaptation and learning.[67] It suggests that even as China has accepted change, the perpetuation of collective memories about past violations of Chinese sovereignty, coupled with ongoing concerns about the fragility of Beijing's rule over China, has made Chinese acquiescence especially tenuous and contingent. In short, to the extent that we think of shifts in Chinese positioning with reference to socialization arguments, the "new learning" that is taking place has occurred within the context of earlier "lessons" that have made Chinese elites particularly sensitive about ceding any aspect of Chinese sovereignty.

Third, the explanation of Chinese behavior put forward here combines elements of the rationalist and ideationalist arguments that have been proposed in the general international studies literature about why states take particular positions on sovereignty and intervention. On the one hand, Chinese behavior has been informed by cost-benefit calculations, as would be expected by proponents of the rationalist argument, but Beijing's perception of Chinese interests was framed by both old ideas (involving the sanctity of sovereignty) and new norms (regarding the legitimacy of humanitarian intervention). On the other hand, ideas explain less of the story than typical ideationalist approaches to sovereignty have contended. International norms have mattered, but their influence was only felt through the prism of older, more deeply entrenched, and largely domestic normative constructs (the living historical memory of past transgressions of Chinese sovereignty) and was offset by more utilitarian considerations. As such, the chapter points to the merits of developing more eclectic explanations of Chinese foreign policy behavior.[68]

Notes

1. This chapter began as a monograph written for the National Committee on United States–China Relations. See Allen Carlson, *Protecting Sovereignty, Accepting Intervention: The Dilemma of Chinese Foreign Relations in the 1990s* (New York: National Committee on United States–China Relations, 2002), www.ncuscr .org/Publications/Full_Text_Booklet%20_Final_Format.pdf (accessed 5 October 2005), and it draws extensively on Allen Carlson, "Helping to Keep the Peace (Albeit Reluctantly): The Recent Chinese Approach to Sovereignty and Intervention," *Pacific Affairs* 77, 1 (Summer 2004): 9–28. I would like to thank Jan Berris, Iain Johnston, two anonymous reviewers of the *Pacific Affairs* article, and the participants in New Directions in the Study of Chinese Foreign Policy: A Conference in Honor of Allen S. Whiting, Harvard University, 7–9 November 2002, for their helpful comments on earlier drafts of this work.

2. See Mortimer Zuckerman, "What Does China Want?" *US News and World Report*, 7 June 1999, 2; Jasper Becker, "The Heart of Chinese Sovereignty," *South China Morning Post*, 12 June 1999, 17; James Srodes, "Anti-Americans of the World

Unite," *Spectator*, 10 July 1999, 16–17; and "Going to Ground," *New Republic*, 19 April 1999, 7.

3. For partial exceptions to this gap in the literature on the Chinese position on intervention, see M. Taylor Fravel, "China's Attitude Toward UN Peacekeeping Operations," *Asian Survey* 36 (November 1996): 1102–22; Jin-Dong Yuan, "Multilateral Intervention and State Sovereignty: Chinese Views on UN Peacekeeping Operations," *Political Science* 49 (1998): 275–95; and Bates Gill and James Reilly, "Sovereignty, Intervention and Peacekeeping: The View from Beijing," *Survival* 42 (Autumn 2000): 41–59. These articles focus primarily on Chinese behavior in the Security Council during the 1990s and as such are valuable resources; they do not, however, examine more recent events or the broader discussions about sovereignty and intervention that have emerged within China since the early post-Tiananmen period.

4. The articles by Fravel, Yuan, and Gill and Reilly cited in the preceding note emphasize various aspects of these principles.

5. The term "norm" is used in this chapter in a way that is consistent with the definition of such a concept as "a standard of appropriate behavior for actors with a given identity" in Martha Finnemore and Kathryn Sikkink, "International Norm Dynamics and Political Change," *International Organization* 4 (1998): 891.

6. I use the term "foreign policy elite" here to refer to the group of scholars affiliated with a short list of prominent government-sponsored research institutes, think tanks, and universities in China that are involved with analyzing China's foreign relations and broader issues of international politics. Such organizations include, but are not limited to, the CASS Institute of World Economics and Politics (Shijie Jingji yu Zhengzhi Yanjiusuo) and American Studies Institute (Meiguo Yanjiusuo), the Foreign Ministry's Institute of International Studies (Guoji Wenti Yanjiusuo), the State Council's Institute of Contemporary International Relations (Xiandai Guoji Guanxi Yanjiusuo), the Shanghai Institute of International Relations (Shanghai Guoji Wenti Yanjiusuo), Peking University's Institute of International Relations, Fudan University's Institute of American Studies, and the Foreign Affairs College. For two recent surveys of the role and influence of these institutions. see Bonnie Glaser and Phillip Saunders, "Chinese Civilian Foreign Policy Research Institutes: Evolving Roles and Increasing Influence," *China Quarterly*, no. 171 (September 2002): 597–616; and David Shambaugh, "China's International Relations Think Tanks: Evolving Structure and Process," *China Quarterly*, no. 171 (Fall 2002): 575–96.

7. See Thomas Risse and Kathryn Sikkink. "The Socialization of International Human Rights Norms into Domestic Practices: Introduction," in *The Power of Human Rights: International Norms and Domestic Change*, ed. Thomas Risse, Stephen Ropp, and Kathryn Sikkink, 1–38 (Cambridge: Cambridge University Press, 1999).

8. This definition of sovereignty is derived from the provisional one proposed by Thomas Biersteker and Cynthia Weber in "The Social Construction of State Sovereignty," in *State Sovereignty as a Social Construct*, ed. id. (Cambridge: Cambridge University Press, 1996), 2. For a more detailed discussion of these issues, see Allen Carlson, *Unifying China, Integrating with the World: Securing Chinese Sovereignty in the Reform Era* (Stanford: Stanford University Press, 2005).

9. For a broad argument about the endemic nature of various "violations" of sovereignty from the 1600s through the present, see Stephen Krasner, *Sovereignty: Organized Hypocrisy* (Princeton, N.J.: Princeton University Press, 1999).

10. For these and other statistics on UN peacekeeping operations, see www.un .org/Depts/dpko/dpko/pub/pko.htm (accessed 5 October 2005).

11. Stephen Garrett, *Doing Good and Doing Well: An Examination of Humanitarian Intervention* (Westport, Conn.: Praeger, 1999), 3.

12. For a comprehensive bibliography of this literature, see International Commission on Intervention and State Sovereignty, *The Responsibility to Protect: Research, Bibliography, Background: Supplementary Volume to the Report of the International Commission on Intervention and State Sovereignty* (Ottawa: International Development Research Centre, 2001), 227–43.

13. Krasner, *Sovereignty*.

14. For radical strands of this claim, see R. B. J. Walker, *Inside/Outside: International Relations as Political Theory* (Cambridge: Cambridge University Press, 1990) and Richard Ashley, "Untying the Sovereign State: A Double Reading of the Anarchy Problematique," *Millennium* 17 (Summer 1988): 227–62. For a less radical ideas-based argument, see Alexander Wendt and Daniel Friedheim, "Hierarchy Under Anarchy: Informal Empire and the East German State," in *State Sovereignty as Social Construct*, ed. Thomas J. Biersteker and Cynthia Weber (New York: Cambridge University Press, 1996), 240–78.

15. Throughout this chapter, the source used in compiling China's voting record in the Security Council was the online United Nations Dag Hammarskjöld Library, http://unbisnet.un.org (accessed 5 October 2005).

16. Samuel Kim, "China's International Organization Behavior," in *Chinese Foreign Policy: Theory and Practice*, ed. Thomas Robinson and David Shambaugh (Oxford: Clarendon Press, 1994), 422–24.

17. See "China Shows Grave Concern over Iraq's Invasion of Kuwait," Xinhua, 4 August 1990, in LexisNexis database. The fact that Iraq had invaded Kuwait gave Beijing rhetorical space for supporting UN involvement in the Gulf conflict, because such multilateral action could be construed as a defensive action taken in response to military aggression by one UN member state against another.

18. "UN Adopts Resolution on Use of Force Against Iraq," Xinhua, 28 November 1990, in LexisNexis database.

19. Wang Kehua, "Ping Li Jieming yu Li Denghui de 'xin zhuquanlun" [Criticism of James Lilly and Lee Teng-hui's "new sovereignty concept"], *Taiwan Yanjiu* 4 (1991): 2.

20. Personal interview, Foreign Affairs College, 17 June 1997.

21. Deng Xiaoping, *Selected Works*, vol. 3: *1982–1992* (Beijing: Foreign Languages Press, 1994), 344–45.

22. Personal interview, Chinese Institute of Contemporary International Relations, 21 April 1998. The interviewee actually expressed a good deal of frustration about this tendency, arguing that it tended to cloud Chinese thinking about national interests, and handicapped cost-benefit analysis in the making of Chinese foreign policy. He advocated the development of a more objective, scientific approach to these issues.

23. However, when the Security Council moved to place more pressure on the Cambodians through the enactment of economic sanctions, Beijing showed its opposition through abstaining on the resolution (792) proposed by other Security Council members.

24. See "China's Participation in UN Peacekeeping Operations," http://english .pladaily.com.cn/special/e-peace/txt/11.htm (accessed 5 October 2005). According to the *People's Liberation Daily*, the Chinese armed forces' official newspaper, the UNTAC deployment constituted the "first Chinese peacekeeping force." See "China's First Peacekeeping Force," http://english.pladaily.com.cn/special/e-peace/txt/05 .htm (accessed 5 October 2005).

25. "Foreign Ministry Spokesman on the Issue of Rwanda," Xinhua, 23 June 1994, in LexisNexis database.

26. See Fravel, "China's Attitude Toward UN Peacekeeping Operations," 1110–15, for a detailed discussion of these resolutions. In an interesting contrast, and one that reflects the shift in China's approach to intervention and sovereignty discussed in this chapter, in 2004 Beijing sent observers to the UN peacekeeping mission in Haiti.

27. The most vocal spokesman of such a position was Liu Wenzong, a senior international legal scholar and professor at the Foreign Affairs College in Beijing. The frequency with which Liu's editorials appeared in official publications in the early 1990s suggests that his views represented the orthodox position on sovereignty, intervention, and human rights at that juncture. However, many of the international legal scholars in Beijing I spoke with in the late 1990s expressed the view that Liu's opinions were particularly conservative and actually well outside the mainstream of both policy and academic circles in China.

28. A CASS researcher who was among the first to talk about challenges to sovereignty's traditional role in international politics is widely seen among Chinese foreign policy elites as having gone from being a marginal figure within Beijing's foreign policy establishment in the mid 1990s to a well-connected individual within the Ministry of Foreign Affairs at the end of the decade. Another scholar who also staked out a flexible stance on sovereignty, whom I interviewed on a number of occasions in the mid 1990s, made an even more dramatic move, from teaching English to undergraduates to briefing China's top leadership on international issues. Yet another example is Xia Yong, a CASS scholar who began publishing relatively liberal interpretations of international human rights law in the early 1990s, who later became head of CASS's Law Institute, and is now apparently an advisor to President Hu Jintao. I thank William Alford for bringing my attention to this last example.

29. Xu Guojin, "Guojia luxing guoji renquan yiwu de xiandu" [The limits on state performance of human rights obligations], *Zhongguo Faxue* 2 (1992): 18.

30. Li Ming, "'Lianheguo xianzhang' zhong de renquan yu bu ganshe neizheng wenti" [The issue of noninterference in internal affairs in the U.N. Charter], *Zhongguo Faxue* 3 (1993): 39.

31. Li Buyun, "Renquan de liangge lilun wenti" [Two theoretical human rights issues], *Faxue Yanjiu* 3 (1994): 38–39.

32. Wang Yizhou, *Dangdai guoji zhengzhi xilun* [An analysis of contemporary international politics] (Shanghai: Shanghai Renmin Chubanshe, 1995), 81–82.

33. Wang Shuliang, "Guojia zhuquan yu renquan" [State sovereignty and human rights], *Shehui Kexueyuan Xueshu Jikan* (Shanghai) 1 (1996): 68.

34. Ibid., 69.

35. Zeng Lingliang, "Lun lengzhan hou shidai de guojia zhuquan" [A discussion of state sovereignty in the post–Cold War era], *Zhongguo Faxue* 1 (1998). For a more extensive discussion of these articles, see Carlson, *Unifying China, Integrating with the World*, ch. 5.

36. All those interviewed were members of the elite foreign policy community identified earlier in this article. Thirty-four interviewees rejected the possibility of change and staunchly defended a static interpretation of sovereignty. Seventeen interviewees did not comment on this issue.

37. "Qian Qichen Urges Further Promotion of International Human Rights," Xinhua, 20 October 1998, in LexisNexis database.

38. "China: Kosovo Issue Strictly an Internal Affair of Yugoslavia," Xinhua, 10 March 1998, in LexisNexis database.

39. See "China Opposes Interference in Yugoslavia's Affairs," Xinhua, 24 October 1998, in LexisNexis database.

40. See the statement of Shen Guofang (China's deputy permanent representative to the United Nations) featured quite prominently in an article entitled "China on Establishing UNTAET in East Timor," Xinhua, 25 October 1999, in LexisNexis database.

41. This term, *ganshe*, in contrast with the more neutral *ganyu*, is so laden with negative connotations that it virtually precludes consideration of any relative merits of the action being described. To *ganshe* is to get involved in something that is not one's business, whereas to *ganyu* in something may, under certain circumstances, be considered appropriate. The widespread use of the former term to characterize the Kosovo campaign was indicative of the fact that there was no room in published Chinese analysis of the conflict for the expression of a less critical stance. Indeed, as one informant noted, during the Kosovo campaign, and especially after the embassy bombing, the only way to express a dissenting view on the operation was simply to be silent (confidential source, 8 January 2002).

42. Fan Guoxiang, "Renquan, zhuquan, baquan" [Human rights, sovereignty, hegemony], in *Xin tiaozhan: guoji guanxi zhong de "rendaozhuyi ganyu"* [A new challenge: humanitarian intervention in international relations], ed. Yang Chengxu (Beijing: Zhongguo Qingnian Chubanshe, 2001), 1.

43. The workshop, "Sovereignty in Contemporary International Relations," was sponsored by Fudan University and led by one of its top international relations scholars. While it was not particularly large, many of the major figures in China's academic foreign policy community were present. Indeed, elites with close ties to the PLA's top think tanks, the Ministry of Foreign Affairs, and the State Council's Institute of Contemporary International Relations were present (confidential interview and email contact, January 2002).

44. Cheng Shuaihua, "Guojia zhuquan yu guoji renquan de ruogan wenti" [Several issues involving international human rights and state sovereignty], *Ouzhou* 1 (2000): 34.

45. Shi Yinhong, "Lun 20 shiji guoji guifan tixi" [A discussion of the system of international norms in the twentieth century], *Guoji Luntan* 6 (2000): 8.

46. Li Zhenguang, "Renquan yu zhuquan guanxi de lishi kaocha yu sikao" [An investigation and reflection on the historical relationship between sovereignty and human rights], *Taipingyang Xuebao* 1 (2001): 63. For a more detailed discussion of these sources, see Carlson, *Unifying China, Integrating with the World*, ch. 5.

47. "Peacekeeping Must Observe U.N. Charter: Jiang," Xinhua, 7 September 2000, in LexisNexis database.

48. Pang Zhongying, "China's Changing Attitude to UN Peacekeeping," *International Peacekeeping* 1 (2005): 87–104; and Tang Yongshang, "Zhongguo he Lianheguo weihe xingdong" [China and UN peacekeeping operations], *Shijie Jingji yu Zhengzhi* [World Economics and Politics], no. 9 (2002).

49. People's Republic of China, State Council, 2000 Defense White Paper, "Participation in UN Peace-Keeping Operations," www.china.org.cn/e-white/2000/20-6.htm#c (accessed 21 October 2005).

50. See Banning Garrett and Jonathan Adams, *U.S.-China Cooperation on the Problem of Failing States and Transnational Threats*, Special Report 126 (Washington, D.C.: United States Institute of Peace, September 2004), and David M. Lampton and Richard Daniel Ewing, *U.S.-China Relations in a Post–September 11th World* (Washington D.C.: Nixon Center, 2002).

51. Personal interview, Peking University, 20 December 2001.

52. Personal interview, 26 December 2001.

53. Personal interview, Chinese Institute of International Studies, 21 December 2001.

54. For a more detailed report on these meetings, and a list of participants, see Carlson, *Protecting Sovereignty, Accepting Intervention*.

55. Chu Shulong, "China, Asia and Issues of Sovereignty and Intervention" (paper presented at International Intervention and State Sovereignty Conference, Beijing, 14–15 January 2002).

56. Ibid.

57. Fan Guoxiang, "Zen yang kan de xifang renquan sixiang" [How to regard Western human rights ideology], *Zhongguo Dang Zheng Ganbu Luntan* (2003): 4.

58. Zhou Yongkun, "Quanqiuxing shidai de renquan" [Human rights in an era of globalism], *Jiangsu Shehui Kexue* 3 (2002): 163–64. See Carlson, *Unifying China, Integrating with the World*, for a more extensive discussion.

59. Risse and Sikkink, "Socialization of International Human Rights Norms."

60. Tang Yongshang, "Zhongguo he Lianheguo."

61. "China's Position Paper on Enhanced Cooperation in the Field of Non-Traditional Security Issues," www.fmprc.gov.cn/eng/wjb/zzjg/gjs/gjzzyhy/2612/2614/t15318.htm (accessed 5 October 2005).

62. Pang, "China's Changing Attitude to UN Peacekeeping."

63. Ibid.

64. "Chinese Peacekeeping Troops Ready to Set for the DRC," http://english.chinamil.com.cn/site2/special-reports/2004-09/13/content_13034.htm (accessed 21 October 2005).

65. "Chinese Peacekeeping Troops Leave for Liberia," http://english.chinamil
.com.cn/site2/special-reports/2004-09/13/content_13085.htm (accessed 21 October 2005). This being the case, Beijing did not support all the humanitarian operations that have been proposed in the Security Council since the fall of 2001. For example, China has repeatedly expressed reservations about UN involvement in the Sudan conflict, where Beijing has cultivated a growing industry in that war-torn country's oil reserves.

66. See Peter Van Ness, "China as a Third World State: Foreign Policy and Official National Identity," in *China's Quest for National Identity*, ed. Lowell Dittmer and Samuel Kim (Ithaca, N.Y.: Cornell University Press, 1993), 194–215.

67. See Alastair Iain Johnston, "Learning Versus Adaptation: Explaining Change in Chinese Arms Control Policy in the 1980s and 1990s," *China Journal*, no. 35 (January 1996): 27–61.

68. For more on this argument see J. J. Suh, Peter Katzenstein, and Allen Carlson, eds., *Rethinking Security in East Asia* (Stanford: Stanford University Press, 2004). To a certain extent, such a call resonates quite well with the integrative analysis of the first generation of post-1949 China watchers, as exemplified by the work of Allen S. Whiting.

9 *China in Geneva*

LESSONS FROM CHINA'S EARLY YEARS
IN THE WORLD TRADE ORGANIZATION

Margaret M. Pearson

The accession of the People's Republic of China (PRC) to the World Trade Organization (WTO) in December 2001 has provided scholars of international relations behavior with a new crucible for examining the behavior of a major new entrant into a multilateral institution. Is China proving to be a "system maintainer," a "system reformer," or a "revisionist power"? The evidence presented in this chapter suggests that China is far from revisionist. Rather, for the most part, China has been a system maintainer, the exception being its behavior on issues seen to impinge on its sovereignty and dignity. This is largely consistent with the conclusion of previous studies of Chinese behavior in international organizations that the PRC is, by and large, a status quo power.[1]

Notwithstanding this general conclusion, though, China exhibits a complex pastiche of behaviors across a range of substantive, coalitional, and governance issues. The complexity of China's behavior stems from a variety of sources, including: (a) China is in the early stages of determining its interests in this body; (b) Beijing is in no great hurry to take on a central leadership role in the WTO, despite willingness to posture on some issues; (c) the domestic political mechanisms for determining interests and converting them into positions within the WTO are relatively weak; and (d) Chinese diplomacy has to account for a much more diverse set of economic interests, political interests, and domestic expectations than is often recognized.

This chapter's empirical focus is the first two years of China's WTO membership, from December 2001 to December 2003, with some reference to events in subsequent years. Although to some degree the first two years were a time of learning, they also laid the groundwork for China's positioning on subsequent issues, particularly drawing a line as to where it would be flexible and where it would not, and defining its relationship with other WTO members. These first years also offer glimpses into how Beijing views its trade interests and the strategies that would be undertaken to pursue those interests.

The chapter proceeds as follows. The first section presents background information useful for comprehending the machinations of the WTO, as well as an analysis of China's trade interests and trade politics. The second section considers the "exceptional" issues—those that focus on matters of Chinese sovereignty—on which China is most sensitive and in many ways least cooperative with the WTO: treatment of Taiwan in the organization and the Transitional Review Mechanism. The third section analyzes China's coalition-building behavior at the WTO, focusing on its relations with developing countries. The fourth section examines China's ambivalent posture with regard to its own leadership potential in the WTO. Together, the third and fourth sections raise the question of PRC attitudes toward the elitist structure of the WTO and its perception of its place in that structure, as well as in the world. The fifth section turns to China's behavior with respect to two substantive areas central to the country's economic interests—agriculture and textiles. The final section discusses what the evidence presented suggests about China's goals in the WTO, about the degree of "cooperative" behavior China exhibits in Geneva, and about its propensity to proactive leadership behavior in the organization.[2]

Background Issues

Key to any analysis of China's behavior in the WTO is an understanding of the WTO as an organization, and of China's place in it. It is also important to understand the nature of China's trade interests, and that, as in other countries, trade politics in China is primarily domestic. This section expands upon these background issues.

THE NATURE OF THE WTO AS AN ORGANIZATION

Multilateral talks to liberalize trade consist of a series of highly detailed, multilayered negotiating games, carried out across many substantive issues. The internal dynamics of the WTO, and the ongoing Doha Round, initiated in December 2001, are no different. In Geneva, trade negotiations are played out in a series of constantly shifting alliances; while there are some rather long-standing coalitions (such as the "Quad" and the Cairns Group),[3] most are more fractious groups whose members do not proceed in lockstep. For example, U.S. steel politics often pits the United States against its European and Japanese "allies," European agricultural subsidies often pit the European Union against the United States, Canada, and so on. The negotiations that occur within the WTO are serious, and the stakes are high; nevertheless, because coalitions shift from issue to issue, there is often a certain "wink-and-nod" quality about disputes as well; it is well understood that narrow domestic purposes will insert themselves into the negotiations, and that they will usually dominate.

Moreover, although the WTO promotes a rules-driven global trade regime, and although it has a formal structure of councils and committees for negotiation, consultation, dispute resolution, and other formal decision-making, it is in fact a "member-driven" organization, in which decision-making remains poorly institutionalized.[4] Eventually, all members who have a significant interest in an issue will have a chance to be involved in consensus-building meetings. But it is those who are most interested in an issue that initially structure the debate and frame an agreement. Agenda-setting for council meetings is, not surprisingly, driven by the most powerful members. Just as significantly, negotiations frequently occur in the context of informal meetings, often in the infamous "green room" gatherings of invited participants. Other meetings take place informally, by invitation only, away from Geneva. U.S. trade negotiators routinely use what they term "friendlies" to try to build coalitions.[5] Only when a consensus is formed will a formal decision be taken in the appropriate council or committee. The consensus decision rule, which has the potential to threaten stalemate, is softened significantly by the practice of involving all interested parties at some point in the deliberations. Those who have no significant interest are expected simply to "go along" with the decisions reached by interested parties, and to avoid being spoilers. These informal qualities—which to some degree create a game of intrigue—reflect, in part, the fact that the organization is new and underfunded, and that the WTO secretariat's staff is quite small. This informal nature also has the complicity of the largest members, including China, despite some controversy over governance, discussed below.[6]

It is useful to note two further characteristics of the WTO process—characteristics that distinguish the WTO from the Asia-Pacific Economic Cooperation forum (APEC), and that pose challenges to China. First, negotiations operate on a "request and offer" principle. Unless a member is prepared to offer a concession, it cannot seriously make a request; members may request a concession absent a counteroffer, but it is not considered credible as a formal negotiating stance. Second, Doha Round negotiations are linked across issues. The agreement for a "Single Undertaking" means in essence that members will have to sign onto the whole package rather than accept or veto portions of it.[7] The linkage across issues is a deliberate strategy to make the round comprehensive and to force negotiations forward rather than allowing a country to be intransigent in one issue area.

CHINA'S DELEGATION TO THE
WORLD TRADE ORGANIZATION

China has observed the WTO closely since it was formed in 1995, and maintained negotiating teams there as it worked on its accession agreement. Once it gained membership in 2001, China established a formal diplomatic mission. China's interlocutors at the WTO are uniformly complimentary about the quality of personnel in China's delegations. The diplomats, including Ambassador Sun Zhenyu, are respected for their intellect, hard work, and—despite their inexperience—for their professionalism. Chinese members of the mission and involved trade officials are the first to acknowledge, however, that they do not yet have the staff, expertise, budget, or comfort level with the organization to operate effectively as a major player on a wide variety of issues. The Chinese mission grew from ten diplomats in 2002 to fifteen in 2004. It is not as big as the U.S., Japanese, or EU delegations and has fewer members who are WTO "experts," so it has had to rely heavily on personnel dispatched from Beijing.[8] Chinese trade officials have contrasted the PRC delegation's capabilities with that of India; whereas India has a professional staff of only eight or nine, its members are seen as "highly qualified" and "much more active."[9] Echoing these views, foreign observers regard the Chinese participants as "neophytes" in their ability to maneuver within the WTO, and as "overwhelmed." Despite having spent many years in Geneva negotiating China's accession agreement, the delegation's focus during those years was not on what they would do once China became a member. As we shall see, inability to operate at full capacity hinders the PRC delegation from playing the "insider's" game characteristic of much WTO activity. They are characterized, moreover, as having "no coattails," for they cannot yet with any regularity bring others along; even if their voice is important, it still amounts to only one vote.

The makeup of the PRC delegation reflects certain ministerial interests, and particularly the effort of the Ministry of Foreign Trade and its successor, the Ministry of Commerce, to control the mission. Most of the diplomats are from the Ministry of Commerce. One slot each has been reserved, apparently, for the ministries responsible for agriculture, finance, customs, and foreign affairs, with the latter diplomat handling issues related to Taiwan. As was the case at important times in China's accession negotiations, having expansive bureaucratic representation in Geneva potentially inserts narrower domestic interests directly into the WTO process rather than keeping the delegation at arm's length from bureaucratic interference.[10] As for any country, there is a need to aggregate domestic interests and define a consistent negotiating position that can be operationalized by the delegation in Geneva. The Chinese delegation to Geneva is on a short tether to Beijing, moreover. The delegation is empowered to do little more than gather information and send it to Beijing for comment, which tends to hinder quick turnaround. This is in part a function of the lack of manpower in Geneva. Nevertheless, the relative lack of autonomy is the norm for PRC missions in international organizations, and there is no indication that the WTO will be any different.

Many of the difficulties faced by the PRC delegation in Geneva are a reflection of the domestic political atmosphere at home. Indeed, much about any country's trade policy can be explained by domestic politics.[11] Partly a function of leadership transition surrounding the Sixteenth Party Congress in November 2002, domestic politics dominated the political agenda during the first year of China's membership in the WTO. The comparatively great control of the Geneva mission by Beijing, combined with the relatively low priority WTO issues have in Beijing, conspires to keep China's Geneva delegation relatively quiet.

Finally, the domestic political backlash to WTO accession and the political need for leaders to respond to the idea that China had been "sold out" by the stringent concessions to which its negotiators agreed are significant for China's behavior in WTO. After accession, it became de rigueur in China to indicate that the country would not just incur obligations from WTO membership but also would "gain rights and benefits."[12] As will be seen, the need to respond to domestic criticism about China's weakness in its WTO negotiations, the need to stand up to the United States in particular, and the need to use the "rights" afforded China by membership are key to many of the public positions China has taken at the WTO.

CHINA'S TRADE INTERESTS

So, what are China's trade interests? The determination of substantive interests is complicated, and questions of complementarity with other economies depend on the specific sectors and even products concerned. Although a detailed discussion of China's trade interests is beyond the scope of this chapter, it can be said that China has extraordinarily diverse economic interests. It is useful to simplify this question into two dimensions. The first is the question of how open the Chinese economy is to trade and investment. Although economists debate precisely how open China's economy is, it is generally recognized to be more open than the economies of most developing countries and many newly industrialized countries. On many dimensions, China's economy as a whole is more open than the economies of Japan, Korea, Mexico, Brazil, and India.[13] Far more than most developing countries, since the mid 1990s, China has been a "sink" for foreign investment. Even though China maintains protectionist barriers in important sectors, expansion of trade is a central part of its economic strategy. Put differently, as the world's third largest exporting country in 2005 (after Germany and the United States, having recently displaced Japan and Canada), China has a strong interest in opening the economies of other countries to Chinese products.[14] China has export interests in Asia (such as agricultural specialty goods), the United States (notably in textiles), and the European Union. Chinese trade officials also recognize that the tariffs China agreed to upon joining WTO are significantly below those of many countries, especially in Asia, to which it might export. Finally, particularly in agriculture, there is a recognition that China needs to diversify its trade networks so that it is not reliant upon the United States.[15]

China's trade interests are also broad. This diversity distinguishes China from other developing countries, even large ones. China does not have one dominant, overriding interest, such as Argentina does with agriculture or Bangladesh does with textiles. Even India's trade interests are quite asymmetrical. China also has broader trade interests than Australia and the newly industrialized economies of East and Southeast Asia. In the range of interests, in fact, China is increasingly like the United States and the European Union. Most relevant to China's behavior in the WTO is the fact that, in addition to its *offensive* interests in opening markets for its exports, China has *defensive interests* in protecting its own markets.

The Sensitive Exceptions: Taiwan's Status in the World Trade Organization and the Transition Review Mechanism

TAIWAN

Chinese behavior in international organizations is predictable as it pertains to issues regarding sovereignty. Many scholars and observers, including scholars and observers from Taiwan and the PRC, have hoped that the WTO will provide a constructive framework for cooperation between Taiwan and the mainland. Our ultimate interest in this chapter, though, is the degree to which the institutional context of the WTO shapes China's behavior toward Taiwan. Indeed, PRC-Taiwan interaction presents the toughest test for the idea that PRC membership in international institutions shapes the government's behavior. In the first years of China's and Taiwan's respective memberships, China adjusted some of its behavior in line with WTO norms, but at the same time, it has launched an effort to downgrade Taiwan's status and have the organization deny any sovereignty implications of Taiwan's membership. While some of these hostile actions are attributable to the extreme level of tension between Beijing and the Chen

Shui-bian administration in Taipei, the underlying dynamic bears the hall-marks of what has been seen at other times and in other international organizations.

On the accommodative side of the ledger, behind-the-scenes contact has been taking place, with an apparent effort on the part of the top members of the Taiwanese and PRC delegations to build personal relationships. Given the fact that WTO–Geneva is a relatively small community, members of the two delegations see each other frequently. This mirrors what has occurred in the APEC process, with interactions occurring primarily at social events held in tandem with sector-specific meetings.[16] Until a blowup at the APEC Leaders' Meeting in Shanghai in October 2001 over the acceptability of a representative sent by Taiwan's President Chen Shui-bian, the two sides reportedly worked at the meetings in a nonobstructionist manner.

In addition to informal interactions, there have been a few high-profile, formal meetings between the two delegations. Interactions on both substantive negotiations and on symbolic issues concerning nomenclature and status are illustrative of positive and negative trends. One substantive issue concerned contacts between Taiwanese and PRC delegates over Taiwanese steel exports following Beijing's imposition of quotas and tariff barriers on imported Taiwanese steel in March 2002. The PRC invited the Taiwanese steel industry association to Beijing for informal consultations. It also established a new Cross-Strait Trade and Economic Promotion Association (Liang An Jingmao Guanxi Chujing Xiehui) to help coordinate such contacts, and suggested that Taiwan do the same. Furthermore, Beijing informed Taipei of its desire for association-level consultation in Chinese for use of cross-Strait channels rather than formal procedures in Geneva. Beijing hinted that after the problem had been addressed at the level of industry associations, it might be brought to formal discussions at Geneva. Taipei refused to deal at the association level, seeing Beijing's overtures as a strategy to avoid the sovereignty implications of Taiwan's WTO membership and believing the offer of possible future WTO interaction to be disingenuous.[17] Taiwan instead requested formal consultations in Geneva. The PRC initially refused, reiterating that "Beijing will not hold trade and economic consultations with Taiwan under the WTO framework unless the 'one-China' issue is solved by both sides of the Taiwan Strait."[18]

Beijing subsequently made some conciliatory moves. In July 2002, the PRC mission used WTO channels to inform Taiwan's WTO chief delegate, Yen Ching-chang, of its position on consultations, and it did the same with subsequent notification of an investigation into ethanol dumping. Still, these communications were in Chinese rather than in English, the official WTO language.[19] More significantly, in December 2002—and contrary to the earlier statements precluding direct discussions at Geneva—members of the two delegations conducted a direct three-hour bilateral consultation on steel, albeit in a Geneva hotel rather than at WTO headquarters.[20] For those hoping that the norms of WTO interaction would rapidly change China's behavior toward Taiwan, the direct meeting appeared significant. But if the meeting did break new ground, its effect was temporary; the PRC delegation canceled several subsequently scheduled consultations, prompting complaints from the Taiwan delegation to the WTO secretariat.[21]

Members of the two delegations held face-to-face formal contacts on still another substantive issue—the Transitional Review Mechanism (TRM), the forum for monitoring Chinese compliance to its WTO accession agreement (discussed below). In September 2002, the PRC delegation answered complaints from Taiwan concerning Chinese tariffs on beer and photographic equipment, as well as import licensing and tariff administration. Consistent with China's cantankerous attitude toward the TRM process as a whole, it indicated it would pursue some of these issues only outside of the WTO setting.[22]

The dance between the PRC and Taiwan over substantive interactions was replicated with regard to issues of nomenclature and the status of the Taiwanese mission.[23] Specifically, the PRC has tried to insist that reference to Taiwan's membership in the WTO and its organizations not imply sovereignty. With regard to Taiwan's pursuit of membership in the WTO's plurilateral Government Procurement Agreement (GPA), for example, China (not yet a member) asked other GPA members to include a footnote in Taiwan's membership documents to the effect that use of the term "central government of the Republic of China" has no sovereignty implications.[24] This dynamic recurred on a grander scale in early 2003. On the heels of disputes over Taiwan's status in the World Health Organization at the time of the SARS outbreak, Taiwan made public that the WTO Director-General Supachai Panitchpakdi had approached the head of the Taiwanese delegation in February 2003 with several requests. The essence of the requests was to downgrade Taiwan's WTO status from "permanent mission," which in diplomatic parlance most often implies an independent country, to "office of permanent representative," and for Taiwan to "affirm that the actions regarding WTO representation of Taiwan have no implications for sovereignty." Another report noted that Supachai urged Taiwan to consider not listing its delegation as a "permanent mission" in the WTO's internal telephone directory; when Taiwan failed to agree, the publication of the directory was put on hold.[25] Although Supachai voiced these initiatives, it is inconceivable that he would have taken on this issue except at the behest of Beijing. The PRC apparently asked for a longer list of items, but Supachai declined to approach Taiwan's delegation on them.[26]

THE TRANSITIONAL REVIEW MECHANISM (TRM)

All WTO members are subject to a periodic Trade Policy Review (TPR) of their trading practices. China in addition agreed in its accession protocol to be reviewed during each of the first eight years of membership, with a final review in the tenth year.[27] Whereas TPRs typically take place solely within the WTO secretariat's office, each of the WTO's functional councils is involved in China's transitional review. This "WTO-plus" commitment was justified by the fact that China was to be admitted *before* it was in full compliance with the terms of membership.

The TRM is widely unpopular in China. It invokes images of foreigners, especially the United States (which has driven the TRM process), snooping into China's affairs, even though China's leaders have repeatedly vowed to comply with the accession terms. The TRM is a focus point for PRC concerns about national humiliation and sovereignty, and it is all the more aggravating to many Chinese citizens because their leaders agreed to it. It also is evocative of the annual Most Favored Nation (MFN) debate over China trade in the United States. However, China has more influence over the direction of the TRM debate than it ever did over the MFN debate.

The first TPR was to be completed within one year of China's accession (by 11 December 2002). The basic dynamic in the first year was characterized by U.S. government efforts (with substantial EU and Japanese support) to initiate discussion of compliance problems in the various substantive subcommittees several months prior to the formal review in December. The PRC's official response was threefold: compliance issues should not be brought up significantly before the formal date of the one-year review; China would respond to issues raised, but only to the letter of the law, and as such would only provide oral answers; and any other discussions about compliance should take place in informal or bilateral settings. The delegation further communicated informally to U.S. officials that to the extent that its responses required information forthcoming from ministries at home, it was having trouble getting that information. Whether or not officials of China's Ministry of Foreign Trade and Economic Cooperation (MOFTEC) had the information is debatable, but they were clearly under pressure from ministries in Beijing not to provide what data they had.[28] China also tried to mobilize support for its position from other WTO members. The U.S. delegation at the WTO was informed by a "big power and neighbor of China" (presumably India) that the United States "cannot approach us" for support on the TRM.

China's efforts to contain the TRM process required substantial resources and attention on the part of its diplomats. The issue also led to some highly acrimonious behavior from the Chinese delegation. In one meeting, a senior member of the PRC delegation (not Sun Zhenyu) reportedly "made a pounding-the-table type of speech," directed at the United States, that linked the TRM process to "neo-imperialism"—an echo of speeches delivered in the Maoist era. In late September, the dispute continued as members of the Quad (the United States, the European Union, Canada, and Japan, joined for questioning by Australia and Taiwan) complained that China had not provided any written answers to questions they had posed in the context of the Market Access Committee on compliance. China, while asserting that "some countries" were being "troublemakers," offered to discuss the issues with the Quad informally, but withdrew the offer after the United States and Japan said that this was not acceptable and reiterated the demand for written answers. China then stated that the committee's compliance review was over, a view that the committee's Lesothan chair concurred with by his comments that he could not force China to engage in discussion, and that he would forward a factual summary to the superior General Council for its year-end review on 11 December.[29] The Chinese delegation also appeared to bristle at the sense that the Quad countries were ganging up on it.

A MOFTEC official deeply involved in the TRM process claimed that the process had left "a lot of bad feelings" among his colleagues, especially against the United States and Japan, and led to a desire to shun U.S. embassy officials in Beijing.[30] This official also was concerned about the attention diverted from other substantive negotiations and indicated that China would continue to try to contain the TRM process, particularly by compressing the timeframe. Happily for the PRC delegation, its obfuscating tactics were successful in relieving pressure from the TRM in subsequent years. A PRC diplomat, viewing the backing off of the United States as a victory, concluded that the United States recognized that the wording of the TRM requirement as written into China's accession protocol was relatively weak.[31]

The Politics of Coalition Building: China's "Bridge" to the Developing World

The PRC government used the occasion of its first major speech as a WTO member to declare it would serve as a "bridge" between the developed and developing worlds. This designation is usually dismissed as rhetoric, and in significant ways this dismissal is accurate. Yet China's verbal commitment to support developing countries' concerns and its actual behavior in building coalitions highlight important questions about China's goals in the WTO and its self-definition vis-à-vis the developed and developing worlds.

Consistent with the moniker "Doha *Development* Round," the Doha Ministerial Declaration that launched the round in 2001 makes a strong statement about the need to meet certain developing country demands.[32] The core substantive elements of the developing country agenda are: maintenance of distinct categories and preferential treatment for developing countries, especially the least developed ("special and differential treatment"); guaranteed export markets for products from less developed countries; special consideration of the impact of the intellectual property agreement on prices, particularly of pharmaceuticals (primarily HIV/AIDS drugs); and aid for Trade Related Technical Assistance needs, such as capacity building and WTO implementation. There is also, secondarily, a governance reform agenda to ensure that developing countries have a fuller voice in the WTO and are more involved in agenda-setting.

In the WTO, "developing country" is a self-designated term. South Korea in many instances terms itself "developing," for example. In its accession negotiations, China's negotiators tried, unsuccessfully, to be recognized as a developing country as a means of garnering longer compliance phase-in schedules and other special treatment. Even so, consistent with its concrete trade interests, China does not put itself in the developing country camp. How are we thus to understand the consistent rhetorical support, in China's first years of membership, for developing country interests, and the strong language about serving as a bridge? These efforts are said by those close to the process to have been a deliberate tactic to lay a foundation for future negotiating leverage.[33] Ultimately, China has not been a forceful advocate of the development agenda. Rather, its "development" positions have been closely linked to its own economic interests. This is evident, for example, in a typical speech by China's ambassador to the WTO, Sun Zhenyu. Sun listed the "developing country goals for the Doha Round" as reduced agriculture tariffs and subsidies (China already has reduced tariffs, wishes to export to higher tariff areas, and says it cannot afford subsidies),[34] curbs on excessive use of anti-dumping charges (China is the most frequent target of such claims), the opening of services to developing countries' labor, progress on liberalization of rules for temporary entry of persons to a WTO member country to provide a service (termed "movement of natural persons"), greater flexibility in services negotiations (so that developed countries can offer more without China having to "give" more), and additional concessions by industrialized countries in areas such as textiles and apparel (where China wished to guarantee expanded exports, perhaps at the expense of other developing countries [see below]). The one area mentioned by Sun that is on the developing agenda but not high on China's agenda is technical assistance and capacity building. Presumably, China will not be asked to foot the bill for technical assistance to developing countries.[35]

China appeared "development-minded" in some early initiatives on governance issues within the WTO. Governance issues are intriguing because, as discussed further below, members expect China to be part of the WTO governing elite. Yet on two occasions, both occurring in its first month of membership, the PRC was outspoken on procedural reform proposals that would rein in the authority of the secretariat and committee chairs, seen as dominated by developed countries, and would influence agenda-setting. The first occasion was when the PRC joined with a large group of developing countries to demand that the chairmanship of the Trade Negotiations Committee (TNC) for the Doha Round be rotated among member ambassadors rather than be the permanent prerogative of the director general (DG) of the WTO.[36] China also joined with a group of developing countries advocating restrictions on the discretion of the chairs of the six TNC subcommittees to decide which alternative positions are included for consideration in draft proposals. The aim was to prevent compromise texts that do not reflect the positions of developing countries and to bring a more open deliberation process to the choice of language.[37] Although it is argued below that China has generally been a follower of others' initiatives, the PRC was apparently quite influential in this latter decision.[38] As actions on governance have subsided into the background in favor of substantive negotiations, however, China's early commitment to rejiggering the governance structure has not been further tested. Rather, governance issues appear marginal to China's overall agenda in the WTO. China's support for these two rule changes appears to have been to gain easy and costless tactical wins rather than being a serious gambit to alter the power structure.

Deeper consideration of China's long-term prospects for leadership of the developing world requires a sense of the developing countries' views of China. In specific situations, such as with the governance issues noted previously, developing countries have found China's support useful. But many developing countries have been at least as concerned with the threats China poses to their substantive interests and feel their interests more often compete with than complement China's. Foreign officials involved in China's WTO negotiations frequently observe that developing countries, at the same time as making plaintive *public* comments that China's terms of accession "set the bar too high" for developing countries, *privately* have supported strict terms—such as safeguards on textiles and the other inexpensive, labor-intensive goods—to restrain Chinese competition to their exports.[39] When the United States initiated textile safeguards against China in 2005, developing countries that stood to benefit were supportive of U.S. moves.[40]

The depiction of China's concrete economic interests laid out previously, and China's reluctance to adopt the "developing country" label, have led to skepticism that China will find enduring complementary interests that can form the basis of substantial alliances with developing countries.[41] Rather, it is likely that China will carefully choose where it can take low-stakes stands on issues it attributes to developing countries, but that its commitment will be less deep than commonly expected. Chinese trade officials also recognize the fractious nature of the developing country group; as one Chinese trade official commented, it is a group that, because of its divergent interests, "cannot be led."[42] As will be seen below, and has been shown consistently in China's behavior in international organizations, China has been relatively aloof from established coalitions within the WTO.[43] When it has joined coalitions, it does not play an active role but, rather, uses its membership primarily to improve its image. The idea that it is a "bridge" is a way to maintain maximum flexibility for maneuver between the developed and developing agendas.

This effort to cover both sides of the developed-developing country agenda played out repeatedly throughout China's early WTO tenure. China at times appeared to tilt toward the developed countries, with the direction of influence across China's "bridge" toward the south from the industrialized world. This was evident, for example, in U.S. Trade Representative Robert Zoellick's attribution of credit to the Chinese (before China was formally admitted) for using the Shanghai APEC meetings in 2001 to launch the Doha Round itself, including its successful efforts to convince reluctant Southeast Asian nations—particularly Malaysia—of the value of the round. Chinese trade officials, too, have expressed pride in China's help to the United States on this matter.[44] It also is evident in specific negotiations on agricultural liberalization, as discussed below.

At other times, China has appeared to side with the developing world. This face of China is consistent with the country's recent outreach toward Southeast Asia. China is engaged in a strategy to upgrade the quality of its diplomatic attention to Southeast Asia through unusually proactive diplomacy and substantial sensitivity to poorer neighbors' concerns about Chinese economic competition.[45] The pro-development face reached new heights in September 2003 in the context of China's first WTO ministerial conference, held in Cancun, Mexico. But what initially appeared to be a strong gambit into the developing country camp later revealed itself to be another instance of negotiating a unique path between the developed and developing camps. Given China's general avoidance of coalitions, it was contrary to expectations that China joined the Group of Twenty (G20) developing countries in putting forth a counterproposal on agriculture and services to the U.S.-EU proposal in Cancun.[46] In large part as a result of the stalemate, the meetings failed to produce a needed agreement on how to proceed with agricultural negotiations. The G20 complained that the

U.S.-EU draft did not go far enough to commit to cuts in agricultural subsidies by wealthy exporters, while at the same time asking for tariff reductions by (and providing only a modicum of "special and differential treatment" for) developing countries. Recall that China's concrete interests are
split between a desire to increase its own agricultural exports and a desire
to reduce subsidies, which it cannot afford, by its competitors.

The initiative for the coalition clearly lay with Brazil and India, notwithstanding the fact that China's name appeared routinely in reports about the
coalition. China's willingness to allow itself to be called a "leader" on this
issue appeared to be an important stand and was leveraged by the G20 to
lend credibility to its cause. Yet, ultimately, China's role in this coalition was
to lend support, not to lead it or act seriously to advance its agenda. Indeed,
it appeared quite aloof. For example, China's delegation to Cancun, led by
Minister of Commerce Lu Fuyuan, did not seek headlines for itself concerning the G20 moves. When the talks fell apart, Chinese diplomats moved
into crisis management mode, attempting to reduce the vituperative tenor
of rhetoric from the true leaders, Brazil and India, toward the United States
and European Union. Lu's comments to the media conference where the
G20 made its major statements were much more conciliatory than those
of other participants, saying China "*hoped* the Ministers would *consider*
the G20 text even as they are considering the Chairman's draft" (emphasis
added). In contrast, the Argentinean minister said the paper "must" be ac-
corded the same basis as the chair's text, while the Brazilian foreign minister stated that it was essential that the group's paper be taken as a basis for
negotiations.[47] As discussions among ministers were becoming particularly
tendentious, moreover, Lu intervened to point out, to no avail, that stalemate was in nobody's interest.[48]

At home, China's media barely reported the activities of China in the G20.
The reports that did appear were descriptive and factual. The domestic press
carried no significant analysis of the coalition and China's concrete role in
Cancun. There was no effort to use the failure of the meetings to undermine
the legitimacy of WTO processes or to promote the idea that China is a
developing country working against the interests of the United States and
European Union. Indeed, a PRC Ministry of Commerce WTO analyst appeared to backtrack when, in an *Asian Wall Street Journal* op-ed piece published shortly after the failure at Cancun, he claimed that China "belongs to
no trade group" and operates according to self-interest—which in practice
means that China will adopt a strategy that is "different from both the developed and developing country members of the WTO."[49] Consistent with
this aloof position, while China has remained a member of the G20 and has
attended subsequent meetings, it is virtually never mentioned as a leader or
as having made significant contributions to the group's deliberations.

China Inside the Power Center?

What does the discussion of China's concrete economic interests, and the expected limits on coalitional activity vis-à-vis the Third World, suggest about China's posture toward the WTO's power center—the United States and the European Union? Chinese support for mild revisions on governance has the potential to shift power slightly toward developing countries. But despite the mild revisionism implicit in these moves, China does not seriously reject the status quo power structure of the WTO. Rather, its post-accession behavior suggests that it wishes to join the power center without wresting control of it. In turn, representatives of the countries that dominate the WTO assume that China will necessarily play a major role on many issues and believe that the idea that China might be excluded is ludicrous. For example, no non-Chinese interviewee indicated that China should be excluded from "green room" discussions, although some added the qualification that China's purposes in such settings should be serious and the PRC should be tractable.

Consistent with China's participation in the UN Security Council, then, there is no substantial evidence that the Chinese reject the dominant rules and operative norms of the WTO. They do not yet feel comfortable in it, but, according to Chinese officials who have spent time in Geneva, they are busy learning about it. They take note of when Chinese participants are not included in informal meetings and have been pleased to be invited when they are, including to a small number of Quad meetings. More generally, Chinese trade officials agree that there is a need for the WTO's ubiquitous informal meetings that allow the most interested parties to work out disagreements before bringing issues to a more formal setting. One Chinese trade official spoke in positive terms of the U.S. and EU discussions (which excluded China) about differences in their approaches to agricultural talks, for example, and contended more generally that China "would not support any major overhaul of the decision-making structure" in Geneva.[50]

The question of style of behavior also came up frequently in discussions with Chinese trade officials. They often attempted to distance themselves from India, expressing annoyance at India's grandstanding and "uncooperative" behavior in Geneva. Style also translates into deeper behavioral characteristics. U.S. and EU trade officials observe that China does not like to be ostracized from the majority. Rather, the Chinese delegation tends to watch to see where coalitions are forming and then to lend verbal support to the coalitions after they have taken basic shape.[51] This occurred, for example, when China joined the 2002 complaint initiated by the European Union and Japan against U.S. steel tariffs, but only after the basic coalition was in place. China's move came after most of the international attention to the steel complaint had died down, but still allowed China to gain substantial do-

mestic publicity for its move. (U.S. delegates may try to defuse Chinese opposition by presenting them with a pre-arranged coalition, or by asking
third countries seen by China as more neutral to voice views in favor of the
U.S. position.)

With regard to China's potential for leadership, Chinese diplomats have
on most issues adopted a learning posture. Thus far, Chinese attempts at
leadership are primarily exhibited as a desire to host major meetings, much
as they will do for the Olympics in 2008. They received strong praise for
successfully staging the APEC Shanghai year, culminating in the 2001 Leaders' Meeting in Shanghai. Though the Chinese APEC planners reportedly
were not proactive on the substantive side, they were organizationally
extremely adept.[52] With APEC Shanghai successfully completed and, undoubtedly, with the 2008 Olympics in mind, they have continued their offers to host. For example, China quietly offered to host the midterm review
of the Doha Round in the fall of 2003. There was, however, little enthusi-
asm for China's offer, and Mexico stepped in and was given the job. Perhaps
as a compromise, Hong Kong was chosen to host the next Doha Ministerial
meeting at the end of 2005.

If China is not a deal broker, is it likely to be a deal breaker? Once again,
the answer must depend on its concrete interests at the time. As noted previously, any major participant can block any major move that is not in its
interest. China's behavior in the first years since its accession suggests that
the PRC "goes along to get along" unless strong economic or sovereign interests are threatened.

The Substance of Doha: Liberalization

Two major conclusions about China's trade interests have emerged
from the previous discussion. First, China cannot afford deep support for
developing countries' agendas, because its interests are fundamentally different from theirs. Second, China's interests do not permit it to be a major
obstructionist power in terms of further liberalization in key areas on the
Doha agenda. This is not to suggest that China will be a major liberalizing
force; it cannot be expected to pursue liberalization for liberalization's sake.
Overall, however, it is mistaken to presume that China will consistently be
on the opposite side of any group of countries; rather, it will often find partners from among the developed nations and will often favor further liberalization of trade barriers. This section discusses the unfolding Chinese position on two sectors that are central to China's export agenda and that are
thus poised to form the core of its offensive position in the Doha Round: agriculture and textiles.

Before discussing these two concrete issues, it is useful to recall the existence of the "request and offer" system and the Single Undertaking mandate. For China, as for all countries, the "request and offer" format and the "Single Undertaking" built into the Doha Round mean that narrow, tit-for-tat negotiations will not be productive. Although PRC officials have frequently claimed that the depth of China's accession commitments means it has nothing left to offer, foreign observers counter that "no one is maxed out."[53] While both these positions are tactical, the foreign position is undergirded by the request and offer modality. Each member is forced to take a broad view of its interests and formulate a comprehensive strategy involving many issue areas. And in fact the Chinese delegation has put forth some requests in major areas, notably agriculture and services, but has offered little.[54] This is not surprising, given China's domestic political need to be seen as "reaping the benefits" of WTO membership, and given the fact that the Doha Round has not yet reached the end-game of negotiation.[55]

AGRICULTURE

The ongoing negotiations on the WTO Agreement on Agriculture (AoA) are extremely complex and contentious. They are, moreover, so contentious and so central to the Doha agenda that—under the Single Undertaking rule—their failure would threaten the success of the entire round.[56] Broadly speaking, negotiations are occurring between three somewhat loosely defined groupings. The United States and the Cairns Group of seventeen agricultural exporting countries (see n. 3) have, since the Uruguay Round negotiations (1986–94), tended to favor fundamental liberalization of agriculture markets.[57] (Note that the Cairns Group is made up of both developed and developing countries.) The European Union, supported by a so-called G10 ("Group of 10") that includes Japan, Korea, Norway, and Switzerland, has opposed drastic reductions in domestic supports and seeks to protect the "multifunctionality" of agriculture (e.g., environmental concerns).[58] The third major grouping, developing countries, has sought to open developed country markets to its members' commodity exports, to end price-suppressing domestic supports by developed countries, and to protect food security and enhance rural development through "special and differential treatment" that allows slower trade liberalization in developing countries. The G20, formed prior to the Cancun Ministerial, is joined in this grouping by the G33—led by Indonesia and the Philippines and containing mostly African countries. Since the Cancun failure, the main negotiations have occurred within a grouping known as the Five Interested Parties (FIPs)—the United States, the European Union, Brazil, India (these two from the G20), and Australia (Cairns). China is not included. The G20 continues to meet and is presumably informed on the FIPs progress by Brazil and India.

China from the beginning was unlikely to play a major role in the success or failure of the agricultural negotiations, both because the negotiating space is dominated by the other coalitions and because of resource constraints and the absence of an authoritative mandate from Beijing. However, China's position in the unfolding of these talks suggests how it is defining its trade interests and offers further insight into its coalitional behavior. China did put forth a proposal in 2002 but, as expected, it did not contain any offers of substantive concessions on China's part.[59] It was framed as a call on behalf of developing countries, and one of its major goals was the reduction of European and U.S. domestic subsidies and other trade-distorting supports. Yet, in substance, China left quite a bit of room for cooperation with other agricultural exporting countries, particularly the Cairns Group and the United States, and for a coalition against the European Union, Japan, and South Korea. Indeed, China quietly indicated at least some support for the U.S. initiatives.[60]

Moreover, over the course of several months of early Doha Round agricultural talks, China increasingly moved away from its rhetorical position of support for developing country interests to a more explicit congruence with the United States and the Cairns Group. During the summer of 2002, China's former chief negotiator Long Yongtu (by then a vice minister) appeared on the scene in Geneva to attend a TNC discussion of agriculture issues. Long made what U.S. officials considered a very helpful intervention; while portraying China as a leader of the developing world, he made statements about the value of further liberalization of agricultural export markets. On the issue of export subsidies, which China committed to reduce to zero in its own accession agreement, it took on the mantle of liberalizer, particularly against the European Union and Japan. This, of course, can be seen as helping developing countries—and China. But China did not feel it necessary to frame its argument as in opposition to the United States. Moreover, a key MOFTEC official involved in framing China's position on agriculture indicated that the basic argument was between a Cairns Group–U.S. coalition—which he asserted China's position was most like—versus the European Union, Switzerland, Japan, and Korea. He did not mention a "developing country" interest.[61] While China's problems with rural unemployment might suggest that it would lead the charge for an expansive definition of a "development box" in agriculture, it has been quite muted on the issue.[62]

The following discussion outlines the three agreed-upon areas ("pillars") for AoA negotiations in the Doha Round, and China's basic position on them.[63]

Agricultural import tariff liberalization (market access).   These negotiations revolve around lowering tariffs and tariff quotas on agricultural goods. China agreed at the time of its WTO accession to reduce average tariffs on agricultural imports to 15 percent by January 2004, far lower than those of nearly all developing countries, including others in Asia. (Korea's and Japan's are about 50–60 percent.)[64] China already exports many fruits and vegetables and has a trade surplus in vegetables, mostly exported to Asian countries (Chinese agricultural production in specialty items is on too small a scale to be competitive with that of Europe or the United States). It has large export-oriented fish and shrimp-processing industries. PRC agricultural officials understand that China stands to gain export markets if other countries' barriers come down, and that exports could have a positive employment effect in the countryside. A U.S. proposal in July 2002 called for further lowering of the average tariff level to 15 percent (from 62 percent). The Chinese seem to have quietly accepted this proposal. The PRC, United States, and Cairns Group proposals are generally consistent in calling for a phased-in lowering of tariffs, with longer periods for the developing countries (six years in the PRC proposal) than in the developed (three years). Disagreement among them has arisen over China's own poor record of implementing tariff-rate quota commitments in its accession. In contrast, the EU proposal, broadly by the G10, including Japan, Korea, Norway, and Switzerland, calls for a 36 percent cut in existing tariffs.[65]

Domestic supports.   These negotiations focus on how to reduce domestic production subsidies, which are judged to distort trade. In meetings in the fall of 2002, the United States, China, India, and the Cairns Group— all agricultural exporters—called for the eventual elimination of trade-distorting domestic subsidies ("amber box" spending),[66] while the European Union, Japan, South Korea, Switzerland, and Taiwan have argued that elimination of these subsidies—which account for about 40 percent of all domestic subsidies—is too ambitious. The European Union called for a 55 percent reduction in domestic production-linked subsidies.[67]

Export subsidies.   China committed to reduce export subsidies to zero upon WTO entry, a liberalization substantially beyond the current U.S. and EU levels.[68] The Chinese government has claimed it cannot afford subsidies and has called for "fair trade" by the United States and, especially, the European Union.[69] The formal PRC proposal is for a three-year phase-in for developed countries and six years for developing countries.[70] The United States has proposed multilateral elimination of all export subsidies by 2010. There is therefore overlap between China, the Cairns Group, and the United States on this issue. There has been resistance from the European Union, which has proposed instead a 45 percent reduction in export subsidies.

There are therefore several key issues on which China has significant complementary interests with liberalizing exporting countries. In part because China sees agricultural exports as a future export strength,[71] and because its WTO accession agreement commits it to terms more stringent than those that apply to other developing countries, as well as, in some cases, to the United States and Europe, it clearly has identified an interest in global liberalization of agriculture. Arguing against the durability of such a coalition is the fact that the United States can be expected to attempt to keep some form of export supports off the table, both by manipulating the "box" categories and by trying to avoid the inclusion of export credits (which it relies upon heavily).[72]

TEXTILES

As with agriculture, the Chinese position on liberalization of textiles trade says much about China's trade behavior. Unlike agriculture, though, textiles are likely to be a major source of conflict with the United States. There are several key dimensions of this issue. First, China is the world's dominant export power in textiles and apparel. As early as 1996, even while restricted by quotas (and including Hong Kong re-exports), China accounted for 12.5 percent of the world's exports and was the world's largest textiles and apparel producer.[73] In the United States, in contrast, the textile industry supplies a few niche markets, but has not been able to withstand competition from lower-cost producers such as China, India, Pakistan, Mexico, and Bangladesh, despite substantial political clout. The WTO Agreement on Textiles and Clothing (ATC) provides that restrictions on the growth of China's market share be lifted through the phasing out of all quantitative restrictions on textiles and clothing—quota arrangements ensconced primarily in the Multifiber Arrangement (MFA)—by the end of 2004.

Second, China is subject to two conflicting international agreements, both signed by the United States as well. One is the ATC. The other is the 1999 Sino-U.S. bilateral agreement, which provides the U.S. government with two tools—the textiles safeguards mechanism (until 2008) and the product specific safeguards mechanism (for twelve years after accession)—to protect the U.S. textile and apparel market against Chinese imports deemed excessive or harmful.[74]

Third, although China would like to gain political leverage at the WTO by claiming that it is upholding international rules, it is unlikely to be able to form a strong coalition with other developing countries on this issue, because most developing countries worry about Chinese competition to their own textile exports. There is disagreement about what the exact impact of China's ability to expand its exports will be for other textile-producing developing countries, such as India, Pakistan, and Bangladesh. But the bigger issue is the *perception* of those countries that the reduction of quotas for China harms their textile exports. Although MFA quotas originally had the effect of curbing imports to developed countries, these quotas also gave many developing countries a share of the large U.S. and EU markets they would not have gotten had market share been determined by competitive market forces. In other words, the MFA protected not only U.S. producers but other low-cost developing country textile exporters as well. U.S. trade officials involved in China's accession negotiations contend that developing countries, except for India, never strenuously objected to the U.S. inclusion of safeguards in its bilateral agreement. Even India's objections were considered merely rhetorical, because it has also indicated privately a desire to see U.S. safeguards in place.[75] Other developed countries that are theoretically opposed to quotas, because they hinder the credibility of a rules-based system, such as Australia and the European Union, have not become active on this issue.[76]

Finally, the textile issue is of such importance—both symbolic and substantive—that Chinese trade officials have sometimes suggested that China will attempt to link it to other issues in order to get what it wants in textiles and apparel. If the United States "is difficult on this issue after 2005, it will unravel everything," one PRC official said.[77] China's other option is to creatively play the role of an upholder of liberalizing agreements—against the United States.

Tensions over rising Chinese textile exports came to the fore in the spring of 2005, when exports to the United States and the European Union surged quickly following the MFA's expiration. As was widely anticipated, the United States launched safeguard actions against China in May 2005.[78] China reacted with sharp language but did not immediately attempt to retaliate either bilaterally or in the WTO. The European Union threatened to follow suit with its own quotas in June, but the two reached a deal providing for China's voluntary restraints on exports to European countries.[79] In the early stages of the dispute over surging Chinese textile and apparel exports, then, China has attempted to avoid throwing oil onto the fire, apparently wishing instead to preserve steady markets.

Conclusions

What insights does analysis of China's first years in the WTO provide about likely Chinese behavior in this and other multilateral institutions in the future, and about its trade interests? In this final section, I focus on the broader implications of China's role, framed around three issues central to the question of China's emergence on the world stage: (1) Chinese political and economic interests in the organization; (2) China's propensity for leadership and coalition-building, including in relation to the developing world; and (3) China's "cooperative"—as opposed to "revisionist"—behavior.

What are China's priorities in the WTO? Beijing's greatest challenge in effectively maneuvering within the WTO process in Geneva is to set clear priorities and to give its diplomats in Geneva the resources and authority to be able to act quickly and effectively. This challenge is dictated in large part by the complexity of trade negotiations and vastness of the trade agenda, the Single Undertaking, and the reality of shifting coalitions. The multiplicity of China's goals is in turn dictated by the diversity of its economic interests, combined with its security and sovereignty goals and its image concerns. Thus, not even accounting for the domestic side of WTO compliance, China is trying to pursue multiple goals related to:

- Sovereignty (Taiwan, TRM)
- A trade strategy (build and diversify export markets)
- Substantive sector-by-sector economic interests
- International relations with the developing world and, especially, Southeast Asia
- Global image—a desire to be a player at the table with significant leverage, but not a troublemaker (except on sovereignty-related issues), unlike India

China's public strategy has been to pursue all of these goals without giving up any of them. But it has spent most of its time on the issues related to sovereignty and (Taiwan relations aside) on guarding its international image (through Third World bridge rhetoric and by following the lead of other countries). Moreover, China is no different from other countries in which domestic politics is the primary driver of trade policy. Hence, attention to the agricultural negotiations is driven by the domestic political attention now focused on problems in the rural sector and links to social stability, plus the common popular feeling that China was "duped" on its agricultural commitments. Attention to Taiwan's status, much as in other international organizations where Taiwan has a presence, is attributable to the regime's continuing sensitivity to denying any potential implications of Taiwanese sovereignty.

But though domestic politics and economic interests set China's priorities, they are not yet played out in an effective process. There is an absence of clear and effective processes to parse PRC interests and prioritize them such that they are actionable by the negotiators.[80] For China to identify clearly, prioritize, and then make operational its trade policy issues is a complicated undertaking, which requires effective leadership at home. Thus far, neither the domestic interest aggregation process nor the empowerment of the negotiators has occurred, contributing to the gap between the high natural stature predicted for China and its low level of leadership in practice.

China's leadership and coalitional behavior.   Might China in the future take on a proactive leadership role on particular issues, much as the United States or Cairns Group (or even Australia) has done in agriculture? Here, the answer is no, not yet, and not for some time—except in defense of its own singular sovereignty concerns. Interviewees with long experience in the WTO routinely say it would be unusual for China to try to assert leadership at this point—it is simply too early. There is a more fundamental problem with China's leadership potential at this early stage, however. Politically, China has designated itself only as active on behalf of the developing world, and even its "Third World bridge" rhetoric is devoid of implications of true leadership. At the same time, China's core economic interests increasingly lie as much, if not more, with the developed world (or with specific developed countries on specific issues, especially as concerns exports). It cannot lead what it is not and does not wish to be.

In the longer term, China's effectiveness as a great power will be measured in terms of its vision for future WTO rounds and its ability to build coalitions and bring others along. Moreover, in the WTO context, to be proactive also means aggressively engaging in the game of shifting coalitions on an issue-specific basis, and actively pursuing coalitions. To do this, trade policy leaders once again need to have a strong sense of a country's offensive interests, to work actively to build consensus between interested parties at home and in Geneva, and to move an agenda ahead in the WTO. China has shown itself willing to work on general statements with other countries, especially developing countries, or to suggest quiet support (such as to the Cairns Group and U.S. agricultural initiatives). But for the most part, it seems to either go it alone, or to react to already formed coalitions (such as on the steel complaint against the United States). Deep and enduring coalitions are not part of the WTO, but the ability to use coalitions nimbly to serve domestic interests is important. China does not yet play this role well. Domestic politics that hamper the identification of offensive interests in multiple trade areas, as well as the Geneva delegation's weakness as a satellite decision-maker, also are constraining.

Is China a "cooperative" power in the WTO?   There are several fundamental difficulties with the question of whether a nation is a "cooperative" member of an international organization.[81] Too often, cooperation is judged in terms of agreement with the United States. In the WTO, the measure of cooperative behavior must be specifically tied to the formal and informal norms and rules of the organization.

At the level of participation in the institution in Geneva, the answer to the question of whether China is a cooperative power in the WTO is by and large yes. We can look at this question through two lenses. First, how can we characterize China's support for pursuing the Doha Round trade agenda— which is mainly designed to liberalize trade and investment flows but also contains a number of commitments to developing countries? Beijing could in theory coalesce with and even lead a more extreme New International Economic Order (NIEO) southern agenda against the more status quo agenda. But China is not "revisionist" in this dimension. The developing country agenda at Doha is itself hardly revisionist of the whole trading system, although it challenges aspects of it at the edges. Moreover, China has spent much more energy launching and advancing the Doha Round than it has criticizing it. Since the beginning of the Doha Round negotiations, in fact, China has consistently called for talks to move forward on the basis of the existing agenda, notably when the process was on the brink of disaster at Cancun.

Second, and more significantly, does China uphold the formal and informal norms and rules of the organization: consulting formally and informally with other members, avoiding throwing up obstacles to consensus reached by others (unless it is a core interest), understanding that it is a game of shifting coalitions, and so forth? Put another way, does China adhere to the "rules about rules" of the organization? A country that clearly violates rules about how an organization is to be governed cannot be considered cooperative.[82] Again, the answer when posed this way is basically positive. At the level of day-to-day negotiations, cooperation cannot be defined by an absence of conflict with other nations, since conflict over trade interests is assumed and built into the process. Indeed, patterns of disputes in the WTO suggest that conflict between trading nations is more a function of trade volume than fundamental opposition; the huge volume of U.S. trade with Canada and Europe means that the United States routinely conflicts with these allies. Furthermore, because coalitions shift from issue to issue, China cannot therefore be considered uncooperative, because it warmed somewhat to the United States on agricultural negotiations and at that same time joined the steel safeguard complaint against the United States.[83] If so, then the European Union and Japan are also uncooperative. Obviously, at the level of specific issues, the notion of cooperation is quite fluid. China may be hindered in its ability to maneuver nimbly in this system, but it does not challenge this fundamental structure.

Moreover, China has made no sustained effort to change the conservative consensus rules of the WTO. The informal processes to which the consensus rules give life are also accepted by China. China's acceptance of the consensus-related norm of noninterference in issues where core interests are not involved is evident too. In this, China is often contrasted (and contrasts itself) to India, which has been seen as the WTO's resident troublemaker, often criticized for taking ideological positions rather than interest-based ones. Chinese trade officials recognize that India often marginalizes itself and wish to avoid doing so.

Where China has routinely come closest to breaching the "rules about rules" is on the issues of Taiwan and the TRM; these are perhaps the most interesting cases to watch—precisely because they pose the greatest challenges for the idea that institutions shape members' interests and behavior. Both the PRC and Taiwan entered the WTO as full participants in the organization, yet subordinating Taiwan's membership in global forums has been important to China's claim to sovereignty over Taiwan. Beijing's efforts to downgrade Taiwan's status to that of Hong Kong, using the WTO's director general as an agent, contrary to the understanding of members who admitted both parties, indicates an attempt to change some basic terms of the organization. The promise that China will continue to resist the TRM process in future years further suggests that China will continue to rub up against the edges of the rules of the organization on issues connected with sovereignty. Still, even here China more or less abides by the letter, if not the spirit, of the TRM.

Where China has not fully embraced the rules, is there evidence that China is nonetheless being socialized into the WTO's dominant mode of operation? Precisely because China is rather "far out" on the issue of Taiwan, it will be a fruitful place to watch in the future for socialization on the part of China into the norms of the organization.[84] Recall some of China's conciliatory gestures toward the Taiwanese delegation, namely, the willingness—after initial resistance—to hold official meetings with Taiwan over steel and the greater propensity to use English in its interactions. Although at this point, these accommodative signs appear to be more tactical than a result of any genuine persuasion, and while these issues are likely to be a significant source of friction in the future, this could change. Such behavior is an irritant to other members and may produce social opprobrium, perhaps providing a feedback loop for a socialization process that image-conscious China will find difficult to resist. Indeed, seeking to use the WTO's director general as an agent, while itself remaining silent, suggests that Beijing is trying to gain its political goals but also preserve its image.

With the exception of these sovereignty-regarding areas, though, China has not challenged the rules and norms of the WTO. China lent support to a minor reemphasis in the WTO power structure toward developing countries, but this is not central to China's agenda and appears rather to have been a small bone tossed to supporters of the idea of China as a bridge to the Third World. Rather, China is emerging as an upholder of the status quo in areas where this is in its interest. As it is in the case of the United Nations, its stake in the WTO's legitimacy is high. This makes sense, given all China conceded to in order to be admitted, the political costs paid at home, and the domestic understanding of these costs. And it makes sense in light of the concrete interests China brings to the organization—especially opening the export markets of developing countries.

Notes

1. See Alastair Iain Johnston, "Is China a Status Quo Power?" *International Security* 27, 4 (2003): 5–56; Margaret M. Pearson, "China's Integration into the International Trade and Investment Regime," in *China Joins the World: Progress and Prospects*, ed. Elizabeth Economy and Michel Oksenberg (New York: Council on Foreign Relations Press, 1999), 161–205; and Samuel S. Kim, "China and the United Nations," ibid., 42–89.

2. This chapter is primarily empirical and its conclusions are inductive. The data used are drawn primarily from interviews with PRC officials knowledgeable about China's role in Geneva and with foreign observers (mostly trade officials) of China's WTO behavior. The chapter also draws on trade weeklies as the major documentary basis for these findings. The question of China's behavior in the WTO examined in this chapter is conceptually separate from the question of how China is complying with its WTO accession agreement, which is not considered systematically here.

3. The Quad consists of the United States, the European Union, Canada, and Japan. The Cairns Group, a formal organization, comprises seventeen agricultural exporting countries, both developed and developing, committed to a market-based trading system for agriculture. Its members are Argentina, Australia, Bolivia, Brazil, Canada, Chile, Colombia, Costa Rica, Guatemala, Indonesia, Malaysia, New Zealand, Paraguay, the Philippines, South Africa, Thailand, and Uruguay.

4. On the institutional culture of the WTO, see John Braithwaite and Peter Drahos, *Global Business Regulation* (Cambridge: Cambridge University Press, 2000); Anne O. Krueger, ed., *The WTO as an International Organization* (Chicago: University of Chicago Press, 1998); and Gary P. Sampson, ed., *The Role of the World Trade Organization in Global Governance* (Tokyo: UN University Press, 2001).

5. "Friendlies" are also at times used by the United States to achieve another strategy (also common in the APEC), which is to find another country to take the lead on an issue so that it does not immediately alienate those who might quickly oppose what they perceive to be a U.S. initiative.

6. Some observers find this informality to be highly functional and warn against "creeping legalism" in the WTO. See Razeen Sally, *Whither the WTO? A Progress Report on the Doha Round*, Trade Policy Analysis, No. 23 (Washington, D.C.: Cato Institute, 2003), 7.

7. Ibid., 10.

8. In addition to the diplomats, the mission includes drivers, chefs, and servants. Information from interviews with Chinese scholar, Beijing, September 2002; and

MOFTEC official, Beijing, November 2002. See also Gong Wen, "Changes Take Place over the Past Half Year Since China's WTO Entry," *People's Daily* online, 12 July 2002, http://english.peopledaily.com.cn/other/archive.html (archive date 20020711 [11 July] (accessed 27 October 2005).

9. Interview with MOFTEC official, November 2002, and with member of the Chinese delegation in Geneva, New York, 6 February 2004.

10. On bureaucratic interference in China's WTO accession negotiations, see Margaret M. Pearson, "The Case of GATT/WTO," in *The Making of Chinese Foreign and Security Policy in the Era of Reform*, ed. David M. Lampton (Stanford: Stanford University Press, 2001).

11. Obedience to domestic political calculations of economic interest are the expected norm within the WTO and other international organizations. See Judith Goldstein, "International Institutions and Domestic Politics: GATT, WTO, and the Liberalization of International Trade," in *The WTO as an International Organization*, ed. Krueger, 133–52; and I. M. Destler, *American Trade Politics: System Under Stress*, 3d ed. (Washington, D.C.: Institute for International Economics, 1995). On China's domestic trade politics, see Margaret M. Pearson, "The Institutional, Political, and Global Foundations of China's Trade Liberalization," in *Japan and China in the World Political Economy*, ed. Saadia Pekkanen and Kellee S. Tsai (New York: Routledge Press, 2005).

12. See Minister of Foreign Trade Shi Guangsheng's comments in Gong, "Changes . . . Since China's WTO Entry."

13. Nicholas R. Lardy, *Integrating China into the World Economy* (Washington, D.C.: Brookings Institution Press, 2002).

14. Zhang Jin, "Nation Jumps to be World Third Largest Trader," *China Daily*, 11 January 2005, www.chinadaily.com.cn/english/doc/2005-01/11/content _407979.htm (accessed 7 October 2005).

15. Interview, Australian embassy economic officer, Beijing, November 2002. The desire to diversify away from the United States in grain is particularly acute in some quarters, and is a key reason for China's recent pursuit of regional trade agreements, particularly with Southeast Asia.

16. On the informal contacts among top leaders of the delegations, personal communication from business association official, Washington D.C., May 2003. These informal meetings are said to outnumber the formal meetings, and to take place in Chinese.

17. The PRC also apparently hoped to rally Taiwan business pressure on the government to accept such informal, industry-level channels of contact. The use of industry associations to handle business-to-business relations when the PRC firm is state-owned is increasingly common. For example, industry associations frequently handle anti-dumping cases.

18. Trade negotiator Long Yongtu is quoted in "Taiwan Petitions Beijing to Respect WTO," *Central News Agency* (CNA), 4 September 2002.

19. "Changes in Taipei, WTO Dealings," *Central News Agency* (CNA), 11 September 2002. The steel and ethanol actions were directed at several members, not just Taiwan.

20. See Mure Dickie, "China and Taiwan Officials Discuss Trade," *Financial Times*, 16 December 2002, and "China Accepts Talks with Taiwan over Steel Tariffs," *Kyodo News Service*, 4 December 2002.

21. Communication from trade association official, Washington, D.C., 20 May 2003.

22. "China's Refusal to Answer Quad Queries Shuts Down Compliance Review Session," BNA *International Trade Reporter*, 26 September 2002 (online trade journal, available by subscription only).

23. A senior U.S. official who worked extensively on the Shanghai meetings reported that the two sides worked very well together, and that the Taiwan officials who were allowed to come to the mainland, many for the first time, were visibly "giddy" and "thrilled." Ultimately, though, the Chinese delegation refused to call Taiwanese ministers "minister" in either written or oral contexts, deeply annoying members of the Taiwan delegation. Interview with U.S. APEC official, Washington, D.C., August 2002.

24. Interview, Office of the U.S. Trade Representative, August 2002.

25. On 12 February 2003, Supachai is reported to have made five requests of Taiwan. In addition to the two listed above, it was asked that Taiwan change diplomatic titles on name cards and letterheads; that the WTO secretariat use only "sovereignty-neutral terminology when referring to Taiwan," avoiding the terms "country" and "state"; and that Supachai reserve the right to change any terminology in documents that was not sovereignty-neutral. Charles Snyder, "Supporters in US More Pessimistic," *Taipei Times*, 31 May 2003. See also Observer, "Vexed Directory," *Financial Times*, 28 May 2003.

26. The PRC mission had itself once previously tried to use downgraded nomenclature for the Taiwan representative. In the steel talks of December 2002, noted above, the Chinese originally used the title "Taiwan Economic and Trade Office" (TECRO) to refer to Taiwan, implying that Taiwan's delegation held a similar status to those of Hong Kong and Macao. At the meetings themselves, however, China switched to the official terminology of the WTO, the "Separate Customs Territory of Taiwan, Penghu, Kinmen and Matsu" (Dickie, "China and Taiwan Officials Discuss Trade"). It appears that Supachai's later requests were a continuation of Beijing's previous efforts, but under an institutional cover.

27. The TRM is set forth in Paragraph 18 of China's accession protocol. After the TRM expires, China will be subject to a four-year review cycle. The European Union and the United States are reviewed every two years because of their larger trade volume. Lardy, *Integrating China into the World Economy*, 104.

28. Interview, U.S. trade official, Washington, D.C., August 2002. This official contrasted MOFTEC's prickly TRM response to its normally "helpful" attitude.

29. China also clashed with the United States, Canada, and Japan in the first Agriculture Committee TRM discussion, with China answering only part of the questions (orally) and saying it would follow up bilaterally. The dialogue in the Committee on Import Licensing (24 September 2002) was similar to the market access talks, although China did supply some written answers in that venue. The review process went smoothly on intellectual property, a topic on which U.S.

government officials at the time felt China was genuinely responding. Sources for this paragraph are: "China Rejects U.S. Push for More Review of Market Access Commitments," *Inside US-China Trade*, 27 September 2002; "China's Refusal to Answer Quad Queries Shuts Down Compliance Review Session"; Daniel Pruzin, "China Chafes at Dumping Panel Agenda for Excessive Focus on Accession Issues," *BNA International Trade Reporter*, 26 April 2002; "China Refuses to Discuss WTO Trade Review in Farm, SPS Committees," *Inside US-China Trade*, 3 July 2002, 5; "China Agrees to Allow Trade Remedy Review; Balks on Procedures," ibid., 15 May 2002, 1, 4; Daniel Pruzin, "China Review Woes Continue in WTO as Agriculture Meeting Questions TRQS," *BNA International Trade Reporter*, 3 October 2002; and interview, USTR official, Washington, D.C., August 2002.

30. Interview with MOFTEC official, November 2002, Beijing. A U.S. embassy official confirmed this "cold shoulder treatment" in an interview in Beijing in November 2002.

31. Interview, PRC diplomat to the WTO, New York, 6 February 2004.

32. See preamble to the "Ministerial Declaration" (WT/MIN(01)/DEC/W/1, 14 November 2001, paras. 2 and 3, at www.wto.org/english/thewto_e/minist_e/min01_e/mindecl_e.htm (accessed 27 October 2005). On the developing country agenda, see Sally, *Whither the WTO?* 18–22, and Rubens Ricupero, "Rebuilding Confidence in the Multilateral Trading System: Closing the 'Legitimacy Gap,'" in *Role of the World Trade Organization*, ed. Sampson, 37–58.

33. Interviews with a senior MOFTEC official deeply involved in WTO accession, Washington, D.C., May 2002; and a Chinese scholar, Beijing, September 2002.

34. This is also the position of the United States. Nobody would argue that the U.S. support here puts it in the development camp.

35. These comments were made by then Foreign Trade Minister Shi Guangsheng, and are quoted in *Inside US-China Trade*, 1 May 2002, 3–4. See also the comments of Vice Minister Long Yongtu quoted in "Speed Urged for Global Trade Talks," *China Daily* online, 20 July 2002, www.chinadaily.com.cn/en/doc/2002-07/20/content_128755.htm (accessed 1 November 2005). China also calls for technical assistance to developing countries at IMF board meetings.

36. This effort in January 2002 was pushed by a broad coalition, including most African countries and many in Central America and the Caribbean, plus Pakistan, and opposed by the Quad countries, Southeast Asian countries, and India. A complicating twist that helped split developing countries was that the incoming director general, Supachai Panitchpakdi, who is Thai, had been backed for the position by many developing countries. See D. Ravi Kanth, "China: The New and 'Pushy' Boy on the Block," *Asia Times* online, 7 February 2002, and *Inside US-China Trade*, 25 January 2002. The effort was not successful in the short term, but China indicated that it was conceding only for this round. The proposal was linked to a preference (which was adopted) that the six TNC subcommittee chairs be from member countries.

37. *Inside US-China Trade*, 8 February 2002, and Kanth, "China: The New and 'Pushy' Boy."

38. "China Takes Lead Role in Shaping WTO Negotiating Procedures," *Inside US-China Trade*, 6 February 2002, 1, 4.

39. This view was repeated in interviews with various former and current U.S. trade officials, Washington, D.C., and Beijing, August–September 2002. Argentina was said to have been quite vocal in its view of China as a competitor.

40. Greg Rushford, "Washington's Dirty War on Chinese Clothing," *Far Eastern Economic Review* 168, 1 (2005): 31–36.

41. One assessment of China's trade interests from the developing country perspective argues that the prospective picture for competitive exports from China is mixed, and shows that it must be discussed on a sector- and country-specific basis. S. M. Shafaeddin, *The Impact of China's Accession to WTO on the Exports of Developing Countries*, UNCTAD Discussion Paper No. 160 (Geneva: United Nations Conference on Trade and Development, 2002), www.unctad.org/en/docs/dp_160.en.pdf (accessed 7 October 2005). See also Lardy, *Integrating China into the World Economy*, 126–27.

42. Interview with Chinese trade official, Washington, D.C., August 2002.

43. In the APEC, for example, China is seen as avoiding coalitions and does not engage in or form alternatives to the Buick Group (including the United States, Australia, New Zealand, Hong Kong, Singapore, Canada, and Chile).

44. Interviews with U.S. and PRC trade officials, Washington, D.C., and Beijing, August and September 2002. China's efforts on the Doha Round in Shanghai can be seen in the context of Beijing's willingness to channel the most significant portion of the agenda to security issues raised after the events of 11 September 2001.

45. China is acutely aware of this sensitivity and often acts to downplay actions that might further deepen the notion that its economic growth will come at the expense of its Southeast Asian neighbors.

46. The working draft used as the basis for negotiations had been submitted by the General Council chairman, Uruguay's Ambassador Carlos Perez del Castillo. This draft was seen by the G20 as too similar to the draft the United States and European Union had agreed to several weeks earlier in meetings in Montreal and as ignoring concerns raised in a paper submitted in response by the G20 in August.

47. See Martin Khor, "Developing Countries Prepare for Agricultural Battle at Cancun Ministerial," *TWN Report*, 9 September 2003.

48. Peter Wonacott and Neil King, "China Moves Quietly to Push Trade Goals: Beijing, Balancing Needs to Its Farmers, Factories, Treads Softly at WTO Talks," *Wall Street Journal*, 15 September 2003.

49. Ma Yu, "China Belongs to No Trade Group," *Asian Wall Street Journal*, 25 September 2003, A11.

50. Interview, Chinese trade official, Washington D.C., August 2002.

51. Various interviewees noted this not only with regard to China's behavior in the WTO (such as on some of the governance issues noted previously), but also in the APEC and at the International Telecommunications Union (ITU).

52. Interviews with U.S. officials involved at both the leaders' level and various sectoral ministers' meetings, Washington, D.C., July and August 2002. On substantive trade issues, the Chinese planners were reportedly reluctant to put forward their own proposals and eventually accepted the U.S. government's proposal for and the substance of the "Shanghai Accord" that became the main work of the meeting.

53. "China's WTO Entry Could Hurt Developing Country Interests," *Inside US-China Trade*, 7 November 2001, 5. One argument made by both U.S. and EU trade officials is that, because most of China's commitments will be phased in as of 2005, and because the Doha Round is not expected to conclude before that, it will be in a position to offer more.

54. Overall, China's trade barriers still remain higher than those of the United States, European Union, Canada, etc., and in areas of keen interest to these countries. So despite the fact that barriers have come down fast and are lower than many other developing countries (two points China emphasizes), they still exist (the point the developed economies emphasize).

55. It is noteworthy that China's proposals, while request-heavy, are nevertheless said to be detailed and fairly well thought through, in contrast to India's strategy. Interview with EU delegation representative, Beijing, October 2002.

56. During the second half of 2002, the United States, the European Union, and even China offered proposals on agricultural liberalization. The differences between these proposals were substantial, and the first major deadline by which the interested parties were to have agreed on negotiating modalities, 31 March 2003, passed without agreement. Elizabeth Becker, "Negotiators Fail to Agree on Agricultural Subsidies," *New York Times*, 1 April 2003, C1.

57. U.S. agricultural production has, of course, relied heavily on domestic supports for agriculture, a fact that seriously undermines trust in the United States as an agricultural liberalizer. Nevertheless, compared to the EU-based coalition, and particularly in the Doha Round, U.S. trade policy has increasingly favored restricting the special exemption that agricultural trade has had in the GATT. An account that categorizes the main players in two camps—a development perspective and a trade-liberalizer perspective—is David Orden, Rashid S. Kaukab, and Eugenio Diaz-Bonilla, *Liberalizing Agricultural Trade and Developing Countries*. Carnegie Endowment TED Policy Brief No. 6 (Washington, D.C.: Carnegie Endowment for International Peace, 2003), summary at www.carnegieendowment.org/publications/index.cfm?fa=view&id=1202&prog=zgp&proj=zted (accessed September 27, 2005).

58. The G10 also includes Taiwan.

59. China's proposal was written by the Ministry of Agriculture, but it appears to be derivative of work by the OECD. Interview, Canadian trade official, October 2002, Beijing.

60. Interview, USTR official, August 2002. Recall also Long Yongtu's comment, noted above, that developing countries should go along with agricultural liberalization.

61. Interview, MOFTEC official, Beijing, November 2003. This official did note that on GMO labeling, China's position is closer to that of the European Union, and that Switzerland has articulated some reasonable positions on a formula for tariff reduction.

62. Key among the developing country proposals for what should constitute "special and differential treatment" is the idea of adding a "development box" in agriculture, which would target low-income and resource-poor farmers (particularly

to ensure rural employment) and would provide exemptions for crops deemed necessary for secure "food security" in these countries. "WTO Members Split on 'Development Box' and S & D," *Bridges Weekly Trade News Digest*, 12 February 2002.

63. On the Doha positions, see Daniel Pruzin, "Harbison Calls on WTO Members to 'Change Gears' in Agricultural Talks," BNA *International Trade Reporter*, 3 October 2002. The agricultural goals of the Doha Round are expressed in the Ministerial Declaration of 2001. In addition to these main pillars, the developing countries are to receive "special and differential treatment" to take account of food security issues and the needs of rural development. "Non-trade concerns," such as animal welfare and consumer protection, also are to be considered, largely at the behest of the European Union. Sally, *Whither the WTO?* 15.

64. Lardy, *Integrating China into the World Economy*, 75–76. The TRQ commitments lower import quotas to below this for designated agricultural products. Global food and agricultural tariffs average about 62 percent. U.S. average agricultural tariffs are about 12 percent.

65. Sally, *Whither the WTO?* 15.

66. Domestic agricultural supports are classified into three "boxes": amber box (trade-distorting, and subject to reduction commitments), green box (non–trade distorting, exempt from reduction commitments), and blue box (production-limiting supports, also exempted from WTO reduction commitments) subsidies. See www.wto.org/english/tratop_e/agric_e/agboxes_e.htm (accessed 21 October 2005). There is much contention over the exemption of "blue box" and "green box" supports, used heavily by the United States, the latter because their sheer volume is said by some, including the Cairns Group, to be distorting. See Pruzin, "Harbison Calls on WTO Members."

67. The U.S. position unveiled in the summer of 2002 called for simplification of trade-distorting domestic subsidies (phased in over a five-year period) to 5 percent of a country's total value of agricultural production (i.e., equalizing this for all countries) and then moving to eventual elimination; see www.fas.usda.gov/itp/wto/proposal.htm (accessed 3 November 2005). At present, according to the U.S. Department of Agriculture, Europe is at 25 percent, Japan at 40 percent, and United States at 10 percent (Ann Veneman, press conference, 29 July 2002). China agreed in its WTO accession, after much last-minute dispute, to domestic supports of no greater than 8.5 percent. Lardy, *Integrating China into the World Economy*, 92.

68. Lardy, *Integrating China into the World Economy*, 94. Developed countries had previously agreed to reduce the value of their agricultural export subsidies by 36 percent by 2005, and developing countries by 24 percent.

69. See Shi Guangsheng's comments in Wen, "Changes Take Place over the Past Half Year Since China's WTO Entry." These comments were echoed by Long Yongtu, *China Daily*, 20 July 2002. More than 80 percent of all agricultural export subsidies are accounted for by the European Union, whereas only 25 of the 134 WTO members (as of February 1999) were entitled to use export subsidies—and most of these were developed countries. "Export Subsidies: Detrimental to Developing Country Exports" (undated Cairns Group fact sheet), www.cairnsgroup.org/factsheets/export_subsidies.pdf (accessed 31 October 2005).

70. *Inside US-China Trade*, 21 June 2002. This was in fact quite similar to an earlier Cairns Group proposal.

71. Daniel H. Rosen, Scott Rozelle, and Jikun Huang, *Roots of Competitiveness: China's Evolving Agricultural Interests* (Washington, D.C.: Institute for International Economics, 2004).

72. Under the U.S. proposal, the United States would maintain certain "green boxed" domestic supports (such as direct payments to farmers to not grow crops or income insurance). On export credit negotiations, see "Agriculture," *Doha Round Briefing Series* 1, 2 (Geneva: International Center for Trade and Sustainable Development, 2003), at www.ictsd.org/pubs/dohabriefings/doha2-agric.pdf (accessed 31 October 2005).

73. Lardy, *Integrating China into the World Economy*, 123.

74. Ibid., 123–25.

75. Interviews with former U.S. trade officials involved in China's WTO accession agreements, July 2002. On developing countries textile exporters' support for U.S. safeguards against China, see Rushford, "Washington's Dirty War on Chinese Clothing."

76. Interview with non-U.S. trade official, Beijing, October 2002.

77. Interview, Chinese trade official, Washington, D.C., August 2002.

78. U.S. protectionism was also evident in the imposition in 2003 of quotas on certain types of Chinese imports. See Rushford, "Washington's Dirty War on Chinese Clothing."

79. Lucy Hornby, "EU, China Clinch Deal to Avert Textiles Showdown," Reuters, 10 June 2005, www.reuters.com/newsArticle.jhtml?storyID=8759653&type=businessNews (accessed 10 June 2005).

80. Some of the agency problems between Beijing and its trade negotiators that were evident in China's WTO accession negotiations continue to be relevant. In those negotiations, the inability of China's trade officials to gain consensus (both at home and with foreign interlocutors) meant that the Chinese timing was often "off." By the time Chinese negotiators were ready to address and resolve an issue, the negotiators on the other side had already moved on to something else. Interviews with U.S. and EU trade negotiators, Washington, D.C. and Beijing, August and September 2002.

81. A relevant question is *whose* definition of the norms of the WTO are to be used: those of intellectuals (primarily liberal trade economists and their counterparts in IGOs and NGOs), on the one hand, or those of member states, as evidenced in their actual behavior, on the other? Despite the existence of a well-thought-out free trade paradigm and probably the most theoretically robust underpinning for cooperative behavior found anywhere in the international arena in the late twentieth and early twenty-first centuries, the fact that the WTO itself is driven by member states with interests that only sometimes support free trade is the more significant marker of the true norms. Those who routinely deal with the WTO as bureaucrats or negotiators suggest the great power of the interest-driven paradigm.

82. A classic statement about cooperation with rules and norms of an organization is Abram Chayes and Antonia Handler Chayes, "On Compliance," *International Organization* 47, 2 (1993).

83. Elizabeth Becker, "W.T.O. Rules Against U.S. On Steel Tariff," *New York Times*, 27 March 2003, C1.

84. China's WTO membership could conceivably change its behavior toward interactions with Taiwan in international organizations by changing the material incentives facing China, by altering the distribution of power among the relevant constellation of actors at home (in the PRC), or by socializing China to more cooperative behavior. See Alastair Iain Johnston, "Treating International Institutions as Social Environments," *International Studies Quarterly* 45 (2001): 487–515. There is not at this point any evidence that the first two processes are relevant. Thus, socialization into acceptable norms of behavior and the processes by which socialization occurs seem to be the places to look for explanations of change in China's behavior toward Taiwan in the WTO context.

10 Chinese Foreign Policy Faces Globalization Challenges

Samuel S. Kim

> Who are our enemies? Who are our friends? This is a question of the first importance for the revolution. The basic reason why all previous revolutionary struggles in China achieved so little was their failure to unite with real friends in order to attack real enemies.
>
> —Mao Zedong, 1926

> Opening to the outside world is a long-term basic state policy. Confronted with the globalization trend in economic, scientific, and technological development, we should take an even more active stance in the world by improving the pattern of opening up in all directions, at all levels and in a wide range, developing an open economy, enhancing our international competitiveness, optimizing our economic structure and improving the quality of our national economy.
>
> —Jiang Zemin, 1997

> Globalization has an immense potential to improve people's lives, but it can disrupt—and destroy—them as well. Those who do not accept its pervasive, all-encompassing ways are often left behind. It is our task to prevent this; to ensure that globalization leads to progress, prosperity and security for all. I intend that the United Nations shall lead this effort.
>
> —UN Secretary-General Kofi Annan, 1998

Introduction

At the turn of the new millennium, globalization seemed to have morphed into all things in the eyes of theorists and practitioners of international politics—a fait accompli, a myth, a rallying cry, a journalistic buzzword, and a theoretical puzzle. Like a tidal wave sweeping across the world, the acceleration and intensification of globalization in the last decade of the twentieth century has spewed new opportunities and new dangers to national security, well-being, and identities in both developed and developing countries. At least until 9/11, no subject or phenomenon had elicited as much interest, controversy, and even protest as had globalization among people in the street, ivory-tower academics, political activists, and elites, all advancing conflicting claims about the forces and processes of contemporary globalization. In addition, globalization suddenly has found its way clear to becoming the hottest topic of a "global community" structured and symbolized by the United Nations and its affiliated specialized agencies.[1]

Where does the People's Republic of China stand in the controversial discourse and politics of globalization? This chapter proceeds from the premise that by dint of what it *is* and what it *does*, the PRC is inescapably part of both the world-order problem and the world-order solution. Indeed, as the world's most populous country, enjoying the world's fastest economic growth in the past two decades, rising China holds one of the master keys to the future of globalization in the post–Cold War world. The globalization trope thus offers a useful but relatively underutilized analytical lens with which to track and explain the new thinking and directions in China's foreign policy, especially its global policy. As China is increasingly integrated into the global community, how it wields whatever power it holds—and how the outside world and particularly the East Asian states adapt to the emergence of a global China—provides a new empirical basis for exploring the relationship between globalization and sovereignty, especially the impacts and consequences of globalization for the shaping of Chinese thinking and practices on state sovereignty.

This chapter is organized in four sections to provide an overview of how China is coping with the forces of globalization in the post–Cold War era. The first section briefly appraises the debate over globalization in order to develop an alternative conceptual framework to facilitate a more synthetic assessment of the thinking and practice of globalization in post–Cold War Sino-global interactions. The second section scans the Chinese globalization discourse, especially how the promises and perils of globalization are actually conceived of and addressed by key pundits and decision-makers. The third section explores the complex and evolving interplay between globalization dynamics and China's post-Mao global policy, particularly with respect to the questions of unilateralism versus multilateralism, state sovereignty versus global interdependence, and national security versus cooperative—human—security. The final section sketches out several challenges to both Chinese foreign policy itself and the advancement of Chinese foreign policy studies in the coming years.

China in the Global Discourse

Globalization is a socially constructed and politically contested concept. Despite the burgeoning literature, there is as yet no dominant theory of globalization that commands much theoretical excitement, let alone paradigmatic status.[2] While globalization is mentioned as one of the four leading post–Cold War international relations (IR) theories in the Chinese scholarly discourse,[3] the scholarly discourse in the United States is dominated by the continuing turf war of contending realist, liberal, and constructivist theories.[4]

The globalization debate has remained sterile, dominated by two extreme views. At one extreme, hyperglobalists advance a Panglossian claim that globalization heralds the emergence of a truly open and integrated global economy, the rise of a new post-Westphalian global order, and the functional demise of the state system.[5] At the other extreme, neorealist skeptics argue that there is nothing new in today's world economy, and that all the frenzy about globalization amounts to nothing more than "globaloney." Relying on a wholly economistic conception of globalization, neorealist skeptics argue that the historical evidence at best confirms only the existence of heightened levels of interaction between predominantly national economies. The postwar growth of international economic transactions is seen as representing internationalization or regionalization rather than the emergence of a truly global economy, and the current levels of international trade are seen as comparable to—or even lower than—those during the classical gold-standard period (c. 1870–1914). Moreover, skeptics assert that the state is as robust as it ever was, with an impressive array of political options.[6] "The claim that globalization is undermining sovereignty," according to a neorealist skeptic, "is exaggerated and historically myopic."[7]

Much of the globalization debate in the worlds of academia and punditry, dominated by the hyperglobalization and globaloney schools, has been marred by tenuous conceptualizations, ideological presuppositions and polemics, and inattention to the full range of available empirical evidence. Both schools are misconceived, proceeding from the dubious premise of globalization as an ideal end—a fully globalized economy—rather than as an ongoing process with ups and downs. Globalization is better seen as a continuum. The either/or conceptions of globalization that underlie the current debates, suggesting either that a paradigmatic change has already occurred, heralding a new post-Westphalian global order, or that there is nothing new in contemporary international life, stand on shaky ground historically and empirically.

The neoliberal hyperglobalization school commits the fallacy of premature specificity of and optimism regarding the benefits of globalization and the demise of the putatively obsolescent state. All the same, there is considerable evidence to rebut the neorealist claim that the contemporary international economy is not so very different from that of the gold-standard era. New tools of communication, new markets, new actors (both state and nonstate), and new rules and institutions have all combined to fuel globalization dynamics. The scope, intensity, speed, sheer numbers, modalities, and impact of human relations and transactions have radically increased regionally and globally, eroding the boundaries between hitherto separate economic, political, and sociocultural entities throughout the world.

An appraisal of the interplay between globalization and Chinese foreign policy requires a broad conceptual framework that shies away from hyperglobalist assumptions about the functional demise of the state, while also avoiding the neorealist and neomercantilist critique that does not adequately take into account new patterns and dynamics. The concept of globalization suggested here follows the "transformationalist thesis,"[8] which refers to an interactive and interpenetrating process that relates multiple levels and facets of modern life—economics, politics, society, culture, security, and ecology. Globalization is defined as a boundary-expanding or boundary-penetrating and boundary-weakening process that intensifies the levels of interconnectedness and interpenetration within and among states and societies—a worldwide revolution with far-reaching but differing consequences for people's security, well-being, and identities. As a consequence, the separation between the local and the global, between "domestic" and "foreign" affairs, has become increasingly blurred. Perhaps the most salient feature of globalization is this intensification of domestic and external linkages. This transformational perspective seems best suited to capture the new thinking, new directions, and new behavioral tendencies in Chinese foreign policy.

China's Evolving Views

Deng Xiaoping's reform and opening in 1978, while not explicitly understood or recognized at the time as a response to the emerging challenges of globalization, may in practice be considered exactly that.[9] There was a drastic reformulation (and relegitimation) of China's future in terms of such hitherto proscribed concepts as the open door, international interdependence, division of labor, and specialization. China's backwardness and stunted modernization were attributed, not to Western imperialism, but to China's own isolationism, going back to the Ming dynasty. For Deng, Chinese nationalism and globalization were defined in virtuous and mutually complementary terms: the so-called "grabbing with two hands" approach. With one hand, China would grasp reform and opening (economic globalization) as necessary to grow strong and prosperous, while at the same time suppressing all kinds of ideological and cultural pollutants from abroad (cultural globalization) with the other hand.[10]

From a diachronic perspective, it is worth noting that only four years before the advent of Deng's reforms, Chinese UN Ambassador Huang Hua, using a vivid Chinese metaphor, declared to the global audience at the Sixth Special Session of the General Assembly that "interdependence" in the contemporary world economy was a fig leaf obscuring the asymmetrical inter-dependence "between a horseman and his mount."[11] Indeed, for the *dependencia* and world-system theorists, Mao's China was the exception—an anti-center model, as it were—that supported their thesis about the global political economy of center-periphery capitalism. Johan Galtung argued in 1976, for example, that the center countries were "not only on the decline in terms of power, but also as *models*—which, of course, is one aspect of their total power decline" and then argued that "if any country is a model, it would rather be China."[12]

The heated and short-lived debate on "global citizenship" (*qiuji*) that the *World Economic Herald* (Shanghai) initiated in 1988 is representative of the Chinese debate on globalization. The meaning of "global citizenship" that came out of this debate seems clear enough. Acknowledging that the new wave of scientific and technological revolution was creating complex global networks of mutual influence and infiltration, it was said that China could choose either not to emancipate its political-economy thinking—thereby falling behind in the technological race, forfeiting its "global citizenship" in the process—or to more fully integrate itself into the world market and make more creative use of the global economy—whereby the country could leap into the front ranks of world power.[13]

In the wake of the Tiananmen carnage, the concept of "global citizenship" or the notion of "global village consciousness" was denounced as one source of the ideas behind the uprising of 4 June.[14] Even President George H. W. Bush's call for a "new world order" was attacked in China as the invisible integrationist hand of the conspiratorial "peaceful evolution" strategy of seeking to establish a "'free' federation or a federation of 'democratic countries' on the basis of a common principle and common outlook and values." The Chinese view at the time was that such a scheme involved a hidden American agenda of bringing the entire world under hegemonic U.S. rule.[15]

By the mid 1990s, the word "globalization" had found its way clear into Chinese discourse. Li Shenzhi, former vice president of the Chinese Academy of Social Science (CASS), advances the most liberal "think globally, act locally" proposition. According to Li, transnational, supranational, and global forces are at work, multiplying global problems and defying national solution; hence it behooves all nations to seek common solutions through multilateral cooperation. "If China chooses chauvinism," Li argues, "it will be China's and the world's disaster; if China chooses globalism, it will be China's and the world's fortune." In an era of globalization, the solution to the perennial Chinese *ti-yong* quest should be "treating the universal laws of globalization as 'essence' (*ti*) and Chinese characteristics as 'utility' (*yong*), thus turning the well-known axiom of Chinese learning for essence, Western learning for utility" on its head.[16]

Other scholarly works published since 1995 explore how globalization dynamics are impacting and reshaping the traditional notion of a state-centric international order. The mainstream scholarly discourse converges on the notion of globalization as simultaneously empowering and constraining. Contrary to the hyperglobalization and globaloney schools of thought, globalization dynamics have not so much replaced the Westphalian state-centric international order as they have transformed the context and conditions under which states compete for power and plenty.[17]

Also in the Chinese discourse on globalization, there has been a subtle and significant shift in mainstream thinking about world order. Previously, the notion that a strong China was an irreducible prerequisite to international order was central to Deng's reform and opening to the world: "The stronger China grows, the better the chances are for preserving world peace," Deng asserted.[18] The concept of the responsibility of the great powers, though still underexplored in Western IR theory, has in recent years suddenly come to the fore in the Chinese debate on globalization.[19] The rise of China as a responsible great nation in the international community—the notion that China's sense of responsibility to the world is commensurate with its status as a great nation—is said to be a major change in Chinese foreign policy.

Gone apparently is the rooted Sinocentric view of the world justified by the tyrannies of the past and the abiding quest for national identity via civilizational autonomy and political self-sufficiency. In the long stretch of China's encounter with the outside world, foreign (barbarian) technical, commercial, religious, educational, and military advisors have come and gone without making much of a dent in Chinese world-order thinking.[20] China today belongs to the world, and we are now told that the world does not belong to China alone. "China cannot afford to pay the price that the destruction of the existing international system will entail. Nor can it afford the huge cost of setting up a separate system." China should then shy away from an ultranationalist policy or the expansionist policy of hegemony. Should China pursue a revisionist policy, three anti-China consequences would follow: (1) China would face containment by the United States and its Western allies; (2) the security environment in the surrounding region and the world would be damaged; and (3) neighboring countries could be pushed into forming an alliance against China.[21]

The Chinese incremental multilateralism that has emerged in place of revisionism has come about as a result of some changes in Sino-global interaction since the end of the Cold War. However, China is far from the hyperglobalist example par excellence. Based on extensive field interviews in Beijing, Banning Garrett describes opposition to globalization that comes from a loose and shifting coalition of nationalists in the party, media, military, and academia, and also an apparently growing number of vocal ultraleftists in academic institutions and the party. These groups all share a

TABLE 10.1

Globalization in China's "State of the World Message" in the General Assembly's Grand Debate, 1994–2002

Date Doc Symbol Speaker	Number of References	Key Remarks
09/28/94 A/49/PV.8 Qian Qichen	Multipolarity = 1 WTO = 2	"Globalization" is not mentioned, but the speech does say, in urging developed countries to take measures to share their wealth with other countries and to strengthen economic cooperation, that "the world economy is an interdependent whole."
09/27/95 A/50/PV.8 Qian Qichen	N/A	The closest mention is the phrase "The worldwide tendency towards economic integration, regionalization and the formation of economic groupings has accelerated."
10/24/95 A/50/PV.39 Jiang Zemin	N/A	Jiang speaks of the "internationalization of economic life" and mentions the need for international cooperation on global issues like the environment and population control.
09/25/96 A/51/PV.8 Qian Qichen	Multipolarity = 3 Globalization = 3	The first mention of economic globalization occurs in this speech; it is cited as a "tide" and as a rare opportunity for all countries to enhance cooperation. China also speaks of the need to address noneconomic global issues through international cooperation.
09/24/97 A/52/PV.9 Qian Qichen	Multipolarity = 1 Globalization = 1	Here China approves that the "economic links and mutual penetration among countries and regions are on the constant increase" but warns of the risks of the "highly globalized" international financial market. A paragraph is also devoted to "transboundary issues."
09/23/98 A/53/PV.11 Tang Jiaxuan	Multipolarity = 1 Globalization = 3 WTO = 2	The trends of multipolarity and economic globalization are cited as indications of a readjustment of international relations. The 1997 crisis occurred "in the overall context of globalization," but China pledges to "keep abreast of the trend of globalization" and expresses its wish to join the WTO. The "accelerated democratization" of international relations (IR) is first mentioned in this speech.
09/22/99 A/54/PV.8 Tang Jiaxuan	Multipolarity = 1 Globalization = 1 WTO = 1	Wealthy countries are asked to share in the responsibility of contributing to the growth of developing countries because "the world economy is an interrelated and indivisible whole." China requests that the UN hold a conference to discuss the globalization of the world economy and other global issues such as poverty, the environment, population, etc.

TABLE 10.1   *(continued)*

Date Doc Symbol Speaker	Number of References	Key Remarks
09/06/00 A/55/PV.3 Jiang Zemin	Multipolarity = 2 Globalization = 3	"The trends towards multi-polarization and economic globalization are gaining momentum" opens this speech. China points out that the fruits of economic globalization and modern technology are not shared by all, as well as mentioning the need to address the environment, drugs, and refugees internationally.
11/11/01 A/56/PV.46 Tang Jiaxuan	Globalization = 5 WTO = 2	For the first time, China describes the question of security as becoming globalized and points to the positive and negative aspects of globalization; it is "neither a panacea for development nor a monster causing disaster," the speech reads. The need to "democratize" IR comes up again.
09/13/02 A/57/PV.5 Tang Jiaxuan	Globalization = 2	China speaks of the need to "strengthen guidance and management of the globalization process." Following on the security issue, the speech reads, "countries have come to realize that they have common security interests and feel a greater sense of interdependence."

common belief that entry into the World Trade Organization (WTO) is a threat to China's political, cultural, and economic sovereignty.[22] In the wake of China's accession to the WTO in November 2001, however, the anti-globalization groups shifted from outright opposition to a discussion of how best to meet the new challengers, new rules and norms, and new governing procedures imposed by China's WTO commitments.[23]

And as compared to the hyperglobalist ideal, most Chinese observers and policymakers conceive of globalization in state-centric and state-empowering terms. The official understanding, as made evident in the annual "state of the world messages" given to the UN General Assembly over the past decade, is that economic globalization is not only state-centric but also largely one-dimensional. As Table 10.1 shows, the first mention of "economic globalization" occurs in Foreign Minister Qian Qichen's state of the world message delivered on 25 September 1996, a year earlier than President Jiang Zemin's political report to the Fifteenth Chinese Communist Party (CCP) Congress invoked the phrase "economic globalization" to the domestic audience for the first time. Content analysis of China's annual state of the world messages also reveals that the term "globalization" is often used in connection with "multipolarization," cited as a reason for the changing trend of international relations, and described as a double-edged sword to call attention to the need for the "standardization and management of globalization."

The real surprise in Table 10.1 has to do with the 2001 "state of the world message" that for the first time describes "security" as becoming increasingly globalized, indicating an extra-economic concept of globalization. Simultaneously, the concept of multipolarization that had remained as a recurring theme and claim in Chinese foreign policy pronouncements since the early 1980s seems to have suffered a disconnect from the concept of globalization. In a similar vein, the annual frequency of the term "multipolarization" (*duo-jihua*) in the *People's Daily* in 1990–2000 appears to be on the steady decline relative to the term "globalization" (*quanqiuhua*).[24] The strategic implications of such a shift in China's global policy pronouncements are not self-evident, but the two terms at the very least assume very different means and ends of seeking what the Chinese call "comprehensive national strength" (*zonghe guoli*).

China's Evolving Strategy

In the post–Cold War world, which is becoming simultaneously increasingly interdependent and fragmented, it is one thing for a state to announce a positive view of globalization and quite another for a state to engage substantively with globalization. Even though Chinese leaders and scholars may publicly claim in general terms that there is no necessary or inevitable conflict between globalization and sovereignty-bound concepts (e.g., traditional security, multipolarity, independence), there is growing recognition, albeit more often outside of China, that globalization by any definition requires a strategic choice about the basic structure and goals of the economy and the society, a choice that will determine the nature and direction of their developmental trajectory. It is important, therefore, to break down the areas in which China is more or less fully engaging with globalization.

ECONOMIC GLOBALIZATION

China clearly is a big winner in the (economic) globalization game. Beijing's generally positive view of and response to globalization are fueled by impressive economic accomplishments, which in turn reinforce the belief that the country is well positioned to take further advantage of globalization in the future. As early as 1991, the World Bank had singled out post-Mao China as having garnered an all-time global record in doubling per capita output in the shortest period (1977–87).[25] China's GDP growth rate during the first decade of the globalization era (1990–2001) is even more impressive. China easily won the global race in economic growth rate and ranking, with the nearest peer competitor being the tiny city-state of Singa-

TABLE 10.2

China's GDP growth rate in comparative perspective,
1990–2001

Country	Average Annual Growth Percentage, 1990–2001
China	10.0%
Singapore	7.8%
India	5.9%
South Korea	5.7%
Hong Kong	3.9%
United States	3.5%
France	1.8%
Germany	1.5%
Japan	1.3%
North Korea	−2.0%
Russia	−3.7%
World Average	2.7%

Sources: Adapted from World Bank, *World Development Report,*
2003 (New York: Oxford University Press, 2003), table 3, 238–39; North
Korea's GDP is based on the Bank of Korea (Seoul).

pore—one of the fastest runners in the globalization race, as shown in
Table 10.2 above.

China's trade exploded, from about $20 billion in the late 1970s to
$1.15 trillion in 2004, as trade as a percentage of GDP—a widely used
measure of a country's integration into the global economy—more than
doubled once every decade, from 5.2 percent in 1970 to 12.9 percent in
1980 to 26.8 percent in 1990 and then 44 percent in 2000, compared to
11 percent for North Korea, 18 percent for Japan, 19 percent for India, and
21 percent for the United States in 2000. In 2004, the rate of China's foreign trade dependence witnessed a steep rise, reaching an all-time high of 70
percent, an increase of 58 points since the end of the Mao era.[26] The country is the world's third-largest trading state after the United States and Germany and is 3.5 times as integrated into the world economy as the United
States or Japan. China is also the world's largest recipient of foreign direct
investment ($60.6 billion in 2004)[27] and the world's second-largest holder
of foreign exchange reserves ($609.9 billion in 2004). All of this has con-
tributed to China having a $7.2 trillion gross national income on a purchas-
ing power parity (PPP) basis (as of 2004).

Foreign direct investment has gone into bolstering China's position as the
world's primary assembly line. China now produces more steel than Japan
and the United States combined, and it is also a leader in almost every category of manufactured goods, from shoes to semiconductors.[28] In the early

twenty-first century, without much fanfare, China began bridging the digital divide to become a significant player in the information-technology (IT)
industry. In 2000, China surpassed Taiwan as the world's third-largest
producer of computer hardware.[29] In 2001, China surpassed the United
States to become the world's largest mobile phone user and market and also
became the world's third-largest maker of IT products, after the United
States and Japan.

The downside of China's political economy in the post-Mao era is rapid
growth in income inequality. As measured by the Gini coefficient, this income inequality had risen to 0.458 by 2000, up from 0.424 in 1996.
China's ranking in the UN Development Programme's human development
index dropped from 82d (out of 160) in 1990 to 96th (out of 173) in 2000,
although the human development index itself registered an improvement
from 0.614 to 0.726. Rapid growth helped lift some 200 million Chinese
out of poverty between 1978 and 1995, but the poor (under the World
Bank's international poverty line of $1 a day) still made up 18.8 percent of
China's population (i.e., 239 million people) as of the end of 2001, down
from 22 percent in 1995.[30] The PRC remains a poor global power in per
capita terms: in 2004, national income per capita was only $1,290 (or
$5,530 on a PPP basis).[31]

Despite being enmeshed in the Asian-Pacific economic matrix and bur-
dened by enormous debt, China emerged relatively unscathed from the
1997–98 Asian financial crisis. China's relative immunity was due to the
nonconvertibility of its currency, substantial foreign exchange reserves to
defend against speculative attacks on the yuan, and a large inflow of FDI,
only a small percentage of which is portfolio investment, which is more vulnerable than capital investment to quick withdrawal in a panic.

Beijing's response to the Asian financial crisis shows a variety of considerations are at work in shaping China's policy and behavior, including
China's integration into the global community as a responsible great power,
which seems to be the primary factor. China's policy elites seldom fail to
cite Beijing's refusal to devalue the renminbi (RMB) as positive proof of its
status as a responsible great power. Beijing's decision not to devalue the
RMB is explained again in "grabbing with two hands" terms: "On the one
hand, the non-devaluation of the renminbi demonstrated to the world community China's formidable economic muscle. On the other hand, China has
impressed its neighbors as a country that does not take advantage of others'
misfortune or hit a person when he is down. It also shows that as a great
nation, China feels a sense of responsibility for the stability of the international system as well as the regional order in Asia."[32]

Responsible great powerdom aside, it was not in China's own interest to
devalue the RMB. Although devaluation would have made finished Chinese

goods cheaper on the world market, it would also have raised the price of imports. According to most estimates, about 50 percent of China's total exports depend on the processing of imported raw materials. China's integration into the world economy has complicated the calculation of relative and absolute gains, making it non-zero-sum. Indeed, the Asian financial crisis is said to have strengthened China's resolve to maintain the momentum of its reform and opening to meet the challenges of globalization and to more fully integrate into the global economy.[33] Beijing must increasingly define its interests in the context of its position as a responsible economic power and according to how its behavior could sire instability contrary to its own national interests.

By any reckoning, the WTO has become a lightning rod for anti-globalization protests. As protests against the WTO became frequent, China completed its protracted struggle to gain WTO entry. Despite significant opposition at home and major sovereignty-diluting preconditions imposed by the United States, China's leadership arrived at the conclusion that economic globalization was indeed irresistible and that China could either join the trend or be left behind. As explained by Jiang Zemin, "Joining the WTO is a strategic policy decision by the Chinese government under the situation of economic globalization; it is identical with China's objective of reform, opening up, and establishing a socialist market economic structure."[34]

After fourteen years of often difficult negotiations, in late 2001, China finally became a member of the WTO under terms that hewed to the long-standing Western demands not only for reducing tariff and nontariff barriers but also for opening up long-closed sectors such as telecommunications, banking, and insurance. In a few important areas, China assumed obligations that exceed normal WTO standards—the so-called WTO-plus commitments.[35] There is no denying that Beijing's determination to gain WTO entry at almost any price represents a big gamble in the checkered history of China's engagement with the global community. Why then did Beijing take some unprecedented sovereignty-diluting steps to gain WTO entry?

While there is no simple or single answer, China's WTO entry nonetheless underscores the extent to which the forces of globalization have blurred the traditional divide between the international and the domestic, confronting China's leadership with "intermestic" challenges. As Joseph Fewsmith argues, what really convinced the Chinese leadership to proceed with the deal, despite or perhaps even because of the mounting domestic opposition, was the commitment of Jiang Zemin and Zhu Rongji to globalization and a fundamental restructuring of Chinese industry. Politically, failure to reach an agreement would have left Jiang in a passive position vis-à-vis his domestic adversaries, including Li Peng. Jiang would have faced a large and inefficient government-owned enterprise sector with no way to address its problems.[36]

Indeed, Jiang and Zhu seem to have assigned an almost impossible multi-tasking social and economic mission to foreign trade, especially exports: alleviating the growing unemployment problem, increasing tax revenues and the state's foreign exchange reserves, fueling steady economic growth, accelerating technology transfer, and above all enhancing the competitiveness and productivity of domestic enterprises. China's participation in the WTO is also seen not only as providing one of the most important channels to participation in economic globalization but also as allowing Beijing more space to exert its influence on the management of economic globalization. Status drive, not as a hegemonic or revisionist power but as a responsible great power, is preprogrammed in the form of mutual legitimation—the WTO needs China; China needs the WTO. The not-so-subtle subtext of China's status drive is clear enough: "The rise in a country's economic status will bring about a corresponding rise in its political status."[37]

As revealed in Jiang Zemin's major speeches since 1997, the forces that most define China's national identity now are those associated with globalization.[38] This shows the extent to which China has shifted from ideological or nationalistic legitimation to performance-based legitimation. Such performance-based legitimation can be generated over the long term only through increased trade, foreign investment, and the more disciplined and rule-bound domestic economy that WTO membership is expected to bring about. And yet the question of how to bring nationalistic legitimation in sync with performance-based legitimation is left unmentioned and unresolved, opening the door, if only in principle, to other claimants to legitimacy.

SECURITY GLOBALIZATION

What does it mean for the Chinese state and people to be or feel "secure" in an era of globalization? With the clarity, simplicity, and apparent stability of the Cold War gone, the agency and the scope of "threat" as well as the sources and effects of security globalization have become more complex and diverse than ever. The most common characterization of the relationship between globalization and security is the "outside-in" premise—that is, that globalization impinges upon the state from the outside and transforms the security environment within which it operates. However, security is also affected by internal transformations of the state.[39] The new security environment is increasingly being shaped and defined by the "intermestic" interconnection and interpenetration between the international and domestic spheres. This has been the case in no small part because globalization affects not only external sovereignty choices but also internal sovereignty in terms of relations between the public and private sectors.[40] Security effects of globalization inevitably translate into certain behavioral tendencies in a state's foreign policy.

Although the term "security globalization" (*anquan quanqiuhua*) is seldom used in the Chinese globalization discourse, the question of security is inevitably smuggled into both scholarly writings and policy pronouncements. Some conservative analysts argue that globalization is the functional equivalent of a Hobbesian war-of-all-against-all: "economic wars, commodity wars, technology wars, and wars over talented people—between developed and developing countries and among developing countries."[41] Other Chinese military analysts see globalization as the functional equivalent of "unlimited war." They argue that for a relatively weak country like China to stand up to a powerful country like the United States, it is strategically imperative to resort to compensatory devices such as terrorism, drug trafficking, environmental degradation, and computer virus propagation.[42]

At the other end of the conceptual and normative spectrum, more liberal Chinese scholars have been breaking new ground in defining globalization as more than just an economic phenomenon. In the post–Cold War globalization era, security is seen and defined more broadly and multidimensionally than ever before. Security "refers not only to 'safety' in the military and diplomatic senses, but also to economic and technological security, including financial, trade and investment security, the avoidance of big rises and falls, the ability to have stronger competitive methods and a grasp of information factors."[43] The new security concept has also given rise to the notion of cooperative or collective security. Cooperative security is said to have no common enemy, contrary to Maoist fundamentalism; it only has the need to deal with a potential threat through political dialogue and multilateral arrangements. Cooperative security seeks to increase transparency, deepen mutual understanding, and build institutional ties among the member states to deal with transnational security problems such as drugs, crime, terrorism, and ecological damage, so as to minimize the factors that may prompt one country to go to war against another.[44]

The policy prescription that flows from this liberal and increasingly mainstream discourse on the relationship between globalization and security is that China should pay more attention to the economic, social, and political aspects of security. Hence global human rights and environmental thinking and practices have become part of Chinese thinking on "security globalization." Indeed, China's grand strategy for the new millennium is now said to require placing economic and internal security broadly defined higher than external and military security as conventionally defined.[45] As a result of China's growing global interdependence, economic and social security have come to enjoy a preferred position in Chinese security thinking. Military security is still important but is progressively downplayed in favor of nonmilitary security.[46]

With the rise of a new security concept in 1996, Chinese foreign policy has been slowly and steadily shifted toward a direction of greater multilateral cooperative security. Although the People's Liberation Army has been involved in nine wars and armed conflicts—fought for ideological reasons and for the protection of national sovereignty and territorial integrity—most of these actions were taken in the 1950s and 1960s, and no war involving China took place in the 1990s. This reflects the peaceful settlement of territorial disputes with Russia, Mongolia, the Central Asian republics, Burma, Pakistan, and Vietnam, as well as the demise of the ideological basis for war.[47]

To focus on "war" is perhaps to miss the larger picture of Chinese conflict behavior and crisis management. Yet Johnston's empirical analysis of China's militarized interstate dispute behavior from 1949 to 1992 concludes that "China will be more likely to resort to force—and relatively high levels of force—when disputes involve territory and occur in periods where the perceived gap between desired and ascribed status is growing or larger."[48] Thus the growth seen in Chinese power is not likely per se to translate into a more aggressive use of that power. In fact, China may be less involved in conflicts, as long as its territorial integrity and international status are afforded proper respect. The combined interactive effects of several factors in Chinese foreign relations augur well for the peace and stability of the East Asia region and beyond: (1) the fact that economic globalization sharply increases the costs of the use of force; (2) the successful settlement of territorial disputes with most of China's neighbors, with the corresponding sense of enhanced state sovereignty; (3) the demise of ideological conflict; and (4) the substantial accomplishment of China's status drive to be recognized as a great power.

There is little evidence that China is seeking regional hegemony in East Asia; most Asian nations do not see China as dangerous or threatening. A major multinational citizens' opinion survey, jointly sponsored by *Tong-a Ilbo* (Seoul) and *Asahi Shinbun* (Tokyo), conducted in October and November 2000 and involving national samples of 2,000 in South Korea, 3,000 in Japan, 1,024 in the United States, and 1,000 in China, suggests that China is not generally viewed as a threat. As Table 10.3 shows, the China-threat theory (*Zhongguo weixie lun*) is almost exclusively an American elite perception, especially strong among right-wing Republicans. The survey found that 38.1 percent of the American respondents in the survey singled out China as most militarily threatening, compared to only 7.7 percent of South Koreans. What is most surprising is that only 9.4 percent of Japanese singled out China as most militarily threatening.

Equally revealing are the responses of South Korean, Japanese, and American citizen respondents to the question, "Which country do you think will become the most influential in Asia in ten years [by 2010]? Please select one country, whether it is an Asian country or not." The fact that 52.6 percent of South Korean respondents singled out China as the most influential Asian

TABLE 10.3
Multinational citizens' perceptions of threat and influence in Asia
(late 2000)

		ROK	Japan	U.S.	China
Q-1: By which country do you feel most militarily threatened? Please select one country	1. U.S.	12.4	13.2	—	62.8
	2. Russia	4.0	9.5	20.9	1.2
	3. **China**	**7.7**	**9.4**	**38.1**	—
	4. Japan	20.7	—	2.5	12.4
	5. ROK	—	1.1	0.1	0.4
	6. North Korea	53.7	44.2	6.0	0.2
	7. Do not know/No response	0.3	8.0	10.0	13.7
Question 2: Which country do you think will become the most influential in Asia in ten years? Please select one country, whether it is an Asian country or not.	1. U.S.	8.1	13.7	54.9	9.6
	2. Russia	2.1	1.1	4.7	1.4
	3. **China**	**52.6**	**47.2**	**18.9**	**73.2**
	4. Japan	23.3	8.4	3.8	7.7
	5. ROK	10.7	4.3	0.9	1.1
	6. North Korea	1.0	2.3	2.1	0.1
	7. India	0.1	0.9	1.8	0.4
	8. Vietnam	—	0.3	1.3	—
	9. Others	1.2	0.6	2.0	1.9
	10. None	0.1	7.3	—	—
	11. Do not know/No response	0.8	13.9	9.6	4.6

Source: "Multinational Citizens' Poll on Current States Surrounding Korean Peninsula," *Tong-a Ilbo* (Seoul), 4 December 2000.
Note: South Korea: $N = 2,000$, survey conducted 25 October–18 November 2000. Japan: $N = 3,000$, 19–20 November 2000. United States: $N = 1,024$, 13–18 November 2000. China: $N = 1,000$, 1–10 November 2000.

power in ten years, while only 23.3 percent chose Japan, was to be expected. What is particularly surprising and revealing, however, is that 47.2 percent of Japanese respondents selected China, as against only 8.4 percent for their own country as the most influential Asian power in ten years. Almost five times as many Americans (18.9 percent) selected China, compared to only 3.8 percent for Japan, as the most influential Asian power in ten years, show-ing the extent to which the familiar "Japan as Number One" chorus of the 1980s has vanished from American collective memory.

The post-Mao era witnessed the acceleration and intensification of Sino-UN linkages and interactions, as China's membership and participation in all the remaining UN-related regimes increased steadily, as did Chinese ac-cession to UN-sponsored multilateral treaties. This growing and widening engagement with the UN-centered global community has produced some nontrivial feedback and spillover effects, facilitating certain adjustments and shifts in Chinese multilateral diplomacy and also in the policymaking and policy-reviewing processes and institutions within China.[49]

China's growing multilateralism is made evident in the sensitive domain of arms control and disarmament. As Michael Swaine and Alastair Johnston point out, the Chinese perspective has shifted significantly over the post-Mao years, especially in the 1990s, from a view of arms control as largely irrelevant to China's national security concerns to a broader conception of security that recognizes the benefits to be derived from more active cooperative participation. Whereas Beijing had signed about 10 to 20 percent of all arms control agreements it was eligible to sign in 1970, by 1996, this figure had jumped to 85 to 90 percent. Much of this cooperative behavior had to do with China's determined drive to be seen as a responsible great power.[50]

Despite its absence from conventional security studies, the protection of the environment is a quintessential challenge of the epoch of globalization. It is central to "human security" and "cooperative security," just as it is integral to China's global policy. Indeed, China is rapidly becoming one of the most important if not yet completely unproblematic players in global environmental politics. Beijing plays an active role as a concerned but responsible environmental giant in the preparation and implementation of international environmental conventions. China has already ratified all relevant environmental conventions, including the Kyoto Protocol, the Montreal Protocol, the UN Framework Convention on Climate Change, the UN Convention on Biological Diversity, and the UN Convention to Combat Desertification. The ratification and implementation process itself seems to have worked its way clear to placing environmental issues on the national agenda.[51] However, the discrepancies between promise and performance are perhaps greater in this issue area than in any other area of China's global policy.[52]

Although the question of human rights is conspicuously absent in the Chinese globalization discourse, it deserves brief analysis, given that the concepts of human rights and "human security" are organically interlinked and that China's human rights diplomacy highlights one crucial and contentious dimension of Sino-global interaction as well as the relationship between sovereignty and globalization.

China's human rights diplomacy in the post–Cold War and post-Tiananmen era has proved to be most confusing, turbulent, and significant, marked by a series of unprecedented events.[53] Although the human rights clock was set back after the Tiananmen carnage, China returned to global human rights politics with a divide-and-conquer strategy, combining sovereignty-bound defense and resistance with selective but progressively expansive concessions. China has been nudged along a meandering path that has led to a slow but steady involvement in the global human rights regime, consequently locking the Chinese government into discursive human rights formulations—not irrevocably but to a degree sufficient to demonstrate that China remains an integral part of the global human rights solution.[54]

The year 1998, as the fiftieth anniversary of the Universal Declaration of Human Rights, conceptually and normatively marked the most significant turning point in Beijing's acceptance of the universality of human rights, with all the accompanying legal accountability and obligations. The International Bill of Rights and the international human rights regime engendered various "second-image reversed" consequences already evident in the emergence of a human rights epistemic community, the publication of a flurry of white papers, the enactment of a series of criminal justice laws, and the incremental lessening of the scope of political repression. Participation in the human rights regime linked China's international legal behavior and its legislative politics at home. The two keystone human rights covenants that Beijing signed in 1997 and 1998 provide a legitimating platform for China's emerging labor union and democratic movements to prod their government to carry out its new legal obligations.[55] China's willingness to sign the two principal covenants of the International Bill of Rights, rather than walk away from the human rights regime, is an acknowledgment that human rights are a valid subject of international dialogue, as well as a sign of Beijing's willingness to respond to international concerns. In the Chinese case, there is also the normative/behavioral requirement of great power status: a great power abroad is and becomes what a great power does at home. Despite such status-driven forward moves, China's human rights practices have not progressed far enough for domestic norm diffusion and internalization.

China's participation in the UN Security Council (UNSC), the cockpit of global security politics, provides an empirical basis for assessing the extent to which the security effects of globalization are translated into certain behavioral tendencies of China's global policy. Despite its "principled opposition" to a wide range of sovereignty-related issues in the Security Council, China has generally expressed its opposition in the form of "nonparticipation in the vote" in the early post-entry years and abstention in the 1990s.

As shown in Table 10.4, in more than three decades, from late 1971 to the end of 2004, China cast only 4 vetoes out of a total of 138 (2.9 percent), as against 14 by the Soviet Union / Russia (10.1 percent), 14 by France (10.1 percent), 27 by the United Kingdom (19.6 percent), and 79 by the United States (57.2 percent).[56] The first two vetoes were cast in 1972. One was on the question of Bangladesh membership and was in effect a proxy veto cast on behalf of an ally (Pakistan), but two years later in 1974 Beijing reversed itself by giving full and unqualified support for Bangladesh's UN membership. The second veto was cast along with the Soviet Union on an amendment to a three-power draft resolution (S/10784) on the Middle East question. The impact of the second Chinese veto was substantially diluted by three facts: (1) it was a non-solo veto; (2) it was on an amendment, not a draft resolution; and (3) the original draft resolution itself was vetoed by another permanent

TABLE 10.4
Voting in the Security Council, 1971–2004

Year	Total Passed	Unanimous	Nonaligned Permanent Members	Nonaligned Unanimous	Total Vetoes Cast	Vetoes Cast by Permanent Five
1971	6	2	2	6	4	SU = 2, UK = 1
1972	17	3	3	17	8	**Cn = 2**, UK = 4, U.S. = 1, SU = 1
1973	20	7	7	19	4	U.S. = 3, UK = 1
1974	22	11	11	17	4	F = 1, SU = 1, UK = 1, U.S. = 1
1975	18	10	10	13	8	U.S. = 6, F = 1, UK = 1
1976	18	9	9	12	9	U.S. = 6, F = 2, UK = 1
1977	20	13	13	17	9	F = 3, UK = 3, U.S. = 3
1978	21	7	7	21	0	
1979	18	3	3	17	2	SU = 2
1980	23	8	8	22	3	SU = 2, U.S. = 1
1981	15	10	10	15	13	U.S. = 5, F = 4, UK = 4
1982	29	21	21	28	9	U.S. = 8, UK = 1
1983	17	10	12	15	3	U.S. = 2, SU = 1
1984	14	7	8	12	3	U.S. = 2, SU = 1
1985	21	16	16	21	9	U.S. = 7, UK = 2
1986	13	10	10	13	12	U.S. = 8, UK = 3, F = 1
1987	13	10	10	13	4	UK = 2, U.S. = 2
1988	20	17	17	20	7	U.S. = 6, UK = 1
1989	20	18	18	20	9	U.S. = 5, F = 2, UK = 2
1990	37	29	36	29	2	U.S. = 2
1991	42	36	40	36	0	
1992	74	64	65	67	0	
1993	93	85	87	89	1	Ru = 1
1994	77	65	70	67	1	Ru = 1
1995	66	60	60	66	1	U.S. = 1
1996	57	50	50	57	0	
1997	54	50	50	53	3	U.S. = 2, **Cn = 1** (S/1997/18)
1998	73	69	69	73	0	
1999	65	57	58	62	1	**Cn = 1** (S/1999/201)
2000	50	44	49	48	0	

TABLE 10.4 (*continued*)

Year	Total Passed	Unanimous	Nonaligned Permanent Members	Nonaligned Unanimous	Total Vetoes Cast	Vetoes Cast by Permanent Five
2001	52	50	50	52	2	U.S. = 2
2002	68	63	66	64	2	U.S. = 2
2003	67	62	64	63	2	U.S. = 2
2004	59	52	51	53	3	U.S. = 2; Ru = 1
1971-2004	1,279	1,028	1,060	1,197	138	**China (Cn) = 4 (2.9%)**; USSR (SU)/Russia (Ru) = 14 (10.1%); France (F) = 14 (10.1%); United Kingdom (UK) = 27 (19.6%); United States (U.S.) = 79 (57.2%)

Sources: Adapted from UN docs. s/pv.1599 (23 November 1971)–s/pv.5107 (22 December 2004).

member.[57] The third and fourth vetoes were cast in 1997 and 1999 on sui generis Taiwan-connected cases: a draft resolution (S/1997/18) authorizing a small UN peacekeeping mission for Guatemala, because of that country's pro-Taiwan activities—but here again Beijing reversed itself eleven days later by allowing the Council to approve the UN Human Rights Verification Mission in Guatemala (MINUGUA)—and another draft resolution (S/1999/201) to extend the mandate of the UN Preventive Deployment Force (UN-PREDEP) in the former Yugoslavia Republic of Macedonia for a period of six months, as a punitive strike at Macedonia for establishing diplomatic relations with Taiwan in the previous month (January 1999). None of the four Chinese vetoes had any paralyzing consequences for the UNSC's decision-making process.

Given its long-standing assault on the veto as an expression of hegemonic behavior, China tried hard not to allow itself to be cornered into having no choice but to cast its solo veto. In the post–Cold War era, however, "abstention" has become in most cases a kind of normative veto and an expression of "principled opposition" without standing in the way of the majority will in the UNSC. From August 1990 to December 1999, for example, China registered no fewer than 41 abstentions as an expression of its principled opposition on such issues as the use of force, humanitarian intervention, and the establishment of international criminal tribunals.[58] Thus China is sometimes forced to affirm a resolution (as in the case of resolution 827 on the international war crimes tribunal in Bosnia) that violates its most cherished principle of the nonviolability of state sovereignty, with nothing more than the habit-driven ritualistic pronouncement of a "principled position."[59]

The most obvious explanation for such behavior on the part of China is the country's desire to retain maximum leverage as part of its indeterminate strategy of becoming all things to all nations on the many issues intruding upon the Security Council agenda. As with nuclear weapons, the real power of the veto lies not so much in its actual use as in the threat of its use or non-use. To abstain is to apply the Chinese code of conduct of being firm in principle but flexible in application, or to find a face-saving exit with a voice in those cases that pit China's realpolitik interests against idealpolitik normative concerns for China's international reputation. Barry O'Neill has argued, with some exaggeration, that China is the most powerful permanent member of the UNSC, because it wields its veto power from an extreme political position, standing alone.[60] Use of China's veto power in the UNSC remains the quickest way to project its identity as a great power. With the recent and unexpected revival of Taiwan's UN bid, the veto power has also been publicly touted as the powerful sword and impregnable shield that defend the integrity of the People's Republic as the only legitimate Chinese government in the world organization.

China's position on UN peacekeeping operations (UNPKOs) has evolved over the years in a dialectical situation-specific way, as China has balanced its realpolitik interests with concerns for its international reputation as the champion of Third World causes. During the pre-entry period as a whole (1949–71), both ideology (in the form of the Maoist theory of just war) and experience (the trauma of the UN intervention in the Korean War) conditioned China's negative attitude toward UN peacekeeping activities. Once on the Security Council, China's position shifted and metamorphosed through three discernible stages: (1) principled opposition/nonparticipation (1971–80); (2) support/nonparticipation (1981–89); and (3) support/incremental and situation-specific participation (1990–present). In December 1981, China voted for the first time for the extension of a UN peacekeeping force (UNFICYP, in Cyprus). In November 1989, in another shift, the Chinese government decided to dispatch five Chinese military observers to serve in the UN Truce Supervision Organization (UNTSO) in the Middle East and twenty Chinese civilians to serve as members of the UN Transitional Assistance Group (UNTAG) to help monitor the independence process in Namibia.[61]

Some recent Chinese writings show a greater willingness to evaluate UNPKOs according to their contributions to regional stability. It is worth noting in this connection that Pang Zhongying, one of the leading scholars on globalization, publicly criticized Chinese abstention votes in the Security Council: "Casting an abstention ballot is equal to abandoning one's responsibility. China should consider how to select between safeguarding national interests and safeguarding the world, or think of a way to integrate them organically. . . . As a world power, China has a responsibility toward world peace."[62] Pang is apparently not alone in this thinking. There is a sense among some Chinese IR scholars that abstentions imply that China has no special message or soft power to project, or that China refuses to bear the responsibility and requirement as one of the Permanent Five (P5) in global security politics. Another scholar joins Pang in an indirect attack on Chinese abstentions by playing up the notion that China's great power status as one of the P5 requires nothing less than the corresponding responsibility and requirement of more proactive participation in UNPKOs. Working positively in UNPKOs is then not only China's responsibility as a great power but also a requirement and effective means for China to join the global security mechanism.[63]

Recent Chinese writings and Chinese multilateral diplomacy show a greater willingness to evaluate UNPKOs according to their contributions to the "conditions of peace and stability." With the lesson of Kosovo (where China got badly burned) fresh in Chinese minds, Beijing opted for a more flexible conflict management approach in East Timor, where China for the first time contributed its civilian police in a UN peacekeeping and peace-making role. One indicator of Beijing's incremental multilateralism with respect to UNPKOs has been the establishment and expansion of training programs for peacekeepers in China through the Office of Peacekeeping in China, located under the General Staff Headquarters of the People's Liberation Army (PLA).[64] Another indicator of Beijing's greater commitment to UNPKOs is that in 1997 China decided in principle to take part in the UN's standby arrangements for UNPKOs and in 2002 actually joined the Class-A standby arrangements system.

China actively participated in two major UNPKOs—Cambodia and East Timor—because of a number of situation-specific factors: geographical proximity, initial involvement with the authorization process in the Security Council, and host-nation consent (one of the two conditions for the first generation of UNPKOs). Where similar conditions are present, and the Taiwan factor absent, Beijing's slow yet steady support for UNPKOs is likely to continue unabated in coming years.

As if to showcase Beijing's growing interest and willingness in expanding its influence beyond the "home region," China announced in February 2003 that it would send 218 "peacekeepers"—175 engineers and 43 medical personnel—from the PLA to the Democratic Republic of the Congo in support of the UN Peacekeeping Mission (MONUC), thereby more than doubling the number of its peacekeepers from 137 to 355. In an apparent victory for the Ministry of Foreign Affairs and more progressive elements in the PLA, Beijing was demonstrating its desire and willingness to boost its international role and reputation as a responsible great power, at a time when the United States was pressuring the United Nations—without success—to demonstrate its "relevance" by legitimizing America's preventive war against Iraq.

Conclusions

Taken together, Chinese foreign policy in the post–Cold War globalization era leads to one obvious and somewhat paradoxical conclusion: China's growing integration into the global community, aided and abetted by the forces of globalization, is having paradoxical effects that at once confirm and constrain Chinese sovereignty. On the one hand, the confluence of domestic and external forces has made it necessary for China's post-Mao leadership to accelerate its reform and opening to the outside world in order to modernize its economy, to enhance its international reputation, and to increase its comprehensive national strength. As a result, China's external sovereignty is more secure in the global community today than ever before. On the other hand, post-Mao China has allowed the camel's nose of globalization to enter the tent of China's internal sovereignty, constraining the Chinese state with all kinds of global norms and rules, and releasing enormous entrepreneurial energies of sovereignty-free "intermestic" actors that have transformed the process of economic development with their own pace, logic, and direction.

While sovereignty remains central to Chinese foreign policy rhetoric, its underlying premises have been progressively softened and chipped away by the functional and normative requirements of China's integration into the global economy. Unless directly challenged, Beijing has been remarkably willing to compromise or shelve sovereignty-bound issues in the pursuit of national economic interests. With the growing globalization of the Chinese political economy, the devolution of power at home, and the fragmentation of authority and decision-making structures at the apex, the center has made a series of decentralizing decisions "enabling" the central planners to maintain the appearance that they are still controlling the economic reforms and opening to the outside world.

The sound and fury of a sovereignty-based international order has been receding in Chinese foreign policy pronouncements in recent years, highlighting a new global reality that almost everywhere today sovereignty is either in voluntary or forced retreat or in a highly perforated condition. Even powerful states command only shared or compromised sovereignty in a system of multiple power centers and overlapping spheres of authority. According to former U.S. Deputy Secretary of State Strobe Talbott, even the world's lone superpower, faced with the globalization challenge of doing more and more with less and less, has had to leverage scarce resources by forming coalitions with nonstate actors—multinational corporations (MNCs), nongovernmental organizations (NGOs), and such global inter-governmental organizations as the United Nations, the World Bank, and the International Monetary Fund (IMF)—since such coalitions help the United States "to work not only multilaterally, but multi-multilaterally, through several organizations and institutions at the same time."[65]

That said, however, China faces at least three major challenges in the coming years, each of which will be a decision on how best to cope with the multiple dangers and opportunities of globalization, more specifically, on how to deal with the twin pressures of globalization from above and with-out and localization/fragmentation from below and within. First, a silent revolution of global information and transparency is under way in China, even in the remote hinterlands. The Chinese state has lost its hegemonic power to control the flow of information. This revolution reflects and af-fects the globalization of increasingly intertwined political, economic, so-cial, and normative structures and values, even as it fosters the rapid mobi-lization of people's needs, demands, frustration, and intolerance—indeed, the second "revolution of people power." Although its full impact is diffi-cult to assess, especially if the Chinese economy continues to grow at 8 per-cent or a higher rate, this silent revolution nonetheless undergirds the critical social forces for change in emerging Chinese civil society. This type of frag-mentation from within could emerge from the growing economic gaps be-tween the regions and also through the eruption of ethnonational identity conflicts in Tibet and Xinjiang or a war between Beijing and Taipei.

Second, the fact that China has come to interact with the global com-munity in more ways, with more depth and complexity, and on more fronts than ever before has several unsettling consequences for the Chinese decision-making process. As China's integration continues apace, different "intermestic" actors, with different interests, will seek to "participate" in the making and implementation (or nonimplementation) of foreign policy goals, with their own agendas and rules. The conduct of Chinese foreign policy can no longer be contained within a state-to-state bilateral strait-jacket. Like it or not, the globalization challenge requires fast responses at a time when China's foreign policy decision-making process is becoming diffuse because of its multilevel bargaining across multiple issue areas both at home and abroad. China thus faces the daunting challenge of establish-ing a fruitful congruence between domestic and foreign policies amid the changing functional requirements of globalization.

Third, coping with the twin pressures of globalization and localization is likely to remain a central challenge for China's leadership. The primal force behind often nationalistic posturing, especially in the early post-Tiananmen years, was not any military threat from without but the leadership's resolve to project China's national identity as an up-and-coming great power—and more recently as a responsible great power—in the Asia-Pacific region, so as to make up for domestic legitimation and security deficits. Indeed, the main threat to China's security comes from within, not from without. Hence the antinomies between globalization from above and without and fragmentation (deglobalization) from below and within can be seen as entering full force into China's multiple and competing role conceptions, with significant implications for matching the means and ends of foreign policy as well as for establishing a healthy and stable domestic order. The most fundamental challenge ahead lies in seeking not grandiose schemes but more synergistic coalition formation with many types of "intermestic" actors, including NGOs and transnational corporations (TNCs) to leverage scarce resources for more effective prevention, regulation, and resolution of potentially deadly conflict, as well as for the creation of a more peaceful, prosperous, stable, and just China.

The globalization template is ready-made for advancing the study of Chinese foreign policy in a number of different but mutually complementary ways. Although diagnosis and prescription are seldom matched in foreign policy, globalization opens a large menu of questions and puzzles for tracking any new thinking, new directions, and new behavioral tendencies in China's foreign policy in the post–Cold War globalization era. The effects of globalization on Chinese foreign policy can be traced and explained by posing and addressing several key questions. What is the relationship between globalization and the state, more specifically the impact of globalization on state sovereignty, state security, state power, and state identity? Does Beijing define the relationship between globalization and sovereignty in mutually constitutive or conflicting terms, and with what consequences for the conception and conduct of Chinese foreign policy? How is China's national identity constructed, deconstructed, and reconstructed and with what behavioral consequences? Has the very meaning of "sovereignty," "power" and "security" changed in the course of Chinese discourse and response to the globalization challenge? Does globalization foster or inhibit the incidence of China's militarized disputes and armed conflicts? These are questions of both theoretical and real-world significance that have not received sufficient attention in the field of Chinese foreign policy studies. As it pushes beyond Robert Putnam's two-level game approach,[66] globalization can serve as a bridge-building template, generating more concrete theoretical multilevel games questions of real-world significance and thus allowing Chinese foreign policy specialists and IR theorists to speak to each other profitably. More multidimensional and interdisciplinary research is needed on the complex interplay of the global, regional, and local forces that are impacting upon and shaping the patterns of China's behavior of conflict or cooperation.

Notes

I am grateful to Iain Johnston for valuable comments on an earlier version of this chapter, and I thank Matthew Winters for his superb and dedicated research assistance. The chapter epigraphs are drawn respectively from *Selected Works of Mao Tse-Tung*, vol. 1 (Peking: Foreign Languages Press, 1965), 13; Jiang Zemin, "Hold High the Great Banner of Deng Xiaoping Theory: Carrying the Cause of Building Socialism with Chinese Characteristics to the Twenty-First Century," *Xinhua*, 21 September 1997, in Foreign Broadcast Information Service (hereafter cited as FBIS), CHI-97–266; UN Secretary-General Kofi Annan, Annual Report of the Secretary-General on the Work of the Organization, UN doc. A/53/1 (3 September 1998), par. 168.

1. In 1998 alone, three major discussions were held under UN auspices on the opportunities and dangers of globalization for the global community. That year, for the first time, the UN secretary-general's annual report (a state of the world message) declared that the world organization would take up the challenge of ensuring that "globalization leads to progress, prosperity and security for all." The second half of 1999 witnessed the UN Development Programme (UNDP) and the World Bank turning their primary attention for the first time to globalization, presenting in their annuals—*Human Development Report, 1999* and *World Development Report, 1999/2000*—empirically rich and generally balanced accounts of the new benefits and threats globalization poses to human security, broadly defined. See UNDP, *Human Development Report, 1999* (New York: Oxford University Press, 1999), and World Bank, *World Development Report, 1999/2000: Entering the 21st Century* (New York: Oxford University Press, 2000).

2. The literature on globalization is too plentiful to list here. Suffice it to say that the most comprehensive and definitive scholarly work on globalization remains David Held et al., *Global Transformations: Politics, Economics and Culture* (Stanford: Stanford University Press, 1999), a product of ten years of collaborative research by four leading British social scientists. For overview readers, see David Held and Anthony McGrew, eds., *The Global Transformations Reader: An Introduction to the Globalization Debate* (Cambridge: Polity Press, 2000) and Patrick O'Meara, Howard D. Mehlinger, and Matthew Krain, eds., *Globalization and the Challenges of a New Century: A Reader* (Bloomington: Indiana University Press, 2000). For discussion of globalization in the East Asian context, see Samuel S. Kim, ed., *Korea's Globalization* (New York: Cambridge University Press, 2000), and *East Asia and Globalization* (Lanham, Md.: Rowman & Littlefield, 2000); and Catarina Kinnvall and Kristina Jonsson, eds., *Globalization and Democratization in Asia: The Construction of Identity* (London: Routledge, 2002).

3. In a remarkable speech delivered at Qinghua University in Beijing, Pang Zhongying argued that the demise of the Soviet Union and the end of the Cold War

have fundamentally changed world politics, giving rise to a series of new IR theories in the West, especially in the United States: Francis Fukuyama's theory of "the end of history"; Huntington's theory of "the clash of civilizations"; the "democratic peace theory," which he claims is in part directed at China; and "the theory of globalization," of which there are many schools, but the mainstream school is "new liberalism." See Pang Zhongying, "China's International Status and Foreign Strategy After the Cold War," in FBIS-CHI-2002-0506 (5 May 2002). For a more comprehensive treatment of the Chinese understanding and analysis of the globalization debate (although often more outside than inside of China), see Pang Zhongying, ed., *Quanqiuhua, fanquanqiuhua yu Zhongguo: lijie quanqiuhua de fuzaxing yu duoyangxing* [Globalization, anti-globalization, and China: understanding the complexity and diversity of globalization] (Shanghai: Shanghai People's Press, 2002).

4. A few notable exceptions include the prominent IR theorists Joseph Nye, Robert Keohane, and James Rosenau. See Joseph S. Nye and John D. Donahue, eds., *Governance in a Globalizing World* (Washington, D.C.: Brookings Institution Press, 2000); James N. Rosenau, *Along the Domestic-Foreign Frontier: Exploring Governance in a Turbulent World* (New York: Cambridge University Press, 1997), *Distant Proximities: Dynamics Beyond Globalization* (Princeton, N.J.: Princeton University Press, 2003); and Ian Clark, *Globalization and International Relations Theory* (New York: Oxford University Press, 1999). For a succinct summary of the three dominant IR theories (from a realist perspective), see Steven M. Walt, "International Relations: One World, Many Theories," *Foreign Policy*, no. 110 (Spring 1998): 29–46.

5. Kenichi Ohmae, *The Borderless World* (London: Collins, 1990); Kenichi Ohmae, *The End of the Nation-State: The Rise of Regional Economies* (New York: Free Press, 1995); Robert Reich, *The Work of Nations* (New York: Vintage Books, 1992); and Susan Strange, "The Defective State," *Daedalus* 124, 2 (1995): 55–74, and *The Retreat of the State: The Diffusion of Power in the World Economy* (New York: Cambridge University Press, 1996).

6. Peter Beinart, "An Illusion for Our Time: The False Promise of Globalization," *New Republic*, 20 October 1997, 20–24; Paul Hirst and Grahame Thompson, *Globalization in Question?* (Cambridge: Polity Press, 1996); and Stephen Krasner, "Compromising Westphalia," *International Security* 20, 3 (1995): 115–51.

7. Stephen Krasner, "Globalization and Sovereignty," in *States and Sovereignty in the Global Economy*, ed. David A. Smith, Dorothy J. Solinger, and Steven Topik (London: Routledge, 1999). See also Stephen Krasner, *Sovereignty: Organized Hypocrisy* (Princeton, N.J.: Princeton University Press, 1999).

8. For the most authoritative articulation of the transformationalist thesis, see Held et al., *Global Transformations*, 7–10.

9. Stuart Harris, "China and the Pursuit of State Interests in a Globalizing World," *Pacifica Review* 13, 1 (February 2001): 15–29.

10. Christopher Hughes, "Globalisation and Nationalism: Squaring the Circle in Chinese International Relations Theory," *Millennium: Journal of International Studies* 26,1 (1997): 103–24.

11. Samuel S. Kim, *China, the United Nations, and World Order* (Princeton, N.J.: Princeton University Press, 1979), 265.

12. Johan Galtung, "Conflict on a Global Scale: Social Imperialism and Sub-

Imperialism—Continuities in the Structural Theory of Imperialism," *World Development* 4, 3 (March 1976): 162; emphasis in original.

13. See Lu Yi et al., eds., *Qiuji: yige shijiexing de xuanze* [Global citizenship: a worldwide choice] (Shanghai: Baijia Chubanshe, 1989), and Samuel S. Kim, *China in and out of the Changing World Order* (Princeton, N.J.: Center of International Studies, Princeton University, 1991), 48–49.

14. *Renmin Ribao*, 26 November 1990, 5.

15. Kim, *China in and out of the Changing World Order*, 42–49.

16. See Yong Deng, "Conception of National Interests: Realpolitik, Liberal Dilemma, and the Possibility of Change," in *In the Eyes of the Dragon: China Views the World*, ed. Yong Deng and Fei-Ling Wang (Lanham, Md.: Rowman & Littlefield, 1999), 55.

17. See Pang, "China's International Status" and *Quanqiuhua, fanquanqiuhua yu Zhongguo*; Wang Yizhou, ed., *Quanqiuhua shidai de guoji anquan* [International security in an era of globalization] (Shanghai: Shanghai People's Press, 1998); Wang Yizhou, "New Security Concept in Globalization," *Beijing Review*, no. 7 (11–15 February 1999): 7; Wang Yizhou, *Dangdai guoji zhengzhi xilun* [Analysis of contemporary international politics] (Shanghai: Renmin Chubanshe, 1995), esp. 19–46; and Hu Angang, Yang Fan, and Zhu Ning, *Daguo zhanlue: Zhongguo de liyi yu shimin* [China's grand strategy: missions and interests] (Shenyang: Liaoning People's Press, 2000).

18. Deng Xiaoping, "A New Approach Towards Stabilizing the World Situation, February 22, 1984," in *Fundamental Issues in Present-Day China* (Beijing: Foreign Languages Press, 1987), 97.

19. For a wide-ranging discussion involving Australian, British, and Chinese scholars on the notion of China as a responsible great power, see Yongjin Zhang and Greg Austin, eds., *Power and Responsibility in Chinese Foreign Policy* (Canberra: Asia Pacific Press, 2001). See also Samuel S. Kim, "China's Path to Great Power Status in the Globalization Era," *Asian Perspective* 27, 1 (March 2003): 35–75.

20. This thesis is eloquently argued and developed in Jonathan Spence, *To Change China: Western Advisers in China, 1620–1960* (New York: Penguin Books, 1980).

21. Chen Quansheng and Liu Jinghua, "China and the World amid Globalization," in *Ta Kung Pao* (Hong Kong), FBIS-CHI-1999-0306, 3 March 1999.

22. Banning Garrett, "China Faces, Debates, the Contradictions of Globalization," *Asian Survey* 41, 3 (May–June 2001): 415.

23. Personal communication with and from Dr. Wang Yizhou of the Institute of World Economics and Politics of the Chinese Academy of Social Science (CASS), 13 May 2003.

24. See Alastair Iain Johnston, "China's International Relations: The Political and Security Dimension," in *The International Relations of Northeast Asia*, ed. Samuel S. Kim (Lanham, Md.: Rowman & Littlefield, 2004).

25. World Bank, *World Development Report, 1991: The Challenge of Development* (New York: Oxford University Press, 1991), fig. 1.1, 12.

26. *People's Daily Online*, 10 January 2005, http://english.peopledaily.com.cn.

27. In 2003, for the first time, China overtook the United States as the world's largest recipient/destination of foreign direct investment (FDI). While FDI into the

United States declined to $40 billion in 2003 from $72 billion in 2002 and $167 billion 2001, FDI into China declined only slightly to $53 billion in 2003 from $55 billion in 2002. See Laurent Frost, "China Overtakes U.S. as Investment Target," Associated Press, June 28, 2004. For the 2004 figure, see *People's Daily Online*, 25 January 2005, http://english.peopledaily.com.cn.

28. Joseph Kahn, "China's Hot, at Least for Now," *New York Times*, 16 December 2002.

29. Peggy Pei-chen Chang and Tun-jen Cheng, "The Rise of the Information Technology in China: A Formidable Challenge to Taiwan's Economy," *American Asian Review* 20, 3 (Fall 2002): 125–74.

30. World Bank, *China, 2020: Development Challenges in the New Century* (Washington, D.C.: World Bank, 1997), 50–51; UNDP, *Human Development Report, 1991* (New York: Oxford University Press, 1991), 120, and *Human Development Report, 2002* (New York: Oxford University Press, 2002), 150.

31. World Bank, *World Development Report 2006: Equity and Development* (New York: Oxford University Press, 2005), 292.

32. Chen and Liu, "China and the World amid Globalization."

33. Pang Zhongying, "Globalization and China: China's Response to the Asian Economic Crisis," *Asian Perspective* 23, 1 (1999): 111–31.

34. "Seize Opportunity, Meet Challenge, and Participate in Economic Globalization," *Renmin Ribao*, 19 December 2001, in FBIS-CHI-2001–1220.

35. Nicholas Lardy, *Integrating China into the Global Economy* (Washington, D.C.: Brookings Institution Press), 2.

36. Joseph Fewsmith, "The Politics of China's Accession to the WTO," *Current History* 99, 638 (September 2000): 273. For a comprehensive and authoritative analysis of how international institutions and commitments can be used by domestic reformers to tie hands in order to force domestic change, see Daniel W. Drezner, ed., *Locating the Proper Authorities: The Interaction of Domestic and International Institutions* (Ann Arbor: University of Michigan Press, 2003).

37. *Jingji Ribao* [Economic Daily], "The World Trade Organization Needs China, China Needs the World Trade Organization," in FBIS-CHI-2000–0121.

38. For this line of reasoning, see Thomas Moore, "China's International Relations in Northeast Asia: The Economic Dimension," in *The International Relations of Northeast Asia*, ed. Samuel S. Kim (Lanham, Md.: Rowman & Littlefield, 2004) and George T. Crane, "Imagining the Economic Nation: Globalisation in China," *New Political Economy* 4, 2 (July 1999): 215–32.

39. Clark, *Globalization and International Relations Theory*, 107–26.

40. Wolfgang Reinicke, "Global Public Policy," *Foreign Affairs* 76, 6 (1997): 127–38.

41. Liu Ji, a CASS researcher, in *Ta Kung Pao*, 25 January 1999, in FBIS-CHI-99–025.

42. See Qiao Liang and Wang Xianghui, *Chaoxian zhan* [Unlimited war] (Beijing: Liberation Army Literature and Art Press, 1999).

43. Wang Yizhou, "New Security Concept in Globalization," 7. See also id., *Dangdai guoji zhengzhi xilun*, esp. 19–46, and "Mianxiang ershi shiji de Zhongguo waijiao: sanzhong xuqiu de xunqiu jiqi pingheng" [China's diplomacy for the

twenty-first century: seeking and balancing three demands], *Zhanlue yu Guanli* [Strategy and Management], no. 6 (1999): 18–27.

44. Chen and Liu, "China and the World amid Globalization."

45. Wang, "Mianxiang ershi shiji de Zhongguo waijiao."

46. For an elaboration of the new concept of economic security enjoying a preferred position, see the *White Paper on China's National Defense*, issued 27 July 1998, in FBIS-CHI-98-208.

47. You Ji, "The PLA, the CCP and the Formulation of Chinese Defense and Foreign Policy," in *Power and Responsibility in Chinese Foreign Policy*, ed. Zhang and Austin, 119–20. For a list of territorial disputes peacefully resolved in the 1990s, see *Defense White Paper, 2000*, in FBIS-CHI-2000–1016, 16 October 2000.

48. Alastair Iain Johnston, "China's Militarized Interstate Dispute Behaviour, 1949–1992: A First Cut at the Data," *China Quarterly*, no. 153 (March 1998): 29.

49. Samuel S. Kim, "China and the United Nations," in *China Joins the World: Progress and Prospects*, ed. Elizabeth Economy and Michel Oksenberg (New York: Council on Foreign Relations Press, 1999), 42–89.

50. Michael D. Swaine and Alastair Iain Johnston, "China and Arms Control Institutions," in *China Joins the World: Progress and Prospects*, ed. Elizabeth Economy and Michel Oksenberg (New York: Council on Foreign Relations Press, 1999), 101.

51. See Stockholm Environment Institute and UN Development Programme, *China Human Development Report, 2002: Making Green Development a Choice* (New York: Oxford University Press, 2002).

52. See Elizabeth Economy, "China's Environmental Diplomacy," in *Chinese Foreign Policy Faces the New Millennium*, ed. Samuel S. Kim (Boulder, Colo.: Westview Press, 1998), 264–83, and Lester Ross, "China and Environmental Protection," in *China Joins the World: Progress and Prospects*, ed. Elizabeth Economy and Michel Oksenberg (New York: Council on Foreign Relations Press, 1999), 296–325.

53. For detailed discussion of China's human rights diplomacy, see Ann Kent, *China, the United Nations, and Human Rights: The Limits of Compliance* (Philadelphia: University of Pennsylvania Press, 1999); Rosemary Foot, *Rights Beyond Borders: The Global Community and the Struggle over Human Rights in China* (New York: Oxford University Press, 2000); Ming Wan, *Human Rights in Chinese Foreign Relations: Defining and Defending National Interests* (Philadelphia: University of Pennsylvania Press, 2001); Samuel S. Kim, "Human Rights in China's International Relations," in *What If China Doesn't Democratize?* ed. Edward Friedman and Barrett McCormick (Armonk, N.Y.: M. E. Sharpe, 2000), 129–62; Andrew J. Nathan, "China and the International Human Rights Regime," in *China Joins the World: Progress and Prospects*, ed. Elizabeth Economy and Michel Oksenberg (New York: Council on Foreign Relations Press, 1999), 136–60; and James D. Seymour, "Human Rights in Chinese Foreign Relations," in *China and the World: Chinese Foreign Policy Faces the New Millennium* (Boulder, Colo.: Westview Press, 1998), 217–38.

54. For the argument along this line, see Foot, *Rights Beyond Borders*.

55. For instance, an incipient Czech human rights movement issued "Charter

77" in January 1977, drawing its legitimacy from the incorporation of the two human rights covenants into the domestic laws of communist Czechoslovakia.

56. These figures exclude a 1981 Sino-U.S. "veto war" during closed-door deliberations on a recommendation on the appointment of a secretary-general; they do not show up in official records of the Security Council.

57. Kim, *China, the United Nations, and World Order*, 206–8.

58. Sally Morphet, "China as a Permanent Member of the Security Council, October 1971–December 1999," *Security Dialogue* 31, 2 (June 2000): 161–62.

59. Nigel Thalakada, "China's Voting Pattern in the Security Council, 1990–1995," in *The Once and Future Security Council*, ed. Bruce Russett (New York: St. Martin's Press, 1997), 94–95.

60. Barry O'Neill, "Power and Satisfaction in the Security Council," in *Once and Future Security Council*, ed. Russett, 59–82.

61. Liu Enzhao, "Lianheguo weichi heping xingdong" [UN peacekeeping forces], *Guoji Wenti Yanjiu* [Journal of International Studies], no. 2 (1989): 53–61.

62. Pang, "China's International Status."

63. Tang Yongsheng, "Zhongguo yu Lianheguo weihe xingdong," *Shijie Jingji yu Zhengzhi* [World Economics and Politics], no. 9 (2002): 39–44. See also Wang Yizhou, "Mianxiang ershi shiji de Zhongguo waijiao."

64. Bates Gill and James Reilly, "Sovereignty, Intervention and Peacekeeping: The View from Beijing," *Survival* 42, 2 (2000): 41–59.

65. Strobe Talbott, "Globalization and Diplomacy: A Practitioner's Perspective," *Foreign Policy*, no. 108 (Fall 1997): 79.

66. Robert Putnam, "Diplomacy and Domestic Politics: The Logic of Two-Level Games," *International Organization* 42 (Summer 1988): 427–60.

Part **Three**

DOMESTIC POLITICS

11 *Identity and Conflict in Sino-American Relations*

Peter Hays Gries

What do you see? A cuddly panda or a menacing dragon? Americans interpreting the People's Republic of China, like subjects staring at inkblots during a Rorschach test, frequently reveal much more about themselves than they do about the PRC itself.

Both panda and dragon seers are likely motivated by a complex mixture of sense and sensibility: cold calculations of their own self-interest are intertwined with deep-seated "gut feelings" about China. But post-Enlightenment Westerners are loathe to admit that we are influenced by our emotions. As the Italian sociologist Vilfredo Pareto noted long ago, while we frequently act irrationally, we are masters at post facto rationalizations of our behavior.[1] We rarely admit to ourselves—let alone to others—that we may have been moved by anything other than enlightened reason.

Rationalizing our China policy preferences, analysts frequently infer Chinese intentions from Chinese capabilities. Engagement advocates depict China as a cuddly panda—nothing threatening about a furry vegetarian— to argue that China is benign. Meanwhile, containment advocates depict China as a menacing dragon: its scales and fire-breathing speak for themselves. This is an aggressive fighting creature.

As Gulf War II has recently revealed, the causal arrows can run the other direction as well: capabilities can be inferred from presumed intentions. The Cheney–Rumsfeld argument for war was that since Saddam Hussein was a "bad guy" with sinister intentions, he must have weapons of mass destruction (WMD)—even if the facts belied that inference. "Blue Team" China-bashers on Capital Hill are frequently driven by a similar logic. In their 1998 book *Year of the Rat: How Bill Clinton Compromised U.S. Security for Chinese Cash*, Edward Timperlake and William Triplett II, who view both the Clinton administration and China as "bad guys," infer an anti-American Clinton-China conspiracy, despite a lack of compelling evidence to support their inference.[2]

Can international relations (IR) theory help analysts to move beyond such inkblot-gazing? Can we interrogate the intentions that actually drive the makers of China's foreign policy? When will they, like a cuddly panda, choose cooperation? And when will they, like a fierce dragon, choose confrontation?

Realists like Paul Kennedy have argued that rising powers and hegemons tend to go to war.[3] Secretary of State Condoleezza Rice and the University of Chicago's John Mearsheimer have drawn on such arguments to suggest that China is a revisionist power destined to clash with America.[4] Aaron Friedberg has argued along these lines as well. Some China IR scholars have also suggested that under certain conditions the likelihood of China's using force against the United States is not insubstantial. Tom Christensen has declared China the "high church of realpolitik" today.[5] Iain Johnston has similarly argued that the hard realpolitik elements of Chinese strategic culture would support "hitting hard and hitting first."[6]

IR theorists in the liberal tradition, by contrast, have been more optimistic. Traditional liberals like Woodrow Wilson viewed human nature as fundamentally good; nations, therefore, could coexist without conflict. Today, neoliberals maintain that international institutions and interdependence restrain state aggression. In the U.S.-China case, liberals like Mike Lampton point to economic interdependence and common security concerns as ensuring bilateral cooperation.

This chapter joins a new controversy in the old IR debate over cooperation and conflict. Constructivist IR theorists have focused on the social— rather than material—side of the debate. In a 1992 article, Alexander Wendt proclaimed in his title that "Anarchy Is What States Make of It." It may "lead to competitive power politics," he explained, but it "also may not." To Wendt, structural realists were wrong to assume self-help a priori from the material structure of the world system: "Self-help and power politics do not follow either logically or causally from anarchy."[7] In asserting that the relations among nations are not inherently conflictual, Wendt provided ammunition for liberal critics of realism.

Drawing on social psychology to defend realism, in 1995, Jonathan Mercer took issue with Wendt's critique of self-help. In an essay titled "Anarchy and Identity," Mercer argued that ethnocentrism explains the group egoism that neorealists take for granted. Conflict, in his view, is "an *inescapable* feature of intergroup and interstate relations."[8] Mercer in effect uses social identity theory (SIT) to create a primordial superrealism, providing neorealism with the psychological foundation Kenneth Waltz had cast aside in 1979. Samuel Huntington has made a similar argument at the even broader level of "civilizations": with the end of the Cold War, the major civilizations of the world—each with its own distinct identity—are destined to clash.[9]

Identity dynamics, Mercer and Huntington assert, make intergroup conflict inevitable.

In his 1999 monograph *Social Theory of International Politics*, Wendt defends himself against Mercer's critique, arguing that the "in-group bias" Mercer cites does not predetermine enmity. Wendt provides no empirical support for this position, however. Furthermore, his book provides few clues as to *when* intergroup conflict will occur.[10]

So, when will states clash? This chapter argues that intergroup identity dynamics do *not* inexorably lead to conflict. The social psychology literature Mercer drew on in his effort to refute Wendt does not support his pessimistic conclusion that interstate conflict is inevitable. I thus join Wendt in questioning the inevitability of anarchy and self-help in international politics. However, unlike Wendt, I highlight contingency: the specific conditions that promote conflict in international affairs, and those that militate against it. Depending on circumstances, states may lock horns, but they also may not. Neoliberals and neorealists both have it right some of the time. The problem is that a narrow focus on material interests alone usually cannot tell us when states will do battle. By redirecting our gaze to the very real realm of ideal interests, social psychology provides insights into when the world of absolute gains will dominate and when the world of relative gains will.

Based on recent findings in social psychology, I make concrete predictions about the conditions under which identification with the nation will lead to international conflict. In brief, we all identify with our nations and imbue our national identities with positive value. When that positivity is challenged, leading to consequential, relative comparisons with salient external nations, we *promote* competition, a stage that necessarily precedes international conflict. However, the absence of a single one of these conditions will inhibit competition. Furthermore, there are five different ways in which comparisons may be framed that *reduce* the likelihood of international competition: social mobility ("exit" from a national identity) and four different forms of social creativity (shifting the dimension under comparison, changing the values of the attributes, changing the target of comparison, and self-deception). The cards are thus stacked against a competitive outcome.

Of course, identity is only one possible cause of conflict. This paper only addresses the Wendt-Mercer debate over the nature of interstate competition in the symbolic realm; it can say nothing about the dispute between neorealists and neoliberals over competition in the material realm. And it only treats identity as an independent variable (as a possible cause of conflict); identity conflict can also be a dependent variable—the result, for example, of objective conflicts of interest.

To illustrate my analysis, I use examples from Sino-American relations, and I deliberately use that term rather than speaking of "U.S.-China relations." My focus is decidedly Sinocentric: on what recent Chinese nationalist writings about America can tell us about the likelihood of conflict in the Asia-Pacific region. Therefore, in addition to joining a debate over conflict in international relations theory, this chapter also seeks to contribute to the stalemated debate in the China field over the existence of a "China threat." Specifically, I suggest that Iain Johnston and Tom Christensen may be right about the Chinese tendency to resort to force—some of the time.[11] Social psychology can provide insights into when the Chinese will choose cooperation and when they will choose conflict.

By focusing on the recent high tide of Chinese nationalism rather than a representative sample of Chinese foreign policies over the years, I stack the cards against my case. If nationalist writings can be used to support my argument that conflict is a *contingent* outcome, I shall have made a "crucially hard case" theoretically.[12] I do not, however, seek to make any substantive claims about the relative weight of nationalism vis-à-vis other Chinese attitudes to foreign affairs. Furthermore, because I bracket cultural differences and history in an attempt to apply universal social psychological insights to IR theory, I cannot make strong substantive claims about the future of Sino-American relations.[13] To repeat: the Chinese examples are used to *illustrate* the theory; they do not seek to *prove* anything.

The Social Psychology of Intergroup Relations

For most social psychologists today, groups do not act; individuals act. Although "group psychology" approaches were once popular in America, the days of "groupthink" are over.[14] Social psychology today focuses on the impact of groups on individuals. Therefore, when James Fearon and David Laitin dismiss psychological approaches as "group-level" to advocate their own "individual interactions" approach, they mischaracterize psychology, in the process doing themselves and political science a disservice.[15]

Theories of intergroup relations in social psychology parallel the debate in IR over conflict. The first major approach, realistic (group) competition theory (RCT), supports the rationalist position. Based on a 1954 study at a summer camp in Robbers Cove, Oklahoma, Muzafer Sherif and his colleagues found that the introduction of material competition was sufficient to divide an otherwise homogeneous group of boys into rival groups. Conversely, the introduction of a joint task (extracting a "stuck" bus) led the two groups to cooperate.[16] Such findings led to the development of RCT, which maintained that objective relations of material interest determine group formation and intergroup relations. In other words, patterns of resource interdependence drive cooperation or conflict. RCT is the implicit social psychology of rationalist views of IR.

Further experimental work soon revealed, however, that the direction of causality implied by RCT was unclear: Yes, material competition could lead to group formation, but simply categorizing people into separate groups could also lead to in-group identification and bias. Material competition, therefore, was a sufficient but not necessary condition for group formation.[17] The development of social identity, according to the now dominant social identity theory (SIT), was not the epiphenomenal by-product of patterns of resource interdependence, but the result of self-categorization. John Turner even found that concern about social identity could take precedence over the individual's pursuit of material self-interest.[18] The SIT challenge to RCT thus parallels the constructivist challenge to earlier rationalist approaches in IR, in that both involve a shift in focus from objective conflicts of interest to identity dynamics.

Group categorization and comparison do not inevitably lead to intergroup competition and conflict.[19] Recent experimental evidence indicates that group membership is indeterminate in this respect. As the social psychologist Marilynn Brewer notes, "any relationship between in-group identification and out-group hostility is progressive and contingent rather than necessary and inevitable." Two stages intervene between the formation of in-group identity and intergroup conflict: in-group positivity and intergroup competition. Conflict is thus the last stage of a four-stage process constituted by (1) in-group identification; (2) in-group positivity; (3) intergroup competition; and (4) intergroup conflict.

Although all humans, as social beings, likely engage in the first two processes, the latter two stages are indeterminate: They are not inevitable but require the impetus of additional conditions.[20]

The question is *what* these conditions are and *when* in-group positivity leads to intergroup competition. In this chapter, I focus on this transition between stages 2 and 3, only turning to the equally contingent transition between stages 3 and 4 in the conclusion. I argue that the issue of social comparison lies at the juncture of stages 2 and 3. When national positivity is challenged, we compare our nations with other nations. Internation comparisons only lead to competition under certain conditions, however. Specifically, the comparisons must be (a) salient; (b) consequential, and (c) zero-sum.

All three of these conditions must hold for competition to ensue (each is a necessary but not a sufficient cause). If *any* of the following occur during comparison processes, however, competition will be avoided:

- Social mobility: "exit" from a social identity
- Social creativity 1: changing the dimension of comparison

- Social creativity 2: changing the meaning of the value being compared
- Social creativity 3: changing the target of comparison
- Social creativity 4: self-deception

Each of these five conditions, in other words, is sufficient by itself to prevent competition. No competition thus seems to be the most likely outcome of internation comparison, a prediction supported by James Fearon and David Laitin's empirical findings on the relative nonoccurrence of ethnic conflict.[21] These social psychological variables, I argue, help explain whether we inhabit a realist world of relative gains or a liberal community of absolute gains.

In-group Identification and Positivity: When "Good" is Good Enough

Experimental work in the SIT tradition has convincingly demonstrated (a) that we identify with groups and (b) that we privilege them. First, we associate ourselves with groups that, in effect, become part of our identities. SIT posits two mutually exclusive aspects of the self: personal identity and social identity. Henri Tajfel defined social identity as "that part of an individual's self-concept which derives from his knowledge of his membership in a social group . . . together with the value and emotional significance attached to that membership."[22] When social identity is salient, the self is extended out and into the group prototype, a process involving self-stereotyping. The group becomes represented in the individual's self-concept: its concerns become the individual's concerns.[23]

Once we have identified with groups, we look to others to better understand our social identities. A century ago, the sociologist Charles Cooley called this the "looking-glass self" and argued: "Our ideal self is constructed chiefly out of ideas about us attributed to other people."[24] George Mead concurred, noting that "the individual experiences himself . . . only indirectly . . . by taking the attitudes of other individuals towards himself."[25] In 1954, the psychologist Leon Festinger similarly proposed that when we are uncertain about our beliefs or social standing, we engage in "social reality testing" through comparison with reference groups.[26] Festinger's social comparison theory holds for both personal and social identities. When personal identity is salient, we undertake interpersonal comparisons; when social identity is pertinent, we engage in intergroup comparisons. We gain knowledge about our personal and social identities through comparisons with other individuals and groups.[27] As Yu Xinyan writes in a 1995 patriotic education handbook entitled *Waiguoren kan Zhongguo*

(Foreigners' views of China): "If you want to know if your dress is correct, you can look in a mirror. If you want to know if your behavior is appropriate, you can listen to what other people say about it. If you want to know your own nationality, your own nation-state, it is necessary to listen to the views of foreigners."[28] Constructivists in IR share Yu's insight: Wendt, for instance, argues that a need for "ontological security" drives states to seek the recognition of other states.[29] We look to others to understand our personal and social identities.

Why do we assimilate ourselves into groups? Social psychologists have explored a number of motives, including uncertainty reduction,[30] desires for inclusion,[31] belonging,[32] and existential distress.[33] However, it is the motive of self-esteem that has received the greatest attention.[34] At first, SIT researchers thought that desire for self-esteem drives us to join groups. Evidence of the opposite process has been more robust, however: to the extent that we associate with certain groups, we gain (and lose) "collective self-esteem" from those groups' accomplishments and failures.[35] One group of social psychologists, for instance, found that students tended to wear their school colors more often following a football victory than after a loss, a finding they explained as a desire to "bask in reflected glory."[36] The same is true of our national identities. In another experiment, women who were shown a clip from an altered *Rocky IV*, in which the American boxer (Sylvester Stallone) lost to the Russian, were found to have lost national self-esteem.[37]

In addition to identifying with groups, research in the SIT tradition has demonstrated that we see the groups we associate ourselves with as basically good, and favor our fellow in-group members over out-group members. Indeed, the mere mention of in-group signifiers like "we," "us," and "our" is sufficient to generate positive affect.[38] And experimental studies have overwhelmingly demonstrated that in-group favoritism is robust even when the individual has nothing to gain.

Desires to maintain in-group positivity motivate intergroup social comparisons.[39] We want others to confirm our positive views of ourselves.[40] The 1990 *A Pictorial History of the War of Resistance Against America in Aid of Korea*, which mixes actual photographs with cartoons to tell the "history" of the Korean War to young Chinese readers, is an arresting example of this project. It is not enough that the authors unilaterally proclaim Chinese heroism and condemn American evil: both friends and enemies must verify those claims. For example, frame 1000 is a famous photograph of an old Korean woman embracing a Chinese soldier: Korean gratitude toward China confirms Chinese beneficence. In frame 696—a cartoon of a Caucasian singing with a group of Chinese soldiers—an American similarly verifies Chinese rectitude. The caption explains: "This American prisoner's name is Larry. The policy of superior treatment of prisoners quickly dissolved his antagonistic mentality toward us. He frequently sang: 'Hailalalala, hailalalala . . . The Chinese and Korean people's strength is great, and has defeated the American devils!'"[41]

"Larry" thus confirms the Chinese authors' claim to in-group positivity. "When we are accepted as we present ourselves," the sociologist Thomas Scheff suggests, "we usually feel rewarded by the pleasant emotions of pride and fellow feeling."[42] I concur, with a single amendment: it is our *perception* of others' acceptance of our claims—rather than their actual views of us (as the pictorial history's far-fetched cartoon makes clear)—that determines our emotional response.

Such affect is no "mere" emotional matter, however: It has highly instrumental implications. When we believe that our claims to positive in-group identity are affirmed, we not only feel good, we gain confidence. One group of social psychologists found, for instance, that in subjects for whom being a fan of a particular team was an important aspect of their social identity, assessments of personal efficacy (like their ability to get a date with an attractive member of the opposite sex, win a game of darts, etc.) were significantly higher after a team victory than after a team loss.[43] Pride in past accomplishments translates into confidence about the future.[44] Basking in "victory" over America in Korea, for example, is an important psychological resource when confidence in China's prospects in confronting the United States is again required. The pictorial history of the Korean War discussed above was issued in 1990, when the Beijing elite, facing American-led international sanctions following the Tiananmen massacre, took advantage of the fortieth anniversary commemorations of the onset of the Korean War to bolster Chinese self-confidence. The role of the war as a psychological resource is often explicit. For instance, war veteran Yang Dezhi is blunt: "The spiritual riches [*jingshen caifu*] that the war has left me are precious. I am *confident* that China will prosper."[45] In 1996, following the deployment of two U.S. aircraft carriers near Taiwan, Chinese nationalists again drew on "victory" in Korea to revive what appears to have been a shaken confidence about future confrontations with America. The cover of a 1996 *Shenzhen Zhoukan* (Shenzhen Panorama Weekly), for instance, shows a large photograph of a Korean War veteran sternly waving his finger, accompanied by a large caption warning: "We have squared off before." Pride in the past can bolster confidence in an uncertain future.

Perhaps the most fascinating example of the desire for external confirmation of in-group positivity among contemporary Chinese nationalists involves their infatuation with Henry Kissinger. Kissinger's words of praise for China's past and current leadership, and predictions of China's future rise, are popular enough among Chinese nationalists to be dubbed a "Kissinger complex."[46] Kissinger's praise of Mao Zedong and Zhou Enlai is a favorite theme in nationalist treatments of the 1972 establishment of diplomatic relations between China and America. In a 1998 interview, for example, the *People's Daily* correspondent Li Yunfei claims that Kissinger gushed: "I cherish deep feelings for Zhou Enlai . . . [he] was a man of noble character who towered above the rest in intelligence and had profound knowledge and extensive learning. He was an outstanding politician. . . . The profundity of Zhou Enlai's understanding of the world situation was amazing."

Li also lingers in his article over the minutiae of Kissinger's etiquette in receiving him: "He hurried over to shake hands with this reporter, saying sincerely: 'If you were not a reporter from China, I would not be able to find time to do your interview.' Then, he showed me into his Park Avenue office."[47] Li and his *People's Daily* editors clearly enjoyed both "basking in the reflected glory" of Zhou's greatness and Kissinger's obsequious praise of China.

This "Kissinger complex" involves more than just creating pride in China's past: it is also about creating confidence in the future. Kissinger's recent writings on international relations have been extremely popular among Chinese nationalists, because they are seen as predicting America's decline and China's imminent rise. Tang Zhengyu, for example, concludes his section of the 1996 sensation *Zhongguo keyi shuobu* (China can say no) with the question: "Some say that the nineteenth century was the English century, and that the twentieth century is the American century. What about the twenty-first century?" Tang supports his answer—"The twenty-first century will be China's"—by appending a translation of a 1996 Kissinger speech, the gist of which is that America will not be able to contain China.[48] Kissinger is featured even more prominently predicting America's demise on the back cover of Xi Yongjun and Ma Zaihuai's 1996 book *Chaoyue Meiguo: Meiguo shenhua de zhongjie* (Surpassing America: the end of the American myth).[49] Kissinger helps these Chinese nationalists relieve any doubts they might have about China's future glory.

When our desires for positive self-confirmation are not met, however, we are not pleased. Social psychologists have found that if a member of another group is perceived to impugn one's own group, one's sense of personal self-esteem may be threatened as well. Collective and personal self-esteem are intertwined.[50]

Chinese nationalists' anger at being denied international affirmation is perhaps best symbolized by their "Nobel Prize complex": a resentment that Chinese achievements have been denied their rightful confirmation by the West. Chinese economists believe that they should be awarded a Nobel Prize for China's "economic miracle."[51] One Chinese scholar explained that "with Deng's 1992 Southern tour and the new spurt of economic development, Chinese are increasingly proud of their accomplishments. They thus

find it increasingly hard to bear the disregard and affronts of others."[52] To
add insult to injury, when the first Nobel Prize was awarded to a Chinese in
2000, it was given to Gao Xingjian, who is considered a dissident writer—
a traitor living in Paris. Even the nationalist Gu Qingsheng, whose section
of the anti-American *Zhongguo keyi shuobu* includes headers like "We
Don't Want MFN, and in the Future, We Won't Give it to You," agrees that
the "Nobel complex" indicates that "we have a psychological problem. . . .
Although we say that there is nothing special about foreigners, we are very
sensitive [about their views]."[53] The Nobel complex, I argue, is the flip side
of Chinese nationalists' Kissinger complex: they are the two sides of the
same coin of desire for international affirmation.

In sum, the need for confirmation of in-group positivity motivates intergroup comparisons. When in-group positivity is affirmed, social competition is avoided; if it is not, anger and competition may ensue. In the Chinese
case, Kissinger is beloved for providing high-status confirmation of Chinese
nationalists' claims of superiority; the Nobel Prize Committee, by contrast,
is reviled for withholding such validation.

That "we" must be good does not, however, require that "they" must be
bad. Allen Whiting recognized this distinction in a 1995 exploration of Chinese nationalism: "Affirmative nationalism centres exclusively on 'us' as a
positive in-group referent with pride in attributes and achievements. Assertive nationalism adds 'them' as a negative out-group referent that challenges the in-group's interests and possibly its identity."[54] Attitudes toward
self and other are not necessarily zero-sum, but can vary independently. Discriminating in favor of an in-group does not necessitate discriminating
against an out-group. Studies of racism in the United States and Europe, for
instance, have found evidence of a "symbolic"[55] or "aversive"[56] racism that
involves pro-white, rather than anti-black, attitudes and behavior. In-group
positivity reserves trust and sympathy for one's own, withholding such positive sentiments from the out-group. In-group love does not necessarily lead
to out-group hate.[57]

Intergroup Competition: When
"Better" is Better than "Good"

So, when will in-group identification (stage 1) and positivity (stage 2)
lead to intergroup competition (stage 3) and conflict (stage 4)? When, in
short, does in-group love lead to out-group hate?

Social comparison processes lie at the heart of any answer to this question. Comparison is not inherently competitive. First, it is only when comparisons are made with salient others, are consequential, and are framed in

zero-sum terms that competition may ensue. Second, the presence of any one of five forms of social mobility or social creativity is sufficient by itself to prevent competition.

Necessary but Not Sufficient Causes of Intergroup Competition

For competition to follow, comparisons must (a) be made with salient others, (b) be consequential, and (c) be framed in zero-sum terms. Each is a necessary but not a sufficient cause of intergroup competition.

First, *whom* do we compare ourselves to? Comparisons must be made with *salient others* to lead to competition. For instance, it is only when a comparison is made with external groups that intergroup competition becomes a possible outcome. Interpersonal and intragroup comparisons will not lead directly to intergroup competition. The proximity, availability, and similarity of other in-group members makes them ideal objects of comparison. For example, in most circumstances, individual Chinese will compare their lot with that of their neighbors—other Chinese—and not with Americans across the Pacific Ocean. This generates a tendency toward interpersonal and against intergroup comparisons, militating against intergroup competition.

Intragroup comparisons also inhibit competition between groups. For example, temporal comparisons—Are we better off than we were before?—militate against international competition.[58] Chinese cultural conservatives today, for instance, construct themselves as "realists" and "pragmatists" against the foil of China's recent past: the "radicals" of the late 1980s and even the Cultural Revolution (1966–76).[59] Interethnic comparisons will not lead to international competition either. When Han chauvinists exoticize Chinese minorities as infantile, feminine, and barbaric to flatter themselves as mature, masculine, and civilized, they seek to construct a Han vision of Chinese national identity.[60] They may generate domestic tensions in the process, but such "otherization" will not directly lead to internation competition.

In addition to being *external*, the salient other must also be a *desirable* object of comparison. National histories, like all "auto-biographies," usually tell the story of the nation in relation to other nations. Nationalist historians turn complex pasts into Manichean histories pitting a good "we" against an evil "them."[61] These histories can help us identify who the desired object of comparison is. In Chinese histories, it is usually the West in general and the United States in particular. The West, capitalized as a proper noun to signify its reification, has become China's alter ego. Following Edward Said's discussion of Orientalism, this phenomenon has been labeled "Occidentalism."[62]

In Chinese eyes, however, Americans are racially and culturally different from Chinese. They are not, therefore, ideal objects for comparison. Identity involves both similarity and difference, and "Western devils" are too different for most Chinese to identify with. It is the more proximate and similar Japan, instead, that has served as a more ideal object of self-other dialectics.[63] An assumption of fundamental difference underlying most Chinese writings about the West forces Chinese writers to be explicit about the basis of similarity that justifies comparison at all. The back cover of a special 1996 issue of *Ai Wo Zhonghua* (Love Our China) on the "Sino-American Contest," for instance, constructs a framework of Sino-American equivalence with the line "China and America are both world powers," but then highlights difference: China is kind, America is barbaric, China is a superman, America is a bandit, and so on.[64]

So, why force comparison with the United States? Because comparisons with the United States are *desirable*. When Chinese nationalists choose to compare China to the otherwise dissimilar United States, they clearly seek to depict themselves *to themselves* as a superpower. Upward comparisons, psychologists have shown, serve to inspire self-improvement.[65] This helps explain why many Chinese nationalists obsessively compare China to America. Samuel Huntington's "clash of civilizations" argument probably created a sensation among numerous Chinese nationalists less out of opposition to his view of a Confucian threat to the West than out of a glee that some Westerners feel threatened by China. Writing in Beijing's influential magazine *Dushu* (Reading), for instance, Li Shenzhi argued that China "should take Huntington's perspectives seriously, because they represent a kind of deep [racial] fear."[66] Huntington's argument is celebrated because it confirms Chinese nationalists' claims to great power status.

Conversely, those who reject Chinese claims to greatness are despised. For instance, the late Gerald Segal relegated China to "middling power" status in a 1999 *Foreign Affairs* article.[67] He promptly drew the ire of the *Beijing Review*'s most prominent nationalist, Li Haibo, who retorted that "Chinese feel insulted when their strength is underestimated."[68] In sum, it is only comparisons with salient others that will generate competition. Specifically, those others must be external and desirable objects of comparison.

Second, *what* do we compare? The object of comparison must be *consequential* to the self-concept for it to induce competition. As the sociologist Charles Cooley has noted, it is only when the injurious thought we impute to another is "regarding something which *we cherish as part of our self*" that anger is awakened.[69] What we compare is determined by what we care about; we do not compete over things that do not matter to us.

Language is a consequential issue because it is central to national identity. Fearing that English is a threat to the Chinese language, some Chinese nationalists compete over it. In a 1996 letter printed in *Beijing Fazhibao* (Beijing Legal News), for instance, one man complained about Chinese employees of foreign companies speaking to him in English. Restaurant menus, to add insult to injury, sometimes put English first and list their prices in U.S. dollars: "It's a disgrace!"[70] Xiao Tong and Du Li's 1997 book *Longli, 1978–1996: Zhuanxingqi Zhongguo baixing xinjilu* (Dragon history, 1978–1996: the true feelings of the Chinese people during a time of transition), a psycho-autobiography written by members of the "fourth generation" of thirty-something Chinese, reveals a similar angst. In a section entitled "Whitey, Please Study Chinese," the author tells of feeling "suffocated and resentful" on reading in a Chinese-language textbook written for foreigners: "I'm determined to study English well. If I don't learn it well, I won't be able to find a spouse." He comments: "The sentence would clearly be much more enchanting if you just replaced the word 'English' with the word 'Chinese.'"[71] What he wants is an inversion of hierarchies, with China in the superior position.[72]

Such popular anger has even found public expression. In the spring of 1996, legislation was proposed in the National People's Congress that would eliminate the "poison" of foreign words from the Chinese language.[73] That fall, China's Ministry of Foreign Affairs suspended English interpreting at its press conferences, thereby demanding that all foreign journalists learn Chinese.[74] We compete when the object of comparison is consequential to our self-concept.

When the object of comparison is inconsequential to our self-concept, however, there is no need to compete. As Marilynn Brewer notes, "As long as the in-group feels superior on dimensions that are important to the group's identity, members can tolerate or acknowledge out-group superiority on dimensions of lesser importance. But when groups hold common values and adopt a common measure of relative worth, the search for positive distinctiveness becomes competitive."[75] Sino-American relations in the 1970s reveal a pair of examples of the former dynamic of tolerance. Although Nixon and Kissinger had been working hard toward establishing diplomatic relations with China in the early 1970s, Zhou Enlai stole credit for the breakthrough with a brilliant gambit: inviting a U.S. ping-pong team to China. Because few Americans cared much about ping-pong, defeat was inconsequential to them. For those Chinese who care greatly about their national game, however, victory must have been satisfying. This may have helped Mao and Zhou sell their about-face on policy toward the "American imperialists" to the Chinese people. Deng Xiaoping then returned the favor in 1979, inviting an American basketball team to Beijing as part of the normalization of diplomatic relations. Although the "world champion" Washington Bullets' victory over the Chinese national team (with their huge center, Mu) was enormously satisfying to this young American basketball fan, at the time, few Chinese likely cared much about losing a game of basketball.[76] In other words, because these two sports competitions were each only consequential to one side, they did not promote intergroup competition. One side could gain collective self-esteem without threatening the other.

Third, and finally, *how* is the comparison framed? Is the social comparison construed in zero-sum or positive-sum terms? Zero-sum comparisons induce competition. Such is the case whenever an issue is perceived as a question of status. As a matter of relative ranking, status is a zero-sum resource.[77] This makes the quest for greater status highly competitive.[78]

In China, status issues are often discussed in the language of "face." The zero-sum nature of face and China's history of victimization at the hands of the West combine to make many contemporary Chinese view diplomacy as a fierce competition between leaders who win or lose face for the nations they embody. Chinese nationalist depictions of Richard Nixon also reveal a zero-sum view of Sino-American relations. Ironically, many of the same Chinese nationalists who adore Kissinger also revel in denigrating Nixon, to the same end of enhancing their national self-esteem at America's expense. They delight, for instance, in constructing "victories" over Nixon at the United Nations in 1971 and at Beijing Airport in 1972. Although Nixon and Kissinger clearly desired rapprochement with the PRC and greater Chinese involvement in world affairs to balance against the Soviet Union,[79] recent Chinese narratives of the PRC's 1971 entry into the United Nations ignore such geopolitics to depict the events in Manichean terms: China's victory was America's loss. An October 1996 *People's Daily* article, for instance, commemorated the twenty-fifth anniversary of the "restoration" of the PRC's UN seat with the lines: "The resolution was passed by an overwhelming majority . . . thunderous applause burst out in the assembly hall . . . and many could not refrain from dancing. . . . Certain people of course felt very embarrassed."[80] Chen Feng et al.'s popular 1996 history *ZhongMei jiaoliang daxiezhen* (The true story of the Sino-American contest) is both more explicit about who these "certain people" are and more creative in describing their "embarrassment." One photograph shows the UN General Assembly scene in October 1971 accompanied by the caption: "Delegates applauded heartily, and America was utterly discomfited." Chapter 3, "Feeling Proud and Elated at the UN," elaborates on American "impotence," "humiliation," and "anger." American impotence is conveyed by asserting American opposition and then denying American actors agency to highlight the actions of China's "chin up and chest out" delegation. The authors "quote" the then U.S. ambassador to the United Nations, George H. W. Bush, "despondently" admitting that "this was a loss of face" for America. Construed American anger at this humiliation, however, is revealed in an even more fanciful portrayal of Nixon's reaction to the UN vote, which he apparently watched, "still hoping for a miracle," on television in the White House library: "The room was perfectly quiet. Nixon burned with anger, and the blue veins on his forehead protruded suddenly. 'Unbelievable! . . . to perform so poorly at an international forum.'"[81]

Although *ZhongMei jiaoliang daxiezhen* was produced by the China Institute of Contemporary International Relations (CICIR), a think tank under the State Security Bureau (China's equivalent of the FBI), I suspect that this detailed description of the White House scene was less a product of Chinese intelligence gathering than of the authors' fertile imaginations. They project their view of the situation onto Nixon: because face is a zero-sum game, China's win must be America's loss, and American humiliation at defeat is represented in Nixon's red-faced fury.

Recent Chinese accounts of the 1972 handshake between Nixon and Zhou Enlai also depict it as a zero-sum competition over status. In the special 1996 issue of *Ai Wo Zhonghua* (Love Our China) mentioned above, for example, the PLA writers revel in denigrating Nixon to elevate Zhou and China. Chapter 1 is triumphantly entitled "Nixon Put His Hand Out First." Although handshakes are usually understood to signify conciliation, the authors clearly interpret "the handshake" as a Chinese victory. A tone of pride and vanity permeates their ensuing discussion of Nixon's further humiliation upon discovering no red carpet or masses awaiting at Beijing Airport: "Nixon had hoped for cheering crowds. This plain and simple welcome made Nixon think of the American opinion poll that had predicted that he would be ridiculed and fall into a trap when he visited China."[82] The PLA authors clearly delight in imagining Nixon's chagrin.

When framed as an issue of relative status or face, therefore, Sino-American relations come to approximate the winner-takes-all world of Hobbesian realism. "A 'zero-sum' mentality holds that America's gains (or losses) are China's losses (or gains)," Wang Yuesheng noted in the 1997 volume *Zhongguo ruhe miandui xifang* (How China faces the West).[83] Such zero-sum comparisons promote competition.

In sum, when internation comparisons are made with salient foreign nations, are consequential, and are framed in zero-sum terms, competition may ensue. The absence of any one of these three conditions, however, will inhibit competition.

Causes Sufficient to Prevent Intergroup Competition

The presence of any one of five additional psychological processes, furthermore, is sufficient by itself to inhibit a competitive outcome. These fall under two headings: individual mobility and social creativity. Individual mobility refers to the option of "exit" from a threatened or negative social identity. One can, for example, seek upward social mobility by dis-identifying with a low-status group in favor of identification with a high-status group.

Chinese nationalists often seem keenly aware of the temptations of "exit" from their national identity. In the spring of 1999, the *China News Digest*'s U.S. service (CND-US), a listserv providing news for the mainland Chinese community in America, printed a letter from Zheng Anderson, a Chinese-Canadian, who wrote of being mistreated by an INS agent in Detroit Airport. "I have lived in Canada for 14 years and . . . have treated Canada as my home," she writes. But "despite all the hard work I have done to contribute to my community and my country [Canada] . . . I am still regarded as Chinese."[84] The next issue of CND-US contained four responses to the story. Two were supportive of Anderson's anger with the INS and its discrimination against Chinese. The other two, however, accused her of aspiring to "individual mobility," or "exit" from her national identity. Li Jie asks, "Is she ashamed of BEING a Chinese? I think that this experience should teach her a lesson not to think that she is superior to her own people. She is always a Chinese no matter how many years she has been a Canadian citizen."[85]

Guo Danqun surmises from her name that Anderson is probably married to a "non-Chinese" and then similarly asserts that she has an attitude of "supremacy over other Chinese."[86] Chinese like Li and Guo reject the option of exit from their national identity.

Like such social mobility, social creativity militates against social comparison processes leading to intergroup competition. In general, social creativity involves the reframing of comparisons that threaten one's collective self-esteem into comparisons that allow for positive distinctiveness. Tajfel and Turner suggest that social creativity can take three forms: (a) introducing a more favorable dimension of comparison, (b) changing the values assigned to the attributes, and (c) changing the target of comparison.[87] I would add a fourth: (d) self-deception.

First, when comparisons are framed along a single zero-sum dimension, they can lead to head-to-head competition. However, if a new and more significant dimension of comparison is introduced, the comparison can generate positive distinctiveness for the in-group, thus diffusing competition. Rather than compare our inferior X_1 to their superior X_2, the framework is tweaked: "They may be good at X, but we are good at Y—and Y is more important." Chinese Occidentalism is full of examples of this first type of social creativity. In their 1997 psycho-autobiography *Disidairen de jingshen* (The spirit of the fourth generation), for example, Song Qiang et al., who include contributors to the 1996 hits *Zhongguo keyi shuobu* (China can say no) and *Zhongguo haishi neng shuobu* (China can still say no), juxtapose "Western materialism" with "Eastern harmony" and Westerners' "impersonal coldness" with Easterners' "warm-heartedness." They then borrow from Max Weber to argue that although Western materialism is ascendant, it is an iron cage: it is Easterners who have made "the greater contribution to humanity."[88] Such "othering" of America creates positive distinctiveness for China, but because it does so on separate dimensions, it militates against direct competition.

A second type of social creativity involves what Nietzsche called the "transvaluation of values": a "negative" attribute is changed into a "positive" one, or vice versa. The "black is beautiful" movement in the United States is an example of how social creativity can resolve threats to collective self-esteem: activists successfully argued that "black" was not ugly or evil, but beautiful. A letter published in *Yangcheng Wanbao* (Canton Evening News) in 1998 provides a parallel example of this process involving the valuation of the very term "Chinese." The writer, a U.S. resident, claims that Americans use the word "Chinese" as a "racial epithet." As evidence, he cites an experience he had in Cincinnati when a homeless person taunted him saying, "Chinese, Chinese." He therefore advocates reverting to the Sinocentric "Zhongguoren," literally "person from the Middle Kingdom," rather than using the "pejorative" English "Chinese." To his mind, doing this would restore Chinese to their proper position of superiority.[89] A more consequential example of this second form of social creativity is the recent mainland Chinese reevaluation of the Confucian tradition. Lambasted under Mao as "feudal" and "backward," nationalists now praise Confucianism as the heart of China's glorious civilization. Its meaning transvalued, "Confucianism" now bolsters rather than threatens the national self-esteem of Chinese cultural nationalists.

A third form of social creativity involves changing the comparison target: switching to a lower-status out-group allows for a more favorable comparison. Downward comparisons, psychologists have shown, enhance self-esteem, especially under conditions of threat.[90] In a 1996 piece titled "Chongjian Zhongguo youxi guize" (Rewriting China's rules of the game), for instance, Li Fang first speaks soberly about continued Western hegemony: "The West's power is shaken, but its control of the game has not been." He then finds solace by shifting to a more favorable target of comparison: China's "ancient neighbors," Li writes, worshiped China as "elegant and poised" and "just and fair." "They found glory in drawing close to China and feared distancing themselves from China and reverting to ignorance."[91] This downward comparison (to China's East Asian neighbors) seems to cheer Li up, relieving his earlier anger against the West. Changing the object of comparison can diffuse competition.

Self-deception is the fourth and final form of social creativity. Social comparison occurs along a single dimension, the standards of "good" and "bad" are not challenged, and the target of comparison does not change. Instead, the perception of each party's relative standing is simply distorted. For all their disagreements, social psychologists share the belief that man is not the passive object of social influence, but rather actively interprets his social environment. They thus follow Kant, who argued that we do not see things as they "are," but actively construct our universe.[92] In their desire to see China triumph over America, Chinese nationalists often confuse description and prescription: what is and what ought to be are conflated. Because of the lengthy history of the WTO talks, trade has become an issue of status. Chinese nationalists who wish that China's economy is stronger than America's often simply assert that it is. For instance, the authors of *Chaoyue Meiguo* (Surpassing America) argue that the United States is dependent on the Chinese economy: "If America drops out of the China market . . . the blow to America would be huge and unprecedented." Americans, they write, "cannot do without Chinese products twenty-four hours a day."[93] This view of American economic dependence on China is remarkably widespread, laments China Economics and Trade University's Chong Ling.[94] In a broader critique, PLA writer Jin Hui depicts 1990s Chinese nationalists as suffering from an "Ah Q–style blind optimism." Ah Q is the protagonist of a modern Chinese novel famous for his talent for turning defeats into psychological victories.[95] "For over 100 years," Jin writes, "generation after generation of Chinese have been dreaming that since we were once strong, although we are now backward, we shall certainly become strong again." Such "illusions," he warns, are "even worse than spiritual opiates."[96] However delusional, such Ah Q–style self-deception has the positive side effect of diminishing the threat of direct social comparison.

Any one of these psychological processes, in sum, is sufficient by itself to prevent intergroup comparisons from generating competition.

Sino-American Apology Diplomacy, 1999 and 2001

Two recent examples of Sino-American apology diplomacy illustrate the utility of social identity theory in explaining Chinese foreign policy.

At midnight on 8 May 1999, an American B-2 bomber dropped five precision guided missiles over Belgrade. All five hit their intended target. But it was not a Serbian arms depot: it was the Chinese embassy. Three exploded near the embassy's intelligence operations center. Three Chinese were killed in the blast, and twenty-three others were injured. In Washington, President Bill Clinton proclaimed the bombing a "tragic mistake" due to outdated maps and extended his "regrets and profound condolences" to the Chinese people. In Beijing, however, Chinese officials rejected American explanations as "sophistry" and declared NATO apologies to be "insufficient" and "insincere." The Chinese media did not publicize Clinton's public apologies until 11 May. Instead, they proclaimed the bombing a "barbaric" and intentional "criminal act."[97]

After lengthy negotiations, Beijing and Washington agreed on compensation packages for both sides. When money finally changed hands nearly two years later in January 2001, however, Chinese Foreign Ministry spokesman Zhu Bangzao again demanded that the United States "conduct a comprehensive and thorough investigation into the bombing, severely punish the perpetrators and give satisfactory account of the incident to the Chinese People."[98]

A few months later, on 1 April 2001, a Chinese F-8 jet fighter and an American EP-3 surveillance plane collided over the South China Sea. The EP-3 made it safely to China's Hainan Island; the F-8 tore apart and crashed, and the Chinese pilot, Wang Wei, was killed. A few days later, China's Foreign Minister Tang Jiaxuan and President Jiang Zemin demanded an American apology. The United States balked: viewing the aggressiveness of the Chinese jet as the cause of the collision, Americans did not feel responsible. As Senator Joseph Lieberman said on CNN's *Larry King Live*, "When you play chicken, sometimes you get hurt."

The impasse was only broken after eleven days of intensive negotiations. U.S. Ambassador Joseph Prueher gave a letter to Foreign Minister Tang: "Please convey to the Chinese people and to the family of pilot Wang Wei that we are very sorry for their loss. . . . We are very sorry the entering of China's airspace and the landing did not have verbal clearance." Having extracted an "apology" from Washington, Beijing released the twenty-four American servicemen being held on Hainan Island.

What accounts for the willingness of Chinese and American leaders to choose confrontation over these two issues? And why does the 1999 affair remain unresolved, while the 2001 incident has largely been diffused?

Rationalist and symbolic approaches to IR provide complementary— not competing—answers to these questions. Rationalist approaches highlight the instrumental dimension of China's apology diplomacy. But symbolic approaches also carry causal weight in explaining Chinese behavior. Specifically, SIT proves indispensable to answering the questions of why Chinese and Americans choose competition, and when they choose to compete and when they choose not to. These two case studies can thus further illustrate the utility of SIT to an understanding of Chinese foreign policy. To repeat, I am *not* testing rationalist against symbolic hypotheses, because I believe that both realms are integral to explaining the genesis and resolution of each incident.

I have discussed the Chinese reaction to the Belgrade bombing at length elsewhere.[99] Here, suffice it to say that with the reemergence in the mid 1990s of a victimization narrative of Chinese suffering at the hands of Western imperialism, most Chinese understood the Belgrade bombing as yet another in a long history of Western insults. Chinese thus experienced the bombing as an assault on their collective self-esteem as "Chinese."

Chinese refusals to accept apologies from President Clinton in 1999 thus had both instrumental and emotional dimensions. Chinese and American diplomats were jockeying for position in post–Cold War East Asia. A rationalist analysis of post–Belgrade bombing Chinese diplomacy would rightly point to an instrumental motivation: restoring China's position in the East Asian hierarchy of power. Like a father refusing his son's repeated prostrations of forgiveness, refusing America's repeated apologies was one of the few ways China's leadership could seek to restore China's status in the eyes of the Chinese people.

But social identity was also a big part of the problem. All three of the necessary conditions for competition were present. America, as noted above, is a highly *salient* peer competitor against which Chinese define their social identity. Had it been the Serbs who had mistakenly bombed the Chinese embassy, Chinese would not have been as distraught. The death of three Chinese was obviously a *consequential* issue, and because status is a *zero-sum* resource, post–Belgrade bombing diplomacy was primed for competition. Furthermore, none of the five conditions that can prevent competition were readily available. The bombing was clearly a Sino-American issue, so social mobility was not an option. And the death of three Chinese was not something that any amount of social creativity could easily explain away.

Both rationalist and social psychological variables thus help explain why Chinese diplomats could not resolve the Belgrade bombing incident through cool diplomacy: the instrumental stakes were too high, and the assault on Chinese self-esteem was too acute. Chinese nationalists were moved to take to the streets in protest, and Chinese diplomats had to resort to a public posture of rejecting American apologies and explanations.

The 2001 plane collision incident was both similar and different. From a rationalist perspective, 2001, like 1999, implicated China's instrumental concern with maintaining its position in post–Cold War East Asia. On the symbolic side, 2001 was also similar to 1999 in that all three necessary conditions for intergroup competition were present: once again, Chinese understandably framed the comparison with the United States in salient, consequential, and zero-sum terms.

The crucial difference between 1999 and 2001, however, seems to have been that in 2001 both sides were able to utilize social creativity to diffuse Sino-American competition. Specifically, both sides engaged in self-deception over the meaning of the two "very sorrys" to declare victory in bilateral diplomacy. The reality, of course, is that both sides suffered from the incident. Ah Q–style self-deception, however, allowed them to diffuse the crisis.

Cross-cultural differences in responsibility assessment and the meaning of apologies help explain how both sides could simultaneously claim victory.[100] Chinese tend toward a consequentialist view of responsibility. A Chinese pilot, Wang Wei, was dead, so an American apology was necessary to restore the relationship. Americans, in contrast, tend to focus on intentionality in assessing responsibility, hence our legal distinctions, for instance, between first- and second-degree murder. Was the act premeditated? Because Americans viewed the incident as a "tragic accident"—not something Americans had chosen to do or had done with premeditation—no apology was necessary.

The intensive negotiations over the wording of the letter Ambassador Prueher gave to Foreign Minister Tang reflected these cultural differences. Chinese were able to claim that Americans had admitted responsibility for the incident, while Americans could claim that the two "I'm sorrys" were mere gestures of condolence—not an admission of culpability. As Secretary of State Colin Powell explained after the release of the American crew, "There is nothing to apologize for. To apologize would have suggested that we have done something wrong or accepted responsibility for having done something wrong. And we did not do anything wrong."

Hawks on both sides were adept at face-saving self-deception. In Beijing, many boasted of how President Jiang had planned America's humiliation from the start and had "taught Bush Jr. a lesson." Qinghua University's Yan Xuetong, for instance, declared that "China stuck to principle" and "did a better job of dealing with the incident."[101] In this Chinese view, Jiang, "diplomatic strategist extraordinaire," had won a major diplomatic victory.[102] In Washington, meanwhile, Bush was widely praised for having handled the situation masterfully, winning the day. For instance, the *Nelson Report* newsletter offered a parody of the American "we're sorry" letter: "We're sorry the world is now seeing your leaders as the xenophobic, clueless thugs that they really are. We're sorry you are losing so much *face* over this."[103] Ironically, it was such Ah Q–style self-deception that helped to diffuse the 2001 crisis.

Conclusions

Drawing on experimental findings in social psychology, I have argued that our basic human tendency to identify with groups and imbue them with positive meaning does not inevitably lead to competition between groups.

It is only when comparisons are made with salient others, are consequential, and are framed in zero-sum terms that competition may ensue. Each of these three conditions is a necessary, but not sufficient, cause of competition. Furthermore, each of five forms of social mobility and social creativity is sufficient on its own to inhibit against a competitive outcome. Intergroup competition, in sum, is a highly contingent outcome.

International competition is no different. Although we all, to varying degrees, assimilate ourselves into our national groups and favor our fellow nationals over foreigners, we do not invariably pit our nations against other nations. Anti-foreignism is neither in our blood nor hardwired into our psyches. International competition is not—as Jonathan Mercer suggests—the inexorable product of our identification with national groups. James Fearon and David Laitin's quantitative findings on the relative *nonoccurrence* of ethnic conflict support this argument.

Assuming that competition precedes conflict, this chapter has focused on the transition from in-group positivity to intergroup competition, the second and third stages of the four-stage model of the progression from in-group identification to intergroup conflict. It has not, therefore, said much about the equally contingent transition between intergroup competition and intergroup conflict, stages 3 and 4. Rogers Brubaker and Laitin are right that this transition is a "phase shift": it is not a change in degree, but a change in kind demanding separate theoretical attention.[104]

I disagree with Brubaker and Laitin, however, when they assert that psychological theories cannot account for aggression.[105] Just as I located comparison at the juncture between in-group positivity and intergroup competition (stages 2 and 3), I suggest that emotion lies at the juncture between intergroup competition and conflict (stages 3 and 4).[106] I thus join Mercer and Neta Crawford in calling for emotion to be brought back into the study of IR.[107] The psychologies and sociologies of emotion in particular can teach us a great deal about when international competition will lead to war—and when it will not.

Although a persuasive case for the pivotal role of affect in transforming competition (stage 3) into violent conflict (stage 4) requires separate treatment, a brief discussion of one specific emotion—anger—is warranted here to defend psychology from Brubaker and Laitin's critique. Anger can restore status after it has been taken away unfairly. It "seems designed to rectify injustice," one group of psychologists writes: "to reassert power or status, to frighten the offending person into compliance, to restore a desired state of affairs."[108] In *Injustice: The Social Bases of Obedience and Revolt*, Barrington Moore similarly argues that "vengeance means retaliation. It also means a reassertion of human dignity or worth, after injury or damage. Both are basic sentiments behind moral anger and the sense of injustice."[109] Where

Moore highlights the emotional, J. M. Barbalet stresses the instrumental: "Vengefulness is an emotion of power relations. It functions to correct imbalanced or disjointed power relationships. Vengefulness is concerned with restoring social actors to their rightful place in relationships."[110] It is such ethical anger, I suggest, that impels sustained conflict and violence.[111]

Indeed, Chinese nationalists frequently speak of injustice. Xiong Lei, for instance, writes in the passionate 1996 anti-American bestseller *Yaomohua Zhongguo de beihou* (The plot to demonize China) that "we do not seek to foment hatred of Americans, only to restore justice."[112] The Chinese who threw bricks at the U.S. embassy in Beijing after the bombing of their embassy in Belgrade in May 1999 were also impelled by an ethical anger that sought to right a wrong. They were genuinely angry—not, as Western pundits generally suggested, playthings in the hands of communist puppet masters. Chinese protestors sought retributive justice: to restore China's proper place in international society.[113] Righteous anger can help transform intergroup competition into violent protest.

In this chapter I have attempted to advance the theoretic debate over conflict in IR by bringing in agency and contingency. Nations do not act: individuals act. Like all peoples, Chinese are neither innately pacifist nor hardwired for conflict. Instead, history and culture shape how individual Chinese will construe the events of world politics. The social psychology of intergroup relations can then help explain whether they will choose cooperation or conflict in a given situation. Sino-American relations in the twenty-first century will *not*, therefore, inevitably be conflictual. Individual agency plays a vital role. It is the actions of individual Chinese and Americans that will determine whether our need to view our nations positively will lead to Sino-American conflict. By suggesting which conditions promote intergroup conflict and which diffuse it, social identity theory (SIT) can help us learn to live together in peace.

Notes

1. Vilfredo Pareto, *Trattato di sociologia generale* (Florence: G. Barbèra, 1916), trans. Andrew Bongiorno et al. under the title *The Mind and Society: Trattato di sociologia generale*, ed. Arthur Livingston (1935; New York: AMS Press, 1983), pt. 1.

2. Edward Timperlake and William C. Triplett, *Year of the Rat: How Bill Clinton Compromised U.S. Security for Chinese Cash* (Washington, D.C.: Regnery, 1998).

3. Paul Kennedy, *The Rise and Fall of the Great Powers: Economic Change and Military Conflict from 1500 to 2000* (New York: Random House, 1987).

4. Condoleezza Rice, "Promoting the National Interest," *Foreign Affairs* 79, 1 (January–February 2000): 45–62; John Mearsheimer, *The Tragedy of Great Power Politics* (New York: Norton, 2001).

5. Thomas Christensen, "Chinese Realpolitik," *Foreign Affairs* 75, 5 (September–October 1996): 37n9.

6. Johnston makes valuable contributions both in debunking the myth of a pacifist Chinese strategic culture (Chinese can and do frequently use force) and by bringing culture into the analysis. As Johnston himself notes, however, his approach to culture makes the same deterministic predictions about Chinese behavior as a "simple structural realpolitik model" would. Alastair Iain Johnston, *Cultural Realism: Strategic Culture and Grand Strategy in Chinese History* (Princeton, N.J.: Princeton University Press, 1995).

7. Alexander Wendt, "Anarchy Is What States Make of It: The Social Construction of Power Politics," *International Organization* 46, 2 (Spring 1992): 395, 394.

8. Jonathan Mercer, "Anarchy and Identity," *International Organization* 49, 2 (Spring 1995): 233.

9. Samuel Huntington, "The Clash of Civilizations?" *Foreign Affairs* 72, 3 (Summer 1993): 22–49.

10. Although Wendt proposes a "social structural" approach to IR, his view of the state is often surprisingly asocial: international society, he asserts, has a "low density," because "states are by nature more solitary than people." This leads Wendt to concede pessimistically to the materialists that "states are predisposed to define their objective interests in self-interested terms . . . the international system contains a bias toward 'Realist' thinking." On the other hand, Wendt is remarkably optimistic in asserting that the relationship among his three "international political cultures"—Hobbesian, Lockean, and Kantian—is progressive, or at least "unidirectional." Such passages leave the reader wondering whether to be optimistic or pessimistic about interstate relations. Because his focus is on the macro, systemic level, Wendt can provide little insight into when specific states will spar. Alexander Wendt, *Social Theory of International Politics* (New York: Cambridge University Press, 1999), 276, 21, 267, 241, 312.

11. Johnston, *Cultural Realism*; Christensen, "Chinese Realpolitik."

12. Harry Eckstein, "Case Study and Theory in Political Science," in *Strategies of Inquiry*, ed. Fred I. Greenstein and Nelson W. Polsby (Reading, Mass.: Addison-Wesley, 1975), 79–137.

13. For a brief discussion of the role of culture in the Sino-American dispute over the April 2001 spy plane collision, see Peter Hays Gries and Peng Kaiping, "Culture Clash? Apologies East and West," *Journal of Contemporary China* 11, 30 (2002): 173–78.

14. E.g., Irving Janis, *Groupthink: Psychological Studies of Policy Decisions and Fiascoes* (Boston: Houghton Mifflin, 1983).

15. James Fearon and David Laitin, "Explaining Interethnic Cooperation," *American Political Science Review* 90, 4 (December 1996): 717.

16. Muzafer Sherif, *In Common Predicament: Social Psychology of Intergroup Conflict and Cooperation* (Boston: Houghton Mifflin, 1966).

17. Roger Brown, *Social Psychology* (New York: Free Press, 1986), 543.

18. John Turner, *Differentiation Between Social Groups: Studies in the Social Psychology of Intergroup Relations* (London: Academic Press, 1978).

19. Given that SIT *challenges* RCT's material self-interest argument about group formation and intergroup relations, Mercer's use of SIT to *support* realist assumptions about self-help and relative gains is particularly surprising. I disagree with his assertion that "SIT provides theoretical and empirical support for the neorealist assumption that states are a priori self-regarding." Mercer, "Anarchy and Identity," 251n3.

20. Marilynn B. Brewer, "Ingroup Identification and Intergroup Conflict: When Does Ingroup Love Become Outgroup Hate?" In *Social Identity, Intergroup Conflict, and Conflict Resolution*, ed. R. Ashmore, D. Jussim, and L. Wilder (Oxford: Oxford University Press, 2000), 17–41.

21. Fearon and Laitin, "Explaining Interethnic Cooperation," *American Political Science Review* 90, 4 (December 1996): 717.

22. Henri Tajfel, *Human Groups and Social Categories* (Cambridge: Cambridge University Press, 1981), 255.

23. Turner makes this point especially clear in an elaboration of SIT that he calls self-categorization theory, See John Turner, *Rediscovering the Social Group: A Self-Categorization Theory* (Oxford: Blackwell, 1987).

24. Charles Cooley, *Human Nature and the Social Order* (1902; New York: Scribner, 1922), 397.

25. George Mead, *Mind, Self, and Society* (1934; Chicago: University of Chicago Press, 1965), 138.

26. Leon Festinger, "A Theory of Social Comparison Processes," *Human Relations* 7 (1954): 117–40.

27. Work on "prototypes" in person perception also addresses this issue of the role of comparison processes in understanding our social world. See, e.g. Nancy Cantor and Walter Mischel, "Prototypes in Person Perception," *Advances in Experimental Social Psychology* 12 (1979): 3–52.

28. Yu Xinyan, *Waiguoren kan Zhongguo* [Foreigners' views of China] (Beijing: Zhongguo Shaonian Ertong Chubanshe, 1995).

29. Alexander Wendt, "Collective Identity Formation and the International State," *American Political Science Review* 88, 2 (June 1994): 384–96. The critical constructivists Naeem Inayatullah and David Blaney go even further in maintaining that "the deepest motivation for human contact is self-knowledge." See Naeem Inayatullah and David Blaney, "Knowing Encounters: Beyond Parochialism in International Relations Theory," in *The Return of Culture and Identity in IR Theory*, ed. Yosef Lapid and Friedrich Kratochwil (Boulder, Colo.: Lynne Rienner, 1996), 81. I borrow the label "critical constructivism" from Ted Hopf, "The Promise of Constructivism in International Relations Theory," *International Security* 23, 1 (Summer 1998): 171–200.

30. Michael Hogg and Dominic Abrams, "Towards a Single-Process Uncertainty-Reduction Model of Social Motivation in Groups," in *Group Motivation: Social Psychological Perspectives*, ed. id. (New York: Harvester Wheatsheaf, 1993), 173–90.

31. Marilynn B. Brewer, "The Role of Distinctiveness in Social Identity and Group Behavior," in *Group Motivation: Social Psychological Perspectives*, ed. id. (New York: Harvester Wheatsheaf, 1993), 1–16.

32. Émile Durkheim, *Suicide* (1897; New York: Free Press, 1963); Roy Baumeister and Mark Leary, "The Need to Belong: Desire for Interpersonal Attachments as a Fundamental Human Motivation," *Psychological Bulletin* 117, 3 (1995): 497–529.

33. Emmanuel Castano et al., "I Belong, Therefore, I Exist: Ingroup Identification, Ingroup Entitativity, and Ingroup Bias," *Personality and Social Psychology Bulletin* 28, 2 (February 2002): 135–43.

34. Almost two centuries ago, American President John Adams (1805) wrote that "a desire to be observed, considered, esteemed, praised, beloved, and admired by his fellows is one of the earliest as well as the keenest dispositions discovered in the heart of man." John Adams, *Discourses on Davila* (Boston: Russell & Cutler, 1805), cited in William Swann, *Self-Traps: The Elusive Quest for Higher Self-Esteem* (New York: W. H. Freeman, 1996), 35.

35. Jennifer Crocker and Riia Luhtanen, "Collective Self-Esteem and In-group Bias," *Journal of Personality and Social Psychology* 58, 1 (January 1990): 60–67.

36. Robert Cialdini et al., "Basking in Reflected Glory: Three (Football) Field Studies," *Journal of Personality and Social Psychology* 34, 3 (September 1976): 366–75.

37. Collective self-esteem was restored, however, if the subjects were subsequently allowed to derogate Russians. Nyla Branscombe and Daniel Wann, "Collective Self-Esteem Consequences of Outgroup Derogation When a Valued Social Identity Is on Trial," *European Journal of Social Psychology* 24, 6 (November–December 1994): 641–57.

38. Charles Perdue et al., "Us and Them: Social Categorization and the Process of Intergroup Bias," *Journal of Personality and Social Psychology* 59, 3 (September 1990): 475–86.

39. Henri Tajfel and John Turner, "The Social Identity Theory of Intergroup Behavior," in *Psychology of Intergroup Relations*, ed. Stephen Worshel and William Austin (Chicago: Nelson Hall, 1986), 7–24.

40. Social psychologists have done a better job of *demonstrating* the existence of desires for in-group positivity, however, than of *explaining* them.

41. *KangMei yuanChao zhanzheng huajuan* [A pictorial history of the war of resistance against America in aid of Korea], Liang Qianxiang, chief ed. (Beijing: KangMei YuanChao Jinianguan, 1990), 366.

42. Thomas Scheff, "Shame and Conformity: The Deference-Emotion System," *American Sociological Review* 53 (1988): 396.

43. Edward Hirt et al., "Costs and Benefits of Allegiance: Changes in Fans' Self-Ascribed Competencies After Team Victory Versus Defeat," *Journal of Personality & Social Psychology* 63, 5 (1992): 724–38.

44. J. M. Barbalet, *Emotion, Social Theory, and Social Structure: A Macrosociological Approach* (New York: Cambridge University Press, 1998), 87.

45. Yang Dezhi, "Qianyan" [Preface], in *KangMei yuanChao de kaige* [A paean to the war to resist America and aid Korea] (Beijing: Zhongguo Da Baike Quanshu Chubanshe, 1990), 3.

46. Kissinger's "China complex" is a separate issue.

47. Li Yunfei, "Zhou Enlai Was the Most Outstanding Politician—Interviewing Former US Secretary of State Dr. Kissinger," *Renmin Ribao*, 3 March 1998, 6, trans. in Foreign Broadcast Information Service (hereafter cited as FBIS), CHI-98-089, 30 March 1998.

48. Song Qiang, Zhang Zangzang et al., *Zhongguo keyi shuobu* [China can say no] (Beijing: Zhonghua Gongshang Lianhe Chubanshe, 1996), 199, 202–5.

49. Xi Yongjun and Ma Zaihuai, *Chaoyue Meiguo: Meiguo shenhua de zhongjie* [Surpassing America: the end of the American myth] (Huhehaote: Neimenggu Daxue Chubanshe, 1996), 228.

50. Crocker and Luhtanen, "Collective Self-Esteem and Ingroup Bias," n. 36. The exact nature of the relationship between personal and collective self-esteem is not yet clear, however.

51. Zhao Suisheng, "Chinese Intellectuals' Quest for National Greatness and Nationalistic Writing in the 1990s," *China Quarterly*, no. 152 (December 1997): 731.

52. Jin Niu, "Zhongguo ruhe shuobu?" [How should China say no?], in *Zhongguo ruhe shuobu?* [How should China say no?], special edition of *Meiguo daguan* [America the Beautiful] (Beijing: Chinese Academy of Social Science, Institute of American Studies, 1996), 5.

53. Song et al., *Zhongguo keyi shuobu* [China can say no], 285n48.

54. Allen Whiting, "Chinese Nationalism and Foreign Policy After Deng," *China Quarterly*, no. 142 (June 1995): 295–316.

55. Donald Kinder and David Sears, "Prejudice and Politics: Symbolic Racism Versus Racial Threats to the Good Life," *Journal of Personality & Social Psychology* 40, 3 (1981): 414–31.

56. Audrey Murrell et al., "Aversive Racism and Resistance to Affirmative Action: Perceptions of Justice Are Not Necessarily Color Blind," *Basic & Applied Social Psychology* 15, 1–2 (1994): 71–86.

57. Brewer, "Ingroup Identification and Intergroup Conflict," n. 15.

58. See the political science literature on relative deprivation, e.g. Ted Gurr, *Why Men Rebel* (Princeton, N.J.: Princeton University Press, 1970).

59. Xu Ben, "Contesting Memory for Intellectual Self-Positioning: The 1990s' New Cultural Conservatism in China," *Modern Chinese Literature and Culture* 11, 1 (Spring 1999): 157–92.

60. Louisa Schein, "Gender and Internal Orientalism in China," *Modern China* 23, 1 (January 1997): 69–98.

61. Sudipta Kaviraj, "The Imaginary Institution of India," in *Subaltern Studies VII*, ed. Partha Chatterjee and Gyanendra Pandley (New York: Oxford University Press, 1992), 6.

62. E.g., Chen Xiaomei, *Occidentalism: A Theory of Counter-Discourse in Post-Mao China* (New York: Oxford University Press, 1995).

63. In the modern period, indeed, Japan has arguably served as "China's Occident."

64. "Zhongguo qizhi shuobu: ZhongMei jiaoliang" [China shouldn't just say no: the Sino-American contest], *Ai Wo Zhonghua* [Love Our China] (Hefei), special issue, 1996.

65. E.g., Shelley Taylor and Marci Lobel, "Social Comparison Activity Under Threat: Downward Evaluation and Upward Contacts," *Psychological Review* 96, 4 (1989): 569–75.

66. Li Shenzhi, "Fear Under Numerical Superiority," *Dushu* [Reading] (Beijing), no. 6 (June 1997); 31–38, trans. in FBIS-CHI-97-296 (23 October 1997).

67. Gerald Segal, "Does China Matter?" *Foreign Affairs* 78, 5 (September–October 1999): 24–37.

68. Li Haibo, "China and Its Century," *Beijing Review* 42, 42 (18 October 1999): 11–16.

69. Cooley, *Human Nature and the Social Order*, 266n23.

70. "Wo tuoqi nazhong Zhongguoren" [I detest that kind of Chinese], *Beijing Fazhibao* [Beijing Legal News], 29 May 1996.

71. Xiao Tong and Du Li, *Longli, 1978–1996: Zhuanxingqi Zhongguo baixing xinjilu* [Dragon history, 1978–96: the true feelings of the Chinese people during a time of transition] (Beijing: Gaige Chubanshe, 1997), 287–88.

72. In the context of African decolonization, Franz Fanon argued that the "native's minimum demand" is that "the last shall be first and the first last." He is "ready at a moment's notice to exchange the role of the quarry for that of the hunter." *The Wretched of the Earth* (1961; New York: Grove Press, 1968), 37, 53.

73. "Top Advisors Call for Regulations to Purify Chinese Language," Xinhua, 6 March 1996.

74. Not all Chinese, of course, share this view of the English language. The linguist Chen Guanglei, for instance, has urged restraint. There is "no need to either fear or worship the Western," Chen counsels; Chinese should "absorb foreign words while maintaining self-respect and love of our own language." See "Gaige kaifang zhong hanyu cihui de biandong" [Changes in the Chinese vocabulary under reform and opening], *Yuyan Jiaoxue yu Yanjiu* (Beijing) 2 (1997): 21, 16.

75. Marilynn Brewer, "The Psychology of Prejudice: Ingroup Love or Outgroup Hate?" *Journal of Social Issues* 55, 3 (Fall 1999): 435.

76. Today's Chinese are more likely to care about basketball. China now has its own professional basketball association, the CNBA, and millions of aspiring Michael Jordans.

77. The problem is one of inflation. If everyone gets "A's," for example, an "A" would lose its value.

78. Manipulating status, furthermore, is very difficult. "Located" in other people's minds, status is highly elusive. Attempting to buy or coerce status, for instance, is usually self-defeating, reducing one's prestige. Rather than being bought or acquired by force, status is instead earned through conformity to social norms and association with those of high status. See Murray Milner Jr., *Status and Sacredness: A General Theory of Status Relations and an Analysis of Indian Culture* (New York: Oxford University Press, 1994).

79. Rosemary Foot makes a persuasive case that the Nixon administration's formal opposition to Beijing's UN bid was half-hearted: they were going through the motions for the sake of Taiwan and domestic American opinion, which supported PRC entry but remained loyal to the Nationalists in Taiwan. See *The*

Practice of Power: U.S. Relations with China Since 1949 (Oxford: Clarendon Press, 1995).

80. Fu Hao, "A Ruling Given by History—Marking the 25th Anniversary of China's Restoration of Its Legitimate Seat in United Nations," *Renmin Ribao*, 23 October 1996, 6, trans. in FBIS-CHI-96–212, 23 October 1996.

81. Chen Feng et al., *ZhongMei jiaoliang daxiezhen* [The true story of the Sino-American contest], vol. 2 (Beijing: Zhongguo Renshi Chubanshe, 1996), 322.

82. "Zhongguo qizhi shuobu: ZhongMei jiaoliang" [China shouldn't just say no: the Sino-American contest], 12n67.

83. Wang Yuesheng, "Shehui qingxu, wenming jiaowang yu gongtong jiazhi" [Social sentiment, the exchange of civilizations, and common values], in *Zhongguo ruhe miandui xifang* [How China faces the West], ed. Xiao Pang (Hong Kong: Mirror Books, 1997), 131.

84. Zheng Anderson, " 'He Was Treating Me Like a Criminal'—A Chinese Canadian's Experience at Detroit Airport," *China News Digest—US*, 20 March 1999, www.cnd.org/CND-US/CND-US.99/CND-US.99-03-20.html (accessed 2 October 2005).

85. Li Jie, "She Is Not Superior to Her Own People," *China News Digest—US*, 3 April 1999, www.cnd.org/CND-US/CND-US.99/CND-US.99-04-03.html (accessed 2 October 2005).

86. Guo Danqun, "Chinese Holding Foreign Passport Superior to Other Chinese?" *China News Digest—US*, 3 April 1999, www.cnd.org/CND-US/CND-US.99/CND-US.99-04-03.html (accessed 3 November 2005).

87. Tajfel and Turner, "Social Identity Theory of Intergroup Behavior," 19–20n40.

88. Song Qiang et al., *Disidairen de jingshen: xiandai Zhongguoren de jiushi qingjie* [The spirit of the fourth generation: the savior complex of the modern Chinese] (Lanzhou: Gansu Wenhua Chubanshe, 1997), 246–49.

89. "Wo shi 'Zhongguoren,' bushi 'Chinese' " [I am a "person from China," not a "Chinese"), *Yangcheng Wanbao* [Canton Evening News], 4 October 1998. My thanks to Regina Abrami for this reference.

90. E.g., Thomas Ashby Wills, "Similarity and Self-Esteem in Downward Comparison," in *Social Comparison: Contemporary Theory and Research*, ed. Jerry Suls and Thomas Ashby Wills (Hillsdale, N. J.: Lawrence Erlbaum, 1991), 51–78.

91. Li Fang, "Chongjian Zhongguo youxi guize" [Rewriting China's rules of the game], *Zuojia Tiandi* [Writer's World], special issue (1996): 23.

92. Immanuel Kant, *Critique of Pure Reason* (1781; New York: Cambridge University Press, 1998). See also Shelley Taylor, "The Social Being in Social Psychology," in *The Handbook of Social Psychology*, 4th ed., ed. Daniel Gilbert et al. (Boston: McGraw-Hill, 1998), 1: 52, 70.

93. Xi and Ma, *Chaoyue Meiguo* [Surpassing America], 228, 231n50.

94. Chong Ling, "Guanyu yibenshu de duozhong shengyin" [On the many voices about a single book], *Beijing Wanbao*, 18 August 1996, reprinted in Jia Qingguo, *Zhongguo bu jinjin shuobu* [China should not just say no] (Beijing: Zhonghua Gongshang Lianhe Chubanshe, 1996),265–67.

95. For a perceptive analysis, see Lu Junhua, *Lun Ah Q jingshen shenglifa de zheli he xinli neihan* [On the philosophical and psychological meaning of Ah Q's psychological victory technique] (Xi'an: Shaanxi Renmin Chubanshe, 1982).

96. Jin Hui, "Geng zhongyao de shi minzu jingshen shijie de chongjian" (More important is the reconstruction of a national psychological world), in *Zhongguo ruhe miandui xifang* [How China faces the West], ed. Xiao Pang (Hong Kong: Mirror Books, 1997), 182–98.

97. Ta Kung Pao editorial 1999, trans. in FBIS-CHI-1999–0512.

98. "China Acknowledges U.S. Payment for Belgrade Embassy Bombing," Kyodo News Service, 20 January 2001.

99. See Peter Hays Gries, "Tears of Rage: Chinese Nationalism and the Belgrade Embassy Bombing," *China Journal*, no. 46 (2001): 25–43.

100. For a more detailed discussion, see Peter Hays Gries and Peng Kaiping, "Culture Clash? Apologies East and West," *Journal of Contemporary China* 11, 30 (2002): 173–78.

101. Yan Xuetong, "Experts on Jet Collision Incident and Overall Situation in Sino–U.S. Relations," *Liaowang*, 2001. Cited in FBIS-CHI-2001–042616, 6–8.

102. Willy Wo-Lap Lam, "Behind the Scenes in Beijing's Corridors of Power," CNN, 11 April 2001.

103. *Nelson Report*, April 2001. I thank Rick Baum and Chinapol for this reference.

104. Rogers Brubaker and David Laitin, "Ethnic and Nationalist Violence," *Annual Review of Sociology* 24 (1998): 426.

105. Ibid., 438.

106. This is not meant to imply that emotion does not play a role in other intergroup dynamics. Indeed, sociologists of emotion make the broader argument that emotion is the vital link between social actor and social structure; see, e.g., Barbalet, *Emotion, Social Theory, and Social Structure*, 27n39. SIT and especially social categorization theory, however, have shied away from motivation in favor of a focus on the cognitive dimensions of intergroup behavior.

107. Jonathan Mercer, "Approaching Emotion in International Politics" (paper presented at the International Studies Association annual meeting, 25 April 1996); Neta Crawford, "The Passion of World Politics: Propositions on Emotion and Emotional Relationships," *International Security* 24, 4 (Spring 2000): 116–56.

108. Phillip Shaver et al., "Emotion Knowledge: Further Exploration of a Prototype Approach," *Journal of Personality & Social Psychology* 52, 6 (1987): 1078, cited in Brenda Major, "From Social Inequality to Personal Entitlement: The Role of Social Comparisons, Legitimacy Appraisals, and Group Membership," *Advances in Experimental Social Psychology* 26 (1994): 343.

109. Barrington Moore, *Injustice: The Social Bases of Obedience and Revolt* (Boston: Beacon Press, 1978), 17.

110. Barbalet, *Emotion, Social Theory, and Social Structure*, 136n39.

111. Moore and Barbalet's argument about anger seeking to restore status overlaps with prospect theorists' findings that we are more averse to loss than desirous of gain. Beyond just being angered by status loss, therefore, we are also more willing to take risks to restore it. On "prospect theory," see Daniel Kahneman and

Amos Tversky, "Prospect Theory: An Analysis of Decision Under Risk," *Econometrica* 47 (1979): 263–91.

112. Li Xiguang, Liu Kang et al., *Yaomohua Zhongguo de beihou* [The plot to demonize China] (Beijing: Zhongguo Shehui Kexue Chubanshe, 1996), 83.

113. Peter Hays Gries, "Tears of Rage: Chinese Nationalist Reactions to the Belgrade Embassy Bombing," *China Journal*, no. 46 (July 2001): 25–43.

12 The Correlates of Beijing Public Opinion Toward the United States, 1998–2004

Alastair Iain Johnston

Introduction

In the past public opinion has never really been an important issue in Chinese foreign policy studies for obvious reasons. The People's Republic of China is not, after all, a country where the people can vote to recall poorly performing political leaders. Foreign policy is one of the last and most sensitive "forbidden zones" where unapproved or sharp public dissent and criticism can still be politically risky.[1] And the PRC's political system is still a dictatorship.

Yet in recent years there has been more talk from both U.S. observers and Chinese analysts about the constraints that public opinion—meaning, at its simplest, the opinions of some representative sample of the entire politically aware population—places on Chinese leaders.

Moreover, there is evidence that the Chinese leadership is increasingly sensitive to and constrained by the opinion of "attentive publics" (primarily urban political, economic, and military elites) on issues running from Taiwan to Japanese reparations to the treatment of ethnic Chinese in Indonesia. Joseph Fewsmith and Stanley Rosen suggest that public intellectuals in particular have a growing impact on foreign policy through consulting with relevant bureaucracies,[2] high-profile writing in an increasingly commercialized press, and efforts to mobilize broader sectors of the public, whose views may then be reflected in public opinion polling by the state or the Chinese Communist Party (CCP),[3] even though they do not address mobilization on foreign policy issues per se.

It is not unreasonable to believe that just as the cultural, political, and economic preferences of various sectors of the Chinese public may increasingly influence the domestic policies of the central government, so too their foreign policy preferences may increasingly constrain the options of China's leaders. Just which sectors will matter is unknown, of course, but one suspects that the preferences of urbanites and the burgeoning middle class will predominate. This may be even more likely in the event that political reform leads to limited democratization. As it is, with Jiang Zemin's decision in 2001 to sanction the induction of capitalists and entrepreneurs into the CCP, it is plausible to expect that a wider range of voices will increasingly be heard within the Party itself.[4]

If this general impression in punditry and scholarship is true, then it is important to learn more about public opinion on international relations and foreign policy questions.[5] This raises two basic questions about which we know relatively little. First, what is Chinese public opinion? Second, how does it affect the leadership's foreign policy decisions? Even if we had good measures of public opinion, it may be that how Chinese leaders understand public opinion differs from actual opinion. For instance, some argue that U.S. national security elites overestimate the degree of casualty-aversion and isolationism in the post–Cold War U.S. public.[6] It is possible that Chinese national security elites wrongly estimate anti-Americanism among the Chinese public.

This paper is a first cut at the first question: what is Chinese public opinion about the United States? What is its structure? How does it vary? The second question is harder to answer without detailed interviewing inside, and data from, the foreign policy process. U.S. studies of the impact of public opinion on foreign policy reveal very complex relationships. Some research suggests, for example, that there is a spiral relationship between opinion polls, media coverage of an issue, elite responses to that coverage, and then government policy.[7] New research on the impact of U.S. infotainment suggests that instant and graphic media coverage of relatively low-stakes foreign policy crises mobilizes public opinion, which in turn limits the political space for decision-makers to back down in crises. This constrains decision-makers from getting into such crises in the first place through risk-acceptant, escalatory policies.[8] Some research suggests that incumbents, in particular, will anticipate public reactions to foreign policy successes and failures and thus adjust their policy choices accordingly while in office. Massive public relations campaigns behind new foreign policies— such as the one the Reagan administration engaged in to shift opinion in favor of the Contra war against the Sandinista government of Nicaragua— also suggest that politicians believe it is important to change public opinion, thus implying that they regard it as a potential constraint on their options.[9] There is some evidence that foreign policy decision-makers themselves believe that they are influenced by public opinion, although they tend to conflate congressional opinion, media opinion, and special interest opinion with public opinion.[10] Other studies show that the degree to which opinion influences decision-makers depends on the decision-maker's a priori normative belief in the legitimacy and desirability of public opinion as an input in decisions.[11]

Anecdotally, it seems that in the Chinese case, there are channels through which public opinion is reflected and refracted. These include inner Party communications networks, such as the internal reference materials system (*nei can*); classified polling; an increasingly commercialized punditry (TV talking heads, sensationalist publications and books, etc.); viewer call-ins; and interactive Internet talks with officials, among other sources. Future work on Chinese public opinion and foreign policy would probably benefit from a careful translation of the hypothesized causal mechanisms from U.S. and western European literature into a marketized Leninist system. Needless to say, I cannot do this here.[12]

Previous Research on Chinese Public Opinion About the United States

There is a general impression in the U.S. policy and punditry worlds that whatever Chinese public opinion is, it is increasingly anti-American and nationalist. After the Belgrade embassy bombing in May 1999 and the collision between a Chinese fighter and a U.S. EP-3 surveillance plane in April 2001, a number of analyses argued, for instance, that the PRC leadership could not afford to take a soft line on the United States, because public opinion might turn against the CCP.[13]

However, the conclusions about "rising" Chinese nationalism and anti-Americanism come mostly from anecdotal evidence from foreign media reporting, relatively unsystematic reliance on high-profile, popular publications in China, or individual interactions between U.S. scholars and officials and Chinese scholars and officials.

The sources that the U.S. media rely upon to make these inferences about public opinion, however, are severely biased (in a sampling sense). An analysis of U.S. newspaper articles from October 2000 to July 2001 that mentioned Chinese nationalism shows that in the fifteen papers that had such articles, almost 30 percent of the citations were to interviews with non–randomly selected Chinese students, while another 22 percent were to young Chinese professionals. Only 12 percent were to U.S. (non-PRC) China specialists (see Fig. 12.1).[14]

Books such as Song Qiang et al.'s 1996 nationalist screed *Zhongguo keyi shuobu* (China can say no) are often held up as evidence of a rising tide of anti-Americanism. However, another best seller in this time frame was Qian Ning's 1997 *Liuxue Meiguo* (Studying in America), written by the son of

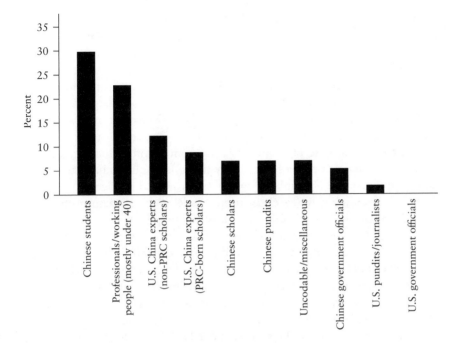

FIGURE 12.1. Sources on "rising Chinese nationalism" in U.S. newspapers, October 2000–July 2001. Sources: See endnote 14.

the senior foreign policy figure Qian Qichen, which both American and Chinese readers considered a balanced and fair treatment of the United States, often contrasted positively in it with China.[15]

There is no reason to doubt the accuracy of U.S. scholars' impressions of Chinese scholars' views of Chinese public opinion, nor to doubt that Chinese scholars may have a better sense of this opinion than American scholars. But elites can often misjudge popular opinion. Moreover, the total number of different scholars with whom U.S. specialists on Chinese politics and foreign policy interact is, of course, exceedingly small and likely to be unrepresentative of popular attitudes.

In short, all three sources of information need to be treated cautiously, just as we would urge caution for Chinese colleagues who drew inferences about U.S. opinion from nonrandom interviews with U.S. college students, a small selection of elite scholars, or a couple of best-selling books (such as, say, *The China Threat* by Bill Gertz).

In recent years, a fourth source of information about public opinion and attitudes toward international relations (IR) and the United States has become available, namely, quantitative polling data, which have proved to be of varying representativeness and reliability. The *China Youth Daily* polls from the mid 1990s that claimed that the United States was the most disliked country among Chinese youth are perhaps the best known of these surveys.[16] This poll is sometimes invoked as evidence of growing anti-Americanism and nationalism among Chinese youth, even though it did not meet any social scientific sampling criteria.[17]

There are several studies now of which I am aware that use more conventional random sample survey-type methods to extract attitudes toward the United States. One of these was a randomly sampled survey of 720 Beijing residents' perceptions of military threat from the United States and Japan, conducted in November 1999 by Chen Jie and the People's University's Public Opinion Research Institute (PORI).[18] Chen reports that this study found that an overwhelming majority of respondents agreed or strongly agreed that the United States had the intent (75 percent) to threaten China and believed or strongly believed that it had the capabilities (85 percent) to do so. The study also linked these perceptions to a number of other political attitudes, namely, support for the PRC regime, attitude toward China's future role in international politics, and degree of attention to political issues. These were all positively correlated with the belief that the United States constituted a threat. As far as I could tell from the report on this study, no socioeconomic or demographic controls were used, however. The study only gave respondents a choice between these two external threats to Chinese security.[19]

A second study on attitudes toward the United States was run by scholars at Zhejiang University and Valparaiso University, Indiana. The survey, conducted after the 1999 embassy bombing, sampled around 750 better-educated (*dazhuan* and above) people from Hangzhou, Ningbo, and Wenzhou and asked questions about attitudes toward the United States and U.S. China policy. Sixty percent of respondents believed that the main U.S. foreign policy goal was to preserve America's hegemonic status, although 26 percent said U.S. foreign policy reflected the interests of domestic political groups. The overwhelming majority of respondents (62 percent) were optimistic about U.S.-China relations over the next five years. A small portion of the sample (12 percent) saw the United States as China's main enemy. The plurality (49 percent) thought that relations were unfriendly, but that the United States was not an enemy. A small majority (51 percent) thought that the main goal in U.S. China policy was to influence China's development in ways that were more advantageous to the United States. The largest portion of respondents (44 percent) believed that Europe would be the most important source of help in China's development over the next ten years, but 39 percent chose the United States. However, it is unclear how to interpret many of these data. For one thing, the report on the data analysis provides only the raw percentages of responses, without any tests of association, difference, or correlation.[20] In addition, the report on the survey is unclear about sampling procedures. The sample was overwhelmingly made up of well-educated young male students, and it was thus not especially representative of society at large. Finally, many of the questions used highly charged political terms common to Chinese discourse on IR—such as alluding to the "threat" posed to world peace by "U.S. hegemonism"—that could have had certain cueing effects. The data report only supplies a handful of socioeconomic and demographic controls and does not look at other views about international relations to determine whether there are correlates with views about the United States. Still, the polling procedures and questions appear to be far more reliable and valid than the previous *China Youth Daily* polling.

In the past few years, a number of polls have suggested that despite the ups and downs in the U.S.-China relationship, a substantial portion of the Chinese public still has relatively positive feelings about the United States and Sino-American relations. The well-known Horizon Group, for instance, has data showing that in 2003, among urban Chinese, overwhelmingly the most liked country was, not surprisingly, China (53.6 percent). France was second (6.3 percent), and the United States placed third (6.1), ahead of Canada (5.1 percent).[21] And in a comparison of between 1999 and 2004 polls, Horizon found that the percentage of respondents who had a positive view of the United States had increased from 60.9 percent to 63 percent over the intervening five years. The data also showed that the United States was still the preferred destination for overseas study—22.1 percent of respondents chose the United States, while the next most popular destination was Australia (19.6 percent).[22] On the other hand, when choosing which country was the friendliest toward China, the United States ranked sixth in 1999 (9.8 percent) but had dropped to tenth place (7.2 percent) in 2004. In both years, the United States was chosen as the country least friendly to China (70.3 percent and 74.4 percent respectively).

More recently, a multi-city poll conducted by the Chinese Academy of Social Science's Institute of American Studies has attracted a fair amount of attention for its relatively positive view of the United States. The full data are not yet available, but according to news reports, 71 percent of Chinese respondents were satisfied with the state of Sino-U.S. relations; 66 percent said that they liked Americans; and 35.6 percent said that the United States was a cooperative partner. American support for Taiwan was given as the main reason for complaints about the U.S. government by 37.6 percent of respondents, but 31.7 percent cited the U.S. war against Iraq.[23]

Still, none of these surveys provide times-series data, and none of the institutes have published any findings controlling for socioeconomic and demographic variables.

The Beijing Area Study Survey

The analysis I present below is based on yet another survey project, the Beijing Area Study (BAS) survey of Beijing citizens, which has been conducted annually since 1995 by the Research Center on Contemporary China (RCCC) at Peking University, perhaps the most authoritative and sophisticated academic social science survey institute in China today.[24] My analysis draws from a unique subset of the 1998 through 2004 BAS data sets on attitudes toward international relations, including specific questions about the United States. Sampling was done according to probability proportional to size, a form of stratified random sampling, to ensure as representative a sample of the Beijing population as possible. The polling involved lengthy face-to-face interviews with respondents by trained graduate students associated with the RCCC. For the most part, the interviews were done in December or January at the end of each year.[25] Some of the questions were modeled on those used in the 1994 and 1998 Chicago Council of Foreign Relations surveys. Some questions were experimental, designed to test measures of in-group identification and the degree of "othering" of national out-groups. Some were designed to tap into attitudes related to China's growing participation in international institutional life. The questions on foreign affairs were only a small part of a large list of annual questions on a range of socioeconomic indicators. Overall, the BAS is modeled on the University of Michigan's Detroit Area Study.[26]

The data collection process was also separated by some very important events, or "shocks," in U.S.-China relations. The BAS 1998 and 1999 data collections were separated by the U.S. bombing of the Chinese embassy in Belgrade in May 1999. The 2000 and 2001 data collections were separated by the EP-3 incident. The 2001 and 2002 data were separated by 9/11 and the start of Sino-U.S. anti-terror cooperation. These episodes allow one to test the volatility in overall worldview and in specific attitudes in response to major events in Chinese foreign policy. Moreover, they allow for some insights into the degree to which there is an interactive effect in Sino-U.S. relations. Some analysts in the United States discount the possibility that U.S. actions have negative consequences for Chinese understandings of the United States, except where there are deliberate PRC government efforts to whip up anti-Americanism. Pre- and post-Kosovo and pre- and post-EP3-incident data may tap into responses that are independent of direct government cueing,[27] and they are thus useful for testing this assumption.

In sum, these are, as far as I am aware, among the first systematic, social scientific, nongovernmental *time-series* data on the contemporary Chinese public's attitudes on a wide range of international issues.

There are, of course, many problems with public opinion polling, let alone polling in the PRC: the susceptibility of responses to word choice and order, to respondent deception, to unrelated exogenous conditions in the interview situation, and to questions that have low construct validity; the meaning of "don't knows"; the shoe-horning of people's complex and often contradictory attitudes into categories of analysis determined by an outside scholar, among others. But in addition to all its standard advantages (relative transparency, reproducibility, capturing the attitudes of representative samples, etc.), polling is also a way to provide a voice to individuals when they may have few opportunities to express opinions.[28] These data are an additional method for tapping into Chinese preferences and attitudes on foreign policy that can be analyzed alongside qualitative and more impressionistic data. Indeed, findings that are similar across sources and methods should be considered especially robust. Findings that are inconsistent should compel us to rethink conventional wisdom, whether derived from qualitative or quantitative sources.

That said, the analysis that follows should not be considered a definitive study of urban Beijing opinion, let alone urban Chinese opinion. This study is about the "correlates," not the causes or the deep structure. The problem with *explaining* opinion is twofold. First, I am not developing or testing a theory of opinions, so I have no particular reason to posit some variables as critical independent variables. I hazard guesses about direction of influence between control variables and opinion toward the United States, but these should be taken as heuristic at best. Second, except for some basic socioeconomic data, I do not have access to other questions on the BAS that one might use to model causes of these beliefs about the United States (e.g., one might expect a liberal ideology or support for domestic political reform to be part of the explanation for attitudes toward the United States, but I lack such information). So I only explore the correlates between the standard socioeconomic and demographic characteristics of respondents, rather than hypothesizing about general socioeconomic and ideational causes of U.S. attitudes in a multivariate model.

BAS Questions Used to Measure
Attitudes Toward the United States

The chapter examines three main sets of questions that pertain to attitudes toward the United States as dependent variables. As set out in more detail below as a first step in explaining these attitudes, the chapter looks at the relationship between six basic socioeconomic and demographic control variables.

The three measures of attitudes toward the United States are:

Level of amity.   "Feelings" about the United States are measured on a standard 1–100 degree feeling thermometer for the years 1998 to 2004. Feeling thermometers are common in U.S. and European public opinion polling (for instance, they are used on the Chicago Council of Foreign Relations quadrennial survey of U.S. foreign policy attitudes). Respondents were given a 100° scale and asked to assign a temperature to a named country corresponding to their general degree of amity toward that country. Anything below 50° signified coolness (*meiyou hao gan*) toward that state, anything above 50° signified warmness (*you hao gan*), with 50° indicating neutral feelings. A list of states was provided so that, in effect, people were not just being asked to rate their discrete feelings about states, but were being encouraged to think comparatively. In essence, they were being asked where they would rank a particular state affectively in relation to other states.

Identity and "othering."   How a social group describes its own traits and those of other groups appears to be a critical indicator of how it will behave toward the other. The differences in these characterizations matter, and they are not necessarily epiphenoma of prior conflicts of material interest. Based on some very robust empirical findings, social identity theory (SIT) argues, for example, that the construction of in-group identity generally leads to the construction of different and often devalued notions of out-group identity, in order to consolidate the legitimacy of the group's internal order. This process is commonly if awkwardly referred to as "othering." The degree of devaluation of the out-group will vary depending on the requirements for in-group identity construction. Less differentiation and thus less devaluation is hypothesized to be associated with less competitiveness directed at the out-group.[29] The boundaries between in-group and out-group are messier, allowing people to hold marginal (liminal) identities, creating more situations where individuals may sometimes share an identity with some members of the erstwhile out-group. Conversely, more differentiation, ceteris paribus, can lead to more devaluation and this is associated with more competitive views of an even more threatening out-group.[30]

The 2000–2004 BAS surveys asked questions about self and other using what are called Osgood semantic differential scales.[31] These are common in social psychology and are used to determine the traits that different identities are associated with, and the degree to which differences within and across identity groups are salient. Basically, respondents are asked to assess where on a 5-,7-, or 9-point scale anchored by polar opposite adjectives they would classify a subject (e.g., peaceful–warlike; moral–immoral). Means and the spread or dispersion of responses are used to determine differences between groups and degree of in-group identification.[32]

For this study, I constructed an othering scale for the 2000–2004 data using the peaceful–warlike and moral–immoral scales (1–7). Respondents were asked to determine where on these scales they would consider "the Chinese" to be and where they would situate "Americans."[33] To capture the degree of difference that any given respondent believed existed between Chinese and Americans in terms of their inherent traits and characteristics,[34] I constructed an othering scale, calculated by averaging the multiple scales into one identity score and then subtracting the Chinese composite score from the American composite score. The lower this figure, the narrower the perceived identity difference and the more "like us" the Americans are considered by Chinese respondents. The higher this figure, the wider the difference, and the less "like us," and hence potentially competitive or threatening, Americans are considered by Chinese respondents.

The main threat to Chinese national security. This question was only asked in the 2001, 2002, and 2003 surveys. Respondents were asked to chose one of the following options: Taiwan independence, the revival of Japanese militarism, global economic decline, domestic social unrest, U.S. military power, Russian military power (in 2002 and 2003), global problems (e.g., drugs, terrorism) (in 2002 and 2003), or none of the above. As far as I am aware, there are no publicly available polling data from China that provide this range of options for respondents. Most other polls provide a limited list of countries that could pose security threats (e.g., Russia, the United States, Korea, Japan) and asked respondents to chose which was most threatening. Given that national security problems need not be limited to countries, this BAS question enables respondents to choose among internal and external threats.

The Structure of Attitudes Toward the United States: Socioeconomic and Demographic Correlates

I use various socioeconomic and demographic control variables in order to do some descriptive "brush clearing" concerning which factors at least appear to matter in accounting for variations in attitudes toward the United States. I do not use other ideational or attitudinal questions as controls, for a couple of reasons. First, it is often hard to determine the causal direction of attitudes as predictors of other attitudes. For instance, one could argue that attitudes toward military spending reflect fundamental conceptions of levels of external threat, from which derive levels of othering of the United States. One could also argue that othering of the United States determines the degree to which one believes that there is a threatening external environment and thus one's views on military spending. Second, and related, the BAS questions to which I have access do not include attitudes toward domestic politics. There may be some attitudes about domestic politics (support for democracy, for instance) that would predict foreign policy attitudes (lower levels of hostility toward other democracies).

For these reasons (e.g., omitted variable bias) and because I do not have a theory of attitudes toward the United States that can be tested on these data, I do not try to develop a comprehensive multivariate explanatory model of respondents' attitudes. Instead, I first look at bivariate relationships between views of the United States and these sociodemographic variables. This helps determine which variables might matter in a multivariate analysis. Moreover, one can examine whether there is much variation within these control variables—for example, are respondents who "came of age" politically after Tiananmen really more anti-American than the pre-Tiananmen political generation? So it makes sense first to determine which nonattitudinal variables may account for some of the variation in attitudes toward the United States.

I used the following control variables to determine the degree to which these attitudes about the United States varied:

Income level. One should expect those with higher incomes to demonstrate relatively higher levels of amity and lower levels of othering toward the United States compared to those from lower income groups. This could be a reflection of their respective positions vis-à-vis benefits from integration with the outside world.[35] For the purposes of this analysis, I have used the criteria for determining income groups developed by two Chinese analysts, Ming Ruifeng and Yang Yiyong. In their 1997 study, what they termed the "middle class" in 1995 was the socioeconomic group with annual household earnings of 30,000 RMB (U.S.$3,600 at 1996 exchange rates) or more.[36] At the time of their study, this constituted 9 percent of urban families. I divided the BAS sample into three groups using the income categories suggested by Ming and Yang. The "middle class" is constituted by respondents whose monthly household income is 3,000 RMB or more. The "potential middle class" has household incomes from 800–2,999 RMB, and the "poor" respondents have monthly household incomes of less than 800 RMB.[37] Until recently, inflation was very low, and in some years negative, so it is reasonable to use the same income group thresholds for the 2000–2004 period.[38]

Foreign travel. One should expect that those who have gone abroad in some capacity will tend to express lower levels of anti-Americanism than those who have not been abroad. This might reflect a higher income or education level (in other words, those going abroad are a self-selected group). Or it might reflect a more critical eye toward self and a more empathetic eye toward others as a result of travel. In the 2001, 2002, 2003, and 2004 BAS, the questionnaire asked whether respondents had traveled abroad.

Education levels.   One would expect higher levels of education to be related to lower levels of anti-Americanism, because exposure to more information about the outside and to more sophisticated modes of analysis and thought contribute to a more critical or nuanced view of one's own group. Education levels are tapped by a clustered "level of achieved education" variable (do respondents have at least some primary, some secondary, or some university education?).

Age and political generation.   I developed a "political generation" variable that codes for membership in the post-Tiananmen generation. Respondents who were twenty-one years old or younger in 1989 are coded as members of the post-Tiananmen generation (thus thirty-five or younger in 2004). This is designed to test the general impression that the post-1989 generation has, in particular, been successfully targeted by a state effort to whip up anti-Americanism and nationalism in an effort to repair the damaged legitimacy of the CCP.[39] I also use age as of the year in which the respondent is interviewed.

Gender.   This variable is a standard demographic variable in polling on foreign relations. In the United States, at least, there is evidence that women tend to adopt somewhat more "liberal" and "internationalist" attitudes on international conflict issues.[40] But unfortunately the literature on gender and foreign policy preferences is still too underdeveloped to produce any testable hypotheses.

Interest in international news.   Respondents were asked whether they followed international news closely through to not following this news at all. The assumption here is that this variable should tap into levels of awareness of the outside world and possibly levels of amity and othering toward the United States and Americans. A low interest in international news should correlate with lower levels of amity and higher levels of othering.

Table 12.1 provides a summary of the dependent variables, the socioeconomic and demographic control variables, and years in which these are available.

The Correlates of Amity Toward the United States

Turning now to the first variable of interest, amity toward the United States has been relatively volatile compared to all other states, except for Japan.[41] In 1998, the mean temperature on the 100° feeling thermometer

TABLE 12.1
Dependent and socioeconomic/demographic control variables,
and the BAS survey years for which there are data

Dependent variable	Amity	Othering	Main national security threat
Control variable			
Income (class)	1998		
	1999		
	2000	2000	
	2001	2001	2001
	2002	2002	2002
	2003	2003	2003
	2004	2004	
Education	1998		
	1999		
	2000	2000	
	2001	2001	2001
	2002	2002	2002
	2003	2003	2003
	2004	2004	
Foreign travel	1998		
		2000	
	2001	2001	2001
	2002	2002	2002
	2003	2003	2003
	2004	2004	
Age/political	1998		
generation	1999		
	2000	2000	
	2001	2001	2001
	2002	2002	2002
	2003	2003	2003
	2004	2004	
Interest in international news	1998		
	2000		
Gender	1998		
	1999		
	2000	2000	
	2001	2001	2001
	2002	2002	2002
	2003	2003	2003
	2004	2004	

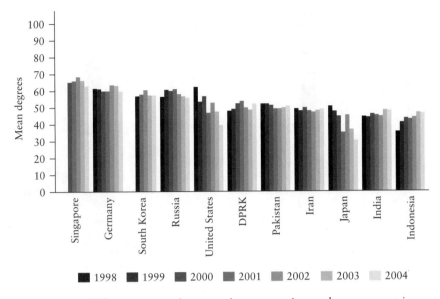

FIGURE 12.2 U.S. temperature in comparison across time and across countries (y axis is mean degrees). Source: Beijing Area Study data.

was highest for the United States, and the U.S. mean was significantly greater than the mean for all states (see Fig. 12.2). The levels of amity dropped substantially in 1999 and 2001, possibly due to the Belgrade embassy bombing and the EP-3 incident. But from 2001 to 2002, it climbed again. Then it dropped in 2003 and again in 2004. The trend, therefore, appears to be a downward one, the slope of which may be steepening. The United States has gone from a country with one of the highest levels of amity as late as 1998 to a level that is roughly similar to that of Japan over the past few years. Indicative of this shift over the past seven years is the distribution of amity levels in the 1998 and 2004 data. They are, in essence, mirror images (see Fig. 12.3).

What then were the relationships between the level of amity expressed toward the United States and the various socioeconomic and demographic control variables listed above?[42]

Amity and income level. The BAS data indicate that levels of amity toward the United States have consistently been higher among the middle class than among other social groups. While the wealthiest sector of the population had mean temperatures consistently above the average, only in 2000 and 2003 was the association between income level and amity statistically significant at the $p = 0.05$ level.

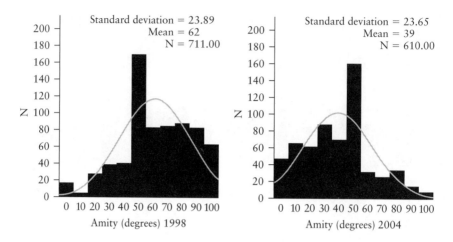

FIGURE 12.3. Distribution of levels of amity to the United States, 1998 and 2004. (*N* = number of respondents). Source: Beijing Area Study data.

Amity and education. Those with more education consistently express warmer feelings toward the United States.[43] In four of the years, the ANOVA measure indicated that this *overall* relationship is statistically significant. But in 1998, 2002, 2003, and 2004, the Tukey HSD statistic indicates that the numerical difference between those with some secondary and some university education was not statistically significant. In 1998, the significant difference was between those with some tertiary and some primary education.

Amity and interest in international news. The data indicate that in the two years this question was asked, those who followed international affairs closely had higher degrees of amity than those who did not. In 1998, the difference in mean levels of amity was statistically significant at the $p = 0.1$ level, with the main significant difference being between those who were very interested and those who were hardly interested at all (Tukey HSD $p = 0.08$). In 2000, the overall difference was statistically significant at the $p = 0.05$ level. These findings suggest that those who are better informed about the outside world are less anti-American than those who are less well informed.[44]

Amity and gender. In general, there do not seem to be any clear trends in gender and amity. In 1999, 2000, 2001, 2003, and 2004, women expressed a lower level of amity than men. But the difference is only significant at the .05 level in 2001 and at the 0.1 level in 2004. In all other years gender differences were virtually nonexistent.

Amity and foreign travel. In the years in which this question was asked, foreign travel appears to be associated with high levels of amity. In 1998 and 2004, this relationship was not statistically significant, but in 2001, 2002, and 2003, it was significant ($p = 0.02$, $p = 0.017$, and $p = 0.00$ respectively).

Amity and political generation. There does not seem to be any evidence that those who came of political age after Tiananmen are any more hostile to the United States than older political generations are. In two of the years, 2000 and 2001, the post-Tiananmen generation did show statistically significantly lower degrees of amity than the pre-Tiananmen generation ($p = 0.07$ and $p = 0.09$ respectively). But in the other years, the differences are not significant. As for age in years, the results also suggest that the assumption that youth are more hostile to the United States is incorrect. From 1998 to 2001, age is negatively related to amity—the younger one is, the higher the level of amity—and this relationship is statistically significant. From 2002 to 2004, the relationship is not statistically significant, although the signs on the coefficients are again negative.

In sum (see Table 12.2), it would appear that, in general, the wealthier, better educated, better traveled, younger, and better informed (or more interested in the external world) one is, the higher one's positive or warm feelings toward the United States are likely to be. Gender does not appear to be linked to amity toward the United States. And, contrary to the conventional wisdom, the post-Tiananmen generation, and younger people in general, do not express markedly more hostile views of the United States than older generations.

The Correlates of Identity Difference
Between Chinese and Americans

Do these patterns hold up when it comes to the degree to which Chinese respondents see their identity traits as different from Americans'? First of all, Chinese respondents clearly perceive a fairly large degree of identity difference. Figure 12.4 shows the mean perception on the semantic differential scale for BAS respondents. I have included a comparison with perceptions of identity difference between Chinese and Japanese so as to provide some context for the level of othering directed at Americans. It is clear that Chinese respondents perceive Chinese people to be much more peaceful and moral by nature than Americans and Japanese.[45] This suggests considerable in-group–out-group differentiation by Chinese respondents. However, it is important to note that the perceived identity difference (scores given to

TABLE 12.2

Summary of results concerning levels of amity toward the United States

Variable	Effect on amity	1998 Results in predicted direction?	1998 Statistically significant?	1999 Results in predicted direction?	1999 Statistically significant?	2000 Results in predicted direction?	2000 Statistically significant?	2001 Results in predicted direction?	2001 Statistically significant?	2002 Results in predicted direction?	2002 Statistically significant?	2003 Results in predicted direction?	2003 Statistically significant?	2004 Results in predicted direction?	2004 Statistically significant?
Income	Income should be positively associated with amity	Yes	No	Yes	No	Yes	Yes	Yes	No	Yes	Yes	Yes	No	Yes	No
Education	Education should be positively associated with amity	Yes	Yes[1]	Yes	Yes	Yes	Yes	Yes	Yes	Yes	No	Yes	No	Yes	No
Interest in international news	Interest in international news should be positively associated with amity	Yes	Yes[2]	n/a	n/a	Yes	Yes	n/a	n/a	n/a	n/a	n/a	n/a	n/a	n/a
Gender	?	Women express higher level of amity	No	Women express lower level of amity	No	Women express lower level of amity	No	Women express lower level of amity	Yes	Women express higher level of amity	No	Women express lower level of amity	No	Women express lower level of amity	Yes[3]

Variable	Hypothesis													
Foreign travel	Travel abroad should be positively associated with amity	Yes	No	n/a	n/a	n/a	n/a	Yes	Yes	Yes	Yes	Yes	Yes	Yes	No
Political generation	Post-Tiananmen generation should be negatively associated with amity	No	No	No	No	No	Yes	Yes	Yes[4]	Yes	No	No	No	Yes	No
Age in years	Age should be positively associated with amity	No[5]	Yes	No	Yes	Yes	Yes	No	Yes	No	No	No	No	No	No

[1] Between those with some tertiary and those with some primary education.

[2] At the 0.1 level.

[3] At the 0.1 level.

[4] At the 0.1 level.

[5] The younger the respondent, the higher the expressed level of amity.

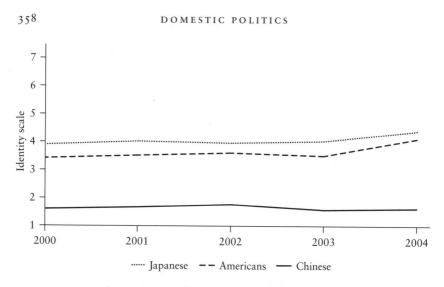

FIGURE 12.4. Average respondent perception of Chinese, Americans, and Japanese on combined peaceful (1) to warlike (7) and moral (1) to immoral (7) scales. Source: Beijing Area Study data.

Americans and Japanese minus scores given to Chinese) did not change much between 2000 and 2004, except for the last year (Fig. 12.5). In other words up until 2004, othering of Americans and Japanese appears to have been relatively stable, perhaps reflecting somewhat deeply rooted assumptions about the other, regardless of specific ups and downs in political relationships. It is unclear, of course, whether the movement toward convergence in Chinese othering of the United States and Japan in 2004 represents a basic shift in the trend. It certainly bears watching; if the shift does represent a new trend, then it suggests a more fundamental reevaluation of the degree of perceived compatibility between Chinese and Americans.

Othering and income. The BAS suggests that as we might expect, middle-class respondents perceived a lower level of difference between Chinese and Americans. The ANOVA shows that these differences in means were statistically significant in 2000, 2002, 2003, and 2004.[46]

Othering and education. Education is clearly related to perceived difference between Chinese and Americans with regard to peacefulness and morality traits. Those respondents with at least some university education perceived a lower degree of difference than those with less education. These differences are statistically significant across the years, except in 2001 and 2004.

Othering and travel abroad. The data show that those who had traveled abroad consistently perceived much lower degrees of identity

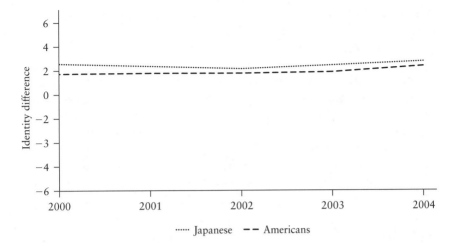

FIGURE 12.5.   Identity difference scores for Americans and Japanese, 2000–2004. Source: Beijing Area Study data.

difference between Chinese and Americans. The ANOVA statistic shows that these differences were significant at the p = 0.01 level in all four years in which the question was asked.[47]

Othering and political generation.   The BAS data indicate that in almost all years, there is no statistical difference in the degree of othering of Americans between the pre-Tiananmen and post-Tiananmen generations. In one year, 2002, the difference is significant, but it indicates that the post-Tiananmen generation perceived a *lower* degree of identity difference than the pre-Tiananmen generation. These findings about political generation and othering are analytically interesting, because they run counter to the strong assumption in U.S. policy and punditry discourse that younger Chinese are more anti-American than older Chinese.

Othering and age.   There does not appear to be a clear pattern across the years in the relationship between these two variables. In 2000, for instance, age was positively associated with identity difference. The younger the respondent, the lower the degree of othering. This relationship was statistically significant. This runs contrary to what one might expect, given the patriotic education campaign aimed at Chinese youth. On the other hand, in 2004, the relationship was the reverse: the younger the respondent, the higher the degree of othering. In all other years, the relationship was not statistically significant.

Othering and gender.   The BAS data show that the perceived identity difference between Chinese and Americans differs between males and

females, and that the gender difference is statistically significant for all years
except for 2004. Females perceived greater levels of identity difference between Chinese and Americans than males did.[48]

In sum, the degree of othering or perceived identity difference between
Chinese and Americans does vary considerably (see Table 12.3). In general
greater wealth, higher levels of education, and travel abroad are all associated with a lower degree of othering of Americans. This is generally consistent with the findings about levels of amity. As with levels of amity, there is
no evidence of any systematic relationship between youth or membership in
the post-Tiananmen political generation, on the one hand, and higher levels of othering of Americans, on the other.

Perceptions of the American Threat

The third dependent variable is the perceived main threat to Chinese
national security. The first point to make is that there is no uniform opinion on this in the Beijing sample (see Fig. 12.6). In 2001, the largest portion
of the respondents who expressed a choice picked Taiwan independence
(27.5 percent) and domestic social unrest (28 percent). Only a fifth of the
respondents chose U.S. military power as the main threat (20.8 percent). A
very small percentage (9 percent) chose a revival of Japanese militarism. In
2002 there was not much change in the portion choosing Taiwan independence, although there was a decline in the percentage choosing domestic
social unrest. In both 2002 and 2003, additional national security threat
choices were listed, including Russian military power and global problems
such as AIDs, crime, environmental problems, drugs, and so forth. This latter option appears to have soaked up a fair amount of choice that might
have gone to another threat, so the 2002–3 years are not entirely comparable with 2001. However, note that even with this additional option,
perceptions of a Taiwan independence threat increased from 2002 to
2003 (from 26.3 percent to 35.8 percent), while the number of those choosing U.S. military power declined from 16.5 percent to 12 percent (indicating that respondents did not see these two choices as mutually substi-
tutable). In short, while amity toward the United States was declining, as of
2003, U.S. military power was not the threat that preoccupied most of the
respondents.[49]

Threat and income. In 2001, income and class status were not statistically related to threat perception. This appears to be a result of the fact
there is little difference across income groups in the identification of Taiwan,
Japan, and a global economic downturn as threats. The major differences
appear, however, in the choices of domestic unrest and U.S. military power.

TABLE 12.3

Summary of findings about "identity difference"

Variable	Effect on identity difference	2000 Results in predicted direction?	2000 Statistically significant?	2001 Results in predicted direction?	2001 Statistically significant?	2002 Results in predicted direction?	2002 Statistically significant?	2003 Results in predicted direction?	2003 Statistically significant?	2004 Results in predicted direction?	2004 Statistically significant?
Income	Income is negatively related to othering	Yes	Yes	Yes	No	Yes	Yes	Yes	Yes	Yes	Yes
Education	Education is negatively related to othering	Yes	Yes	Yes	No	Yes	Yes	Yes	Yes[6]	Yes	No
Travel abroad	Travel abroad is negatively related to othering	n/a	n/a	Yes	Yes	Yes	Yes	Yes	Yes	Yes	Yes
Gender	?	Women show higher levels of othering	No	Women show higher levels of othering	No	Women show higher levels of othering	Yes	Women show higher levels of othering	Yes	Women show higher levels of othering	No
Political generation	Post-Tiananmen generation expresses higher level of othering	No	No	No	No	No[7]	Yes	No	No	Yes	No
Age	Age is negatively related to othering	No[8]	Yes	No	No	Yes	No	Yes	No	Yes	Yes[9]

[6]Between those with some tertiary and some secondary education.

[7]Post-Tiananmen generation expresses significantly lower level of othering.

[8]The younger the respondents the lower the level of othering.

[9]At the 0.1 level.

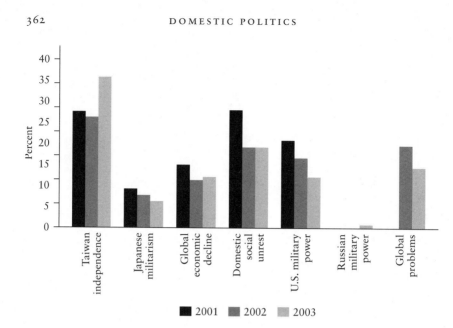

FIGURE 12.6.   The perceived main threat to Chinese national security, 2001–2003 (% of sample). Source: Beijing Area Study data.

Middle-class respondents were less likely than non-middle-class respondents to choose U.S. military power (24.7 percent versus 17.4 percent) and more likely to choose domestic unrest (30.9 percent versus 24 percent) as a threat. A multinomial logit analysis indicates that this particular difference is statistically significant. In 2002, the interincome group differences were even smaller, with virtually no difference between the two income groups with respect to any of these threats. In 2003, overall differences appear slight, with no statistical difference in the choice of the U.S. threat across the two.

Threat and education.   In 2001, those who chose the United States as the main threat were disproportionately likely to be less educated. Altogether, 21 percent of the sample chose the U.S. threat. However, 45.8 percent of those with some primary education chose the U.S. threat, whereas only 16.2 percent of those with some post-secondary education did. The chi square indicates that the association between education and threat choice overall is statistically significant at the 0.02 level. The multinomial logit analysis essentially suggests that the main difference is that those without university education (especially those with only some primary education) are more likely than those with some university education to choose the U.S. threat over domestic social unrest or global economic decline. In 2002, there is no overall statistical relationship between education and threat, and the multinomial logit analysis shows that there is no statistical relationship specifically with respect to the likelihood of choosing the United States as the main threat (though the "sign" is in the right direction, with 23 percent of those with some primary education only choosing the U.S. threat, and only 15 percent of those with some tertiary education making that choice). In 2003, the association between education and threat reappears (X^2 = 21.9; p = 0.039). Those with some tertiary education, however, were more likely to choose the U.S. threat than those with only some primary education. In this regard, education seems to have had the opposite effect than it did in 2002. For all educational levels, the main perceived threat was Taiwan independence, not U.S. military power.

Threat and travel.   In 2001, there was no statistical relationship between experience abroad and choice of main threat, although the "signs" are, again, in the right direction: the proportion of those who had traveled abroad who picked the United States as the main threat was smaller than that of those who chose global economic and domestic unrest as major threats. Those who had traveled abroad also appeared to downplay the Japan and Taiwan threats. In 2002, the association between these two variables was statistically significant (p = 0.014), although there was no statistical difference when it came to likelihood of choosing the United States as the main threat. Again, the "signs" are in the right direction, with 12.6 percent of those with foreign travel experience choosing this option, while 17.1 percent of those with no travel experience choosing the U.S. threat. The main statistical difference between the two groups had to do with the threat of internal social unrest, with those who had traveled abroad being more likely to choose this threat than those who had not. In 2003, there is no statistical relationship between travel abroad and perception of main threat. Indeed, when it comes to the likelihood of choosing U.S. military power as the main threat, the proportion of those with travel abroad making this choice is precisely identical with the proportion of those with no travel abroad (12 percent).

Threat and gender.   In 2001, gender is significantly associated with threat choice (p = 0.04). The multinomial logit analysis shows that women are more likely than men to choose the United States as the main threat. In 2002, again, gender is associated with threat choice (p = 0.001), but when it comes to the likelihood of choosing the United States as the main threat, there is virtually no difference across genders. In 2003, the overall association between the two variables is not significant.

Threat and political generation.   As for political generation, in 2001, respondents of the post-Tiananmen generation were more worried about Taiwan independence and global economic decline than those of the pre-Tiananmen generation but they were less likely than the latter to choose U.S.

military power as the main threat. In 2002, the overall association between the two variables was statistically significant (p = 0.048), but there was no major difference in the likelihood of choosing the U.S. threat as the main challenge to China's national security. In 2003, the chi square statistic of association was not significant, nor was there any statistical difference in the likelihood of either political generation choosing the United States as the main threat.

In sum, there was no obvious pattern across the three years of data in the variables most closely associated with choosing the United States as the main threat (see Table 12.4). Education is associated in opposite directions: in 2001, some university education predicts a lower likelihood of choosing the U.S. threat, while in 2003, it predicts a higher likelihood. In 2001, higher income, more education, and being female were all associated with a lower likelihood of choosing the United States as the main threat. Over the next two surveys, these relationships essentially disappear. It is important to note, given the conventional wisdom about anti-Americanism among the Chinese youth, that the political generation had no relationship to perceiving U.S. military power as the main threat to China. The only thing that can be said is that as of 2003, perceptions of the U.S. military threat were declining somewhat, while perceptions of the threat from Taiwan independence were increasing.

Some Tentative Conclusions

With three major requisite caveats in mind (namely, that Beijing is not representative of the rest of China; that there are a number of likely relevant omitted variables in the BAS questions; and that it is unclear what influence popular opinion has on Chinese decision-makers), the BAS data suggest a number of conclusions.

First, the trend line in amity toward the United States suggests a decline between 1998 and 2004.[50] Surprisingly, though, in contrast to high-profile Chinese polls and much punditry and scholarly opinion, amity toward the United States was quite high even by the late 1990s. The declines in amity toward the United States, both in terms of mean temperature and in the portion of people who express "warm" feelings (Fig. 12.7) appear to be a cumulative result of reactions to the Belgrade embassy bombing, the EP-3 incident, continuing tension over the Taiwan issue, and a more general concern about American "hegemony" in the wake of the stepped-up tempo of U.S. military interventions in the post–9/11 period. Given the relatively high starting point in 1998, the data also suggest that it has been these short-term, recent events rather than some long-term cumulative effect of

TABLE 12.4

Summary of findings about the "main threat to China's national security"

Variable	Hypothesized effect on choice of U.S. threat	2001		2002		2003	
		Results in predicted direction?	Statistically significant?	Results in predicted direction?	Statistically significant?	Results in Predicted direction?	Statistically significant?
Income	wealthy less likely to choose U.S. threat	Yes	Yes	Yes	No	No	No
Education	those with some university education less likely to choose U.S. threat	Yes	Yes	Yes	No	No	Yes
Travel abroad	those with foreign travel less likely to choose U.S. threat	Yes	No	Yes	No	No	No
Gender	?	women more likely to choose U.S. threat	Yes	women less likely to choose U.S. threat	No	women more likely to choose U.S. threat	No
Political generation	post-Tiananmen generation more likely to choose U.S. threat	No	No	Yes	No	No	Yes

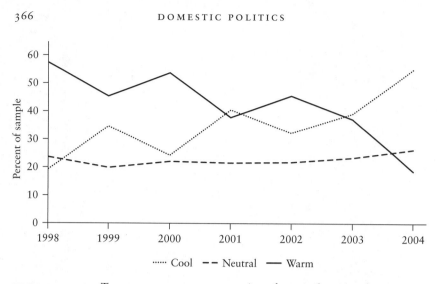

FIGURE 12.7. Temperature category as portion of respondents (cool = 0–49 degrees, neutral = 50 degrees; warm = 51–100 degrees). Source: Beijing Area Study data.

state propaganda that are largely responsible for the decline.[51] Indeed, there is wide diversity in opinions of the United States, again suggesting that whatever unified state effort there is to inculcate a particular view, it is not especially successful, especially among those who are better educated, wealthier, better traveled, and so on. Despite this decline in amity, until 2004, a sizable portion of respondents held warm views of the United States.

Most interesting here is the composition of this "pro-American" group. It is generally wealthier, better educated, and more traveled than those who hold "cool" feelings.[52] The bad news from the U.S. perspective is that it has shrunk over the past few years, but the good news is that, barring any major shocks to Sino-U.S. relations, economic development should increase its size and political influence over time, to the extent that development creates constituencies with these characteristics. This constituency or pool of less hostile views of the United States might wield more influence at the top under some limited domestic political reform and external security scenarios (e.g., gradual diversification of inner-Party interests and continued economic development, in the absence of major conflict with the United States). It would appear that the development of a middle class, educated, and traveled urban elite is in U.S. interests—a socioeconomic process that is likely to be sped up by multilateral and bilateral economic engagement or slowed down by economic downturn in China and conflict with the United States. In short, to push these findings further (perhaps a bit too far!), the data would suggest that the commonly heard argument that democratization in China will lead to a more nationalistic and anti-American foreign policy needs to be stated in much more conditional terms.[53] Whether democratization brings greater nationalism or greater integrationist impulses will depend in part on whose interests are mobilized. Much more research needs to be done on how different scenarios for political change in China would mobilize different socioeconomic and ideological constituencies, given what we are beginning to learn about their foreign policy attitudes.

Second, despite this slight decline in amity, only from 10 to 20 percent of respondents saw U.S. military power as the main threat to China. This does not appear to be consistent with the claim made by many U.S. and Chinese analysts alike that Chinese see the United States as their main threat or as their number one adversary. When respondents were given the option of a range of external and internal threats, U.S. military power ranked third overall in 2001 and fourth in 2002 and 2003.

Third, the degree of othering of Americans as people has been relatively constant over the years covered here. Basically, those who are wealthier, better educated, and have traveled abroad express lower degrees of othering toward Americans. Moreover, this degree of othering has mostly been significantly lower than that expressed toward Japanese as people. While the real-world implications of social identity theory for international relations are relatively understudied, in principle, stability in perceptions of identity difference should suggest stability in basic levels of hostility toward another country and its people. This has been the good news. However, the shift in the BAS 2004 data in identity difference levels toward a greater degree of othering of Americans is something to watch. There is some evidence that anti-Japanese sentiment is a real constraint on the options that the Chinese leadership has in its foreign policy toward Japan; in particular, it has hindered the implementation of "new thinking" (*xin siwei*) whereby the history question is downplayed for the sake of a less emotional engagement strategy.[54] All things being equal, if the level of othering of Americans reaches the level of othering of Japanese, one might expect similar public opinion constraints on China's policy toward the United States.

Fourth, foreign travel matters. In both years in which this question was asked, travel was related to higher levels of amity and lower levels of othering. Of course, the causal arrows are not entirely clear. Are those with lower levels of othering more likely to wish to go abroad? Or does travel abroad contribute to lower levels of othering? A plausible case can be made for the latter, since many Chinese (at least those interviewed by the BAS) go abroad for educational, economic, or official business opportunities. It is unlikely that those who are given these opportunities are mostly predisposed to lower degrees of othering. The findings on this question are consistent with the Zhejiang University–Valparaiso survey finding that those who had been abroad were much less likely to completely agree that U.S. hegemonism threatened world peace than those who had not gone abroad. They were also much more likely to have positive impressions of the United States than those who had not gone abroad. They were also more likely to believe that the U.S. bombing of the Belgrade embassy was an accident.[55] This suggests that building a constituency with more positive attitudes toward interaction with the United States requires providing Chinese citizens with more opportunities to travel abroad.

Fifth, there appears to be a gender gap problem in Chinese perceptions of the United States. Compared to men, women generally expressed higher degrees of othering, and in at least one of the years, they were more likely than men to identify U.S. military power as the main national security threat. It is not entirely clear why this is the case. Indeed, it seems inconsistent with the literature that suggests that in many contexts women hold more "liberal" foreign policy attitudes. But, as I have noted, the question of gender and foreign policy preferences is an understudied one, so it may be that the Chinese responses are not unusual.

Sixth, while the numbers in the total sample were fairly small, there is not much evidence that students have different views about the United States than non-students. In other words, the much commented upon anti-Americanism of Chinese students does not show up in these data. Sampling that can stratify by student so as to increase the size of the student sample would be an important next step in any survey. It can be said, however, that there is no evidence in the BAS surveys that those who came of age after Tiananmen, and after the implementation of a patriotic education campaign, are more hostile to Americans than those who are older.

Finally, I want to address the "so what" question—the question of the substantive impact of these attitudes. Since the attitudes toward the United States are not being used as independent variables, I have not tested for their effects on other attitudes or on behavior. Obviously, to do so would matter in the long run, since these differences—even those that are statistically significant—will not matter if there is no substantive influence on other attitudes or behavior. Does it matter whether, say, the propensity to other the United States is lower for highly educated citizens, or for the middle class, or for those who have traveled abroad?

The "so what" question is hard to answer at this stage, because "substantive significance" can mean different things. It can mean, in a statistical sense, whether a change in an independent variable causes a large change in the dependent variable in some version of a regression equation. Another meaning, of course, is whether these differences matter for political and policy outcomes in China. Since the Chinese political system is not an electoral democracy, without better information about the impact of popular opinion on decision-making, this is a hard question to answer at the moment. It should be noted, however, that over a large voting population, even small differences in the positions of two or more groups can translate into large numbers of votes. Depending on the form of the institutions that translate these votes into political power (parliamentary, presidential, first-past-the-post, proportional representation, etc.), these small differences can translate into large political effects. Obviously, there is no way of knowing at this point whether the differences in attitudes toward the United States across, say, socioeconomic groups or levels of education will have any political effect. But, to the extent that, as in the United States, the urban educated and wealthier groups are likely to be more politically active than poorer and less educated groups, and to the extent that the current Chinese leadership realizes that the urban entrepreneur and white-collar citizen is a social, economic, and political force to be incorporated into the system, some of these differences may come to matter in internal policy debates. To those used to studying countries with large social, economic, and political cleavages manifested in open political systems, some of the differences reported in this chapter may appear as a glass half empty. To those who study closed societies where the intent of the state socialization systems has been to inculcate uniform attitudes toward major public policies—especially foreign policy—these emergent differences in the Chinese data could be likened to a glass half full.

Notes

1. When the regime has not clearly articulated a policy or when it has signaled that it wants to generate ideas for policy, the public debates among scholars and pundits can be quite sharp. In recent years, these debates have flared over whether Deng Xiaoping's judgment that this is an epoch of peace and development still applies and over the pros and cons of WTO membership. Comparatively speaking, hard-line punditry in China has more political space than soft-line punditry. Nonetheless, there is still little space for direct criticism of the Chinese leadership's handling of foreign relations.

2. The Foreign Ministry, for instance, has regulations on the books that allow academics to be paid consultants to the ministry.

3. Joseph Fewsmith and Stanley Rosen, "The Domestic Context of Chinese Foreign Policy: Does 'Public Opinion' Matter?" in *The Making of Chinese Foreign and Security Policy in the Era of Reform, 1978–2000*, ed. David M. Lampton (Stanford: Stanford University Press, 2001), 151–87.

4. Jiang Zemin, "Speech at the Meeting Celebrating the 80th Anniversary of the Founding of the Communist Party of China" (1 July 2001), www.china.org.cn/english/features/35725.htm (accessed 14 November 2005). See Fewsmith and

Rosen, "Domestic Context," 151–87, for an explanation of why the requirements of China's integration into global politics and economics has created space for attentive public, expert, and subelite opinion.

5. In a sense, this research question extends Allen Whiting's lifelong concern about the foreign policy images of Chinese decision-makers lower down the political hierarchy. Public opinion research in China may be increasingly important for two related reasons. First, elites may themselves become more sensitive to popular images. Second, popular images may be articulated at decision-making levels through the diversification of interests within the main political institutions in China, such as the Party.

6. On elite misperceptions of casualty aversion, see Charles K. Hyde, "Casualty Aversion: Implications for Policy Makers and Senior Military Officers," *Aerospace Power Journal*, Summer 2000, 17–27, www.airpower.maxwell.af.mil/airchronicles/apj/apj00/sum00/hyde.pdf (accessed 10 October 2005). On misperceptions of public isolationism, see Steven Kull and I. M Destler, *Misreading the Public: The Myths of a New Isolationism* (Washington, D.C.: Brookings Institution Press, 1999), online at http://brookings.nap.edu/books/0815717652/html/index .html (accessed 10 October 2005).

7. Justin Lewis, *Constructing Public Opinion: How Political Elites Do What They Like and Why We Seem to Go Along With It* (New York: Columbia University Press, 2001).

8. See Matthew A. Baum, "Soap Opera Wars: The Mass Media, Public Opinion, and the Decision to Use Force Abroad" (Ph.D diss., University of California, San Diego, 2000).

9. On these arguments see Ole R. Holsti, "Public Opinion and Foreign Policy: Challenges to the Almost-Lippman Consensus," *International Studies Quarterly* 36 (1992): 439–66.

10. On the self-reported impact of public opinion on the decision-elite's choices, see Richard Sobel, *The Impact of Public Opinion on U.S. Foreign Policy Since Vietnam: Constraining the Colossus* (New York: Oxford University Press, 2001).

11. See Douglas Foyle, "Public Opinion and Foreign Policy: Elite Beliefs as a Mediating Variable," *International Studies Quarterly* 41 (1997): 141–69.

12. For one of the few efforts to understand how China's leaders might be constrained by popular opinion on foreign policy issues, see Fewsmith and Rosen, "Domestic Context," 172–75.

13. See CNN, 10 May 1999; *National Interest*, Winter 2000–2001; CNN, 3 April 2001; *Newsweek*, 16 April 2001; Al Hunt on CNN, 21 April 2001; David Shambaugh, testimony, U.S. Congress, Senate, East Asian and Pacific Affairs Sub-Committee, 107th Cong., 1st sess., 1 May 2001; and *Newsweek*, 7 May 2001, to list a few sources. In fact, a search of congressional sources, transcripts, Washington-based newsmagazines, and other pundit outlets (*National Interest, National Review, New Republic, US News and World Report, Washington Quarterly, Foreign Affairs, Newsweek, Washington Post* magazine, *Weekly Standard, Insight on the News*, and CNN) from 1996 to 2002 found twenty-three references to public opinion in China, fifteen of which suggested that public opinion is mostly increasingly nationalist, and that the Chinese leadership cannot ignore this content. Six references suggest the

reverse—that the leadership, rather than being constrained by public opinion. either ignores it or is whipping up nationalism and anti-Americanism. Both groups of analysis, though, tend to agree about the content of this opinion. My thanks to Manjari Miller for her excellent research assistance on this question.

14. A keyword search of LexisNexis for the phrase "Chinese nationalism" came up with fifty-seven identified, quoted sources in fifteen different newspapers, the *Baltimore Sun, Houston Chronicle, Washington Post, Boston Herald, Milwaukee Journal Sentinel, Boston Globe, USA Today, Chicago Sun-Times, St Petersburg Times, Atlanta Constitution, Star Tribune, San Diego Union-Tribune, New York Times, Los Angeles Times*, and *Seattle Times*. My thanks to Michael Griesdorf for collecting these articles.

15. For an analysis of the impact on its readers' views of Song Qiang et al.'s *Zhongguo keyi shuobu* [China can say no] (Beijing: Zhonghua Gongshang Lianhe Chubanshe, 1996), see Fewsmith and Rosen, "Domestic Context," 434–35n40.

16. See *Zhongguo qingnian bao*, 14 July 1995.

17. For an extensive analysis of the methodology used in this poll, based on interviews in Beijing, see Fewsmith and Rosen, "Domestic Context," 433–34n30. In fact, the survey polled readers' voluntary responses and thus did not represent a random sample of Chinese youth. The 1995 survey was designed by Song Qiang et al., the authors of the 1996 volume *Zhongguo keyi shuobu* [China can say no]. See also, more recently, Fang Ning, Wang Xiaodong, and Song Qiang, *Quanqiuhua yinying xia de Zhongguo zhi lu* [China's road under the shadow of globalization] (Beijing: Chinese Academy of Social Science Press, 1999), 92–93.

18. See Chen, Jie, "Urban Chinese Perceptions of Threats from the United States and Japan," *Public Opinion Quarterly* 65 (2001): 254–66.

19. See also Yu Gouming, "Zhongguo ren yanzhong de Riben he Riben ren," *Guoji Xinwen Jie*, no. 6 (1997): 58–65, which reported that 40 percent of respondents chose the United States as the country most likely to become a threat to China, while 21 percent chose Japan (p. 63).

20. See Yu Sunda et al., "Zhong Mei guanxi: lai zi minzhong de kanfa" [Sino-U.S. relations: views from the masses], *Shijie Jingji yu Zhengzhi* [World Economics and Politics], no.6 (2001): 33–38.

21. Zhang Hui, "2003 nian Zhongguo ren yanzhong de shijie zhuanti diaocha zhi er—Zhongguo ren kan Meiguo: shiyongzhuyi + bentuhua qingjie zong di 594 qi suo shu fenlei: shehui wenti yanjiu" [The second 2003 survey of Chinese views of the world—Chinese view the United States: pragmatism and localization]. Vol. 594, social science research, 14 November 2003. www.horizonkey.com/showart.asp?art_id=274&cat_id=6 (accessed 14 November 2005).

22. See Tan Qing, "Zhongguo ren kan Meiguo de ganshou hen fuza, zong di 724 qi, suo shu fenlei: shehui wenti yanjiu" [The feelings with which Chinese view Americans are very complicated]. Vol. 724: social science research, April 11, 2005. www.horizonkey.com/showart.asp?art_id=418&cat_id=6 (accessed 14 November 2005).

23. CASS Institute of American Studies poll, www.people.com.cn/GB/paper68/14196/1264756.html (accessed 10 October 2005).

24. The sample sizes were as follows: 1998, 756; 1999, 712; 2000, 757; 2001, 615; 2002, 662; 2003, 551; 2004, 617. On the sampling procedures, see Hao Hong-sheng, "The Sampling Design and Implementation for the 1995 Beijing Area Study" (Research Center for Contemporary China, Peking University, 7 March 1996).

25. The interviews for the 2004 BAS were done in early 2005.

26. See the *BAS Data Report* (Beijing: Zhongguo Shehui Kexue Chubanshe, forthcoming).

27. That is, to the extent that respondents take positions independent of government on other foreign policy issues, there is less reason to believe that a rise in anti-Americanism reflected in these data is the direct effect of anticipating the state's official position toward the United States.

28. See Lewis, *Constructing Public Opinion*.

29. See Henri Tajfel and John Turner, "An Integrative Theory of Intergoup Conflict," in *Intergroup Relations: Essential Readings*, ed, Michael A. Hogg and Dominic Abrams (Philadelphia: Psychology Press, 2001). See also Peter Gries's chapter in this volume for a discussion of the scope conditions under which this differentiation leads to competition and then to conflict.

30. On SIT, see Henri Tajfel, *Social Identity and Intergroup Relations* (Cambridge: Cambridge University Press, 1982); Dominic Abrams and Michael Hogg, eds., *Social Identity Theory* (New York: Harvester Wheatsheaf, 1990); John C. Turner, *Rediscovering the Social Group* (Oxford: Basil Blackwell, 1987). On its application to political science and international relations, see Jonathan Mercer, "Anarchy and Identity" *International Organization* 49, 2 (1995): 229–52; William Connolly, *Identity/Difference* (Ithaca, N.Y.: Cornell University Press, 1991); Paul Kowert, "The Construction of National Identity," in *International Relations in a Constructed World*, ed. Vendulka Kubalkova et al. (Armonk, N.Y.: M. E. Sharpe, 1998), 101–22.

31. On the logic behind Osgood semantic differential scales, see Charles E. Osgood, George J. Suci, and Percy H. Tannenbaum, *The Measurement of Meaning* (Urbana: University of Illinois Press, 1957). In contrast to Likert scales (e.g., strongly opposed, somewhat opposed, etc.), semantic differential procedures allow respondents to make more active judgments/assessments of a wider range of possible responses: since they are being asked to place self (and/or other) on a logically inclusive range of possibilities, respondents are more likely to tap into an internally generated concept of self than they are with Likert scales.

32. For examples of the Osgood semantic differential scale in assessing identity, see Peter J. Burke and Judy C. Tully, "The Measurement of Role Identity," *Social Forces* 55, 4 (June 1977): 881–97, and Peter J. Burke and Donald C. Reitzes, "The Link Between Identity and Role Performance," *Social Psychology Quarterly* 44 (1981): 83–92. It should be noted again that in the Chinese foreign policy field, Allen Whiting early on in his work understood the centrality of these kinds of bipolar value-judgements in determining images of the "other." See his discussion along these lines in *China Eyes Japan* (Berkeley: University of California Press, 1989), 18.

33. A separate question asked how respondents would rate the United States as a great power. This was designed to determine if respondents differentiated between

a people and their state. In general, respondents did differentiate between state and people in the U.S. case, consistently considering the U.S. state to be more warlike than American people. Respondents, however, did not make a significant distinction between the peacefulness of the Chinese people and the Chinese state.

34. Unfortunately, I have no data on the othering of China in U.S. public opinion. The interactive effects of this process—mediated by the news media and punditry on both sides—is a critical topic that deserves more research.

35. For a discussion of hypotheses about the foreign policy preferences of high-income groups, see Alastair Iain Johnston, "Chinese Middle Class Attitudes Towards International Affairs: Nascent Liberalization?" *China Quarterly*, no. 179 (September 2004): 603–28.

36. Ming Ruifeng and Yang Yiyong, "Yi ye chun feng: chengli ren de shouru chu tu xiu se" [An evening of spring breezes: urban population income], in *Gongping yu xiaoyi: dangdai Zhongguo de shouru fenpei wenti* [Equality and efficiency: the issue of distribution of income in contemporary China], ed. Yang Yiyong (Beijing: Jinri Zhongguo Chubanshe, 1997), 133. I thank Zhang Ming for pointing out this source. For a more detailed discussion of who or what constitutes a middle class, see Johnston, "Chinese Middle Class Attitudes."

37. I report mostly on the views of the first two social groups. The *N* of the "poor" is quite small in the sample, so inferences about their views are more unstable and less reliable.

38. China's inflation rate from 1999 through to 2003 ranged from -1.5% to 1.2%. See www.worldwide-tax.com/china/chi_inflation.asp (accessed 14 November 2005).

39. "The generation of young Chinese who began to come of age after 1989 is notably more xenophobic, anti-democratic, and confrontational than its immediate predecessors," according to Arthur Waldron, "The Chinese Sickness," *Commentary*, July–August 2003.

40. This does not hold for all regions of the world, nor for all issues, of course. One study of Middle Eastern women found no association between gender and support for peaceful resolution of conflicts. Rather, liberal attitudes toward women's rights, whether held by men or women, were a good predictor. See Mark Tessler et al., "Further Tests of the Women and Peace Hypothesis: Evidence from Cross-National Survey Research in the Middle East," *International Studies Quarterly* 43 (1999): 519–31. U.S. data suggest that women are more protectionist than men. See Brian J. Burgoon and Michael A. Hiscox, "The Mysterious Case of Female Protectionism: Gender Bias in Attitudes Toward International Trade" (paper presented at the Annual Meeting of the American Political Science Association, Philadelphia, 28–31 August 2003). www.people.fas.harvard.edu/~hiscox/BurgoonHiscoxFemaleProtectionism.pdf (accessed 11 October 2005).

41. Indeed, there is a very high positive correlation between change in amity for the United States and for Japan (Pearson's r = 0.9).

42. When the dependent variable is continuous or interval data (temperature, othering), I used a one-way ANOVA (analysis of variance) technique with the Tukey's Honestly Significant Differences (HSD) test to determine which pairs of means are in fact statistically different when there are multiple groups being compared. When the

dependent variable is categorical data ("main threat") I use a chi square test of as-sociation, supplemented by multinomial logit regression to determine which control variable responses matter. To avoid clutter, I do not provide the cross tabs or pa-rameter estimates. The statistical analysis also excludes the "don't know" (DK) re-sponses. There is much debate over what these responses mean, whether or not a DK is in fact an legitimate opinion, and how to handle DKs in data analysis. I took the advice of those who run the BAS to exclude the DKs from the analysis. For the most part, there were relatively few DK responses.

43. This relationship holds if one uses years of education or a more detailed breakdown of level of graduation.

44. This result is consistent with the analysis of anti-Americanism in Europe by Giacomo Chiozza in "Love and Hate: Anti-Americanism and the American Order" (Ph.D diss., Department of Political Science, Duke University, 2004), whose find-ings, using a feeling thermometer as the measurement instrument, suggest that those who show higher levels of political knowledge about the outside world have more pro-American views (p. 138).

45. The difference between Japanese and American scores is statistically signi-ficant in all years (using a standard paired difference of means t-test).

46. Unless stated differently, when I note that the differences in perceived iden-tity difference are statistically significant, I mean that the between-group means as measured by the ANOVA F statistic are significant at or below the $p = 0.1$ level.

47. It is unclear, of course, what the causal direction might be here. Are those who travel abroad more likely a priori to have a lower perception of difference (due perhaps to wealth or education qualifications that enable travel in the first place), or does travel abroad help create a less black-and-white perception of the other? It is not altogether clear why travel abroad is statistically related to lower levels of anti-Americanism. That is, why does travel abroad matter for othering? There are at least a number of hypotheses. One is that those who travel are self-selecting (they are more cosmopolitan, therefore less likely to "other" Americans than those who do not wish to go abroad. Therefore travel per se has no particular causal effect on levels of nationalism. This hypothesis is not entirely convincing. Take the BAS 2003, for example. The plurality of those who reported having gone abroad said they had traveled as tourists. But this group of respondents does not express statistically significantly lower levels of othering compared to others who go abroad. That is, there is no reason to believe that the people who go abroad for travel are self-selecting in terms of levels of othering (e.g., more cosmopolitan to begin with). An-other possibility is that those who go abroad are wealthier, hence it is their middle-class status that explains their more nuanced view of others. And indeed, of those who have gone abroad, 85 percent are from the middle class, versus 48 percent for those who have not gone abroad. The average monthly family income for those who have been abroad is about twice that of those who have not been abroad. So going abroad may be a rough proxy for income category. But, as the regression equation suggests, being middle class is not always significantly related to lower levels of othering. A third hypothesis is that opportunities to go abroad may be a reflection of higher levels of education. And it is education that best explains levels of other-ing. This seems plausible. Eighty-one percent of those who have been abroad have

some university education, compared to 34 percent for those who have not gone abroad. Of those who have not been abroad, only 34 percent have some university education. Finally, a very different hypothesis is that travel abroad is transformative; it has an impact on how people see the world and others, and it should lead to more empathy. Unfortunately, the BAS is not a panel study, so one cannot ask people's views of national out-groups before travel and after travel. However, the fact that there are a wide range of reasons for travel abroad—tourism, short-term training, visiting relatives, studying abroad, official visits, and commercial business, among others—suggests that overall, this group may not be especially self-selecting. This opens the door to the possibility that travel has socialization effects. Suffice it to say that the relationship is most likely endogenous in many cases. Unfortunately, the BAS data do not allow sorting through this relationship, since the respondents change from year to year. A panel study, of course, might help settle the question.

48. It is unclear, however, why gender matters so consistently, and why, generally, women other Americans more? Gender is not masking for age, since there is no statistical difference in age of males (43.3 years old) and females (44.4 years old). Gender is also not masking for years of education. The average number of years of education for men was 12.34, and for women it was 12. It is possible that achieved level of education helps explain the gender difference. Compared to men in the sample, women are underrepresented when it comes to having some university education (37.5 percent versus 45.4 percent for men) and overrepresented in terms of having some high school education (59.3 percent versus 50.4 percent for men). The chi square test of association, however, is borderline ($p = 0.113$). Nor is gender a mask for more "liberal" and therefore tolerant foreign policy attitudes among men. The BAS asks a battery of questions about foreign policy preferences and about domestic spending preferences. Basically, there is no statistical difference between men and women when it comes to spending on education, the military, unemployment insurance, UN payments, fighting terrorism, support for free trade, or support for the belief that eco-interdependence will reduce conflict. Gender is also not a cover for realpolitik preferences. Indeed, women are more likely to agree with the view that military spending should be reduced in order to improve economic welfare (42.7 percent of women versus 32.4 percent of men supported a reduction in military spending for this purpose, chi square $p = 0.08$). Clearly, the question of gender and foreign policy preferences deserves further study. For some exploratory work on why women in the United States appear to be less supportive of free trade than men, see Burgoon and Hiscox, "Mysterious Case of Female Protectionism," cited in n. 40 above.

49. This finding appears to be in considerable tension with the PORI report that 75 percent of respondents in the 1999 survey of Beijing residents strongly agreed or agreed with a statement that the United States had threatening intentions toward China and believed that it had the capabilities to threaten China. There are two critical differences in the BAS and PORI surveys, however. First, the BAS offered respondents a choice among different kinds of security threats. Second, the PORI questions do not ask directly if respondents believe that a particular country is the main threat. Rather, they ask whether that country has the intention or capability of threatening China. It is logically possible that a country could have this intention

and capability but still be discounted as a threat (perhaps as a result of confidence in one's own capabilities). In any event, it would be worth exploring these differences further. It is possible that there is a consistent underlying two-part attitude, namely, that the United States has the intention and capability to threaten China, but that in the long list of internal and external threats China faces, the United States is not the primary one.

50. In contrast to a widely cited 2000 survey by a Korean newspaper, the *Tong-a Ilbo*, the BAS data show that from 1998 to 2000, those who had warm feelings toward the United States (perhaps roughly equivalent to the *Tong-a Ilbo* category "like") constituted a clear majority of respondents; it was only in 2001 that the majority had cool feelings (equivalent to the *Tong-a Ilbo* category "dislike"). The number of those with neutral feelings has remained a constant in the BAS data and has never reached the 33 percent reported in the *Tong-a Ilbo* survey for those who neither like or dislike the United States.

51. I do not mean to say that state propaganda has had no impact on opinion. Clearly the highly negative views of Japan are partly a product of the construction of historical memory by the state. The propaganda system is still responsible for issuing specific instructions about how various topics are to be covered in the media and the education system. But the fact is that despite what has been perceived to be a high degree of anti-American propaganda in China over many years, Beijing citizens as late as 1998 (and again in 2000) held quite warm feelings toward the United States, compared to feelings toward a wide range of other countries. Moreover, 42.3 percent of respondents in the Zhejiang-Valparaiso survey (overwhelmingly male students) believed that Chinese media coverage of the United States was not correct or fair. See Yu et al., "Zhong Mei guanxi," 36. This suggests there is at least some degree of skepticism about official messages regarding the United States. The extensive Maryland survey of images of the United States in the PRC media coverage suggests that in recent years, at least, the messages about the United States have been quite varied on a wide range of topics. See Deborah A. Cai, principal investigator, "Perspectives Toward the United States in Selected Newspapers of the People's Republic of China" (Institute for Global Chinese Affairs and the Department of Communication, University of Maryland, 30 May 2002), www.uscc.gov/researchpapers/2000_2003/pdfs/chinmed.pdf (accessed 14 November 2005).

52. It is also more supportive of free trade and more opposed to increases in military spending. This conclusion is based on an analysis of the relationship between a suite of questions that tap into "liberal" internationalist versus "conservative" realpolitik attitudes toward international relations. I have not looked at attitudinal predictors of attitudes toward the United States here for a couple of reasons. First, the questions only tap into foreign policy attitudes. These may themselves be rooted in domestic politics and policy attitudes that are very sensitive and are not asked in the BAS. The risk, therefore, of looking at ideological correlates of views of the United States is omitting key variables having to do with domestic political and ideological predilections. Second, predicting attitudes with attitudes can be risky, because the causal direction of the relationships can be difficult to determine.

53. For references to this and similar arguments about the danger of democratization in China, see the summary of the Institute of International and Strategic

Studies Annual Conference, Manila, 14–17 September 2000, by David Dickens, www.vuw.ac.nz/css/docs/reports/IISS.html (accessed 2 October 2005); June Dreyer's testimony to the House Armed Services Committee, "Testimony of Dr June Teufel Dreyer. The U.S. Response to China's Increasing Military Power: Eleven Assumptions in Search of a Policy" (19 July 2000), www.house.gov/hasc/testimony/106thcongress/00-07-19dreyer.html (accessed 11 October 2005); Barrett McCormick, "Introduction," in *What If China Doesn't Democratize: Implications for War and Peace*, ed. Edward Friedman and Barrett L. McCormick (Armonk N.Y.: M. E. Sharpe, 2000), 11; David Bachman, "China's Democratization and U.S.-China Relations," ibid., 196; Harvey Nelsen, "Caution: Rough Road Ahead," ibid.,279; Ying Ma, "China's America Problem," *Policy Review*, no. 111 (February–March 2002), www.policyreview.org/FEB02/ma.html (accessed 11 October 2005). Many of these sources uncritically accept the Mansfield-Snyder argument and evidence about the relationship between democratization and nationalist external aggressiveness. See Edward D. Mansfield and Jack Snyder, "Democratization and the Danger of War," *International Security* 20, 1 (Summer 1995): 5–38, and "Democratic Transitions, Institutional Strength, and War," ibid. 56, 2 (Spring 2002): 297–337. In fact, there are some problems in their analysis. Among other things, in their first article the cross-tab analysis actually shows that it is a change in regime type— whether toward democracy or autocracy—that correlates with war-proneness, not democratization per se. In both articles, the primary dependent variable in their data (war-proneness) is not the dependent variable implied by their theory (aggressively nationalist and assertive foreign policies). When they use war initiation as a dependent variable in the second article, the statistical findings do not really support their theoretical claims. Finally, the statistical analysis shows that democratization is destabilizing only when it is accompanied by weak central political institutions. Democratization per se is unrelated to more conflictual behavior. For critiques of the first article, see Michael D. Ward and Kristian S. Gleditsch, "Democratizing for Peace," *American Political Science Review* 92, 1 (March 1998): 51–61, and William R. Thompson and Richard Tucker, "A Tale of Two Democratic Peace Critiques," *Journal of Conflict Resolution* 41, 3 (June 1997): 428–54. As Ward and Gleditsch put it, "The first efforts in this area have not presented the accumulated, supporting replications that allow sweeping generalizations. It is clear more work is needed and that the current findings seem especially fragile" (p. 54). See, finally, Bear Braumoeller, "Hypothesis Testing and Multiplicative Interaction Terms," *International Organization* 58, 4 (Fall 2004): 807–20.

54. Author interview, Beijing, February 2004. On the power of anti-Japanese sentiment as a constraint on new thinking in China's Japan policy, see Peter Gries, "China's New Thinking on Japan," *China Quarterly*, no. 184 (December 2005).

55. Yu et al., "Zhong Mei guanxi," 37. Unfortunately, the report on this survey does not include any tests to determine whether these associations are statistically significant.

13 *Conclusions and Future Directions*

Thomas J. Christensen, Alastair Iain Johnston, and Robert S. Ross

The chapters in this volume reveal the depth and breadth that is now possible in the field of Chinese foreign policy. In terms of the substantive issues they cover, the range of methods and theories that they employ, and the variety of sources used, they reveal the great strides the field has made in recent years. Together, these chapters indicate just how much one can and should consider the systematic study of Chinese foreign policy to be a part of the larger disciplinary fields of history, foreign policy analysis, and international relations. We summarize the implications of the research here for a substantive research agenda, for the incorporation of new methods and theories, and for the use of new sources with a view to pointing out what more needs to be done.

Implications for Substantive Issues
in Chinese Foreign Policy

Allen Whiting has taught us a tremendous amount about the foreign relations of the People's Republic of China. What is even more important for the future of the field, he has taught us how to approach the study of the PRC's interactions with other states. Today's China is quite different from the China of Mao or even of Deng Xiaoping, the topics of three of Whiting's classic studies.[1] As Avery Goldstein argues in his chapter on Chinese policy toward Korea, Maoist ideology has vanished from China's foreign policy calculations, and China has expansive economic and political ties with former enemies like South Korea. Nevertheless, Whiting's basic lessons about deterrence and security politics in the PRC endure. The chapters of this volume and Whiting's own work on more contemporary issues in China's foreign relations demonstrate that fact quite convincingly.[2]

Whiting has long argued that China's government pursues its international goals with basic rationality. He believes that this applies not only to contemporary leaders in the reform era, like Hu Jintao, but to much more ideologically fundamentalist actors, like Mao himself. But this basic rule of rationality does not mean that we can therefore simply apply abstract models to China without attention to the specific historical, domestic, and ideational context within which Chinese elites pursue those goals. Moreover, rationality is conditioned by perceptions and misperceptions of China's international and domestic environment as held by Chinese elites and by foreign elites designing policies toward China.

In comparison to the Mao era and the early reform era, today we find a China much more integrated economically with the region and the world and a China increasingly enmeshed in and active in international institutions. China is also arguably much more pluralistic in its views on the outside world, with important, wide-ranging debates within the country and within the government about how Beijing should address the world. This means China's future is far from determined. The new and dynamic setting in which Chinese foreign policy is formed only places a higher premium on what Whiting has taught us all along: try to see China and the world the way that influential Chinese see China and the world and you will be not only a much better scholar but a much more effective advisor to those creating policies toward Beijing in the United States and elsewhere. Empathy, not sympathy, is critical.

THE INTERNAL-EXTERNAL SECURITY CALCULATIONS OF THE PRC AND THE CENTRAL ROLE OF THE TAIWAN ISSUE

Whiting has long emphasized the role of historical legacies and their link to CCP domestic legitimacy as a central driving force in China's foreign relations. In this context, he appreciates the central role that the Taiwan issue plays in linking the domestic and international political challenges facing the CCP leadership and in influencing PRC relations with actors other than Taiwan. For example, to our knowledge Whiting was the first scholar to recognize explicitly the importance of U.S. intervention in the Taiwan Strait in June 1950 to Mao's decision to cross the Yalu and fight U.S. troops in Korea in October.[3] He was also among the first in the mid 1990s to explore how China's missile exercises in the Taiwan Strait were helping to redefine ASEAN and PRC relations in new ways.[4]

Consistent with an overall problem-solving theme in his work, Whiting has always adopted a cautiously optimistic tone about the prospects of maintaining the peace in the Taiwan area and preventing a U.S.-China war over Taiwan. One of the central themes in his writings is that no matter how complex and difficult an issue appears, understanding the complexity and difficulty always points one in the direction of a solution. So, while Thomas

Christensen portrays the Taiwan deterrence problem as quite complicated and Robert Ross portrays it as tending toward stability (especially in comparison to North Korea), both chapters are consistent with Whiting's work in one key regard: the problems are, in the end, manageable. No one in this volume claims that war across the Strait or across the Pacific is inevitable.

THE ROLE OF HISTORY, EMOTIONS, AND NORMS
IN A RATIONAL ANALYTIC FRAMEWORK

Along the same lines of cautious optimism, Whiting never considered problems and challenges in China's foreign relations as necessarily permanent and beyond repair. This point comes through in *China Eyes Japan*, where Whiting traces Beijing's negative attitudes about and mistrust of Japan based on the bitter history of the 1930s and contemporary treatment of that history in Japan and China.[5] Few problems might appear more intractable and permanent than this one, given the legacy of the Pacific War, yet Whiting counsels that we need not view this problem from such a fatalistic point of view. Not only can emotional elements of policy be contained within a rational policy framework, but deepening contacts and exchanges can reduce mutual misperceptions and mistrust. Several chapters in this book demonstrate not only Whiting's concern for the role of emotion and historical legacies in China's foreign relations but also his hope for positive change in these factors that might make relations with regional actors and the United States more stable and constructive over time.

Samuel Kim's and Allen Carlson's chapters both touch on a core issue: how does Beijing view international sovereignty, and how flexible is China's interpretation of it? The general description of China's post-Maoist leadership in the early and mid 1990s as "realist" or "realpolitik" owed much to China's apparent obsession with defending a strict Westphalian definition of sovereignty. This normative view of sovereignty is common in the postcolonial developing world (although not exclusive to that world, as the U.S. case makes clear) and leads to suspicion, not only of great power intentions, but also of multilateral institutions. Kim's chapter tracks in rigorous detail the softening of the PRC's traditionally hard attitudes about sovereignty toward an acceptance of "incremental multilateralism" and "conditional multilateralism."

In his chapter, Allen Carlson discusses what might be a truly core issue on this score: gradual but important changes in China toward international norms regarding human rights and peacekeeping. Chinese attitudes are evolving even in this inner core of values related to sovereignty. If these trends were to progress, it might become easier to imagine more creative proposals in negotiations across the Taiwan Strait and more creative solutions to territorial disputes in the South China Sea and East China Sea. Our point is not that Beijing's attitudes toward humanitarian intervention elsewhere naturally lead to compromises on these island disputes in some mechanistic fashion, but rather that a more flexible attitude toward sovereignty and its meaning in one area can lead to more flexible approaches elsewhere, with potentially wide-ranging effects on China's foreign relations.

Margaret Pearson's chapter explores China's early and important interactions with the WTO and shows the same combination of progress conditioned by caution and nationalist emotion in response to perceived slights to PRC national pride. In her very rich study, one sees how China's lack of experience in international forums is a technical hurdle to China's participation in the WTO, how the Taiwan issue complicates and shapes China's approach to the organization, and how "special treatment" of China through the transitional review mechanism is viewed through the lens of the "century and a half of humiliation." Still, given where the PRC started in its relationship to the global economy, the reader will find in Pearson's account real signs of a momentum in China's engagement with international economic organizations.

All of these works underscore the multiple forms of nationalism that can affect Chinese foreign policy. China will almost certainly be nationalistic as its power grows, but there are multiple forms that nationalism can take. Some are jealous, reactive, and fraught with zero-sum thinking (what Whiting described in 1983 as "assertive nationalism"), and some are more confident, characterized by positive-sum thinking, and fully consistent with cooperation and confidence-building in the security and economic realms.[6] Whiting is a pioneer in systematically addressing the role of legacies of history and emotion in the development of Chinese nationalism in the reform era. This is most prominent in his classic work *China Eyes Japan*. Whiting focused in the same spirit on how policies toward history textbooks were in many ways as potentially volatile an issue in China-Japan relations as issues more commonly studied by security analysts, such as weapons systems, alliances, and territorial disputes.

What form Chinese nationalism will take will depend in large part on whether or not China's leaders and public view themselves as under pressure from the outside world or as gaining respect and acceptance in the international community. As Peter Gries's chapter shows, the possibility that alleged examples of disrespect for China in the United States and elsewhere and Chinese frustration and anger can lead to belligerence, but Gries concludes that such an outcome is far from predetermined. Yong Deng's chapter argues somewhat counterintuitively that "the China threat theory" and China's concerns about it have been major motivations behind Beijing's efforts to reassure the world, especially its neighbors, of its benign intent. In other words, a factor that easily could have fed the security dilemma—international assumptions of China as a threat—has, via China's remedial actions, tended to reduce the security dilemma in the region.

The shoring up of the U.S.-Japan alliance and the U.S. defense commitment to Taiwan in 1995–96 could well have resulted in similar Chinese sensitivity to the security dilemma. These tough U.S. policies might have led the
PRC to reach out multilaterally to its neighbors in Southeast Asia and Central Asia. That is not to say that Chinese acceptance of multilateralism is
purely a response to a perceived threat from the United States, but rather
that the inability of China to deal with the perceived U.S. threat head on and
coercively might have increased the influence of the more creative "positive-
sum" thinkers who already existed within the Chinese system.

Also apropos of potentially positive changes in Chinese attitudes, norms,
and preferences, Iain Johnston's chapter tries to track the evolution of
China's attitudes toward the outside world among relatively well-off urbanites, many of whom are exposed to that outside world socially and economically. It is a mantra in the study of China's foreign relations that engagement of China is more constructive than containment. Scholars and
pundits alike predict that China will feel less threatened by and more
benefited by the international order as a result of engagement and will therefore be more pacific and less neurotic than otherwise. But few have explored
in any depth how this process might actually occur. Johnston's analysis of
the Beijing Area Survey strongly suggests that relatively economically secure
and cosmopolitan citizens of China are less negatively disposed to the outside world, particularly the United States, and more supportive of liberal
foreign policies, such as free trade, than many of their compatriots. This
suggests that engagement and the domestic economic development that it
helps encourage do more than reduce misperceptions; they help socialize at
least some significant segments of China's population into a positive-sum
view of the international arena.

THE DEATH OF MAOIST IDEOLOGY, THE GROWTH
OF INTERDEPENDENCE, AND SOME ENDURING
SECURITY PROBLEMS IN NORTHEAST ASIA

Avery Goldstein's chapter on China's security strategy toward the
Korean peninsula is a fine encapsulation of how much has changed in
China's foreign relations in recent years, and yet also of how well Whiting's
analytic lessons endure in the new era. Goldstein discusses how, given the
economic reforms within China and Beijing's early rejection of anything
even vaguely akin to Kim Il Sung's original *juche* self-reliance strategy in international economic policy, China now has almost no ideological stake
in the North Korean regime. If there is any such stake, it is in the hope
that North Korea will borrow China's post-Mao marketized development
model and thus survive as a modernizing "pragmatic" state. Moreover,
China has a very deep economic relationship with South Korea and views it

as a regional partner, not an enemy. Goldstein asserts, however, that China still wants to maintain North Korea as a buffer and does not want precipitous change on the peninsula, especially violent change, which would increase the number of refugees and bring an American ally, and perhaps U.S. forces, up to China's Yalu River border. Goldstein argues that China might still be willing to threaten the use of force against U.S. forces in order to prevent the collapse of North Korea under U.S. pressure. But it would be more likely to do so if it feels insecure at home and abroad as it observes developments on the peninsula that it views as negative. On the other hand, Goldstein also suggests that if Beijing becomes more confident in the region and in its domestic security, it may become more concerned about the destabilizing effects of Pyongyang's behavior, and less concerned about the implications of Seoul or the United States gaining the upper hand over Pyongyang.

One area where China's internal economic reforms and external engagement have not done very much yet to change Chinese foreign policy is Sino-Japanese relations. All things being equal, economic engagement is certainly a good thing for bilateral relations, but Michael Yahuda's polling data suggest that anti-Japanese sentiments are still very strong in China.[7] Yahuda argues that in the absence of a sustained security dialogue and deeper social and political interaction, economic interdependence alone may not solve the problems in this basic relationship.

One wonders about what role growing economic interdependence will play in the Taiwan Strait as well. As Ross and Christensen agree, there is little doubt that economic interdependence between the mainland and Taiwan is a factor for caution in cross-Strait relations in both Taipei and Beijing. But in the absence of cross-Strait political dialogue and in the presence of highly emotional differences of interpretation over past history and current sovereignty, it is unclear whether economic interdependence can create the foundation for a political settlement. In contrast to the Sino-Japanese relationship discussed by Yahuda, one might argue that close blood and cultural ties across the Taiwan Strait will facilitate the process of political reconciliation. There is, however, a strong and growing Taiwanese nationalist movement that has its own emotional and negative involvement with mainland Chinese nationalism.

LOOKING BEYOND EAST ASIA IN THE
STUDY OF CHINA'S FOREIGN RELATIONS

Allen Whiting was among the very first to break the exclusive focus on East Asia in China studies. In *Sinkiang: Pawn or Pivot* (1958) and in *Chinese Calculus of Deterrence* (1975), Whiting focused on issues related to China's western frontier, often neglected by students of China's foreign relations.

Whiting demonstrated that Beijing's concerns about the PRC's west were often related to simultaneous concerns about domestic politics at home and the challenges posed by Taiwan, Southeast Asia, the former Soviet Union, and so forth. So, even if we were to accept that China's main foreign policy focus has been on its south, east, and north, we must recognize that Chinese elites have not had the luxury of ignoring the western frontier. John Garver's carefully researched chapter on the rivalry of India and China over their common and disputed border and in South Asia more generally shows how Chinese misperceptions of Indian intentions had dramatically unconstructive long-term effects on Sino-Indian relations. While Sino-Indian détente in the past decade or so may be based on better information about each other's intentions and capabilities, Garver's work suggests that a future topic for research ought to be if, how, and why these perceptions persist.

CHALLENGES FOR THE FUTURE

As with any good collection of academic essays on an important topic, these essays beg more questions than they answer. One wonders about the degree to which China's economic integration in the region and with the broader world will prevent conflict, particularly conflict over the sensitive issue of Taiwan. Political science does not have a tremendously strong grip on how economic integration affects security decisions. Scholarship is basically divided into three views: that bilateral economic interdependence reduces bilateral conflict; that general economic openness is associated with reduced conflict proneness, although not necessarily reduced bilateral conflict in any particular dyadic relationship; and that there is no relationship between economic interdependence and conflict, and that the proper focus is not interdependence, but relative dependence. The problem only grows if we move from the question of economic incentives in maintaining the peace across the Strait to the potential role of economics in fostering a permanent cross-Strait settlement. Despite the one still partial example of the European Union, there is little precedent for economic integration leading to political integration.

Most essays in this book point in the direction of further Chinese economic growth, further integration with the international community, including economic and security institutions, and a more cooperative relationship between China and its neighbors and China and the United States over time. But there is fairly widespread recognition in the essays that integration to date is still a relatively new phenomenon, and that China is not yet fully comfortable in its new institutional and regional roles. This might be changing quickly under the new leadership of Hu Jintao, who has shown confidence and a proactive approach to diplomacy both in handling the

North Korean crisis and in diplomacy toward Southeast Asia. But this progress may not continue smoothly. The chapters do not wrestle in much detail with the potential consequences of a potential major disappointment in Chinese domestic politics or foreign policy. This might take the form of a sharp economic downturn in the region or in China itself, or the failure of a Chinese multilateral initiative, perhaps in North Korea, or increased tensions in the Taiwan Strait and between the United States and China. Would such outcomes set back the progress we have seen to date and to what degree? Would regional actors continue to see China as a partner in that changed setting? Would the politics of emotion and historical legacies rise to the fore in Beijing or other capitals under those conditions or would China and its neighbors become more insular and self-absorbed?

Chapters in this book also do not deal systematically or in detail with the prospect of significant domestic political change on the mainland over time. If we consider a scenario in which China were to democratize, for example, many questions arise regarding whether the outcome would be a "confident" or an "assertive" Chinese nationalism. As Edward Mansfield and Jack Snyder's work suggests, a stable and developed Chinese democracy might be quite confident and moderate in its interactions with other states, particularly other democracies, but the democratization process is fraught with danger, specifically with the possibility of nationalism-driven conflicts in its early phases, as long as there are no strong governmental and societal institutions that can buffer politics from cruder versions of hypernationalism and emotional politics (Whiting's "assertive nationalism").[8] Institutional development needs to precede or, at a minimum, accompany the opening of the electoral system for a smooth process of democratization to occur.

One question for scholars is whether China will democratize at all in the foreseeable future? If so, will it first develop the rule of law, a marketplace of ideas, and more open media before it does so, thus reducing the likelihood that hypernationalist attitudes to Taiwan and Japan might rise to the fore? How would we as social scientists measure the progress toward such institutionalization, and what public and elite attitudes in China would lead us to believe that Chinese democratization was likely to start and end successfully? We raise these questions, not to criticize what has been done here, but to point out that much more needs to be done to understand a nation that is changing quickly and is growing in regional and international importance.

Implications for Theory and Methodology

The chapters in this book demonstrate a very wide range of theoretical and methodological orientations. Not that the book is representative of all the major schools of theory and methods in international relations (IR) studies, or even in Chinese foreign policy studies. Indeed, throughout its history, Chinese foreign policy studies has had a fairly wide range of implicit and explicit positions on theory and methods. In terms of theory, the field has made use of various stripes of realist thought, including structural, classical, and neoclassical arguments;[9] interdependence and institutionalist arguments;[10] arguments based on domestic politics and political and factional bargaining;[11] second image reversed arguments;[12] theories of perception, image, and belief systems;[13] theories of ideology;[14] and theories from the "sociological turn" in IR theory.[15]

In terms of research methodology, the field has actually been quite eclectic as well. One can find examples of Pekingological analysis of statements and discourse;[16] historical analysis;[17] qualitative and quantitative behavioral analysis;[18] content analysis;[19] interviews;[20] surveys and structured interviews;[21] and formal modeling.[22]

So it is not that the Chinese foreign policy field taken as a whole has been atheoretical or methodologically narrow and parochial.[23] But it is probably accurate to say that in much of the research, the major or the default theoretical and methodological choices are roughly realist and roughly historical/descriptive, particularly when focusing on post–Cultural Revolution (1966–69) foreign policy. In some cases of research, one finds a theoretical eclecticism that often stretches the degree of compatibility or commensurability across theories. It is also safe to say that, in general, the subfield has been a consumer but not a producer of theory and methods.

This volume does not, therefore, claim to introduce theories or methods that have been hitherto absent from the study of Chinese foreign policy. But, taken as a whole, the chapters here—in the intellectual style started by Allen Whiting—are more theoretically self-conscious, more theoretically consistent, and more likely to take advantage of new materials and new research opportunities compared to past collections of research. As such, collectively, they deepen and sharpen the theoretical and methodological repertoire available to scholars of Chinese foreign policy. The chapters show, also, where Chinese foreign policy studies can position themselves along the cutting edge of IR theory.

REALIST APPROACHES

Recent critiques of realism from within the realist tent have focused on the neglected importance of perceptions of power and opportunity, and on the domestic constraints in mobilizing resources for dealing with security threats. Even this realist loyal opposition agrees that a simplistic focus on rational unitary actor calculations of how to maximize security under conditions of uncertainty generated by anarchy are often insufficient to explain much of the variation in state behavior. Together, five chapters in this book show the complexity of applying realist arguments to the China case.

On the one hand, both Ross and Goldstein focus on instances where Chinese leaders have correctly understood the constraints on their power and more or less correctly estimated the options open to them. Stable deterrence between the United States and China on the Taiwan issue, Ross argues, can essentially be explained by accurate estimates on both sides of the costs of using military force. In this context, the likelihood of mistakes in the use of force or of provocative challenges to the status quo are unlikely. Goldstein notes that Chinese leaders have more or less clear (and certainly not unique) national interests in economic development in a peaceful environment and preserving territorial integrity (the Taiwan issue), as well as a more or less clear sense of the power constraints on pursuing this interest (i.e., limited military modernization in a unipolar era). This constrains their options toward the Korean peninsula, creating a strong status quo interest there too.

On the other hand, Christensen, Garver, and Yong Deng in one form or another show that under some circumstances, the decisions of Chinese leaders cannot be modeled by using unitary rational actor, security-maximizing assumptions. They show that despite the fact that Chinese leaders have been well schooled in realpolitik views of the world, Chinese foreign policy has not been an unbroken record of the successful management of security threats. That is, it is a mistake to treat the Chinese leadership as if it were always capable of rationally understanding and more or less accurately assessing power distributions, the intentions and capabilities of adversaries, and other constraints in the international system, and then acting in ways that maximize China's own security.

Rather, they note that Chinese leaders have in fact made choices that helped create some of these security threats. These choices have been biased by some very basic pathologies of decision-making: poor estimations of trends in the international balance of power and in domestic politics in China and in other states (Christensen); lack of recognition of security dilemma dynamics; ideology, historical identity, and an inordinately high valuation of the symbolic importance of territory (Garver). Attribution errors have been a key obstacle to correctly reading "structural" signals, particularly in Maoist foreign policy, Garver notes. Such errors are especially common among those with cognitively simplistic, binary worldviews and are typical of authoritarian personality types and of fundamentalist political movements. So, we may ask, was Maoist misreading of international signals a function of Mao's personality or of his Marxist-Leninist ideology?

Yong Deng's work starts from the premise that such distortions have existed in Chinese foreign policy, but that they can also be ameliorated. He notes that Chinese leaders have recently recognized the presence and logic

of security dilemmas in external relationships. He shows how strategic dilemma theory can illuminate Chinese behavior, where China rationally tries
to alleviate the strategic dilemma through rhetorical strategies designed to
undermine China threat theory. Chinese leaders' recent effort to grasp the
potential for the "peaceful rise" (*heping jueqi*) of China is further sugges-
tive of Chinese efforts to ameliorate the security dilemma. This suggests, for
one thing, that strategic dilemmas, while pernicious and dangerous sources
of conflict—essentially from a realist understanding of international relations—do not ineluctably entrap rational actors, and that there are conditions under which they may contribute to reducing security dilemma
effects (Gorbachev's policy of perestroika is one example). *If* the motivation is precisely to head off a strategic dilemma (rather than simply to strategically reduce an obstacle to China's expansion, for example), then this
suggests that in a very short time, there has been some "learning" about
how China's own behavior affects the behavior of other countries. This
would represent a basic breakthrough in understanding international politics, since recognizing strategic dilemmas, as Robert Jervis points out, is extremely hard for decision-makers to do. Yong Deng's work raises some key
questions—what factors obstruct, disrupt, or moderate security dilemmas,
and when? Since the security dilemma is central to defensive realist claims
about the sources of conflict under anarchy, understanding how it is ameliorated or moderated is crucial to revealing the conditions under which
conflict is created. The Soviet Union's contribution to the peaceful end of
the Cold War under the leadership of Mikhail Gorbachev involved transnational interaction and persuasion[24] of an elite that was particularly motivated to understand its security environment.[25] How does the Chinese case
support or challenge arguments about transnational epistemic communities
and the relative strength of states and societies in the transmission of
transnational ideas?

Together, these chapters suggest that a major step forward in Chinese foreign policy studies (and in IR theory in general) would be to show whether
there is any systematic variation in the conditions under which Chinese leaders do and do not rationally pursue their material interests under different
distributions of power.

INTERDEPENDENCE ARGUMENTS

Margaret Pearson shows that China's integration into the global
economy has helped create domestic and policy constituencies with a stake
in preserving international institutions. Such a stake increases the value of
economic exchange with the outside world relative to other interests that
might lead to conflict with other states. The thrust of Pearson's argument is

certainly not inconsistent with the large literature on the stabilizing effects of cross-national economic linkages, and she provides invaluable details about how precisely these linkages do or may influence foreign policy. Much of the interdependence literature to date relies on large-N statistical models. The microprocesses by which interdependence might constrain behavior, however, really only come through in detailed empirical work.

Michael Yahuda's work adds to the list of hypotheses about the requirements of economic interdependence, at least in bilateral relationships. His examination of the Sino-Japanese relationship suggests that in this instance, the standard interdependence arguments about economic integration and the amelioration of security dilemma effects do not work. To borrow from James Rosenau, we might ask, "Of what is this an instance?" Is it a case where economic interdependence is not accompanied by political and cultural integration and exchange? Yahuda suggests that economic integration is only possible in the context of political and cultural exchanges. Economic interdependence by itself does not suffice to break down historical memories that reduce trust. Yahuda's work thus points to historical memory and identity construction as critical variables when thinking about the political effects of economic integration. Thus far, there is little in the international political economy or economic interdependence literature per se that speaks to this question. Rather, interdependence and economic interaction are assumed to reduce political conflicts by creating constituencies that have a stake in economic exchange, or by changing domestic balances of power. Karl Deutsch was one of the first to suggest that the intensity or quality of exchange—economic and cultural—predicts shared identity and thus the emergence of security communities.[26] Extending Yahuda's chapter, it would suggest that Chinese foreign policy students might test this hypothesis further by comparing the effects of economic integration in the Sino-Japanese case with the Sino-ROC, Sino-U.S., and Sino-ASEAN cases.

PSYCHOLOGY AND SOCIOLOGY

The work in this volume also shows the importance of using concepts from psychology and sociology—identity, belief systems, and status concerns, among others. These factors do not amount to a deus ex machina. They are produced through socialization processes within states and between states. Moreover, there is variation in the strength and importance of these kinds of variables over time. For instance, the conditions under which Chinese nationalism shifts in content and intensity, and how nationalism works as an independent variable, remain puzzling. The so-called sociological turn in IR theory brings a number of new tools and concepts to the analysis of these sorts of questions. For example, as Gries points out, theories of identity construction and intergroup conflict appear critical to understanding the conditions under which elites try to manipulate and are manipulated by nationalism.

Allen Carlson shows how ideational constructs—in this case, sovereignty—constrain how leaders conceptualize China's interests. He demonstrates that Chinese constructs of sovereignty have changed, as the literature on ideational variables would suggest, but also that they are very sticky. Obvious follow-up questions include: What explains the stickiness? Socialization? Institutionalization? Or coercion? Carlson's work shows how Chinese resistance to perceived global norms is based on national experience and socialization in memories of it, something that is a perpetual source of contestation in international politics. His work thus contributes to a developing interest in IR theory to the degree to which there is an endogenous relationship among four processes: the presence of external norms; state resistance to those norms; the internalization and hybridization of those norms at the state or regional level; and then the return impact of this localization on the external norms.[27]

FUTURE DIRECTIONS IN THEORY AND METHODS

Despite the progress in theorizing about and studying Chinese foreign policy, a number of lacunae remain. These involve issues where the integration of Chinese foreign policy analysis with wider debates in the international relations field could benefit both. We list them in no particular order.

First, there is a need to integrate the field of comparative foreign policy studies more fully into the study of Chinese foreign policy. Comparative foreign policy typically focuses on political leadership and foreign policy decision-making processes. While it comes naturally for students of Chinese foreign policy to focus on the impact of individual leaders (Mao, Deng, Jiang, and now Hu) on foreign policy orientation, we have tended to do it without the benefit of the literature on personality type, on leadership type, on decision-making unit type, and so forth.[28] The information requirements for testing many of the hypotheses from this literature are quite daunting. But there has been and will continue to be a growing amount of information about decision-making, particularly in the Mao period, as more documents become available, from both Chinese and Soviet sources.

Second, there is a need for more self-conscious research designs in the study of Chinese foreign policy. China has certain "natural" advantages for testing some kinds of hypotheses. One can hold regime type constant (Leninist dictatorship) throughout the history of the PRC (which makes for useful longitudinal comparisons with India, for instance). One can hold constant or vary particular qualities of decision-makers (personality, risk-acceptance, operational codes, decision-making unit), since so many of the major decisions about strategic and developmental orientation were made by the same people or by small numbers of people (Mao, Deng, Jiang). One can hold constant the effects of geography and geographic contiguity for much of PRC history. As a major power whose leaders were particularly sensitive to relative power trends in an era of bipolarity (in ways that British or French leaders, say, were not, since they were subordinate allies of the United States throughout the postwar era), one can test for the effects of changes in subjective or objective assessments of power distributions on state foreign policy (e.g., the subjective assessment that the "East wind prevailed over the West wind" in the late 1950s, and the objective change in polarity with the collapse of the Soviet Union in 1991). Holding ruling party, political structures, and even some personalities constant, China is a state where development strategies shifted from a Stalinist command to a Maoist mobilizational to a state capitalist/socialist market strategy. China is, therefore, also a good case to test for the independent effects on foreign policy of economic integration with the global market economy. In short, there are a number of puzzles in Chinese foreign policy where factors can be controlled or varied to test the effects of independent variables of interest to the subfield, as well as to IR scholarship in general.

Third, the subfield needs to explore a wider range of methods more self-consciously than in the past. Of course, all methods have their problems, and this is not the place to debate them. But a large amount of data about China's behavior in international relations is now available in standard quantitative databases,[29] making it possible to use standard statistical methods for time series and cross-national comparisons. One relatively new method—vector autoregression—could be very useful in testing for endogenous or highly interactive relationships with other actors across time (e.g., is there an emerging security dilemma between the United States and China where the interaction of conflictual actions by each side leads to an increase in frequency and intensity over time?).[30] There are also various new electronic textual sources (journals, documents from the policy process, public statements in international institutions, etc.) that are more easily amenable to computer-based content analysis, harnessing more powerful text analysis programs than in the past (e.g., Chinese language–capable content analysis programs for frequency counts, key-word-in-context analysis, dictionary-aided discourse analysis, semantic space analysis, etc.).[31] There are a number of reasons for the field to develop these sorts of skills, in addition to their value in the production of new research on Chinese foreign policy. Perhaps the most important is that in order to integrate IR theorizing into the field of Chinese foreign policy and vice versa, scholars of Chinese foreign policy will need to be more attuned to the methodological problems of some of the literature that is being imported into the subfield.

In addition to more traditional social scientific tools, there are new methodologies appearing that ought to be explored. One is agent-based modeling (ABM), where computer simulations of multiple artificial worlds can help us understand how minor changes in agent characteristics can have major macro effects on the environment in which agents act.[32] What does this mean concretely? ABM could be used to model the interactive effects of multiple actors in the foreign policy decision-making process. Or it could be used to model the interactive effects of multiple states in the creation of normal/social constraints on state behavior. For example, one can test different models of how a state might be influenced by, and in turn influence, human rights norms, free trade norms, or arms control norms, among other things. Given that China is a major power, both its compliance with and resistance to major international regimes and associate norms ought to have an impact on the content and efficacy of those regimes and norms, just as they have an impact on Chinese behavior. ABM modeling helps one to understand this mutual constitutive process. Carlson raises this question in his work on sovereignty—the impact of Chinese discourse on global discourse. Since this needs to be observed across time, the logical way of modeling this interactivity is via ABM, even if the actual empirical work is done qualitatively.

Fourth, the field needs to pay more attention to the explicit use of multiple methods. Often work on Chinese foreign policy will use at most two different sets of methods, although for different parts of the research puzzle. Sometimes this is dictated by the nature of the research question. Reconstructing policy process requires interviews, especially when documentary evidence is unavailable. As a general rule, however, it is important to compare the findings about a puzzle using multiple methods: interviews, document analysis (both open source and internal source), behavioral data (large N and case studies), and formal theory. This is especially critical when one method suggests something counter to the conventional wisdom. For example, the survey data about anti-Americanism and nationalism presented in Johnston's chapter raise questions about the validity and reliability of anecdotal accounts of Chinese scholars' opinions or Western journalists' interviews. Conclusions about the nature of the independent foreign policy line of 1982 (that this signaled a shift toward a more equidistant posture between the two superpowers) based on open document analysis do not fit with conclusions based on analysis of internal circulation documents (e.g., in some cases the internal documents stressed that there was no fundamental shift in China's anti-Soviet orientation).

Fifth, and related, the subfield needs to conduct more explicit comparisons with other countries. China could be seen as one of a number of "types" of states—a major power; a Marxist-Leninist state; a transitioning economy; an authoritarian regime; a developing state; an East Asian state; a nuclear weapons state, and so on. These identity types beg comparisons with other states. This is beginning to happen. The number of plausible comparisons will change, obviously, depending on the type and one's research design. But explicit comparisons with states in the same typology will help with both the confirmation and revision of theory. Take major power type. If China's behavior is similar to that of other major powers, then China cases will be an important confirmation of theory. If China's behavior as a major power is unique and challenges conventional theories, say, of major power balancing, then this suggests that the international politics literature should revisit the theory to explain why China is such an outlier and thus to explain the scope conditions under which the theory does or does not work.

From the perspective of subfield building, there is also a strategic need to be more comparative. This will make those who are not China specialists more aware of the Chinese case, and thus more used to including it in their own research or in edited volumes, which will in turn help reduce the isolation of the Chinese foreign policy field from the rest of the discipline.

Finally, there is the problem of balancing rigor and relevance. How does one both be true to an increasingly specialized and technical field of political science as well as responsible for constructive contributions to public and policy debates. This is a problem that Allen Whiting recognized and on which, in his own work, he struck an ideal balance. But the problem remains and has in some sense become more acute. As scholars become more plugged into disciplines—both for good intellectual reasons and for regrettable but real career strategy motives—research becomes less user-friendly, especially for the policy world. This is not entirely the fault of the academic side—the policy world needs to be less dismissive of theorizing and of rich, complex empirical work. But the problem does require some thought as to how to translate research into policy-friendly language.

The Question of Sources

The chapters in this volume demonstrate that the study of Chinese foreign policy today has benefited from a greater access to and use of a wider range of Chinese-language primary and secondary materials than in the past. It has also benefited from an increasing theoretical self-consciousness and greater sophistication in political science research methods. The result, we hope, is a higher degree of confidence in the research findings and a greater ability to address specialized and nuanced aspects of Chinese foreign policy behavior.

From 1949 to 1979, research on Chinese foreign policy primarily depended on analysis of news stories in dispatches from the Xinhua News

Agency and articles, commentaries, and editorials in *Renmin Ribao* (*People's Daily*), the official newspaper of the Chinese Communist Party, and the *Peking (Beijing) Review*, a publication for foreign consumption. Frequently, articles in Hong Kong newspapers provided the only substantive, albeit unreliable, window on the Chinese leadership's strategic perspective and any leadership differences over policy preferences. Given the paucity of Chinese-language research materials, scholars often relied on U.S. government translations of the Chinese media distributed by the Foreign Broadcast Information Service (FBIS) or British government translations in the BBC's Selected World Broadcasts series. In this era, it was not difficult for the U.S. government to offer a comprehensive translation service of the Chinese media. Allen Whiting's use of the Chinese Foreign Ministry publication *Shijie Zhishi* (World Knowledge) in *China Crosses the Yalu* reflected the outer limits of innovative research on Chinese foreign policy.

CHINA'S PUBLICATION EXPLOSION:
MEMOIRS, DIPLOMATIC HISTORIES,
AND DOCUMENT COLLECTIONS

After the death of Mao Zedong in 1976 and the emergence of Deng Xiaoping as China's paramount leader in late 1978, China's publishing industry gradually broadened. In the mid 1980s, memoirs written by Chinese foreign policy leaders and increasingly detailed diplomatic histories became available, and specialized academic and policy journals emerged. By the mid 1990s, a wealth of materials was available from many different Chinese institutions, including government ministries, universities, think tanks, and military research organizations. All of these publications remain a part of the state-controlled Chinese media and thus cannot cover controversial aspects of Chinese political history or adequately reflect the range of foreign policy views within the Chinese policy-making community. To some extent, the semi-commercialization of the Chinese media has created some space for more independent commentary. Nonetheless, there are political limits on the critical analysis of China's own foreign policy. This remains a serious impediment to research of important subjects in Chinese foreign policy, including the domestic politics of policy-making. Still, the result of China's publication explosion has been a substantial broadening of the Chinese foreign policy research agenda.

Chinese document collections, leadership memoirs, and detailed historical studies now enable scholars to make careful studies of Chinese use of force. Many of these materials are internally circulated (e.g., *neibu faxing* or *junnei faxing*) and offer especially informative accounts of Chinese diplomatic and military history. As John Garver writes, these newly available sources enable scholars to go "inside" China's decision-making process to some degree. The chapters written by Thomas Christensen and Garver in this book make extensive use of the internally circulated *Jianguo yilai Mao Zedong wengao* (Mao Zedong's manuscripts since the founding of the republic) and *Zhou Enlai waijiao wenxuan* (Diplomatic documents of Zhou Enlai). These contain telegrams to foreign leaders and Chinese military officers during crises, official writings, and transcripts of their meetings with foreigners. Similarly, the collection of Liu Shaoqi's papers, *Jianguo yilai Liu Shaoqi wengao* (Liu Shaoqi's manuscripts since the founding of the republic), provides insights into the early years of Sino-Soviet relations.

In addition to the collected writings of Mao Zedong and Deng Xiaoping, the collected writings of other senior officials, including Zhou Enlai, Wang Jiaxiang, and Peng Dehuai, are also useful. Although these collections of documents are not nearly as comprehensive as the U.S. government series *Foreign Relations of the United States*, they nonetheless offer a critical perspective on elite decision-making.

A related research source is the Chinese *dashiji* (chronology) and the *nianpu* (chronicle). Chronologies of Chinese political and military history, such as *Zhonghua renmin gongheguo waijiao dashiji* (Chronology of the diplomacy of the People's Republic of China), *Zhou Enlai waijiao huodong dashiji* (Chronology of Zhou Enlai's diplomatic activities), and *Renmin jiefangjun liushinian dashiji, 1927–1987* (Chronology of sixty years of the People's Liberation Army, 1927–1987) can provide key factual information regarding elite meetings and leadership statements. Chronicles of leaders' lives, such as the *Zhou Enlai nianpu: 1949–76* (Zhou Enlai's chronicle: 1949–76) and the *Deng Xiaoping nianpu: 1975–1997* (Deng Xiaoping's chronicle, 1975–1997), can also be important sources of information.

Recent studies of Chinese foreign policy have also made extensive use of the Chinese memoir literature. Vice Premier Bo Yibo's memoir *Ruogan zhongda juece yu shijian de huigu* (Reminiscences of several monumental decisions and events), which was one of the first of the leadership memoirs, provides insights into many episodes in Chinese diplomacy. Wu Lengxi's memoir of his experience as an editor of the *Renmin Ribao*, *Shi nian lunzhan, 1956–1966: Zhong Su guanxi huiyilu* (Ten-year polemical war, 1956–1966: a memoir of Sino-Soviet relations), provides insights into Chinese leadership meetings on critical foreign policy issues. Recent case studies of Chinese foreign policy have also made use of memoirs of important diplomats and foreign policy officials, such as Wang Bingnan, Wu Xiuquan, Yang Gongsu, Liu Xiao, Shi Zhe, and Xiong Xianghui. Former Foreign Minister Qian Qichen's memoir *Waijiao shiji* (Ten stories of a diplomat) is also a valuable resource. Chinese military memoirs are equally important. Marshal Peng Dehuai and Generals Lei Yingfu and Ye Fei have all written memoirs that help us understand the PRC's military chain of command and the triggers for and goals of China's use of force. General Liu Huaqing's 2005 memoir offers insights into more recent Chinese military activities, including China's naval engagement with Vietnam in the South China Sea in the 1980s. The Chinese Foreign Ministry's Office of Diplomatic History has published various multivolume series of chapter-length memoirs written by former Chinese diplomats, such as *Xin Zhongguo waijiao fengyun* (Diplomatic storms of new China). These volumes cover not only China's relations with the great powers and key events and conflicts in post-1949 Chinese diplomacy, but also Chinese relations with Southeast Asian, European, Latin American, and African countries, for example. The weekly magazine *Shijie Zhishi* is also a frequent outlet for the memoir literature.

Most Chinese diplomatic archives remain closed to foreign scholars and to most Chinese scholars. But select Chinese historians at the Central Party School, the Chinese Communist Party Central Committee's Central Documents Research Office, the Research Office of the Chinese Communist Party, the Foreign Ministry's Diplomatic Office, the Institute of Contemporary History, and various PLA research organizations, as well as select university-based scholars, have "clearance" and thus are able to write highly informative (yet still politically constrained) diplomatic histories. Scholars such as Zhang Baijia, Yang Kuisong, Gong Li, Li Jie, Li Danhui, Shen Zhihua, and Zhao Weiwen have all written Chinese archive-based studies that cover such subjects as U.S.-China relations from 1949 through normalization of relations in 1979, the origins and development of the Sino-Soviet conflict, the Sino-Indian border conflict, and China's policy on the Vietnam War. Historians at China's National Defense University and the Academy of Military Sciences have similar access to Chinese military archives and have written valuable histories of the PLA. Xu Yan and Chen Pingsheng have written archive-based studies of the Sino-Indian war. Xu Yan has also written a study of the Taiwan Strait crises of the 1950s. Wang Zhongchun and other PLA historians have written on China's participation in the Vietnam War and in the Sino-Soviet border conflict. Works by these and other Chinese scholars frequently appear as articles in specialized Party history journals such as *Dang de Wenxian* (Party Literature), *Bainian Chao* (Hundred-Year Trend), *Dangdai Zhongguo Shi Yanjiu* (Studies of Contemporary Chinese History), and *Zhonggong Dangshi Yanjiu* (Research on Chinese Communist Party History). Official Chinese diplomatic histories also include helpful materials based on Chinese archives, such as *Dangdai Zhongguo waijiao* (Contemporary Chinese diplomacy) and *Zhonghua renmin gongheguo waijiao shi* (Diplomatic history of the People's Republic of China).

While foreign scholars therefore mostly have to rely on the very limited and often indirect release of Chinese archival material, this situation may be changing to some degree. The Foreign Ministry, for instance, has just opened up its archives to foreigners, but limits the materials to the pre-1955 period. Provincial archives remain an underexplored but potentially useful source. For instance, in the Jiangsu provincial archives, one can find materials related to briefings of provincial officials on major foreign policy issues of the day through to the mid 1960s, to Sino-Indian relations, and to war preparations in 1965 in the face of the expanding Vietnam War. These materials include some Politburo transcripts and instructions on how local levels should handle foreign affairs.[33]

Another extraordinarily rich source of archival materials covering China's relations with the Soviet bloc, Vietnam, the DPRK, and the U.S.-China normalization process are the archives of eastern European states. These tend to be divided into Foreign Ministry and Communist Party archives. The former include information about China gathered by the country's diplomats and transcripts of talks with Chinese leaders. The latter include reports on bilateral and multilateral Party meetings. The ease of access to these archives varies across countries and archives, but they remain underexplored by China specialists.[34] In 2001, the Japanese Foreign Ministry made many of its records of the normalization process with Japan available, including transcripts of discussions between Zhou Enlai and Prime Minister Tanaka Kakuei.[35]

Official biographies of Chinese diplomats and military leaders have also become valuable research resources. There are numerous archive-based biographies of such leaders as Chairman Mao Zedong, Premier Zhou Enlai, President Liu Shaoqi, Foreign Minister Chen Yi, and PLA Marshals Ye Jianying, Nie Rongzhen, and Xu Xiangqian. Biographies of Chinese diplomats, including Wang Zhen and Qiao Guanhua, are helpful sources regarding U.S.-China relations. These biographies and recent Chinese political histories must necessarily reflect the official Chinese Communist Party interpretation of PRC history. Nonetheless, not only do they offer insights into Chinese diplomacy, but their analyses of the roles of Chinese leaders and diplomats in Chinese domestic political conflict, such as the factional conflict involving Zhou Enlai and Chen Yi during the Cultural Revolution, provide an important window into the domestic politics of Chinese foreign policy.

Recent scholarship has benefited not only from the publishing explosion in China and the gradual opening of the Chinese archives but also from improved scholarly access to archives in other countries. U.S. government archives and presidential libraries, as well as the memoirs of U.S. government officials and *Foreign Relations of the United States*, have long been important primary sources for scholars studying China's policy toward the United States. The National Security Archive has provided a very valuable service by obtaining highly informative declassified documents on selected topics, such as U.S. assessments of Chinese nuclear capabilities; the Sino-U.S. normalization process; and more recent events, such as the crackdown on the democracy movement in 1989. But now scholars have access to diplomatic documents from other countries as well. John Garver's chapter makes effective use of English-language Indian archive–based scholarship in order to better understand both Chinese decision-making and the sources of the 1962 Sino-Indian border war. Both Garver's and Christensen's chapters make extensive use of Soviet archival materials to understand Chinese policy toward the Soviet Union and the development of the Sino-Soviet conflict. And Christensen's chapter uses archival documents of Sino-Vietnamese meetings to analyze Chinese policy toward Indochina. The research with Soviet and Vietnamese materials relies on the important translation series published by the International Cold War History Project based at George Washington University. By combining research into Chinese-language materials with translated documents and authoritative histories from other countries, scholars now have unprecedented opportunities to develop a broad and nuanced understanding of the bilateral dynamics of Chinese foreign policy, including the bilateral sources of conflict and cooperation. Another source of declassified Soviet documents that has yet to be fully mined by China foreign policy specialists is the Harvard Project on Cold War History (HPCW).[36]

CHINA'S PUBLISHING EXPLOSION:
SPECIALIZED JOURNALS AND MONOGRAPHS
AND POPULAR LITERATURE

China's publishing explosion and the general opening of Chinese society have not only been helpful in the use of historical case studies to understand Chinese foreign policy. They have also contributed to a greater understanding of the role of key variables and concepts in contemporary China's international behavior. The traditional think tank and academic literature on foreign policy have become sufficiently rich and complex to enable research on Chinese attitudes to various IR concepts. Samuel Kim has used influential journals such as *Zhanlue yu Guanli* (Strategy and Management) and *Guoji Wenti Yanjiu* (International Studies), the journal of the Foreign Ministry research institute, to research Chinese approaches to globalization and the growing popularity of liberal IR concepts, such as cooperative security. In order to track the changes in China's understanding of the limits of sovereignty, Allen Carlson uses such sources as *Shijie Jingji yu Zhengzhi* (World Economics and Politics), China's most influential journal on IR theory, and *Waijiao Xueyuan Xuebao* (Journal of the College of Foreign Affairs). Yong Dong's chapter similarly reveals the wide range of academic materials now available to researchers. His analysis of China's conceptual and foreign policy responses to heightened foreign concern about the China threat makes effective use of *Zhanlue yu Guanli, Taipingyang Xuebao* (Pacific Journal), and *Dangdai Sichao* (Contemporary Trends of Thought), as well as of the increasing richness of materials in such official publications as *Shijie Zhishi* and *Renmin Ribao*. Book-length studies by Chinese specialists in IR theory are also important research materials. Studies by such scholars as Wang Yizhou, Qin Yaqing, Yan Xuetong, and Ni Shixiong contribute to an active Chinese discourse on IR theory.[37]

The increasing volume and richness of writing by analysts in China's military have similarly improved research into contemporary Chinese security policy. Robert Ross's chapter uses writings by specialists at China's National Defense University and the Academy of Military Sciences to study China's understanding of deterrence dynamics and its implications for Chinese behavior in crises in the Taiwan Strait and on the Korean peninsula. Sophisticated writings by PLA scholars such as Chen Zhou, Yao Yunzhu, Wang Baocun, Wang Pufeng, and other authors from the PLA Academy of Military Sciences (AMS) are important research materials on issues of nuclear and conventional deterrence and war-fighting, and information warfare.

There are more and more military textbooks and journals available to scholars as well. Of particular value is *Zhanyi xue* (Military Campaign Studies), a recently published textbook used at the National Defense University.[38] This book for internal circulation in the PLA provides new insights into the kinds of operational scenarios for which the branches of the PLA need to train. The 55-volume *Junshi kexue yuan shuoshi yanjiusheng xilie jiaocai* (Academy of Military Sciences MA graduate student teaching materials), which covers strategy, operations, tactics, military theory, Chinese and foreign military history, and military command, among other things, is also now available, helping us understand how the PLA trains its military strategists. *Zhongguo Junshi Kexue* (Chinese Military Science), China's most prestigious open journal of military affairs, is a valuable resource for analyzing Chinese approaches to deterrence, the analysis of and policy response to developments in high-technology warfare, and the PLA's understanding of the defense strategies of other countries. The journal also publishes case-study analyses of early PRC uses of force. Increasingly, Chinese civilian scholars are conducting research on defense and security topics. Journals such as *Zhanlue yu Guanli* and *Shijie Jingji yu Zhengzhi* and civilian publishing houses have published the works of university-based scholars, including Zhu Feng, Zhang Wenmu, Tang Shiping, Yan Xuetong, and Wu Chunsi, on traditional security subjects.

Contemporary research materials and techniques also enable more sophisticated analysis of Chinese policy toward particular countries. Avery Goldstein's chapter examines a wide range of Chinese journals to examine China's policy toward the Korean peninsula and its assessment of the risks of Korean unification. Journals such as *Shijie Jingji yu Zhengzhi*, *Xiandai Guoji Guanxi* (Contemporary International Relations), the publication of the international relations think tank of China's Ministry of Public Security, and *Taipingyang Xuebao* provide insights not only into China's Korea policy but also into its policies toward a wide range of countries and issues. The area studies journals published by the research institutes of the Chinese Academy of Social Science, including *Dangdai Yatai* (Contemporary Asia-Pacific), *DongOu ZhongYa Yanjiu* (Studies on Eastern Europe and Central Asia), and *Taiwan Yanjiu* (Taiwan Studies) often enable more nuanced assessment of Chinese foreign policy and identification of emerging trends in Chinese foreign policy perspectives. *Guoji Zhanlue Yanjiu* (International Strategic Studies), the journal of the PLA's China Institute of International Strategic Studies, can provide a window on the policy perspectives of Chinese military analysts and, in particular, those in military intelligence.

Peter Gries's chapter makes extensive use of the popular "nationalist" literature in contemporary China to establish the applicability of Western social-identity concepts to Chinese culture and to develop a multidisciplinary approach to the social-identity content of Chinese nationalism and the implications for U.S.-China conflict. Gries's examination of the high tide of anti-American nationalism in the mid 1990s reflects the sentiment of such widely read works as *Zhongguo keyi shuobu* (China can say no), *Zhong-Mei jiaoliang daxiezhen* (The true story of the Sino-American contest), and *Yaomohua Zhongguo de beihou* (The plot to demonize China). Popular Chinese writings on Japanese politics and "militarism" are important sources for research on contemporary China's anti-Japanese nationalism.

INTERVIEWS AND SOCIAL SURVEYS AS RESEARCH TOOLS

The research in this volume underscores the growing importance of interviews in complementing text-based research in carrying out focused and in-depth research on Chinese foreign policy. Indeed, for some issues, such as the policy-making process, interviews are *the* primary materials. Avery Goldstein uses interviews to probe Chinese assessments of the risks of Korean unification, an issue addressed only superficially in the open media. Similarly, Michael Yahuda's work on Sino-Japanese relations relies on interviews with foreign policy intellectuals in China and Japan to understand the sources and content of enduring conflict in Sino-Japanese relations, including the role of nationalism and power considerations. Such interviews can be useful for gauging the impact of nationalism on China's Japan policy. Allen Carlson's chapter on China's evolving approach to sovereignty is based in part on his systematic interviews with 109 Chinese foreign policy intellectuals. To supplement his formal interviews, Carlson incorporates the oral contributions by Chinese IR specialists at an international conference on changing attitudes toward sovereignty and intervention in international politics.

Despite the importance of interviews, their value can vary dramatically. Interviews with academic and think tank analysts are easier to set up than those with officials, but are often at least a couple of levels removed from the policy process. Usually, interviews with senior officials are short in length, and these officials rarely stray from the official line. Interviews with the functional and regional specialists within foreign policy institutions are even harder to arrange than those with senior officials. Usually, the most useful individual interactions take place when the interlocutor is relatively young, has been educated abroad, has known the interviewer for some time and is personally comfortable with her or him, and when the interviewer makes it clear she or he is already fairly knowledgeable about the topic. There are a number of useful aids to learn more about interviewing and ethnographic techniques so as to make interviewing more systematic.[39]

Paralleling the case-study research on Chinese use of force, in which Russian, Indian, and Vietnamese documents are useful in explaining Chinese behavior, interviews with officials from other countries can complement the value of interviews with Chinese officials. Interviews with U.S. government officials have long been important to research on China's U.S. policy. The U.S. State Department's collection of oral histories from some of the key players in the making of U.S. China policy also provides insights into China's own decision-making process. Margaret Pearson's chapter shows that interviews with foreign officials can also address important questions regarding China's role in international institutions. Pearson's interviews in Beijing and Geneva with Chinese trade officials and with trade officials from the United States, Canada, Europe, and Australia enable her to analyze China's role in the World Trade Organization to consider such issues as the implications of China's "rise" for its role in the international economic order, China's relationship with developing countries, and the role of domestic politics and economic and security interests in its global alignment strategies. Similar research methods are essential for scholarship on Chinese participation in regional multilateral organizations, including in the ASEAN Regional Forum and in the ASEAN+3 meetings. Taken together, this research and earlier research by Samuel Kim on China's role in the United Nations permit comparative analyses of China's participation in international organizations and multilateral diplomacy.

Iain Johnston's chapter utilizes quantitative public-opinion polling techniques with social science measures to assess attitudes among Beijing residents toward key countries in Chinese foreign policy and key Chinese foreign policy choices over a six-year period and to associate variation in such attitudes with socioeconomic measures. Complementing Gries's research, Johnston's research employs multidisciplinary measures, including social-psychology measures of identity (Osgood semantic differential scales), to correlate measures of identity and "othering" with foreign policy attitudes. Johnston's chapter suggests that despite the political sensitivity of foreign policy issues in China, collaboration with Chinese social scientists can facilitate reliable data collection, enabling effective use of quantitative social science methodologies to reach conclusions regarding the societal bases of Chinese foreign policy. Such formal polling techniques and social science methodologies complement interview-based research in gauging the intensity and trends in Chinese nationalism.[40]

The Digital Revolution and Research on Chinese Foreign Policy

All of these studies of contemporary Chinese foreign policy use traditional research materials, including printed resources—newspapers, journals, and books—and interviews and opinion polling. In addition to these sources, the Internet has become an important source of research material. Its most common role is in expanding access to traditional Chinese research materials.[41] Comprehensive research is far more possible today than ever before. Many of the chapters in this volume used the Internet to access such newspapers as *Renmin Ribao*, *Guangming Ribao* (Enlightenment Daily), *Jiefangjun Bao* (Liberation Army Daily), *Beijing Qingnian Bao* (Beijing Youth Daily), and *Nanfang Zhoumo* (Southern Weekend), and to access documents at the Chinese Foreign Ministry's web site. More specialized Chinese publications on international politics are increasingly available at independent Chinese web sites, such as "The Strategist," at http://www.laocanmou.net. In this respect, Chinese-language search engines, including http://cn.yahoo.com, have become valuable research tools.

Digital editions of Chinese newspapers and journals with powerful search engines have also become widely available. Full collections of such periodicals and journals, including *Renmin Ribao*, *Jiefangjun Bao*, *Dang de Wenxian*, and the *International Forum* column in *Huanqiu Shibao* (Global Times), the weekend IR newspaper published by *Renmin Ribao*, are now increasingly available on CD-ROMs in China and at major research libraries outside of China, and now online. In addition, the online China Academic Journals Full-Text Database allows powerful searches of nearly three million Chinese-language articles in the social sciences and humanities published since 1994. Most of the academic and policy journals used in this volume are accessible at this site.

But the Internet also allows for more innovative research on society and foreign policy. Gries's work on Chinese nationalism would not be nearly as rich if he had not made use of Chinese postings on a Chinese-language Internet listserv. In addition, Chinese online bulletin boards, including those sponsored by newspapers, Internet portals, such as http://www.sohu.com, and those based at universities, can provide insights into public attitudes toward Chinese foreign policy and attitudes toward other countries. As an outlet for the more activist and more discontented voices in Chinese society, Internet chat rooms can be a useful research window on an important segment of informed Chinese public opinion.

The digital revolution offers a daunting yet ultimately exciting challenge to the field of Chinese foreign policy. On the one hand, the ever-expanding access to research materials suggests that scholars will find it increasingly difficult to do comprehensive research on any given subject. More than ever before, it is possible for a scholar truly never to be able to complete his or her research and thus begin writing. On the other hand, digital resources enable increasing access to Chinese materials right from the scholar's desk, thus facilitating expanded use of primary research materials outside of China. Second, even local libraries will have the space and financial resources to acquire digital collections of specialized Chinese-language materials. Third, powerful keyword search engines allow effective management and use of large amounts of primary sources by enabling efficient identification of relevant materials. For all of these reasons, traditional research agendas can only benefit from the exponential expansion of Chinese-language research materials.

Equally important, the combination of powerful search engines with CD-ROM databases and Internet collections of Chinese newspapers and authoritative journals (such as the China Academic Journals Database) can facilitate the use of sophisticated large-N content analysis methodologies to study Chinese foreign policy. Nearly all of the discipline's traditional fields of study could benefit from digital research materials. Our understanding of Chinese crisis signaling and the sources of threat perception would benefit from the ability to trace gradual and nuanced changes in Chinese diplomatic language in authoritative government publications. Similarly, large-N analyses of Chinese journals and newspapers could contribute to sophisticated process tracing methodologies, enabling higher confidence in our ability to track changes in Chinese behavior and to associate these changes with changes in selected independent variables, including such variables as international forces, domestic political and economic change, and evolving Chinese understanding of such concepts as the sources of international conflict and acceptance of international norms of cooperation.

Conclusions

The agenda for the Chinese foreign policy field is rich and varied. The chapters in this volume have by no means exhausted the topics, methods, and sources available to scholars. But together they do suggest a number of issues that could use more attention as the field develops further. Below we draw together some of the suggestions for further research from this chapter and from the other chapters in the book. These represent *an* agenda, not *the* agenda, for the field. We list them in no particular order.

First, we need a better handle on China's uses of force. There are enduring debates among scholars about whether there are obvious patterns in China's political and military signaling, how defensive or offensive Chinese military strategy has been, whether China is more or less likely to use force as a "normal" tool of diplomacy, and how risk-averse or risk-acceptant Chinese leaders are or have been.[42] These topics are obviously not yet exhausted. But now is the time to start cross-national comparisons. The PRC has a complex history of use of force—during the Cold War, it was the second most militarized dispute-prone major power, after the United States. The fact that it has far more contiguous states than most other major powers has also meant that territorial disputes are a particularly important feature of China's geopolitics. But comparisons with other countries might be useful. For instance, comparison with India would allow one to control for levels of development, to see how variations in colonial and postcolonial histories and contrasts between democratic and authoritarian governments can explain the frequency, scope, scale, and risk-averseness of leaders. Comparisons with the USSR and Vietnam allow one to hold regime type constant.

Chinese attitudes and behavior toward spheres of influences are another topic that needs to be further explored. This issue will come to the fore as China becomes even more proactive in setting up regional institutions in East Asia and in increasing the economic and political depth of its relations with surrounding countries. How precisely does the PRC deal with the asymmetries—or perceived asymmetries—in economic, military, and political power vis-à-vis its neighbors? Again, comparisons with the U.S. and Soviet concepts of limited sovereignty in their respective spheres of influence—Latin America and eastern Europe—could explain the sources of Chinese behavior.

The impact of public opinion on Chinese foreign policy is also a critical but understudied topic. Most foreign and Chinese analysts of Chinese foreign policy accept that Chinese leaders are more sensitive to public opinion today than at any other time since 1949. Most agree that on some issues—such as the relationship with Japan—mass, not just elite, opinion has prevented the leadership from exploring ways of downplaying the history question.

On other bilateral relations (Sino-U.S., China-Taiwan), however, there are debates among China specialists as to whether public opinion matters, and, if so, whose opinion: urban entrepreneurs'? regional political and economic leaders'? urban youth's? party elites'? the military's? How is opinion articulated in the decision-making process in a system where there is limited freedom of the press, where there is no electoral recall of leaders, and where organized interest groups can be politically threatening to the regime? This is obviously a rich set of topics, though if it is anything like the study of the influence of public opinion on U.S. foreign policy, it will be a frustratingly complex question.

How precisely has China's interaction with international institutions evolved over time, or compared across issue area and institution. Margaret Pearson's work in this book, Ann Kent's work on China and international legal institutions such as the International Labour Organization (ILO), and Johnston's and Medeiro's forthcoming works on China in arms control institutions help fill some of the gaps.[43] But we need more of these micro-focus studies in order to see how institutions affect and are affected by China's foreign policy.

Relatedly, more work needs to be done to understand the Chinese foreign policy process. There is some pathbreaking work out there,[44] but it covers only a relatively limited or somewhat dated range of China's foreign policy behaviors. There is still a dearth of studies on the policy process of bilateral relations (e.g., Sino-U.S.; Sino-Indian; Sino–Soviet/Russian; Sino-Japanese), despite the fact that these are the focus of much of the field's research. Apart from the field's focus on patterns in Chinese deterrence strategy, there has been limited work on Chinese crisis behavior. More research on the policy process may tell us more about the varying effects of other factors, such as public opinion, bureaucratic interest, and the constraints of technology.

Decision-making strategies and habits are an important related topic. Is there any systematic variation in the conditions under which Chinese leaders rationally pursue their material interests under different distributions of power? How do Chinese leaders make trade-offs among conflicting interests? Should we assume that there is indeed a "grand strategy" that guides these decisions?

Relatedly, how do Chinese leaders decide on policy trade-offs? Usually, decision-makers have to choose among competing "national interests." It is simply not obvious that "security," traditionally defined, always trumps any other interest, such as development, domestic political legitimacy, personal psychological well-being, or political power and privilege, or that it always trumps normative concerns. And when security is invoked, it is not obvious that different sets of decision-makers across similar structural conditions would define it in the same way.[45] What factors predict when international status matters, as opposed to material security, normative preferences, or domestic political longevity? Thinking in these terms will help the Chinese foreign policy field develop something to say about the relative importance of material structure and normative structure versus domestic political material motivations and domestic normative motivations. It is this question of relative importance that is at the heart of some of the main theory and empirical debates in IR scholarship today.

There is a growing and sophisticated literature on contemporary Chinese nationalism. But for the most part, these are standard and unquestioned tropes that still need to be problematized. Perhaps the most common trope is rising Chinese nationalism. Yet without baselines and benchmarks, it is impossible to tell whether something is rising, falling, or remaining constant. Moreover, little of the work on nationalism has looked across time from the beginning of the PRC to the present to see what precisely has changed in terms of the content, intensity, and targets of Chinese nationalism.

Another topic that directly relates to some essential features of Chinese foreign policy is the question of how economic dependence, interdependence, and conflict relate. First, do Chinese policymakers understand the distinction between dependence and interdependence? Do they even think about interdependence, or are they focused on relative capabilities and the issue of "who needs whom more?" To the extent that China's leaders focus on dependence relations, how does Chinese policy respond to China's dependence on others? Alternatively, how have Chinese leaders manipulated the dependence on China of other states, such as Vietnam, South Korea, and Taiwan, to achieve political objectives? That is, how does China use economic coercion or incentives? On the other hand, as China's economy continues to grow, it may well find itself interdependent (mutually dependent) with other large economies, such as with the United States, Japan, and the European Union. This issue concerns not only bilateral trade relationships but also the stability of the international economic order. Research suggests that there is a great deal of variation between economic interdependence, on the one hand, and its apparent political effects, on the other. It has been a standard argument to point to pre–World War I Europe as evidence that economic interdependence does not prevent conflict. More sophisticated research suggests that the effects of interdependence are conditional on anticipated change in streams of benefits.[46] Others might argue that it depends on the value leaders place on legitimacy via development versus legitimacy via nationalism. Others contend that the interdependence of the early twenty-first century—featuring transnational production and large flows of foreign direct investment, in addition to complex trade relationships—differs markedly from the more simple trade interdependence of the early twentieth century, and is, therefore, more stabilizing politically.[47] Others argue that the level of bilateral interdependence is not a particularly good predictor of levels of conflict between states, compared to the overall openness of the economy. The more open the economy, the less conflict-prone the state is.[48] In other words, there are a lot of hypotheses that could be tested to throw some light on the scope conditions under which economic interdependence does or does not introduce elements of restraint into China's bilateral and multilateral relationships.

How has the Chinese foreign policy system reacted to major setbacks in Chinese domestic and foreign policies, such as large-scale socioeconomic unrest, a major legitimacy crisis, the loss of a major ally, and large-scale conflict on its borders? China has faced all these in the past—the Great Leap Forward, the Cultural Revolution, the Sino-Soviet dispute, and the Korean War—as well as other shocks, such as the Tiananmen massacre. And it may well face them in the future in the shape of an implosion of North Korea, military defeat in a Taiwan conflict, or an explosion of class and ethnic resentments, among other possibilities. We cannot predict the future, but we can venture more educated guesses and forecasts by examining major setbacks in the past, and by examining how other major powers have responded to such internal and external shocks.

Related to this question, how has Chinese foreign policy responded to major domestic change in the mainland? Has there been enough variation in the political process—from consensus among top leaders, to rule by Maoist charisma, to a system where the Party chairman is more equal than others, to a more institutionalized consensus, where politics is relatively less dangerous—to see how leadership types have affected foreign policy?

The question of Chinese foreign policy under severe resource constraints —the effects of severe stresses on water, energy, and the environment—is also understudied. David Zweig and Bi Jianhai have started looking at how one conceptualizes the foreign policy of a resource hungry state. As they point out, this is a "new characteristic that drives much of China's current foreign policy behavior."[49] As one example, it sets up conflicts with the United States, not only because of competition over access to resources, but also because the PRC is willing to deal politically with regimes that the United States believes are potential sources of terrorism or regional instability.

Demography and foreign policy should also be put on the agenda. This is not necessarily a new issue. Due in part to the enormous human losses of the Great Leap Forward, China established foreign trade relations that persisted even during the domestic upheavals of the Cultural Revolution. But there are some interesting new hypotheses out there that require more rigorous testing. For instance, it has been argued that China's surplus male population could be a source of domestic social conflict and hypernationalism.[50] One could imagine testing for some of the observable empirical implications of this hypothesis through the combined use of random sample surveys and anthropological/ethnographic research methods. It is important to know, both intellectually and from a policy perspective, whether this argument has any legs at the individual level.

Another demographic issue concerns Chinese population growth. Historians have observed that population growth and corresponding land pressures have contributed to the growth of the Chinese state. In the contemporary era, in which sovereignty limits expansion and borders are more fixed, how do population pressures and associated resource problems influence Chinese foreign policy, especially foreign economic policy and attitudes toward self-sufficiency and dependency? Another related issue is the foreign policy implications of an aging population. Due to improved standards of living and population control, China's population is aging rapidly. By 2030, according to the United Nations, the proportion of China's population that will be over sixty years old could be greater than that in the United States.[51] The costs of providing adequate social support for this population will be enormous. This could lead to a number of policies with foreign policy implications—for example, a guns versus butter debate, or opening the door to greater immigration from the region. Japan's aging population will also likely require liberalization of its immigration policies. If there is a large-scale influx of Chinese immigrants who retain close ties to their homeland, how will this affect Sino-Japanese relations? These are all speculative questions, but comparative and historical analyses could be useful for understanding the potential stresses and strains on Chinese foreign policy.

Other hypotheses related to demography worth testing have to do with the middle class and foreign policy. Some democratic peace research posits that middle classes generally have more cautious foreign policy preferences, owing to the benefits of economic interdependence and the costs of sacrificing blood and treasure on foreign policy adventures. Moreover, because of their preference for social safety nets, the middle classes are more likely to help encourage guns versus butter debates. This may be even more likely as China's population both gets richer and older.

How has China responded to emerging international norms? It is hard to predict precisely what norms will "take off" at any particular moment in global politics (few predicted the virtually global endorsement of a landmine ban in a short two-year period). But in macrohistorical terms, many Western scholars believe that there is a certain trajectory in the evolution of international norms—that is to say, traditional notions of state sovereignty and autonomy will be increasingly challenged by packages of norms stressing the right of individuals to the maximum protection of body and sociopolitical choices: humanitarian intervention; democratization; women's rights; and environmentalism.[52] If accurate, this poses problems for the current regime in China. There is some pioneering research on China's understandings of sovereignty,[53] but much more needs to be done, across a wider range of normative arenas.

What is the effect of the Chinese diaspora on Chinese foreign policy? We are not referring here to the role of generations of overseas Chinese, but to the impact of the post-Maoist brain drain and return. Diasporic studies and foreign policy is not yet a field.[54] Preliminary work on India's diaspora suggests that overseas talent can affect domestic politics through the transfer of investment, management skills, and political preferences. In the Indian case, these preferences tend to be politically and economically conservative (or classically liberal).[55] Except for David Zweig's pioneering research on the Chinese brain drain and returning students, there is virtually no other literature on this topic in the Chinese case.[56] Zweig shows that the Chinese leadership has finally realized that this circulation of human capital is essential for the development of China's comprehensive national power.[57] It is still not clear, however, what, if any, political and economic preferences the diaspora will bring directly or indirectly to the foreign policy process. As Yossi Shain and Ahron Barth suggest, in principle, the effect of the diaspora on foreign policy will depend on how permeable the policy process is and how much control the state can exercise over the diaspora. Yet we have no way of conceptualizing, let alone measuring, this notion of permeability in the Chinese policy process, in part because homeland attitudes toward the diaspora can be so complex and contradictory.

The effect of regional interests on the center's foreign policy is also understudied. In an era of globalization, economic decentralization, and the diffusion of information, regions in extant states are developing distinctive foreign policy interests. What are the implications for the ability of central governments to manage interstate relations? IR specialists in eastern Europe are paying increasing attention to this issue in the Russian Federation.[58] There so far has been only a limited amount of work on regional economic interests and Chinese foreign policy.[59]

In the face of perforated sovereignty—a function mainly of economic integration—there is wide variation in how states have defined citizenship, in the mechanisms they use for creating identification with the state, and the implications for foreign policy. Citizenship issues have become a battleground for conflicting interests between those wanting to encourage economic growth and those wanting to strengthen national identity. The Chinese territory-based legal definition of citizenship and the unofficial but powerful ethnicity-based perception of who is Chinese are often in tension. We have little understanding of how ethnic preferences affect Chinese foreign policy—for example, is the Chinese leadership's response to interaction with countries with large ethnically Chinese populations affected by the belief that these populations have or ought to have special empathy or sympathy for the PRC?

Relatedly, what role do racial stereotypes play in the formulation and execution of foreign policy? This is a neglected topic in international relations in general. Yet there is no reason to believe that racial stereotypes do not matter. They have mattered enormously in the domestic histories of major powers, and there is little reason to believe that these effects stop at the border. We know that cultural and racial stereotyping has an important effect on how decision-makers carry out net assessment processes when estimating the overall military power and competence of other states.[60] There is interesting, if controversial, evidence that American racial stereotypes militated against the construction of deep multilateral security cooperation with Asians during the Cold War.[61] We know that in China, popular and elite hatred of Japan and the Japanese is often baldly framed in racist terms.

In addition to these more micro-process-focused research topics, the field could use an updated macrohistorical account of the evolution of Chinese foreign policy since 1949. Not only have Yahuda's masterful volumes been useful for teaching undergraduates and graduates, but they embody themes and arguments about what drives the totality of China's foreign policy. Despite new research methods, theories, and sources (including new Chinese materials and declassified materials on foreign policy in the 1950s and 1960s, and transcripts and notes from the China-U.S. and China-Japan normalization processes), we have seen nothing comparable in the past decade that rethinks the "big questions" such as the role of Marxist-Leninist ideology, nationalist ideology, perceptions of power realities, the impact of external actors and opportunities, and so on. How does one explain the quite radical change in China's foreign policies from the Maoist to the post-Maoist periods, from what Samuel Kim has referred to as a system transformer role to a system preserver role? The fact that this shift from Maoist anti-engagement to Dengist engagement with global capitalist institutions occurred in the absence of any change in regime type, and was carried out by many of the people who had been in power before the shift, has very few historical analogues.

In sum, the study of Chinese foreign policy over the past ten or so years has made noticeable advances in its understanding of past and current Chinese behavior, in its integration of empirical research with the theoretical literature and the methodologies in the international politics discipline, and in its use of the ever-expanding amount of Chinese-language research materials. Through better scholarship and through better training of future policymakers, the field has also, it may be hoped, made a contribution to the practice of the China policy of the United States and other countries, to the amelioration of manageable bilateral conflicts, and to the realization of the potential for a mutually beneficial and cooperative bilateral relationship with China. It is beginning, as well, to make contributions to the testing and development of IR theory.

At the same time, the study of Chinese foreign policy has yet to fully realize its potential. In all facets of scholarship, students of Chinese foreign policy still have much to accomplish. As our partial list suggests, there remain many unanswered questions about China's international behavior and many unexplored theoretical and methodological approaches that could yet answer many of these questions. There are also many underutilized research materials that could contribute to knowledge of China's international behavior through traditional as well as more contemporary approaches to international relations. The China foreign policy community itself is still very small, especially in light of the sheer number of topics that need to be covered in greater depth and sophistication and the demand for information from the policy world. It is clear, too, that as it develops and grows, the field of Chinese foreign policy studies holds to the path that Allen Whiting first blazed thirty-five years ago, and that its debt to his groundbreaking scholarship is undiminished.

Notes

1. Allen S. Whiting, *China Crosses the Yalu: The Decision to Enter the Korean War* (Stanford: Stanford University Press, 1960); *The Chinese Calculus of Deterrence: India and Indochina* (Ann Arbor: University of Michigan Press, 1975); and *China Eyes Japan* (Berkeley: University of California Press, 1989).

2. For two examples, see Allen S. Whiting, "ASEAN Eyes China: The Security Dimension," *Asian Survey* 37, 4 (April 1997): 299–322, and "China's Use of Force, 1950–96, and Taiwan," *International Security*, 26, 2 (Fall 2001): 103–31.

3. Whiting, *China Crosses the Yalu*. Subsequent research findings confirmed Whiting's early analysis of this problem. See Thomas J. Christensen, *Useful Adversaries: Grand Strategy, Domestic Mobilization, and Sino-American Conflict, 1947–58* (Princeton, N.J.: Princeton University Press, 1996), ch. 5.

4. Whiting, "ASEAN Eyes China."

5. Whiting, *China Eyes Japan*. On this issue, see also Allen S. Whiting, "Assertive Nationalism in Chinese Foreign Policy," *Asian Survey* 23, 8 (August 1983): 913–33.

6. Whiting, "Assertive Nationalism in Chinese Foreign Policy."

7. Johnston's own data are not entirely reassuring on this score either, because negative feelings toward Japan persist despite the high level of bilateral economic interdependence and Japan's relatively restrained security posture in the region.

8. Edward D. Mansfield and Jack Snyder, "Democratization and the Danger of War," *International Security* 20, 1 (Summer 1995): 5–38.

9. Michael Ng-Quinn, "The Effects of Bipolarity on Chinese Foreign Policy," *Survey* 26, 2 (Spring 1982): 116–30; Lowell Dittmer, *Sino-Soviet Normalization and Its International Implications, 1945–1990* (Seattle: University of Washington Press, 1992); Andrew J. Nathan and Robert S. Ross, *The Great Wall and the Empty Fortress: China's Search for Security* (New York: Norton, 1997); and Denny Roy, *China's Foreign Relations* (Basingstoke, Eng.: Macmillan, 1998).

10. Harold Jacobson and Michel Oksenberg, *China's Participation in the IMF, the World Bank, and GATT: Toward a Global Economic Order* (Ann Arbor: University of Michigan Press, 1990); Elizabeth Economy and Michel Oksenberg, eds., *China Joins the World: Progress and Prospects* (New York: Council on Foreign Relations Press, 1999); Margaret M. Pearson, "The Major Multilateral Economic Institutions Engage China," in *Engaging China: The Management of an Emerging Power*, ed. Alastair Iain Johnston and Robert S. Ross (London: Routledge, 1999), 207–34.

11. Lucian Pye, *The Spirit of Chinese Politics* (Cambridge, Mass.: Harvard University Press, 1992); Kenneth Lieberthal, "Domestic Politics and Foreign Policy," in *China's Foreign Policy in the 1980s*, ed. Harry Harding (New Haven, Conn.: Yale University Press, 1984), 43–70; and Robert Ross, "From Lin Biao to Deng Xiaoping: Elite Instability and China's US Policy," *China Quarterly*, no. 118 (June 1989): 265–99.

12. David Zweig, *Internationalizing China: Domestic Interests and Global Linkages* (Ithaca, N.Y.: Cornell University Press, 2002)

13. Whiting, *China Eyes Japan*; Jianwei Wang, *Limited Adversaries: Post–Cold War Sino-American Mutual Images* (New York: Oxford University Press, 2000); David Shambaugh, *Beautiful Imperialist: China Perceives America, 1972–1990* (Princeton, N.J.: Princeton University Press, 1991).

14. Bruce D. Larkin, *China and Africa, 1949–1970: The Foreign Policy of the People's Republic of China* (Berkeley: University of California Press, 1971).

15. Alastair Iain Johnston, "The Social Effects of International Institutions on Domestic (Foreign Policy) Actors," in *Locating the Proper Authorities: The Interaction of Domestic and International Institutions*, ed. Daniel Drezner (Ann Arbor: University of Michigan Press, 2002), and Allen Carlson, "Constructing a New Great Wall: Chinese Foreign Policy and the Norm of State Sovereignty" (Ph.D. diss., Yale University, 2000).

16. Shambaugh, *Beautiful Imperialist*.

17. Michael D. Swaine and Ashley J. Tellis, *Interpreting China's Grand Strategy: Past, Present, and Future* (Santa Monica, Calif.: Rand Corporation, 2000); Nathan and Ross, *Great Wall*.

18. Samuel S. Kim, *China, The United Nations and World Order* (Princeton, N.J.: Princeton University Press, 1979); Peter Van Ness, *Revolution and China's Foreign Policy* (Berkeley: University of California Press, 1972); Alastair Iain Johnston, "China's Military Interstate Dispute Behavior: A First Cut at the Data," *China Quarterly*, no. 153 (March 1998): 1–30.

19. John Garver, *China's Decision for Rapprochement with the United States, 1968–1971* (Boulder, Colo.: Westview Press, 1982).

20. Thomas J. Christensen, "Posing Problems Without Catching Up: China's Rise and Challenges for U.S. Security Policy," *International Security* 25, 4 (Spring 2001): 5–40; Johnston, "Social Effects"; Michael Pillsbury, *China Debates the Future Security Environment* (Washington, D.C.: National Defense University Press, 2000); Margaret M. Pearson, "China in Geneva: Lessons from China's Early Years in the World Trade Organization" (this volume); Jacobson and Oksenberg, *China's Participation*.

21. Wang, *Limited Adversaries*; Davis B. Bobrow, Steve Chan, and John A. Kringen, *Understanding Foreign Policy Decisions: The Chinese Case* (New York: Free Press, 1979).

414   CONCLUSIONS AND FUTURE DIRECTIONS

22. Bruce Bueno de Mesquita, David Newman, and Alvin Rabushka, *Red Flag over Hong Kong* (Chatham, N.J.: Chatham House, 1996); Emerson Niou and Peter C. Ordeshook, "A Game-Theoretic Interpretation of Sun Tzu's *The Art of War*," *Journal of Peace Research* 31, 2 (May 1994): 161–74.

23. An excellent example of a theoretically (though not so methodologically) diverse collection on Chinese foreign policy is Thomas W. Robinson and David Shambaugh, eds., *Chinese Foreign Policy: Theory and Practice* (New York: Oxford University Press, 1994).

24. Matthew Evangelista, *Unarmed Forces: The Transnational Movement to End the Cold War* (Ithaca, N.Y.: Cornell University Press, 1999).

25. Janice Gross Stein, "Political Learning by Doing: Gorbachev as an Uncommitted Thinker," *International Organization* 48, 2 (Spring 1994): 155–84.

26. Karl W. Deutsch et al., *Political Community and the North Atlantic Area: International Organization in the Light of Historical Experience* (Princeton, N.J.: Princeton University Press, 1957).

27. Amitav Acharya, "How Ideas Spread: Whose Norms Matter? Norm Localization and Institutional Change in Asian Regionalism," *International Organization* 58, 2 (April 2004): 239–75.

28. Margaret Hermann and Charles Hermann, "Who Makes Foreign Policy Decisions and How: An Empirical Inquiry," *International Studies Quarterly* 33, 4 (December 1989): 361–87; Paul A. Kowert and Margaret G. Hermann, "Who Takes Risks? Daring and Caution in Foreign Policy Making," *Journal of Conflict Resolution* 41, 5 (October 1997): 611–37; Daniel L. Byman and Kenneth M. Pollack, "Let Us Now Praise Great Men (and Women): Restoring the First Image," *International Security* 25, 4 (Spring 2001): 107–47; Joe D. Hagan, "Domestic Political Systems and War Proneness," *Mershon International Studies Review* 38, 2 (October 1994).

29. For example, the Correlates of War Militarized Interstate Dispute data set, the International Crisis Behavior data set, and the Kansas Events data set, among others.

30. For an example of vector auto-regression and its application to Chinese foreign policy, see Kuofeng Su, "Taiwan's Democratization and Its Foreign Policy: The Impact of Taiwan's Elections on Its China Policy" (Ph.D. diss., University of Michigan, 2000).

31. For a review of different computer-aided content analysis programs, see Kimberly Neuendorf and Paul Skalski, "Quantitative Content Analysis and the Measurement of Collective Identity," in *Measuring Identity*, eds. Rawi Abdelal, Yoshiko Herrera, Alastair Iain Johnston, and Rose McDemott (forthcoming); Will Lowe, "Software for Content Analysis: A Review" (Harvard Identity Project paper), www.wcfia.harvard.edu/misc/initiative/identity/publications/content_analysis.pdf (accessed 14 October 2005).

32. Robert Axelrod, *The Complexity of Cooperation: Agent-Based Models of Competition and Collaboration* (Princeton, N.J.: Princeton University Press, 1997); John L. Casti, *Would-Be Worlds: How Simulation Is Changing the Frontiers of Science* (New York: Wiley, 1997); Lars-Erik Cederman, *Emergent Actors in World Politics: How States and Nations Develop and Dissolve* (Princeton, N.J.: Princeton University Press, 1997); Joshua M. Epstein and Robert Axtell, *Growing Artificial Societies: Social Science From the Bottom Up* (Cambridge, Mass.: MIT Press, 1996);

John H. Holland, *Hidden Order: How Adaptation Builds Complexity* (Reading, Mass.: Addison-Wesley, 1995).

33. Our thanks to Wang Dong for discovering the foreign policy holdings in provincial archives, and to Manjari Miller, Andy Kennedy, and Lorenz Luthi for providing information on the contents of these archives.

34. Our thanks to Lorenz Luthi for the information about the eastern European archives.

35. See, e.g., Naoto Ito, "China's Decision and Strategy Toward the Normalization with Japan" (MA thesis, Harvard University, Regional Studies East Asia, 2005).

36. The HPCW, for instance, organized a major conference on "The Cold War and Its Legacy in Tibet" in April 2002. A considerable amount of Soviet archival material on China's role in the Korean War has been translated into Chinese and published in Taiwan. See Zhihua Shen, ed., *Chaoxian zhanzheng: Eguo dang'anguan de jiemi wenjian* [The Korean War: declassified documents from the Russian archives], Historical Material Collection No. 48 (Taipei: Academia Sinica, Institute of Modern History, 2003).

37. Ni Shixiong, *Dangdai xifang guoji guanxi lilun* (Shanghai: Fudan University Press, 2001); Yan Xuetong and Sun Xuefeng, *Guoji guanxi yanjiu shiyong fangfa* [Practical methods of international studies] (Beijing: People's Publishing House, 2001); Wang Yizhou, *Xifang guoji zhengzhi xue: lishi yu lilun* [Western international politics studies: history and theory] (Shanghai: Shanghai Renmin Chubanshe, 1998); Wang Yizhou, *Dangdai guoji zhengzhi xilun* [An analysis of contemporary international politics] (Shanghai: Shanghai Renmin Chubanshe, 1995).

38. Wang Houqing and Zhang Xingye, chief eds., *Zhanyi xue* [Military campaign studies] (Beijing: Guofang Daxue Chubanshe, 2000).

39. See e.g., Grant McCracken, *The Long Interview* (Beverly Hills, Calif.: Sage Publications, 1988); Herbert J. Rubin and Irene S. Rubin, *Qualitative Interviewing: The Art of Hearing Data* (Thousand Oaks, Calif.: Sage Publications, 2004); Jaber F. Gubrium and James A. Holstein, *Handbook of Interview Research: Context and Method* (Thousand Oaks, Calif.: Sage Publications, 2001).

40. The Research Center on Contemporary China at Peking University, the Public Opinion Research Institute at People's University, the Survey and Statistics Institute at the China Communications University, and Horizon Group are among the reputable social survey organizations that have done some polling on topics related to foreign policy (e.g., attitudes toward the United States or Japan).

41. For comprehensive analysis of these new sources, see Taylor Fravel, "Online and on China: Research Sources in the Information Age," *China Quarterly*, no. 163 (September 2000): 821–42; Evan Medeiros, "Undressing the Dragon: Researching the PLA Through Open Source Exploitation," in *A Poverty of Riches: New Challenges and Opportunities in PLA Research*, ed. James C. Mulvenon and Andrew N. D. Yang (Santa Monica, Calif.: Rand Corporation, 2003); Taylor Fravel, "The Revolution in Research Affairs: Online Sources and the Study of the PLA," in ibid.

42. See, e.g., Gerald Segal, *Defending China* (Oxford: Oxford University Press, 1985); Andrew Scobell, *China's Use of Military Force: Beyond the Great Wall and the Long March* (New York: Cambridge University Press, 2003); Thomas Christensen in this volume; Allen Whiting, *China's Calculus of Deterrence: India and*

Indochina (Ann Arbor: University of Michigan Press, 1975); id., "China's Use of Force, 1950–96, and Taiwan," *International Security* 26, 3 (Fall 2001): 103–31.

43. Ann Kent, *China, the United Nations, and Human Rights: The Limits of Compliance* (Philadelphia: University of Pennsylvania Press, 1999); Alastair Iain Johnston, *Social States: China in International Security Institutions, 1980–2000* (forthcoming); Evan Medeiros, *Shaping Chinese Foreign Policy: The Evolution of Chinese Policies on WMD Nonproliferation and the Role of U.S. Policy, 1980–2004* (Stanford: Stanford University Press, forthcoming).

44. Lu Ning, *The Dynamics of Foreign-Policy Decisionmaking in China* (Boulder, Colo.: Westview Press, 2000), and David M. Lampton, ed., *The Making of Chinese Foreign and Security Policy in the Era of Reform, 1978–2000* (Stanford: Stanford University Press, 2001).

45. The relativity in definitions of core interests and concepts in international relations was stated forcefully by the godfather of modern realist theory, Hans Morgenthau. See his third principle of political realism, *Politics Among Nations: The Struggle for Power and Peace*, 5th ed. (New York: Knopf, 1978), 8–9.

46. Dale Copeland, *The Origins of Major Power War* (Ithaca, N.Y.: Cornell University Press, 2000).

47. Stephen Brooks, "The Globalization of Production and the Declining Benefits of Conquest," *Journal of Conflict Resolution* 43, 5 (October 1999): 646–70.

48. Soo Yeon Kim, "Structure and Change in International Trade and Militarized Conflict: When Is Engagement Constructive?" (unpublished paper, 1999).

49. David Zweig and Bi Jianhai, "The Foreign Policy of a 'Resource Hungry' State" (unpublished paper, 2005).

50. Valerie M. Hudson and Andrea Den Boer, "A Surplus of Men: A Deficit of Peace Security and Sex Ratios in Asia's Largest States," *International Security* 26, 4 (Spring 2002): 5–38.

51. Richard Jackson and Neil Howe, "The Graying of the Middle Kingdom: The Demographics and Economics of Retirement Policy in China" (presentation at the Center for International and Strategic Studies, 25 May 2004).

52. Anti-terrorism may undermine some of these norms (e.g., democratization) while strengthening others (e.g., humanitarian intervention to alleviate socioeconomic conditions that breed support for terrorism).

53. See Allen Carlson, "More Than Just Saying No: China's Evolving Approach to Sovereignty and Intervention Since Tiananmen," ch. 8 in this volume.

54. For one of the only studies on conceptualizing the relationship between diasporas and foreign policy, see Yossi Shain and Ahron Barth, "Diasporas and International Relations Theory," *International Organization* 57, 3 (July 2003): 449–79.

55. Our thanks to Devesh Kapur for his insights on the Indian diaspora.

56. David Zweig, "'Parking at the Doorstep?': Mainland Professionals in Hongkong" (prepared for "New Directions in Chinese Foreign Policy: A Conference in Honor of Allen S. Whiting," Fairbank Center for East Asian Research, Harvard University, 8–9 November 2002).

57. David Zweig and Chung Siu-Fung, "Redefining the Brain Drain: China's 'Diaspora Option'" (unpublished paper, March 2005)

58. Jeronim Perovic, *Internationalization of Russian Regions and the Consequences for Russian Foreign and Security Policy*. Regionalization of Russian Foreign and Security Policy Project, Working Paper No. 1 (Zurich: Center for Security Studies and Conflict Research, 2000).

59. See, e.g., Gale Christoffersen, "Xinjiang and the Great Islamic Circle: The Impact of Transnational Forces on Chinese Regional Economic Planning," *China Quarterly*, no. 133 (March 1993): 130–51; Peter T. Y. Cheung and James T. H. Tang, "The External Relations of China's Provinces," in *The Making of Chinese Foreign and Security Policy in the Era of Reform,* ed. David M. Lampton (Stanford: Stanford University Press, 2001), 91–120. Jean-Marc Blanchard has also done research on the foreign economic interests of China's northeastern provinces. See his essay in *Locating the Proper Authorities: The Interaction of Domestic and International Institutions,* ed. Daniel W. Drezner (Ann Arbor: University of Michigan Press, 2002).

60. Michael Fischerkeller, "David Versus Goliath: The Influence of Cultural Judgments on Strategic Preference" (Ph.D. diss., Ohio State University, 1997).

61. David Capie, "Power, Identity and Multilateralism: The United States and Regional Institutionalism in the Asia-Pacific" (Ph.D. diss., York University, 2002).

REFERENCE MATTER

Select Bibliography

Abrams, Dominic, and Michael Hogg, eds. *Social Identity Theory*. New York: Harvester Press, 1982.

Acharya, Amitav. "How Ideas Spread: Whose Norms Matter: Norm Localization and Institutional Change in Asian Regionalism." *International Organization* 58, 2 (Spring 2004): 239–75.

Adams, John. *Discourses on Davila*. Boston: Russell & Cutler, 1805.

Adler, Emanuel, and Michael Barnett, eds. *Security Communities*. Cambridge: Cambridge University Press, 1998.

Allen, Kenneth W. "China and the Use of Force: The Role of the PLA Air Force." Unpublished paper, 2000.

———. "PLA Air Force Operations and Modernization." In *People's Liberation Army After Next*, ed. Susan M. Puska, 189–254. Carlisle, Pa.: Strategic Studies Institute, U.S. Army War College, 2001.

Alport, F. H. *Social Psychology*. Boston: Houghton Mifflin, 1924.

An Wei, and Li Dongyan, eds. *Shizi lukou shang de shijie: Zhongguo zhuming xuezhe tantao 21 shiji de guoji jiaodian* [World at the crossroads: famous Chinese scholars explore international central issues of the twenty-first century]. Beijing: Zhongguo Renmin Daxue Chubanshe, 2000.

Anderson, Zheng. "'He Was Treating Me Like a Criminal'—A Chinese Canadian's Experience at Detroit Airport." *China News Digest—US*, 20 March 1999. www.cnd.org/CND-US/CND-US.99/CND-US.99-03-20.html (accessed 2 October 2005).

Armstrong, J. D. *Revolutionary Diplomacy: Chinese Foreign Policy and the United Front Doctrine*. Berkeley: University of California Press, 1977.

Arpi, Claude. *The Fate of Tibet: When Big Insects Eat Small Insects*. New Delhi: Har-Anand, 1999.

Ashley, Richard. "Untying the Sovereign State: A Double Reading of the Anarchy Problematique." *Millennium* 17 (Summer 1988): 227–62.

Axelrod, Robert. *The Complexity of Cooperation: Agent-Based Models of Competition and Collaboration*. Princeton, N.J.: Princeton University Press, 1997.

Bachman, David. "China's Democratization and U.S.-China Relations?" In *What if China Doesn't Democratize: Implications for War and Peace*, ed. Edward Friedman and Barrett L. McCormick. Armonk, N.Y.: M. E. Sharpe, 2000.

Barbalet, J. M. *Emotion, Social Theory, and Social Structure: A Macrosociological Approach*. New York: Cambridge University Press, 1998.

Baum, Matthew A. "Soap Opera Wars: The Mass Media, Public Opinion, and the Decision to Use Force Abroad." Ph.D. diss., University of California, San Diego, 2000.

Baumeister, Roy F., and Mark R. Leary. "The Need to Belong: Desire for Interpersonal Attachments as a Fundamental Human Motivation." *Psychological Bulletin* 117, 3 (1995): 497–529.

Becker, Elizabeth. "Negotiators Fail to Agree on Agricultural Subsidies." *New York Times,* 1 April 2003.

———. "W.T.O. Rules Against U.S. on Steel Tariff." *New York Times,* 27 March 2003.

Beijing Area Study (BAS) data report. Annual survey by the Peking University Research Center on Contemporary China (RCCC), 1998–2004. Beijing: Zhongguo Shehui Kexue Chubanshe, forthcoming.

Beinart, Peter. "An Illusion for Our Time: The False Promise of Globalization." *New Republic,* 20 October 1997, 20–24.

Bennett, Bruce. "The Emerging Ballistic Missile Threat: Global and Regional Implications." In *Emerging Threats, Force Structures, and the Role of Air Power in Korea,* ed. Natalie Crawford and Chung-in Moon, 181–217. Santa Monica, Calif.: Rand Corporation, 2000.

Betts, Richard K. *Nuclear Blackmail and Nuclear Balance.* Washington, D.C.: Brookings Institution Press, 1987.

Betts, Richard K., and Thomas J. Christensen. "China: Getting the Questions Right." *National Interest,* 22 December 2000, 17–29.

Biersteker, Thomas J., and Cynthia Weber. "The Social Construction of State Sovereignty." In *State Sovereignty as Social Construct,* ed. Thomas J. Biersteker and Cynthia Weber, 1–22. Cambridge: Cambridge University Press, 1996.

Blanchard, Jean-Marc. "Giving the Unrecognized Their Due: Regional Actors, International Institutions, and Multilateral Economic Cooperation in Northeast Asia." In *Locating the Proper Authorities: The Interaction of Domestic and International Institutions,* ed. Daniel W. Drezner, 49–76. Ann Arbor: University of Michigan Press, 2002.

Bleiker, Roland. "Neorealist Claims in Light of Ancient Chinese Philosophy: The Cultural Dimension of International Theory." In *Culture in World Politics,* ed. Dominique Jacquin-Berdal, Andrew Oros, and Marco Verweij, 89–115. New York: St. Martin's Press and *Millennium,* 1998.

Bobrow, Davis B., Steve Chan, and John A. Kringen. *Understanding Foreign Policy Decisions: The Chinese Case.* New York: Free Press, 1979.

Boorman, Howard L., and Richard C. Howard, eds. *Biographical Dictionary of Republican China.* 5 vols. New York: Columbia University Press, 1967–79.

Braithwaite, John, and Peter Drahos. *Global Business Regulation.* Cambridge: Cambridge University Press, 2000.

Branscombe, Nyla R., and Daniel L. Wann. "Collective Self-Esteem Consequences of Outgroup Derogation When a Valued Social Identity Is on Trial." *European Journal of Social Psychology* 24, 6 (1994): 641–57.

Braumoeller, Bear. "Hypothesis Testing and Multiplicative Interaction Terms." *International Organization* 58, 4 (Fall 2004): 807–20.

Brewer, Marilynn B. "The Role of Distinctiveness in Social Identity and Group Behavior." In *Group Motivation: Social Psychological Perspectives*, ed. Michael A. Hogg and Dominic Abrams, 1–16. New York: Harvester Wheatsheaf, 1993.

———. "The Psychology of Prejudice: Ingroup Love or Outgroup Hate?" *Journal of Social Issues* 55, 3 (1999): 429–444.

———. "Ingroup Identification and Intergroup Conflict: When Does Ingroup Love Become Outgroup Hate?" In *Social Identity, Intergroup Conflict, and Conflict Resolution*, ed. R. Ashmore, L. Jussim, and D. Wilder, 17–41. New York: Oxford University Press, 2000.

Brooks, Stephen. "The Globalization of Production and the Declining Benefits of Conquest." *Journal of Conflict Resolution* 43, 5 (October 1999): 646–70.

Brown, Lester R. *Who Will Feed China? Wake-Up Call for a Small Planet*. New York: Norton, 1995.

Brown, Michael E., Sean Lynn-Jones, and Steven Miller, eds. *Debating the Democratic Peace*. Cambridge, Mass.: MIT Press, 1996.

Brown, Roger. *Social Psychology*. 2d ed. New York: Free Press, 1986.

Brown, Rupert, and Gabi Haeger. "'Compared to What?' Comparison Choice in an Internation Context." *European Journal of Social Psychology* 29, 1 (1999): 31–42.

Brubaker, Rogers, and David D. Laitin. "Ethnic and Nationalist Violence." *Annual Review of Sociology* 24 (1998): 423–52.

Bueno de Mesquita, Bruce. *The War Trap*. New Haven, Conn.: Yale University Press, 1981.

Bueno de Mesquita, Bruce, David Newman, and Alvin Rabushka. *Red Flag over Hong Kong*. Chatham, N.J.: Chatham House Publishers, 1996.

Burgoon, Brian J., and Michael A. Hiscox. "The Mysterious Case of Female Protectionism: Gender Bias in Attitudes Toward International Trade." Paper presented at the Annual Meeting of the American Political Science Association, Philadelphia, 28–31 August 2003. www.people.fas.harvard.edu/~hiscox/BurgoonHiscoxFemaleProtectionism.pdf (accessed 11 October 2005).

Burke, Peter J., and Donald C. Reitzes. "The Link Between Identity and Role Performance." *Social Psychology Quarterly* 44 (1981): 83–92.

Burke, Peter J., and Judy C. Tully. "The Measurement of Role Identity." *Social Forces* 55, 4 (June 1977): 881–97.

Burnstein, Eugene, Mark Abboushi, and Shinobu Kitayama. "How the Mind Preserves the Image of the Enemy." In *Behavior, Culture, and Conflict in World Politics*, ed. William Zimmerman and Harold K. Jacobson. Ann Arbor: University of Michigan Press, 1993.

Burr, William. "Sino-American Relations, 1969: The Sino-Soviet Border War and Steps Toward Rapprochement." *Cold War History* 1, 3 (2001): 73–112.

Byman, Daniel L., and Kenneth M. Pollack. "Let Us Now Praise Great Men (and Women): Restoring the First Image." *International Security* 25, 4 (Spring 2001): 107–47.

Cai, Deborah A., principal investigator. "Perspectives Toward the United States in Selected Newspapers of the People's Republic of China." Institute for Global Chinese Affairs and the Department of Communication, University of Maryland,

30 May 2002. www.uscc.gov/researchpapers/2000_2003/pdfs/chinmed.pdf (accessed 22 November 2005).

Campbell, David. *Writing Security: United States Foreign Policy and the Politics of Identity*. Minneapolis: University of Minnesota Press, 1998.

Cantor, Nancy, and Walter Mischel. "Prototypes in Person Perception." *Advances in Experimental Social Psychology* 12 (1979): 3–52.

Capie, David. "Power, Identity and Multilateralism: The United States and Regional Institutionalism in the Asia-Pacific." Ph.D. diss., York University, 2002.

Carlson, Allen. "Constructing a New Great Wall: Chinese Foreign Policy and the Norm of State Sovereignty." Ph.D. diss., Yale University, 2000.

———. "Helping to Keep the Peace (Albeit Reluctantly): The Recent Chinese Approach to Sovereignty and Intervention." *Pacific Affairs* 77, 1 (Summer 2004): 9–28.

———. *Protecting Sovereignty, Accepting Intervention: The Dilemma of Chinese Foreign Relations in the 1990s*. China Policy Series No. 18. New York: National Committee on United States–China Relations, 2002. www.ncuscr.org/Publications/Full_Text_Booklet%20_Final_Format.pdf (accessed 5 October 2005).

———. *Unifying China, Integrating with the World: Securing Chinese Sovereignty in the Reform Era*. Stanford: Stanford University Press, 2005.

Carter, Ashton B., and William J. Perry. *Preventive Defense: A New Security Strategy for America*. Washington, D.C.: Brookings Institution Press, 1999.

Castano, Emanuele, et al. "I Belong Therefore I Exist: Ingroup Identification, Ingroup Entitativity, and Ingroup Bias." Forthcoming.

Casti, John L. *Would-Be Worlds: How Simulation Is Changing the Frontiers of Science*. New York: Wiley, 1997.

Cederman, Lars-Erik. *Emergent Actors in World Politics: How States and Nations Develop and Dissolve*. Princeton, N.J.: Princeton University Press, 1997.

Cha, Victor D. "Hawk Engagement and Preventive Defense on the Korean Peninsula." *International Security* 27, 1 (2002): 40–78.

Chai Chengwen, and Zhao Yongtian. *Banmendian tanpan* [Panmunjon negotiations]. Beijing: Liberation Army Press, August 1989.

Chan, Gerald. *China and International Organizations*. Hong Kong: Oxford University Press, 1989.

Chanda, Nayan. *Brother Enemy: The War After the War*. San Diego: Harcourt Brace, 1986.

Chang, Peggy Pei-chen, and Tun-jen Cheng. "The Rise of the Information Technology in China: A Formidable Challenge to Taiwan's Economy." *American Asian Review* 20, 3 (2002): 125–74.

"Changes in Taipei, WTO Dealings." Central News Agency (CNA), 11 September 2002.

Chayes, Abram, and Antonia Handler Chayes. "On Compliance." *International Organization* 47, 2 (1993): 175–205.

Chen Bojiang. "Xinxi shidai Meiguo junshi liliang jianshe yu yunyong de jishuhua" [Buildup and use of U.S. military strength in the information age]. *Zhongguo Junshi Kexue*, no. 2 (1999).

———. "Cong 'he wupin san' dao 'xinxi san'" [From "nuclear weapons umbrella" to "information umbrella"]. *Guangming Ribao*, 23 January 2001. www.gmw.com.cn/0_gm/2001/01/20010123/GB/01^18674^0^GMC1-218.htm (accessed 17 October 2005).

Chen Feng, Huang Zhaoyu, et al.; Chai Zemin, consultant. *ZhongMei jiaoliang daxiezhen* [The true story of the Sino-American contest]. Vol. 2. Beijing: Zhongguo Renshi Chubanshe, 1996.

Chen Guanglei. "Gaige kaifang zhong hanyu cihui de biandong" [Changes in the Chinese vocabulary under reform and opening]. *Yuyan Jiaoxue yu Yanjiu* [Language Teaching and Linguistic Studies] 2 (1997): 15–23.

Chen Hegao, Li Siyang, and Gao Haorong. "Li Peng weiyuanzhang huijian Jin Dazhong zongtong" [NPC Standing Committee Chairman Li Peng meets with President Kim Dae Jung]. Xinhua, 25 May 2001. www.people.com.cn/GB/shizheng/16/20010525/474888.html (accessed 2 October 2005).

Chen, Jian. *The Sino-Soviet Alliance and China's Entry into the Korean War*. Working Paper No. 1. Washington, D.C.: Cold War International History Project, Woodrow Wilson International Center for Scholars, 1991.

———. *China's Road to the Korean War: The Making of Sino-American Confrontation*. New York: Columbia University Press, 1994.

———. "China's Involvement in the Vietnam War, 1964–69." *China Quarterly*, no. 142 (June 1995): 356–87.

Chen, Jie. "Urban Chinese Perceptions of Threats from the United States and Japan." *Public Opinion Quarterly* 65 (2001): 254–66.

Chen, King C. *China's War with Vietnam: Issues, Decisions, and Implications*. Stanford, Calif.: Hoover Institution Press, 1987.

Chen Pingsheng, chief ed. *Yindu junshi sixiang yanjiu* [Research on Indian military thinking]. Beijing: Academy of Military Sciences, 1992. Internally circulated.

Chen, Xiaomei. *Occidentalism: A Theory of Counter-Discourse in Post-Mao China*. New York: Oxford University Press, 1995.

Chen Youyuan. "Junshi jishu geming yu zhanyi lilun de fazhan" [The revolution in military technology and the development of campaign theory]. In *Gao jishu Tiaojian xia zhanyi lilun yanjiu* [Research on theory of local war under high-technology conditions], ed. Campaign Teaching and Research Office of the National Defense University. Beijing: Guofang Daxue Chubanshe, 1997.

Chen Zhou. *Xiandai jubu zhanzheng lilun yanjiu* [A study of modern local war theories]. Beijing: Guofang Daxue Chubanshe, 1997.

Cheng Shuaihua. "Guojia zhuquan yu guoji renquan de ruogan wenti" [Several issues involving international human rights and state sovereignty]. *Ouzhou* 1 (2000).

Cheung, Peter T. Y., and James Tang. "The External Relations of China's Provinces." In *The Making of Chinese Foreign and Security Policy in the Era of Reform, 1978–2000*, ed. David M. Lampton, 91–120. Stanford: Stanford University Press, 2001.

"China Accepts Talks with Taiwan over Steel Tariffs." Kyodo News Service, 4 December 2002.

"China Agrees to Allow Trade Remedy Review; Balks on Procedures." *Inside US-China Trade*, 15 May 2002.

"China Refuses to Discuss WTO Trade Review in Farm, SPS Committees." *Inside US-China Trade*, 3 July 2002, 5.

"China Rejects U.S. Push for More Review of Market Access Commitments." *Inside US-China Trade*, 27 September 2002.

"China Takes Lead Role in Shaping WTO Negotiating Procedures." *Inside US-China Trade*, 6 February 2002.

"China's Refusal to Answer Quad Queries Shuts Down Compliance Review Session." *BNA (online)*, 26 September 2002.

"China's WTO Entry Could Hurt Developing Country Interests." *Inside US-China Trade*, 7 November 2001.

Chiozza, Giacomo. "Love and Hate: Anti-Americanism and the American Order." Ph.D. diss., Duke University, 2004.

Chong Ling. "Guanyu yibenshu de duozhong shengyin" [On the many voices about a single book]. *Beijing Wanbao* [Beijing Evening News], 18 August 1996. Reprinted in Jia Qingguo, *Zhongguo bu jinjin shuobu* [China should not just say no], 265–67. Beijing: Zhonghua Gongshang Lianhe Chubanshe, 1996.

Chong Zi. "Japan Seeks Bigger Military Role." *Beijing Review* 46, 7 (13 February 2003): 11–12.

Christensen, Thomas J. "Threats, Assurances, and the Last Chance for Peace: The Lessons of Mao's Korean War Telegrams." *International Security* 17, 1 (Summer 1992): 122–54.

———. "Chinese Realpolitik." *Foreign Affairs* 75, 5 (September–October 1996): 36–52.

———. *Useful Adversaries: Grand Strategy, Domestic Mobilization, and Sino-American Conflict, 1947–58*. Princeton, N.J.: Princeton University Press, 1996.

———. "China, the U.S.-Japan Alliance, and the Security Dilemma in East Asia." *International Security* 23, 4 (Spring 1999): 49–80.

———. "Posing Problems Without Catching Up: China's Rise and the Challenges for U.S. Security Policy." *International Security* 25, 4 (Spring 2001): 5–40.

———. "China." In *Strategic Asia, 2002–2003: Asian Aftershocks*, ed. Aaron L. Friedberg and Richard Ellings, 51–94. Seattle: National Bureau of Asian Research, 2002.

———. "The Contemporary Security Dilemma: Deterring a Taiwan Conflict." *Washington Quarterly* 25, 4 (2002): 7–21.

———. "Worse than a Monolith: Disorganization and Rivalry in East Asian Communist Alliances and U.S. Containment Challenges, 1949–69." *Asian Security* 1, 1 (January 2005): 80–127.

Christensen, Thomas J., and Michael Glosny. "Sources of Stability in U.S.-China Security Relations." In *Strategic Asia, 2003–2004*, ed. Richard Ellings and Michael Wills. Seattle: National Bureau of Asian Research, 2003.

———. "Why U.S.-PRC Security Relations Are So Stable." In *Fragility and Crisis: Strategic Asia, 2003–2004*, ed. Aaron Friedberg, Richard Ellings, and Michael Wills. Seattle: National Bureau of Asian Research, 2003.

Christoffersen, Gale. "Xinjiang and the Great Islamic Circle: The Impact of Transnational Forces on Chinese Regional Economic Planning." *China Quarterly*, no. 133 (March 1993): 30–151.

Chu Shulong. "Lengzhanhou Zhongguo anquan zhanlüe sixiang de fazhan" [The development of China's thinking about security strategy after the Cold War]. *Shijie Jingji yu Zhengzhi* [World Economics and Politics], no. 9 (1999): 11–15.

———. "Zhongguo de guojia liyi, guojia liliang, he guojia zhanlue" [China's national interest, national strength and national strategy]. *Zhanlue yu Guanli*, no. 4 (1999).

———. "China, Asia and Issues of Sovereignty and Intervention." Paper presented at International Intervention and State Sovereignty Conference, Beijing, 14–15 January 2002.

Chu Shulong, and Wang Zaibang. "Guanyu guoji xingshi he wo duiwai zhanlüe ruogan zhongda wenti de sikao" [Reflections on some important questions about the international situation and our external strategy]. *Xiandai Guoji Guanxi*, no. 8 (1999): 16–21.

Cialdini, Robert B., et al. "Basking in Reflected Glory: Three (Football) Field Studies." *Journal of Personality and Social Psychology* 34, 3 (September 1976): 366–75.

Clark, Ian. *Globalization and International Relations Theory*. New York: Oxford University Press, 1999.

Cole, Bernard D. *The Great Wall at Sea: China's Navy Enters the Twenty-First Century*. Annapolis, Md.: Naval Institute Press, 2001.

Conboy, Kenneth, and James Morrison. *The CIA's Secret War in Tibet*. Lawrence: University of Kansas Press, 2002.

Connolly, William E. *Identity/Difference: Democratic Negotiations of Political Paradox*. Ithaca, N.Y.: Cornell University Press, 1991.

Cooley, Charles. *Human Nature and the Social Order*. 1902. New York: Scribners, 1922.

Copeland, Dale. "Do Reputations Matter?" *Security Studies* 7, 1 (Autumn 1997): 33–71.

Cote, Owen R. Jr. *The Future of the Trident Force: Enabling Access in Access-Constrained Environments*. Cambridge: MIT, Security Studies Program, 2002.

Council on Foreign Relations. *Chinese Military Power*. Report of an Indepedent Task Force Sponsored by the Council on Foreign Relations Maurice R. Greenberg Center for Geoeconomic Studies. Washington, D.C.: Council on Foreign Relations, 2003. www.cfr.org/pdf/China_TF.pdf (accessed 1 October 2005).

Crane, George T. "Imagining the Economic Nation: Globalization in China." *New Political Economy* 4, 2 (July 1999): 215–32.

Crawford, Neta C. "The Passion of World Politics: Propositions on Emotion and Emotional Relationships." *International Security* 24, 4 (Spring 2000): 116–56.

Crocker, Jennifer, and Riia Luhtanen. "Collective Self-esteem and Ingroup Bias." *Journal of Personality and Social Psychology* 58, 1 (January 1990): 60–67.

Cronin, Bruce. *Community Under Anarchy: Transnational Identity and the Evolution of Cooperation*. New York: Columbia University Press, 1999.

Dalvi, Brigadier J. P. *Himalayan Blunder: The Curtain-Raiser to the Sino-Indian War of 1962*. Bombay: Thacker, 1969.

Deng, Xiaoping. "A New Approach Towards Stabilizing the World Situation, February 22, 1984." In *Fundamental Issues in Present-Day China*. Beijing: Foreign Languages Press, 1987.

———. *Selected Works*. Vol. 3: *1982–1992*. Beijing: Foreign Languages Press, 1994.

Deng, Yong. "Conception of National Interests: Realpolitik, Liberal Dilemma, and the Possibility of Change." In *In the Eyes of the Dragon: China Views the World*, ed. Yong Deng and Fei-Ling Wang, 47–72. Lanham, Md.: Rowman & Littlefield, 1999.

———. "Hegemon on the Offensive: Chinese Perspectives of the U.S. Global Strategy." *Political Science Quarterly* 116, 3 (Fall 2001): 343–65.

Deng, Yong, and Thomas G. Moore, "China Views Globalization: Towards a New Great Power Politics." *Washington Quarterly* 27, 3 (Summer 2004): 117–26.

Deng, Yong, and Fei-ling Wang, eds. *China Rising: Power and Motivation in Chinese Foreign Policy*. Lanham, Md.: Rowman & Littlefield, 2005.

Destler, I. M. *American Trade Politics: System Under Stress*. 3d ed. Washington, D.C.: Institute for International Economics, 1995.

Deutsch, Karl W., et al. *Political Community and the North Atlantic Area: International Organization in the Light of Historical Experience*. Princeton, N.J.: Princeton University Press, 1957.

"Developing Countries and Agricultural Trade Liberalization." *Cairns Group Papers*, February 1999.

Dickie, Mure. "China and Taiwan Officials Discuss Trade." *Financial Times*, 16 December 2002.

Ding Shichuan, and Li Qiang. "Chaoxian bandao heping jizhi ji qi qianjing" [A peace mechanism for the Korean peninsula and its prospects]. *Xiandai Guoji Guanxi*, no. 4 (1999): 42–44.

Dittmer, Lowell. *Sino-Soviet Normalization and Its International Implications, 1945–1990*. Seattle: University of Washington Press, 1992.

Dittmer, Lowell, and Samuel Kim, eds. *China's Quest for National Identity*. Ithaca, N.Y.: Cornell University Press, 1993.

"Doha Round Briefing Series." *International Centre for Trade and Sustainable Development* 1, 2 (2003).

Dong Lixi. "Fu Quanyou Meets with the DPRK People's Army Goodwill Mission." Xinhua, FBIS-CHI. WNC Document No. 0H40Z0502GX9RH. 11 October 2002.

Downs, Erica Strecker, and Phillip C. Saunders. "Legitimacy and the Limits of Nationalism: China and the Diaoyu Islands." *International Security* 23, 3 (Winter 1998): 114–46.

Dreyer, June T. "Testimony of Dr June Teufel Dreyer. The U.S. Response to China's Increasing Military Power: Eleven Assumptions in Search of a Policy." U.S. Congress, House Armed Services Committee, Washington, D.C., 19 July 2000. www.house.gov/hasc/testimony/106thcongress/00-07-19dreyer.html (accessed 11 October 2005).

Drezner, Daniel W., ed. *Locating the Proper Authorities: The Interaction of Domestic and International Institutions*. Ann Arbor: University of Michigan Press, 2003.

Drifte, Reinhard. *Japan's Quest for a Permanent Security Council Seat: A Matter of Pride or Justice*. New York: St. Martin's Press, 2000.

————. "US Impact on Japanese-Chinese Security Relations." *Security Dialogue* 31, 4 (December 2000): 449–62.

————. *Japan's Security Relations with China Since 1989: From Balancing to Bandwagoning?* New York: RoutledgeCurzon, 2003.

Durkheim, Émile. *Suicide.* 1897. New York: Free Press, 1963.

Eckstein, Harry. "Case Study and Theory in Political Science." In *Strategies of Inquiry*, ed. Fred I. Greenstein and Nelson W. Polsby, 79–137. Reading, Mass.: Addison-Wesley, 1975.

Economy, Elizabeth. "China's Environmental Diplomacy." In *Chinese Foreign Policy Faces the New Millennium*, ed. Samuel S. Kim, 264–83. Boulder, Colo.: Westview Press, 1998.

Economy, Elizabeth, and Michel Oksenberg, eds. *China Joins the World: Progress and Prospects.* New York: Council on Foreign Relations Press, 1999.

Eliades, George. "Once More unto the Breach: Eisenhower, Dulles, and Public Opinion During the Offshore Islands Crisis of 1958." *Journal of American–East Asian Relations* 2, 4 (Winter 1993): 343–67.

Epstein, Joshua M., and Robert Axtell. *Growing Artificial Societies: Social Science from the Bottom Up.* Cambridge, Mass.: MIT Press, 1996.

Evangelista, Matthew. *Unarmed Forces: The Transnational Movement to End the Cold War.* Ithaca, N.Y.: Cornell University Press, 1999.

Evans, Robert. "China, at First WTO Meeting as Member, Pleads for Poor." Reuters newswire (online), 19 December 2001.

————. "WTO Chief Warns Trade Round Deadline under Threat." Reuters newswire (online), 22 January 2002.

Fan Guoxiang. "Renquan, zhuquan, baquan" [Human rights, sovereignty, hegemony]. In *Xin tiaozhan: guoji guanxi zhong de "rendaozhuyi ganyu"* [New challenges: "humanitarian intervention" in international relations], ed. Yang Cheng. Beijing: Zhongguo Qingnian Chubanshe, 2001.

————. "Zen yang kan de xifang renquan sixiang" [How to regard Western human rights ideology]. *Zhongguo Dang Zheng Ganbu Luntan* [China Party State Cadre Forum] 4 (2003): 59–61.

Fang Hua. "Yatai anquan jiagou de xianzhuang, qushi ji Zhongguo de zuoyong" [The current Asia-Pacific security framework, trends, and China's role]. *Shijie Jingji yu Zhengzhi* [World Economics and Politics], no. 2 (2000): 11–15.

Fang Ning, Wang Xiaodong, and Song Qiang. *Quanqiuhua yinying xia de Zhongguo zhi lu* [China's road under the shadow of globalization]. Beijing: Chinese Academy of Social Science Press, 1999.

Fearon, James, and David Laitin. "Explaining Interethnic Cooperation." *American Political Science Review* 90, 4 (December 1996): 715–35.

Feng Xiao. "Dui guoji xingshizhong jige redian wenti de kanfa" [Perspective on several hot issues in the international situation]. *Xiandai Guoji Guanxi* 12 (1999): 1–3.

Festinger, Leon. "A Theory of Social Comparison Processes." *Human Relations* 7 (1954): 117–40.

Fewsmith, Joseph. *China Since Tiananmen.* New York: Cambridge University Press, 2000.

———. "The Politics of China's Accession to the WTO." *Current History* 99, 638 (September 2000): 268–74.

Fewsmith, Joseph, and Stanley Rosen. "The Domestic Context of Chinese Foreign Policy: Does 'Public Opinion' Matter?" In *The Making of Chinese Foreign and Security Policy in the Era of Reform, 1978–2000*, ed. David M. Lampton, 151–87. Stanford: Stanford University Press, 2001.

Finnemore, Martha, and Kathryn Sikkink. "International Norm Dynamics and Political Change." *International Organization* 52, 4 (1998): 887–917.

Fischerkeller, Michael. "David Versus Goliath: The Influence of Cultural Judgments on Strategic Preference." Ph.D. diss., Ohio State University, 1997.

Foot, Rosemary. *The Practice of Power: U.S. Relations with China Since 1949.* Oxford: Clarendon Press, 1995.

———. *Rights Beyond Borders: The Global Community and the Struggle over Human Rights in China.* New York: Oxford University Press, 2000.

———. "Chinese Power and the Idea of a Responsible Power." *China Journal*, no. 45 (January 2001): 1–19.

Foyle, Douglas. "Public Opinion and Foreign Policy: Elite Beliefs as a Mediating Variable." *International Studies Quarterly* 41 (1997): 141–69.

Fravel, M. Taylor. "China's Attitude Toward UN Peacekeeping Operations." *Asian Survey* 36, 11 (November 1996): 1102–22.

———. "Online and on China: Research Sources in the Information Age." *China Quarterly*, no. 163 (September 2000): 841–42.

———. "The Long March to Peace: China and the Settlement of Territorial Disputes." Ph.D. diss., Stanford University, 2003.

———. "The Revolution in Research Affairs: Online Sources and the Study of the PLA." In *A Poverty of Riches: New Challenges and Opportunities in PLA Research*, ed. James C. Mulvenon and Andrew N. D. Yang. Santa Monica, Calif.: Rand Corporation, 2003.

French, Howard W. "Bush and New Korean Leader to Take up Thorny Issues." *New York Times*, 21 December 2002, A9.

———. "Threats and Responses: Asian Arena; Shifting Loyalties: Seoul Looks to New Alliances." *New York Times*, 26 January 2003, A15.

Freud, Sigmund. *Civilization and Its Discontents*. 1930. New York: Norton, 1961.

Fu Hao. "A Ruling Given by History—Marking the 25th Anniversary of China's Restoration of Its Legitimate Seat in United Nations." *Renmin Ribao*, translated in FBIS-CHI 96, 212, 23 October 1996, 6.

Funabashi, Y. "Tokyo's Depression Diplomacy." *Foreign Affairs* 77, 6 (November–December 1998): 26–36.

Galtung, Johan. "Conflict on a Global Scale: Social Imperialism and Sub-Imperialism—Continuities in the Structural Theory of Imperialism." *World Development* 4, 3 (March 1976): 153–65.

Gao Qiufu, ed., *Xiaoyan wei san: Kesuowo zhanzheng yu shijie geju* [The smoke did not disperse: the war in Kosovo and the world structure]. Beijing: Xinhua Chubanshe, 1999.

Gao Tian. "US Nuclear Submarines on Guam Target China." *Renminwang*, translated in FBIS-CHI, 29 March 2002. WNC Document No. 0GTY14D00R608T.

Garrett, Banning. "China Policy and the Strategic Triangle." In *Eagle Entangled: American Foreign Policy in a Complex World*, ed. Kenneth Oye. London: Longman, 1979.

———. "China Faces, Debates, the Contradictions of Globalization." *Asian Survey* 41, 3 (May–June 2001): 409–27.

Garrett, Banning, and Jonathan Adams. *U.S.-China Cooperation on the Problem of Failing States and Transnational Threats*. Special Report 126. Washington, D.C.: United States Institute of Peace, September 2004.

Garrett, Banning, and Bonnie S. Glaser. "Looking Across the Yalu: Chinese Assessments of North Korea." *Asian Survey* 35 (June 1995): 528–45.

———. "Chinese Apprehensions About Revitalization of the U.S.-Japan Alliance." *Asian Survey* 37, 4 (April 1997): 383–402.

Garrett, Stephen. *Doing Good and Doing Well: An Examination of Humanitarian Intervention*. Westport, Conn.: Praeger, 1999.

Garver, John W. *China's Decision for Rapprochement with the United States, 1968–1971*. Boulder, Colo.: Westview Press, 1982.

———. "The Chinese Communist Party and the Collapse of Soviet Communism." *China Quarterly*, no. 133 (March 1993): 1–26.

———. *Protracted Contest: Sino-Indian Rivalry in the Twentieth Century*. Seattle: University of Washington Press, 2001.

———. "The Restoration of Sino-Indian Comity Following India's Nuclear Tests," *China Quarterly*, no. 168 (December 2001): 865–89.

———. *The China-India-U.S. Triangle: Strategic Relations in the Post-Cold War Era*. Seattle: National Bureau of Asian Research, 2002.

———. "Sino-American Relations in 2001: The Difficult Accommodation of Two Great Powers." *International Journal* 57, 2 (Spring 2002): 283–310.

George, Alexander L., and Richard Smoke. *Deterrence in American Foreign Policy: Theory and Practice*. New York: Columbia University Press, 1974.

Gertz, Bill. *The China Threat: How the People's Republic Targets America*. Washington, D.C.: Regnery, 2000.

Gill, Bates. "Two Steps Forward, One Step Back: The Dynamics of Chinese Nonproliferation and Arms Control." In *The Making of Chinese Foreign and Security Policy in the Era of Reform, 1978–2000*, ed. David M. Lampton, 257–88. Stanford: Stanford University Press, 2001.

Gill, Bates, and James Reilly. "Sovereignty, Intervention and Peacekeeping: The View from Beijing." *Survival* 42, 2 (2000): 41–59.

Gilpin, Robert. *War and Change in World Politics*. Cambridge: Cambridge University Press, 1981.

Glaser, Bonnie, and Phillip Saunders. "Chinese Civilian Foreign Policy Research Institutes: Evolving Roles and Increasing Influence." *China Quarterly*, no. 171 (September 2002): 597–616.

Glaser, Charles L. "The Security Dilemma Revisited." *World Politics* 50, 1 (1997): 171–201.

Glosserman, Brad. "Troubling Signs for Japan-China Relations." *Pac Net* 37 (2 September 2004): 1–2.

Goldstein, Avery. "Discounting the Free Ride: Alliances and Security in the Postwar World." *International Organization* 49, 1 (Winter 1995): 39–72.

———. "Great Expectations: Interpreting China's Arrival." *International Security* 22, 3 (Winter 1997–98): 36–73.

———. *Deterrence and Security in the 21st Century: China, Britain, France, and the Enduring Legacy of the Nuclear Revolution.* Stanford: Stanford University Press, 2000.

———. "The Diplomatic Face of China's Grand Strategy: A Rising Power's Emerging Choice." *China Quarterly*, no. 168 (December 2001): 835–64.

———. *Rising to the Challenge: China's Grand Strategy and International Security.* Stanford: Stanford University Press, 2005.

Goldstein, Judith. "International Institutions and Domestic Politics: GATT, WTO, and the Liberalization of International Trade." In *The WTO as an International Organization*, ed. Anne O. Krueger. Chicago: University of Chicago Press, 1998.

Goldstein, Lyle. "Research Report: Return to Zhenbao Island: Who Started Shooting and Why Does It Matter." *China Quarterly*, no. 168 (December 2001): 985–97.

Goldstein, Steven M. "Nationalism and Internationalism: Sino-Soviet Relations." In *Chinese Foreign Policy: Theory and Practice*, ed. Thomas W. Robinson and David Shambaugh, 224–65. Oxford: Clarendon Press, 1994.

Goncharov, Sergei, John Lewis, and Xue Litai. *Uncertain Partners: Stalin, Mao, and the Korean War*, 76–130. Stanford: Stanford University Press, 1993.

Gong, Li. "Chinese Decision Making." In *Re-examining the Cold War: U.S.-China Diplomacy, 1954–73*, ed. Robert S. Ross and Jiang Changbin. Cambridge, Mass.: Harvard University Asia Center, 2001.

———. "Tension Across the Taiwan Strait." In *Re-examining the Cold War: U.S.-China Diplomacy, 1954–73*, ed. Robert S. Ross and Jiang Changbin. Cambridge, Mass.: Harvard University Asia Center, 2001.

Gong Wen and Shi Guangsheng. "Changes Take Place over the Past Half Year since China WTO Entry." *Renmin Ribao* online, 12 July 2002, http://english.peopledaily.com.cn/200207/11/eng20020711_99541.shtml (accessed 3 October 2005).

Goodman, David S. G. "The New Middle Class." In *The Paradox of Post-Mao Reforms*, ed. Merle Goldman and Roderick MacFarquhar. Cambridge, Mass.: Harvard University Press, 1999.

Green, Michael J. *Japan's Reluctant Realism: Foreign Policy Challenges in an Era of Uncertain Power.* New York: Palgrave, 2001.

Green, Michael J., and Patrick Cronin, eds. *The U.S.-Japan Alliance: Past, Present, and Future.* New York: Council on Foreign Relations Press, 1999.

Gries, Peter Hays. "A 'China Threat'? Power and Passion in Chinese 'Face Nationalism.' " *World Affairs* 162, 2 (Fall 1999): 63–75.

———. "Tears of Rage: Chinese Nationalist Reactions to the Belgrade Embassy Bombing." *China Journal*, no. 46 (2001): 25–43.

———. *China's New Nationalism: Pride, Politics, and Diplomacy.* Berkeley: University of California Press, 2004.

———. "China's 'New Thinking' on Japan." *China Quarterly*, no. 184 (December 2005): 831–50.

Gries, Peter Hays, and Peng Kaiping. "Culture Clash? Apologies East and West." *Journal of Contemporary China* 11, 30 (2002): 173–78.

Gries, Peter Hays, and Stanley Rosen. *State and Society in 21st Century China: Crisis, Contention, and Legitimation.* New York: RoutledgeCurzon, 2004.

Gubrium, Jaber F., and James A. Holstein, eds. *Handbook of Interview Research: Context and Method.* Thousand Oaks, Calif.: Sage Publications, 2001.

Guo Dafang. "Kexue jishu shi gao jishu jubu zhanzheng shouyao de zhisheng yinsu" [Science and technology is the first factor in subduing the enemy in high-technology local war]. *Zhongguo Junshi Kexue*, no. 6 (2000).

Guo Danqun. "Chinese Holding Foreign Passport Superior to Other Chinese?" *China News Digest—US*, 3 April 1999. www.cnd.org/CND-US/CND-US.99/CND-US.99-04-03.html (accessed 2 October 2005).

Guo Ming, ed. *ZhongYue guanxi yanbian sishinian* [Forty-year evolution of Sino-Vietnamese relations]. Nanning: Guangxi People's Publishers, May 1992. Internally circulated.

Gurr, Ted. *Why Men Rebel.* Princeton, N.J.: Princeton University Press, 1970.

Gurtov, Melvin, and Byong-Moon Hwang. *China Under Threat: The Politics of Strategy and Diplomacy.* Baltimore: Johns Hopkins University Press, 1980.

Haas, Ernst B., and Allen S. Whiting. *Dynamics of International Relations.* New York: McGraw-Hill, 1956.

Hagan, Joe D. "Domestic Political Systems and War Proneness." *Mershon International Studies Review* 38, 2 (October 1994).

Han Deqiang. *Pengzhuang: quanqiuhua xianjin yu Zhongguo xianshi xuanze* [Collusion: the trap of globalization and China's realistic choices]. Beijing: Economic Management Publishing House, 2000.

Hao, Yufan, and Zhai Zhihai. "China's Decision to Enter the Korean War: History Revisited." *China Quarterly*, no. 121 (March 1990): 94–115.

Harris, Stuart. "China and the Pursuit of State Interests in a Globalizing World." *Pacifica Review* 13, 1 (February 2001): 15–29.

He, Di. "The Evolution of the People's Republic of China's Policy Toward the Offshore Islands (Quemoy, Matsu)." In *The Great Powers in East Asia, 1953–60*, ed. Warren I. Cohen and Akira Iriye, 222–45. New York: Columbia University Press, 1990.

Heer, Paul. "A House United." *Foreign Affairs* 79, 4 (July–August 2000): 18–25.

Heinzig, Dieter. "Stalin, Mao, Kim and Korean War Origins, 1950: A Russian Document Discrepancy." *Cold War International History Project Bulletin* [Woodrow Wilson International Center for Scholars, Washington, D.C.], no. 8–9 (Winter 1996–97).

Held, David, and Anthony McGrew, eds. *The Global Transformations Reader: An Introduction to the Globalization Debate.* Cambridge: Polity Press, 2000.

Held, David, Anthony McGrew, David Goldblatt, and Jonathan Perraton. *Global Transformations: Politics, Economics and Culture.* Stanford: Stanford University Press, 1999.

Hemmer, Christopher, and Peter Katzenstein. "Why Is There No NATO in Asia?

Collective Identity, Regionalism and the Origins of Multilateralism." *International Organization* 56, 3 (Summer 2002): 575–607.

Hermann, Margaret, and Charles Hermann. "Who Makes Foreign Policy Decisions and How: An Empirical Inquiry." *International Studies Quarterly* 33, 4 (December 1989): 361–87.

Hirshman, Albert O. *National Power and the Structure of Foreign Trade.* Berkeley: University of California Press, 1980.

Hirst, Paul, and Grahame Thompson. *Globalization in Question?* Cambridge: Polity Press, 1996.

Hirt, Edward R., Dolf Zillmann, Grant A. Erickson, and Chris Kennedy. "Costs and Benefits of Allegiance: Changes in Fans' Self-Ascribed Competencies After Team Victory Versus Defeat." *Journal of Personality & Social Psychology* 63, 5 (1992): 724–38.

Hoffman, Steven A. *India and the China Crisis.* Berkeley: University of California Press, 1990.

Hogg, Michael A., and Dominic Abrams. "Towards a Single-Process Uncertainty-Reduction Model of Social Motivation in Groups." In *Group Motivation: Social Psychological Perspectives*, ed. Hogg and Abrams, 173–90. New York: Harvester Wheatsheaf, 1993.

Holland, John H. *Hidden Order: How Adaptation Builds Complexity.* Reading, Mass.: Addison-Wesley, 1995.

Hong Xuezhi. *KangMei yuanChao zhanzheng huiyi* [Recollections of the war to resist U.S. aggression and to aid Korea]. Beijing: Liberation Army Literature and Art Publishing, 1990.

Holsti, Ole R. "Public Opinion and Foreign Policy: Challenges to the Almost-Lippman Consensus." *International Studies Quarterly* 36 (1992): 439–66.

Hopf, Ted. "The Promise of Constructivism in International Relations Theory." *International Security* 23, 1 (Summer 1998): 171–200.

Hornby, Lucy. "EU, China Clinch Deal to Avert Textiles Showdown." Reuters, 10 June 2005. www.reuters.com/newsArticle.jhtml?storyID=8759653&type=businessNews (accessed June 10, 2005).

Hu Angang, Yang Fan, and Zhu Ning. *Daguo zhanlue: Zhongguo de liyi yu shimin* [China's grand strategy: missions and interests]. Shenyang: Liaoning People's Press, 2000.

Hu Guanping. "Kexue jishu shi diyi zhandouli" [Science and technology are the primary combat power]. *Zhongguo Junshi Kexue*, no. 3, 2000.

Hu, Hsien-chin. "The Chinese Concepts of 'Face.'" *American Anthropologist* 46 (1944): 45–64.

Hu, Weixing. "Beijing's Defense Strategy and the Korean Peninsula." *Journal of Northeast Asian Studies* 14, 3 (1995): 50–67.

Hudson, Valerie M., and Andrea Den Boer. "A Surplus of Men: A Deficit of Peace Security and Sex Ratios in Asia's Largest States." *International Security* 26, 4 (Spring 2002): 5–38.

Hughes, Christopher. "Globalisation and Nationalism: Squaring the Circle in Chinese International Relations Theory." *Millennium: Journal of International Studies* 26, 1 (1997): 103–24.

Hunt, Michael. "Beijing and the Korea Crisis." *Political Science Quarterly* 107, 3 (Autumn 1992): 453–78.

Huntington, Samuel P. "The Clash of Civilizations?" *Foreign Affairs* 72, 3 (Summer 1993): 22–49.

Huth, Paul K. *Extended Deterrence and the Prevention of Local War*. New Haven, Conn.: Yale University Press, 1988.

———. "Reputations and Deterrence: A Theoretical and Empirical Assessment." *Security Studies* 7, 1 (Autumn 1997): 72–99.

Hyde, Charles K. "Casuality Aversion: Implications for Policy Makers and Senior Military Officers." *Aerospace Power Journal*, Summer 2000, 17–27. www .airpower.maxwell.af.mil/airchronicles/apj/apj00/sum00/hyde.pdf (accessed 10 October 2005).

Inayatullah, Naeem, and David Blaney. "Knowing Encounters: Beyond Parochialism in International Relations Theory." In *The Return of Culture and Identity in IR Theory*, ed. Yosef Lapid and Friedrich Kratochwil, 65–84. Boulder, Colo.: Lynne Rienner, 1996.

Institute of International and Strategic Studies. Summary of Institute of International and Strategic Studies 42nd Annual Conference, Manila, 14–17 September 2000, by David Dickens. www.vuw.ac.nz/css/docs/reports/IISS.html (accessed 2 October 2005).

Institute of National Affairs, Delhi. *Dalai Lama and India: Indian Public and Prime Minister on Tibetan Crisis*. New Delhi: Hind Book House, 1959.

International Commission on Intervention and State Sovereignty. *The Responsibility to Protect: Research, Bibliography, Background: Supplementary Volume to the Report of the International Commission on Intervention and State Sovereignty*. Ottawa: International Development Research Centre, 2001.

Ito, Naoto. "China's Decision and Strategy Toward the Normalization with Japan." MA thesis, Harvard University, Regional Studies East Asia, 2005.

Jackson, Richard, and Neil Howe. "The Graying of the Middle Kingdom: The Demographics and Economics of Retirement Policy in China." Presentation at the Center for International and Strategic Studies, 25 May 2004.

Jacobson, Harold, and Michel Oksenberg. *China's Participation in the IMF, the World Bank, and GATT*. Ann Arbor: University of Michigan Press, 1990.

Jain, R. K. *China and South Asian Relations, 1947–1980*. Vol. 1. New Delhi and Brighton, Eng.: Harvester Press, 1981.

Janis, Irving L. *Groupthink: Psychological Studies of Policy Decisions and Fiascoes*. Boston: Houghton Mifflin, 1983.

Jencks, Harlan W. "China's 'Punitive' War on Vietnam: A Military Assessment." *Asian Survey* 19, 8 (August 1979): 801–15.

Jervis, Robert. "Hypotheses on Misperception." *World Politics* 20, 3 (April 1968): 454–79.

———. *The Logic of Images in International Relations*. Princeton, N.J.: Princeton University Press, 1970.

———. *Perception and Misperception in International Politics*. Princeton, N.J.: Princeton University Press, 1976.

———. "Cooperation Under the Security Dilemma." *World Politics* 30, 2 (January 1978): 167–214.

———. "Deterrence and Perception." In *Strategy and Nuclear Deterrence*, ed. Steven E. Miller. Princeton, N.J.: Princeton University Press, 1984.

———. *The Illogic of American Nuclear Strategy*. New York: Columbia University Press, 1984.

———. "Theories of War in an Era of Leading-Power Peace." *American Political Science Review* 96, 1 (March 2002): 1–14.

Jia, Qingguo. *Zhongguo bu jinjin shuobu* [China should not just say no]. Beijing: Zhonghua Gongshang Lianhe Chubanshe, 1996.

———. "Frustrations and Hopes: Chinese Perceptions of the Engagement Policy Debate in the U.S." *Journal of Contemporary China* 27 (2001): 321–30.

Jiang Zemin. "Speech at the Meeting Celebrating the 80th Anniversary of the Founding of the Communist Party of China." 1 July 2001. http://news.xinhuanet .com/english/ztbd/cpc80/ (accessed November 22, 2005).

Jin Hui. "Geng zhongyao de shi minzu jingshen shijie de chongjian" [More important is the reconstruction of a national psychological world]. In *Zhongguo ruhe miandui xifang* [How China faces the West], ed. Xiao Pang, 182–98. Hong Kong: Mirror Books, 1979.

Jin Niu. "Zhongguo ruhe shuobu?" [How should China say no?]. In *Zhongguo ruhe shuobu?* [How should China say no?]. Special edition of *Meiguo Daguan* [America the Beautiful]. Beijing: Chinese Academy of Social Science, Institute of American Studies, 1996.

"Jiu Zhong-Han guanxi, Zhongguo dui chaoxian bandao zhengce wenti, Li Peng jieshou Hanguo jizhe caifang" [On China-ROK relations, Li Peng takes questions from visiting ROK reporters about China's policy toward the Korean peninsula and other matters]. *Renmin Ribao*, 26 February 1995.

Johnston, Alastair Iain. *Cultural Realism: Strategic Culture and Grand Strategy in Chinese History*. Princeton, N.J.: Princeton University Press, 1995.

———. "Learning Versus Adaptation: Explaining Change in Chinese Arms Control Policy in the 1980s and 1990s." *China Journal*, no. 35 (January 1996): 27–61.

———. "Engaging Myths: Misconceptions About China and Its Global Role." *Harvard Asia Pacific Review*, Winter 1997–98, 9–12.

———. "China's Militarized Interstate Dispute Behaviour, 1949–1992: A First Cut at the Data." *China Quarterly*, no. 153 (March 1998): 1–30.

———. "Realism(s) and Chinese Security Policy in the Post-Cold War Period. " In *Unipolar Politics: Realism and State Strategies After the Cold War*, ed. Ethan B. Kapstein and Michael Mastanduno, 261–318. New York: Columbia University Press, 1999.

———. "Treating International Institutions as Social Environments." *International Studies Quarterly* 45 (2001): 487–515.

———. "The Social Effects of International Institutions on Domestic (Foreign Policy) Actors." In *Locating the Proper Authorities: The Interaction of Domestic and International Institutions*, ed. Daniel Drezner. Ann Arbor: University of Michigan Press, 2002.

———. "Is China a Status Quo Power?" *International Security* 27, 4 (2003): 5–56.

———. "China's International Relations: The Political and Security Dimension." In *The International Relations of Northeast Asia*, ed. Samuel S. Kim, ch. 2. Lanham, Md.: Rowman & Littlefield, 2004.

———. "Chinese Middle Class Attitudes Towards International Affairs: Nascent Liberalization?" *China Quarterly*, no. 179 (September 2004): 603–28.

———. *Social States: China in International Security Institutions, 1980–2000.* Forthcoming.

Johnston, Alastair Iain, and Paul Evans. "China's Engagement in International Security Institutions." In *Engaging China: Management of an Emerging Power*, ed. Alastair Iain Johnston and Robert Ross, 235–72. London: Routledge, 1999.

Jones, Edward E. "Major Developments in Five Decades of Social Psychology." In *The Handbook of Social Psychology*, 4th ed., ed. Daniel Gilbert, Susan Fiske, and Gardner Lindsey, vol. 1. Boston: McGraw-Hill, 1998.

Kahneman, Daniel, and Amos Tversky. "Prospect Theory: An Analysis of Decision Under Risk." *Econometrica* 47 (1979): 263–91.

Kalathil, Shanthi. "Dot Com for Dictators." *Foreign Policy*, no. 135 (March–April 2003): 43–49.

Kalkhoff, William, and Christopher Barnum. "The Effects of Status-Organizing and Social Identity Processes on Patterns of Social Influence." *Social Psychology Quarterly* 63, 2 (2000): 95–115.

Kan, Shirley A. *China: Ballistic and Cruise Missiles.* CRS Report for Congress, 97–391 F. Washington, D.C.: Congressional Research Service, Library of Congress, 2000.

Kang, David. "North Korea's Military and Security Policy." In *North Korean Foreign Relations in the Post-Cold War Era*, ed. Samuel Kim. New York: Oxford University Press, 1998.

———. "The Dog That Didn't Bark: Why North Korea Hasn't Attacked in Fifty Years and What International Relations Theorists Can Learn." Unpublished paper, n.d.

Kant, Immanuel. *Critique of Pure Reason.* 1781. Translated and edited by Paul Guyer and Allen W. Wood. New York: Cambridge University Press, 1998.

Kanth, D. Ravi. "China: The New and 'Pushy' Boy on the Block." *Asia Times* (online), 7 February 2002. www.atimes.com/china/DB07Ad01.html (accessed November 22, 2005).

Katzenstein, Peter, ed. *The Culture of National Security: Norms and Identity in World Politics.* New York: Columbia University Press, 1996.

Kaufmann, William W. "The Requirements of Deterrence." In *Military Policy and National Security*, ed. William W. Kaufmann. Princeton, N.J.: Princeton University Press, 1956.

Kaviraj, Sudipta. "The Imaginary Institution of India." In *Subaltern Studies VII*, ed. Partha Chatterjee and Gyanendra Pandley, 1–39. New York: Oxford University Press, 1992.

Kennedy, Paul M. *The Rise and Fall of the Great Powers: Economic Change and Military Conflict from 1500 to 2000.* New York: Random House, 1987.

Kent, Ann. *China, the United Nations, and Human Rights: The Limits of Compliance.* Philadelphia: University of Pennsylvania Press, 1999.

Keohane, Robert O., and Joseph Nye. *Power and Interdependence: World Politics in Transition.* Boston: Little, Brown, 1977.

Khong, Yuen Foong. *Analogies at War: Korea, Munich, Dien Bien Phu, and the Vietnam Decisions of 1965.* Princeton, N.J.: Princeton University Press, 1992.

Khor, Martin. "Developing Countries Prepare for Agricultural Battle at Cancun Ministerial." *TWN Report,* 9 September 2003.

Kim Ji-ho. "China's Envoy to ROK: US Troops in Korea Must Not Pose Threat to Neighbors." *Korea Herald,* 21 August 2002. FBIS-EAS, Article Id: KPP20020821000113.

"Kim Jong-Il Visits China, Meets Jiang." *Xinhua,* 1 June 2000. FBIS-CHI, WNC Document No. 0FVJ2AX01T3OZN.

Kim, Kyoung-Soo. "North Korea's CB Programs: Threat and Capability." *Korean Journal of Defense Analysis* 14, 1 (Spring 2002): 69–95.

Kim, Samuel S. *China, the United Nations, and World Order.* Princeton, N.J.: Princeton University Press, 1979.

——. *China In and Out of the Changing World Order.* Princeton, N.J.: Center of International Studies, Princeton University, 1991.

——. "China's International Organization Behavior." In *Chinese Foreign Policy: Theory and Practice,* ed. Thomas Robinson and David Shambaugh. Oxford: Clarendon Press, 1994.

——. "China and the United Nations." In *China Joins the World: Progress and Prospects,* ed. Elizabeth Economy and Michel Oksenberg, 42–89. New York: Council on Foreign Relations Press, 1999.

——. *East Asia and Globalization.* Lanham, Md.: Rowman & Littlefield, 2000.

——. "Human Rights in China's International Relations." In *What If China Doesn't Democratize?* ed. Edward Friedman and Barrett McCormick, 129–62. Armonk, N.Y.: M. E. Sharpe, 2000.

——. *Korea's Globalization.* New York: Cambridge University Press, 2000.

——, ed. *China and the World: Chinese Foreign Policy Faces the New Millennium.* Boulder, Colo.: Westview Press, 1998.

——, ed. *The International Relations of Northeast Asia.* Lanham, Md.: Rowman & Littlefield, 2004.

Kim, Soo Yeon. "Structure and Change in International Trade and Militarized Conflict: When Is Engagement Constructive?" Unpublished paper, 1999.

Kinder, Donald R., and David O. Sears. "Prejudice and Politics: Symbolic Racism Versus Racial Threats to the Good Life." *Journal of Personality & Social Psychology* 40, 3 (1981): 414–31.

Kinnvall, Catarina, and Kristina Jonsson, eds. *Globalization and Democratization in Asia: The Construction of Identity.* London: Routledge, 2002.

Kissinger, Henry A. *The Necessity for Choice: Prospects of American Foreign Policy.* New York: Harper & Brothers, 1960.

Klein, Donald W., and Anne B. Clark. *Biographic Dictionary of Chinese Communism, 1921–1965.* 2 vols. Cambridge, Mass.: Harvard University Press, 1971.

Knaus, John K. *Orphans of the Cold War: America and the Tibetan Struggle for Survival.* New York: Public Affairs, 1999.

Kokubun, Ryosei, ed. *Challenges for China-Japan Cooperation.* Tokyo: Japan Center for International Exchange, 1998.

Kowert, Paul A. "The Construction of National Identity." In *International Relations in a Constructed World*, ed. Vendulka Kubalkova et al., 101–22. Armonk, N.Y.: M. E. Sharpe, 1998.

Kowert, Paul A., and Margaret G. Hermann. "Who Takes Risks? Daring and Caution in Foreign Policy Making." *Journal of Conflict Resolution* 41, 5 (October 1997): 611–37.

Krasner, Stephen. "Compromising Westphalia." *International Security* 20, 3 (1995): 115–51.

———. "Globalization and Sovereignty." In *States and Sovereignty in the Global Economy*, ed. David A. Smith, Dorothy J. Solinger, and Steven Topik, 34–52. London: Routledge, 1999.

———. *Sovereignty: Organized Hypocrisy.* Princeton, N.J.: Princeton University Press, 1999.

Krueger, Anne O., ed. *The WTO as an International Organization.* Chicago: University of Chicago Press, 1998.

Kull, Steven, and I. M. Destler. *Misreading the Public: The Myths of a New Isolationism.* Washington, D.C.: Brookings Institution Press, 1999. brookings.nap.edu/books/0815717652/html/index.html (accessed 2 October 2005).

Lampton, David M., ed. *The Making of Chinese Foreign and Security Policy in the Era of Reform, 1978–2000.* Stanford: Stanford University Press, 2001.

Lampton, David M., and Richard Daniel Ewing. *U.S.-China Relations in a Post–September 11th World.* Washington, D.C.: Nixon Center, 2002.

Lardy, Nicholas R. *China in the World Economy.* Washington, D.C.: Institute for International Economics, 1994.

———. *Integrating China into the Global Economy.* Washington, D.C.: Brookings Institution Press, 2002.

Larkin, Bruce D. *China and Africa, 1949–1970: The Foreign Policy of the People's Republic of China.* Berkeley: University of California Press, 1971.

Latham, Robert. *The Liberal Moment: Modernity, Security, and the Making of Postwar International Order.* New York: Columbia University Press, 1997.

Le Bon, Gustave. *The Crowd: A Study of the Popular Mind.* London: Ernest Benn, 1896.

Lee, Chung Min. "Coping with the North Korean Missile Threat: Implications for Northeast Asia and Korea." In *Emerging Threats, Force Structures, and the Role of Air Power in Korea*, ed. Natalie Crawford and Chung-in Moon. Santa Monica, Calif.: Rand Corporation, 2000.

Lei Yingfu. *Zai zuigao zongshuaibu dang sanmo—Lei Yingfu jiangjun huiyilu* [Serving on the staff of the high command—memoir of General Lei Yingfu]. Nanchang: Baihuazhou Wenyi Chubanshe, 1997.

Levine, Steven I. "Perception and Ideology in the Study of Chinese Foreign Policy." In *Chinese Foreign Policy: Theory and Practice*, ed. Thomas W. Robinson and David Shambaugh, 30–46. Oxford: Clarendon Press, 1994.

Levy, Jack S. "Declining Power and the Preventive Motivation for War." *World Politics* 40, 1 (October 1987): 82–107.

Lewis, Justin. *Constructing Public Opinion: How Political Elites Do What They Like and Why We Seem to Go Along With It*. New York: Columbia University Press, 2001.

Li Buyun. "Renquan de liangge lilun wenti [Two theoretical human rights issues]. *Faxue Yanjiu* 3 (1994).

Li Danhui. "ZhongSu guanxi yu Zhongguo de yuanYue kang Mei" [Sino-Soviet relations and the Aid Vietnam, Resist America War]. *Dangshi Yanjiu Ziliao*, no. 251 (June 1998): 1–18. Internally circulated.

Li Fang. "Chongjian Zhongguo youxi guize" [Rewriting China's rules of the game]. *Zuojia Tiandi* [Writer's World], special issue (1996): 21–30.

Li Haibo. "China and Its Century." *Beijing Review* 42, 42 (18 October 1999): 11–16.

Li, Jian, and Niu Xiaohan. "The New Middle Class in Beijing: A Case Study." Centre for East and Southeast Asian Studies, Lund University. Unpublished paper, 2001.

Li Jie. "She Is Not Superior to Her Own People." *China News Digest—US*, 3 April 1999. www.cnd.org/CND-US/CND-US.99/CND-US.99-04-03.html (accessed 2 October 2005).

Li Ming. " 'Lianheguo xianzhang' zhong de renquan yu bu ganshe neizheng wenti" [The issue of noninterference in internal affairs in the UN Charter]. *Zhongguo Faxue* 3 (1993).

Li Shenzhi. "Fear Under Numerical Superiority." *Dushu* [Reading] (Beijing), no. 6 (June 1997), 31–38. Translated in FBIS-CHI-97-296 (23 October 1997).

Li Xiguang, Liu Kang, et al. *Yaomohua Zhongguo de beihou* [The plot to demonize China]. Beijing: Zhongguo Shehui Kexue Chubanshe, 1996.

Li Yueran. *Waijiao wutaishang de xin Zhongguo lingxiu* [The leaders of new China on the diplomatic stage]. Beijing: Liberation Army Press, 1989.

Li Yunfei. "Zhou Enlai Was the Most Outstanding Politician—Interviewing Former U.S. Secretary of State Dr. Kissinger." *Renmin Ribao*, 3 March 1998, 6. Translated in FBIS-CHI-98-089 (30 March 1998).

Li Zhenguang. "Renquan yu zhuquan guanxi de lishi kaocha yu sikao" [An investigation and reflection on the historical relationship between sovereignty and human rights]. *Taipingyang Xuebao* [Pacific Journal] 1 (2001).

Liang Qianxiang, chief ed. *KangMei yuanChao zhanzheng huajuan* [A pictorial history of the war of resistance against America in aid of Korea]. Beijing: KangMei YuanChao Jinianguan and Zhongguo Wenlian Chuban Gongsi, 1990.

Lieberthal, Kenneth. "Domestic Politics and Foreign Policy." In *China's Foreign Policy in the 1980s*, ed. Harry Harding, 43–70. New Haven, Conn.: Yale University Press, 1984.

Lindsay, James M., and Michael E. O'Hanlon. *Defending America: The Case for Limited National Missile Defense*. Washington, D.C.: Brookings Institution Press, 2001.

Liu Aimin. "Xinxihua zhanzheng tezheng tantao" [Inquiry into the characteristics of the information transformation of war]. *Zhongguo Junshi Kexue* [China Military Science], no. 3 (2000): 72.

Liu Enzhao. "Lianheguo weichi heping xingdong" [UN peacekeeping forces]. *Guoji Wenti Yanjiu* [Journal of International Studies] 2 (1989): 53–61.

Liu Jianyong. "China and the Renewal of the U.S.-Japan Security Treaty." In *Japan and China: Rivalry or Cooperation in East Asia?* ed. Peter Drysdale and Dong Dong Zhang, 95–114. Canberra: Australia-Japan Research Centre, 2000.

Liu Xiao. *Chu shi Sulian ba nian* [Eight years as ambassador to the Soviet Union]. Beijing: Zhonggong Dangshi Ziliao Chubanshe, 1986.

Liu Yijian. "Zhongguo weilai de haijun jianshe yu haijun zhanlue" [China's future naval construction and naval strategy]. *Zhanlue yu Guanli*, no. 5 (1999): 99–100.

———. *Zhi haiquan yu haijun zhanlue* [Command of the sea and strategic employ-ment of naval forces]. Beijing: Guofang Daxue Chubanshe, 2000.

Liu Zhengxue, and Wang Linchang. "Zhu Rongji tong Jin Dazhong huitan, shuang-fang jiu shuangbian guanxi he diqu wenti jiaohuanle yijian" [Zhu Rongji and Kim Dae Jung hold talks, the two sides exchange opinions on bilateral relations and regional issues]. *Renmin Ribao*, 19 October 2000, 1.

Lowe, Will. "Software for Content Analysis: A Review." Harvard Identity Pro-ject paper, 2002. www.wcfia.harvard.edu/misc/initiative/identity/publications/content_analysis.pdf (accessed 19 October 2005).

Lu Junhua. *Lun Ah Q jingshen shenglifa de zheli he xinli neihan* [On the philo-sophical and psychological meaning of Ah Q's psychological victory technique]. Xi'an: Shaanxi Renmin Chubanshe, 1982.

Lu Yi, et al., eds. *Qiuji: yige shijiexing de xuanze* [Global citizenship: a worldwide choice]. Shanghai: Baijia Chubanshe, 1989.

Lu Youzhi. "Chongxin shenshi Zhongguo de anquan huanjing" [A fresh examina-tion of China's security environment]. *Shijie Jingji yu Zhengzhi* [World Econom-ics and Politics], no. 1 (2000): 56–61.

Luhtanen, Riia, and Jennifer Crocker. "Self-Esteem and Intergroup Comparison: Towards a Theory of Collective Self-esteem." In *Social Comparison: Contempo-rary Theory and Research*, ed. Jerry Suls and Thomas Ashby Wills, 211–36. Hillsdale, N.J.: Lawrence Erlbaum Associates, 1991.

Lum, Thomas. "The Marginalization of Political Activism in China." Paper pre-pared for the American Political Science Association Annual Meeting, San Francisco, 30 August–2 September 2001.

Ma, Ying. "China's America Problem." *Policy Review*, no. 111 (February–March 2002). www.policyreview.org/FEB02/ma.html (accessed 11 October 2005).

Ma, Yu. "China Belongs to No Trade Group." *Asian Wall Street Journal*, 25 Sep-tember 2003, A11.

MacFarquhar, Roderick. *The Origins of the Cultural Revolution: The Coming of the Cataclysm, 1961–1966*. Vol. 3. Oxford: Oxford University Press; New York: Columbia University Press, 1997.

Major, Brenda. "From Social Inequality to Personal Entitlement: The Role of Social Comparisons, Legitimacy Appraisals, and Group Membership." *Advances in Experimental Social Psychology* 26 (1994): 293–55.

Mansfield, Edward D., and Jack Snyder. "Democratization and the Danger of War." *International Security* 20, 1 (Summer 1995): 5–38.

————. "Democratic Transitions, Institutional Strength, and War." *International Organization* 56, 2 (Spring 2002): 297–337.

Mansourov, Alexandre Y. "Stalin, Mao, Kim, and China's Decision to Enter the Korean War, September 16–October 15, 1950: New Evidence from the Russian Archives." *Cold War International History Project Bulletin* [Woodrow Wilson International Center for Scholars, Washington, D.C.], no. 6–7 (Winter 1995–96): 94–119.

Mao Xuncheng. "Chaoxian bandao jushi de fanfu ji qi yuanyin" [The causes of the recurrent situation on the Korean peninsula]. *Shanghai Shifan Daxue Xuebao*, 1996, 100–102.

Mao, Zedong. *Selected Works of Mao Tse-Tung.* Vol. 1. Peking: Foreign Languages Press, 1965.

————. "Mao Zedong sixiang wansui" (Long live Mao Zedong thought). In *Miscellany of Mao Tse-tong Thought (1949–1968)*, no. 61269 (20 February 1974). Joint Publications Research Service.

————. *Jianguo yilai Mao Zedong wengao* [Mao's manuscripts since the establishment of the country]. Beijing: Zhongyang Wenxian Chubanshe 1987–.

Mastanduno, Michael. "Incomplete Hegemony and Security Order in the Asia-Pacific." In *America Unrivaled: The Future of the Balance of Power*, ed. G. John Ikenberry, 181–210. Ithaca, N.Y.: Cornell University Press, 2002.

Mastanduno, Michael, ed. *Unipolar Politics: Realism and State Strategies After the Cold War.* New York: Columbia University Press, 1999.

Maxwell, Neville. *India's China War.* New York: Random House, 1970.

May, Ernest R. *"Lessons" of the Past: The Use and Misuse of History in American Foreign Policy.* New York: Oxford University Press, 1973.

McCormick, Barrett. "Introduction." In *What If China Doesn't Democratize: Implications for War and Peace*, ed. Edward Friedman and Barrett L. McCormick. Armonk, N.Y.: M. E. Sharpe, 2000.

McCracken, Grant. *The Long Interview.* Beverly Hills, Calif.: Sage Publications, 1988.

McDevitt, Michael. "Engagement with North Korea: Implications for the United States." In *North Korea's Engagement—Perspectives, Outlook, and Implications*, ed. United States National Intelligence Council. Washington, D.C.: National Intelligence Council, 2001.

Mead, George H. *Mind, Self, and Society.* 1934. Chicago: University of Chicago Press, 1965.

Mearsheimer, John. *The Tragedy of Great Power Politics.* New York: Norton, 2001.

Medeiros, Evan S. "Undressing the Dragon: Researching the PLA Through Open Source Exploitation." In *A Poverty of Riches: New Challenges and Opportunities in PLA Research*, ed. James C. Mulvenon and Andrew N. D. Yang. Santa Monica, Calif.: Rand Corporation, 2003.

————. *Shaping Chinese Foreign Policy: The Evolution of Chinese Policies on WMD Nonproliferation and the Role of U.S. Policy, 1980–2004.* Forthcoming.

Medeiros, Evan S., and M. Taylor Fravel. "China's New Diplomacy." *Foreign Affairs* 82, 6 (November–December 2003): 22–35.

"Memorandum of Conversation of N. S. Khrushchev with Mao Zedong, Beijing, 2 October 1959." *Cold War International History Project Bulletin* [Woodrow Wilson International Center for Scholars, Washington, D.C.], no. 12–13 (Fall–Winter 2001).

Mendl, Wolf. *Issues in Japan's China Policy.* London: Macmillan for Royal Institute of International Affairs, 1978.

Mercer, Jonathan. "Anarchy and Identity." *International Organization* 49, 2 (Spring 1995): 229–52.

———. "Approaching Emotion in International Politics." Paper presented at the International Studies Association annual meeting, San Diego, 25 April 1996.

———. *Reputation and International Politics.* Ithaca, N.Y.: Cornell University Press, 1996.

———. "Reputation and Rational Deterrence Theory." *Security Studies* 7, 1 (Autumn 1997): 100–113.

Miller, Steven E., Sean M. Lynn-Jones, and Stephen Van Evera, eds. *Military Strategy and the Origins of the First World War.* Rev ed. Princeton, N.J.: Princeton University Press, 1991.

Milner, Murray Jr. *Status and Sacredness: A General Theory of Status Relations and an Analysis of Indian Culture.* New York: Oxford University Press, 1994.

Ming Ruifeng, and Yang Yiyong. "Yi ye chun feng: chengli ren de shouru chu tu xiu se" [An evening of spring breezes: urban population income]. In *Gongping yu xiaoyi: dangdai Zhongguo de shouru fenpei wenti* [Equality and efficiency: the issue of distribution of income in contemporary China], ed. Yang Yiyong. Beijing: Jinri Zhongguo Chubanshe, 1997.

Moeller, Kay. "China and Korea: The Godfather Part Three." *Journal of Northeast Asian Studies* 15 (Winter 1996): 35–48.

Moore, Barrington. *Injustice: The Social Bases of Obedience and Revolt.* Boston: Beacon Press, 1978.

Moore, Richard, Bruce Pirnie, and John Stillion. *Aerospace Operations Against Elusive Ground Targets.* Santa Monica, Calif.: Rand Corporation, 2001.

Moore, Thomas. "China's International Relations in Northeast Asia: The Economic Dimension." In *The International Relations of Northeast Asia*, ed. Samuel S. Kim, 101–34. Lanham, Md.: Rowman & Littlefield, 2004.

Morgan, Patrick M. "Saving Face for the Sake of Deterrence." In *Psychology and Deterrence*, ed. Robert Jervis, Richard Ned Lebow, and Janice Gross Stein. Baltimore: Johns Hopkins University Press, 1985.

Morgenthau, Hans. *Politics Among Nations: The Struggle for Power.* 4th ed. New York: Knopf, 1967.

Morphet, Sally. "China as a Permanent Member of the Security Council, October 1971–December 1999." *Security Dialogue* 31, 2 (June 2000): 161–62.

Mou Weimin, ed. *Waiguo zhengyao yanzhong de Zhongguo* [China in the eyes of foreign VIPs]. Beijing: Zhongguo Shehui Chubanshe, 2000.

Mullik, B. N. *My Years with Nehru: The Chinese Betrayal.* Bombay: Allied Publishers, 1971.

Mulvenon, James. *Missile Defenses and the Taiwan Scenario.* Report No. 44. Washington, D.C.: Henry L. Stimson Center, 2002.

Murrell, Audrey J., Beth L. Dietz-Uhler, John F. Dovidio, and Samuel L. Gaertner, et al. "Aversive Racism and Resistance to Affirmative Action: Perceptions of Justice Are Not Necessarily Color Blind." *Basic & Applied Social Psychology* 15, 1–2 (1994): 71–86.

Nathan, Andrew J., and Robert S. Ross. *The Great Wall and the Empty Fortress: China's Search for Security*. New York: Norton, 1997.

Nau, Henry R. *At Home Abroad: Identity and Power in American Foreign Policy*. Ithaca, N.Y.: Cornell University Press, 2002.

Nelsen, Harvey. "Caution: Rough Road Ahead." In *What if China Doesn't Democratize: Implications for War and Peace*, ed. Edward Friedman and Barrett L. McCormick. Armonk, N.Y.: M. E. Sharpe, 2000.

Neuendorf, Kimberly, and Paul Skalski. "Quantitative Content Analysis and the Measurement of Collective Identity." In *Measuring Identity*, ed. Rawi Abdelal, Yoshiko Herrera, Alastair Iain Johnston, and Rose McDemott, forthcoming.

Ng-Quinn, Michael. "The Effects of Bipolarity on Chinese Foreign Policy." *Survey* 26, 2 (Spring 1982): 116–30.

Ni Shixiong. *Dangdai xifang guoji guanxi lilun* [Contemporary Western international relations theory]. Shanghai: Fudan University Press, 2001.

Niou, Emerson, and Peter C. Ordeshook. "A Game-Theoretic Analysis of Sun Tzu's *The Art of War*." *Journal of Peace Research* 31, 2 (May 1994): 161–74.

Noland, Marcus. *Avoiding the Apocalypse: The Future of the Two Koreas*. Washington, D.C.: Institute for International Economics, 2000.

"North Korea This Week, No. 338 (March 31)." *Yonhap*, 31 March 2005. FBIS, NewsEdge Document No. 200503311477.1_42d30d5f153fc36d.

Nye, Joseph S. Jr. *The Paradox of American Power: Why the World's Only Superpower Can't Go It Alone*. New York: Oxford University Press, 2002.

Nye, Joseph S. Jr., and John D. Donahue, eds. *Governance in a Globalizing World*. Washington, D.C.: Brookings Institution Press, 2000.

Oberdorfer, Don. *The Two Koreas: A Contemporary History*. New York: Basic Books, 1997.

O'Dowd, Edward. "The Last Maoist War: Chinese Cadres and Conscripts in the Third Indochina War, 1978–1991." Ph.D. diss., Princeton University, 2004.

O'Hanlon, Michael. "Stopping a North Korean Invasion: Why Defending South Korea Is Easier Than the Pentagon Thinks." *International Security* 22, 4 (Spring 1998): 135–70.

———. "A Flawed Masterpiece." *Foreign Affairs* 81, 3 (May–June 2002): 47–63.

Ohmae, Kenichi. *The Borderless World*. London: Collins, 1990.

———. *The End of the Nation-State: The Rise of Regional Economies*. New York: Free Press, 1995.

Oksenberg, Michel. "China's Confident Nationalism." *Foreign Affairs* 65, 3 (1987): 501–23.

O'Meara, Patrick, Howard D. Mehlinger, and Matthew Krain, eds. *Globalization and the Challenges of a New Century: A Reader*. Bloomington: Indiana University Press, 2000.

O'Neill, Barry. "Power and Satisfaction in the Security Council." In *The Once and Future Security Council*, ed. Bruce Russett, 59–82. New York: St. Martin's Press, 1997.

Orden, David, Rashid S. Kaukab, and Eugenio Diaz-Bonilla. *Liberalizing Agricultural Trade and Developing Countries*. Carnegie Endowment TED Policy Brief No. 6. Washington, D.C.: Carnegie Endowment for International Peace, 2003. Summary at www.carnegieendowment.org/publications/index.cfm?fa=view&id=1202&prog=zgp&proj=zted (accessed September 27, 2005).

Organski, A. F. K., and Jacek Kugler. *The War Ledger*. Chicago: University of Chicago Press, 1980.

Osaki, Yuji. "China and Japan in the Asia Pacific." In *Challenges for China-Japan Cooperation*, ed. Ryosei Kokubun, 90–113. Tokyo: Japan Center for International Exchange, 1998.

Osgood, Charles E., George J. Suci, and Percy H. Tannenbaum. *The Measurement of Meaning*. Urbana: University of Illinois Press, 1957.

Owen, John M. IV. "Transnational Liberalism and U.S. Primacy." *International Security* 26, 3 (Winter 2002): 117–52.

Palit, D. K. *War in High Himalaya: The Indian Army in Crisis, 1962*. New Delhi: Lancer, 1991.

Pang, Zhongying. "Globalization and China: China's Response to the Asian Economic Crisis." *Asian Perspective* 23, 1 (1999): 111–31.

———, ed. *Quanqiuhua, fanquanqiuhua yu Zhongguo: lijie quanqiuhua de fuzaxing yu duoyangxing* [Globalization, anti-globalization, and China: understanding the complexity and diversity of globalization]. Shanghai: Shanghai Renmin Chubanshe, 2002.

———. "China's Changing Attitude to UN Peacekeeping." *International Peacekeeping* 1 (2005): 87–104.

Pape, Robert A. *Bombing to Win: Air Power and Coercion in War*. Ithaca, N.Y.: Cornell University Press, 1996.

Paul, T. V. *Asymmetric Conflicts: War Initiation by Weaker Powers*. Cambridge: Cambridge University Press, 1994.

Pearson, Margaret M. "China's Integration into the International Trade and Investment Regime." In *China Joins the World: Progress and Prospects*, ed. Elizabeth Economy and Michel Oksenberg, 161–205. New York: Council on Foreign Relations Press, 1999.

———. "The Major Multilateral Economic Institutions Engage China." In *Engaging China: The Management of an Emerging Power*, ed. Alastair Iain Johnston and Robert S. Ross, 207–34. London: Routledge Press, 1999.

———. "The Case of GATT/WTO." In *The Making of Chinese Foreign and Security Policy in the Era of Reform*, ed. David M. Lampton, 337–70. Stanford: Stanford University Press, 2001.

———. "The Institutional, Political, and Global Foundations of China's Trade Liberalization." In *Japan and China in the World Political Economy*, ed. Saadia Pekkanen and Kellee S. Tsai. New York: Routledge Press, 2005.

Peng Dehuai. *Memoirs of a Chinese Marshal*. Beijing: Foreign Languages Press, 1984.

———. *Peng Dehuai junshi wenxuan* [Selected military writings of Peng Dehuai]. Beijing: Zhongyang Wenxian Chubanshe, 1988.

Peng Qian, Yang Mingjie, and Xu Deren. *Zhonguo weishenme shuobu? Lengzhanhou Meiguo duiHua zhengce de cuowu* [Why does China say no? Mistakes in post–Cold War American China policy]. Beijing: Xinshijie Chubanshe, 1996.

People's Republic of China. Ministry of Foreign Affairs. "The Signing of the International Convention on Civil and Political Rights by the Chinese Government." 17 November 2000. www.fmprc.gov.cn/eng/ziliao/3602/3604/t18041.htm (accessed 1 October 2005).

People's Republic of China. People's Liberation Army. General Staff. Military Teaching Department. *Junshi gao jishu zhishi jiaocai* [Teaching materials on knowledge about military high technology]. 2d ed. Beijing: Jiefangjun Chubanshe, 1996.

Perdue, Charles, et al. "Us and Them: Social Categorization and the Process of Intergroup Bias." *Journal of Personality and Social Psychology* 59, 3 (September 1990): 475–86.

Perovic, Jeronim. *Internationalization of Russian Regions and the Consequences for Russian Foreign and Security Policy.* Regionalization of Russian Foreign and Security Policy Project, Working Paper No. 1. Zurich: Center for Security Studies and Conflict Research, 2000.

Pillsbury, Michael. *Chinese Views of Future Warfare.* Washington, D.C.: National Defense University Press, 1997.

———. *China Debates the Future Security Environment.* Washington, D.C.: National Defense University Press, 2000.

Platkovskiy, Alexander. "Nuclear Blackmail and North Korea's Search for a Place in the Sun." In *The North Korean Nuclear Program: Security, Strategy, and New Perspectives from Moscow*, ed. James C. Moltz and Alexander Y. Mansourov. New York: Routledge, 2000.

Pollack, Jonathan. "Perception and Action in Chinese Foreign Policy: The Quemoy Decision." Ph.D. diss., University of Michigan, 1976.

Powell, Robert. "Anarchy in International Relations Theory: The Neorealist-Neoliberal Debate." *International Organization* 48, 2 (Spring 1994): 313–45.

———. *In the Shadow of Power: States and Strategies in International Politics.* Princeton, N.J.: Princeton University Press, 1999.

"PRC Delegation Offers Suggestions on Korean Peace Accord." Xinhua, 22 January 1999.

"PRC Outlines 5 Principles to Reduce Tension in Koreas." Xinhua, 22 January 1999. FBIS-CHI-99–022, article drchio1221999001557.

"PRC Spokesman: Beijing Hopes for Negotiations on Korea." Agence France-Presse, 18 April 1996. FBIS-CHI-96–076, WNC document No. 0DQ4PPO047 NXHJ.

Pruzin, Daniel. "China Chafes at Dumping Panel Agenda for Excessive Focus on Accession Issues." *BNA International Trade Reporter*, 26 April 2002.

———. "China Review Woes Continue in WTO as Agriculture Meeting Questions TRQS." *BNA International Trade Reporter*, 3 October 2002.

———. "Harbison Calls on WTO Members to 'Change Gears' in Agricultural Talks." *BNA International Trade Reporter*, 3 October 2002.

Putnam, Robert. "Diplomacy and Domestic Politics: The Logic of Two-Level Games," *International Organization* 42, 3 (Summer 1988): 427–60.

Pye, Lucian. *The Spirit of Chinese Politics*. Cambridge, Mass.: Harvard University Press, 1992.

Qi Deliang, and Tang Shuifu. "Li, Yi Yong-Tok Discuss Economic Ties." Xinhua, 1 November 1994. FBIS-CHI-94–212, article drchi212_d_94007.

Qiang, Zhai. *China and the Vietnam Wars, 1950–1975*. Chapel Hill: University of North Carolina Press, 2000.

Qiao Liang, and Wang Xianghui. *Chaoxian zhan* [Unlimited war]. Beijing: Liberation Army Literature and Art Press, 1999.

Qu Aiguo. "Zhongguo zhiyuan budui yuan Yue kang Mei junshi xingdong gaishu" [A narrative of the military activities of the Chinese volunteer units in the Assist Vietnam Oppose America War]. *Junshi Shi Lin* [Military History Circles], no. 6 (1989): 38–44.

Reich, Robert. *The Work of Nations*. New York: Vintage Books, 1992.

Reinicke, Wolfgang. "Global Public Policy." *Foreign Affairs* 76, 6 (1997): 127–38.

Reiter, Daniel. "Exploding the Powderkeg Myth: Preemptive Wars Almost Never Happen." *International Security* 20, 2 (Autumn 1995): 5–34.

Rice, Condoleezza. "Promoting the National Interest." *Foreign Affairs* 79, 1 (January–February 2000): 45–62.

Ricupero, Rubens. "Rebuilding Confidence in the Multilateral Trading System: Closing the 'Legitimacy Gap.'" In *The Role of the World Trade Organization in Global Governance*, ed. Gary P. Sampson, 37–58. Tokyo: United Nations University Press, 2001.

Risse, Thomas, and Kathryn Sikkink. "The Socialization of International Human Rights Norms into Domestic Practices: Introduction." In *The Power of Human Rights: International Norms and Domestic Change*, ed. Thomas Risse, Stephen Ropp, and Kathryn Sikkink, 1–38. Cambridge: Cambridge University Press, 1999.

Risse-Kappen, Thomas. *Cooperation Among Democracies: The European Influence on U.S. Foreign Policy*. Princeton, N.J.: Princeton University Press, 1995.

Robinson, Thomas. "China Confronts the Soviet Union: Warfare and Diplomacy Along China's Inner Frontier." In *Cambridge History of China*, vol. 15, ed. Roderick MacFarquhar and John K. Fairbank, 218–304. Cambridge: Cambridge University Press, 1991.

Robinson, Thomas W., and David Shambaugh, eds. *Chinese Foreign Policy: Theory and Practice*. New York: Oxford University Press, 1994.

"Roh Stresses S. Korea's Balancing Role in Regional Security." *Yonhap*, 22 March 2005. FBIS, NewsEdge Document No. 200503221477.1_e7cd003a99afad38.

"ROK NSC Official Expounds on 'Balancer Role' in Northeast Asia Interview with Yi Cho'ng-So'k, Deputy Chief of the National Security Council." *JoongAng Ilbo*, 15 April 2005. FBIS, NewsEdge Document No. 200504151477.1_06640406b8d72b9c.

Rosecrance, Richard, ed. *The New Great Power Coalition*. Lanham, Md.: Rowman & Littlefield, 2001.

Rosen, Daniel H., Scott Rozelle, and Jikun Huang. *Roots of Competitiveness: China's Evolving Agricultural Interests*. Washington, D.C.: Institute for International Economics, 2004.

Rosenau, James N. *Along the Domestic-Foreign Frontier: Exploring Governance in a Turbulent World*. New York: Cambridge University Press, 1997.

———. *Distant Proximities: Dynamics Beyond Globalization*. Princeton, N.J.: Princeton University Press, 2003.

Rosenthal, Elisabeth. "7 North Koreans Allowed to Leave China." *New York Times*, 29 June 2001, A10.

———. "More Koreans Give China the Slip, Invading Embassy School." *New York Times*, 4 September 2002, A6.

———. "North Korean Asylum Seekers Leave China." *New York Times*, 24 June 2002, A6.

———. "U.N. Group Backs North Korean Asylum Seekers in China." *New York Times*, 15 March 2002, A8.

Ross, Lester. "China and Environmental Protection." In *China Joins the World: Progress and Prospects*, ed. Elizabeth Economy and Michel Oksenberg, 296–325. New York: Council on Foreign Relations Press, 1999.

Ross, Robert S. *The Indochina Tangle: China's Vietnam Policy, 1975–79*. New York: Columbia University Press, 1988.

———. "From Lin Biao to Deng Xiaoping: Elite Instability and China's US Policy." *China Quarterly*, no. 118 (June 1989): 265–99.

———. "The Geography of the Peace: East Asia in the Twenty-First Century." *International Security* 23, 4 (Spring 1999): 81–118.

———. "The 1995–96 Taiwan Strait Confrontation: Coercion, Credibility, and the Use of Force." *International Security* 25, 2 (Fall 2000): 87–123.

———. "Navigating the Taiwan Strait: Deterrence, Escalation Dominance, and U.S.-China Relations." *International Security* 27, 2 (Fall 2002): 48–85.

Roy, Denny. "The 'China Threat' Issue: Major Arguments." *Asian Survey* 36, 8 (August 1996): 758–71.

———. *China's Foreign Relations*. Basingstoke, Eng.: Macmillan, 1998.

Rubin, Herbert J., and Irene S. Rubin. *Qualitative Interviewing: The Art of Hearing Data*. Thousand Oaks, Calif.: Sage Publications, 2004.

Ruble, Diane N., and Karin S. Frey. "Changing Patterns of Comparative Behavior as Skills Are Acquired: A Functional Model of Self-Evaluation." In *Social Comparison: Contemporary Theory and Research*, ed. Jerry Suls and Thomas Ashby Wills, 79–113. Hillsdale, N.J.: Lawrence Erlbaum, 1991.

Ruggie, John. "Introduction: What Makes the World Hang Together? Neo-Utilitarianism and the Social Constructivist Challenge." In *Constructing the World Polity: Essays on International Institutionalization*, by John Ruggie, 1–39. New York: Routledge, 1998.

Rushford, Greg. "Washington's Dirty War on Chinese Clothing." *Far Eastern Economic Review* 168, 1 (2005): 31–36.

Sa Benwang. "Woguo anquan de bianhua ji xin de pubian anquanguan de zhuyao tezheng" [The change in our country's security and the main features of the new concept of universal security]. *Shijie Jingji yu Zhengzhi Luntan* [Forum on World Economics and Politics], no. 1 (2000): 50–52.

Saiget, Robert J. "North Korean Premier in Beijing amid Renewed Nuclear Threats." Agence France-Presse, 22 March 2005. FBIS, NewsEdge Document No. 200503221477.1_2389008b6e6f5d5e.

Sally, Razeen. *Whither the WTO? A Progress Report on the Doha Round.* Trade Policy Analysis, No. 23. Washington, D.C.: Cato Institute, 2003.

Sampson, Gary P., ed. *The Role of the World Trade Organization in Global Governance.* Tokyo: UN University Press, 2001.

Scheff, Thomas. "Shame and Conformity: The Deference-Emotion System." *American Sociological Review* 53, 3 (1988): 395–406.

Schein, Louisa. "Gender and Internal Orientalism in China." *Modern China* 23, 1 (January 1997): 69–98.

Schelling, Thomas C. *The Strategy of Conflict.* New York: Oxford University Press, 1963.

———. *Arms and Influence.* New Haven, Conn.: Yale University Press, 1966.

Schlapak, David A., David T. Orletsky, and Barry A. Wilson. *Dire Strait? Military Aspects of the China-Taiwan Confrontation and Options for U.S. Policy.* Santa Monica, Calif.: Rand Corporation, 2000.

Schulzinger, Robert D. "The Johnson Administration, China and the Vietnam War." In *Re-Examining the Cold War: U.S.-China Diplomacy, 1954–1973,* ed. Robert S. Ross and Jiang Changbin. Cambridge, Mass.: Harvard University Asia Center, 2001.

Scobell, Andrew. *China's Use of Military Force: Beyond the Great Wall and the Long March.* New York: Cambridge University Press, 2003.

Sedikides, Constantine. "Assessment, Enhancement, and Verification Determinants of the Self-Evaluation Process." *Journal of Personality & Social Psychology* 65, 2 (1993): 317–38.

Segal, Gerald. *Defending China.* Oxford: Oxford University Press, 1984.

———. "Does China Matter?" *Foreign Affairs* 78, 5 (September–October 1999): 24–37.

Segal, Leon V. *Disarming Strangers: Nuclear Diplomacy with North Korea.* Princeton, N.J.: Princeton University Press, 1998.

77 Conversations Between Chinese and Foreign Leaders on the Wars in Indochina, 1964–1977. Edited by Odd Arne Westad, Chen Jian, Stein Tonneson, Nguyen Vu Tung, and James Hershberg. Working Paper No. 22. Washington, D.C.: Cold War International History Project, Woodrow Wilson Center for Scholars, 1998.

Shafaeddin, S. M. *The Impact of China's Accession to WTO on the Exports of Developing Countries.* UNCTAD Discussion Paper No. 160. Geneva: United Nations Conference on Trade and Development, 2002. www.unctad.org/en/docs/dp_160.en.pdf (accessed 7 October 2005).

Shain, Yossi, and Ahron Barth. "Diasporas and International Relations Theory." *International Organization* 57, 3 (Summer 2003): 449–79.

Shakya, Tsering. *The Dragon in the Land of Snows: A History of Modern Tibet Since 1947.* London: Pimlico, 1999.

Shambaugh, David. *Beautiful Imperialist: China Perceives America, 1972–1990.* Princeton, N.J.: Princeton University Press, 1991.

———. "China's International Relations Think Tanks: Evolving Structure and Process." *China Quarterly,* no. 171 (Fall 2002): 575–96.

Shaver, Phillip, with Judith Schwartz, Donald Kirson, and Cary O'Connor. "Emotion Knowledge: Further Exploration of a Prototype Approach." *Journal of Personality & Social Psychology* 52, 6 (1987): 1061–86.

Shen, Zhihua. "The Discrepancy Between the Russian and Chinese Versions of Mao's 2 October 1950 Message to Stalin on Chinese Entry in the Korean War: A Chinese Scholar's Reply." *Cold War International History Project Bulletin* [Woodrow Wilson International Center for Scholars, Washington, D.C.], no. 8–9 (1996–97): 237–42. www.wilsoncenter.org/topics/pubs/ACF197.pdf (accessed 22 November 2005).

———. *Mao Zedong, Si Dalin yu Chao zhan: Zhong Su zui gao jimi dang'an* [Mao Zedong, Stalin and the Korean War: the top secret Sino-Soviet Archives]. Hong Kong: Cosmos Books, 1998.

———, ed. *Chaoxian zhanzheng: Eguo dang'anguan de jiemi wenjian* [The Korean War: declassified documents from the Russian archives]. Historical Material Collection No. 48. 3 vols. Taipei: Academia Sinica, Institute of Modern History, 2003.

Sherif, Muzafer. *In Common Predicament: Social Psychology of Intergroup Conflict and Cooperation.* Boston: Houghton Mifflin, 1966.

Shi Bo, ed. *Zhong Yin da zhan jishi* [Record of events in the big China-India war]. Beijing: Da Di Chubanshe, 1993.

Shi Yinhong."Kunnan yu xuanze: dui Taiwan wenti de sikao" [Difficulty and choice: thoughts on the Taiwan issue]. *Zhanlue yu Guanli,* no. 5 (1999).

———. "Guanyu Taiwan wenti de jixiang bixu zhengshi de da zhanlue wenti" [Several great strategic issues regarding the Taiwan issue that must be squarely faced]. *Zhanlue yu Guanli,* no. 2 (2000).

———. "Lun 20 shiji guoji guifan tixi" [A discussion of the system of international norms in the twentieth century]. *Guoji Luntan* 6 (2000).

———. "Meiguo dui Hua zhengce he Taiwan wenti de weilai" [U.S. policy toward China and the future of the Taiwan issue]. *Zhanlue yu Guanli,* no. 6 (2000).

Shirk, Susan. "One-Sided Rivalry: China's Perceptions and Policies toward India." In *The India-China Relationship: What the United States Needs to Know,* ed. Francine R. Frankel and Harry Harding. New York: Columbia University Press, 2004.

Sinha, P. B., A. A. Athale, with S. N. Prasad, chief eds. *History of the Conflict with China, 1962.* New Delhi: History Division, Indian Ministry of Defense, 1992.

Smith, Craig S. "China Reshaping Military to Toughen Its Muscle in the Region." *New York Times,* 16 October 2002, 12.

Snyder, Charles. "Supporters in US More Pessimistic." *Taipei Times,* 31 May 2003, 3.

Snyder, Glenn H. *Deterrence and Defense: Toward a Theory of National Security.* Princeton, N.J.: Princeton University Press, 1961.

Snyder, Glenn H., and Paul Diesing. *Conflict Among Nations: Bargaining, Decision Making and System Structure in International Crises.* Princeton, N.J.: Princeton University Press, 1977.

Snyder, Jack. *The Ideology of the Offensive: Military Decision Making and the Disasters of 1914.* Ithaca, N.Y.: Cornell University Press, 1984.

———. "Anarchy and Culture: Insights from the Anthropology of War." *International Organization* 56, 1 (Winter 2002): 7–45.

Snyder, Scott. *Negotiating on the Edge: North Korean Negotiating Behavior.* Washington, D.C.: United States Institute of Peace, 1999.

Sobel, Richard. *The Impact of Public Opinion on U.S. Foreign Policy Since Vietnam: Constraining the Colossus.* New York: Oxford University Press, 2001.

Song Liansheng. *KangMei yuanchao zai hui shou* [Looking back again on the Korean War]. Kunming: Yunnan People's Press, 2002.

Song Qiang, Qiao Bian, Caiwang Naoru, Xia Jilin, and Liu Hui. *Disidairen de jingshen: xiandai Zhongguoren de jiushi qingjie* [The spirit of the fourth generation: the savior complex of the modern Chinese]. Lanzhou: Gansu Wenhua Chubanshe, 1997.

Song Qiang, Zhang Zangzang, et al. *Zhongguo haishi neng shuobu* [China can still say no]. Beijing: Zhongguo Wenlian Chubanshe, 1996.

———. *Zhongguo keyi shuobu* [China can say no]. Beijing: Zhonghua Gongshang Lianhe Chubanshe, 1996.

"Speed Urged for International Trade Talks." *China Daily,* 20 July 2002.

Spence, Jonathan. *To Change China: Western Advisers in China, 1620–1960.* New York: Penguin Books, 1980.

Stein, Janice Gross. "Political Learning by Doing: Gorbachev as an Uncommitted Thinker." *International Organization* 48, 2 (Spring 1994): 155–84.

Stockholm Environment Institute and United Nations Development Programme, China. *China Human Development Report, 2002: Making Green Development a Choice.* New York: Oxford University Press, 2002.

Stolper, Thomas. *China, Taiwan, and the Offshore Islands.* Armonk, N.Y.: M. E. Sharpe, 1985.

Strange, Susan. "The Defective State." *Daedalus* 124, 2 (1995): 55–74.

———. *The Retreat of the State: The Diffusion of Power in the World Economy.* New York: Cambridge University Press, 1996.

Struck, Doug. "S. Korean Stresses Alliance, Dismisses Differences with U.S." *Washington Post,* 10 April 2003, A21.

Su Guiyou, and Liu Yusheng. "PRC Report on Koreas, Middle East." *Zhongguo Xinwen She,* 26 January 1998. FBIS-CHI-98-026, WNC Document No. 0ENJYOV042H3YJ.

Su, Kuofeng. "Taiwan's Democratization and Its Foreign Policy: The Impact of Taiwan's Elections on Its China Policy." Ph.D. diss., University of Michigan, 2000.

Su Yanrong, chief ed. *Gao jishu zhanzheng gailun* [An overview of wars under high-technology conditions]. Beijing: Guofang Daxue Chubanshe, 1993.

Suh, J. J., Peter Katzenstein, and Allen Carlson, eds. *Rethinking Security in East Asia.* Stanford: Stanford University Press: 2004.

Sun Shao, and Chen Zhibin. *Ximalaya shan de xue: Zhong Yin zhanzheng shilu* [Snows of the Himalaya mountains: the true record of the China-India war]. Taiyuan: Bei Yue Wenyi Chubanshe, 1991.

Swaine, Michael D. *Taiwan's National Security, Defense Policy, and Weapons Procurement Process.* Santa Monica, Calif.: Rand Corporation, 1999.

Swaine, Michael D., and Alastair Iain Johnston. "China and Arms Control Institutions." In *China Joins the World: Progress and Prospects,* ed. Elizabeth Economy and Michel Oksenberg. New York: Council on Foreign Relations Press, 1999.

Swaine, Michael D., and Ashley J. Tellis. *Interpreting China's Grand Strategy: Past, Present and Future.* Santa Monica, Calif.: Rand Corporation, 2000.

Swann, William B. *Self-Traps: The Elusive Quest for Higher Self-Esteem.* New York: W. H. Freeman, 1996.

"Taiwan Petitions Beijing to Respect WTO." Central News Agency [CNA], 4 September 2002.

Tajfel, Henri. *Human Groups and Social Categories.* Cambridge: Cambridge University Press, 1981.

―――, ed. *Social Identity and Intergroup Relations.* Cambridge: Cambridge University Press, 1982.

Tajfel, Henri, and John Turner. "The Social Identity Theory of Intergroup Behavior." In *Psychology of Intergroup Relations,* ed. Stephen Worshel and William Austin, 7–24. Chicago: Nelson Hall, 1986.

―――. "An Integrative Theory of Intergroup Conflict." In *Intergroup Relations: Essential Readings,* ed. Michael A. Hogg and Dominic Abrams. Philadelphia: Psychology Press, 2001.

Talbott, Strobe. "Globalization and Diplomacy: A Practitioner's Perspective." *Foreign Policy,* no. 108 (Fall 1997): 69–85.

Tan Qing. "Zhongguo ren kan Meiguo de ganshou hen fuza, zong di 724 qi, suo shu fenlei: shehui wenti yanjiu" [The feelings with which Chinese view Americans are very complicated]. Vol. 724: social science research, April 11, 2005. www.horizonkey.com/showart.asp?art_id=418&cat_id=6 (accessed November 22, 2005).

Tang Yongshang. "Zhongguo he lianheguo weihe xingdong" [China and UN peacekeeping operations]. *Shijie Jingji yu Zhengzhi* [World Economics and Politics], no. 9 (2002): 39–44.

Tao Wenzhao. "China's Position Towards the Korean Peninsula." Paper presented at the ASEM 2000 People's Forum, Seoul, Korea, 17–20 October 2000.

Taylor, Shelley E. "The Social Being in Social Psychology." In *The Handbook of Social Psychology,* 4th ed., ed. Daniel Gilbert, Susan Fiske, and Gardner Lindsey, 1: 52–95. Boston: McGraw-Hill, 1998.

Taylor, Shelley E., and Marci Lobel. "Social Comparison Activity Under Threat: Downward Evaluation and Upward Contacts." *Psychological Review* 96, 4 (1989): 569–75.

Teaching Department of the Chinese Communist Party Central Party School. *Wuge dangdai jianggao xuanbian* [A compilation of five contemporary lectures]. Beijing: Zhonggong Zhongyang Dangxiao Chubanshe, 2000.

Tessler, Mark, et al. "Further Tests of the Women and Peace Hypothesis: Evidence from Cross-National Survey Research in the Middle East." *International Studies Quarterly* 43 (1999): 519–31.

Tetlock, Philip E. "Social Psychology and World Politics." In *The Handbook of Social Psychology*, 4th ed., ed. Daniel Gilbert, Susan Fiske, and Gardner Lindsey, 2: 868–914. Boston: McGraw-Hill, 1998.

Thalakada, Nigel. "China's Voting Pattern in the Security Council, 1990–1995." In *The Once and Future Security Council*, ed. Bruce Russett. New York: St. Martin's Press, 1997.

Thompson, William R., and Richard Tucker. "A Tale of Two Democratic Peace Critiques." *Journal of Conflict Resolution* 41, 3 (June 1997): 428–54.

Tien, Hung-Mao, and Tun-Jen Cheng, eds. *The Security Environment in the Asia-Pacific*. Armonk, N.Y.: M. E. Sharpe, 2000.

Timperlake, Edward, and William C. Triplett II. *Year of the Rat: How Bill Clinton Compromised U.S. Security for Chinese Cash*. Washington, D.C.: Regnery, 1998; rev. ed., 2000.

"Top Advisors Call for Regulations to Purify Chinese Language." Xinhua, 6 March 1996.

Turner, John. *Differentiation Between Social Groups: Studies in the Social Psychology of Intergroup Relations*. London: Academic Press, 1978.

——. *Rediscovering the Social Group: A Self-Categorization Theory*. Oxford: Blackwell, 1987.

Tyler, Patrick. *A Great Wall: Six Presidents and China*. New York: Public Affairs, 1999.

Ulam, Adam B. *Expansion and Coexistence: The History of Soviet Foreign Policy, 1917–1967*. New York: Frederick A. Praeger, 1968.

United Nations Development Programme. *Human Development Report, 1991*. New York: Oxford University Press, 1991.

——. *Human Development Report, 1999*. New York: Oxford University Press, 1999.

——. *Human Development Report, 2002*. New York: Oxford University Press, 2002.

United States. Central Intelligence Agency. *The World Factbook*. Washington, D.C.: Central Intelligence Agency, 2005. www.cia.gov/cia/publications/factbook (accessed 2 October 2005).

United States. Department of Defense. *The United States Security Strategy for the East Asia–Pacific Region*. Washington, D.C.: Office of International Security Affairs, 1998. www.defenselink.mil/pubs/easr98 (accessed September 27, 2005).

——. *2000 Report to Congress on the Military Situation on the Korean Peninsula*. Washington, D.C.: U.S. Department of Defense, 2000. www.defenselink.mil/news/Sep2000/korea09122000.html (accessed September 27, 2005).

——. *Quadrennial Defense Review Report*. Washington, D.C.: U.S. Department of Defense, 2001. www.defenselink.mil/pubs/qdr2001.pdf (accessed 27 September 2005).

——. *Annual Report to Congress and Performance Plan*. Washington, D.C.: U.S. Department of Defense, 2002. www.defenselink.mil/pubs/chem_bio_def _program/2001_CBDP_Annual_Report.pdf (accessed November 22, 2005).

——. *Annual Report on the Military Power of the People's Republic of China*.

Washington, D.C.: U.S. Department of Defense, 2004. www.defenselink.mil / pubs/d20040528PRC.pdf (accessed September 27, 2005).

United States. Department of State. "Joint Statement of the U.S.-Japan Security Consultation Committee." Washington, D.C., 19 February 2005. www.state.gov/r / pa/prs/ps/2005/42490.htm (accessed 2 October 2005).

Van Evera, Stephen. "Offense, Defense, and the Causes of War." *International Security* 22, 4 (Spring 1998).

———. *Causes of War: Power and the Roots of Conflict.* Ithaca, N.Y.: Cornell University Press, 1999.

Van Ness, Peter. *Revolution and China's Foreign Policy.* Berkeley: University of California Press, 1972.

———. "China as a Third World State: Foreign Policy and Official National Identity." In *China's Quest for National Identity*, ed. Lowell Dittmer and Samuel Kim. Ithaca, N.Y.: Cornell University Press, 1993.

Vernon, Graham D. "Controlled Conflict: Soviet Perceptions of Peaceful Coexistence." In *Soviet Perceptions of War and Peace*, ed. Graham Vernon. Washington, D.C.: National Defense University Press, 1981.

"Vexed Directory." *Financial Times*, 28 May 2003.

Wada, Jun. "Applying Track Two to China-Japan-US Relations." In *Challenges for China-Japan Cooperation*, ed. Ryosei Kokubun, 154–83. Tokyo: Japan Center for International Exchange, 1998.

Waldron, Arthur. "The Chinese Sickness." *Commentary*, July–August 2003.

Walker, R. B. J. *Inside/Outside: International Relations as Political Theory.* Cambridge: Cambridge University Press, 1990.

Walt, Steven M. *The Origins of Alliances.* Ithaca, N.Y.: Cornell University Press, 1986.

———. "International Relations: One World, Many Theories." *Foreign Policy*, no. 110 (Spring 1998): 29–46.

Waltz, Kenneth. *Theory of International Politics.* New York: McGraw-Hill, 1979.

Wan, Ming. *Human Rights in Chinese Foreign Relations: Defining and Defending National Interests.* Philadelphia: University of Pennsylvania Press, 2001.

Wang Baocun. "Shixi xinxi zhan" [On information warfare]. *Zhongguo Junshi Kexue* [China Military Science], no. 4 (1997): 102–11.

Wang Bingnan. *Zhong Mei huitan jiunian huigu* [Recollections of nine years of Sino-American talks]. Beijing: Shijie Zhishi Chubanshe, 1985.

Wang Hongwei. "Zhong Yin bianjie wenti de lishi beijing yu 1962 nian Zhong Yin bianjie zhanzheng" [Historical background of the Sino-Indian border problem and the 1962 Sino-Indian border war]. *Ya Tai Ziliao* [Asia-Pacific Materials] 1 (18 March 1989).

———. *Ximalaya shan qingjie: Zhong Yin guanxi yanjiu* [The Himalayas sentiment: a study of Sino-Indian relations]. Beijing: Zhongguo Zangxue Chubanshe, 1998.

Wang, Hongying. "Multilateralism in Chinese Foreign Policy: The Limits of Socialization." *Asian Survey* 41, 3 (May–June 2000): 475–91.

Wang Houqing, and Zhang Xingye, chief eds. *Zhanyi xue* [Military campaign studies]. Beijing: Guofang Daxue Chubanshe, 2000.

Wang, Jianwei. *Limited Adversaries: Post–Cold War Sino-American Mutual Images*. New York: Oxford University Press, 2000.

Wang Jisi, ed. *Wenming yu guoji zhengzhi* [Civilizations and international politics]. Shanghai: People's Press, 1995.

Wang Kehua. "Ping Li Jieming yu Li Denghui de 'xin zhuquanlun'" [Criticism of James Lilly and Lee Teng-hui's "new sovereignty concept"]. *Taiwan Yanjiu* 4 (1991).

Wang Linchang. "Tang Jiaxuan waizhang baihui Hanguo zongtong Jin Dazhong" [Foreign Minister Tang Jiaxuan Calls on ROK President Kim Dae Jung]. *Renminwang*, 3 August 2002. www.peopledaily.com.cn/GB/shizheng/19/20020803/791325.html.

Wang Linchang, Xu Baokang, and Zhao Jiaming. "Yearender—Korean Peninsula: Peace Process in Motion and Tense Situation Eased." *Renmin Ribao*, 24 December 1997, 6. FBIS-CHI-98–012, article drchio1121998002156.

Wang Qiming, and Chen Feng, eds. *Daying gao jishu jubu zhanzheng: junguan bidu shouce* [Winning high-technology local war: required reading handbook for military officers]. Beijing: Junshi Yiwen Chubanshe, 1997.

Wang Shuliang. "Guojia zhuquan yu renquan" [State sovereignty and human rights]. *Shehui Kexueyuan Xueshu Jikan* [Social science academy academic journal] (Shanghai) 1 (1996).

Wang Xian'gen. *Zhongguo mimi da fabing: yuan Yue kang Mei shilu* [China's secret large dispatch of troops: the real record of the war to assist Vietnam and resist America]. Ji'nan: Ji'nan Publishers, 1992.

Wang Yiwei. "Dui Tai junshi douzheng dui shijie zhanlüe geju de yingxiang chutan" [A preliminary exploration of the effects on the international strategic situation of military action against Taiwan]. *Shijie Jingji yu Zhengzhi Luntan*, no. 6 (1999): 27–29.

Wang Yizhou. *Dangdai guoji zhengzhi xilun* [An analysis of contemporary international politics]. Shanghai: Shanghai Renmin Chubanshe, 1995.

———. *Xifang guoji zhengzhi xue: lishi yu lilun* [Western international politics studies: history and theory]. Shanghai: Shanghai Renmin Chubanshe, 1998.

———. "Mianxiang ershi shiji de Zhongguo waijiao: sanzhong xuqiu de xunqiu jiqi pingheng" [China's diplomacy for the twenty-first century: seeking and balancing three demands]. *Zhanlue yu Guanli* [Strategy and Management], no. 6 (1999): 18–27.

———. "New Security Concept in Globalization." *Beijing Review*, no. 7 (11–15 February 1999).

Wang Yizhou, ed. *Quanqiuhua shidai de guoji anquan* [International security in an era of globalization]. Shanghai: Shanghai Renmin Chubanshe, 1998.

Wang Yuesheng. "Shehui qingxu, wenming jiaowang yu gongtong jiazhi" [Social sentiment, the exchange of civilizations, and common values]. In *Zhongguo ruhe miandui xifang* [How China faces the West], ed. Xiao Pang, 120–35. Hong Kong: Mirror Books, 1997.

Ward, Michael D., and Kristian S. Gleditsch. "Democratizing for Peace." *American Political Science Review* 92, 1 (March 1998): 51–61.

Weathersby, Kathryn. *Soviet Aims in Korea and the Origins of the Korean War,*

1945–50. Working Paper No. 8. Washington, D.C.: Cold War International History Project, Woodrow Wilson International Center for Scholars, 1993.

———. "New Findings on the Korean War." *Cold War International History Project Bulletin* [Woodrow Wilson International Center for Scholars, Washington, D.C.], no. 6–7 (Winter 1995–96).

Wei Cai. "Mei haijun zhunbei jinnian xiaji jiang sansou Luoshanji ji he jianting bushu dao Guandao" [This summer the U.S. Navy will deploy three Los Angeles class nuclear submarines to Guam]. *Huanqiu Shibao* [Global Times], 9 May 2002.

Wendt, Alexander. "Anarchy Is What States Make of It: The Social Construction of Power Politics." *International Organization* 46, 2 (Spring 1992): 391–425.

———. "Collective Identity Formation and the International State." *American Political Science Review* 88, 2 (June 1994): 384–96.

———. *Social Theory of International Politics.* New York: Cambridge University Press, 1999.

Wendt, Alexander, and Daniel Friedheim. "Hierarchy Under Anarchy: Informal Empire and the East German State." In *State Sovereignty as Social Construct*, ed. Thomas J. Biersteker and Cynthia Weber, 240–78. New York: Cambridge University Press, 1996.

Whiting, Allen S. *China Crosses the Yalu: The Decision to Enter the Korean War.* 1960. Stanford: Stanford University Press, 1968.

———. *The Chinese Calculus of Deterrence: India and Indochina.* Ann Arbor: University of Michigan Press, 1975.

———. *The Chinese Calculus of Deterrence: India and Indochina.* Michigan Papers in Chinese Studies, No. 4. Ann Arbor: Center for Chinese Studies, 1981.

———. *China Eyes Japan.* Berkeley: University of California Press, 1989.

———. "Assertive Nationalism in Chinese Foreign Policy." *Asian Survey* 23, 8 (August 1993): 913–33.

———. "Chinese Nationalism and Foreign Policy after Deng." *China Quarterly*, no. 142 (June 1995): 295–316.

———. "ASEAN Eyes China: The Security Dimension." *Asian Survey* 37, 4 (April 1997): 299–322.

———. "China's Japan Policy and Domestic Politics." In *Japan and China: Rivalry or Cooperation in East Asia?* ed. Peter Drysdale and Dong Dong Zhang. Canberra: Australia-Japan Research Centre, 2000.

———. "China's Use of Force, 1950–1996, and Taiwan." *International Security* 26, 2 (Fall 2001): 103–31.

Whitson, William W., with Chen-hsia Huang. *The Chinese High Command: A History of Communist Military Politics, 1927-71.* New York: Praeger, 1973.

Wills, Thomas Ashby. "Similarity and Self-Esteem in Downward Comparison." In *Social Comparison: Contemporary Theory and Research*, ed. Jerry Suls and Thomas Ashby Wills, 51–78. Hillsdale, N.J.: Lawrence Erlbaum, 1991.

Wohlforth, William C. "The Stability of a Unipolar World." *International Security* 24 (Summer 1999): 5–41.

Wohlforth, William C., and Stephen G. Brooks. "American Primacy in Perspective." *Foreign Affairs* 81 (July–August 2002): 20–26.

Wonacott, Peter, and Neil King. "China Moves Quietly to Push Trade Goals: Beijing, Balancing Needs to Its Farmers, Factories, Treads Softly at WTO Talks." *Wall Street Journal*, 15 September 2003.

World Bank. *World Development Report 1991: The Challenge of Development*. New York: Oxford University Press, 1991.

———. *China 2020: Development Challenges in the New Century*. Washington, D.C.: World Bank, 1997.

———. *World Development Report 1999/2000: Entering the 21st Century*. New York: Oxford University Press, 2000.

"Wo shi 'Zhongguoren,' bushi 'Chinese'" [I am a "person from China," not a "Chinese"]. *Yangcheng Wanbao* [Canton Evening News], 4 October 1998.

"Wo tuoqi nazhong Zhongguoren" [I detest that kind of Chinese]. *Beijing Fazhibao* [Beijing Legal News], 29 May 1996.

"WTO Members Split on 'Development Box' and S & D." *Bridges Weekly Trade News Digest*, 12 February 2002.

Wu Lengxi. *Shi nian lunzhan, 1956–1966: Zhong Su guanxi huiyilu* [Ten-year polemical war, 1956–1966: a memoir of Sino-Soviet relations]. 2 vols. Beijing: Zhongyang Wenxian Chubanshe, 1999.

Wu, Xinbo. "U.S. Security Policy in Asia: Implications for China-U.S. Relations." *Contemporary Southeast Asia* 22 (2000): 479–97.

———. "To Be an Enlightened Superpower." *Washington Quarterly* 24, 3 (Summer 2001): 63–71.

Xi Yongjun, and Ma Zaihuai. *Chaoyue Meiguo: Meiguo shenhua de zhongjie* [Surpassing America: the end of the American myth]. Huhehaote: Neimenggu Daxue Chubanshe, 1996.

Xiao Tong, and Du Li. *Longli, 1978–1996: Zhuanxingqi Zhongguo baixing xinjilu* [Dragon history, 1978–96: the true feelings of the Chinese people during a time of transition]. Beijing: Gaige Chubanshe, 1997.

Xiong, Guangkai. "The New Security Concept Initiated by China." *International Security Studies*, no. 3 (2000): 1–5.

Xu, Ben. "Contesting Memory for Intellectual Self-Positioning: The 1990s' New Cultural Conservatism in China." *Modern Chinese Literature and Culture* 11, 1 (Spring 1999): 157–92.

Xu Guojin. "Guojia luxing guoji renquan yiwu de xiandu" [The limits on state performance of human rights obligations]. *Zhongguo Faxue* 2 (1992).

Xu Yan. *Jinmen zhi zhan* [The battle over Quemoy]. Beijing: Zhongguo Guangbo Dianshi Chubanshe, 1992.

———. *Zhong Yin bianjie zhi zhan lishi zhenxiang* [True history of the Sino-Indian border war]. Hong Kong: Cosmos Books, 1993.

———. "ZhongYin bianjie ziwei fanji zuozhan de lishi zhenxiang" [The real history of the self-defense counterattack warfare at the Chinese-Indian border]. In *Junshi miwenlu* [Secret military records]. Beijing: Beijing Shifan Daxue Press, 1993.

Yahuda, Michael B. *China's Role in World Affairs*. London: Croom Helm 1978.

———. *Towards the End of Isolationism: China's Foreign Policy After Mao*. New York: St. Martin's Press, 1983.

————. *The International Politics of the Asia-Pacific*. 1996. Rev. ed. New York: RoutledgeCurzon, 2004.

Yan Xuetong. "Dui Zhongguo anquan huanjing de fenxi yu sikao" [Analysis and thoughts on China's strategic environment]. *Shijie Jingji yu Zhengzhi* [World Economics and Politics], no. 2 (2000): 5–10.

Yan Xuetong, and Sun Xuefeng. *Guoji guanxi yanjiu shiyong fangfa* [Practical methods of international studies]. Beijing: People's Publishing House, 2001.

Yang Chengxu. *Xin tiaozhan: guoji guanxi zhong de "rendaozhuyi ganyu"* [A new challenge: humanitarian intervention in international relations]. Beijing: Zhongguo Qingnian Chubanshe, 2001.

Yang Dezhi. "Qianyan" [Preface]. In *KangMei yuanChao de kaige* [A paean to the war to resist America and aid Korea]. Beijing: Zhongguo Da Baike Quanshu Chubanshe, 1990.

Yang Gongsu. *Zhonghua renmin gongheguo waijiao lilun yu shixian* [The theory and practice of PRC diplomacy]. Beijing: Beijing University, 1996. Internally circulated, limited edition textbook.

Yang, Kuisong. "The Sino-Soviet Border Clash of 1969: From Zhenbao Island to Sino-American Rapprochement." *Cold War History* 1, 1 (August 2000): 21–52.

Yao Yunzhu. *Zhanhou Meiguo weishe lilun yu zhengce* [Postwar U.S. deterrence theory and policy]. Beijing: Guofang Daxue Chubanshe, 1998.

Ye Fei. *Ye Fei huiyilu* [The memoirs of Ye Fei]. Beijing: Liberation Army Press, 1988.

Ye Zicheng. "Zhan yu he, jiaogei Taiwan dangju xuan" [War and peace, give the choice to the Taiwan authorities]. *Huanqiu Shibao*, 22 October 1999.

————. "Zhongguo shixing daguo waijiao zhanlüe shizai bixing" [The imperative for China to implement a great power diplomatic strategy]. *Shijie Jingji yu Zhengzhi* [World Economics and Politics], no. 1 (2000): 5–10.

Ye Zicheng, and Feng Yin. "Dangqian ZhongMei guanxi de ba da tedian" [Eight Key Characteristics of Current Sino-U.S. Relations], *Nanfang Ribao*, 22 February 2002, at www.nanfangdaily.com.cn/zt/zt/009bush/200202220021.asp (accessed 19 February 2006).

Yi Jun, Hua Shan, and Xu Shujun. "Behind the US–South Korea 'RSOI 2001' Exercise." *Jiefangjun Bao*, 30 April 2001, 12. FBIS-CHI-2001–0430, WNC Document No. 0GCNRWY01F5CM5.

You, Ji. "The PLA, the CCP and the Formulation of Chinese Defense and Foreign Policy." In *Power and Responsibility in Chinese Foreign Policy*, ed. Yongjin Zhang and Greg Austin. Canberra: Asia Pacific Press, 2001.

Yu Gouming. "Zhongguo ren yanzhong de Riben he Riben ren." *Guoji Xinwen Jie* 6 (1997): 58–65.

Yu Kaitang, and Cao Shuxin, eds. *Tezhong kongxi mubiao yu duikang lilun yanjiu* [Theoretical research on special air-attack targets and counterattack]. Beijing: Guofang Daxue Chubanshe, 2000.

Yu Sunda, et al. "Zhong Mei guanxi: lai zi minzhong de kanfa" [Sino-U.S. relations: views from the masses]. *Shijie Jingji yu Zhengzhi* [World Economics and Politics], no. 6 (2001): 33–38.

Yu Xinyan. *Waiguoren kan Zhongguo* [Foreigners' views of China]. Beijing: Zhongguo Shaonian Ertong Chubanshe, 1995.

Yuan Zhengling. "Shilun changgui weishe" [On conventional deterrence]. *Zhongguo Junshi Kexue*, no. 4 (2001).

Zeng Lingliang. "Lun lengzhan hou shidai de guojia zhuquan" [A discussion of state sovereignty in the post–Cold War era]. *Zhongguo Faxue* 1 (1998).

Zhai Xiaomin. *Lengzhanhou de Meiguo junshi zhanlue* [American military strategy after the Cold War]. Beijing: Guofang Daxue Chubanshe, 1999.

Zhan Xuexi. "Xiandai zhanyi tedian" [Analysis of the characteristics of contemporary campaigns]. In *Gao jishu tiaojian xia zhanyi lilun yanjiu* [Research on theory of local war under high-technology conditions], ed. Campaign Teaching and Research Office, Research Department, National Defense University. Beijing: Guofang Daxue Chubanshe, 1997.

Zhang Baijia. "Mao Zedong yu Zhong Su tongmeng he Zhong Su fenlie" [Mao Zedong and the Sino-Soviet alliance and the Sino-Soviet Split]. MS presented to the Chinese Communist Party Central Party History Research Office's International Scholars Research Forum. Beijing, 1997.

Zhang Guocheng. "Quadripartite Talks Enter Substantive Stage." *Renmin Ribao*, 29 January 1999, 6. FBIS-CHI-99-030, WNC Document No. 0F6JMO503HYFPI.

Zhang Hui. "2003 nian Zhongguo ren yanzhong de shijie zhuanti diaocha zhi er—Zhongguo ren kan Meiguo: shiyongzhuyi + bentuhua qingjie zong di 594 qi suo shu fenlei: shehui wenti yanjiu" [The second 2003 survey of Chinese views of the world—Chinese view the US: pragmatism and localization] Vol. 594, social science research, 14 November 2003. www.horizonkey.com/showart.asp?art_id=274&cat_id=6 (accessed 14 November 2005).

Zhang Jin. "Nation Jumps to Be World Third Largest Trader." *China Daily*, 11 January 2005. www.chinadaily.com.cn/english/doc/2005-01/11/content_407979.htm (accessed 2 October 2005).

Zhang, Ming. *China's Changing Nuclear Posture: Reactions to the South Asian Nuclear Tests*. Washington, D.C.: Carnegie Endowment for International Peace, 1999.

Zhang, Ming, and Ronald Montaperto. *A Triad of Another Kind: The US, China and Japan*, Basingstoke, Eng.: Macmillan, 1999.

Zhang, Shuguang. *Deterrence and Strategic Culture: Chinese-American Confrontations, 1949–1958*. Ithaca, N.Y.: Cornell University Press, 1992.

———. *Mao's Military Romanticism*. Lawrence: University of Kansas Press, 1995.

Zhang Wannian. *Dangdai shijie junshi yu Zhongguo guofang* [Contemporary world military affairs and China's national defense]. Beijing: Junshi Kexue Chubanshe, 1999.

———. *Dangdai shijie junshi yu Zhongguo guofang* [Contemporary world military affairs and China's national defense]. Beijing: Zhonggong Zhongyang Dangxiao Chubanshe, 2000.

Zhang Xin, and Han Xudong. "Reasons Behind Constant Clashes in Northeast Asia as Viewed from ROK-DPRK Sea Battle." *Liaowang* 28 (2002): 60–61. FBIS-CHI-2002-0718, WNC Document No. 0GZNJ2ToOJ3S5Q.

Zhang, Yongjin, and Greg Austin, eds. *Power and Responsibility in Chinese Foreign Policy*. Canberra: Asia Pacific Press, 2001.

Zhang Zhaozhong. "Meiguo junshi zhanlue zhuanxiang yatai zhendui shei?" [At whom is the U.S. military strategy's move toward the Asia-Pacific aimed?]. *Beijing Qingnian Bao*, 30 August 2001. www.people.com.cn/GB/junshi/192/3514/3646/20010830/547897.html (accessed 2 October 2005).

Zhang Zhirong. *Guoji guanxi yu Xizang wenti* [International relations and the Tibetan problem]. Beijing: Lüyou Jiaoyu Chubanshe, 1994.

Zhao Suisheng. "Chinese Intellectuals' Quest for National Greatness and Nationalistic Writing in the 1990s." *China Quarterly*, no. 152 (December 1997): 725–45.

———. *A Nation-State by Construction: Dynamics of Modern Chinese Nationalism*. Stanford: Stanford University Press, 2004.

Zhao Weiwen. *Yin Zhong guanxi fengyun lu (1949–1999)* [Record of the vicissitudes of India-China relations (1949–1999)]. Beijing: Shi Shi Chubanshe, 2000.

Zhao Xijun. "'Bu zhan er quren zhi bing' yu xiandai weishe zhanlue" ["Victory without war" and modern deterrence strategy]. *Zhongguo Junshi Kexue* [Chinese Military Science], no. 5 (2001).

Zhao Zhongqiang, and Peng Chencang. *Xinxi zhan yu fan xinxi zhan: zema da* [Information war and anti-information war: how to fight]. Beijing: Zhongguo Qingnian Chubanshe, 2001.

"Zhongguo qizhi shuobu: ZhongMei jiaoliang" [China shouldn't just say no: the Sino-American contest]. *Ai Wo Zhonghua* [Love Our China], special issue. Hefei, 1996.

Zhongguo renmin jiefangjun liushinian dashiji (1927–1987) [Record of sixty years of major events of the PLA, 1927–1987]. Beijing: Junshi Kexue Chubanshe, 1988.

ZhongYin bianjiang ziwei fanji zuozhan shi [The battle history of the self-defense counterattack on the Sino-Indian border]. Beijing: Academy of Military Sciences, 1994.

Zhou Enlai. *Zhou Enlai waijiao wenxuan* [Diplomatic documents of Zhou Enlai]. Beijing: Zhongyang Wenxian Chubanshe, 1990.

———. *Zhou Enlai nianpu: 1949–76* [Zhou Enlai's chronicle: 1949–76]. 3 vols. Beijing: Zhongyang Wenxian Chubanshe, 1997.

Zhou Yongkun. "Quanqiuxing shidai de renquan" [Human rights in an era of globalism]. *Jiangsu Shehui Kexue* 3 (2002).

Zhu Feng. "RiChao shounao huitan: Xiaoquan chengle zuida 'ying jia'?" [The Japan-DPRK summit: will Koizumi be the biggest "winner"?]. *Zhongguo Ribao*, 19 September 2002. www.people.com.cn/GB/guoji/24/20020919/826587.html (accessed 2 October 2005).

Zhu Jiamu, and An Jianshe, eds. *Zhenhan shijie de 20 tian: waiguo jizhe bixia de Zhou Enlai shishi* [Twenty days that shook the world: Zhou Enlai's passing in the writings of foreign reporters]. Beijing: Zhongyang Wenxian Chubanshe, 1999.

"Zhu Rongji zongli tong Hanguo zongtong Jin Dazhong juxing huitan" [Premier Zhu Rongji and ROK President Kim Dae Jung Hold Talks]. Xinhua, 18 October 2000.

Zweig, David. *Internationalizing China: Domestic Interests and Global Linkages.* Ithaca, N.Y.: Cornell University Press, 2002.

Zweig, David, and Bi Jianhai. "The Foreign Policy of a 'Resource Hungry' State." Unpublished paper, 2005.

Zweig, David, and Chung Siu-Fung. "Redefining the Brain Drain: China's 'Diaspora Option.'" Unpublished paper, March 2005.

Index

relations, 95; sources in, 415n36; and Tibet, 92, 100; and UN, 296; unification with China of, 21–24; U.S. arms sales to, 19, 38, 62, 76–77, 192; and Vietnam, 73; and WTO, 251, 260, 272n58. *See also* Sino-Taiwanese relations

Taiwan Strait, 397, 400; 1950 crisis in (Korean War), 54, 57, 380; 1954-55 crisis in, 52, 58–61; 1958 crisis in (Quemoy-Matsu), 60–63; 1995-96 crisis in, 19, 21–23, 31–32, 75–76, 135, 171, 175, 179, 198–99, 316, 380; and Chinese use of force, 35, 50–51, 68, 70, 123; deterrence in, 13–24, 30–32, 37–38; islands in, 58–63, 86, 123

Tajfel, Henri, 314, 324
Talbott, Strobe, 298
Tanaka Kakuei, 398
Tang Jiaxuan, 282–83, 327, 329
Tang Shiping, 400
Tang Yongsheng, 233
Tang Zhengyu, 317
tariffs, 165, 247, 272nn54,57; agricultural, 252, 255, 260, 273n64; and quotas, 248, 260, 262; and U.S. steel industry, 256; and WTO, 248–49, 252, 273n64, 287
Tawang region, 113, 122–23
technology, 288, 406; and global citizenship, 280; and globalization, 283, 289; information (IT), 25, 286; Japanese, 164, 177; and military capability, 17, 30, 135, 400; in North Korea, 25
terrorism, 182, 289, 408; and China threat theory, 195, 204–5; Chinese response to, 230–31; and international norms, 416n52; and North Korea, 29, 143, 152; and public opinion, 346, 349; and Sino-Japanese relations, 177; and Sino-U.S. relations, 180, 204–5, 231; and sovereignty *vs.* intervention, 219, 230–31; and Taiwan Strait crises, 76
textiles, 7, 243, 247, 252–53, 258, 261–62
Thagla Ridge, 96, 109, 113–15
Thailand, 61, 68, 267n3
Third World. *See* developing countries
threat perception, 404; and attribution error, 102–3; Chinese, 3–4, 70, 132, 137, 146–48, 173; and deterrence, 146–48; and gender, 363–65, 368;

and globalization, 288; and Korea, 32, 137, 146–48; psychology of, 88–89; and public opinion, 349, 360–65, 367, 375n49; and security dilemma, 187, 189–90; in Sino-Indian relations, 93–105; and Sino-Indian war, 87–88; and social identification, 190–91; U.S., 196, 205. *See also* China threat theory
"three no's policy" (Japan's militarization), 198
"three no's policy" (Taiwan issue), 174
Tiananmen protests (1989), 142, 168, 292, 300, 399, 408; and China threat theory, 192; Chinese isolation after, 218, 222; generation following, 350–51, 355, 359, 363, 368; and global citizenship, 280; sanctions after, 222–23, 316; and Sino-Japanese relations, 167
Tibet: 1959 uprising in, 3, 90, 92–93, 98–100, 102–3, 105; as buffer zone, 89–90, 95–96; Chinese sovereignty in, 92–93, 97–103; CIA in, 3, 92, 100–101; class structure of, 94–95, 101; demonstrators in, 126n17; and domestic instability, 299; imperialism in, 89–91; and India, 3, 91–93, 98–100, 125; and India's Forward Policy, 105; and Mao's attribution error, 88; militarization of, 99, 101; PLA occupation of, 90–91, 105; refugees from, 92–93, 101, 125; resistance in, 92, 96, 100–102; road construction in, 102, 108; 17-point agreement on (1951), 90, 92, 98; and Sino-Indian war, 63, 65, 86–87, 89–103, 105, 115, 118, 120–21, 123
Tilelli, John, 32
Timperlake, Edward, 309
Timurlane, 116
ti-yong (essence and utility), 280
tourism, 162, 165
trade: and China's Korea policy, 134, 149–50; and China threat theory, 192; Chinese, 246–47, 260, 285; and Chinese foreign policy, 136; and domestic politics, 243, 246, 263; and globalization, 278, 285, 288–89; liberalization of, 243, 265; and North Korea, 25, 157n31; offensive *vs.* defensive interests in, 247; Sino-Japanese, 164; Sino-Taiwanese, 22, 76–77; and status, 326; with Tibet, 92–93. *See also* ex-